COMPENSATED EMANCIPATION

IN THE

DISTRICT OF COLUMBIA

Petitions under the Act of April 16, 1862

Dorothy S. Provine

HERITAGE BOOKS
2008

HERITAGE BOOKS
AN IMPRINT OF HERITAGE BOOKS, INC.

Books, CDs, and more—Worldwide

For our listing of thousands of titles see our website
at
www.HeritageBooks.com

Published 2008 by
HERITAGE BOOKS, INC.
Publishing Division
100 Railroad Ave. #104
Westminster, Maryland 21157

Copyright © 2005 Dorothy S. Provine

Other Heritage Books by the author:
Alexandria County, Virginia Free Negro Register, 1797-1861
*Compensated Emancipation in the District of Columbia:
Petitions under the Act of April 16, 1862*
District of Columbia Free Negro Registers
District of Columbia Indentures of Apprenticeship, 1801-1893
*District of Columbia Marriage Records Index
June 28, 1877 to October 19, 1885: Marriage Record Books 11 to 20*
Wesley E. Pippenger and Dorothy S. Provine
District of Columbia Marriage Records, 1870-1877
Index to District of Columbia Wills, 1921-1950

— Publisher's Notice —
Due to a paginaton error, page 148 does not exist. No text is missing.

All rights reserved. No part of this book may be reproduced or transmitted in any form or by any means, electronic or mechanical, including photocopying, recording or by any information storage and retrieval system without written permission from the author, except for the inclusion of brief quotations in a review.

International Standard Book Numbers
Paperbound: 978-0-7884-3183-8
Clothbound: 978-0-7884-7262-6

TO

THE SISTAHS OF THE SUNFLOWER

AIN'T WE GOT FUN

TABLE OF CONTENTS

Introduction vi

Sample Petition xii

Petitions 1

Appendix A: List of servants to whom certificates have been granted under the supplemental act of July 12, 1862, and names of alleged owners 233

Appendix B: List of persons from whom certificates have been withheld on their applications under the supplementary act of July 12, 1862, with the names of alleged owners 237

Appendix C: Disposition of late claims 239

Index 241

Introduction

On Apr. 16, 1862, Congress passed the law entitled "An Act for the Release of Certain Persons Held to Service of Labor in the District of Columbia" which abolished slavery in the nation's capital and provided monetary compensation for the ex-slaveowners. The act provided that "all persons held to service of labor within the District of Columbia by reason of African descent are hereby discharged and freed of and from all claim to such service or labor; and from and after the passage of this act neither slavery nor involuntary servitude, except for crime, whereof the party shall be duly convicted, shall hereafter exist in said District."

The District of Columbia was unique as being the only place the Federal government paid slaveholders after liberating their slaves. Petitioners were required to take an oath of allegiance to the Government of the United States and to swear that they had not borne arms against it or given aid and comfort to its enemies. Those loyal persons claiming ownership were required to submit within 90 days a petition naming and describing their slaves, estimating their value and stating how they obtained title to such persons. Petitioners were required to take an oath of allegiance to the Government of the United States and to swear that they had now borne arms against it or given aid and comfort to its enemies.

The act established a commission of three members appointed by the President to receive the petitions, investigate and determine the validity of the claims and, if approved, set an appropriate amount to be paid the claimants. The President appointed Robert R. Goodloe, Horatio King and Samuel F. Vinton to the commission, but Vinton died in May and John M. Brodhead was appointed to replace him. The commissioners held their first meeting at City Hall on Apr. 28, 1862, to organize themselves. They later placed notices in the newspapers about their meetings and produced a blank form to be filled-in by the petitioners. They also arranged for an "experienced dealer in slaves," B. M. Campbell of Baltimore, to assist them in assessing the monetary value of the freed servants.

There were 966 petitions filed between Apr. 29 and Jul. 15, 1862. Of these the commissioners approved 909, rejected 36 and partly rejected 21. They paid compensation for 2,989 servants, but withheld payment for 111, making a total of 3,100 included in the 966 petitions.

Because some owners had not submitted claims for their slaves, a supplemental act dated Jul. 12, 1862, directed the commissioners to receive statements regarding these African Americans who were qualified to be free under the act of Apr. 16, and to issue certificates attesting to their free status. There were 161 petitions brought under this act, of which the commissioners granted 139 and rejected 22. See Appendix A for a list of cases under the supplementary act.

There were, in addition, 13 late petitions (see Appendix C) that the commissioners found to be worthy of payment and referred to Congress for action.

The commission submitted a detailed report entitled *Emancipation in the District of Columbia* that was published as House Executive Document 42, 38 Congress, 1 session. The printed report discusses how the commissioners proceeded, their disposition of the petitions, and, in some instances, the reasoning behind the rejection of certain claims. The heart of the report is a chart that lists each of the 966 petitions, the number assigned it, total number of slaves for which the petitioner claimed ownership, name of the claimant, names of those held to service or labor, the amount awarded and to whom it was paid. The report also includes tables assembled by the commissioners relating to claims under the supplemental act of July 12 and to the 13 claims filed after the deadline. They prepared a name index to petitioners, but did not create one for those being freed.

The report is quite valuable and should be consulted by anyone interested in this topic. However, one must be careful, for there are errors, especially as regards the names of the slaves. The name "Henny" (the shortened version of "Henrietta") almost always appears in the printed report as "Henry", which misleads one as to gender of the person. There are numerous other mistakes regarding the names of ex-slaves. For example, in Petition No. 846 the name given in the printed report is "Nellie Jennie," but the name in the original document is "Nellie Janifer"; in No. 830, Lewis Hanson's name appears in the printed report as "Lewis Harrison"; in No. 869, Betty Ann Humphreys' name is given as "Betty Ann Hampton;" in No. 526, "Louisa Rigney" is really "Louis Rigney;" and in No. 384, Sarah's and Margaret's last name is clearly "Tills" in the original, not "Lee" as in the commissioners printed report.

The amount awarded by the commission averaged about $300 per slave. The individual grants, however, varied greatly. A young child or a very old person might be valued at less that $50; an unusually valuable male might be appraised at over $700; and an especially valuable female at close to $500. Frank Digges, who had charge of the steam engines in Columbus Alexander's printing plant, was valued at $744.60; Lewis Cammel, whose owner hired him out to the anchor shop at the Washington Navy Yard for $300 a year, was valued at $788.40; Henry Hatton, a free Negro, received $700.80 for his 22-year-old son who was a blacksmith. In many instances, slaves were held to service only for a term of years, after which they were to be manumitted. The amount the commissioners paid to the owner reflected that limited time of servitude.

The owners, of course, usually estimated the monetary value of their slaves far in excess of what the commission came to award them. The petitioners consistently described their slaves as the most skillful, intelligent, talented, trustworthy, moral, honest, obedient, faithful, sober, industrious, cheerful servants to be found in the District. They noted in several instances that the servants had learned to read and write. They usually asked compensations that were at least three or four times more that what they got. Judson Naylor (No. 403) asked $1,400 for 36-year-old Henry Munroe, but received only $372.30; John Little (No. 744) asked $3,000 each for two young men who were butchers, but was given $613.20 each; Fanny Ewell (No. 25) asked $2,000 for Moses Martin who was employed as chief cook at the Ebbitt House, but got only $657; and John Neale asked $2,000 for his cook and servant, Henrietta Lancaster, but was awarded only $525.60.

A few of the claimants were free Negroes and they were compensated for the slaves they owned just as the white owners. In almost every instance, however, this was a case of a family member having purchased a spouse or children and there is no evidence that African Americans in Washington were actively engaged in the slave trade. Mary Hasson (No. 545) was compensated for Henry Hasson, who was probably her husband; James W. McDonald (No. 834) had purchased his wife and daughter from a slave trader and was compensated; Jacob Ross was paid for Keziah Ross whom he had purchased in 1856; Edward Coakley (No. 332) submitted a claim for eight persons named Coakley whom he had purchased; Henry Hatton purchased his three children and was paid $1,839.60; Betsy Roberson (No. 460) was paid $613.20 for her son whom she had bought in 1847 when he was ten years old; and Robert Gunnell of Fairfax, Va. (No. 442), claimed compensation for ten slaves he acquired by purchase or by birth who resided in the District of Columbia.

Some petitions were disallowed by the commissioners because of the Southern loyalties of the petitioner, disputed ownership, failure to produce the slave and in a few instances, an attempt to pass off a free African American as a slave. Jacob Smoot (No. 589) and Smith Minor (No. 386) were denied their claims because they had voted for the Virginia ordinance of secession and Sarah Abbott's claim (No. 179) was dismissed because the title to the servant came from her husband who has taken off for Richmond and a job with the "rebel government."

Allison Nailor asked compensation for William and Joseph Johnson (No. 959) whom he said he had purchased from their mother. A mother may apprentice her children, but certainly not sell them into slavery. William and Joseph were free born persons. The same thing happened when Martha E. Nixon (No. 895) tried to claim money for Isaiah Carter, who was an apprentice not a slave, and a similar situation occurred when William Nottingham (No. 501) tried to claim $300 for his apprentice.

As many historians have noted, slavery in the cities differed greatly from that of the rural farming and plantation system. This certainly shows up in these documents, and no where more clearly than in the hiring-out of slaves by their owners. Many of the males were hired out for wages that typically ranged from a few dollars a month to about $40 a month.

Some general remarks concerningAfrican Americans in the nation's capital seems in order. First of all, historians know that slavery as an institution breaks down in an urban setting and certainly this is true in Washington. In 1820 there were in D.C. 6,377 slaves, being 19.3% of the population. By 1860 the number had declined to 3,185, composing only 4.2% of the population. On the other hand, the number of free African Americans increased from 4,048 (12.2%of the population) to 11,131 (19.9) percent of the population. Slavery did not work in the hustle and bustle of a city, especially one with a large free black population. On city streets those who were legally slaves could seldom be distinguished from their free brethren and a great many slaves lived their lives completely unobserved and unsupervised by their owners.

No where was this more evident than in the common practice of hiring out slaves. Many male slaves were hired out by their owners and became an important source of income. Slaves worked at the Washington Navy Yard, at the city's hotels and restaurants, at its markets. They were household servants, blacksmiths, bakers, bricklayers, carpenters, waiters, upholsterers, tailors, laborers, farm hands, ostlers, porters, cooks, domestics, children's nurses, laundresses, seamstresses and midwives. William H. Beckett (No. 774) was Secretary of State William Seward's carriage driver and had previously served as foreman of Joshua Peirce's extensive gardens and nurseries. Philip Reid worked in the foundry of the architect Clark Mills and was in charge of placing of the statue of freedom on the new Capitol dome. It is important to note, however, the many free blacks resented the competition with slaves and especially protested slaves being hired on government projects.

Three of George Mattingly's slaves (No. 241) worked outside the District. One received $14 a month on a steamboat of the "Potomac Flotilla;"; another was the body servant and waiter for a Union officer at $20 a month; while still a third was a cook on a steamboat at $12 a month. Henry Branson was employed at the Washington Navy Yard at $1.50 a day, of which he paid Mattingly a $1.00 and kept the rest and his overtime. William Pressy hired his slave out as a cart driver at a wood yard for $20 a month. Rebecca Williams of Georgetown (No. 790) hired out two of her female slaves as housekeepers and cooks and received $60 a year from each above the $5 a month she allowed them to keep. Samuel Stevenson, another slave of Williams's had served as head waiter at Willard's Hotel and at the National Hotel at $15 a month, of which he gave Williams $12. In 1862 he was hired to a unit of the New York Volunteers then camped in Washington.

Many of the petitions were from owners who were residents of the neighboring Maryland counties of Prince George's and Montgomery. In a few instances, owners were from more distant places. Mary Watts (No. 767) lived in St. Mary's County, Md., and hired out Margaret Statesman for $6 to $8 a month in D.C.; another petitioner was a resident in Boston, another of New York. These slaves hired out in the District on the date of the emancipation act, Apr. 16, 1862, were freed.

Many slaves in Washington lived totally free from the supervision of their owners. In several cases the petitioners stated they did not know where their slaves were, but that they were working somewhere in D.C. Indeed, some slaves are listed in the Federal census, despite the fact that the census is an enumeration of free persons, not Indians, living in the United States. For example, Samuel Norment's slaves who were living in his house were listed as free persons (see note accompanying no. 83); Sarah Tolson's slave, George Tenney, is probably the same Tenney entered as head of a free household in 1860; Henry Green (No. 250) a slave and a house servant, in Thomas Richard's home, was listed as a free person. (Green's case is curious in that Richard stated that he purchased Green for a term of years from his father, Henry Green, Sr. Since in slavery one's status is determined by one's mother, this indicates that Green's mother must have been a slave while his father was a free person and his legal owner.) And Margaret Smoot of Montgomery County (No. 289) received payment for her slave Frank Herbert, who is listed in the 1860 census as free and living with his wife and four children in Georgetown.

Most owners owned fewer than five slaves, but a few had substantial holdings. George Washington Young (No. 345) claimed compensation for 69 persons, most of whom appeared to work as field hands on his farm; Margaret C. Barber (No. 366), who lived in Washington County, claimed 34 persons; Harriet White (No. 526) owned 21; Peirce Shoemaker was compensated for 20 persons (No. 494); Mary and Elizabeth Queen (No. 627) owned 24; Ann Biscoe, Angelica Chew and Emma Biscoe owned 26; Peter Vonessen (No. 153) owned 20; Catherine Pearson (No. 163) owned 21; and John Harry (No. 1) owned 28.

At least some owners evidenced a certain squeamishness and discomfort with the brutal reality of slavery. Usually they referred to their "servants" rather than their slaves in an obvious attempt to blur the harsh reality of one human being owning another. In several instances, owners asserted that they had purchased the slave solely for benevolent reasons--to prevent the person from being sold South (No. 414), to prevent the breakup of a family (414), or at the request of the slave to enable him to obtain his freedom upon repayment of his purchase price. Hilleary Offut (No. 203) states that for $400 he bought Maria Shiles and her child "to prevent the separation of said Maria from her husband and prevent her from being sold to a trader and carried out of the District of Columbia." Samuel A. H. Marks (No. 145) paid $1,875 to buy Basil Chase, Lucy Chase Magruder, and Lucy's child to prevent their being sold South by their owners; and John E. Neale (No. 170) paid $1,000 or $1,200 to buy John Lancaster to prevent his being carried off to Georgia. This does not mean, however, that the white residents of D.C. supported the emancipation act, even if it contained the compensation provisions. They did not.

EDITORIAL METHOD

The records of the Board of Commissioners for the Emancipation of Slaves in the District of Columbia, 1862-1863, are located in the National Archives where they are assigned to Record Group 217, Records of the General Accounting Office. The records have been microfilmed and the six rolls of film are available as National Archives Microcopy No. 520. The author worked primarily from the microfilm.

The entries in this book are abstracts of the petitions for compensation rather than verbatim transcriptions. Every attempt has been made to include all important information found in the original documents and, for the most part, to paraphrase closely in order to preserve the original flavor of the language. The documents have not been edited to clean up offensive expressions that were sometimes used to describe persons, although the author has made a concession to current practice in capitalizing the word "Negro."

The numbers of the petitions are those assigned by the commission and the index refers to those numbers rather than to page numbers. Information from the printed report has been integrated with the information from the petitions. The material enclosed in brackets at the end of each petition regarding the disposition of the claims is taken from the printed report of the commissioners. The material in italics represents information or comments added by the author.

The index covers petitions 1-966. Appendix A, which is an alphabetical list of servants given certificates of freedom under the supplemental act of July 12, 1862, and Appendix B, relating to some 13 late claims, have not been included in the main index.

The reader needs to be aware that at this time the District of Columbia consisted of three separate jurisdictions: the city of Washington, the city of Georgetown, and the County of Washington which included that area not found in the two cities. The county was predominantly rural and farmland.

Some petitions are missing from the records. In such cases that fact is noted and the information given is that taken from the printed report of the commissioners.

SAMPLE PETITION

To the Commissioners under the act of Congress approved the 16th of April, 1862, entitled "An act for the release of certain persons held to service or labor in the District of Columbia."

Your Petitioner, *John Doe* of *Washington, D.C.*

By this *his* petition in writing, represents and states, that *he* is a person loyal to the United States, who, at the time of the passage of the said act of Congress, held a claim to services or labor against *the following three*

persons of African descent of the name of *William Jones, Julia Lee, and Tom Lee*

for and during the life of said *persons* and that by said act of Congress said *persons* were discharged

said *William Jones, Julia Lee and Tom Lee, Richard Washington*

were of the ages of *18, 35 and 38*

and of the personal description following:
William is 15 years old, mulatto in color and about 5 feet 7 inches tall.
Tom Lee is 38 years old, black in color and about six feet tall. He has a mold on his chin and a scar on his left arm from a burn. Julia Lee, Tom's wife, is 35, has a light complexion and is about 5 feet 5 inches tall.
They are all healthy and robust and of good moral character.

That your petitioner acquired *his* claim to the aforesaid service or labor of said *persons* in the manner following:

William Jones he purchased from B. O. Shekell in Washington on Jan. 1, 1850, for $850. A copy of that bill of sale is attached to this petition. Tom and Julia he inherited under the will of his father, John Doe, Sr., which was proved Feb. 3, 1857, and recorded in Liber J.A.S. No. 5, folio 66.

That your petitioner's claim to the service or labor of said *persons*

was, at the time of said discharge, therefore of the value of *$3,000* dollars in money.

William is a first-rate waiter and has been hired out at the National Hotel for of $20 a month. Value, $1,500. Tom is a good dining room servant. Value, $750. Julia is an excellent cook, servant and washer and ironer value $750.

Your petitioner hereby declares that *he* bears true and faithful allegiance to the Government of the United States, and that *he* has not borne arms against the United States in the present rebellion, nor in any way given aid or comfort thereto.

And your petitioner further states and alleges, that *he* has not brought said *servants* into the District of Columbia since the passage of said act of Congress; and that, at the time of the passage thereof, said *persons* were held to service or labor therein, under and by virtue of your petitioner's claim to such service or labor.

Your petitioner further states and alleges, that *his* said claims to the service or labor of said *persons* does not originate in or by virtue of any transfer heretofore made by any person who has in any manner aided or sustained the present rebellion against the Government of the United States.

And your petitioner prays the said Commissioners to investigate and determine the validity *his* claim of to the service or labor of said *persons* herein above set forth; and if the same be found to be valid, that they appraise and apportion the value of said claim in money, and report the same to the Secretary of the Treasury of the United States, in conformity to the provision of said act of Congress.

(Signed by)

No. 1, Petition of John Harry Filed Apr. 29, 1862

John Harry of Georgetown claims compensation for 28 persons.

1. Grace Butler, aged about 58, is black, of a strong frame but complains of rheumatism. [Value $100]
2. Martha [Butler], her daughter, is aged about 34, black, of good size and in good health. [Value $600]
3. Eliza Ann Butler, Grace's daughter, is aged about 20, black and in good health. [Value $800]
4. Walter Butler, Grace's son, is 16 years old, small sized, black and in good health. [Value $800]

Grace was presented to Harry by Martha Clagett of Georgetown, the mother of his first wife, when Grace was a small girl and she resided in his family until three or four years ago. The children were born in Harry's house.

5. Jane Coney is about 37, in good health, black, of small statue and was born in Harry's house of a slave woman. [Value $500]
6. Lydia Meredith, aged about 43 years, is a mulatto slave in good health. [Value $500]
7. Richard Meredith is aged about 25, a dark mulatto, about 5 feet 7 or 8 inches and in good health. [Value $4,200]
8. John Meredith, aged 23 years, is a dark mulatto.

Petitioner acquired his claim to the service or labor of said slaves in the following manner.

Grace Butler, Jane Coney and Lydia Meredith are explained in the body of this petition

Henrietta Crusey's children were all born in her own hired house in Harry's neighborhood and were always under his care and protection.

Petitioner claims a total of $16,100 in compensation.

Harry says that he has no additional remarks except that Lydia Meredith and her family, as well as Henrietta Crusy [Crusey] and her children, are among the most respectable and moral of their class. He has no knowledge of any other moral, mental or bodily infirmities or defects save those stated.

An attached copy of a bill of sale states that Harriet Williams of Georgetown, in consideration of the sum of one dollar paid by John Harry of Washington County, Md., sells to him one mulatto woman named Nancy and her five children: John, Lydia, Henrietta, Louis and Francis. The woman Nancy, Williams gave to her daughter Harriet Eliza, many years ago and she wishes to confirm the gift. (Signed, May 26, 1825, Harriet Williams)

[Commissioners paid John Harry a total of $8,168.70: Grace Butler, $43.80; Martha Butler, $350.40; Eliza Ann Butler, $481.80; Jane Coney, $219; Walter Butler, $306.60; Lydia Meredith, $131.40; Richard Meredith, $262.80; John Meredith, $569.40; Philip Meredith, $569.40; Lizzie Meredith, $481.80; Adeline Meredith, $438; Henry Meredith, $153.30; Alfred Meredith, $219; Charles Meredith, $43.80; Maria Meredith, $394.20; Kate Meredith, $87.60; Rogers Meredith, $43.80; Henrietta Crusey, $175.20; Eveline Crusey, $438; William Crusey, $569.40; John Lewis Crusey, $657; Martha Crusey, $438; James Crusey, $350.40; Anna Crusey, $306.60; Lydia Crusey, $219; Julius Crusey, $131.40; Frank Crusey, $87.60; Martha Crusey, no value.]

No. 2, Petition of William B. Kibbey Filed Apr. 29, 1862

William B. Kibbey of the city of Washington claims compensation for two female slaves.

1. Mary Lewis is an unmarried woman aged 40, tolerably light in color and most invaluable. Mary Lewis was purchased from George N. Lewis of Prince George's County, Md. [Value $500]
2. Anne Brown, unmarried, aged 18, is a very light mulatto. She was purchased from William Beckett of Baltimore, Md. [Value $500]

[Commissioners paid Kibbey $788.40: $306.60 for Mary Lewis; $481.80 for Anne Brown]

No. 3, Petition of Seth A. Elliott Filed Apr. 29, 1862

Seth A. Elliott of the city of Washington, submits a claim for his slave, Ginnie McPherson, who is a child of Maryland parents. About the middle of March 1861, he hired this little servant girl, who was about ten years old, from Mrs. Plummer, wife of Edward S. Plummer, who was then residing in the District of Columbia, at the rate of $20 a year. The money was to be paid to Plummer's sister because of money he owed her or services she might render to his family. Elliot was obliged to find proper clothing for Ginnie. Subsequently, Plummer, accompanied by his wife's brother, said that because of money difficulties, he wished to sell the girl.

The bill of sale states that Edward S. Plummer, of Maryland, in consideration of $300, sells to Seth A. Elliott of Washington a Negro girl named Ginnie McPherson. Elliott grants to Plummer the right to regain possession of the servant girl within 18 months by paying to Elliott $300 plus interest. Elliott is to remain in possession of McPherson until Jan. 1, 1864, upon the payment of $25 a year dating from Jan. 1, 1862. (Signed Apr. 15, 1861)

Elliott states that there is little chance that Plummer will act to regain possession of McPherson as he is out of the District of Columbia and Maryland. His family has not offered reimbursement either.

Ginnie is dark brown in color, healthy and cheerful. He values her at $370.

[Commissioners paid Elliott $219.00.]

No. 4, Petition of William Thomas
Filed May 1, 1862

William Thomas claims compensation for Kitty. She is aged about 47, black, short and lame in one foot because of a burn she received as a child. She is in good health and is a good house servant, cook, washer and the like.

Thomas purchased Kitty for $300 from Edward N. Roach, administrator of the estate of T. Elwood.

The bill of sale shows that Edward N. Roach, administrator of the estate of Isaac T. Elwood, for $300, sells to William Thomas of Washington, a slave for life named Kitty, who is about 43 years old. (Signed Mar. 9, 1858)

[Commissioners paid Thomas $219.]

No. 5, Petition of Benjamin K. Morsell
Filed May 2, 1862

Benjamin K. Morsell of Maryland claims compensation for William Dodson. Dodson is 32 years old, black, about 5 feet 10 inches to six feet tall and weighs about 160 pounds. He is strong and healthy. [Value $1,000]

His mother belonged to Morsell when he was born a slave in Washington and resided there since then.

Dodson has always been honest (?) . . . He has been in the employ of different bricklayers for . . . some 15 or 16 years (?). *The author is unable to read much of this document.*

[Commissioners paid Morsell $547.50.]

No. 6, Petition of Ann E. Beall
Filed May 2, 1862

Ann E. Beall of Washington submits a claim for Barbery [Barbara] Robinson and her son, Robert.

1. Barbary is 56 years old, dark brown in color, short of statue, stout and strong. She was bequeathed to Beall by the will of Mrs. Rachel W. Turner of Prince George's County, Md. She is healthy, able-bodied and capable of performing labor typical of most women her age. [Value $500]

2. Robert became Beall's property because he was born to Barbery while she was Beall's slave. He is 22 years old, dark brown, about 5 feet 10 inches tall and of a spare build. He is a sprightly man and has been employed as a waiter in hotels and boarding houses in the city at good wages. [Value $1,000]

[Commissioners paid Beall $438: $153.30 for Barbara Robinson and $284.70 for Robert]

No. 7, Petition of John E. Bates
Filed May 2, 1862

John E. Bates of Washington City submits a claim for compensation for Mary Finnick. Mary Finnick is about 18 years old, dark colored and about 5 feet 1 inch tall. She is a stout, healthy girl and has not been confined to her bed a day since he has owned her, which has been upwards of seven years.

Bates purchased Finnick from Alfred Richards of Washington for $350. She was then about 11 years old.

Mary has been in his family since Feb. 14, 1855. She is free from all infirmity and he has never had to call a physician to attend her.

The bill of sale shows that Alfred Richards of the city of Washington, in consideration of $350, sold to John E. Bates, a "coloured girl" named Mary Finick [Finnick]. (Signed Feb. 14, 1855)

[Commissioners paid Bates $481.80.]

No. 8, Petition of Noble Young, M.D.
Filed May 2, 1862

Nobel Young submits a claim for compensation for seven slaves.

1. Lucy Lancaster is about 46 and is the mother of the others. She is light brown, stout, able-bodied and healthy. [Value $800]

2. Henry Lancaster is about 30, dark brown, robust and powerful. [Value $1,600]

3. Nathan [*he is called "Matthew" at one time in this statement*] is about 24, dark brown, medium sized, able-bodied and healthy. [Value $1,500]

4. Rachel Lancaster is about 20 years old, light brown, of good size, active and healthy. [Value $1,300]

5. Henny Lancaster is about 18, light brown, of medium size, active and healthy. [Value $1,300]

6. Eliza Lancaster is about 16, light brown, well-grown and tall for her age, active and healthy. [Value $1,100]

7. John Lancaster is about 12, light brown, well-grown for his age, active and healthy. [Value $1,000]

They were all servants born in his father's family and were acquired by Young for a nominal consideration. The bill of sale is recorded in D.C. Liber J.A.S. No. 17, folio 163. They were his share of his father's personal estate.

Young says his estimated values are moderate market values, for the slaves are invaluable. "What peculiarly enhances their value is their strict & scrupulous honesty; cheerful and affectionate dispositions; willingness to work;

capacity to learn and fidelity." Lucy is an excellent cook; the men are perfect waiters and the girls know nursing (?), washing and cooking.

[Commissioners paid Young $2,737.50: Lucy, $219; Henry, $438; Rachel, $438; Nathan, $438; Henny, $525.60; Eliza, $372.30; John, $306.60.]

No. 9, Petition of Edgar H. Bates   Filed May 2, 1862

Edgar H. Bates submits a claim for compensation for his female slave, Adaline, who is held for a term of four years, two months and 20 days. Adaline is about 20 years and nine months old, dark chestnut in color; about 5 feet 2 inches tall, and is intelligent and smart. He is paying her $6 a month.

Bates acquired Adaline by the will of his father, Edward Bates, of Fairfax County, Va., dated Jan. 27, 1857, and recorded in the D.C. Orphans' Court. She was to be freed when she reached age 25. Adaline was born Jul. 4, 1841, and thus would have been free in 1866. She was a part of the personal property of his father and came into his hands with the consent of the other heirs and his brother, John E. Bates, who was the administrator of the will.

Adaline is mentally and physically one of the best servants in D.C. He values her at $300.

[Commissioners paid $87.60 to Bates.]

No. 10, Petition of Josiah Melvin   Filed May 5, 1862

Josiah Melvin of Washington City submits a claim for compensation for Sarah Taylor and her son, John Wallace.
1. Sarah Taylor is a black woman, 30 years old, thick set and healthy.
2. John Wallace is ten months old, well-built and very healthy and intelligent.

Melvin acquired title to them by his marriage to Maria (?) Louisa Williams of Prince William County, Va., who inherited Sarah from her father. Sarah's son was born while living in Melvin's residence.

Melvin claims $1,200 for the slaves.

[Commissioners paid Melvin $438: $394.20 for Sarah and $43.80 for her son.]

No. 11, Petition of Alexander Sword   Filed May 5, 1862

Alexander Sword of Washington, D.C., claims compensation for Rachel Truxson. Truxson is 35 years old, a copper colored and 5 feet 4 inches tall. She is missing two front teeth.

Truxson was willed to his wife, Mary E. Sword, by her father, Thomas Bean, in a will dated about 1830 and recorded in Leonardtown, St. Mary's County, Md.

Sword states that Truxson has been in his family for about 22 years and he has always trusted her as an honest and faithful servant. He knows of no moral, mental or bodily defect in her. He values her at $600.

[Commissioners paid $262.80 to Melvin.]

No. 12, Petition of Ann J. Brown   Filed May 5, 1862

Ann J. Brown of Washington claims compensation for a slave named Cecelia C. Stewart. Stewart is 19 years old, has a dark complexion, is about five feet tall and has short curly hair. She is very stout and is generally considered a good looking girl. She is healthy and has no moral defect. [Value $1,200.]

Brown purchased her for $600 from Alexander Maddox, Mary Jane Maddox and John Green of Washington City.

The bill of sale, dated Feb. 25, 1837, shows that Alexander Maddox, Mary Jane Maddox and John Green of Washington, in consideration of $600 received from William Brown of Washington, sell to him a Negro girl named Cecelia Caroline Stewart, who is about 14 years old. (Signed Feb. 25, 1857)

Ann J. Brown signed the petition with her mark.

[Commissioners paid $503.70 to Brown.]

No. 13, Petition of Sarah Jane O'Brien   Filed May 5, 1862

Sarah Jane O'Brien of Washington submits a claim for compensation for two persons.
1. Ellen Nora Bell is aged about 25, dark colored, about 5 feet 3 or 4 inches tall, healthy and a good worker.
2. Caroline Bell is a mulatto, six months old and in good health.

Ellen Nora was left to O'Brien by her mother, Susannah Armstead of Washington. Caroline is her offspring and was born in Washington.

She claims $1,200 for the two. Ellen Nora is young and healthy. She is a good cook, washer, and ironer and generally a good worker. Neither Ellen Nora nor her child has any moral defects.

[Commissioners paid O'Brien $394 for "Ellenora" Bell and $43.80 for Caroline.]

No. 14, Petition of James Tucker   Filed May 5, 1862

James Tucker of Washington City claims compensation for a woman named Caroline. Caroline is about 48 years old, tall and has a dark, almost black, complexion. She is a good house servant and a good cook and washer. She is healthy and has a good moral character. [Value $500]

Tucker states he purchased her in the fall of 1831 from the estate of John Adams, deceased. He does not remember the price paid, but the sale is recorded among the records of the Orphans' Court.

[Commissioners paid Tucker $197.10.]

No. 15, Petition of Joseph Harbaugh   Filed May 5, 1862

Joseph Harbaugh of Washington submits a claim for compensation for a female slave, Letty Carter. Carter is 39 years old, a dark mulatto, about 5 feet 6 inches tall, rather slim and tolerably good-looking. Her health is good except for a cough which is sometimes troublesome but not considered dangerous. She has had two children, but they are dead. Her physician believes she has a disease of the womb which will prevent her from having more children. She is a useful and valuable servant and he estimates her value at $500.

Harbaugh purchased her for $400 in 1850 from the estate of the late Col. William Brent.

John Carroll Brent, attorney and son of the late Col. Brent, testifies to the purchase by Harbaugh.

[Commissioners paid $350.40 to V. Harbaugh, executor of Joseph.]

No. 16, Petition of Sarah Boarman   Filed May 5, 1862

Sarah Boarman of Georgetown claims compensation for Rose. Rose is 23 years old, copper colored, with black hair, black eyes and is 5 feet 4 inches tall.

Boarman states that she purchased Rose for $200 about 15 years ago in Maryland from her brother to prevent her from going south because she was in Boarman's family. [Value $1,100]

Boarman says that she is poor and the hire of Rose was her only source of income. Boarman states that she was very much attached [to Rose] and freed her promptly. (Boarman signs with her mark.)

[Commissioners paid Boarman $438 by her attorney R.P. Jackson.]

No. 17, Petition of Samuel Drury   Filed May 5, 1862

Samuel Drury of the city of Washington submits claim for compensation for Mary E. Thomas. Thomas is 26 years old, 5 feet 5 inches tall, a bright mulatto and has black eyes and black hair.

Drury states he got her from his father's estate about 20 years ago and raised her as one of his family. He says that Mary refuses to leave her old home. He says that before the rebellion he was offered $1,500 for her. She had charge of the entire house and was often in charge of his money. She is very honest and has no defects.

[Commissioners paid $481.80 to Drury.]

No. 18, Petition of Hugh W. Throckmorton   Filed May 5, 1862

Hugh W. Throckmorton of Washington City submits claim for compensation for eight persons.

1. Lewis Scipio, aged 30 is light colored. [Value $1,200]
2. Solomon Ford, aged 29 is dark colored. [Value $1,400]
3. Henry Weaver, aged 26 is dark colored. [Value $400]
4. Patsy Jackson, aged 22 is dark colored. [Value $1,000]
5. John Jackson, aged eight months is light colored. [Value $100]
6. Dennis Weaver, aged 18 is dark colored. [Value $1,150]
7. Winney Ford, aged 16 is dark colored. [Value $1,100]
8. Joseph Ford, aged 15 is dark colored. [Value $1,000]

They are all very healthy and have no defects, except Henry Weaver who has a broken leg and is walking on crutches, but he is improving.

Hugh received them by inheritance and by purchase from his father, Mordecai Throckmorton, who died in Loudoun County, Va., leaving the Negroes to him. He paid his father's debts and thereby partly received them by inheritance and partly by purchase.

They are good workers and are free of defects, except for Henry as noted above.

[Commissioners paid Throckmorton $2,715.60: Lewis Scipio, $394.20; Solomon Ford, $525.60; Henry Weaver, no value; Patsy Jackson, $438; John Jackson, $43.80; Dennis Weaver, $569.40; Winney Ford, $394.20; Joseph Ford, $350.40.]

No. 19, Petition of Jennings Pigott　　　　　　　　　　　　　　　　　　　　　　　　　　　Filed May 5, 1862

Jennings Pigott submits a claim for compensation for Nancy Page and Evelyn.

1. Nancy Page is 17 years old, short, stout and has a dark complexion. She limps slightly, but this is thought to be from habit according to examining physicians. She is a pretty good plain cook and seamstress and a good house servant. She is in perfect health and has never had a day's sickness in her life, except for measles or something of the kind. She is also a good washer and ironer. [Value $800]

2. Evelyn is between six and seven years old and has a dark complexion. She is healthy, intelligent and very sprightly. [Value $375]

Jennings got title to them by virtue of his marriage to Anne E. Moseley (?) of North Carolina on Dec. 1, 1857.

[Commissioners paid Pigott $525.60: 394.20 for Nancy Page and $131.40 for Evelyn]

No. 20, Petition of Julia A. Bryan　　　　　　　　　　　　　　　　　　　　　　　　　　　　　Filed May 5, 1862

Julia A. Bryan of Washington City claims compensation for Mary Shields. Mary is 24, copper colored, about 5 feet 3 or 4 inches tall and robust. She weighs about 150 pounds, has a full suit of hair and is in good health.

Bryan acquired Shields by inheritance from her mother about nine years ago. She knows of no public record of her title and no written evidence because Mary Shields was raised by her family.

She claims Shields value is $800, and believes she could have sold Shields for that amount before the present rebellion. She knows of no defects or infirmities that would impair her value.

[Commissioners paid Bryan $481.80.]

No. 21, Petition of William H. Langley　　　　　　　　　　　　　　　　　　　　　　　　　　Filed May 5, 1862

William H. Langley of Washington City submits a claim for compensation for Minnie Ann Johnson. Johnson is 56 years old, dark colored and about 4 feet 10 inches tall. She is sound and healthy in every particular, has good features and a pleasant disposition.

He purchased Johnson from Judson F. Richardson of Maryland for $500 about a year and ten months ago.

Langley values Johnson at $800. She is a most valuable servant, of a sound mind, free from all vices and of good moral habits. .

Attached is a copy of a bill of sale signed Aug. 8, 1860, by which Judson F. Richardson, agent to John H. Sainsbury of Prince George's County, Md., in consideration of $500 paid by William H. Langley of Washington City, sells to him Negro women Minty as a slave for life.

[Commissioners paid Langley $131.40.]

In the published report of the commissioners Johnson's name is given as "Winnie" Ann Johnson.

No. 22, Petition of James Rhodes　　　　　　　　　　　　　　　　　　　　　　　　　　　　　Filed May 5, 1862

James Rhodes of Washington claims compensation for two persons.

1. James Crampton is about 45 or 50 years old. He is about 5 feet 6 inches tall, has a scar on his left hand between the forefinger and thumb extending two inches up his wrist and also a scar across the back of the fingers of his right hand. He is gray-headed and has a dark copper colored complexion. [Value $400]

2. Eliza Carroll is 13 years old, about five feet tall, of a dark copper color and short with a flat nose. She has a pleasant countenance and is large for her age. [Value $1,000]

Crampton was purchased from James Carbery, Esq., for $300 by a bill of sale dated Nov. 14, 1835, and recorded in D.C. Liber W.B. No. 92, folio 461. Eliza was born his property.

Rhodes has taught Crampton the trade of butcher. He is a good hand and does the work of a journeyman. If he was in business now, he would consider Jim worth from $12 to $15 a month. He is strong, stout and healthy and has no defects. He will have to pay $7 a month for a substitute. Eliza Carroll is a strong, healthy girl and has never had any complaints other than those to which children are subject.

[Commissioners paid Rhodes 613.20: $175.20 for Crampton and $438 for Carroll.]

No. 23, Petition of John Dickson　　　　　　　　　　　　　　　　　　　　　　　　　　　　　　Filed 5 May 1862

John Dickson claims the services of Andrew Montgomery, the slave of Watkins Addison of Georgetown, who was by him conveyed to Walter S. Cox by a bill of sale dated Aug. 6, 1860, and recorded in D.C. Liber J.A.S No. 203, folio 70, in trust to secure a note of $540 of the said Addison in favor of Dickson upon which Richard S. Cox was accommodation endorser. There remains a balance of $375.66 with interest on the debt dating from Apr. 17 and he claims that amount for the Negro.

Montgomery is black, 5 feet seven or 8 inches tall and 19 years old. He is strong and capable. [Value $1,200 or $1,500]

In an attachment Walter S. Cox swears that he knows the boy Andrew and that his mother was a servant for a number of years in his house and was partially brought-up there. They were both the property of his grandfather, the late Col. John Cox and Andrew was given by him to his daughter, the wife of Watkins Addison, and was always regarded as her property by the rest of the family. Andrew is a strong, healthy boy, very smart, understands cooking and waiting and all that pertains to household management. Cox thinks he would command as high a price as any house servant of his age. He does not think $1,500 to be too high a valuation. Cox says he was a trustee in the deed given by W. Addison referred to in the petition. (Signed by Cox, May 5, 1862)

[Commissioners compensated Dickson $375.76.]

No. 24, Petition of Mildred E. Ewell   Filed May 5, 1862

Mildred E. Ewell of Washington City claims compensation of $4,800 for the following persons.

1. Charity Smith is aged 29, dark-colored and of medium size. She is healthy and smart, and possesses every qualification for a desirable servant. [Value $1,000]

2. Eveline Moore aged 25, is of a dark color and genteel in her manner. She has an intelligent mind, and good disposition. She is a useful servant and a woman of unusual capabilities. [Value $1,000]

3. Benjamin Moore is 20 years old. He is a dark man, large and healthy, of a good appearance and character and has the capacity to discharge the most responsible position as a servant. [Value $1,600]

4. Sallie Moore is aged six. She is light colored and an unusually bright and healthy child. [Value $500]

5. Frederick Moore is aged four. He is light colored, has dark eyes and is strong and healthy. [Value $400]

6. Helen Smith is three years old, dark colored, rather small but healthy and smart. [Value $500]

Ewell says she acquired the slaves in 1848 from her parents, Jesse and Mildred Ewell of Prince William County, Va. She also states that she moved to Washington with her slaves from Virginia in 1851 and had the slaves registered in the clerk's office of the D.C. Circuit Court.

[Commissioners paid John Dickson $1,839.60 on Mildred Ewell's behalf: Charity Smith, $394.20; Eveline Moore, $525.60; Benjamin Moore, $613.20; Sallie Moore, $131.40; Frederick Moore, 87.60; Helen Smith, $87.60.]

No. 25, Petition of Fanny B. Ewell   Filed 5 May 1862

Fanny B. Ewell of Washington City claims the services of the following eight persons of African descent:

1. Fanny Martin, aged about 60, is a small woman of light color who is well and active. [Value $300]

2. Davy Martin, aged about 58 or 59, is a small man of dark color. He is a very efficient porter and has been a bricklayer for William Orme for the past eight years and has received good wages. [Value $800]

3. Moses Martin, aged 24, has a bright countenance and a pleasing manner. He is employed as chief cook at the Ebbitt House and receives good wages. [Value $2,000]

4. Louisa Curtis is 39 (?) years old and is an efficient servant. She has been sick but is now quite improved in health. [Value $400]

5. Frances Curtis is 17, light colored and lively. She has pleasing manners, a good disposition and character. She is a very good servant. [Value $900]

6. Margaret Curtis, aged 15, is light colored and a capable and efficient servant. [Value $700]

7. George Curtis, aged 11, is a small boy for his age, but uncommonly smart and useful. [Value $600]

8. Mary Curtis is dark colored, aged seven and healthy and smart. [Value $300]

Ewell acquired title to the slaves in 1848 from her parents, Jesse and Mildred Ewell of Prince William County, Va. In the winter of 1851 she and her slaves moved to the city of Washington and she had the slaves registered in the clerk's office of the Circuit Court.

[Commissioners paid $2,430.90: Fanny Martin, $43.80; Davy Martin, $131.40; Moses Martin, $657; Louisa Curtis, $350.40; Francis Curtis, $481.80; Margaret Curtis, $438; George Curtis, $219; Mary Curtis, $109.50.]

No. 26, Petition of Edward Deeble   Filed 5 May 1862

Edward Deeble of Washington City submits a claim for compensation for his female slave named Elizabeth. Elizabeth is a mulatto, aged 24, 5 feet 2 inches tall, stout built and good-looking. Her health has always been good. She had smallpox several years ago, but she speedily recovered and the only remains of the disease are the marks that usually attend from that disease. He knows of no moral, mental or bodily defects that impair her value.

He purchased Elizabeth on Oct. 5, 1843, from Eliza A. Hopkins of Accomac County Va. [Value $800]

Bill of sale attached shows that Deeble purchased Negro woman Milly and her child, Elizabeth, from E. A. Hopkins for $550 on Oct. 5, 1843.

[Commissioners paid $569.40 to Deeble.]

No. 27, Petition of George Bender — Filed May 5, 1862

George Bender of Washington City submits a claim for compensation of $2,900 for the following:

1. Caroline Wood is aged 29, of a light brown complexion with long black hair. Caroline was acquired by inheritance from his wife's father, Richard S. Briscoe, who died in Washington in January of 1843. He believes Caroline could have been sold two years ago for $l,000. She is a very waitress and is handy at all work.

2. Melinda Dyer, aged 42, has a dark brown complexion and short black hair. He purchased her in Washington on Nov. 21, 1843, from Miss Ann Briscoe for $800. She is an excellent cook.

3. Julia Dyer is Melinda's child and was purchased for $800 from Miss Briscoe at the same time and place as Melinda. She is 23, has a light brown complexion and long black hair.

4. Rose Dyer, daughter of Melinda, aged 17, was born in his house and purchased for $300. She has a black or very dark complexion and black hair. She is partially blind, but very strong and healthy.

None of the above is intemperate and they have no mental or bodily defects except as mentioned above.

[Commissioners paid Bender $1,598.70: 569.40 for Caroline Wood; $438 for Melinda Dyer; $569.40 for Julia Dyer; $21.90 for Rose Dyer.]

No. 28, Petition of Sally T. Mathews — Filed May 5, 1862

Sally T. Mathews of Washington City submits a claim for $2,200 compensation for the following:

1. Lydia Sampson, aged 36, is an intelligent looking mulatto about 5 feet three or 4 inches tall and of a slender build. She has a felling on one of her thumbs which somewhat disfigures it, but no other marks. [*A note on the front of the petition states that Mathews thinks Lydia lives with A. Moxley, a barber under Washington House on Pennsylvania Ave.*]

2. Jinney Sampson, aged 12, is the daughter of Lydia. She is a good-looking, copper colored girl, stout for her age and perfectly healthy.

3. Laura Sampson, aged ten, daughter of Lydia, is a bright mulatto, the usual size for her age and is healthy.

4. Gertrude Sampson, aged six, daughter of Lydia, is a very dark mulatto, rather stout for her age and healthy.

5. Maria Sampson, aged three, daughter of Lydia, is a very dark mulatto. She has had her back injured from an accidental fall and looks delicate, but is healthy.

6. Florence Sampson, aged 18 months, daughter of Lydia, is a fine, dark mulatto child and is healthy.

Mathews inherited Lydia's mother from the estate of her father, William T. Ringgold of Maryland.

They are valuable servants and have no defects except for Maria's back injury.

[Commissioners paid Mathews a total of $936.31 and J. H. Johnson, the attorney for A. Moxley, $49.19, as follows: Lydia Sampson, $350.40; Jinney Sampson, $284.70; Laura Sampson, $153.30; Gertrude Sampson, $131.40; Maria Sampson, no value; Florence Sampson, $65.70.]

An attachment dated Oct. 28, 1862 states that with regard to the award by the Commissioners, that $350 with interest is to be awarded to Mrs. Matthews and the remainder to the estate of the late A. Moxley. (Signed by attorney for Matthews and by attorney for Moxley.)

Articles of Agreement between Mrs. Sally T. Mathews and Alberry Moxley dated Apr. 16, 1862, provided that Mathews will sell Lydia Sampson and her daughter, Florence to Moxley for $100 in cash and a note for $150 payable on Jan. 1, 1863, and another note for $250 payable Jan. 1, 1864. It is further agreed that should these slaves gain their freedom by act of Congress that any money received as compensation by Mathews shall be credited to Moxley's account. Mathews also agrees to hire to Moxley the slaves at a rate of $2.00 monthly until the promissory notes are paid. (Signed Apr. 5, 1862, by Moxley (his x mark) and Mathews.) In a document dated May 20, 1862, Moxley designates John H. Johnson as his attorney to assert his claims under the act of Apr. 16, 1862.

The Washington Directory of 1860 lists Alberry Moxley, "col'd", as being a hairdresser at Pennsylvania Ave., near 3rd, with his house at 29 Jackson Alley. Sally's last name is spelled both with one "t" and two.

No. 29, Petition of Eliza W. Ringgold — Filed May 5, 1862

Eliza W. Ringgold of Washington claims compensation of $1,500 for her slave, Perry Goodwin. Goodwin is 28 and 5 feet 9 inches tall. He is very intelligent, of "good address". He is an upholsterer and is also a good rough carpenter and very handy at any kind of work. He has no known infirmity or defect.

Ringgold acquired title to Goodwin as a gift from her sister who is now deceased.

A note on the front of the petition states that Goodwin's residence is not known by the petitioner, but that he can be readily found, unless removed from the city, if the commissioners will notify her.

[Commissioners paid $569.40 to Ringgold.]

No. 30, Petition of Mary Ann and Henrietta Kerr   Filed May 5, 1862

Mary Ann Kerr and Henrietta Kerr, residing in Washington, state that they inherited a colored man named Robert Wilkinson from their father, the late Alexander Kerr, and that Wilkinson still lives in their household as a servant.

Wilkinson is about 70 years old and is still of much service to them in their domestic affairs. They will be compelled to pay him hire should he choose to remain with them or have to seek another servant in his place.

[Commissioners paid $32.85 to Mary A. Kerr and Mary A. Kerr, executor of Henrietta, by Leonard C. Gunnell, attorney.]

No. 31, Petition of Eglantine Randolph   Filed May 5, 1862

Eglantine Randolph of the city of Washington submits a claim for $1,000 in compensation for a bright mulatto girl, aged 13, named Louisa. She is very smart and a useful domestic. Randolph acquired title to her in 1858 upon the death of her sister, Affrays Beverly, in Richmond, Va.

[Commissioners paid Randolph $262.80.]

No. 32, Petition of Jesse Williams, Guardian   Filed May 5, 1862

Jesse Williams of Washington City submits a claim for $1,200 for Sophronia Chase. Chase is 28, dark brown in color, 5 feet 6 inches tall and of quite "prepossing" appearance. She has no scars of any kind. She is an excellent house servant, as well as a good laundress and faithful domestic.

Chase is being held in trust for his minor children by virtue of a letter of guardianship from the Orphans' Court of Charles County, Md. According to a copy of documents from the Orphans' Court dated Feb. 8, 1851, the appraised value of Sophronia was $700. Also attached are copies of guardianship papers from that court dated Dec. 30, 1850, that appoint Jesse Williams guardian of Joseph Williams, Ann Dorinda Williams, John Marsellas Williams and William Elias Williams of Washington, D.C.

[Commissioners paid Jesse Williams $459.90.]

No. 33, Petition of Elias Travers   Filed May 5, 1862

Elias Travers of Washington City submits a claim for $400 in compensation for Henrietta Queen. Queen is about 48 years old and is a likely black woman. She is a good house servant in his own family.

Travers purchased Queen on Feb. 2, 1859, from Alfred Richards of Washington.

The bill of sale shows that Alfred Richards of Washington, having received $400 from Elias Travers, sells to him Henrietta Queen, a Negro woman aged about 45 years. (Signed Feb. 2, 1859)

[Commissioners paid Travers $87.60]

No. 34, Petition of Rufus H. Speake   Filed May 5, 1862

Rufus H. Speake of Washington City submits a claim for $1,500 for Harriet Johnson, aged 30 years and three months. Harriet is of a chestnut color, about five feet five inches tall, with rather full eyes and tolerably thick lips. She has a strong constitution and is remarkably healthy. She has never had any sickness except the common childhood diseases such as scarlet fever, measles and whooping cough. Her front teeth are much decayed which is very perceptible when she laughs.

Speake states that he once refused $1,500 for Harriet offered by Samuel C. Wroe of Washington. She was a very honest, sober, and trustworthy nurse and house woman and a good cook. She has no defects except a toothache. She has been his cook and general house servant since July 1853.

His claim is based on the fact that Harriet's mother was given to his first wife in February of 1830 by his wife's mother, Mrs. Ann Vinson of Montgomery County, Md. Harriet was born a slave in that county on Nov. 15, 1831, and when Speake moved to Washington in 1849, Harriet came with him. He names several persons who can vouch for his title to Harriet: Joseph B. Newlin of the Metropolitan Police, George Stabler and William V.W. Weaver, his brother-in-law.

[Commissioners paid Speake $569.40.]

No. 35, Petition of Thomas Donoho   Filed May 5, 1862

Thomas Donoho of Washington submits a claim for a total of $5,500 for his nine slaves.
1. Selina Williams, aged 51, of a black color. She is sound and healthy. [Value $300]
2. James, son of Selina, aged 30, a bright mulatto. [Value $650]
3. Lydia, daughter of Selina, aged 24, a dark mulatto. [Value $1,200]
4. Lewis, son of Selina, aged 15 years and six months, a bright mulatto. [Value $1,200]
5. Marion, daughter of Selina, aged 20, a dark mulatto. [Value $1,000]
6. Gertrude, daughter of Marion, aged six years, a bright mulatto. [Value $400]
7. Laura, daughter of Marion, aged three, a bright mulatto. [Value $200]
8. Edward, son of Lydia, aged six, dark mulatto. [Value $400]
9. Albert, son of Lydia, aged 18 months, a bright mulatto. [Value $150]

Donoho states that he has refused to sell some of these slaves at prices above what he is claiming. They are obedient servants and have no mental or bodily defects, except for James who is slightly knock-kneed, but that does not impair his value to Donoho.

He purchased "Cline" and child in 1833. The bill of sale shows that Donoho paid $325 to Joshua Albert of Washington County D.C., for Negro woman Cline and her boy child named John Henry. (Signed Apr. 13, 1833)

[Commissioners paid Donoho $2,562.30, as follows: Selina Williams, $197.10; James, $569.40; Lydia, $438; Lewis, $438; Marion, $481.80; Gertrude, $175.20; Laura, $87.60; Edward, $131.40; Albert, $43.80.]

No. 36, Petition of Charles Vinson   Filed May 6, 1862

Charles Vinson submits a claim for $9,700 in compensation for the following nine persons. He acquired title to them from the will of his father.
1. Robert Meekins is aged 38, dark colored, about 5 feet nine or 10 inches tall, temperate and honest. He is now hired to a farmer in Maryland for the present year for annual wages of $100 and clothing. [Value $1,500]
2. Alexander Meekins, aged 25, black complexion is 5 feet 6 or 7 inches tall. He is a dining room and house servant of "No. 1 qualifications." He is temperate and honest. He receives wages of $10 a month and clothing. [Value $1,500]
3. Harrison Meekins is aged 22, black complexion, round face and full eyes and 5 feet 8 or 9 inches tall. He has been serving for some time to a married daughter in Maryland, but her title belongs to Vinson. He has been here since the middle of March. [Value $1,500] *This claim was later withdrawn after he wrote the Commissioners that Harrison was born in the service of his daughter and she claims him as a gift to her.*
4. Lila Powell, aged 70, has been serving as a cook in Vinson's family. She is not very dark, has regular features and a good face and is faithful and honest. [Value $300]
5. Phillis Noland, aged 39, is a washer and ironer in his family. She is 5 feet 8 or 9 inches, has a dark complexion, regular features, a good face and a "good personal aspect.". She is faithful and honest. [Value $1,000]
6. Basil Noland, aged 19, is a waiter and dining room servant now hired in a boarding house. He has a dark complexion and is 5 feet 6 or 7 inches tall. His wages are $10 (?) a month. [Value $1,500]
7. Milley Noland, aged 17, has a dark complexion and is honest in character. She is now hired out as a house and chamber maid at wages of $36 (?) a year and clothing. [Value $800]
8. Betsy Noland, aged 12, has a dark complexion and a handsome face and features. She is sprightly and intelligent and is a waiter and chamber maid in his family. [Value $800]
9. Hanson Noland, aged ten, has a dark complexion, good features and a good face. He is now [hired]out for his clothes and support. [Value $800]

[Commissioners paid Vinson $2,956.50, as follows: Robert Meekins, $372.30; Alexander Meekins, $569.40; Harrison Meekins, not allowed; Lila Powell, $21.90; Phillis Noland, $350.40; Basil Noland, $613.20; Milley Noland, $438; Betsy Noland, $350.40; Hanson Noland, $240.90]

No. 37, Petition of George Savage   Filed May 6, 1862

George Savage claims the service of Sallie Collins, aged 22. She is quite dark, over 5 feet tall, has a pleasant look when spoken to and is stout and healthful. [Value $1,000]

Savage purchased Collins from Mrs. Emma L. Berry of Prince George's County, Md., through her agent, William W. Hill, about ten years ago.

The bill of sale dated Mar. 6, 1852, shows that Savage paid $525 for Collins as a slave for life.

[Commissioners paid Savage $525.60]

No. 38, Petition of Mary Moore   Filed May 6, 1862

Mary Moore of Washington, D.C. claims the services of Harriet Hanson, a dark mulatto girl aged 16 ½ years. She is 5 feet 3 ½ inches tall and is rather stout. Hanson has no infirmities and she can read. She has black eyes and wooly hair. Moore acquired title by a gift from Patty Jenkins, now deceased, in July of 1849. [Value $800]

[Commissioners paid Moore $481.80]

No. 39, Petition of Thomas Carbery   Filed May 6, 1862

Thomas Carbery claims compensation for 12 persons.
1. Mary, aged 65, a dark mulatto. She is Carbery's faithful cook and is very valuable. [Value $1,000]
2. Sally, aged 45, a dark mulatto. She is a first-rate cook and house (?) woman. [Value $1,000]
3. Jane Minor, aged 30, black. She is a good house woman and good farm hand. [Value $800]
4. William, aged 43, a dark mulatto. He is a first-class farm hand. [Value $1,800]
5. Jane Scott, aged 25, black. She is a first-class house servant. [Value $600]
6. Sarah Prior, aged 18, a dark mulatto. She is a first-class house servant and seamstress (?). [Value $1,500]
7. Marcellus, aged 15, a dark mulatto. He is a healthy and willing boy. Cost (?) last fall $600. [Value $600]
8. Dominick, aged 12, black. He is a strong and healthy boy. Cost (?) last fall $600. [Value $600]
9. George Minor, aged 21, black. He is a very good farm hand. [Value $1,800]
10. Mary Bryan, aged 12, dark mulatto. She is a healthy and good girl. [Value $500]
11. Rose Scott, aged seven, light mulatto. She is a first-class (?) _____. [Value $400]
12. Mary Ann Scott, aged four, black, is a very strong and healthy child. [Value $300]

These Negroes are all honest, moral and correct (?). They are healthy and free from disease and have no moral, bodily or mental defects. A year ago they would have sold for $18,000 or $20,000.

Carbery acquired numbers 1, 2, 4, 7 and 8 by purchase as slaves for life. Numbers 3, 5 and 9 were willed to him by a relation. Numbers 6, 11 and 12 were born as slaves to him. Number 10, Mary Bryan, was manumitted by Carbery when she arrived at 21 years of age.

[Commissioners paid Carbery $3,295.95: Mary, $43.80; Sally, $109.50; Jane Minor, $262.80; William, $306.60; Jane Scott, $328.50; Sarah Prior, $438; Marcellus, $438; Dominick, $284.70; George Minor, $613.20; Mary Bryan, $120.45; Rose Scott, $219; Mary Ann Scott, $131.40.]

No. 40, Petition of Robert Prout   Filed May 6, 1862

Robert Prout of Charles County, Md., claims the services of Landonia and Charity.
1. Landonia is aged 17 years, black, about 5 feet tall and likely and healthy. [Value $700]
2. Charity is 13 years old, black, about 4 feet high and likely and healthy. [Value $300]

Prout acquired title by virtue of his marriage to Sarah Dyson of Charles County, who inherited them from her mother, Sarah Dyson of Charles County.

[Commissioners paid Prout $895.90, as follows: $525.60 for Landonia and $372.30 for Charity]

No. 41, Petition of Joseph Follansbee   Filed May 6, 1862

Joseph Follansbee of Washington County claims the services of Harriet Boyd and her son
1. Harriet Boyd is an unmarried cook and general house servant. She is about 40, dark brown and healthy.
2. William Thomas Clinton Boyd, her son, is about 11 years old a bright mulatto color.

Follansbee claims a value of $1,400 for the two slaves.

Follansbee acquired title by purchasing Harriet Boyd from Zachariah Hazle of Washington City on May 24, 1834, for $375. Harriet's son was born after Follansbee purchased her.

Attached is the bill of sale recorded Oct. 24, 1834, in D.C. Liber WB 52, folio 211, by which Hazle sold "Follansby" his Negro slave named Harriet who was then in the possession of "Follansby." The purchaser paid $50 at the time of the signing (May 24, 1834) and periodically paid the balance on the note.

[Commissioners paid Follansbee/Follansby $525.60: Harriet Boyd, $262.80; William Thomas, $262.80]

No. 42, Petition of Marinus Willett   Filed May 6, 1862

Marinus Willett of Georgetown claims the services of Harriet, who is about 26 years old. She is short, thick set and not more than five feet tall. She is solid and compactly made, full, strong and well proportioned. She is dark mulatto or copper in color and has a full oval face. She has no mental or bodily imperfections except the loss of a joint from one of her fingers some years ago by a bone fallon.

Harriet is strong and healthy and capable of most of the duties of household labor. She is the most efficient one for that purpose in his small family and she has been in his family for the last seven or eight years. [Value $600]

Harriet was purchased by his wife, Mrs. Sarah Willett for $250 from George Washington Young, administrator. At the time, Harriet was about 13 years old and the property of the late Mrs. H.M.L. Young. Bill of sale dated Aug. 3, 1848.

[Commissioners paid $438]

No. 43, Petition of Louisa Kearney   Filed May 6, 1862

Louisa Kearney of Georgetown claims the following:

1. Agnes Bennett, aged 22, a dark mulatto woman is about five feet tall. Her two front teeth are out.

2. Anne Bennett, aged five, a bright mulatto child, is about four feet tall.

Agnes was bought by her husband from Richard Mason about 1843 or 1844. Anne is the child of Agnes and was born since her mother was purchased by Richard. Louisa inherited them from her husband.

Kearney states that Agnes has been in her family for the last 16 years. She is a faithful servant who is honest and correct. Anne is a smart child to whom the family is much attached. [Value for both: $1,000]

[Commissioners paid Kearney a total of $569.40: Agnes Bennett, $481.80; Anne Bennett, $87.60]

No. 44, Petition of Thomas Carbery, executor of R. N. Boarman   Filed May 6, 1862

Thomas Carbery, executor of Ralph H. Boarman of Charles County, Md., claims the services of:

1. Maria, aged 56, a very fine cook and house servant. [Value $800]

2. Sey, aged 55, a first-class farm hand. [Value $1,500]

3. Stephen, aged 22, a very good farm hand. [Value $1,500]

These Negroes are of good quality and very valuable. Stephen was taken from the farm of Thomas Carbery in D.C. by the 10th Regiment Mass. Vols. and carried to Fortress Monroe, Va., about the time of the passage of the act to manumit the slaves in D.C. The estate of Captain Boarman will sustain a total loss unless the Commissioners pay for these slaves.

[Commissioners paid Carbery a total of $832.20: Maria, $131.40; Sey, $153.30; Stephen, $547.50]

No. 45, Petition of Margaret A. Goddard   Filed May 6, 1862

Margaret A. Goddard of Washington, D.C., claims the services of Eliza Jones, aged 18 years. She is about 5 feet 2 inches tall, stout built, light mulatto in color. She is healthy and free of infirmities. [Value $1,200]

Goddard inherited Eliza from her grandmother, E.A.C. Goddard, in Jan. about two years ago. She was valued at $1,200.

[Commissioners paid $$481.80 to Margaret A. Goddard by Francis M. Goddard, her attorney]

No. 46, Petition of Jonathan Prout   Filed May 6, 1862

Jonathan Prout of Washington City claims the following three men:

1. Isaac Brown, aged six, is small, active and intelligent. He is a good gardener and carriage driver. [Value $300]

2. Joshua Johnson, aged 55, is large and stout. He is a first-rate farm hand. [Value $500]

3. Henry Lee, aged 35, black, is large and stout. He is a good farm hand. [Value $1,000]

Prout acquired title through his wife who inherited them from her father, Thomas T. Gantt, of Prince George's County, Md., in 1839.

Attached is a statement dated Dec. 31, 1857, signed by Jon. Prout and addressed to Mrs. (?) Kirkwood. Prout instructs her in the future to pay Joshua his wages directly. Prout says he sold him to Mrs. Thomas T. Gantt who, in consideration of his long services, set him free.

Prout also says that Henry Lee has been living in Maryland for more than six months and that he was set free at the same time as Joshua.

[Commissioners paid Prout a total of $635.10, as follows: Isaac Brown, $87.60; Joshua Johnson, not allowed; Henry Lee, $547.50]

No. 47, Petition of Ann E. Robertson   Filed May 6, 1862

Ann E. Robertson of Georgetown claims compensation for Henry Burgess, aged 20, who is healthy and strong. Robertson inherited Burgess from her mother, Matilda Drummond, whose will is filed in D.C. [Value $1,000]

[Commissioners paid Robertson $481.80]

Matilda Drummond of Georgetown died Jul. 4, 1848. Her will provided that her daughter, Ann Eliza, inherit mulatto slave, Henny and her issue, who were to descend to Ann's children. See Wesley E. Pippenger, District of Columbia Probate Records. Will Books 1 through 6, 1801-1852 and Estate Files, 1801-1852 p. 322 and note. Hereinafter cited as Pippenger, D.C. Probate Records, 1801-1852. Ann Eliza's surname is given as "Robinson" in Pippenger's entry.

No. 48, Petition of Ann Robertson   Filed May 6, 1862
Ann Robertson of Georgetown claims compensation for Isaac Clark, aged 23, who is healthy and strong. [Value $1,500]

[Commissioners paid Ann Robertson, her x mark, $569.40.]

No. 49, Petition of John E. Carter   Filed May 6, 1862
John E. Carter of Georgetown claims compensation for the following:
1. James Thomas, male, aged 18. [Value $1,500]
2. Jinney, female, aged 15. [Value $500]
3. Winney Butler, female, aged 65. [Value $100]

All of the above are healthy and sound.

He purchased James Thomas on Oct. 13, 1855, for $750 from Henry C. Matthews; purchased "Jenny" from Robert C. Jones of Montgomery County, Md. on Nov. 27, 1861, for $225. He also purchased Winney Butler.

[Commissioners paid Carter a total of $963.60, as follows: James Thomas, $569.40; Jinney, $394.20; Winney Butler, no value]

The attached bill of sale for Jimmy gives the date of the sale as Nov. 13, 1855.

No. 50, Petition of John M. Williams   Filed May 6, 1862
John M. Williams of Georgetown claims compensation for Nace Claxton. Claxton is 58 years old and is in sound health with a good body and mind. [Value $400]

Williams purchased Claxton for $600 about 20 years ago.

[Commissioners paid Williams $87.60]

No. 51, Petition of Charles Myers   Filed May 6, 1862
Charles Myers of Georgetown claims compensation for the following.
1. Henrietta Young is aged 35 years. [Value $600]
2. Henry Young, aged 14 years, is the son of Henrietta. [Value $600]

Myers states that he purchased Henrietta Young and that her child was born after the purchase.

[Commissioners paid Myers a total of $810.30: Henrietta Young, $372.30; Henry Young, $438]

No. 52, Petition of John Davidson   Filed May 6, 1862
John Davidson of Georgetown claims compensation for the following 15 persons:
1. Grace Digges, aged about 62 years. [Value $200]
2. Wesley Digges, aged about 23 years. [Value $1,000]
3. Charles Tilman, aged about 47 years. [Value $300]
4. July, or Juliet, Tilman, aged 24 years. [Value $600]
5. John Tilman, aged about six years. [Value $400]
6. Eliza Tilman, aged two years. [Value $200]
7. John Carter, aged about 25 years. [Value $1,000]
8. Andrew Carter, aged about 22 years. [Value $1,000]
9. Robert Carter, aged about 15 years. [Value $600]
10. William Carter, aged about 10 years. [Value $500]
11. Susan Green, about 25 years. [Value $600]
12. Ann Green, aged about 11 years. [Value $500]
13. Samuel Green, aged about nine years. [Value $500]
14. Mary Green, aged about five years. [Value $200]
15. Martha Green, aged about 10 months. [$100]

All of the above are healthy and sound in their limbs. Davidson purchased their parents and the children were born since that time.

[Commissioners paid Davidson $4,270.50: Wesley Digges, $613.20; John Carter, $569.40; Andrew Carter, $525.60; Robert Carter, $394.20; William Carter, $262.80; Samuel Green, $219; John Tilman, $131.40; Charles Tilman, $87.60; Grace Digges, $43.80; July Tilman, $481.80; Susan Green, $481.80; Ann Green, $262.80; Mary Green, $87.60; Martha Green, $43.80; Eliza Tilman, $65.70.]

No. 53, Petition of Thomas B. Dawson   Filed May 6, 1862

Thomas B. Dawson of Alexandria County, Va., claims compensation for two persons.
1. Maria Jenkins, aged 40 years. [Value $800]
2. Henrietta Jenkins, aged 38 years. [Value $800]

The above persons are healthy and sound. Dawson acquired them by the will of Mrs. Elizabeth Dawson of Montgomery County, Md.

[Commissioners paid Dawson a total of $613.20: Maria Jenkins, $262.80; Henrietta Jenkins, $350.40]

No. 54, Petition of Drusilla Gray   Filed May 6, 1862

Drusilla Gray of Georgetown claims compensation for four persons.
1. Eliza Evans, aged about 22 years. [Value $600]
2. Juliet Parker, aged about 17 years. [Value $600]
3. Alexander Evans, aged about nine years. [Value $300]
4. Sally Evans, aged about three years. [Value $100]

All of the above are healthy and sound. They came to Gray by partition of her late husband's (Benjamin Gray of Maryland) property.

[Commissioners paid Gray by her attorney, R. P. Jackson, a total of $1,204.50: Eliza Evans, $481.80; Juliet Parker, $438; Alexander Evans, $197.10; Sally Evans, $87.60]

No. 55, Petition of Jenkin Thomas   Filed May 6, 1862

Jenkin Thomas of Georgetown claims compensation for his female slave, Priscilla, who is about 60 years old. Priscilla is sound in body limbs. [Value $100]

Thomas purchased Priscilla for $250 from Henry Trunnell. Trunnell had purchased Negro woman Priss from Robert Evans for $175 on Jun. 18, 1838.

[Commissioners paid Thomas by his attorney, R. P. Jackson, $43.80]

No. 56, Petition of Benjamin J. Fenwick   Filed May 6, 1862

Benjamin J. Fenwick of Washington County claims compensation for four slaves.
1. Joseph Shorter, a blacksmith, unmarried, aged about 42, of a dark copper color. He is healthy, but lamed (?) in both arms (?), but this does not prevent him from working. [Value $540]
2. Michael Shorter, field hand, unmarried, aged about 38, healthy, of a bright yellow color. [Value $540]
3. Charles Shorter, field hand, married, aged about 36, healthy, of a light copper color. [Value $540]
4. Isaac Shorter, field hand and gardener, married, about 34 years old, healthy, of a light copper color. [Value $540]
5. Nancy Lee, cook and general house servant, married, aged about 40, healthy, of a light copper color. [Value $540]

Fenwick got title to the above slaves through acquisition of their mother, Nancy Shorter, who was presented to him by his uncle, Rev. Notley Young of Washington City.

[The Commissioners paid Fenwick a total of $1,927.20: Joseph Shorter, $262.80; Michael Shorter, $394.20; Charles Shorter, $438; Isaac Shorter, $569.40; Nancy Lee, $262.80]

No. 57, Petition of Sarah Ann Beall   Filed May 6, 1862

Mrs. Sarah Ann Beall of Washington claims compensation for two slaves.
1. Ann Velinda Henderson, aged 45, of a chestnut color, 5 feet tall. She has a scar from a burn on her left arm above the elbow. She is an old and faithful servant and Beall could not fill her place.
2. John Randoy, aged 18, black, 5 feet 7 inches tall, with a scar on his right ankle. He is a truthful and faithful servant who is always honest and correct.

Beall purchased them 11 years ago from the sale of her late husband and paid $750 for the woman and $375 for the boy. The bill of sale is recorded in Rockville, Md.

[Commissioners paid Beall a total of $700.80: $175.20 for Ann "Verlinda"; $525.60 for John Randoy.]

No. 58, Petition of James N. Ball
Filed May 6, 1862

James N. Ball of Washington claims compensation for slave Sallie Soper. She is an old and faithful servant whom Ball can trust with any thing and his family is much attached to her. Soper is sound and healthy and has no moral, mental or bodily infirmities. She is 57 years old, of a dark chestnut color, 4 feet 9 inches tall, with round shoulders. [Value $300]

Ball's wife was given Soper by the D.C. Orphans' Court with the distribution of the personal property of her husband, the late Reuben Brown.

[Commissioners paid Ball $43.80.]

No. 59, Petition of David Rawlings
Filed May 6, 1862

David Rawlings of Washington City claims compensation for six persons.

1. Minty Colbert, aged 65, black, 5 feet 2 inches tall.
2. Adeline Jones, aged 37, black, 5 feet 4 inches tall. She has been in Rawlings' family for about ten years and is healthy, capable and particularly valuable. The four named below are her children.
3. Martha Bowman, aged ten, dark, 4 feet 6 inches tall.
4. Julia Jones, aged eight and one-half years, mulatto, 4 feet 1 inch tall.
5. Christiana Jones, black, aged six years seven months, 3 feet 5 inches tall.
6. Caroline Jones, black, aged six years seven months, 3 feet 6 inches tall.

Rawlings purchased Colbert by a bill of sale dated Feb. 11, 1853, for $125 from James G. Webster of Prince George's County, Md. He purchased Adeline Jones and her child for $650 from John C. Thompson in a document dated Mar. 31, 1853.

[Commissioners paid Rawlings $1051.20: Colbert, no value; Adeline Jones, $306.60; Martha Bowman, $262.80; Julia Jones, $219; Christiana Jones, $131.40; Caroline Jones, $131.40.]

No. 60, Petition of John H. Wise
Filed May 6, 1862

John H. Wise of Washington City claims compensation for Susan Brown, aged about 55, black, about medium height and healthy. She is a good house servant and Wise pays her $5 a month for her services. [Value $300]

Wise purchased her in Alexandria City about 30 months ago.

[Commissioners paid Wise $65.70.]

No. 61, Petition of Henry Hatton, colored
Filed May 6, 1862

Henry Hatton of Prince George's County, Md., claims compensation for three persons.

1. Martha Hatton, aged 24, mulatto, medium height. She is an excellent seamstress.
2. Henry Hatton, 22, dark, tall and stout. He is a good blacksmith.
3. George Hatton, 19, mulatto, medium height and stout. He is an excellent servant.

Elsworth Bayne of Prince George's County, for $120 paid by Henry Hatton of Washington City, sold to him a girl named Martha, aged about three, and a boy named Henry, aged about ten months. (Signed Nov. 13, 1841)

A bill of sale dated Jun. 23, 1847, shows that Henry Hatton paid $100 to purchase his son, George, about three years old, from Elsworth Bayne.

[Commissioners paid Hatton $1,839.60: Martha Hatton, $569.40; Henry Hatton, $700.80; George Hatton, $569.40.]

No. 62, Petition of Thomas Scrivener

Thomas Scrivener of Washington City claims compensation for two slaves.

1. Linda Harris, aged about 30, of an olive brown complexion, with a full suit of hair. She is free spoken and intelligent. She has been in his family 21 years and is intelligent, honest and has been carefully taught. She is an excellent cook, washerwoman or nurse. During the past year she has had occasional attacks of rheumatism and at intervals is troubled with weakness of the breast, but has never been compelled to abandon her usual duties. Linda was assessed on the books of Washington City for $600 in 1861. [Value $800]

2. Edward Maddox, aged about 17, of a very dark complexion, with a long and narrow head and face. He has

short knotty hair and is slow in speech. For the past three years he has been taught and employed as an assistant in Scrivener's store and for general domestic purposes. He is intelligent and trustworthy, strong and healthy. He was assessed on the books of Washington City for $600 in 1861. [Value $1,000]

Both still voluntarily live in Scrivener's house at 16 A St., North Capitol Hill, where they may be inspected or summoned.

Scrivener purchased Harris on Jul. 15, 1840, for $200 as recorded in D.C. Liber W.B. No. 80, folios 73-74. He purchased Maddox on Jul. 26, 1859, from Sarah Ann Landreth for $300 as recorded in D.C. Liber J.A.S. No. 189, folio 37.

[Commissioners paid Thomas "Scrivenner" Jr., attorney for Thomas "Scrivenner", $766.50: $306.60 for Linda Harris; $459.90 for Edward Maddox.]

Boyd's Directory for 1864, p. 245, shows that Scrivener had a grocery on Delaware Ave. on Capitol Hill.

No. 63, Petition of Benjamin Berry   Filed May 6, 1862

Benjamin Berry claims compensation for four slaves.

1. Ann Williams is a black woman who is 65 years old. She is slightly lame from corns and one of her upper teeth is missing. She is a good cook and washer and quite sound for her age, except for the corns. [Value $200]

2. Louisa Saunders is a light copper colored woman aged 19. She is a good house servant and perfectly sound and healthy. [Value $1,000]

3. Jack Saunders, light copper colored, is the son of Louisa and is two years seven months old. He is sound and healthy. [Value $150]

4. Albert Hollyday is a copper colored boy, aged seven years, who has a very flat nose and large eyes. He is a sound and healthy boy and is being raised as a house servant. [Value $450]

Ann Williams was acquired by marriage 40 years ago from the estate of William Sasser of Maryland. Louisa Saunders was bought at the sale of the estate of Mrs. Elizabeth Selby in June of 1855, in Maryland. Jack is the son of Louisa and was born while his mother was owned by Berry. Albert is the grandson of Ann Williams and was born while his mother (Eliza, since sold) was owned by Berry.

[Commissioners paid Berry $766.50: Ann, $43.80; Louisa, $481.80; Jack, $65.70; Albert, $175.20.]

No. 64, Petition of William T. Doniphan   Filed May 6, 1862

William T. Doniphan of Washington claims compensation for Lewis Diggs, who is 54 years old, a dark copper color, 5 feet 4 inches tall, with gray nappy hair. Diggs is Doniphan's only house servant and is trustworthy and free from any defects. [Value $500]

Doniphan acquired Diggs as the heir to his mother, Catherine P. Doniphan, who died in 1844. There is also a deed of gift on file in the Clerk's Office that he believes was recorded in 1840.

[Commissioners paid Doniphan $131.40]

No. 65, Petition of James Riordan   Filed May 6, 1862

James Riordan of Washington City claims compensation for Martha Ann Blaxton. Blaxton is 28 years old, has African features, is about 5 feet tall and of a robust form. She is a model servant with a taciturn disposition and is trustworthy in every way. She has always been treated as one of the family and they have confidence in her truth and honesty. No temptation would induce Riordan to sell her. Martha has been trained in the principles of strict morality. Her manners are pure and she does not associate with people of her color. She attends church every Sunday and accompanies her mistress to the communion table. She loves Riordan's children and is entrusted with the keys of his desk. [Value $800]

Riordan acquired title to Blaxton from his father-in-law, Bartholomew Rochfort, Esq., of Alexandria, which was then in the District of Columbia. Martha was born in Rochfort's home of his domestic slaves Joe and Eliza Blaxston, who were in lawful wedlock. Martha Anne was presented by Rochfort to Riordan's wife after her marriage and has continued to live with the family since that time, which is about 20 years.

[Commissioners paid Riordan $481.80.]

No. 66, Petition of Lucy A. M. Counselman, now Connell   Filed May 6, 1862

Lucy A. M. Counselman of Montgomery County, Md., claims compensation for Lucinda Martin. Martin has been living in Georgetown for the past two years and is still in that city. She is 24 years old, a black woman, 5 feet 2 inches tall, with large eyes and a wide mouth. She has been living out since a child and is a good housekeeper. She is healthy, has no defects, and Counselman has had no trouble with her. [Value $800]

Martin was willed to Counselman by her grandfather, Samuel Counselman, six years ago. That will is recorded in Rockville, Md.

[Commissioners paid William G. Connell, Lucy A. M. Connell, late Counselman, $$438.]

No. 67, Petition of George W. Cissel   Filed May 6, 1862

George W. Cissel of Washington City claims compensation for William Snowden. Snowden is about 66, a bright mulatto or copper color, about 5 feet 10 inches tall. He is able to work and is hired out at $100 a year. [Value $300]

George Cissel acquired title to Snowden by inheritance from his father, Thomas "Cissell" of Montgomery County, Md.

[Commissioners paid Cissel $65.70. George "Cissell" signed his x mark.]

No. 68, Petition of Marshall Brown   Filed May 6, 1862

Marshall Brown of Washington City claims compensation for five persons.

1. Henrietta Locke, aged 16, very bright, a handsome mulatto, healthy, is an excellent seamstress and house servant. She was born in the family of the late Jesse Brown and was purchased by Marshall Brown from that estate. [Value $1,200]

2. Harriet Ann Talbott, about 32 years old, of a copper color, is an excellent pastry cook and laundress. He has been offered $1,500 for her. Brown purchased Talbott about 15 years ago from James Gannon, now deceased.

3. Mary Ann Jackson is about 35 years old, copper colored, healthy. She is a valuable seamstress and house servant. Marshall purchased her about eight years ago from Charles Pic of Port Tobacco, Md. [Value $1,000]

4. Patty Simms, is about 60 years old, copper colored. Marshall inherited Simms from his father, the late Jesse Brown. [$50]

5. Jeremiah Jackson, aged about 60, is of a dark copper color. He was purchased many years ago from Slacum of Alexandria, Va. [Value $50]

[Commissioners paid Brown $1.357.80: Henrietta Locke, $525.60; Harriet Ann Talbott, $438; Mary "Jane" Jackson, $394.20; Patty Simms and Jeremiah Jackson, no value.]

Jesse Brown's will is recorded in D.C. Will Book 6. He was the proprietor of the Indian Queen Hotel and died Apr. 7, 1847. See Pippenger, *D.C. Probate Records, 1801-1852*, p. 311 and 311n..

No. 69, Petition of Robert E. Taylor   Filed May 6, 1862

Robert E. Taylor of Washington City claims compensation for Sarah Ann Chandler. Chandler is about 19, light chestnut brown in color, about 5 feet 5 inches tall. She is hale and healthy and has no defects. He has been offered $8 a month for her services. [Value $1,500]

Taylor acquired title from the will of Emeline Ward of Charles County, Md., to his wife, then Mary E. Nash of the same place.

[Commissioners paid Taylor $569.40.]

No. 70, Petition of Mary Ann Haslup   Filed May 6, 1862

Mrs. Mary Ann Haslup of Washington City claims compensation for two male slaves.

1. Casper Hauser Hopkins, aged eight, is 4 feet 2 inches tall, well proportioned and bright mulatto in color. [Value $450]

2. William Henry Snell, aged five years old, 3 feet 6 inches tall, stout built, and quite black. [Value $350]

Both boys are well-grown for their age and are healthy and sound. She inherited them from her father, Griffith White in Anne Arundel County, Md. The grandmother of the boys, named Delilah, belonged to her father and was given to her in 1810 and by his will of 1816 recorded in Anne Arundel County. While in Haslup's service, Delilah had a daughter named Amanda, who is the mother of Casper and William.

Attached is a complete copy of White's will that contained the provision that his daughter, Mary Ann Haslup, inherit a Negro girl called Delilah which she then had in her possession. (Will signed Jul. 10, 1816; proved Sept. 14, 1819, after White's death.)

[Commissioners paid $240.90 to Mary A. Haslup, by J. Waters Haslup, her attorney: Casper Hauser Hopkins, $131.40; William Henry Snell, $109.50.]

No. 71, Petition of Martha Manning   Filed May 7, 1862

Martha Manning of Prince George's County, Md., claims compensation for ten slaves.
1. Judy Harris, aged 50, stout, copper colored, 5 feet 3 inches tall, with gray hair.
2. Sarah Waters, aged 25, dark mulatto, 5 feet 5 inches tall.
3. Mary Clare Waters, aged 27, bright mulatto, stout, 5 feet 6 inches tall.
4. Lucy Waters, aged 12, dark mulatto, 4 feet 6 inches tall.
5. Mary Louise Waters, aged three, bright mulatto, 3 feet tall.
6. Charles Harris, aged 20, 5 feet 10 inches tall, bright mulatto.
7. Lorenzo Waters, aged seven, bright mulatto, 4 feet tall.
8. James Waters, aged nine, bright mulatto, 4 feet 3 inches tall.
9. William Joseph Waters, aged two, black, 2 feet tall.
10. Nicholas Bowie, aged 15, black, 5 feet tall.

Judy Harris was willed to Manning by her father, Henry Diggs, in 1813 and his wil lis recorded in Port Tobacco, Md. Sarah Waters, Mary Clare Waters, Charles Harris, Lucy Waters, Mary Louisa Waters and William J. Waters are her children and grandchildren who were born after Judy Harris was in Manning's possession. Nicholas Bowie is the child of Eliza Bowie and was also willed to her by her father.

All of the above are good, honest servants and Manning has never had any trouble with them. Sarah Waters has asthma. All the others are sound and healthy and have no moral, mental or bodily infirmities. [Value $8,000]

[Commissioners paid Manning $2,058.60: Judy Harris, $43.80; Sarah Waters, $394.20; Mary Clare Waters, $306.60; Lucy Waters, $240.90; Mary Louisa Waters, $65.70; Charles Harris, $525.60; Lorenzo Waters, $175.20; James Waters, $219; William J. Waters, $43.80; Nicholas Bowie, $43.80.]

No. 72, Petition of Jonathan Kirkwood   Filed May 7, 1862

Jonathan Kirkwood of Washington City claims compensation for two persons.

1. Laring Whitaker, aged 22, black in color, 5 feet tall. She is stout and healthy, but has marks from a severe burn she received accidentally some years ago. [Value $800]

2. Marian Whitaker, daughter of Laring, aged one month. She is black in color and healthy. [Value $50]

Kirkwood purchased Whitaker on Mar. 26, 1850, from P. H. C. Gittings of Montgomery County, Md., for $275.

[Commissioners paid Kirkwood $525.60: Laring Whitaker, $503.70; "Marion" Whitaker, $21.90.]

No. 73, Petition of Henry L. Abbot   Filed May 7, 1862

Henry L. Abbot, of the Topographical Engineers of the U. S. Army, claims compensation for Joanna Cole, called Alexander. Cole is about 27 years old, 5 feet 4 inches tall, of a bright mulatto complexion, straight black hair, dark eyes, slender with a good figure. She has no defects or infirmities. [Value $800]

Abbot purchased Cole from Mary Helen McLeod of Georgetown executed on Jun. 19, 1860, for $600 and a conditional agreement for the payment of $200 more. The sale is recorded in D.C. Liber J.A.S. No. 201, folio 1.

At the time of passage of the D.C. emancipation act, Joanna Cole was a fugitive from labor and living in Massachusetts. Abbot was deprived of his property under the terms of the Fugitive Slave Act of 1850 which should have led to Cole's return to him in D.C.

[Commissioners paid $438 to Abbot by his attorney, David A. Burr. Lt. Abbot was at the time in camp at Yorktown, Va.]

For a discussion of the legal issues considered by the commissioners with regard to those slaves who had absconded before Apr. 16, 1862, see pages 8-9 of the printed report.

No. 74, Petition of Thomas Woodward   Filed May 7, 1862

Thomas Woodward of Georgetown claims compensation for Rachael Day. Day is 20 years old, dark brown in color, about 5 feet tall. She is a good cook, washer, ironer and a good nurse. She is industrious, a good working woman and generally healthy. [Value $800]

Woodward acquired title to Day by purchasing her mother. Rachel was born in his family. He was offered $1,200 for her and she was assessed in 1860 at $800.

[Commissioners paid Woodward $525.60.]

No. 75, Petition of Edwin Colton   Filed May 7, 1862

Edwin Colton of Washington claims compensation for two slaves.

1. Archey Morton, aged 35, about 5 feet 8 inches tall, bright mulatto, fine features. He is active and very

intelligent and sound in every particular. [Value $1,500]

2. William, aged about 20, a bright mulatto, 5 feet 6 inches tall, well formed and of sound body and mind. [Value $1,000]

Colton states that he acquired the persons by a bill of sale "hereto annexed to this petition."

An attached document, dated Jan. 1, 1862, Washington City, provides that J. C. Cook on Jan. 1, 1863, pay Colton $300 for the time of Negro man Archy Morton and boy William, together with good and sufficient clothing and board.

[Commissioners paid Colton $1,051.20: Archy Morton, $481.80, William, $569.40.]

The document attached to the petition relates to the hiring out of Archy and William by Colton, not his purchase of the two men. How Colton acquired title to the men is not stated.

No. 76, Petition of Thomas Talbert   Filed May 7, 1862

Thomas Talbert of D.C. claims compensation for four persons.

1. Harriet Williams, aged 27, mulatto, 5 feet 3½ inches tall. She is a good house servant, cook, ironer and washer. She is strong and healthy. [Value $900]

2. Mary Sophia is aged six years, copper colored, 3 feet 9 inches tall. She is the child of Harriet Williams and is strong and healthy. [Value $500]

3. Caroline, copper colored, is aged three years. She is the child of Harriet Williams and is strong and healthy. [Value $200]

4. Charles Brown, a black man, is 19 years old and six feet tall. He is a house servant and field hand and is strong and healthy. [Value $1,400]

Talbert acquired title to Harriet Williams in 1827 from his father, Thomas Talbert, as provided by his father's will, recorded in D.C. Will Book J. H. B. No. 1, folio 434. The two girls were born to Harriet after she became his property. Charles Brown was born of Eliza, a slave woman whom he purchased from Francis Mullikin.

The attached bill of sale signed by Francis Mullikin indicates that Talbert paid him $180 for Negro woman Eliza to serve him nine years. Dated Jan. 8, 18 (?).

[Commissioners paid Talbert $1,314: Harriet Williams, $481.80; Mary Sophia Brown, $153.30; Caroline Brown, $65.70; Charles Brown, $613.20]

The printed report of the Commissioners spells Thomas's surname as "Talbertt", but the original documents give it as "Talbert." Also the printed report gives the surname "Brown" to Mary Sophia and Caroline, although no surnames for them are given in the original documents.

See Pippenger, D.C. Probate Records, 1801-1852, p. 139 for the will of Thomas "Talburt" dated Mar. 21, 1827. In that document Talburt directs that his executor is "to sell slave Harriot and her offspring to her husband, Stepney Marlow, a man of color, at a price at which they are appraised."

No. 77, Petition of Anna Bradley   Filed May 7, 1862

Anna Bradley, widow of Phinious Bradley, of Washington City, claims compensation for two persons.

1. William Richardson is 29 years and three months old, very black and has black hair that is short and curly. He is about 5 feet 10 inches tall, rather slender and of good appearance and manners. He has no scars or marks and is sound and healthy. He is a good cart driver and has been hired out as such by Bradley. He has, however, not been seen by Bradley since January 1862, and she does not know where he is. She believes, however, that he is in Washington where he has lived since his birth. [Value $800]

2. James Richardson, brother of William, aged 26 years and eleven months, is copper colored with black hair. He is about 5 feet 8 or 9 inches tall and compactly built. He has regular teeth and remarkably fine features and the impression of his countenance is intelligent and agreeable. He has good mental capacity and is polite with well-bred manners. He is sound and healthy. He is an excellent waiter or dining room servant and he is hired to Mrs. Holman, who keeps a fashionable boarding house in this city. [Value $1,000]

Bradley acquired title from her mother. William and James's great-grandmother, Patty, was a slave of Bradley's mother, Elizabeth Ann King, long since deceased. Her mother acquired Patty from John Hammond, her father, late of Annapolis, Md. Bradley states that she also became the owner of Jenny, the daughter, and of Mary, the granddaughter of Patty. Mary was the mother of William and James and thus they have belonged to Bradley since their birth.

[Commissioners paid James E. McDonald, adm'r of Anna Bradley, $1,138.80: William Richardson, $525.60; James Richardson, $613.20]

Boyd's City Directory for 1864 shows that a "Mrs. E. Holmead" keeps a boarding house in Washington.

No. 78, Petition of Perry E. Brocchus   Filed May 7, 1862

Perry E. Brocchus of Washington City, temporarily, claims compensation for Rachel Gardner, aged about 28 years. Gardner is very dark brown, of low statue, has fine physical structure and is stout, but not fat. She is of pleasant address, agile motion, strong constitution and fine health. She is a very superior cook and excellent laundress. She is industrious, amiable, honest, truthful and trustworthy. She is of superior intelligence and sagacity for one in her condition and in every respect has the qualities of a most desirable servant. She has no defects except the loss of a few teeth. [Value $1,000]

Brocchus purchased her twelve years ago from Mrs. Amelia T. Young for $360 in the city of Washington. She was in very delicate health.

Attached is a document by which Brocchus, in consideration of $669, assigns any compensation he may receive for Gardner to the firm of Rittenhouse, Fant & Company (Signed May 7, 1862) Rittenhouse, Fant & Co. assigns the above sum of money to Fanny W. Hall. (Signed Jun. 28, 1862)

[Commissioners paid $306.60 to Fanny W. Hall, assignee, by D.A. Hall, attorney.]

No. 79, Petition of James Walters, guardian of George D. Walters   Filed May 7, 1862

James Walters, guardian of George D. Walker, Howard County, Md., claims compensation for Caroline Bell, aged 16, nearly 17 years. She is black, about 5 feet 1 inch tall, large for her age and healthy. She is a cook and house servant. She is very valuable, strong, faithful, honest, obedient and intelligent. [Value $800]

The title is based on the will of Mrs. Mary Moxley that was admitted to probate about 1846 in Howard County. Caroline was born at Walters' residence and he has known her ever since.

Attached is a copy of a document dated Mar. 17, 1858, appointing James Walters guardian of infant George D. Walters.

[Commissioners paid $481.80 to James Walters, guardian for G. D. Walters.]

No. 80, Petition of James Walters   Filed May 7, 1862

James Walters of Howard County, Md., claims compensation for three persons.

1. Margaret Burley, aged 56, copper colored, about 5 feet 2 inches tall. She is a number one cook, washer and ironer.

2. Alexander Burley, aged 24, of a chestnut color, about 5 feet 7 ½ inches tall with a scar on his left cheek. He is one of the best house servants and waiter and is good-looking.

3. Maria Burley, now Maria Johnson, aged about 21. She is married to a man named Johnson. She has never given cause of complaint.

Walters estimates their value at $2,200.

Walters was given Margaret Burley by his father, James Walters, about 1828. The children were born after that time and are slaves for life. He has permitted them to reside in the city of Washington with his father for several years and they are well known in that place.

[Commissioners paid Walters $1,204.50: Margaret Burley, $109.50; Alexander Burley, $613.20; Maria Burley, $481.80.]

No. 81, Petition of Caroline V. Walters   Filed May 7, 1862

Caroline V. Walters of Howard County, Md., claims compensation for Jane Maria Bell. Bell is aged 18, nearly black in color, about 5 feet 1 inch tall. She is an excellent house servant, chambermaid, waiter or nurse. She has served (?) at her places without complaint and is trustworthy, honest, obedient and faithful. She has no defects. [Value $800]

Walters inherited Bell under the will of Mary Moxley of Howard County, which was recorded about 1846.

[Commissioners paid $459.90 to B. H. Brown and Caroline V. Brown, formerly Walters, his wife, by James Walters, their attorneys.]

No. 82, Petition of Caroline V. Spalding   Filed May 7, 1862

Caroline V. Spalding of Washington claims compensation for Angeline Barbour who is 36 years old. She is light brown in color, of medium height, well formed, sound and perfectly healthy. She is a first-class family servant and earns $8.00 a month in wages. [Value $1,200]

Spalding states that Angelina was a gift to her from her uncle, John J. Lambert of Prince George's County, Md., when Angeline was a small child no more than two or three years old.

[Commissioners paid Spalding $372.30]

No. 83, Petition of Samuel Norment   Filed May 7, 1862

Samuel Norment of Washington claims compensation for five persons.

1. Serena, aged 39, of a dark complexion and has a very pleasant disposition. She is hearty, healthy and intelligent. She is an excellent cook, washer and ironer, and is one of the most valuable servants Norment owns. She is the mother of the four servants listed below. [Value $1,300]
2. Truman, aged 12, is active, hearty, healthy and intelligent. [Value $1,000]
3. Alice, aged nine, is hearty, active and serviceable. [Value $600]
4. Sam is six and a most sprightly boy. [Value $500]
5. Louisa, one year old, is a hearty and promising child. [Value $100]

They are all of a dark complexion and free of scars or any defects. They were given to Norment by his father-in-law, Ulysses Ward, five years ago.

[Commissioners paid Norment $919.80: Serena, $262.80; Truman, $262.80; Alice, $219; Sam, $131.40; Louisa, $43.80.]

An examination of the 1860 D.C. Census (Vol. 2, p. 385) shows Samuel Norment, a lumber dealer, living in Ward 4. Listed in his household are the following free Negroes; Serena Stewart, aged 40, William Stewart, aged 45, Truman Stewart, aged ten, and Alice Stewart, aged six. Norment is living in the same house as his father-in-law, Ulysses Ward, a clergyman.

No. 84, Petition of Marial H. Williams   Filed May 7, 1862

Marial H. Williams of Washington City claims compensation for three persons.

1. Kitty Martin, aged 61, 5 feet 4 inches tall, copper colored.
2. Louisa Lee, aged 14, 4 feet 6 inches tall, bright mulatto.
3. Juliet Lee, aged ten, 4 feet tall, copper colored.

The above are all healthy and free of defects. The three are of a value of $1,400. Kitty Martin was inherited from her husband's estate and the children were born Williams's slaves.

[Commissioners paid Williams $657: Kitty Martin, $43.80; Louisa Lee, $350.40; Juliet Lee, $262.80.]

No. 85, Petition of Lewis Brooks   Filed May 7, 1862

Lewis Brooks of Georgetown claims compensation for Hannah and Rachel Ogle.

1. Hannah Ogle, aged 36. [Value $1,000]
2. Rachel Ogle, aged 25. [Value $1,000]

They are dark colored, sound, and in good health.

Brooks acquired title by marriage from the estate of James Davidson of Anne Arundel County, Md., about 20 years ago when they were children.

[Commissioners paid Brooks $1,051.20: Hannah Ogle, $481.80; Rachel Ogle, $569.40.]

No. 86, Petition of Eleazer Lindsley   Fled May 7, 1862

Eleazer Lindsley claims compensation for four persons.

1. Sophia is 52 years old, black, stout built, 5 feet 10 (?) inches tall, with black eyes and black hair. She is a first-rate cook and washerwoman. She is intelligent, industrious and has good habits. She has been troubled occasionally by a sore on one leg, caused, he believes, by a "too full habit," but she is now entirely well. [Value $500]
2. Charles Henry, or Osceola, is 21 years old, black, stout built, 5 feet 8 inches tall and has black hair and black eyes. He is intelligent, a good farmer, gardener, and carriage driver. He is sound and healthy. [Value $1,000]
3. Cecilia is aged 18, black, very large and stout framed, 5 feet 8 inches tall, with black hair and black eyes. She is a likely girl who is sound, hearty, and of good habits. She is a good cook and waiter. [Value $1,000]
4. Thomas Sidney, or Tecumseh, is unusually intelligent, active and strong. He is black in color, with back hair and eyes, and is 4 feet 11 inches tall. He is remarkably intelligent and very active. He is healthy and strong and has a good disposition and good habits. [$600]

Lindsley purchased Sophia from William McL. Cripps (?) of Washington City about 28 years ago for $300. Charles Henry, Cecilia and Thomas Sidney are children of Sophia and were born in his house.

[Commissioners paid Lindsley $1,620.60: Sophia, $175.20; Charles Henry, $613.20; Cecilia, $481.80; Thomas Sidney, $350.40.]

No. 87, Petition of Nathan C. McKnew   Filed May 7, 1862

Nathan C. McKnew of Washington City claims compensation for two persons.

1. Robert Thomas, aged over 50 years, of a copper color, is sound and healthy. He is an excellent house servant and coachman and has been employed by Mr. Fletcher near Georgetown Heights as his body servant at the rate of $300 a year with board and clothing. [Value $1,000]

2. Nancy Thomas, the wife of Robert, aged 45, of a copper color, sound and good-looking. She is a valuable cook, washer and ironer and an excellent house keeper. [Value $1,000]

McKnew purchased them from the estate of his father, Thomas McKnew, deceased, of Prince George's County, Md., about 1857.

[Commissioners paid McKnew $328.50: Robert Thomas, $197.10; Nancy Thomas, $131.40.]

No. 88, Petition of Augustus E. L. Keese   Filed May 7, 1862

Augustus E. L. Keese of Washington City claims compensation for Caroline Gray. Gray is copper colored, about five feet tall, stout, well set, broad across the shoulders and of a lively disposition. Gray is a house servant in his own family and is much liked by all the family. She has a good disposition and no defects of any kind. He purchased Gray for $700 in the city of Washington on Aug. 13, 1861, from Charles Wilson. [Value $800]
Attached is the bill of sale by which Keese purchased Gray. She was then 16 years old.

[Commissioners paid Keese $350.40.]

No. 89, Petition of Robert L. Teel   Filed May 7, 1862

Robert L. Teel of Washington claims compensation for eight persons.

1. Arilla Johnson, is 49 years old, a bright mulatto woman, 5 feet 3 ½ inches tall. [Value $600]
2. Charlotte Johnson is 15 years old, a bright mulatto, 4 feet 10 ½ inches tall. [Value $1,000]
3. Joseph Johnson is aged 11, a bright mulatto, 4 feet 3 ½ inches tall. [Value $900]
4. Charlotte is 25 years old, a bright mulatto, 5 feet 1 inch tall. [Value $1,200]
5. Louisa is seven, a bright mulatto, 3 feet 9 ½ inches tall. [Value $600]
6. Charles is four years old, a bright mulatto, 3 feet 1 inch tall. [Value $300]
7. Edward is three years old, a black boy, 2 feet 7 inches tall. [Value $250]
8. George is four months old, a bright mulatto, 1 foot 11 inches tall. [Value $100]

Teel purchased Arilla, Charlotte and Joseph from Mrs. Haxall (?) in Richmond, Va., eight years ago and paid $1,100 for them. He purchased Charlotte at a sale at Chesterfield Court House, Va., 20 years ago. Louisa, Charles, Edward and George were born of Louisa since he purchased her.

The above persons have been in Teel's family for several years and he has always trusted them and found them to be honest and correct. His entire family is much attached to them.

[Commissioners paid Teel $1,533: Arilla Johnson, $175.20; Charlotte Johnson, $372.30; Joseph Johnson, $219; Charlotte, $459.90; Louisa, $153.30; Charles, $87.60; Edward, $43.80; George, $21.90]

No. 90, Petition of John Thomas and Eliza, his wife   Filed May 8, 1862

John and Eliza Thomas claim compensation for four persons.

1. Martha, who is the mother of Susan, Rose and Henry, is 30 years old, dark in color, 5 feet 2 ½ inches tall. She is a very industrious and good servant who is able and healthy. [Value $1,100]
2. Susan, aged ten years 11 months, dark color, 4 feet 1 inch tall. [Value $600]
3. Rose, aged four years seven months, dark in color, 2 feet 7 inches tall. [Value $200]
4. Henry, aged eight years and nine months, of a dark color, 3 feet 8 ½ inches tall. [Value $500]

These persons were inherited under the will of Benjamin Taylor, deceased, brother of Eliza Thomas.

Regarding the amount of the claim, he states that they were valued a year ago in Alexandria for $2,500.

[Commissioners paid John Thomas and Eliza Thomas $788.40: Martha, $372.30; Susan, $197.10; Rose, $65.70; Henry, $153.30.]

No. 91, Petition of Maria A. Queen   Filed May 8, 1862

Maria A. Queen of the city of Washington claims compensation for Ellen Henson, aged about 48, of a dark copper color, 5 feet tall. She is a superior cook and washer and is sound in body and mind. Queen states that Ellen was given to her at the age of ten by her grandfather, Edward Harding of Montgomery County, Md., and that she has been in her service ever since. [Value $1,000]

[Commissioners paid Maria A. Queen, by E. F. Queen, attorney, $175.20.]

No. 92, Petition of Artimesia Bean   Filed May 8, 1862

Artimesia Bean of Washington City claims compensation for three persons.

1. Charlotte Ann Locke, 22, is a bright mulatto, about 5 feet tall, with her upper lip (?) high in the center. [Value $500]

2. Lewis Washington Locke, son of Charlotte, aged one year, is brighter in color than his mother.

3. Valinda Ann Duskin, aged 83 years, is black in color and bent with age.

Bean says the slaves belonged to her late husband, Benjamin Bean of Washington and she purchased them at the sale of his personal estate for $500 on Apr. 4, 1861. She says that Charlotte would earn $5.00 per month over and above what services she performed at home. Her child was worth in service nothing and Valinda is worth a great deal less than nothing, but still remains in Bean's house. Charlotte and her child have absented themselves since the passage of the act of Apr. 16, 1862.

[Commissioners paid Bean $503.70: Charlotte Ann Locke, $459.90; Lewis W. Locke, $43.80; Valinda, no value.]

No. 93, Petition of Isabella Cissel   Filed May 8, 1862

Isabella Cissel of Howard County, Md., claims compensation for Maria Green, aged 30, copper colored, 5 feet 3 inches tall, is healthy but has two upper front teeth missing. She is an excellent servant and for several years has hired out for $8.00 a month in Washington City. [Value $1,000]

Cissel states that her husband purchased Maria's other from Z. Cesil of Prince George's County, Md., and Maria was born her slave.

[Commissioners paid $394.20 to Cissel by Z. Jones, her attorney.]

No. 94, Petition of Sarah Jones   Filed May 8, 1862

Sarah Jones of Washington City claims compensation for 11 persons.

1. James Countee aged 60, copper colored. Jones makes no monetary claim for him.

2. Richard Wallace, aged 30, copper colored, 5 feet 10 inches tall, has a scar over his eye, is very healthy. [Value $1,200]

3. Thomas Seibert aged 25, mulatto, 6 feet tall. He is a valuable house servant. [Value $1,100]

4. George Jackson aged 21, dark brown, 5 feet 6 inches tall with a little cast (?) in the eyes. He is a valuable servant. [Value $1,000]

5. Charles Hues, aged 15, dark brown, 4 feet 3 inches tall, has a scar in his hand. He is a valuable servant. [Value $450]

6. Otho Hues, aged 13, dark brown. He is a valuable boy. [Value $350]

7. Louisa Seilbert, aged 23, yellow, is healthy and a valuable servant. She has twin children, aged six months. [Value $900]

8. Ida Seilbert, aged five, copper colored, 2 feet 3 inches tall. [Value $300]

9. Matilda Seibert, aged 15, copper colored, valuable and healthy. [Value $900]

10. Harriet

11. Kitty

Jones says that she raised them all, except for James Countee. Their parents were in her husband's family for many years.

[Commissioners paid Jones $3,525.90: James Countee, no value; Richard Wallace $569.40; Thomas Seibert, $657; George Jackson, $613.20; Charles Hues, $372.30; Otho Hues, $306.60; Louisa Seibert, $350.40; Ida Seibert, $131.40; Matilda Seibert, $481.80; Harriet, $21.90; Kitty, $21.90]

No. 95, Petition of Eliza G. Moreland   Filed May 8, 1862

Miss Eliza G. Moreland of Washington City claims compensation for four persons.

1. Leathe Stewart, aged about 62, five feet tall, dark complexion, stout build. [Value $100]

2. William Stewart, about 43 years old, 5 feet tall, dark complexion, tolerably well-built. He makes $1.25 a day

as a laborer. [$700]

3. Jerry Stewart, aged about 32, 5 feet 10 inches tall, copper colored, well-built. He makes $14 a month as a house servant. [Value $1,200]

4. Manuel Stewart, aged 13 last September, 4 feet 9 inches, dark complexion. He has been hired for $30 a year. [Value $700]

Moreland states that Leathe was a verbal gift from her grandfather in 1818. Leathe's children were raised by Moreland's parents while she resided with her parents. She believes that there is in Georgetown a paper signed by her father to the above effect.

[Commissioners paid Moreland $1,664.40: Leathe Stewart, $65.70; William Stewart, $613.20; Jesse [sic] Stewart, $613.20; Manuel Stewart, $372.30]

No. 96, Petition of Benjamin B. Burr — Filed May 8, 1862

Benjamin Burr of the city of Washington claims compensation for William Prather, aged 12, black, about 4 feet 3 inches tall. He has no defects. Prather is an active, intelligent, honest and industrious house servant and waiter. [Value $500]

Burr acquired title to Prather by virtue of his marriage last November with Sarah R. Offut, formerly of Montgomery County, Md. [Value $500]

[Commissioners paid Burr $197.10.]

No. 97, Petition of A. Richards — Filed May 8, 1862

A. Richards of Washington claims compensation of $1,000 for two persons.

1. Francis Ignatius Gardner, aged 45, medium size, rather stout. He is healthy except for an affliction in his right eye. He is a good brickyard hand.

2. German Ignatius Green, aged about 19, about 5 feet 7 inches tall, bright mulatto. He is healthy, active and good-looking.

Gardner was willed by Mrs. Elizabeth Montgomery to Richards' wife. Green was purchased from his father, Henry Green, for a term of ten years. An attached bill of sale signed Mar. 28, 1860, provided that Henry Green of the city of Washington, in consideration of $600 paid to him by Thomas A. Richards, sells to Thomas A. Richards and Alfred Richards, a servant boy named German Ignatius Green, aged about 17, and Henry Robert Green, aged about 15 years. They are to serve for a period of ten years dating from Apr. 1, 1860, after which they are to be manumitted and discharged from slavery. (Henry Green signed with his X mark.)

[Commissioners paid Richards $306.60: Gardiner [sic], $131.40; Green, $175.20.]

No. 98, Petition of Margaret Ann Peirce — Filed May 8, 1862

Margaret Ann Peirce of Montgomery County, Md., claims compensation for two valuable house servants.

1. Mary E. Dorsey, aged 23, a bright mulatto, five feet tall. She is healthy with no defects. [Value $1,000]

2. Rose Dorsey, aged 26, dark brown, five feet tall. She is healthy and has no defects. [Value $800]

Peirce inherited their mother from her grandmother's estate and she raised Mary and Rose.

[Commissioners paid Peirce $941.70: Mary E. Dorsey, $503.70; Rose Dorsey, $438.]

No. 99, Petition of Fannie Parker — Filed May 8, 1862

Fannie Parker of Washington claims compensation for Charles Gordon. Gordon is 35 years old, black (ebony hue), a little over medium height. He is a first-rate servant and has always enjoyed excellent health. He is assessed on the tax books of the Corporation of Washington for 1861 at $800, although Parker considers him worth at least $1,000. [Value $800]

Parker acquired Gordon as a gift from her father, George Parker, Esq., about 18 months ago, although there is no bill of sale or other writing with regard to this.

[Commissioners paid $306.60 to Parker, by George Parker, her attorney.]

No. 100, Petition of Lt. Col. James Edelin — Filed May 8, 1862

Lt. Col. James Edelin of the Marine Corps, of Maryland, claims compensation for Mary Brooks who is about 33 years old. She is black, about 5 feet 6 inches tall, stout, active and in perfect health. She is a very fine looking servant. She is an excellent cook, washer and ironer and, in early life, a good nurse. She is of good moral character, strict fidelity and reliability.

Edelin purchased her in 1843 from the estate of Alfred Jolson, deceased. Edelin states he purchased her at the earnest entreaties of her parents in order to save her from being sold South. No bill of sale or written transfer was received.

[Commissioners paid $438 to Edelin by Richard H. Clarke, attorney.]

No. 101, Petition of Ann Kelley
Filed May 8, 1862

Ann Kelley of Washington claims compensation for Laura who is 13 years old. Laura has a slender form, of a mulatto color, healthy, industrious and obedient. She is faithful and truth telling and Kelley has always had confidence in her. Kelley states that she relies on Laura for domestic comforts and attendance in her infirm state of health. She is Kelley's only companion, attendant and nurse both night and day. She is cheerful, perfectly healthy and happy to be with Kelley. [Value $500]

Kelley purchased Laura in Washington on May 12, 1860, for $400 from Philip Ratchford. The attached bill of sale indicated that Laura was to serve during Miss Ann Kelley's lifetime and then to be free.

[Commissioners paid $219 to Kelley.]

No. 102, Petition of Benjamin T. Thorn
Filed May 8, 1862

Benjamin T. Thorn claims compensation for six persons.

1. Emily Dison aged 37, dark in color, a likely person, excellent cook and washerwoman, and a valuable woman. She suffers from occasional rheumatism. [Value $800]

2. Ann "Dyson", aged 20, black, is a good and valuable servant. She is sound and healthy, except a little deaf. [Value $1,000]

3. Delilah Dison, aged 17, black, is sound and healthy. She is a likely girl and fine servant. [Value $1,000]

4. Thomas Dison, aged 14, dark in color. He is sound and healthy and a first-rate boy. [Value $800]

5. Benjamin Dison, aged eight, is sound and healthy. He is a sprightly lad and will make a good servant. [Value $500]

6. John H. Hawkins, aged 34, black, is sound and healthy. He is well formed, a fine man, and a very valuable servant. [Value $1,400]

The above persons are all well and are more than ordinarily intelligent. Thorn inherited them upon the death of his father, Alexander A. Thorn of St. Mary's County, Md.

Attached is a copy of a document dated Nov. 29, 1842, from the Orphans' Court of St. Mary's that shows the division of Alexander Thorn's slaves among his widow, and two children, Matild and Benjamin. Benjamin received Emily, aged 19, valued a $325, Younger John, aged 15, valued at $400, Ann, aged 19 months, valued at $75, and Lawson, aged 46, valued at $250.

[Commissioners paid Thorn $2,233.80: Emily Dyson, $240.90; Ann Dyson, $438; Delilah Dyson, $438; Thomas Dyson, $350.40; Benjamin Dyson, $197.10; John H. Hawkins, $569.40.]

The printed report of the Commissioners gives the surname of the six persons as "Dyson." For additional information about Alexander Thorn's will, see the original petitions.

No. 103, Petition of Edward Chapman
Filed May 8, 1862

Edward Chapman of Georgetown claims compensation for four slaves.

1. William Duffin, aged about 32, about 5 feet 7 inches tall, dark mulatto, rather bald. He is an active man in the prime of life and a first-rate gardener, house servant and waiter. [Value $1,500]

2. Polly Middleton, aged about 44, black, about 5 feet 3 or four inches tall and healthy. She is a first-rate cook and has an excellent temper and disposition. [Value $700]

3. Minty Middleton, daughter of Polly, aged 22, black, about 5 feet two or 3 inches tall, healthy. Under proper supervision she is a very valuable servant. [Value $1,000]

4. Winny Coates, aged about 40, black, about 5 feet one or 2 inches tall. Both of her feet were burned when she was a child. She is an excellent plain cook, a steady good servant who is trustworthy. [Value $800]

Chapman purchased the first three by a bill of sale dated Mar. 31, 1862, from Mrs. F. J. Dodge and the trustee of her separate estate, Francis Dodge. That bill of sale states that Duffin was employed by Walt (?) Godey. Winny Coates he purchased in 1853 from the late Jeremiah Orme of Georgetown.

[Commissioners paid Chapman $1,160.70: William Duffin, $328.50; Polly Middleton, $175.20; Minty Middleton, $525.60; Winny Coates, $131.40.]

No. 104, Petition of Dickinson Nailor　　　　　　　　　　　　　　　　　　　　　　　　　　Filed May 8, 1862

Dickinson Nailor of Washington City claims compensation for Nace Pitts, a black man about 40 years old who is about 5 feet 6 inches tall. He has no defects. Nailor acquired title to Pitts from John G. Lindsay of Prince George's County, Md., administrator of the estate of the late Samuel D. Lindsay of Maryland. The attached bill of sale from Lindsay to Nailor is dated Jul. 15, 1853. [Value $1,000]

[Commissioners paid Nailor $219.]

No. 105, Petition of Elizabeth E. Cassell, administratrix

Elizabeth E. Cassell, widow of John A. Cassell and administratrix of his estate, claims compensation for two slaves.

1. Milly Jourdan, aged 57, is black and about 5 feet 5 inches tall. She is strong and healthy and a good house servant, cook, washer and ironer. [Value $250]

2. James Dorsey, aged about 60 is a dark mulatto who is about 5 feet 7 or 8 inches tall. He is an honest and industrious servant and has been receiving ten dollars a month at Brown's Hotel as a servant in that house. He is strong and healthy. [Value $250]

John A. Cassell purchased Milly in Washington on Aug. 31, 1844, for $275 from William (?) H. Richards. He purchased James from Frederick J. Greenwell of Maryland for $225 on Dec. 22, 1853.

[Commissioners paid Cassell $219: Milly Jourdan, $87.60; James Dorsey, $131.40.]

No. 106, Petition of Coleby Young and Sarah A. Young, his wife　　　　　　　　　　　　Filed May 8, 1862

Coleby Young and his wife, Sarah A. Young, of Washington City claim compensation for James Newman, who is 16 years old. James is a bright mulatto, about 5 feet 6 inches tall, who is a valuable house or other servant. He has no defects. [Value $1,200]

Sarah Young acquired Newman as a result of the division of the estate of her late father, Martin Hogan of Logan County, Ky., subsequent to her marriage to Young.

[Commissioners paid Coleby and Sarah A. Young $438.]

No. 107, Petition of Christiana Larner　　　　　　　　　　　　　　　　　　　　　　　　Filed May 8, 1862

Christiana Larner of Washington claims compensation for two servants.

1. Martha Marshall, aged 31, of a dark color with dark eyes, 5 feet 6 inches tall, with no marks. She is an excellent cook, washer and ironer. Such a servant could be obtained at eight dollars a month.

2. Ellen Marshall, Martha's daughter, aged five, of a dark color with dark eyes, about 3 feet 2 ½ inches tall. She is bowlegged and very sprightly and is free of distinguishing marks. She was raised in the family and is very useful, being able to wait the table and do many things about the house. She could not have been bought for $600.

Larner values the above at $1,000.

Larner purchased Martha on Jan. 1, 1849, for a term of 15 years from Arian Tweedy of Washington City. Ellen was born during that term of service and is thus a slave for life.

[Commissioners paid Christiana Larner by her attorney, Michael Larner, $142.35: Martha "Marshal", $32.85; Ellen "Marshal", $109.50.]

No. 108, Petition of John T. Kelley　　　　　　　　　　　　　　　　　　　　　　　　　Filed May 8, 1862

John T. Kelley of Georgetown claims compensation for William James, who is held for a term of service of five years (from Apr. 22, 1861 to Apr. 22, 1866.) Jones is 31 years old, dark in color, and 5 feet 8 inches tall. Kelley purchased him at a sheriff's sale in Baltimore County, Md., for $450. Attached is a copy of a judgement of the Circuit Court for Baltimore County wherein William Jones was found guilty of larceny on Mar. 21, 1861, and ordered sold out of the state of Maryland for the balance of his term. [Value $450]

[Commissioners paid Kelley by his attorney, R.P. Jackson, $100.50.]

No. 109, Petition of Thomas A. King　　　　　　　　　　　　　　　　　　　　　　　　Filed May 8, 1862

Thomas A. King of Washington claims compensation for servant girl Rebecca who is nine years old. Rebecca is moderately bright in complexion, intelligent and useful in attendance at the table. She is sound and has no defects. King's wife inherited Rebecca from her father, Henry Garrick of Prince George's County, Md., and she has been in King's possession for upwards of three years. [Value $600]

[Commissioners paid King $219. Thomas A. King signed with X his mark.]

No. 110, Petition of Caroline Mackall Filed May 8, 1862

Caroline Mackall claims compensation for seven persons.

1. Maria Compton, aged 45, is the mother of Henry, William, Lizzie, Eugene and Clarence and the grandmother of Marlborough Wilson. She is a bright mulatto and is a first-rate house servant, cook, washer and ironer. She has been hired out by her former owner for ten dollars a month. Her general health is good but she has suffered occasionally from enlarged veins in one leg, although this has not interrupted her employment. [Value $500]

2. Henry Compton, aged 22, is a bright mulatto about 5 feet 10 inches tall. He is an orderly and well-behaved servant and is an excellent coachman. [Value $1,500]

3. William Compton, aged 21, is copper colored and about the same height as Henry. He is strong, able-bodied, and without defects, sober and honest. He is a good cartman and farm hand. [Value $1,400]

4. Lizzie Compton, aged 17, is a likely mulatto, tall, and of a very good personal appearance and healthy. She is a good house servant. [Value $1,000]

5. and 6. Eugene Compton and Clarence Compton, aged 12, are twins. Both are well-grown, intelligent and very helpful on a farm. They are orderly and easily managed. [Value $1,000 for both]

7. Marlborough Wilson, aged 9, is smart, sound and healthy. He is copper colored and well-grown for his age. [Value $300]

Maria and Marlborough are in the District of Columbia; the others are in Prince George's County, Md.

Mackall acquired title to Maria about 1820 as a paternal gift. The others are descendants of Maria.

[Commissioners paid Caroline Mackall, now Duvall, Matthew E. Duvall, $2,562.30: Maria, $175.20; Henry, $525.60; William, $569.40; Lizzie, $481.80; Eugene, $284.70; Clarence, $306.60; Marlborough Wilson, $219.]

No. 111, Petition of John P. Pepper Filed May 8, 1862

John P. Pepper of Washington claims compensation for two persons.

1. Sarah Ross, aged 56, is solidly and squarely built. She is dark brown or black in color and about 5 feet 6 inches tall. She is healthy, hearty, and strong and is an excellent cook. [Value $300]

2. Joseph Cornelius Dorsey, aged between four and five years, is a dark mulatto, about three feet tall. He is a sprightly and healthy child. [Value $200]

Pepper purchased Sarah for $250 on Jul. 7, 1859, from John B. Young. Joseph was born his property.

[Commissioners paid Pepper $175.20.]

No. 112, Petition of Christopher Cammack Filed May 8, 1862

Christopher Cammack of Washington claims compensation for George Burrell who is ten years eight months old. He is a mulatto, about 4 feet 4 inches tall, healthy and able to do the business required of him. Cammack purchased Burrell from John McKeldin of Washington, who owned his mother, on Oct. 21, 1853, and he has lived in Cammack's family since then. [Value $750]

[Commissioners paid C. Cammack, Sr., $284.70.]

No. 113, Petition of John William Woodward Filed May 8, 1862

John William Woodward of Washington claims compensation for Virginia Napa. She is 12 or 13 years old, dark copper in color and 4 feet 4 ½ inches tall. She is honest and industrious and has been brought up as a dining room servant. She is generally useful about the house and has no infirmities. [Value $600]

Woodward purchased her for $500 from Peter Pulman of Virginia on Apr. 15, 1861.

[Commissioners paid Woodward $306.60.]

No. 114, Petition of Horace S. Johnston Filed May 8, 1862

Horace S. Johnston of Washington City claims compensation for five persons.

1. Fanny Butler, aged 26, copper colored. [Value $1,000]
2. Flora Carter, aged ten, very black. [Value $700]
3. James Butler, aged six, very black. [Value $500]
4. Calvin Jamison, aged 17, light mulatto. [$1,200]
5. Eliza Butler, aged 15 months, light mulatto. [$200]

All of the above are healthy, hardy, strong servants and valuable for their services as working people, except Eliza who is too tiny for service. They are all smart, active and free from any defects.

Johnston inherited them from relations residing here but formerly from Virginia. He has owned them for the past

15 years and a portion of them were born in his family.

[Commissioners paid Johnston $1,116.90: Fanny Butler, $262.80; Flora Carter, $262.80; James Butler, $109.50; Calvin Jamison, $416.10; Eliza Butler, $65.70.]

No. 115, Petition of Catharine Windsor
Filed May 8, 1862

Catharine Windsor of Washington City claims compensation for eight persons.
1. Jemima Brown, aged 73, copper colored, and healthy for a person so advanced in years. [Value $100]
2. Daniel Brown, aged 47, black, healthy, active and very valuable. [Value $1,000]
3. Cornelia Hampton, aged 36, black, very healthy. [Value $1,000]
4. Caroline West, aged 40, black, healthy and a good servant. [Value $1,000]
5. Julia Wallace, aged 16, very healthy. [Value $1,100]
6. Noah Wallace, aged 11, black and healthy. He is a servant boy. [Value $800]
7. Daniel Wallace, aged 11, black, a twin of Noah. He is a servant boy. [Value $800]
8. Lester Wallace, eight, black, healthy. [Value $700]

Windsor inherited the servants and their increase from her father, Richard S. Windsor of Fairfax County, Va., with the exception of Cornelia Hampton and Daniel Brown. Cornelia she purchased from her father's estate and from her mother, Lofton Windsor, about nine years ago, and Daniel Brown from the same about four years ago.

[Commissioners paid Catharine Windsor $1,839.60: Jemima, 21.90; Daniel Brown, $328.50; Cornelia, $175.20; Caroline, $284.70; Julia, $394.20; Noah, $219; Daniel Wallace, $219; Lester, $197.10.]

No. 116, Petition of Sarah Davis, of Abel
Filed May 9, 1862

Mrs. Sarah Davis of Washington City claims compensation for seven persons.
1. Hannah West, about 55, black. No money could have bought Hannah or her children. She has been of no service for a year because she is very heavy and has a sore leg and gout.
2. Aleck, or Alexander, West, son of Hannah, is aged 29 or 30 and bright mulatto. Davis's son has turned down an offer of $1,800 for Aleck by Col. Singleton of Mississippi. He is a valuable house servant and cook.
3. Toby, alias Hampton, son of Hannah, aged 25, bright mulatto. He is more valuable than his brother.
4. Julia, niece of Hannah, aged about 30, black. She is in the prime of life and is an excellent cook.
5. Annie, child of Julia, about eight or nine years old, bright mulatto.
6. Benjamin, child of Julia, black, about one year old.
7. Susan Joyce, about 30, black. She was purchased to keep her from being sold away from her family. Her mistress, Mrs. Wilcoxen, was in indigent circumstances and obliged to part with her.

Hannah and her children were a gift to Sarah Davis and John Davis from her mother, Mrs. Sarah Walker, in a deed of gift. Susan Joyce she purchased from Ellen Wilcoxen in a bill of sale dated Oct. 19, 1842. Julia and her child, called Annie or Amelia, she purchased from her sister-in-law, Mrs. Lucy B. Walker, in payment of a debt due from Davis's deceased brother, Zacharias Walker.

Attached is the deed of gift for Hannah and children from Sarah Walker of Washington City to Sarah Davis and her husband, John Davis. (Signed Nov. 12, 1810) Also attached is a copy of the bill of sale by which Ellen "Willcoxen" of Washington, in consideration of $250 paid by Sarah Davis, sells to her Susan Joyce, then aged about 14 years. (Signed by Ellen Willcoxen, X her mark, Oct. 18, 1842) Also attached is a bill of sale from Lucy B. Walker dated Apr. 8, 1859, by which she sold servant girl Julia and her child, Amelia, for $534 to Sarah Davis.

[Commissioners paid Sarah Davis, of Abel, $2,211.40: Hannah West, no value; Aleck West, $569.40; Hampton West, $613.20; Julia, $481.80; Annie, $175.40; Benjamin, $21.90; Susan Joyce, $350.40.]

No. 117, Petition of Ann Scott
Filed May 9, 1862

Ann Scott of Washington claims compensation for eight persons.
1. Dennis Magruder, aged 60, has a dark complexion, is tall, strong and healthy.
2. Ellen Magruder is aged 45, of a dark complexion and low in statue.
3. Betty Bender, aged 24, mulatto and low in statue.
4. Martha Singleton, aged 18, of a dark complexion, is low in statue.
5. Clara Singleton, aged two years, mulatto, is sprightly.
6. James Tilghman, aged 13, has a dark complexion, is bright and intelligent.
7. Charles Tilghman, mulatto, aged 14, is a sprightly and valuable boy.
8. Michael Parr, mulatto, is aged 70. He is active and capable.

All of the above are valuable and are sound and healthy. Two of the men are carpenters and their labor is valuable to Scott. Scott acquired them by inheritance from her father and most of them are children of old family servants.

[Commissioners paid Scott $1,971: Dennis Magruder, $43.80; Ellen Magruder, $131.40; Betty Bender, $481.80; Martha Singleton, $503.70; Clara Singleton $65.70; James Tighlman [sic] $350.40; Charles Tighlman [sic] $372.30; Michael Parr, $21.90.]

At one point in the original petition, "Charles" Tilghman is referred to as "Thomas" Tilghman, but this is probably in error.

No. 118, Petition of John Downes   Filed May 9, 1862

John Downes of Washington City claims compensation for two persons.
1. Sarah Brown, aged about 14, a light mulatto or copper color, stout and healthy. [Value $700]
2. Rachael Brown, aged about 11, healthy, but stout for her age. [Value $700]

They are stout, healthy and able to do house work. Th oldest also does washing and ironing.

Downes acquired title by inheriting their grandmother from his father, the late Zachariah "Downs" of Montgomery County, Md. The girls and their mother were born and raised in his family.

[Commissioners paid Downes $678.90: Sarah Brown, $394.20; "Rachel" Brown, $284.70.]

No. 119, Petition of William Wilkinson   Filed May 9, 1862

William Wilkinson of Washington City claims compensation for three persons.
1. Eliza Cooper, aged 24, is very black, about 5 feet 3 inches tall, and "quite handsome for a black woman". She is a good cook and washer and is a woman of strict honesty and faithfulness.
2. Kate Luck Cooper, child of Eliza, aged about four years, is black in color.
3. Mary Ellen Cooper, child of Eliza, is six months old and the same color as her mother.

Their total value is $1,200.

Wilkinson purchased Eliza Cooper and her oldest child from the firm of Betts Gieson (?) of Richmond, Va., in January of 1861. Mary Ellen was born since that purchase.

[Commissioners paid Wilkinson $569.40: Eliza Cooper, $438; Kate Luck Cooper, $87.60; Mary Ellen Cooper, $43.80.]

No. 120, Petition of Thomas R. Bird   Filed May 9, 1862

Thomas R. Bird claims compensation for six persons.
1. Henny, aged 28, black, 4 feet 10 inches tall. [Value $1,000]
2. Louisa, daughter of Henny, aged 12, black, 4 feet 6 inches tall. [Value $800]
3. Mariah, daughter of Henny, aged ten, black, 3 feet 6 inches tall. [Value $600]
4. Cora, daughter of Henny, aged eight, 3 feet 6 inches tall. [Value $600]
5. Kate, daughter of Henny, aged two, 2 feet 4 inches tall. [Value $200]
6. Grace, aged eight years, mulatto, four feet tall. [Value $600]

Henny and her children, Louisa and Mariah, Bird purchased about nine years ago from the sheriff of Prince George's County, Md. The other two children were born subsequent to that purchase. Grace is the daughter of a woman named Hannah and she was born after he was purchased Hannah from Mrs. Bassett of the District of Columbia.

[Commissioners paid Bird $985.50: Henny, $262.80; Louisa, $262.80; Mariah, $131.40; Cora, $131.40; Kate, $43.80; Grace, $153.30.]

No. 121, Petition of Martin Buell   Filed May 9, 1862

Martin Buell of Washington claims compensation for two persons.
1. Martha Ann Jackson, about 47 years old, yellow complexion, somewhat fleshy, and about five feet tall. She is healthy, of obliging disposition, honest and industrious. She is a good house servant. [Value $500]
2. Caroline Jackson, daughter of Martha Ann, is of a darker complexion than her mother, about the same height, and with an aquiline nose. She has no defects. [Value $800]

Buell acquired Martha Ann in accordance with a judgement of the Circuit Court of Prince George's County, Md., dated Apr. 12, 1853, in a dispute over Martha Ann's ownership between Buell and Henry A. Pumphrey of Montgomery County, Md. Buell lost the case and paid Pumphrey $756.33 for the slave.

[Commissioners paid Buell $219 for Martha Ann Jackson. The claim for Caroline Jackson was not allowed.]

No. 122, Petition of Joseph Downing   Filed May 8, 1862
Joseph Downing of Washington City claims compensation for John Brooks, aged about 45, a mulatto or copper color, about 5 feet 7 ½ inches tall. He is moderately healthy and able to labor in mechanical pursuits. He is generally healthy but is lame in one hip from its dislocation in infancy or youth. He is a good hand at mechanical work. [Value $400]

Downing acquired title through his marriage to Elizabeth Webster of Prince George's County, Md. His wife had inherited Brooks from her father, the late William Webster.

[Commissioners paid Downing $262.80]

No. 123, Petition of Horatio Moran   Filed May 9, 1862
Horatio Moran of Washington City claims compensation for two persons.

1. John Lewis Webster, aged 27, bright mulatto, healthy and strong. He is a good hackman and has followed that occupation in Washington. [Value $900]

2. Sandy Webster, aged 29, is stout, bright mulatto, healthy and strong. He is a good hackman and has followed that occupation in Washington. [Value $900]

Horatio Moran acquired title by inheritance from his father's, John Moran's, estate in Charles County, Md. He inherited the mother before John Lewis and Sandy were born. Attached is a copy of a document dated Mar. 25, 1843 (?), relating to the disposition of the elder Moran's personal property. Horatio received two slave boys named Morgan (?) and Francis, and a slave woman named Catharine.

Attached is a letter dated Westover, Va., Aug. 5, 1862, to Moran from A. P. Porter (?), Capt., NY Vols. (?), stating that Sandy has been employed by him since the beginning of March. Porter says he had no idea that he belonged to Moran or he would have consulted him before bringing Sandy away. Sandy is an excellent (?)_____ to take care of horses. Porter has allowed him to go to Washington this morning as he has been unwell for a few days, so that the commissioners can see for themselves. He says Sandy is worth at least $1,800. Sandy says that his brother John is on the staff of General McDowell.

[Commissioners paid Moran $1,182.60: John Lewis Webster, $569.40; Sandy Webster, $613.20.]

No. 124, Petition of William Richards   Filed May 9, 1862
William Richards of Washington claims compensation for Henry Dorsey, aged 32 years. Dorsey is 5 feet 5 inches tall, of a dark copper color, stout, and is inclined to be stoop shouldered. Richards is engaged in the brick business and Dorsey is particularly valuable as he was one of the best brick burners in his yard. He has never had a day of sickness since Richards has owned him and has no bodily or mental defects. [Value $1,000]

Richards purchased Dorsey from Richard Wallach for $500 on Feb. 28, 1859. Wallach had purchased Dorsey from Thomas C. Magruder, administrator of the estate of Thomas Boothe, on May 26, 1854.

[Commissioners paid Richards $657.]

No. 125, Petition of Bushrod W. Reed   Filed May 9, 1862
Bushrod W. Reed of Washington City claims compensation for three persons.

1. Lucy Jones, over the age of 27 or 28, is of a copper complexion and about 5 feet 6 inches tall. She has a small scar on her right arm below the elbow from a burn. She was a first-rate chamber maid and attended generally to all the house work. Lucy also kept in order the three rooms Reed rented in his large establishment at the corner of F and 14th. [Value $1,000]

2. Rebecca Henson, aged about 21 or 22, is of a light copper complexion and about 5 feet 5 inches tall. She has no marks. She was an excellent cook and washer and attended to her duties faithfully. [Value $1,000]

3. Jack Jones, aged about eight or nine, is a bright mulatto with straight hair about 3 feet 10 inches tall. He has no scratch or mark on him. He is active, remarkably intelligent and very useful about the house. [Value $500]

All of the above are domiciled in Reed's family and are familiar with the duties of a house servant. They are honest and free from infirmities.

Lucy Jones and Rebecca Henson were inherited by Reed's wife from Richard Piles of Montgomery County, Md. Jack Jones is the son of Rebecca Henson and was born since his mother became the property of Reed. The attached copy of Pile's will, filed in the Montgomery County Orphans' Court on Jan. 17, 1848, bequeathed to Maria Louisa "Read" a Negro boy named Abraham, a Negro girl named Lucy, and a Negro girl named Rebecca.

[Commissioners paid Reed $1,226.40: Lucy Jones, $525.60; Rebecca Henson, $525.60; Jack Jones, $175.20.]
A complete copy of Pile's will was attached to the petition and contains additional information about his bequests to family members.

No. 126, Petition of Owen Leddy   Filed May 9, 1862

Owen Leddy of Washington City claims compensation for two female slaves.

1. Mary Bronaugh, aged 15, brown in color.

2. Emily Bronaugh, aged 12, black in color.

Both are well-grown for their ages and have no marks and scars. The girls were raised as household servants. They are of good character and have no infirmities or defects. [Value $1,600]

The girls were born into slavery, of slaves Leddy purchased in Virginia about 23 years ago. This was recorded in D.C. in 1846 when Leddy moved to the District from Virginia.

[Commissioners paid Leddy $657: Mary Bronaugh, $394.20; Emily Bronaugh, $262.80.]

No. 127, Petition of Green Adams   Filed May 9, 1862

Green Adams of the District of Columbia claims compensation for two persons.

1. George, aged 23, a bright mulatto, dark eyes and hair, 5 feet 6 inches tall, well-built. He is intelligent, honest, industrious and valuable as a field hand and house servant.

2. Martha, aged 16, a dark mulatto with dark eyes and hair, rather stout, 5 feet one-half inch tall. She is valuable as a cook and general houseworker, and especially as a nurse for children.

George was purchased Jun. 18, 1851, from Skelton Renfro of Knox County, Ky., who held him under the will of James Renfro, Sr. Martha he acquired under the will of his father, Randolph Adams, who died in 1848 in the county and state aforesaid.

[Commissioners paid Adams $1,073.10: George, $547.50; Martha, $262.80.]

No. 128, Petition of Sally Murray and Martin King   Filed May 9, 1862

Sally Murray and Martin King of Washington claim compensation for two slaves.

1. Margaret will be about 42 years old next July. She has a black complexion, black eyes, woolly hair and is about 5 feet 5 inches tall. She is a cook, ironer and washerwoman and is of excellent moral character.

2. Miranda is 26 years old. She is 5 feet 5 inches tall, has black eyes, wooly hair and a black complexion. She is a chambermaid, seamstress and does general housework. She is of excellent moral character.

They are together valued at $3,000.

Martin King purchased for $500 from Jesse Duvall Negro woman Margaret, aged about 22, and her two children, Thomas, aged about two, and Miranda, aged about six. (Signed Jun. 25, 1842) The two have been in the service of King since that time. On May 4, 1861, King in a bill of sale of his personal property included the aforesaid Margaret and Miranda. See D.C. Liber J.A.S. No. 211, folios 210-212.

[Commissioners paid Sally Murray, Martin King, $700.80: Margaret, $219; Miranda, $481.80.]

No. 129, Petition of T. L. Alexander   Filed May 9, 1862

Col. T. L. Alexander of the U.S. Army claims compensation for the following seven persons.

1. Wesley, about 28 years old, mulatto, 5 feet 9 inches tall, healthy. He is a splendid dining room servant, cook and coachman. [Value $1,500]

2. Louisa, wife of Wesley, aged about 27, light mulatto, about 5 feet 3 inches tall, healthy. She is a good seamstress, cook, washer and ironer. [Value $1,000]

3. Bob, child of Wesley and Louisa, aged about nine, bright mulatto. He is a very smart boy, healthy and waits well on the table. [Value $800]

4. Mary, child of Wesley and Louisa, aged about five, bright mulatto, healthy and very smart. [Value $350]

5. Ellenora, child of Wesley and Louisa, aged about two, bright mulatto, healthy. [Value $250]

6. Kitty, sister of Louisa, about 21 years old, mulatto, healthy. She is a superior seamstress and house servant. [Value $1,000]

7. Ann, an unmarried woman aged about 38 who is delicate. She is a fine cook and house servant and splendid washerwoman. She complains of dyspepsia and headaches. [Value $600]

Alexander inherited Wesley from his father as an infant and raised him. He received Ann as part of his mother's retained interest in his father's estate when she died about two years ago. Kitty and Louisa and Bob were given by the father of his wife several years ago and Mary and Ellenora have been born since the gift.

[Commissioners granted Alexander $2,102,40: Wesley, $525.60; Louisa, $372.30; Bob, $306.60; Mary, $131.40; Ellenora, $65.70; Kitty, $481.80; Ann, $219.]

No. 130, Petition of Milton Garret, for self, and as guardian of the estate of W. C. Caldwell
Filed May 9, 1862

Milton Garrett, for himself, and as guardian of the estate of W. C. Caldwell; Sarah Caldwell, J. H. Caldwell, S. V. Zimmerman, contestants of M. Garrett's claim, claims compensation for seven persons.

Garrett, on behalf of himself and as guardian of the estate of the late William S. Caldwell, claims the following slaves.

1. Grace Payne, aged about 50 years, black, stout, five feet tall, erect in her carriage and intelligent. She is an excellent cook and housekeeper. [Value $200]
2. Maria Casey, daughter of Grace, aged about 25, black complexion, 5 feet 2 inches tall, stout, likely and intelligent and erect in her carriage. She is an excellent cook and domestic servant. [Value $900]
3. Malinda Goins, daughter of Grace, about 32 years old, black complexion, about five feet tall, stout and strong, likely and intelligent. She is an excellent cook and domestic servant. [$600]
4. Rose Goins, daughter of Malinda, aged ten, black, likely and intelligent. [$300]
5. William H. Harrison, aged 22, dark brown in color, about 5 feet 6 inches tall. He is heavy and squarely made. [Value $1,000]
6. John Berkley, aged 20, black, about 5 feet 7 inches tall. He is sound and well set. [Value $1,000]
7. George Goins, son of Malinda, aged about 14, mulatto or yellow in complexion, about 5 feet 1 inch tall. He is stout and able-bodied and strong and intelligent. [$600 or $1,000]

Attached is the copy of a bill of sale from John A. Washington of Jefferson County, Va., to William Caldwell of Christian County Ky., of Negro Grace and her infant born Sept. 21, 1823. (Signed Oct. 9, 1823)

Title to numbers 1, 2, 3, 4, and 7 are by inheritance from William S. Caldwell to his wife and children Mrs. Sarah Caldwell, Naomi J. Turner (formerly Caldwell), John H. Caldwell, A. M. Caldwell, and Sarah Virginia. Zimmerman (formerly Caldwell), and Milton Garrett in right of his wife, formerly Mary L. Caldwell. [Petition filed Jun. 11, 1862]

Another petition, numbered 130 as above and filed Jun, 11, 1862, submits the claim of Milton Garrett of Washington City to William H. Harrison, John Berkley, and George Goins. Title comes from the inheritance from William S. Caldwell, and Garrett claims he owns three-sevenths of these servants in his own right.

[Commissioners paid $1,204.50 to Sarah Caldwell, John H. Caldwell, A. M. Caldwell, S. V. Zimmerman, by Lloyd, their attorney; Naomi J. Turner, by William A. Hall, her attorney, and M. Garrett. The claims to William H. Harrison and John Berkley were not allowed as they were not produced. By agreement the persons received the following: Mrs. Sarah Caldwell, $120.48; Mrs. Naomi J. Turner, $154.86; John H. Caldwell, $154.86; A. M. Caldwell, $154.86; Sarah Virginia Zimmerman, $154.86; Milton Garrett, $464.58]

The above document was extremely difficult to read and very confusing as to its terms.

No. 131, Petition of Sophia M. White
Filed May 9, 1862

Sophia M. White of Washington claims compensation for Louisa Trapnell, aged 13 years. She is a bright mulatto, 4 feet 11 inches tall, with bushy hair. She is a good and faithful servant, honest, and the family is very much attached to her. She is sound and healthy. White received title to Louisa from her aunt, Mary Berry, about six months ago as will be shown by evidence of Margaret Osborn and Susan Osborn. [Value $900]

[Commissioners paid White $328.50]

No. 132, Petition of Elizabeth A. Hilleary
Filed May 9, 1862

Elizabeth A. Hilleary of Washington claims compensation for four persons.
1. Amelia Scott, aged 56, of a yellow complexion, medium sized, with no peculiar marks. [Value $500]
2. Richard Brown, aged 48, black complexion, rather tall. [Value $900]
3. Mary A. Brown, aged 23, yellow complexion. She is very likely and has no particular marks. [Value $1,000]
4. Amelia S. Brannon, 19 months old, has a yellow complexion. [Value $100]

Hilleary obtained title by inheritance from her father.

[Commissioners paid Hilleary $941.70: Amelia Scott, $87.60; Richard Brown, $306.60; Mary A. Brown, $481.80; Amelia S. Brannon, $65.70.]

No. 133, Petition of Sarah A. Hilleary Filed May 9, 1862

Sarah A. Hilleary of Washington claims compensation for four persons.

1. William Allen, aged 25, has a very dark complexion, is of medium size with no particular marks. [Value $1,000]
2. Henderson Pipsico, aged 19, has a dark complexion, is likely with no particular marks. [Value $900]
3. Letitia B. Pipsico, aged seven, has a dark complexion, is likely and has no marks. [Value $350]
4. Louis Cass Pipsico, 15, has a very dark complexion, is intelligent and well-grown for his age. [Value $700]

Hilleary inherited the above slaves from her father.

[Commissioners paid Hilleary $1,664.40: William Allen, $569.40; Henderson Pipsico, $591.30; Letitia B. Pipsico, $131.40; Louis Cass Pipsico, $372.30.]

No. 134, Petition of Leonard Hilleary Filed May 9, 1862

Leonard Hilleary of Washington claims compensation for two slaves.

1. Susan Orme, aged 19, has a dark complexion, is medium in size and very likely. [Value $800]
2. Catharine Orme, aged 27 months, has a dark complexion and no marks. [Value $150]

Hilleary inherited the persons from his father.

[Commissioners paid Hilleary $547.50: Susan Orme, $481.80; Catharine Orme, $65.70.]

No. 135, Petition of Robert P. Dodge Filed May 9, 1862

Robert P. Dodge of Georgetown claims compensation for two persons.

1. Harriet Smoot, aged 50, dark in color, large lips, 5 feet 2 inches tall. She stoops while walking. She has cooked for his family for ten years. She complains of rheumatism at times in one arm but is rarely sick. [Value $400]
2. Samuel Smoot, aged 16, dark color, 5 feet 4 inches tall, has a pleasant countenance. He is smart, very ingenious and useful. He has no defects. [Value $800]

Dodge purchased them in the summer of 1852 at a sale of the estate of George Rhodes, deceased, of Georgetown.

[Commissioners paid Dodge $657: Harriet Smoot, $87.60; Samuel Smoot, $569.40]

No. 136, Petition of John Bayne Filed May 9, 1862

John Bayne of the city of Washington claims compensation for two persons.

1. Mary Jane Queen, aged eight last September, is a stout, black girl, four feet tall, very healthy. [Value $300]
2. Frank Queen, aged six last December, is a stout, black boy who is well made. He is 3 feet 6 inches tall and is healthy. [Value $300]

Bayne acquired title by purchase of their mother, Harriet Williams, which sale is recorded in D.C. Liber J.A.S. No. 49, folio 94. Mary Jane and Frank were born during the period of Harriet's slavery.

[Commissioners paid Bayne $372.30: Mary Jane Queen, $219; Frank Queen, $153.30.]

No. 137, Petition of George McCeney Filed May 9, 1862

George McCeney of Washington County, D.C., claims compensation for 14 persons.

1. Jeremiah Hall, aged 62, black, healthy. He is a valuable gardener and salesman worth $250 a year, which is the wage that he would have to pay for one inferior to replace him. [Value $600]
2. Minta Hall, aged 58, is a good cook, laundress and nurse. She is uniformly healthy. [Value $400]
3. Priscilla Pinkney, aged 48, black, is a good cook and laundress who is very honest and reliable. She has occasional rheumatism, but her general health has been sound. [Value $400]
4. Martha Pinkney, aged 22, black, is a dairy maid and garden hand. She is robust and very healthy. [Value $1,000]
5. Ellen Pinkney, aged 20, black, is a cook and garden hand and generally healthy and well conditioned. [Value $1,000]
6. Priscilla Pinkney, 2d., is aged 18 and brown. She is dairy maid and garden hand and perfectly healthy. [Value $1,000]
7. Maria Pinkney, aged 14, black, is a house servant and is healthy. [Value $600]
8. Caroline Hall is aged 23 and brown. She is a very valuable cook, laundress and chambermaid and general house servant. She is never sick. [Value $1,000]
9. Louisa Allen is aged 21 and dark mulatto. She is a gardener and farm hand who is reliable, valuable and perfectly healthy. She has a fine appearance. [Value $1,000]

10. Rachel Jackson, aged nine, is black. She serves (?) neatly and is generally useful. She is healthy. [Value $300]

11. Jerelina Hall, aged five, female, brown. Her qualities are not yet developed. She is healthy. [Value $250]

12. John Wesley Hall, aged 11 months, black. His qualities are not yet developed. He is healthy. [Value $100]

13. Margaret Allen is aged nine months, dark mulatto in color and healthy. Her qualities are not yet developed. [Value $100]

14. Laura Pinkney is aged six months and black. Her qualities are not yet developed. She is healthy. [Value $100]

McCeney inherited Jeremiah Hall and Priscilla Pinkney from his father, Joseph McCeney of Anne Arundel County, Md. Minta Hall he obtained from T. Randall of Annapolis in exchange for other servants. All of the others were born of parents whom McCeney held as slaves.

Except for the first three, all of the others were reared by McCeney himself for his own uses. They were carefully instructed in their servant duties and are incalculably valuable to him.

[Commissioners paid McCeney $3,963.90: Jeremiah Hall, $153.30; Priscilla Pinkney, no value; Minta Hall, $109.50; Martha Pinkney, $569.40; Ellen Pinkney, $591.30; Priscilla Pinkney, 2d., $569.40; Maria Pinkney, $525.60; Caroline Hall, $481.80; Louisa Allen, $525.60; Rachel Jackson, $197.10; Jerelina Hall, $131.40; John Wesley Hall, $43.80; Margaret Allen, $43.80; Laura Pinkney, $21.90.]

No. 138, Petition of George W. Stewart   Filed May 9, 1862

George W. Stewart of Washington City claims compensation for Reuben Nelson, aged 11, black in color. He is a valuable servant who is hearty, strong and able to labor.

Stewart purchased his mother about 12 years ago from the estate of John Wilson of Anne Arundel County, Md. Reuben was born in Stewart's house and was raised there. [Value $800]

[Commissioners paid $306.60 to Mary E. Stewart, adm'x. of George W. Stewart, by H. Clay Stewart.]

No. 139, Petition of Martha H. McKnight   Filed May 9, 1862

Martha H. McKnight of Washington City claims compensation for a female slave named Rozetta Dorsey. Dorsey is dark colored, of medium size and about 50 years old. She is McKnight's cook and does all her work including washing and ironing. She is assessed at $400 but is worth more to McKnight. She complains at times of a slight dropsical affliction, but is generally well. [Value $400]

McKnight purchased Dorsey about eight years ago. The accompanying bill of sale dated Oct. 10, 1855, shows that W. J. C. Duhamel of Washington City, in consideration of $400, sells to Mrs. Martha McKnight, Negro woman "Resseta".

[Commissioners paid McKnight $153.30]

No. 140, Petition of Rezin Arnold   Filed May 9, 1862

Rezin Arnold of Washington claims compensation for George Crowner. He is aged about 50, mulatto and 5 feet 8 inches tall. He is an honest and industrious servant and is strong and healthy. [Value $500]

Arnold acquired him as a gift from Henry Talbert, deceased, about 1832 and the deed is recorded in D.C. Liber W.B. No. 39, folio 412.

[Commissioners paid Arnold $262.80.]

No. 141, Petition of John Kulp   Filed May 9, 1862

John Kulp of Washington claims compensation for his servant named Julia. She is a bright copper colored girl, aged 11, and is sound and intelligent for her age. She is useful in assisting in all kinds of house work and is honest and reliable. [Value $700]

Kulp states that he raised her from a child in his own family.

[Commissioners paid Kulp $306.60.]

No. 142, Petition of William B. Slack   Filed May 9, 1862

Major William B. Slack, U. S. M. Corps, of the city of Washington, claims compensation for two persons.

1. Frances Duckett, aged 54, about 5 feet 2 inches tall, dark color. She is active and energetic in her movements, polite when spoken to and has very cheerful manners. She is a highly esteemed family servant and a remarkably fine cook. She is sober, industrious and her correct deportment is unsurpassed. [Value $300]

2. Evelina Robertson, aged 23, is about 5 feet 4 inches tall, light complexion, dark eyes. She has a mild disposition and very genteel manners. She is an intelligent, trustworthy domestic and has been raised by Mrs. Slack and always lived with her. She is correct in every relation of life and efficient in every department. [Value $1,000]

Frances was originally the property of Slack's father who sold her to Daniel Kent of Calvert County, Md. Slack purchased her for $300 from Kent in February of 1856. Evelina was inherited by Slack's wife from her father, the late Richard Henry Hall of Baltimore.

[Commissioners paid Slack $657: Frances Duckett, $87.60; Evelina Robertson, $569.40.]

No. 143, Petition of Francis S. Walsh   Filed May 9, 1862

Francis S. Walsh claims compensation for Emily and her six children.

1. Emily, aged about 40, is black, 5 feet 2 inches tall, corpulent and has wooly hair and black eyes. She is cheerful and animated when spoken to. [Value $800]

2. Charlotte, is about 13, mulatto, 4 feet 9 ½ inches tall. She has black, straight hair and dark eyes. [Value $800]

3. Henry, aged about 11, mulatto, 4 feet 5 inches tall. He has wooly hair, dark eyes and is a more than ordinarily active for a boy his age. [Value $800]

4. George, about six years old, 3 feet 7 inches tall, black in color. He is stout and has wooly hair and black eyes. [Value $100]

5. Elvira is about five years old and 3 feet 3 inches tall. She is stout with wooly hair and black eyes. [Value $100]

6. Charles, aged about two-and-a-half, is three feet tall. He is stout with wooly hair and black eyes. [Value $100]

7. Abraham, an infant, is over six weeks old. He is dark in color. [Value $100]

Walsh purchased Emily and Ellen, aged six years, and Arthur, aged 18 months, for $550 from Ruthey Edmonds on Feb. 23, 1847, as recorded in D.C. Liber W.B. No. 132, folios 217-218. Walsh no longer owns Ellen and Arthur.

[Commissioners paid Walsh $1,270.20: Emily, $262.80; Charlotte, $372.30; Henry, $306.60; George, $131.40; Elvira, $98.55; Charles, $76.65; Abraham, $21.90.]

No. 144, Petition of Clement Weeden   Filed May 9, 1862

Charles Weeden of Washington City claims compensation for one woman and her two children.

1. Margaret Ann Price, aged 24, is chestnut colored. She is healthy and a good cook, washer and ironer. [Value $1,000]

2. Benjamin Price is aged four, light mulatto in color and healthy. [Value $300]

3. Joseph Price is aged 18 months, light mulatto in color and healthy. [Value $200]

Weeden acquired them by marriage with Maria Hancock of Alexandria County, Va. (then part of the District of Columbia). She inherited them from Weeden's father, who was then residing in Anne Arundel County, Md. He presented her with Harriet in the year 1856 and the children were born after that time.

[Commissioners paid $613.20: Harriet Ann Price, $438; Benjamin Price, $109.50; Joseph Price, $65.70. Of the total paid, William F. Speake, as per agreement, received $104 and Clement Weeden the residue.]

No. 145, Petition of Samuel A. H. Marks   Filed May 9, 1862

Samuel A. H. Marks of Washington City claims compensation for three persons.

1. Basil Chase, aged 32, 5 feet 4 ½ inches tall, black with black hair and black eyes. He is a good coachman and sound and of good moral character. [Value $1,000]

2. Lucy Magruder, formerly Lucy Chase, aged 28, 5 feet 1 inch tall, black with black hair and black eyes. She is a first-rate house servant and a good cook. She is sound and of excellent moral character. [Value, including her child, Daniel, $500]

3. Daniel Magruder, child of Lucy Magruder, aged eight months, black with black hair and black eyes.

Basil Chase was purchased Mar. 17, 1857, for $1,100, from Charles Digges of Prince George's County, Md. Lucy Magruder was purchased for $775 from Mrs. Anna P. Harvey of Prince George's County, Md., on Jul. 11, 1853. Marks states that he purchased them to prevent their sale South by the parties owning them. Daniel Magruder was born Aug. 28, 1861, and is the offspring of Lucy.

[Commissioners paid Marks $1,007.40: Basil Chase, $547.50; Lucy Magruder, $416.10; Daniel Magruder, $43.80.]

No. 146, Petition of Mary C. Fenwick   Filed May 13, 1862

Mary C. Fenwick of the county of Washington, D.C., claims compensation for six persons.
1. Daniel Fletcher, aged 50, black, married, healthy. He is a field hand.
2. Mary Nelson, aged 28, a bright mulatto, married, healthy. She is a cook and a seamstress and is good in the field.
3. Jane Butler, aged 32, unmarried, of a light copper color. She is a number one cook, washer and ironer and general house servant. She is the mother of the children listed below.
4. Gusty, aged seven, is a dark copper color and is healthy.
5. George, aged three, is a bright copper color and is healthy.
6. Lizzie, aged one (?) year, is a dark copper color and is healthy.

Fenwick claims a value of $4,000 for all six. She claims their services or labor are worth $288 yearly. Fenwick states that Daniel Fletcher with Edward and Frederick were devised to her by marriage as shown by her husband's will. The others came to her about 35 years ago from the estate of her father, Joseph Thurburn of Charles City, Md.

[Commissioners paid Fenwick $1,423.50: Daniel Fletcher, $284.70; Mary Nelson, $372.30; Jane Butler, $394.20; Gusty, $219; George, $109.50; Lizzie, $43.80.]

No. 147, Petition of Richard Butt   Filed May 13, 1862

Richard Butt of Washington County, D.C., claims compensation for five persons.
1. Ellen is aged 20 (?) and mulatto. She is a good house servant and is the mother of the children listed below.
2. Wallis, aged eight, is a mulatto boy. He is sound and free of defects.
3. George, aged four (?), is a dark mulatto. He is sound and free of defects.
4. James, aged three, is a mulatto.
5. Caroline, aged three, is a bright mulatto.

Butt claims their value to be $1,800.

He purchased Ellen from Albert MacDaniel about 15 years ago.

[Commissioners paid Butt $919.80: Ellen, $394.20; Wallis, $197.10; George, $153.30; James, $87.60; Caroline, $87.60.]

No. 148, Petition of Ann E. Newton   Filed May 13, 1862

Mrs. Ann E. Newton of Washington City claims compensation for two persons.
1. Mary Lee, aged 45, has a light complexion, is about 5 feet 1 or 2 inches tall. She has no marks.
2. Louisa Cook, aged 35, has some marks on her face caused by enycephilus (?), which disease attached her about 18 years ago.

They are in good health and are good and faithful servants. They are kind and respectful and are Newton's only support, she being a widow.

She estimates their value at $1,200.

Newman inherited them from her father, the late Richard Smith of Washington City, who died some 19 years ago.

[Commissioners paid Newton $591.30: Mary Lee, $197.10; Louisa Cook, $394.20.]

No. 149, Petition of Thomas J. Carper   Filed May 13, 1862

Thomas J. Carper of Fairfax County, Va., claims compensation for James Thomas, aged 28 years. He is a bright mulatto of good appearance, 6 feet tall, healthy and able to labor. He is a very valuable servant and is now in the employ of the government at $25 a month. He has no moral or other defects. [Value $1,200]

Carper inherited Thomas from the estate of his father, Philip Carper of Fairfax County, Va., when Thomas was a youth.

[Commissioners paid Carper $525.60.]

No. 150, Petition of S. John Thomson   Filed May 13, 1862

S. John Thomson of Washington claims compensation for a woman slave and her son.
1. Margaret Smith, aged about 30, about 5 feet 3 or 4 inches tall, of a copper or chestnut color. She is well-built and active and is the sole household servant in his family. She is expert and trustworthy in business and accustomed to doing all that is usually done by such servants in the same situation. She and her son are remarkably healthy and have no damaging defects. [Value $800]
2. William, or Bill, son of Margaret, was five years old on Jan. 15, 1862. He is about three feet tall and his complexion is a little darker than his mother's. He is healthy and free of defects. [Value $200]

Thomson states that Margaret Smith was the property of his wife, M. Louisa Cross, formerly Miss Duvall. She obtained ownership by dower from the estate of her former husband, Osborn Cross, Esq., of Prince George's County, Md., who purchased her from the estate of the late Col. Kent of Prince George's County, about 1839. Bill was born since then and was raised in the family as a slave.

[Commissioners paid Thomson $613.20: Margaret Smith, $459.90; William, $153.30.]

No. 151, Petition of Joseph Osmun   Filed May 13, 1862

Joseph Osmun of Washington claims compensation for Ellen Sanders, aged about 16. She is five feet tall, of a copper or chestnut color, well-built and sprightly. She has been Osmun's sole household servant and is expert and trustworthy in business and accustomed to doing all that is usually done by such servants in the same situation. She has been remarkably healthy and has no damaging defects. [Value $800]

Osmun purchased the mother of Ellen Sanders from William F. French, Esq., of Prince William County, Va. in 1849 and she has been raised in the family as a slave.

[Commissioners paid Osmun $525.60.]

No. 152, Petition of Eleanor R. Lang   Filed May 13, 1862

Eleanor R. Lang of Georgetown claims compensation for ten persons.

1. Mary Dyer, aged 48, mulatto, 4 feet 11 ½ inches tall. She is an excellent cook, washer and ironer. [Value $600]
2. Lizzie Clark, aged 33, mulatto, 5 feet one-half inch tall. She does chamber work and the like. [Value $1,000]
3. Henry Clark, aged 28, dark copper color, 5 feet 3 3/4 inches tall. He is a house servant and is insured for $1,000. [Value $1,200]
4. George Dyer is 23 years old, mulatto and 5 feet 7 ½ inches tall. He is a house servant and is insured for $1,000. [Value $1,200]
5. Mary Jane Clark, aged 16, mulatto, 5 feet 3 inches tall. She is a good cook. [Value $800]
6. Eliza Ann Clark, aged 14 ½, mulatto, 5 feet 1 inches tall. She is a house servant. [Value $800]
7. William Henry Clark, aged 13, mulatto, 4 feet 5 ½ inches tall. She is a house servant. [Value $500]
8. Alfred Clark, aged ten, mulatto, 4 feet 2 3/4 inches tall. [Value $500]
9. Maria L. Clark, aged eight-and-one-half, mulatto, 4 feet ½ inch tall. [Value $300]
10. Frank Clark, aged two months. [Value $100]

All of the above are healthy and have no defects or bodily infirmities.

Lang purchased Mary Dyer from James F. and Debra (?) Essex in 1824 for $200. Lizzie Clark and Henry Clark are the children of Mary Lingon (?) purchased by Lang from Col. Marbury. George Dyer is the some of Mary Dyer. Mary Jane Clark, Eliza Clark, William Clark, Alfred Clark, Maria Clark and Frank Clark are the children of Lizzie Clark.

Lang states that her claim is subject to a deed of trust dated Jul. 19, 1858, recorded in D.C. Liber J.A.S. No. 158, folio 227, to secure a debt to Peter Vonessen. (Signed Eleanor X her mark Lang)

[Commissioners paid Lang $3,504: Mary Dyer, $175.20; Lizzie Clarke, $372.30; Henry Clarke, $657; George Dyer, $525.60; Mary J. Clarke, $569.40; Eliza Ann Clarke, $481.80; William H. Clarke, $306.60; Alfred Clarke, $219; Maria L. Clarke, $175.20; Frank Clarke, $21.90.]

The original petition gives the name "Clark" as the surname; the printed commissioners' report spells the name as "Clarke."

No. 153, Petition of Peter Von Essen   Filed May 13, 1862

Peter Von Essen of Georgetown claims compensation for twenty persons.

1. Rosanna Lee, aged 45, 4 feet 11 ½ inches tall, black. [Value $500]
2. George Lee, aged 23, 5 feet 7 inches tall, yellow. [Value $800]
3. Addie Lee, aged 20, 5 feet 1 inch tall, yellow. [Value $800]
4. Cornelia Savage, aged 19, 5 feet 3 1/8 inches tall, yellow. [Value $800]
5. Allice Savage, aged 13, 4 feet 10 3/4 inches tall, yellow. [Value $700]
6. Hester Savage, aged 11, 4 feet 2 ½ inches tall, yellow. [$500]
7. Harriet Savage, aged ten, 4 feet 1 1/4 inches tall, yellow. [$300]
8. William Savage, aged six, 3 feet 2 ½ inches tall, yellow. [Value $200]
9. Hamilton Savage, aged five, 3 feet 1 inches tall, yellow. [Value $150]

10. Malinda Hawkins, aged 62, 4 feet 10 inches tall, black. [Value $150]
11. Martha Hawkins, aged 30, 4 feet 10 inches tall, black. [Value $800]
12. Lewis Hawkins, aged 25, 5 feet ½ inch tall, black. [Value $800]
13. Isaac Hawkins, aged 24, 5 feet 2 3/4 inches tall, black. [Value $800]
14. Charles Hawkins, aged 12, 4 feet 2 3/4 inches tall, yellow. [Value $700]
15. Emily Hawkins, aged ten, 3 feet 11 ½ inches tall, yellow. [Value $600]
16. Henry Hawkins, aged eight, 3 feet 10 1/4 inches tall, yellow. [Value $500]
17. George Hawkins, aged seven, 3 feet 8 ½ inches tall, yellow. [Value $450]
18. Ellen Hawkins, aged five, 3 feet 2 1/4 inches tall, yellow. [Value $300]
19. James Hawkins, aged four, 3 feet 1 inch tall, yellow. [Value $300]
20. Mathias Hawkins, nine months, 2 feet 5 inches tall, yellow. [Value $50]

Von Essen states that he purchased Rosannah Lee when she was ten years old and his title to Malinda Hawkins dates from a purchase of many years ago. All of the others are the children or grandchildren of these two. In addition, Von Essen states that he has claim to the labor or service of others of African descent by virtue of a deed of trust from Eleanor Lang dated Jul. 19, 1858, recorded in D.C. Liber J.A.S. No. 158, folio 227. The said persons were conveyed in trust to secure a debt of Eleanor R. Lang, being the sum of $2,645.92 with interest; and an additional sum of $2,066.88 without interest. See Eleanor R. Lang's petition numbered 152.

[Commissioners paid Von Essen $5,256: Rosanna Lee, $350.40; George Lee, $438; Addie Lee, $394.20; Cornelia Savage, $481.80; Alice Savage, $394.20; Hester Savage, $131.40; Harriet Savage, $240.90; William Savage, $131.40; Hamilton Savage, $109.50; Malinda Hawkins, $87.60; Lewis Hawkins, $284.70; Martha Hawkins, $284.70; Isaac Hawkins, $569.40; Charles Hawkins, $262.80; Emily Hawkins, $262.80; Henry Hawkins, $197.10; George Hawkins, $175.20; Ellen Hawkins, $109.50; James Hawkins, $109.50; Matthias Hawkins, $43.80.]

There are some spelling discrepancies between the printed report of the Commissioners and the original documents. For example, Von Essen is spelled "Vonessen" in the printed report, and Mathias Hawkins's first name is given as "Matthias" in the printed document. Boyd's City Directory for 1864, p. 311, shows Von Essen as having a livery stable on Congress St. in Georgetown.

No. 154, Petition of Henry T. Dixon   Filed May 13, 1862

Henry T. Dixon of Georgetown claims compensation for William Johnson, aged about 30, about 5 feet 2 inches tall, with a black complexion. He is erect and spare of form and has a genteel carriage. He is an accomplished dining room servant and one of the most valuable and accomplished servants Dixon has ever known. [Value $1,000]

He purchased Johnson from Mrs. Ellen M. Brooke of Washington on Dec. 2, 1861, and the bill of sale is recorded in the D.C. clerk's office.

[Commissioners paid Dixon $525.60]

No. 155, Petition of Mary Brien, administratrix of Francis Masi   Filed May 13, 1862

Mrs. Mary Brien, administratrix of Francis Masi, late of Washington, claims compensation for two persons.

1. Maria Butler, aged 50, an ordinary-sized woman with a black complexion. She is an excellent cook and a good washer and ironer. She is good, honest, very intelligent and trustworthy. She has no defects. [Value $500]
2. Sam Butler, aged 28, about 5 feet 7 inches tall, black complexion. He has scars on his face from having smallpox when he was a child. He is a good house servant and waiter in the dining room. He is worthy and intelligent and has no defects. [Value $1,500]

Maria was bought by her father, the late Francis Masi, Esq., from Mr. Clement McWilliams, deceased, of Washington, about 35 years ago. The receipt for the money has been lost or mislaid. Samuel was born after the purchase of his mother.

[Commissioners paid Brien, administratix by Seraphim Massi, her attorney, $569.40: Maria Butler, $131.40; Samuel Butler, $438.]

The printed report spelled the surname as "Massi," but the original petition spells it as "Masi."

No. 156, Petition of Thomas T. Everett   Filed July 29, 1862

Thomas T. Everett of Washington claims compensation for two persons:

1. Teresa Smith, aged between 21 and 22, light mulatto, about 5 feet 3 inches tall, with dark hair and dark eyes. She is moderately stout, healthy and hardy and weighs 125 pounds. She is an excellent house servant and can read and write. His tax receipts for 1859 and 1860 show Teresa assessed at $900, that of 1861 has her assessed at $700.

2. Robert, son of Teresa, is between three and four years old. He is of a very light color with light eyes, light hair and is about 3 feet 5 inches tall. He is a bright, fine boy and stout and large for his age.

Everett estimates their value as $1,200.

His wife, Jane H. Everett, purchased them from Stanislaus Murray of Washington for $800 on Nov. 29, 1858.

[Commissioners paid Everett $613.20: Teresa Smith, $481.80; Robert Smith, $141.40.]

No. 157, Petition of Samuel Stott   Filed May 13, 1862

Samuel Stott of the city of Washington claims compensation for William Burrell, aged about 16, brown or mulatto in color, 5 feet 5 inches tall. Burrell is bound to Stott until he reaches age 35. He is a good house servant, is good health, and has no defects. Stott purchased him when he was about 18 months old. [Value $1,000]

[Commissioners paid Stott $175.20.]

No. 158, Petition of Samuel Stott, trustee of estate of William Worthington   Filed May 13, 1862

Samuel Stott, trustee, of the city of Washington claims compensation for two persons.

1. Sarah Cook, aged about 60, a dark mulatto about 5 feet tall. She has a lump under her right jaw about as large as a small hen's egg. Sally is a first-rate cook, washer and ironer. [Value $100]

2. William Cook is the son of Sarah. He is about 32 years old, dark brown in color, 5 feet _____ inches tall. He is a hack driver. [Value $1,500]

Stott makes his claim by virtue of being appointed trustee by the D.C. Circuit Court and at the request of the heirs of the late William Worthington.

[Commissioners paid Stott, trustee, $459.90: Sarah Cook, no value; William Cook, $459.90.]

No. 159, Petition of Walter B. Chew   Filed May 13, 1862

Walter B. Chew of Georgetown claims compensation for five persons.

1. James Albert Brown, aged 20, light complexion, 5 feet 8 inches tall, with straight and dark hair. He has a defect in one eye. [Value $1,000]

2. Charles Brown, aged 16, light complexion, 4 feet 10 inches tall, has straight, dark hair. [Value $800]

3. Cecelia Brown, aged 13, light complexion, 4 feet 4 inches tall, has straight, brown hair and dark eyes. [Value $500]

4. Mary Catharine Brown, aged ten, bright complexion, 4 feet 1 inch tall, has straight, dark hair and dark eyes. [Value $$400]

5. Eugene Brown, aged seven, copper colored, 3 feet 7 inches tall. He has light curly hair and dark eyes. [Value $200]

The five persons listed above are the children of Catharine Brown, now deceased, who was purchased by him. Such is recorded in the county court.

[Commissioners paid Chew $1,292.10: James Albert Brown, $350.40; Charles Brown, $306.60; Cecelia Brown, $262.80; Mary Catherine Brown, $219; Eugene Brown, $153.30.]

No. 160, Petition of John T. Tonge   Filed May 13, 1862

John T. Tonge of Washington claims compensation for three persons.

1. Ann Brown, aged 32, is 5 feet tall and dark brown in color. She is strong and healthy. She is an excellent family servant and is a first-rate cook, washerwoman and ironer. She does all the marketing for our family. [Value $1,000]

2. Sally A. Brown, daughter of Ann, aged ten, is 3 feet 4 inches tall and light brown in color. [Value $600]

3. Charles E. Brown, son of Ann, is seven, 3 feet tall and light brown in color. [Value $400]

Ann Brown belonged to Tonge's wife, Margaret Ellen Butler, whom he married on Sept. 17, 1846. The children was born after she became Tonge's property.

[Commissioners paid Tonge $876: Ann Brown, $438; Sally A. Brown, $262.80; Charles Brown, $175.20.]

No. 161, Petition of Richard J. Ryon   Filed May 13, 1862

Richard J. Ryon of Washington claims compensation for two persons.

1. William Carroll, aged 40, black in color, about 5 feet 8 inches tall, medium sized. He is healthy, sober, industrious, and very intelligent. He has acted as a porter in Ryon's store for the last two years and three months and was worth to Ryon in that capacity over $2,000. [Value $1,200]

2. Mary Carroll, William's wife, aged 38, copper colored, medium sized. She is a first-rate cook, washer and ironer and her services to Ryon's family have been invaluable. [Value $1,000]

They were purchased from the estate of Thomas P. Ryon of Prince George's County, Md. for $1,500 some two years and three months ago. They were sold below their value because they were bid on by the family of Thomas Ryon to prevent their going South. There was no competition in the bidding so the price was low.

[Commissioners paid Ryon $635.10: William Carroll, $372.30; Mary Carroll, $262.80.]

Boyd's Directory for 1864, p. 241, shows that Ryon owned a grocery at 9th and D, NW.

No. 162, Petition of Carlisle P. Patterson   Filed May 13, 1862

Carlisle P. Patterson of the District of Columbia, claims compensation for six persons.

1. Cassy Ann Butler was born at Brentwood, D.C., in 1827, and is 35 years old. She is black, 5 feet 2 ½ inches tall. She is a remarkably finished laundress, house and lady's maid. She is in good health though not very strong. [$1,400]

2. Cassy Ann Butler, Jr., the daughter of Cassy Ann, is nine years old, and was born at Brentwood in 1853. She is a fine, intelligent girl and is strong and healthy. [Value $600]

3. Anthony Butler, is five years old, black and was born in Washington. He is a fine, healthy, strong boy. [Value $350]

4. Hannah Butler, aged three-and one-half, is a strong, healthy girl. [Value $250]

5. Maria Dover was born at Brentwood in 1830 and is 31 years old. She is a dark mulatto, 5 feet 4 inches tall, and healthy. She is a very good house servant. [Value $1,100]

6. Josephine Vallis, daughter of Maria Dover, is 15 years old and was born at Brentwood in 1847. She is 5 feet one-half inch tall, is well-grown, and black in color. [Value $900]

Patterson acquired title to the above by his marriage to Elizabeth Worthington Pearson, the daughter of the late Joseph and Catharine Pearson of Brentwood. See D.C. Will Book No. 1, H. C. N., folio 258.

[Commissioners paid Carlisle Patterson, by his attorney, William H. Philip, $1,730.10: Cassy Ann Butler, $394.20; Cassy Ann Butler, Jr., $197.10; Anthony Butler, $153.30; Hannah Butler, $109.50; Maria Dover, $438; Josephine Vallis, $438.]

See Pippenger, D.C. Probate Records, 1801-1852, p. 193, for Pearson's will. The printed report of the Commissioners gives Patterson's given name as "Carlile" and Cassy Butler's name as "Casey."

No. 163, Petition of Catherine Pearson   Filed May 13, 1862

Catharine Pearson, residing at Brentwood, D.C., claims compensation for 21 persons.

1. Edward Lee was born in Washington in 1807 and is 55 years old, black, and 5 feet 10 inches tall. He has been the family coachman for 30 years and is throughly honest and reliable. He is healthy, through occasionally rheumatic. [Value $1,000]

2. Nelly Mitchell was born in Washington in 1816 and is 46 years old, black, fat, 5 feet 3 ½ inches tall. She is an accomplished cook and washer woman and has been the family cook for 20 years. She is healthy, honest, and trustworthy. [Value $1,000]

3. Mary Smith was born in Georgetown in 1838 and is 24 years old, dark mulatto, and 5 feet one-half inch tall. She is a good house servant and plain seamstress and is perfectly healthy. [Value $1,000]

4. James Dangerfield, six months old, is the infant son of Mary Smith and was born at Brentwood. He is a fine, healthy boy. [Value $300]

5. Kitty Mitchell, the daughter of Nelly Mitchell, was born in Georgetown in 1841. She is 21 years old, 5 feet 1 ½ inches tall, and light black. She is an active, intelligent house servant and seamstress, and is in perfect health. [Value $1,200]

6. Joseph Burnet is 4 months old and the son of Kitty Mitchell and was born at Brentwood in December 1861. He is stout and healthy. [Value $50]

7. John Mitchell, son of Kitty Mitchell, was born in Brentwood in 1842. He is 20 years old, 5 feet 11 ½ inches tall, and black in color. He is strong, healthy and is a first-rate farm hand. [Value $1,200]

8. Anthony Jefferson, the brother of Nelly Mitchell, was born at Brentwood in 1835. He is 27 years old, about 5 feet 8 inches tall, slender, and black in color. He is a first-rate waiter and butler. [Value $1,700]

9. Jenny Butler, born in Georgetown in 1798, is 64 years old. She is very stout, black in color. She is a splendid family cook and is generally in good health although somewhat rheumatic in her legs. [Value $350]

10. William Butler, son of Jenny Butler, was born at Brentwood in 1835 and is 27 years old, dark mulatto, about

5 feet 8 inches tall. He is an accomplished waiter and good coachman. He is healthy and in fine condition. [Value $1,500]

11. George Dover was born at Brentwood in 1825 and is 37 years old, black, 5 feet 7 3/4 inches tall. He is a first-rate farm hand and for the last several years has been the head man on the farm. He is strong, healthy and intelligent. [Value $1,500]

12. Mary Shorter was born at Brentwood in 1824 and is 38 years old, 5 feet 2 ½ inches tall, and black in color. She is the sister of George Dover. She is a good laundress and general cook and is strong and healthy. [Value $1,000]

13. Elizabeth Shorter, daughter of Mary Shorter, was born at Brentwood in 1843. She is 19 years old, dark mulatto, about 5 feet 4 inches tall. She is a good chambermaid and waitress and is strong and healthy. [Value $1,000]

14. Thomas Shorter, son of Mary Shorter, was born at Brentwood in 1845 and is 17 years old. He is 5 feet 5 1/4 inches tall, and black. He is strong, healthy, well grown and a good farm hand. [Value $1,100]

15. Benjamin Shorter, son of Mary Shorter, was born at Brentwood in 1849. He is 13 years old, well grown, healthy and black. He works at the farm. [Value $$900]

16. Lewis Shorter, son of Mary Shorter, was born at Brentwood in 1851. He is 11 years old, brown, strong and tough, but not large for his age. His intelligence suits him for a house waiter. [Value $750]]

17. Henry Shorter, son of Mary Shorter, was born at Brentwood in 1853 and is nine years old and brown in color. He is strong and healthy. [Value $600]

18. Sarah Shorter, son of Mary Shorter, was born at Brentwood in 1855 and is seven years old and brown in color. She is strong and healthy. [Value $350]

19. Jacob Shorter, son of Mary Shorter, was born at Brentwood in 1857 and is five years old. He is brown in color and strong and healthy. [Value $350]

20. Andrew Shorter, son of Mary Shorter, was born at Brentwood in 1859. He is two-and-one-half years old, brown in color, and is healthy and strong. [Value $200]

21. Frank Shorter, son of Mary Shorter, was born at Brentwood in 1861. He is 10 months old and is brown in color. He is healthy and strong. [Value $100]

Pearson acquired title to the slaves under the terms of the will of her husband, Joseph Pearson, recorded in D.C. Will Book No. 1, H. C. N., folio 258.

[Commissioners paid Pearson, by William H. Philip, her attorney, $6,044.40: Edward Lee, $262.80; Nelly Mitchell, $197.10; Mary Smith, $503.70; James Dangerfield, $43.80; Kitty Mitchell, $525.60; Joseph "Burnett", $21.90; John Mitchell, $613.20; Anthony Jefferson, $569.40; Jenny Butler, $21.90; William Butler, $569.40; George Dover, $438; Mary Shorter, $197.10; Elizabeth Shorter, $394.20; Thomas Shorter, $569.40; Benjamin Shorter, $394.20; Lewis Shorter, $175.20; Henry Shorter, $175.20; Sarah Shorter, $131.40; Jacob Shorter, $109.50; Andrew Shorter, $87.60; Frank Shorter, $43.80.]

No. 164, Petition of Elizabeth O'Reiley   Filed May 13, 1862

Elizabeth O'Reiley of Georgetown, claims compensation for three persons.
1. James Smith, aged 38. [Value $1,200]
2. Mary Smith, aged 35. [Value $600]
3. Dick Smith, aged 22. [Value $1,200]

She claims their service by descent.

[Commissioners paid O'Reiley by Eliza Barry, her attorney, $1,182.60: James Smith, $394.20; Mary Smith, $262.80; Dick Smith, $525.60.]

No. 165, Petition of Ann Biscoe   Filed May 13, 1862

Mary Biscoe of Washington claims compensation for four persons.
1. Mary Forrest, aged 32, 5 feet 1 ½ inches tall, black in color. She is of a delicate make but is quite healthy. She is a sound, honest and faithful servant. [Value $750]
2. Elsie Curtis, aged 29, 5 feet 2 inches tall, black. She is stoutly made and able-bodied. [Value $800]
3. Mary Ellen Simms, aged 25, 5 feet 1 ½ inches tall, light brown in color. She is likely and robust. [Value $800]
4. Marion Curtis, aged nine, about 4 feet 9 inches tall, mulatto, She is delicately made, but is lively and healthy. [Value $275]

Ann purchased them for $100 from her father, Bennett Biscoe, by a bill of sale signed Apr. 20, 1840 and recorded in D.C. Liber W.B. No. 80, folios 350-352.

[Commissioners paid Biscoe $1,445.40: Mary Forrest, $438; Elsie Curtis, $394.20; Mary Ellen Simms, $438; Marion Curtis, $175.20.]

The printed report spells the surname as "Bisco," but the original documents give "Biscoe." The provisions of the bill of sale from Bennett state that he sells to his daughter, "one Negro girl named Mary aged about nine years one Negro girl named Alice, aged about seven years one Negro girl named Maria aged about three years."

No. 166, Petition of Richard A. Boarman

Richard A. Boarman of Washington claims compensation for George Curtis, aged 11, 4 feet 7 ½ inches tall, mulatto. He is robust and stout for his age and is remarkably active and honest. [Value $600]

He was purchased by Boarman's wife from Ann Biscoe. The accompanying bill of sale signed Apr. 16, 1858, shows that Ann Biscoe sold to her sister, Eliza Boarman, for $5, her servant boy named George.

[Commissioners paid Boarman $350.40.]

No. 167, Petition of Elizabeth C. Peerce   Filed May 13, 1862

Elizabeth C. Peerce of Washington County, D.C., administratrix of Joseph M. Peerce, deceased, her husband, claims compensation for Henry Wheeler, aged 28. The Orphans' Court granted Elizabeth letters of administration on May 8, 1855. Wheeler is rather tall, of a dark chestnut color, and delicately (?) made. He has a scar on his left cheek caused by a burn. Peerce receives from Wheeler wages of $12 a month for his services as a first-class waiter and dining room servant. [Value $900]

Elizabeth holds title by virtue of being administrator of her husband's will. Joseph Peerce had purchased Henry for $205 from John T. Powers on Jul. 8, 1847.

[Commissioners paid Perce, per Charles M. Matthews, attorney, $350.40.]

No. 168, Petition of David Moore   Filed May 13, 1862

David Moore of Washington claims compensation for Mary Crawford, aged 30, a dark colored woman who is stout built. She has a pleasant countenance and is about 5 feet 3 to 4 inches tall. She is an excellent cook, washer and ironer. She has a good disposition and no infirmities or defects. [Value$1,000]

Moore acquired her from the administrator of the estate of the late Mr. Crawford of Prince George's County, Md., for a purchase price of $451 on Jan. 12, 1841.

[Commissioners disallowed the claim as slave was not produced.]

No. 169, Petition of James W. West and Eliza M. West   Filed May 13, 1862

James W. West and Eliza M. West of the city of Washington claim compensation for 11 persons.

1. Julia Burgess, aged about 48, a bright mulatto woman, well proportioned, of medium size, erect in her carriage, stout and strong. She has a peculiar expression of countenance arising from the fact that one of her lips is thicker than the other and one of her eyes is larger than the other. [Value $300]

2. Jane Walker, or Burgess, daughter of Julia, aged about 24, has a dark brown complexion, is tall and stout. She is quite erect in her carriage and is likely and intelligent. [Value $1,000]

3. Susan Burgess, daughter of Julia, aged about 22, is a dark mulatto woman of medium size. She stoops a little in walking, is tolerably tall but not very stout and is likely and intelligent. [Value $1,000]

4. Sarah Burgess, daughter of Julia, aged about 19, a mulatto woman who is small in statue and erect in her carriage. She has a peculiar expression of countenance from the fact that one of her eyes is larger then the other. She is likely and intelligent. [Value $1,000]

5. Margaret Burgess, daughter of Julia, is about 17 years old, has a black complexion and is tall and stout. She is erect in her carriage, likely and intelligent. [Value $1,000]

6. George Burgess, son of Julia, is about 15, mulatto, of medium height and not very stout. He is erect in his carriage, and likely and intelligent. [Value $1,000]

7. Josephine Walker, daughter of Jane Walker, alias Burgess, is about two years old, light brown in color, not very stout, and is likely. [Value $100]

8. Tempe Burgess, daughter of Susan Burgess, is about four years old, black, rather small in statue with black eyes. She is likely and intelligent. [Value $150]

9. Mille Burgess, daughter of Susan Burgess, aged about two, is a bright mulatto child, well proportioned, rather stout for her age. She is likely and intelligent. [[Value $100]

10. Alice Burgess, daughter of Sarah Burgess, is about four years old, a bright mulatto, well proportioned, and is

likely and intelligent for her age. [Value $150]

11. Cynthia Burgess, daughter of Sarah Burgess, aged about two, is a bright mulatto child, well proportioned, likely and smart for her age. [Value $100]

The will of William Mills, who died in Fairfax County, Va., about 1827, provided that his widow and children, including daughter, Eliza M., now Eliza M. West since her marriage to James W. West, inherit certain servants. The widow, being now advanced in age, has transferred her interests to Eliza M. In addition, the interests of Eliza's brother and sister, John Mills and Nancy Mills, have also passed to Eliza.

[Commissioners paid James W. and Eliza M. West $2,956.50: Julia Burgess, $197.10; Jane Walker, or Burgess, $481.80; Susan Burgess, $481.80; Margaret Burgess, $525.60; George Burgess, $394.20; Josephine Burgess, $65.70; Tempe Burgess, $87.60; Mille Burgess, $65.70; Alice Burgess, $109.50; Cynthia Burgess, $65.70.]

No. 170, Petition of John E. Neale   Filed May 13, 1862

John E. Neale claims compensation for six persons.

1. Henry Lancaster, aged about 37, is of a light complexion, about 5 feet 7 inches tall, very likely, smart and intelligent. He is tolerably stout and erect in his carriage. He is an engineer by trade and is hired out at $32 a month. [Value $3,000]

2. John Lancaster, brother of Henry, aged about 35, black complexion, about 5 feet 6 inches tall, very likely, smart, rather stout in person. He is a blacksmith and is hired out at $39 per month. [Value $3,000]

3. Henrietta Lancaster, wife of John, aged about 33, of a black complexion though somewhat lighter than John, about 5 feet 6 inches tall, tolerably stout and well formed, very likely, intelligent and erect in her carriage. She is a good cook and house help and has been living in the family since she was a small girl. She can demand $9 or $10 per month. [Value $2,000]

4. James Lancaster, son of John and Henrietta, aged about 16, of a black complexion, though somewhat lighter than John, about five feet tall, stout for his age, erect in his carriage, very likely and with a moderate degree of intelligence. He is rather slow. He is a good waiter and can command $12 or $13 for his services. [Value $1,800]

5. Louis Napoleon Bonapart Lancaster, son of John and Henrietta, is about six, of a black complexion although somewhat lighter than John, is about four feet tall, stout for his age and erect in his carriage. He is sprightly, smart and intelligent. He is very useful about the house as a waiter or messenger and could readily command $2 or $3 dollars a month. [Value $1,000]

6. Eliza Lancaster, daughter of John and Henrietta, aged about 14, has a black complexion, although somewhat lighter than John, is about 5 feet tall, tolerably stout for her age, erect in her carriage, very likely and possesses a moderate degree of intelligence. She speaks rather slowly. She is good about the house either as a cook, chambermaid or nurse. She could command $5 a month. [Value $500]

Henry, Henrietta, James, Eliza and Louis Napoleon were inherited by Neale. John was purchased from Dr. J. B. Evelin of Charles County, Md., Neale's nephew, about 18 or 20 years ago for either $1,000 or $1,200. Neale states that the particular object in buying him was to keep him in the family and save him from being carried to Georgia. All of the persons have been in Neale's family from their infancy.

[Commissioners paid Neale $2,934.60: Henry Lancaster, $613.20; John Lancaster, $657; Henrietta Lancaster, $525.60; James Lancaster, $525.60; Louis N. B. Lancaster, $197.10; Eliza Lancaster, $416.10.]

No. 171, Petition of Jesse Sisson and Ann F. Sisson   Filed May 13, 1862

Jesse Sisson and Ann F. Sisson of the city of Washington claim compensation for Mary Guttrich, aged 47, of a copper color, about five feet tall, wooly hair, well formed, with a little scar under one ear (?), usually healthy. She has an amiable disposition and is free of infirmities or defects. They have been residents of Washington for the last 16 years. [Value $500]

Ann Sisson acquired title to Guttrich under the will of her father, Ignatius Ratcliff of Charles County, Md., who died about 1834. At the time of his death she was the widow of John Hall, deceased. Since then she has married Jesse Sisson.

A copy of the will of Ratcliff is attached. Among other things, he willed to Ann F. "one negro Boy called Bob, one girl called Mary and one old woman called also Mary."

[Commissioners paid Jesse and Ann F. Sisson $197.10.]

No. 172, Petition of Rosa O. Gantt   Filed May 13, 1862

Rosa O. Gantt of Washington claims compensation for two persons.

1. Louisa Noble, aged between 45 and 50, 5 feet 5 inches tall, dark color. She has a good disposition and is honest and faithful. She is a good cook, washer and ironer. She was paid $10 a month while on hire.

2. Elisa Noble, daughter of Louisa, aged 16, about five feet tall, dark color. She has an amiable disposition. As to her other qualities Gantt knows nothing, as she has always lived with and been under the control of her mother.

Gantt values them together at $1,000. They are strong and healthy.

Gantt got title from her husband, "Ceasa" A. Gantt, now deceased, who had inherited Louisa Noble from his father. Ceasa transferred title to his wife, Rosa, by a bill of sale that is recorded at Marlborough Court House.

[Commissioners paid Gantt $197.10: Louisa Noble, $197.10; Eliza Noble, no value.]

No. 173, Petition of Margaret A. Loughborough   Filed May 13, 1862

Margaret A. Loughborough of Georgetown claims compensation for six persons.

1. Jeffrey Beall, chestnut colored, is aged about 38 and about six feet tall and lame. He is a most excellent house servant and waiter. He is capable and honest.

2. Mary Lee, aged 29, is a mulatto with dark freckles and about 5 feet 2 inches tall. She is a lady's maid and is intelligent, capable and honest. She is the mother of the children listed below.

3. John Lee, son of Mary, aged eight, is chestnut colored and well-grown for his age.

4. William Lee, son of Mary, aged four, is chestnut colored and well-grown.

5. Loretto Lee, child of Mary, aged two, is light mulatto and well-grown.

6. Male infant child of Mary, is light mulatto and not yet christened.

She values them at $3,200.

She purchased Jeffrey about ten years ago from Mrs. Margaret H. Loughborough of Washington County, D.C., for $1,100. She also purchased Mary Lee and her child, John, about five years ago for $1,500 from Commander S. Bissell, U. S. Navy. Mary's other children weres born after the purchase.

[Commissioners paid M. A. Loughborough $919.80: "Jeffry" Beall, $175.20; Mary Lee, $328.50; William Lee, $131.40; Loretto Lee, $87.60; John Lee, $175.20; infant, $21.90.]

No. 174, Petition of Lucy R. Miller, Maria Miller, Harriet Miller, William Miller   Filed May 13, 1862

Lucy R. Miller, Maria Miller, Harriet Miller and William Miller of the city of Washington claim compensation for five persons.

1. Hannah is aged 21, black, of low statue and well formed. She is a good house servant, cook, washer and ironer and is of a good constitution and free of infirmities.

2. Isabella is aged 26, black and of low statue. She is a superior cook, washer and ironer, a good house servant and healthy.

3. John Joseph Shorter is aged 14, bright mulatto, well formed and likely. He is a house servant and is healthy, capable and efficient.

4. Charles Edwin Shorter, otherwise Charles Edwin Taylor, is aged 11, bright mulatto, well formed and very intelligent. He is a house servant, and is healthy, capable and efficient.

5. Nanc[y] is aged about 56, black, short and stout. She is a good cook, washer and ironer, but of somewhat delicate health.

The above persons are valued at $4,000.

The Millers are heirs under the will of Eliza Ariss Miller, recorded in the D.C. Orphans' Court on May 3, 1856.

Attached is a copy of Eliza Miller's will which, among other things, provided that her brother, William, and her sisters Lucy R., Maria and Harriet should have all of her servants: John Joseph Shorter, Charles Edwin Shorter, Nancy, Isabella, and Hannah and their offspring. She requests her brother never sell any of the servants unless it is their wish to be sold and that they are not to be sold out of the District of Columbia. If sold, they are to have choice of their master and place.

[Commissioners paid Lucy R., Maria, Harriet Miller, by their attorney, William Miller, $1,226.40: Hannah, $438; Isabella, $306.60; John Joseph Shorter, $175.20; Charles Edwin Shorter, $262.80; Nancy, $43.80.]

No. 175, Petition of Maria Miller   Filed May 13, 1862

Maria Miller of the city of Washington, claims compensation for two persons.

1. Louisa Washington is aged 45, mulatto and rather above medium height. She is a first-rate house servant, cook, washer and ironer.

2. Mary Teresa [Washington], daughter of Louisa, is aged 20, has a very light complexion, is above medium

height, finely formed and has long dark brown hair. She is a first-rate ladies' maid, seamstress and house keeper.

Miller values them at $2,600.

Miller's father, in about 1815, gave his daughter Cynthia, who is the mother of Louisa and grandmother of Mary Teresa. Her father obtained Cynthia from his mother-in-law as a gift. Maria states that the ancestors of these Negroes have been in the possession of her family for more than a hundred years.

[Commissioners paid to William Miller, attorney for Maria Miller, $700.80: Louisa Washington, $175.20; Mary Teresa, $525.60.]

No. 176, Petition of Susanna Boarman — Filed May 13, 1862

Susanna Boarman of Charles County, Md., claims compensation for Trecy Harper, a bright, yellow woman about 31 years old. She is about 5 feet 1 or 2 inches tall, has black hair and dark eyes. She is muscular in form, but not fleshy. She is a fine cook, washer and ironer and a valuable house servant. She is likely and in good health and has no defects. She has resided with her brother in Washington for the last eight or ten years. [Value $1,000]

Boarman inherited Trecy under the will of Elizabeth Reeves of Charles County, Md., dated Mar. 14, 1837. A copy of the will is attached which provides that Susanna Boarman, the daughter of Dr. George Boarman, receive the Negro girl, "Trece", the daughter of Cecy. (George Boarman is Susanna's nephew.)

[Commissioners paid Sylvester B. Boarman, administrator, $438.]

For additional information about bequests under Reeves's will, see the attachment to the original petition. Among other things, Reeves gives Mary Boarman, also daughter of Dr. George Boarman, a Negro boy named Baptist, son of Gracy. Other slaves and property were also distributed among nephews, nieces and friends.

No. 177, Petition of Dr. John L. Gibbons — Filed May 13, 1862

John L. Gibbons of Washington City claims compensation for three persons.

1. Rachel Yearby, aged 35, about 5 feet 4 inches tall, stout made, good looking, and sprightly. [Value $1,000]
2. Kate Adams, daughter of Rachel, eight, bright mulatto, about 3 ½ feet tall, active and sprightly. [Value $500]
3. Noble Harris, aged 14, black in color, about 4 feet 8 or 10 inches tall, active and sprightly. [Value $900]

They are all valuable family servants and are in good health.

Gibbons inherited Rachel. Kate was born in his family. He purchased Noble from Dr. William N. Pindle of Talbot County, Md., although he has no written evidence of title.

[Commissioners paid Gibbons $963.60: Rachel Yearby, $394.20; Kate Adams, $219; Noble Harris, $350.40.]

No. 178, Petition of Alfred A. Sloan — Filed May 12, 1862

Alfred A. Sloan of Washington City claims compensation for Negro woman Milly Blake, aged about 46 years. She is about 5 feet 1 inch tall, quite black and stout. She is an excellent house servant and good cook, washer and ironer. Sloan says he has been offered $8 a month for her services. She is sound and healthy and has no defects. [Value $500]

Sloan purchased Blake and Blake's child from the estate of Maria M. McKnew, deceased, the mother of his wife, about Dec. 3, 1857, at a public sale of McKnew's estate. The child has since died

[Commissioners paid "Sloane" $175.20.]

No. 179, Petition of Sarah A. Abbott — Filed May 13, 1862

Sarah A. Abbott of Georgetown claims compensation for Leah Dorman, aged 31, of a quite dark color, about 5 feet 3 inches tall. She is sound, strong and healthy. Dorman was born in the service of Abbott's father, Dr. John Austin, who presented Dorman to Abbott. She has been in Abbott's service for 17 years. [Value $1,500]

[Commissioners did not allow Abbott's claim.]

The printed report of the Commissioners, p. 4, explains that Charles Abbott, Sarah's husband, abandoned his home in D.C. and went to Richmond or elsewhere in Confederate territory and is believed to be in the civil service of the rebel government. Leah Dorman became the property of Charles upon his marriage with Sarah. Abbott's lawyer asserted that Dorman was merely loaned to her by her father who retained title. But the statement in the petition itself contradicts this and, in any case, 17 years of possession would give undisputed title to Charles Abbott.

No. 180, Petition of Eliza A. Gallaher — Filed May 13, 1862

Eliza A. Gallaher of Washington City claims compensation for four persons.

1. Beverly Pullison, mulatto, aged 23. He is a first-class dining room servant and Gallaher has frequently been

offered $1,500 for him. [Value $1,500]

2. Lucy Alexander, aged 38, black, is a valuable family servant. She has a temporary swelling of her ankle. [Value $800]

3. Harriet Cross, mulatto, aged 24. She is a first-class cook and very valuable. [$700]

4. Lucy Cross, nearly white child of Harriet, she is one year old. [Value $300]

Gallaher received Beverly from her father's estate in 1856 and he was valued then at $1,200. Lucy Alexander she acquired in an exchange with her brother for a servant named Randall, who had became Gallaher's property under her father's will. Harriet Cross was purchased from Mr. Cross of Bladensburg, Md., for $477 for a term of 13 years after which she was to be emancipated. The accompanying bill of sale is dated Jul. 1, 1858, and conveys Harriet Cross to John S. Gallaher, Jr., trustee for Mrs. Eliza A. Gallaher, and states that Harriet's term of service was to date from June 28, 1858. Also attached is a copy of a document, dated Jul. 1, 1858, by which Howerton Cross sells to Thomas H. Cross of Washington, his title to Harriet Cross and gives Thomas the right to dispose of her services for a term of 13 years. Eliza Gallaher states that her intent in buying Harriet Cross was to save her from being sent South by her former master. Lucy Cross is the daughter of Harriet.

[Commissioners paid Gallaher $1,160.70: Beverly Pullison, $657; Lucy Alexander, $262.80; Harriet Cross, $219; Lucy Cross, $21.90.]

No. 181, Petition of Mary Ann Hall

Mary Ann Hall of Washington claims compensation for four persons.

1. Rosanna Gordon, aged 24, chestnut colored, about five feet tall. [Value $1,200]

2. William Gordon, child of Rosanna, aged eight, mulatto. [Value $500]

3. Alexander Gordon, child of Rosanna, aged four, mulatto. [Value $300]

4. Caroline Lucas, aged 23 (?), chestnut colored. [Value $1,000]

Hall purchased for $359.81 on Jan. 9, 1846, Rosanna Gordon, who was then about eight years old, from James P. Gannon and Cornelius Cox through K. N. Lambell. She purchased Caroline Lucas for $275 on Feb. 15, 1844, from J. P. Cannon through K. N. Lambell.

[Commissioners paid Hall, per T. E. Lloyd, atty., $1,138.80: Rosanna Gordon, $438; William Gordon, $175.20; Alexander Gordon, $87.60; Caroline Lucas, $438.]

No. 182, Petition of John W. Fitzhugh   Filed May 13, 1862

John W. Fitzhugh of Washington claims compensation for two persons.

1. Mandy Snell, aged 24, black, 5 feet 4 inches tall.

2. Jenny Snell, Mandy's daughter, aged three years four months, black.

Fitzhugh states they are worth $1,500 and that he has been offered that much for the slaves. They are healthy and have no defects.

He purchased them from Mary Ann Haislip of Washington for $1,000 on Apr. 13, 1861. In addition, he states he did some repairs on Haislip's house that amount to about $200.

[Commissioners paid Fitzhugh $613.20: Mandy Snell, $503.70; Jenny Snell, $109.50.]

No. 183, Petition of Daniel Bryan   Filed May 13, 1862

Daniel Bryan of the city of Washington claims compensation for two persons.

1. Milly Goodall, aged about 51, dark mulatto. She is large, stout, likely and healthy. She is a first-rate cook and general servant and is hired to George W. Riggs, Esq., at $8 a month, which Bryan regards as very low wages considering her value. [Value $600]

2. Emily Goodall, daughter of Milly, aged about 23, is lighter in color than her mother. She is not quite as tall or large as her mother, but is a likely, stout, healthy woman. Emily is a first-rate cook and house servant and there could not be found in the District of Columbia a servant of better disposition, or habits, or great efficiency. [Value $900]

Col. Thomas Barbour of Orange County, Va., gave Milly to Bryan's wife many years ago and Emily was born subsequently. Col. Barbour was his wife's father.

Both the servants are honest and free of infirmities and have no impairments except, perhaps, that Milly, like other cooks, may be sometimes a little high-tempered.

[Commissioners paid Bryan $744.60: "Milley" Goodall, $219; Emily Goodall, $525.60.]

No. 184, John Marbury   Filed May 13, 1862

John Marbury of Georgetown claims compensation for four persons.
1. George Martin, aged about 70, 5 feet 7 inches tall, of a dark complexion, in ordinary health, and capable of rendering useful services. He purchased Martin. [Value $100]
2. Henny Morris, aged about 72 or 73, 5 feet 1 or 2 inches tall, of a dark complexion. She is in good health and capable of rendering useful service. He received title to Henny under the terms of the will of his mother, Ann O. Marbury. [Value $100]
3. Kitty Taylor, the elder, is about 70 years old, 5 feet 3 or 4 inches tall, of a dark complexion. She is in delicate health, but is capable of useful service. He acquired title to her by virtue of his marriage to his first wife, Elizabeth Sommervell. [$100]
4. Kitty Taylor, Jr., aged 30, 5 feet 3 or 4 inches tall, dark complexion. She is in good health and capable of rendering useful services. She was born after her slave mother belonged to Marbury.
[Commissioners paid Marbury $569.40: George Martin, $21.90; "Henry" Morris, $65.70; Kitty Taylor $43.80; Kitty Taylor, Jr., $438.]

No. 185, Petition of Joseph N. Fearson   Filed May 13, 1862
Joseph N. Fearson of Georgetown claims compensation for nine persons.
1. Sarah Duglas, aged 68, about five feet tall, bright yellow in color, very hale and hearty. [Value $350]
2. Caroline Gray, aged 46, five feet, very dark black, very hale and hearty. [Value $800]
3. Jennie or Janna Gray, aged 29, 5 feet 2 inches tall, very dark black, hale and hearty. [Value $1,000]
4. Lucy Gray, aged 26, 5 feet 2 inches tall, very dark black, hale and hearty. [Value $1,000]
5. Frank Gray, aged 15, five feet tall, bright yellow, hale and hearty. [Value $1,000]
6. Benjamin Gray, aged 12, 4 feet 6 inches, bright yellow, hale and hearty. [Value $800]
7. Phebe Gray, aged seven, 3 feet 6 inches tall, very dark, hale and hearty. [Value $500]
8. Nebraska Bill Gray, aged nine, four feet tall, bright yellow, hale and hearty. [Value $700]
9. Abraham Dixie Gray, aged 18 months, bright yellow, hale and hearty. [Value $400]
The above have no infirmities or defects, except for Sarah Duglas who has the natural infirmity of old age.
Sarah Duglas was bought by his father, Joseph Fearson, in 1812 from Edmund Shaw of Charles County, Md., and she remained in his service until his death on Sept. 7, 1832. Afterwards she served his mother until she died in Aug. 26, 1854. Sarah was then inherited by Joseph's brother, Samuel S. Fearson, and himself. Samuel sold his interest to Joseph. Joseph purchased Caroline and her two children Jennie and Lucy, from Nacy Griffith, Esq., of Montgomery County, Md., on Dec. 2, 1834, for $600. The others were all born of Jinnie or Janna while in Joseph's service.
[Commissioners paid Fearson $2,146.20: Sarah Duglas, $43.80; Caroline Gray, $284.70; Jennie, or Janna, Gray, $394.20; Lucy Gray, $481.80; Frank Gray, $350.40; Benjamin Gray, $219; Phebe Gray, $131.40; Nebraska Bill Gray, $197.10; Abraham Dixie Gray, $43.80.]

No. 186, Petition of Samuel Fearson
Samuel Fearson claims compensation for three persons.
1. Anna Thomas is the mother of William Henry and Ann Maria and aged about 26 in 1859.
2. William Henry Thomas was aged about nine in 1859.
3. Ann Maria Thomas was aged about four in 1859.
The petition consists of the copy of a bill of sale from Joseph N. Fearson by which he sells for $1,100 to Samuel Fearson, son of Samuel S. Fearson of Georgetown, Negro woman Anna, aged about 26, and her two children, William Henry, aged about nine, and Ann Maria, aged about four. Bill of sale dated Jan. 20, 1859.
[Commissioners paid Samuel Fearson $700.80: Anna Thomas, $350.40; William Henry Thomas, $219; Ann Maria Thomas, $131.40.]

No. 187, Petition of John Moore   Filed May 13, 1862
John Moore of Washington City claims compensation for two persons.
1. Robert S. Thomas, aged seven years and seven months, above three feet tall, dark brown in color. He is an active and intelligent boy.
2. Josephine S. Thomas, aged five years and ten months, light brown in color. She is also active and intelligent.
Moore claims that at the time Robert and Josephine were born, he owned the services of their mother, Susan Thomas. They are both sound, healthy and free of marks or bruises.
[Commissioners did not allow this claim as the persons not produced.]

No. 188, Petition of Margaret Ann Hutchinson Filed May 13, 1862

Margaret Ann Hutchinson of Washington City claims compensation for her man servant, James Shaw. Shaw is 22 years old, of a dark complexion, with black eyes and black hair. He is about 5 feet 7 inches tall, of medium build, and has no visible marks. He is active, intelligent, healthy, honest and trustworthy. He is an excellent house servant and is accustomed to the care and management of horses. [Value $1,200]

Hutchinson acquired him under the will of her brother-in-law, Thomas W. Jones, that was filed in the D.C. Orphans' Court on Jun. 25, 1859. Shaw had been born of a slave woman who belonged to George Bean, Hutchinson's father, and had been allocated to Jones in the division of Bean's estate. Attached is a copy of the will of Jones leaving his estate to his sister-in-law, Mrs. Margaret Ann Hutchinson.

No. 189, Petition of Catharine Osbourn Filed May 13, 1862

Catharine Osbourn of Washington claims compensation for Elizabeth Duviel, who is aged 25, black and five feet tall. She is a good, industrious servant and perfectly sound and healthy. Osbourn was given the woman about 20 years ago, as will be shown by evidence of Mrs. Susan Osbourn and Mary Berry. [Value $1,000]

[Commissioners paid Osbourn $394.20 for Elizabeth "Duiell."]

No. 190, Petition of Fielder Magruder Filed May 13, 1862

Fielder Magruder, a resident of the District of Columbia, claims compensation for six persons.

1. George York, aged 47, is very black and 5 feet 11 inches tall. He has a scar under his eye. [Value $500]
2. Duke Williams, aged 40, a dark yellow man, is 5 feet 8 inches tall. [Value $1,100]
3. Adeline Williams, aged 35, bright mulatto, is 5 feet 3 inches tall. [Value $1,000]
4. Lewis Williams, aged eight, dark mulatto, is 4 feet 8 inches tall. [Value $500]
5. Charles Williams, aged six, dark mulatto, is 4 feet 2 inches tall. [Value $400 (?)]
6. Maria Williams, aged three, dark mulatto, is 3 feet 6 inches tall. [Value $200]

Magruder bought George York for $500 from John Schooler on Jun. 12, 1858. Duke Williams, Adeline Williams, Lewis Williams and Charles Williams he purchased from John A. Throckmorton about six years ago for $2,500. The accompanying bill of sale is dated Oct. 1, 1856, Montgomery County, Md. According to its terms, Fielder paid $2,025 for Duke, Adeline and her two children. Maria was born of Adeline since that purchase.

All of the above servants are healthy, faithful and industrious. George York has been in the District since last June. The others are out of the District temporarily. They were sent to Magruder's farm in Fairfax County, Va., to tend to domestic business a short time before the emancipation act was passed and he intends to bring them back again. Magruder says that Hon. W. (?) Van Horn said he could bring them in any time within nine months of the passage of the bill.

[Commissioners paid Magruder $1,226.40: George York, $219; Duke Williams, $262.80; Adeline Williams, $350.40; Lewis Williams, $175.20; Charles Williams, $131.40; Maria Williams, $87.60.]

No. 191, Petition of Henry Martin Filed May 13, 1862

Henry Martin of Washington County, D.C., claims compensation for two persons.

1. Charlotte Rendler, aged 35, copper colored, 5 feet 2 inches tall. She has one decayed front tooth. [Value $800]
2. Henry Fletcher, aged 32, black, 5 feet 6 inches tall. [Value $1,500]

Both are good and faithful servants who are healthy and free of defects.

Martin purchased them from Elizabeth Walker of Prince George's County, Md. on Jan. 18, 1843. The bill of sale states that Martin paid $5, but he says the agreement he had with Betsy Walker was to pay her $10 a month for her life, and that this amounted to about $1,000. The sale involved four Negroes: Charlotte, Benjamin, Henry and Douglass. Douglass was sold by Martin Jan. 20, 1843, to Ignatius Hutchinson. Walker says that Benjamin ran away, so he retained only Charlotte and Henry.

[Commissioners paid Martin $394.20 for Henry Fletcher. The claim for Charlotte Rendler was not allowed as she was not produced.]

No. 192, Petition of Susannah Harriet Tobias Filed May 13, 1862

Susannah Harriet Tobias of Washington claims compensation for one female slave named Treacy. She is about 38 years old, black in complexion, hair and eyes, about 5 feet 8 inches tall. She is very large and muscular and quite fat, weighing nearly 300 pounds. She is healthy, industrious and intelligent. Among her personal qualities are that she is not liable to maternity, has uncommon strength and is docile and obedient. [Value $1,300]

Tobias got her under the terms of the will of her aunt, Susannah Beck, late of St. Mary's County, Md. Attached is a copy of Beck's will that provided that her niece, Susannah Harriet Keech, shall inherit Negro "Treasy" after the death of Beck's brother, Samuel Keech. (Will proved Mar. 8, 1831)

[Commissioners paid Tobias $394.20.]

Susan H. Keech married John Tobias Jul. 22, 1856. See Wesley E. Pippenger (comp.), District of Columbia Marriage Licenses, Register 1, 1811-1858 (Westminster, Md., Family Line Publications, 1994), p. 595. Hereinafter cited as Pippenger, D.C. Marriage Licenses, 1811-1858.

No. 193, Petition of Christopher N. Thom — Filed May 13, 1862

Christopher N. Thom of Washington County, D.C., claims compensation for Wilson Briscoe, aged nine years and six months. He is four feet and one-half inch tall, has a very dark complexion, and is remarkably healthy, active and intelligent. He is a house servant and has no impairments. [Value $500]

Thom acquired title through his wife, who inherited Wilson from the estate of William Matthews, late of Charles County, Md., in October 1857. He was brought to the District of Columbia in October 1860.

[Commissioners paid Thom $208.05.]

No. 194, Petition of James Dobbyn — Filed May 13, 1862

James Dobbyn of the city of Washington claims compensation for Elizabeth Baily, aged about 57 years. She is about 5 feet 4 inches tall, black complexion and is believed to be a full-blooded African. She is stout, able-bodied, and is a good cook, washer and ironer, and general household servant. She has been employed in Dobbyn's home and if he had to hire a replacement, it would cost him $7 a month. He purchased Elizabeth in April 1854, from Benjamin Taylor for $200. At the time of her purchase, she was in ill health, but is now strong and hearty. [Value $250]

[Commissioners paid Dobbyn $109.50.]

The printed report of the Commissioners erroneously gives Elizabeth's surname as "Bartey."

No. 195, Petition of Emily MacGill — Filed May 13, 1862

Emily MacGill of Washington City claims compensation for Isaac Moore, aged 55, dark brown, 5 feet 1 inch tall. He is a good servant and, although he occasionally complains of rheumatism, it does not affect his services beyond the loss of a few days. He was born a slave to her mother, Amelia Wilson, and was given to her upon her mother's death. [Value $300]

[Commissioners paid no compensation to MacGill as Moore was not produced.]

The printed report of the Commissioners spells Emily's last name as "McGill," but it is clearly spelled MacGill in the original petition.

No. 196, Petition of Michael R. Coombs — Filed May 13, 1862

Michael R. Coombs of Washington claims compensation for James Henry Cole, aged 22. He is of a chestnut color, about 5 feet 8 inches tall and has no marks. He is a waiter and was employed in the restaurant that Coombs formerly kept on Pennsylvania Ave. He subsequently has been employed in the same business for which he receives one dollar a day. He is smart, active, healthy and trustworthy. Coombs has the greatest confidence in him. He received Cole as a gift from his grandfather, Michael Sardo, by a deed of gift dated Aug. 15, 1844. [Value $1,400]

[Commissioners paid Coombs $569.40.]

No. 197, Petition of Robert K. Nevitt — Filed May 13, 1862

Robert K. Nevitt claims compensation for six persons.

1. Mary Jackson, aged 38, is of a dark brown color, about 5 feet 6 inches tall, with a medium build. She is healthy and a good cook, washer and ironer. [Value $1,200]

2. Richard S. Vigall, aged 22, dark brown in color, about 5 feet 8 or 9 inches tall with a stout build. He is a first-class gardener and farm hand and is very healthy. [Value $1,500]

3. Eliza Jackson, aged between 14 and 15, brown, about 5 feet 3 inches tall, stout build and very healthy. She is a good house servant. [Value $1,400]

4. Sarah Jackson, ten, dark brown, well grown, healthy and sprightly. She is a good chambermaid. [Value $800]

5. Alice Jackson, aged seven, dark brown. She is healthy and very sprightly. [Value $500]

6. Andrew Jackson, aged 18 months, is healthy, sprightly and well-grown. [Value $150]

Nevitt acquired title to Mary Jackson through his marriage in 1838 [*sic*]. His wife had acquired title by the will of Capt. John L. Naylor. The others are all children of Mary Jackson and were born in Nevitt's possession.

[Commissioners paid Nevitt $1,730.10: Mary Jackson, $328.50; Richard S. "Vigell", $569.40; Eliza Jackson, $438; Sarah Jackson, $219; Alice Jackson, $131.40; Andrew Jackson, $43.80.]

Pippenger, D.C. Marriage Licenses, 1811-1858, p. 440, shows that Robert K. Nevitt married Lettice [Eleanor] C. Moore on Dec. 20, 1836. Capt. John Lawson Naylor was a Revolutionary veteran who died in 1818. His will may be found in Pippenger, D.C. Probate Records,1801-1852, p. 87 and 87n.

No. 198, Petition of Selby B. Scaggs   Filed May 13, 1862

Selby B. Scaggs claims compensation for 13 persons.

1. Ailsey Steward, aged 75, black, about five feet tall, healthy. She is a good nurse. [Value $50]

2. David Steward, son of Ailsey, aged 45, black, about 5 feet 7 inches tall and healthy. He is a first-class gardener and farm hand. [Value $1,000]

3. John Steward, son of David Steward, aged 20, black, about 5 feet 8 inches tall, healthy, of medium build. He is a good gardener and farm hand. [Value $1,500]

4. Albert Steward, son of David, aged 15, black, about five feet tall, healthy and very sprightly. He is a good carriage driver. [Value $1,200]

5. Lucy Steward, or Scaggs, seven, dark brown, well-grown, healthy and very sprightly. [Value $500]

6. Edward Steward, aged six, dark brown, not very healthy. [Value $400]

7. Maria Gross, aged 35, light brown, about 5 feet 8 inches tall. She is stout built, very strong and healthy. She is a good gardener and field hand. [Value $1,200]

8. Laura Gross, about four, light brown, sprightly and healthy. [Value $250]

9. Margaret Gross, aged two, light brown, sprightly and healthy. [Value $200]

10. Amanda F. Calvert, aged 19, dark brown, about 5 feet 4 inches tall, stout built and healthy. She is a first-class house servant. [Value $1,400]

11. Rachel Jacks, aged 17, dark brown, about 5 feet 6 inches tall, medium build, healthy and likely. She is a good house servant and garden hand. [Value $1,400]

12. Dennis Lowe, aged 35, black. He has both legs cut off just below the knee. He is very healthy and a good oxcart driver and garden hand. [Value $125]

13. Sarah Hues is aged 25. She is afflicted with insanity and fits.

Ailsey Steward was purchased by Scaggs from his sister, Rebecca Gloyd about four years ago. David Steward, son of Ailsey, was inherited under the will of his father, James Scaggs of Prince George's County, Md. John Steward, Albert Steward, Lucy Steward or Scaggs and Edward Steward are children of David Steward and were born while in Scagg's possession. Maria Gross and infant Laura were purchased from his brother, Isaac Scaggs of Prince George's County. Margaret, daughter of Maria, was born in his possession. Amanda Calvert was purchased from the estate of Nathaniel Brady in Prince George's County . Rachel Jacks was born in his possession. Dennis Lowe was purchased about five years ago from Henry Hillary of Prince George's County and Sarah Hues was purchased from the estate of Nathaniel Brady.

[Commissioners paid Scaggs $3,109.80: "Arlsey" Steward, no value; David Steward, $262.80; John Steward, $657; Albert Steward, $328.50; Lucy Steward, $197.10; Edward Steward, $43.80; Maria Gross, $394.20; Laura Gross, $109.50; Margaret Gross, $43.80; Amanda F. "Colvert", $503.70; Rachel Jacks. $525.60; Dennis Lowe, $43.80; Sarah Hues, no value.]

The Census for 1860, Vol. 2, p. 71, lists Scaggs as a farmer in the County of Washington.

No. 199, Petition of Hannah M. Walker   Filed May 13, 1862

Hannah M. Walker of Washington claims compensation for two persons.

1. Louisa Delaney, aged 21, dark brown color, 5 feet 3 inches tall, very stout. She is a sound, healthy and honest servant.

2. Margaret Delaney, aged 19, a bright chestnut color, 5 feet 2 inches tall. She has a scar on her right lower jaw. She is a sound, healthy, good and honest servant.

Both have lived in her family for the past 13 years. [Value $2,000]

Walker's husband, John Walker, bought the slaves for her about 13 years ago. A copy of the attached bill of sale, signed Jun. 19, 1849, shows that James V. Patton of Washington, in consideration of $250, sold Negro children, Margaret and Louisa, children of Dolly who was owned by Patton, to William H. Gunnell. Gunnell delivered the children to Hannah Walker upon payment of one dollar.

[Commissioners paid Walker $919.80: Louisa Delaney, $438; Margaret Delaney, $481.80.]

No. 200, Petition of Philip A. Cawood and Sarah E. Cawood   Filed May 14, 1862

Philip A. Cawood of Washington City claims compensation for Fanny Isabella Bowman, aged 13 years. She is of a dark color, 4 feet 8 inches tall, rather slender, smart, active and healthy. She is a good cook, washer and ironer and is valuable as a house servant. Cawood says that about a year ago he was offered $1,000 for her by Mr. Mattingly of Charles County, Md. [Value $1,000]

Philip Cawood acquired title through his wife, Sarah Cawood, who was bequeathed Fanny under the will of Sarah Green, her mother, which will is filed in the D.C. Orphans' Court.

[Commissioners paid Philip A. And Sarah E. Cawood $350.40.]

No. 201, Petition of Susanna Monroe   Filed May 14, 1862

Susanna Monroe of Washington claims compensation for two persons.

1. Margaret Ann Wheeler, aged about 33, is black, 5 feet 10 inches tall, stout and thick. She is a valuable servant and is a good cook, washer and ironer. She has no marks or blemishes. [Value $1,000]
2. Judy Smith, aged about 60, is of a light copper color and nearly six feet tall. She is a valuable servant and still minds the children and does general light work. She has no marks or blemishes. [Value $100]

Monroe received them by deed from her father, Thomas Monroe, which is recorded in Port Tobacco, Md.

[Commissioners paid Monroe $109.50 for Margaret Ann Wheeler; Judy Smith was judged of no value.]

No. 202, Petition of Joseph Ehrmantrout   Filed May 14, 1862

Joseph Ehmantrout of Georgetown claims compensation for Hannah Davis, aged 45. She is of a dark color with prominent cheekbones and is 5 feet 3 inches tall. He purchased Davis from Phillip Stone of Montgomery County, Md. [Value $400]

[Commissioners paid Ehrmantrout $219, by his attorney, R. P. Jackson.]

No. 203, Petition of Hilleary L. Offutt   Filed May 14, 1862

Hilleary L. Offutt of Georgetown claims compensation for Maria Shiles and her two children.

1. Maria Shiles, aged 40, of a dark copper color. [Value $600]
2. Isabella Shiles, four years four months old, of a bright copper color. [Value $300]
3. Emily Shiles, aged four months, of a bright copper color. [Value $100]

Offutt purchased Maria and her child from John Austin. He states the purpose of the purchase was "to prevent the separation of said Maria from her husband and prevent her from being sold to a trader to be carried out of the District of Columbia." The accompanying bill of sale, dated Georgetown, Dec. 16, 1859, shows that Offut paid $400 to Austin for Maria and her child, Isabella.

[Commissioners paid Offut $525.60: Maria Shiles, $350.40; Emily [sic] Shiles, $131.40; Isabella [sic] Shiles, $43.80.]

No. 204, Petition of Jesse W. Kitchen   Filed May 14, 1862

Jesse W. Kitchen of Georgetown claims compensation for Jane Berry, aged 13. She is of a dark color and about five feet tall. He states that he had been offered $800 for her before the act of Apr. 16, 1862. [Value $800]

He purchased Jane for $260 from L. Thomas on Jul.. 28, 1859 on condition that she not be carried out of the District of Columbia.

[Commissioners paid "Ketchen" $350.40.]

No. 205, Petition of Eliza Lucas   Filed May 14, 1862

Eliza Lucas of Georgetown claims compensation for four persons.

1. Henny Ritter, aged 65, of a dark color. [Value $250]
2. Eliza J. Johnson, aged 11, of a bright color. {Value $700]
3. Charles Johnson, aged seven, of a bright color. [Value $700]
4. Mary Johnson, aged six, of a dark color, [Value $300]

Lucas acquired title by purchase of Henny Ritter many years ago. Eliza, Charles and Mary are her grandchildren and were born in Lucas's house.

[Commissioners paid Lucas $635.10, by her attorney, R. P. Jackson: Henny Ritter, $43.80; Eliza J. Johnson, $262.80; Mary Johnson, $153.30; Charles Johnson, $175.20.]

No. 206, Petition of William H. Simms   Filed May 14, 1862

William H. Simms of Georgetown claims compensation for two persons.

1. Hannah Johnson is aged 22 and copper colored. [Value $1,000]
2. Aloysius Johnson, aged five, is mulatto. [Value $100]

William Simms acquired his title by purchase for $200 of Hannah Johnson from Thomas J. Bowie of Montgomery County, Md., Dec. 4, 1849. The attached bill of sale indicates that Johnson was purchased for a term of service and was to gain her freedom on May 5, 1875. She was not to be sold or removed from the District of Columbia. The terms of the bill of sale did not apply to any of Johnson's offspring born during her term of service.

[Commissioners paid Simms $306.60: Hannah Johnson, $219; Aloysius Johnson, $87.60.]

No. 207, Petition of Ann M. Wood   Filed May 14, 1862

Mrs. Ann M. Wood of Washington claims compensation for three persons.

1. Jane Webb, aged 58, mulatto, five feet tall, with no particular marks. [Value $500]
2. Nancy Reed, aged 38, dark mulatto, 5 feet 4 inches tall, with no particular marks. [Value $500]
3. Henrietta Evans, aged 18, 5 feet 2 inches tall, with no marks. [Value $800]

Wood says that they are all first-class family servants. Jane is an excellent cook and the others are employed as family servants in her family. They are all good seamstresses and are efficient and free of defects.

Wood inherited Jane Webb from her mother, the late Mrs. Margaret Taylor, relict of General Zachary Taylor. Henrietta Evans also came to her by inheritance. She acquired Nancy Reed by deed of gift and inheritance from her late father, General Zachary Taylor.

[Commissioners paid Wood $854.10: Jane Webb, $109.50; Nancy Reed, $175.20; Henrietta Evans, $569.40.]

No. 208, Petition of Margaret Buchignani, guardian of Emily C. Randolph   Filed May 14, 1862

Margaret Buchignani, as guardian of Emily C. Randolph of Washington, claims compensation for Elizabeth Stutley, aged 13. She is a dark mulatto, about five feet tall with black eyes and short hair. She is a domestic in Buchignani's house and is a good, honest, trustworthy and intelligent girl. [Value $800]

She inherited her from her grandmother, Mrs. Breckinborough.

[Commissioners paid Buchignani, guardian, $284.70.]

A note to the document indicates that Emily's mother was Margaret B. Randolph, who died Mar. 23, 1855, at the age of 23 years. See Wesley E. Pippenger, District of Columbia Interments (Index to Deaths), January 1, 1855 to July 31, 1874 (Westminster, Md., Willow Bend Books, 1999), p. 294. Hereinafter cited as Pippenger, D.C. Deaths, 1855-1874.

No. 209, Petition of Joseph P. Taylor   Filed May 14, 1862

J. P. Taylor of Washington claims compensation for five persons.

1. James McGrunder, aged 30, mulatto, 5 feet 5 inches tall, with no particular marks. He is an amiable, efficient man and has a fine mechanical talent. He is a first-rate waiter and dining room servant. [Value $1,200]
2. Patty Brown, aged 28, black, 5 feet 2 inches tall, with no particular marks. She is a fine house servant and valuable for all work in the house. She is healthy and stout. [Value $800]
3. Nelly Jordan, aged 25, light complexion, five feet tall, no particular marks. She is a fine house servant and valuable for all work in the house. She is rather small. [Value $800]
4. Thomas Reynolds, aged 12, jet black, 4 feet 4 inches tall, no particular marks. He is a fine, healthy, sprightly boy. [Value $500]
5. Guy Carlton, aged seven, light complexion, 3 feet 9 inches tall, no particular marks. He is a fine, healthy, sprightly boy. [Value $300]

Taylor inherited Nelly Jordan and the mother of Tom Reynolds and Guy Carlton from his late sister, Mrs. Sarah B. Gray. Tom and Guy were born after he came into possession of their mother, who is deceased. James McGrunder was a family servant and was purchased by Taylor to prevent his being sold. Patty Brown was purchased from Mr. Humphreys when she was a child some 20 years ago.

[Commissioners paid Taylor $1,752: James "McGrundy", $525.60; Patty Brown, $394.20; Nelly Jordan, $438; Thomas Reynolds, $219; Guy Carlton, $175.20.]

No. 210, Petition of Harriet Smith
Filed May 14, 1862

Harriet Smith of Washington City claims compensation for eight persons.
1. Robert Tyler, aged 30, 5 feet 10 inches tall, dark brown color. [Value $1,500]
2. Charles Mathews, aged 22, 5 feet 9 inches tall, dark brown color. [Value $1,500]
3. Sarah Mathews, aged 29, 5 feet 3 inches tall, bright color. [Value $1,000]
4. Hannah Grant, aged 19, 5 feet 7 inches, dark color. [Value $1,000]
5. Richard Mathews, aged 15, 5 feet 1 inch tall, bright color. [Value $800]
6. George Mathews, aged 13, five feet tall, bright color. [Value $700]
7. Maria Mathews, aged six, dark color. [Value $300]
8. Mary Grant, aged one-and-one-half years, dark color. [Value $100]

They are honest, faithful and industrious servants and are free of defects.

Smith inherited them from her mother, Mary Brumley (she having married a second time), and the will is recorded in D.C.

[Commissioners paid Smith, by Benjamin S. Bayley, her attorney, $2,847: Robert Tyler, $569.40; Charles Mathews, $569.40; Sarah Mathews, $350.40; Hannah Grant, $438; Richard Mathews, $438; George Mathews, $306.60; Maria Mathews, $175.20; Mary Grant, no value.]

Mary Brumley died Apr. 19, 1826. Her will provided that "Harriot" receive "negroes Bob, Dick, Jim, Liz and Harriot and her two children, also John and Emely (Violette's children), and Jane the dau. of Mary, Jane to serve until she is 20 yrs. old and no longer." See Pippenger, D.C. Probate Records, 1801-1852, p.133.

No. 211, Petition of Ann Macdaniel
Filed May 14, 1862

Ann "McDaniel" of Washington claims compensation for two persons.
1. Susan Newton, aged 50, mulatto, 5 feet 2 inches tall. She is a house servant, cook, ironer and washer and is honest and industrious. [Value $300]
2. Tony Newton, aged 26, black, 6 feet one-half inch tall. He is a servant who is honest, industrious and free of defects. [Value $1,500]

Susan has been a slave in Macdaniel's family for the last forty years and Tony was born to her while she was in the family.

[Commissioners paid Macdaniel $788.40: Susan Newton, $175.20; "Toney" Newton, $613.20.]

Ann's surname is spelled both "Macdaniel" and "McDaniel" in the original petition.

No. 212, Petition of Warren Waugh
Filed May 14, 1862

Warren Waugh of Prince George's County, Md., claims compensation for two persons.
1. Mary Joyce, aged 17, of a chestnut color, about 5 feet 1 or 2 inches tall. She is an honest, industrious house servant and is healthy. [Value $1,000]
2. Mary, aged 14, of a chestnut color, about five feet tall. She is an honest, industrious house servant and is healthy. [Value $600]

He acquired Joyce by marriage with Susanna Brown, who got them under the terms of the will of her father, George Brown, of Prince George's County. Mary was willed to Waugh's daughter, Eveline Waugh, by John M. Brown. John M.'s will is recorded in Marlborough, Md.

[Commissioners paid Waugh $854.10: Nancy Joyce, $481.80; Mary, $372.30.]

No. 213, Petition of Benjamin P. Smith
Filed May 14, 1862

Benjamin P. Smith of Washington claims compensation for seven persons.
1. Mary Ann Coleman, aged 27, mulatto, about 5 feet 2 inches tall, healthy and strong. She is an honest and industrious servant and a first-rate cook, ironer and washer. [Value $800]
2. Margaret Woodward, aged 25, a bright-colored woman, about 5 feet 2 inches tall, healthy and strong. She is an honest and industrious servant and a good cook, ironer and washer. She was sold some years back for $500, but was only in part paid for.
3. Harriet Guy, aged 34, black, about 5 feet 3 inches tall. She is an honest, industrious servant and a good cook, ironer and washer. She is strong and healthy. [Value $800]

4. Lila [Guy], mulatto, 15 years old, about five feet tall. She is an honest and industrious girl who is strong and healthy. She is a good dining room servant. [Value $600]

5. Martha [Guy], aged ten years, black, about four feet tall. She is a strong and healthy girl and was raised as a house servant. [Value $450]

6. Betty [Guy], aged seven, black, about 3 feet 6 inches tall, is strong and healthy. [Value $300]

7. John Henry [Guy], aged two years and six months, mulatto, about 2 feet 10 inches tall. He is strong and healthy. [Value $250]

Harriet was a present from Mrs. George Price to Smith's wife. Lila, Martha, Betty and John Henry are her children born while she was in Smith's house. Mary Ann Coleman and Margaret Woodward were acquired from the estate of Smith's wife's father, Benjamin Price of Virginia.

[Commissioners paid Matilda B. Smith, administratrix of Benjamin P. Smith, $2,146.20: Mary Ann Coleman, $481.80; Margaret Woodward, $350.40; Harriet Guy, $394.20; Lila, $394.20; Martha, $262.80; Betty, $175.20; John Henry, $87.60.]

No. 214, Petition of Achsey Dorsey   Filed May 14, 1862

Achsey Dorsey of Anne Arundel County, Md., claims compensation for Georgiana Bacon, 13 years six months old, bright mulatto with black hair that is quite straight and glossy, about five feet tall. She is spare and somewhat stooped in the shoulders. She is employed by Rev. B. Peyton Brown of Washington City and was taken there about the middle of last March. She was bound to serve for a term of years and was to be freed when she reached age 20. She is active, smart and healthy and is a good nurse and an excellent chambermaid. [Value $360]

Georgiana was born of slave woman Maria [Bacon (?)], while she was in Dorsey's service. Maria has since been manumitted and is now a free woman in Maryland.

[Commissioners paid $109.50.]

No. 215, Petition of Nicholas S. Shaw   Filed May 14, 1862

Nicholas S. Shaw of Washington City claims compensation for Stephen Owen, aged 34, of a dark color and six feet tall. He is healthy, sober, intelligent and industrious. He is a first-rate carriage driver. Shaw says he has been offered $1,600 for Owen because of his superior qualities. [Value $1,200]

He acquired Owen from the estate of Rezin Shaw of Montgomery County, Md., about five years ago for $850, and that amount was below his real value.

[Commissioners paid Shaw $438.]

No. 216, Petition of George Horseman   Filed May 14, 1862

George Horseman of Washington City claims compensation for two persons.

1. Sharlott Hatton, aged 14 years six months, dark in color, medium sized, very smart and sprightly. [Value $700]

2. Lavinia Hatton, aged nine years and six months, dark in color, about medium size. She is sound, healthy, smart and free of defects. [Value $600]

Horseman states that he raised the mother of Sharlott and Lavinia, as well as the two children.

A supplementary document was filed on Jun. 6, 1862, by William D. Shepherd showing that Shepherd on May 5, 1861, purchased from George Horseman the services of Charlotte for a specified term. The Act of Apr. 16, 1862, deprived him of the servant's services and he claims compensation for $21, being six months unexpired services from Apr. 25 to Oct. 25, 1862. Attached is the agreement between Horseman and Shepherd signed May, 25, 1861, by which Shepherd paid Horseman $60 for Charlotte's services for 17 months. Should she pass out of Shepherd's possession or become disabled, Shepherd was to receive $3.50 per month for the time lost.

[Commissioners paid Jane E. Horseman, widow and devisee of George Horseman, $675.80 for Charlotte Hatton and they paid William D. Shepherd $25. Smith was paid $262.80 for Lavinia Hatton.]

No. 217, Petition of Middleton & Beall   Filed May 14, 1862

Benjamin F. Middleton and Benjamin Beall of Washington claim compensation for four persons.

1. Charlotte, aged 47, dark, 5 feet 3 inches tall. [Value $800]

2. Henry, aged 17, black, 5 feet 1 inch tall. [Value $650]

3. Mary, aged 11, black, 4 feet 2 inches tall. [Value $350]

4. Anna, aged 7, black, 3 feet 8 inches tall. [Value $250]

All of these servants are sound and healthy and have no infirmities

They were purchased about 12 years ago for a cost of $1,000. Mary and Anna are children of Charlotte and were born after their mother was purchased.

[Commissioners paid Middleton & Beall $897.90: Charlotte, $175.20; Henry, $350.40; Mary, $219; Anna, $153.30.]

Boyd's Directory for 1860, p. 113, lists Middleton (Middleton & Beall, and Hooe, Brother & Co.), grocer, on Pennsylvania Ave.

No. 218, Petition of Benjamin Beall   Filed May 14, 1862

Benjamin Beall of Washington claims compensation for four persons.
1. Rachel, 27 years old, 5 feet 4 inches tall, black. [Value $800]
2. Moses, 14 years old, 4 feet 11 inches tall, brown. He is slightly ruptured. [Value $600]
3. Robert, aged 11, four feet tall, brown. [Value $350]
4. Washington, aged 11, is 3 feet 6 inches tall and brown. He is afflicted with scrofula, sore eyes, and has one leg shorter than the other. [No value]

Moses and Robert were born in Montgomery County, Md. Their parents are both slaves and belong to Beall. Rachel he purchased from William Baird of Montgomery County when she was a small girl. Washington is her child.

[Commissioners paid Beall $657: Rachel, $284.70; Moses, $175.20; Robert, $197.10; Washington, no value.]

"Scrofula" is an old term for a disease with glandular swellings, thus probably tuberculosis.

No. 219, Petition of Charles T. Gardner   Filed May 14, 1862

Charles T. Gardner of Washington City claims compensation for three persons.
1. Ann, aged 37, dark mulatto, stout and low. She is a good cook, washerwoman and house servant. She is very smart and industrious and healthy. [Value $750]
2. Jane, Ann's daughter, aged 17 on May 10, 1862, mulatto, medium height and size. She is healthy, well-grown, likely, smart and industrious. [Value $1,150]
3. Kate, Ann's daughter, aged six on May 20, 1862, mulatto, small for her age. She is very useful in the family and is smart and active. [Value $550]

They are all good house servants and are healthy, reliable and honest. Gardner purchased Ann from Duncan McNeil of Fayetteville, N.C., in 1837 or 1838 when Gardner resided there. The bill of sale has been lost or mislaid. The girls were born since he owned the mother. Gardner attached a "certificate of health" from Dr. Jonas Green stating that as a physician in Gardner's family he knows that Ann has not been confined to her bed by indisposition more than five or six days, except on the two occasions when she gave birth to her children. She is healthy, though not a remarkably robust woman. The two children are uniformly healthy. Also attached is a statement signed by R. C. Gardner, Juliet Gardner, Thomas J. Gardner and Julia Gardner as to the characteristics and value of the slaves.

[Commissioners paid Gardner $832.20: Ann, $240.90; Jane, $459.90; Kate, $131.40.]

No. 220, Petition of William H. Morrison   Filed May 14, 1862

William H. Morrison of the city of Washington claims compensation for Maria Lee, aged about 14 years. She is a dark mulatto, about 4 feet 4 inches tall, rather slender and has no marks or defects. She is a good house servant and is healthy in mind and body. [Value $700]

Morrison purchased Lee for $670 in 1859, from James D. Triplett per Smith H. Rixey, his agent, in the city of Washington. The attached bill of sale is signed Sept. 7, 1859.

[Commissioners paid Morrison $262.80.]

No. 221, Petition of Otis W. Marsh   Filed May 14, 1862

Otis W. Marsh of Washington claims compensation for Sophia Davis, aged 19 years. She is quite black and is 4 feet 11 3/8 inches tall. She has a flat nose, thick lips, is stout built and is sound and healthy. She is a nurse for Marsh's children and is an industrious servant who is well-qualified for all domestic house purposes.

Marsh purchased her for $350 on Nov. 4, 1853, from George H. Cockrell of Prince William County, Va. Attached is a copy of the bill of sale which was recorded in D.C. Liber J.A.S. No. 66 (?), folios 22-23.

[Commissioners paid Marsh $525.60.]

No. 222, Petition of Thomas J. Davis   Filed May 14, 1862

Thomas J. Davis of Washington claims compensation for two persons.

1. Francis Thomas, aged 35, is copper colored and 5 feet 1 1/4 inch tall. He is an old and faithful servant.

2. Harriet Thomas, aged 55, black, 5 feet 3/4 inch tall, healthy. She has a scar on the side of her right eye. She is an old and faithful servant and Davis could not fill her place.

Davis gives their value as $750.

He purchased Francis Thomas from Mr. Goodwin for $200 some 19 years ago. Harriet Thomas was willed to his wife, Rose Ann Semmes, by her father, Francis Semmes of Charles County, Md. Attached is a copy of Semmes's will, proved Sept. 29, 1840, that provides that his daughter, Rose Semmes, inherit his servant woman, Harriet. Also attached is a statement from Susan A. Goodwin, widow of Henry R. Goodwin of Charles County, Md., verifying that on Jan. 5, 1843, Davis purchased Francis Thomas from Henry B. Goodwin.

[Commissioners paid Davis $67.70: Francis Thomas, $21.90; Harriet Thomas, $43.80.]

No. 223, Petition of Charles R. Belt Filed May 14, 1862

Charles R. Belt of the county of Washington, D.C., claims compensation for seven persons.

1. Lethea Bowie, about 49 years old, of a dark copper color, healthy, corpulent, very pleasant and polite when spoken to. She has been his cook for many years and was raised in the petitioner's service.

2. George Bowie, son of Lethea, is aged about 18 (?). He is a valuable servant and would command the highest market price as a farm hand. He is healthy, strong and active, not quite six feet tall, a dark copper color.

3. Harriet Bowie, daughter of Lethea, about 19, copper color, 5 feet 6 inches tall and good in appearance She is a faithful and honest servant and a good seamstress.

4. Andrew Bowie, son of Lethea, aged 17, is a valuable servant, farm hand and cobbler. He is about 5 feet 10 inches tall and is polite, but has a hesitation (?) in answering.

5. Hamilton Bowie, son of Leathe, aged 15, dark copper color, seldom speaks, his eyes are a peculiar color. He is quite ingenious and healthy, handles carpentry very well and is a good farm hand.

6. Eliza Bowie, daughter of Leathe, aged about 13, copper colored and well-grown for her age. She stoops a little when walking, but has a good nature and is pleasant when spoken to. She is about five feet tall.

7. Henry Augustus [Bowie], aged 41, dark copper in color, about 5 feet 7 inches tall. He has a drawn look and a speech impediment which gives him the appearance of a want of intelligence. He is, however, smart and a good farm hand and does his full share of the work with fidelity.

Lethea and Henry are brother and sister and the children of Hannah [Bowie (?)] who belonged to his father, the late Joseph Sprigg Belt, and were born his property. Lethea's children were all born in the petitioner's residence after the death of his father in 1819. Belt left two children, Charles and William J. Belt. Charles continued to reside at the home place in the county and Hannah lived with him as his slave. He subsequently purchased his brother's interest in the servants.

Belt claims $5,600 for the servants.

[Commissioners paid Belt $3,109.80: Lethea Bowie, $219; George Bowie, $657; Harriet Bowie, $525.60; Andrew Bowie, $613.20; Hamilton Bowie, $438; Eliza Bowie, $438; Henry Augustus, $219.]

No. 224, Petition of Charles H. Demar, trustee, and Margaret E. Skelley Filed May 14, 1862

Charles H. Demar of Washington City claims compensation for five persons.

1. Lucy, or Lucinda, Key, aged 34, of a very dark chestnut color, 5 feet 4 inches tall. She is a first-rate servant. She is the mother of the four children listed below. [Value $1,000]

2. Catharine Virginia Key, aged ten, of a very dark chestnut color, 4 feet 2 ½ inches tall. [$600]

3. Mary Alice Key, aged eight, dark mulatto, four feet tall. [Value $500]

4. Charles Richard Key, aged six, very dark mulatto, 3 feet 5 inches tall. [Value $400]

5. Avonia Key, aged four, very bright mulatto, 3 feet 2 ½ inches tall. [Value $300]

All of Lucy's children are likely and promising and have no defects that would impair their value.

Demar is acting under a deed of trust from William E. Skelley dated Apr. 3, 1861, that conveyed the above persons to him for the benefit of Margaret E. Skelley, wife of William E. Skelley. William Skelley purchased Lucy Key from the estate of the late Dr. Benjamin Day of Bladensburg, Md., on Jan. 2, 1847. A copy of the receipt shows payment of $550 for "negro girl Lucinda." Lucy's children were born after 1847.

[Commissioners paid Demar, trustee, and Margaret E. Skelley, her x mark; test: William E. Skelley, $1,116.90: Lucy Key, $394.20; Catharine V. Key, $240.90; Mary Alice Key, $197.10; Charles R. Key, $153.30; Avonia Key, $131.40.]

No. 225, Petition of John McDermott   Filed May 14, 1862

John McDermott of Washington City claims compensation for two persons.

1. George, aged 26, dark brown or black in color, 5 feet 4 inches tall, stout. He has been employed for a long time in the coach factory of M. McDermott. He is nearsighted, but this does not impair his value. He is also ruptured partially. [Value $1,000]

2. Elsey, aged 27, dark brown, about 5 feet 4 inches tall, slight in build. She is an excellent house servant and able-bodied, except she has lost part of the finger, or fingers on one of her hands. [Value $700]

McDermott acquired title to George from his marriage. He purchased Elsey from O. C. Harris of Prince George's County, Md., about Dec. 21, 1855.

[Commissioners paid McDermott $613.20: George, $262.80; Elsey, $350.40.]

Boyd's Directory of 1860, p. 106, contains the following listing: M. McDermott (John, James, Francis and Arthur), coach builders, Penn. Ave.

No. 226, Petition of John McDermott, administrator of Michael   Filed May 14, 1862

John M. McDermott of Washington, administrator of the late Michael McDermott, his father, claims compensation for two persons.

1. Josephine, aged 25, dark mulatto, about five feet tall, stout in build. She is a good house servant. [Value $800]
2. Eliza, daughter of Josephine, aged about ten, light mulatto in color. [Value $400]

Josephine and Eliza was born as slaves in his father's house and were the daughter and granddaughter of a slave named Matilda, whom Michael purchased many years ago from Mrs. Lydia Thompson of Washington. Matilda has died.

[Commissioners paid McDermott $613.20: Josephine, $394.20; Eliza, $219.]

No. 227, Petition of Charles Walter, administrator of J. P. Gilroy   Filed May 14, 1862

Charles Walter, administrator of the estate of Dr. John P. Gilroy of Washington, claims compensation for two persons.

1. Mary, aged 36, black, 5 feet 3 inches tall. She is healthy, active and stout. [Value $500]
2. Molly Posey, aged eight, black, 4 feet 2 inches tall. She is remarkably lively and intelligent. [Value $400]

Dr. Gilroy purchased them in Charles County, Md.

[Commissioners paid Walter $438: Mary, $262.80; Molly Posey, $175.20.]

No. 228, Petition of Gustavus Waters   Filed May 14, 1862

Gustavus Waters of Washington claims compensation for five slaves.

1. John H. Karna, aged 23, dark, 5 feet 10 inches tall.
2. Daniel W. Karna, aged 21, dark, 5 feet 11 inches tall.
3. James W. Karna, aged 19, light, 5 feet 5 inches tall.
4. Charles A. Karna, aged 17, light, five feet tall.
5. Mary C. Karna, aged 14, dark, 5 feet 5 inches tall.

Waters values them at $5,000. He says they are all healthy, well-grown and stout. They are handy servants, honest and faithful, and command good wages. They are his only means of support.

The grandmother of the Karna family was the property of his wife, Tabitha Waters, formerly Mead, whom he married Feb. 14, 1823, in Charles County, Md. The family has been his property and inmates of his house ever since.

[Commissioners paid Waters $2,628: John H. Karna, $613.20; Daniel W. Karna, $635.10; James W. Karna, $481.80; Charles A. Karna, $394.20; Mary C. Karna, $503.70.]

No. 229, Petition of John Q. Willson, for Charles H. Willson   Filed May 15, 1862

John Q. Willson of Washington, guardian of his son Charles Horace Wilson, claims compensation for Joseph Clinton Billingslee, aged seven, of a bright copper color. He is intelligent, honest, industrious and able. [Value $500]

Clinton was a gift from his Charles's aunt, Anna M. L. Forrest of Rockville, Montgomery County, Md. Attached is the deed of gift dated Mar. 8, 1861, whereby Charles Horace Willson, son of John Q. and Ellen Willson of Washington, is given a bright mulatto boy named Joseph Clinton Billingslee, aged five.

[Commissioners paid John W. "Wilson", for C. H. "Wilson", $153.30.]

The surname is clearly spelled "Willson" throughout the original documents, although the commissioners' printed report spells the name with one "l".

No. 230, Petition of Charlotte and Isabella Kilgour, of Rockville, Md. Filed May 15, 1862
Charlotte and Isabella Kilgour of Montgomery County, Md., claim compensation for two persons.

1. Hanson Carroll, aged 20, is about 5 feet 6 or 8 inches tall, dark mulatto in color, thick and well-set. He is able-bodied and in full health. [Value $120 per annum]

2. James Carroll, aged 18, is about 5 feet 6 or 7 inches tall, of a copper color, rather more slender than Hanson. He is able-bodied and in good health. [Value $108 per annum]

Miss Martha Kilgour of St. Mary's County, Md., about 1837 or 1838, gave a Negro woman named Anachy (?) to Elizabeth Kilgour and your petitioners. Elizabeth Kilgour, our sister, has died unmarried. Hanson and James are the children of Anachy (?) and were born after she came into the possession of your petitioners.

[Commissioners paid Charlotte and Isabella Kilgour, by J. C. Kennedy, attorney, $1,138.80: Hanson Carroll, $591.30; James Carroll, $547.50.]

No. 231, Petition of Gregory Ennis Filed May 15, 1862
Gregory Ennis of Washington City claims compensation for Caroline R. Butts, aged 36, mulatto, about five feet tall. She is an excellent house servant and is honest, intelligent, faithful and industrious. [Value $1,500]

Ennis purchased Butts about 24 years ago from the late Jabez Rooker, who used to live in Washington.

[Commissioners paid Ennis $306.60.]

No. 232, Petition of Sabra Woodward Filed May 15, 1862
Sabra Woodward of Georgetown claims compensation for Matilda Graham, aged 22 years. She is of a black or dark chestnut complexion, about five feet tall. She has pleasant features and is quick in movement but slow of speech. She is a first-rate cook, washer, ironer, house servant, and lady's maid. She is sound of mind and body and has an excellent disposition. She was raised in the family and her loss would be irreplaceable. [Value $1,000]

H. M. Sweeny of Georgetown sold Graham to Kirby S. Woodward, trustee, on Apr. 18, 1845, and the bill of sale is recorded in D.C. Liber W.B. No. 116, folio 285.

[Commissioners paid Sabra Woodward $525.60.]

No. 233, Petition of William D.C. Murdock Filed May 15, 1862
William D.C. Murdock of Washington County, D.C., claims compensation for nine persons.

1. William Hutchinson, aged 56, black, 5 feet 6 inches tall, of a pleasant countenance. He is handy, honest, good-tempered and has been Murdock's foreman for out-of-doors work. He is a well-trained house servant, gardener, driver and ostler. [Value $900]

2. William H. Lee, aged 20, dark chestnut color, six feet tall, stout build and with a bashful countenance. Is honest, good tempered, trustworthy and is a good driver, ostler, and farm hand. He is strong and capable of hard work but at present has been slightly ruptured. This, however, does not impair his value. [Value $1,100]

3. Francis X. Lee, aged 20, copper color, 5 feet 8 inches tall, stout build, very intelligent and very likely with a serious countenance. He is a well-trained driver, ostler and gardener. He is strong, healthy, honest, trustworthy and good tempered. [Value $1,200]

4. Theodore Lee, 16, dark chestnut color, 5 feet 5 inches tall, likely, well-made, with a pleasant and cheerful countenance. He is trained in house work, driving and gardening. He is strong, healthy and good-tempered. [Value $1,100]

5. Sophia Hutchinson, aged 89, black in color, gray hair, 5 feet 5 inches tall. She is well-preserved for her age, but infirm. Murdock asserts that he "feels duty bound to support her." [No value]

6. Mary C. Lee, 26, copper color, 5 feet 6 inches tall, intelligent, very likely in her face and has a good figure. She is a well-trained house servant and is healthy, honest, good-tempered, trusty and strong. [Value $1,400]

7. Martha A. Lee, aged 20, 5 feet 5 inches tall, good figure, with a pleasant countenance. She is a well-trained cook and house servant who is honest, healthy, strong, good-tempered, moral. [Value $1,400]

8. Margaret Ann Lee, aged 16, copper color, 5 feet 5 inches tall, likely, has a good figure and a pleasant countenance. Is trained to house work. She is honest, strong, healthy, good-tempered and moral. [Value $1,100]

9. Ellen Lee, aged 14, dark chestnut in color, 5 feet 2 inches tall, well-made, very likely with a pleasant countenance. She is trained in house work and nursing and is healthy, honest and good-tempered. [Value $900]

Murdock was the only child and heir of Addison Murdock, who died in 1808, who owned Sophia and William

Hutchinson, Susan Hawkins and others. Susan Hawkins married and had a daughter named Eliza Matthews and Eliza Matthews married John Lee. William H. Lee and the other Lees are children of Eliza and John Lee.

[Commissioners paid Murdock $3,635.40: William Hutchinson, $175.20; William H. Lee, $657; Francis X. Lee, $569.40; Theodore Lee, $306.60; Sophia Hutchinson, no value; Mary C. Lee, $525.60; Martha A. Lee, $525.60; Margaret A. Lee, $481.80; Ellen Lee, $394.20.]

No. 234, Petition of George Ailer Filed May 15, 1862

George Ailer of Washington claims compensation for Mary A. Strabit, aged 41 years. She is below medium height, black, strong and squarely built. She is slightly nearsighted, but has no other defects. She is healthy and is a first-rate domestic servant who is acquainted with all kinds of house work. [Value $700]

Ailer purchased her and her mother from Mrs. Tanner of Washington City about 37 years ago. Mary's mother died many years ago.

[Commissioners paid Ailer $131.40]

No. 235, Petition of Susan K. Williams Filed May 15, 1862

Susan K. Williams of Georgetown claims compensation for three persons.

1. Laura Jackson, aged about 50, dark brown in color, about five feet tall. She is healthy, active, reliable and faithful and is an excellent cook and house servant. [Value $1,000]
2. Mary Hicks, aged 45, dark brown, about five feet tall. In general, her healthy is very good and she is trustworthy and capable and a valuable house servant. [Value $1,000]
3. Jane Compton, about 13, dark, 5 feet 4 inches tall. She is very strong, healthy and active. [Value $800]

Williams states that Laura and Mary were born in her family of slave parents that belonged to her. Jane was purchased about four years ago from the estate of Mrs. Mary Perry of Prince George's County, Md., for $625.

[Commissioners paid Susan K. Williams, by W. E. Redin, her attorney, $700.80: Mary Hicks, $175.20; Jane Compton, $525.60. The claim for Laura Jackson was withdrawn and was later made by William Brenton Boggs. See No. 625.]

No. 236, Petition of George W. Orme Filed May 15, 1862

George W. Orme of Georgetown claims compensation for two persons.

1. Henrietta Slater, 14 years old. [Value $600]
2. Marion Slater, sister of Henrietta, 11 years old. [Value $400]

They are free of any defect or infirmity.

The late Jeremiah Orme, of whose estate George is executor, got their mother about 15 years ago in the division of his father's estate in Montgomery County, Md. She was his slave when the two children were born to her.

[Commissioners paid Orme $525.60: Henrietta Slater, $306.60; Marion Slater, $219.]

No. 237, Petition of John A. Wroe Filed May 15, 1862

John A. Wroe, trustee, of Frederick County, Md., claims compensation for John Smith, aged 36. Smith is a dark chestnut color and about 5 feet 4 inches tall. He has a high forehead, large mouth, fine set of teeth and gray eyes. He is a first-rate servant who is sober, industrious, healthy and strong. Wroe has refused $1,800 for him. [Value $1,400]

John A. Wroe received title by a deed of trust from Samuel C. Wroe, dated May 24, 1845, for the benefit of Samuel's wife, Vanduden Wroe. This is recorded in D.C. Liber W.B. No. 114, folio 323. Samuel Wroe got Smith in 1845 through his wife of Prince George's County, Md.

[Commissioners paid J. A. Wroe, by Everett Wroe, his attorney, $438.]

Samuel C. Wroe married Vanduden Dodson on Apr. 11, 1844. Pippenger, D.C. Marriage Licenses, 1811-1858, p. 658.

No. 238, Petition of Everett Wroe

Everett Wroe of Washington claims compensation for seven persons.

1. Henry Barker, aged 37, black, 5 feet 7 or 8 inches tall. [Value $900]
2. Rachel Barker, aged 35, black, 5 feet 5 or 6 inches tall. [Value 800]
3. Harry Barker, Jr., aged ten, black, 4 feet 4 or 5 inches tall. [Value $737]
4. Mary Ellen Barker, aged 16, dark chestnut color, 4 feet 8 or 9 inches tall. [Value $925]
5. Sarah Ellen Barker, aged 12, dark chestnut, 4 feet 8 or 9 inches tall. [Value $925]

6. Casper Barker, aged six, light mulatto, 4 feet 3 or 4 inches tall. [Value $800]

7. John H. Barker, aged four, black, 3 feet 2 or 3 inches tall. [Value $400]

The above named servants compose one family and are very likely and intelligent. They are healthy, free from blemishes and without infirmities, except Rachel who is not yet well from the effects of her confinement.

Everett Wroe got title by a deed of trust from Samuel C. Wroe for the use of his wife, Vanduden Marcella Wroe and this is recorded in D.C. Liber J.A.S. No. 140, folio 247, dated Aug. 27, 1857. Samuel C. purchased Rachel and her two children, Mary Ellen and Sarah Ellen in January 1853 from Lewis Bell of Washington County, Md., for $900. He purchased Harry Barber from Elias Crampton, administrator of the estate of Elizabeth Green of said county, for $300 (?).

[Commissioners paid Wroe $1,883.40: Henry Barker, $394.20; Rachel Barker, $306.60; Harry Barker, Jr., $109.50; Mary Ellen Barker, $416.10; Sarah Ellen Barker, $372.30; Casper Barker, $175.20; John H. Barker, $109.50.]

A note written by Everett Wroe on the endorsement page of the petition states that "since the probate of this petition the within named Rachel departed this life on Monday last."

No. 239, Petition of Elizabeth Abbott   Filed May 15, 1862

Elizabeth Abbott of Georgetown claims compensation for 11 persons.

1. Matilda Sims, daughter of Venus [Sims (?)], aged about 48, is 5 feet 4 inches tall and dark brown. She is a very good cook and good servant. [Value $500]

2. Henry Sims, aged about 47, is 5 feet 9 inches tall and dark brown. The sight is injured in one of his eyes. He is the son of Venus [Sims (?)]. He is a stout, able-bodied laboring man. [Value $800]

3. James Sims, aged about 38, is about 5 feet 5 inches tall and dark brown. He is the son of Venus [Sims (?)]. He is a first-rate house and dining room servant and a first-rate gentleman's servant. [Value $1,000]

4. Charles Henry Ambush, son of Harriet [Ambush (?)], is aged about 36, 5 feet 5 inches tall and dark brown. He is a good house or dining room servant and also a good carriage driver. He has been suffering for the last three or four months with rheumatism, but at this time has nearly recovered from its effects. [Value $900]

5. Ellen Norris, aged about 45, is 5 feet 4 inches tall and mulatto. She is a first-rate house servant. [Value $600]

6. Adel Frances Davis, child of Ellen Norris, is aged 22 years, six months and 19 days, about 5 feet 2 inches tall and dark brown. She is a twin to Catharine Ann. She is a first-rate house servant and a good seamstress.

7. Catharine Ann Davis, child of Ellen Norris and twin of Adel Frances, is aged 22 years, six months, 19 days, about 5 feet tall and chestnut colored. She is a first-rate house servant. [Value $800]

8. Indiana Davis, child of Ellen Norris, is aged 20 years, three months, and 18 days, and about 5 feet 4 inches tall and chestnut colored. He is a first-rate house servant. [Value $800]

9. Ellen Virginia Norris, child of Ellen Norris, is aged three years five months and chestnut colored. [Value $200]

10. Joseph Davis, child of Catharine Ann Davis, is aged four years, eight months and 23 days and is bright mulatto. [Value $300]

11. Cora Davis, child of Catharine Ann Davis, is aged one year, eight months, 20 days and very bright mulatto. She has an aneurism (?) on her cheek. [Value $100]

Abbott attaches a bill of sale dated Jul. 29, 1823, by which John Abbott, of Georgetown, for $600, sells to Elizabeth Abbott, Negro Venus, about 44 years six months old and her three children: Henry, aged about eight, Gustavus, aged about four, James, aged about eight months; and also Negro woman, Harriet, aged about 28 years, and her child named Robert, aged about two years two months. Charles Henry Ambush is a son of Harriet. Matilda Sims, daughter of Venus, was a gift from her father more than 25 years ago.

Ellen Norris was a gift from her father more than 30 years ago. Abbott is unable to find that deed, but refers the Commissioners to the records of the D.C. County Court which will show that she, in a deed of manumission dated 29 Jul. 1853, and another dated Aug. 21, 1855, emancipated three of Norris's children. (See Manumission Record No. 4, and Manumission Record No. 5) Her brother, George D. Abbot, vouches for her statement. Adel Frances, Catharine Ann, Indiana are children of Ellen Norris by her first husband and Ellen Virginia is her child by her second husband.

In an accompanying statement, Elizabeth's brother, George D. Abbot, swears that Elizabeth has claimed the service of Matilda Sims and Ellen Norris for the last 25 years and that she has for some time hired out Matilda and the children of Ellen Norris, and received money from their hire. He says that he and his brother, Charles, have had the services of Adel, Catharine and Indiana for many years past and have always paid their sister money for the same.

(Statement dated May 15, 1862)

Commissioners paid Abbot $3,197.40: Matilda Sims, $219; Henry Sims, $175.20; James Sims, $438; Charles Henry Ambush, $350.40; Ellen Norris, $284.70; Adel Frances Davis, $438; Catharine Ann Davis, $459.90; Indiana Davis, $569.40; Ellen Virginia Norris, $109.50; Joseph Davis, $87.60; Cora Davis, $65.70.]

The D.C. "Manumission Volumes" are located in the National Archives and have been microfilmed by the Archives. Dorothy Provine has abstracted these documents in two volumes titled <u>District of Columbia Free Negro Registers, 1821-1861</u> (2 vols., Bowie, Md., Heritage Books, Inc., 1996). Registration No. 1381 shows that Elizabeth Abbott of Georgetown sold for $300 to Maj. James Duncan Graham a Negro woman named Rebecca Simms, for a term of ten years after which she was to be free. Registration No. 2369 shows that Abbot manumitted Edward Francis Norris, the son of Adam and Ellen Norris. She states that Edward was born in Georgetown on Jan. 11, 1855, and his father is a free black man who is able to maintain himself and his child.

No. 240, Petition of Nelson Conrad, trustee Filed May 15, 1862

Nelson Conrad, of Georgetown, trustee for his two younger children, Mary L., aged 14, and Eliza D. Conrad, aged 16, claims compensation for three persons.

1. Lucy Bowles is aged 49, 5 feet 4 inches tall, not very dark in color and has dark eyes. Her front teeth are out, but she has a rather pleasant countenance. She is a good cook and has all the necessary qualification for a number one house servant. Conrad states that she is more valuable now than when he bought her. At that time, she was "greatly complaining and at a very critical time of life with her, now she having passed that period of life & her health is much improved". She is occasionally troubled with rheumatism, but that does not prevent here from attending to her daily labors. [Value $300]

2. Hannah Beson, daughter of Lucy Bowles, is aged 22, 5 feet 2 ½ inches tall, not very dark and has dark, round eyes. She has a scar on each side of her mouth and on her forehead caused by a burn when she was a child. She has a slight defect in her left eye. She is well and hardy and a woman of good character and a first-rate house servant. [Value $700]

3. Mary Lucy Beson, daughter of Hannah, is aged four, about three feet tall, a bright mulatto color with large black eyes. She is large for her age and uncommonly sprightly and handsome. She is well and hardy and has never had a day of sickness. [Value $250]

Conrad acquired title to Lucy by a deed of conveyance dated 23 Apr. 1858, from Mary E. Waugh of Berkley County, Va. This is recorded in Baltimore and Lucy was valued at $200 a short time prior to her conveyance. Hannah Beson was acquired by a deed of conveyance from Martha A. Conrad (?) of Berkley County, Va., dated February 1858. Hannah had been purchased by Martha A. for $725 from George W. Hunter, Jr., trustee.

[Commissioners paid Conrad $678.90: Lucy Bowles, $153.30; Hannah Beson, $438; Mary Lucy Beson, $87.60.]

No. 241, Petition of George Mattingly Filed May 15, 1862

George Mattingly of Washington claims compensation for ten persons.

1. Lucy Miles, aged 45, light copper complexion, 5 feet 4 inches tall. She is a first-class cook, washer and ironer as well as general house servant. She is healthy and strong and has no defects except occasional intemperance. [Value $1,000]

2. Ann Miles, daughter of Lucy, aged 18, dark copper, 5 feet 1 inch tall. She is a first-class cook and general house servant. She is healthy and strong and trustworthy and temperate. He "knows of nothing against her morals other than bearing children without being married." [Value $1,000]

3. Adelaide Miles, daughter of Lucy, aged 14, light copper color, 5 feet 3 inches tall. She is a good house servant and child's nurse and is healthy and strong. [Value $800]

4. Dominick Miles, son of Ann Miles, aged two, is light mulatto and 2 feet 6 inches tall. [Value $100]

5. Mary Bass, is aged 29, light mulatto and 5 feet 2 inches tall. She is a first-class house servant and lady's dressing maid. She is healthy and strong. [Value $1,200]

6. James E. Stanford, aged 18, black, 5 feet 7 inches tall. He is a first-class cook and waiter. His services have averaged $14 a month for the last three or four years. Since April 1861 he has been employed in the U.S. naval service on one of the steamboats of the "Potomac Flotilla" at $14 a month. [Value $800]

7. Willis Young, 35, is dark copper and 5 feet 11 inches tall. He has been healthy since Mattingly purchased him, but was previously slightly troubled with hemorrhage. He is a first-rate body servant, waiter and coachman. He has been since August 1861, in the employ of Lt. Col.. Owens of the 3rd Pennsylvania Cavalry as a body servant and waiter at $20 a month. He has not been sick despite being exposed to camp life. [Value $1,000]

8. Henry Lee is aged 32, bright mulatto and 5 feet 6 inches tall. He is a first-rate cook and waiter and is employed on the U. S. Steamboat Baltimore as a cook since April 1861, at $12 a month. According to the terms of purchase from Mrs. D. (?) Washington, his mother should have the right to purchase him for $500, the amount Mattingly paid for him. [Value $500]

9. Paris Green, aged 55, is black and 5 feet 9 inches tall. He is a first-rate farm hand and is strong, healthy, trustworthy and understands all about farm work. [Value $300]

10. Henry Branson, 45, is black and 6 feet 1 inch tall. He works at the Washington Navy Yard at $1.50 a day. Out of his pay, he pays Mattingly one dollar and keeps the remaining 50 cents and whatever else he may make in overtime. There were ten months of service due by him to Mattingly before the expiration of the four year term for which he was purchased. [Value $250]

Mattingly purchased Lucy Miles in 1841 from Fontane Beckham for $600. Ann Miles and Adelaide Mills were born after the purchase of their mother. Dominick is the son of Ann Miles. Mary Bass was purchased in 1855 from A. M. Hoffer for $700. James E. Stanford was purchased in 1847 from Mrs. Penoply [sic] Luckett for $700 for his mother and two of her children. Willis Young was purchased in 1856 from Mrs. D (?) Washington for $500. Paris Green was purchased in 1861 from Edward Plummer and his wife for $200. Henry Branson was purchased in 1859 from Stephen Shinn for $500.

[Commissioners paid Mattingly $3,898.20: Lucy Miles, $372.30; Ann Miles, $525,60; Adelaide Miles, $481.80; Dominick Miles, $43.80; Mary Bass, $481.80; James E. Stanford, $525.60; Willis Young, $569.40; Henry Lee, $569.40; Paris Green, $240.90; Henry Branson, $87.60.]

No. 242, Petition of Elizabeth Birckhead　　　　　　　　　　　　　　　　　　　　Filed May 15, 1862

Elizabeth Birckhead of the District of Columbia claims compensation for eight persons.
1. Sarah Forrest, aged 75, black, 5 feet 1 inches tall. [Value $400.]
2. Clarissa Forrest, aged 40, black, 5 feet 5 inches tall. [Value $900]
3. Elizabeth Forrest, aged 36, black, 5 feet 5 inches tall. [Value $1,000]
4. Lewis Cass, aged 14, black, five feet tall. [Value $1,000]
5. Maria Peel, aged 27, brown, 5 feet 2 inches tall. [Value $1,000]
6. Clara Peel, aged six, brown, 3 feet 4 inches tall. [Value $400]
7. Richard Peel, aged three, three feet tall. [Value $300]
8. Sarah Peel, aged three months, brown. [Value $100]

Birckhead states that she purchased Sarah Forest for $575 and that bill of sale is recorded in Montgomery County Md. She states that her claim "to these persons other than Sarah Forrest is acquired by reason of their being the issue from said Sarah Forrest, while she was held by me to service for life."

Commissioners paid Elizabeth Birckhead, by Oliver H. Birckhead, her attorney, $1,609.65: Sarah Forrest, $10.95; Clarissa Forrest, $219; Elizabeth Forrest, $306.60; Lewis Cass, $438; Maria Peel, $131.40; Clara Peel, $372.30; Richard Peel, $109.50; Sarah Peel, $21.90.]

No. 243, Petition of Frederick Godfrey Hesse　　　　　　　　　　　　　　　　　　Filed May 15, 1862

I Frederick Godfrey Hesse of Washington City claim compensation for 11 persons.
1. Julia Smallwood, aged about 56, mulatto. She is a good house servant.
2. Ann Smallwood, aged about 22, she is a first-class servant in all respects.
3. Henrietta Smallwood, aged about 20. She is a good house servant and is generally useful.
4. Lucy Smallwood, aged about 18. She is a healthy, active girl and generally useful.
5. Mary Smallwood, aged about 16. She is perfectly healthy and a useful servant.
6. William Smallwood is aged about 14. He is a healthy and active boy.
7. Nelly Smallwood is about 12 years old. She is a sound, healthy and smart girl.
8. Henry Smallwood is aged about ten. He is smart, lively and active.
9. Fanny Smallwood is about eight. She is bright and lively.
10. Bernard Smallwood is aged about six. He is a fine, healthy child.
11. William Thomas is aged about 32 and is light brown in color. He is a faithful and reliable servant.

All of the above vary in color from light mulatto to dark copper. None of them is what is usually termed "black". Hesse estimates the total value of the above to be $10,250.

Hesse acquired title by his marriage with Mary Camilla Spalding, who inherited them. Attached is a copy of the will of John Spalding of Charles County, Md., in which he leaves to his daughter Mary Camilla, Negro man William,

Negro woman Julia, and her four children, Ann, Henny, Lucy and Mary and all the natural increase of Julia. (Signed Dec. 13, 1847; proved Mar. 7 and Apr. 4, 1848)

[Commissioners paid Hesse $3,920.10: Julia Smallwood, $131.40; Ann Smallwood, $503.70; Henrietta Smallwood, $438; Lucy Smallwood, $481.80; Mary Smallwood, $525.60; William Smallwood, $328.50; Nelly Smallwood, $350.40; Henry Smallwood, $262.80; Fanny Smallwood, $175.20; Bernard Smallwood, $153.30; William Thomas, $569.40.]

For additional provisions of Spalding's will, see the original petition. Other slaves of his were bequeathed to his daughter, Ann Caroline Spalding and his son, Basil William Spalding. He also had extensive real property that he divided among his children.

No. 244, Petition of Quintin Barker   Filed May 15, 1862

Quintin Barker of Washington claims compensation for Amanda Wallace and her five children.
1. Amanda Wallace, aged 38.
2. Ellen Wallace, aged 13.
3. Joanna Wallace, aged nine.
4. Elizabeth Wallace, aged seven.
5. Emeline Wallace, aged four.
6. Winna Wallace, aged one.

They are all sound, healthy and intelligent and were "raised in my white family and I hope may be able to take care of themselves in [the] future having been faithful and dutiful to me from in so far as they have been able." He estimates their total value as $2,000.

Amanda and her two oldest children were allotted to his wife as a portion of the estate of her father, William Keane of Fairfax County, Va. The allotments were made Jun. 18, 1854, and recorded at the Fairfax County Clerk's Office. Amanda was valued at $650, Ellen at $225, and Joanna at $150. The other children were born since 1854.

[Commissioners paid Barker $1,270.20: Amanda Wallace, $328.50; Ellen Wallace, $372.30; Joanna Wallace $284.70; Elizabeth, $175.20; Emeline Wallace, $87.60; Winna, $21.90.]

No. 245, Petition of Robert Earl   Filed May 15, 1862

Robert Earl of Washington claims compensation for two persons.

1. Sarah Widdecomb, aged about 26, dark brown in color, 5 feet 2 inches tall, stout and well-built. She is an excellent cook, ironer and washer and can perform all the work about the house. She is healthy and sound. [Value $1,000]

2. George Widdecomb, aged between seven and eight, light mulatto, well-grown and likely. He is a very healthy and sprightly boy. [Value $500]

The accompanying bill of sale shows that Earl purchased Ann [*sic*] about Nov. 16, 1854, for $675, from Seth L. Cole. George, her son, was born a short time after the purchase.

[Commissioners paid "Earle" $657: Sarah Widdecomb, $481.80; George Widdecomb, $175.20.]

No. 246, Petition of Margaret Osbourn, guardian of Mary White   Filed May 15, 1862

Margaret Osbourn, guardian for Mary White of Washington, claims compensation for John Dyer. Dyer is aged 25, black in color and 5 feet 10 inches tall. He is a good servant and is sound and healthy. [Value $1,500]

Dyer was inherited from Mrs. Mary White about 10 years ago, and Margaret Osborn was appointed guardian of Mrs. White's only child, Mary. The documents are recorded in the Register of Wills Office in Upper Marlborough in Prince George's County, Md. (Signed Margaret x her mark Osborn.)

[Commissioners paid $569.40 to Margaret Osbourn, guardian for Mary White, by Susan H. Wilson, her attorney.]
Margaret's surname is spelled both "Osbourn" and "Osborn" in the petition.

No. 247, Petition of Susan Osbourn   Filed May 15, 1862

Susan W. Osbourn of Washington claims compensation for three persons.
1. Susan Duviell is aged 27, copper color, 5 feet 5 inches tall, with a large mouth. [Value $1,000]
2. Eliza Stoddard is aged 20, copper colored, 5 feet 3 inches tall and has very large eyes. [Value $1,000]
3. Charlotte Stoddard is aged 17, black and five feet tall. [Value $1,000]

They are all faithful, honest, trustworthy and healthy.
Susan was given to Osbourn by her brother-in-law, Judson Scott, about 20 years ago. Charlotte and Eliza are her

children and she inherited them from her father. His will is recorded in Upper Marlborough, Md.

[Commissioners paid $1,554.90 to Susan Osbourn, by Susan H. Wilson, her attorney: Susan Duviell, $459.90; Eliza "Stoddert", $569.40; Charlotte "Stoddert", $525.60.]

No. 248, Petition of Patrick H. McNantz   Filed May 15, 1862

Patrick H. McNantz of Washington claims compensation for Lucy Brown. Lucy is nine years old, dark brown in color, 5 feet 2 ½ inches tall, with short nappy hair and thick lips. She has the makings of a good servant and is obedient, industrious and healthy. [Value $500]

He holds title through his wife, who was made a present of Brown by her mother when Lucy was about two years old. Mrs. Julia Ann Mudd, McNantz's mother-in-law, owned Lucy's mother and resides in Charles County, Md.

[Commissioners paid McNantz $262.80.]

No. 249, Petition of John Fister   Filed May 15, 1862

John Fister of Washington City claims compensation for three persons.
1. Sophia Barnes, aged 37, dark brown, 5 feet 2 inches tall.
2. Henry T. Barnes, aged 15, dark brown, 4 feet 11 inches.
3. James S. Barnes, aged 13, dark brown, four feet tall.

They are all healthy and sound and free of defects. Estimated value for the three is $1,100.

Fister purchased them for $550 about ten years ago from Zadock Williams of Washington.

[Commissioners paid Fister $1,314: Sophia Barnes, $394.20; Henry T. Barnes, $481.80; James S. Barnes, $438.]

No. 250, Petition of Thomas A. Richards   Filed May 15, 1862

Thomas A. Richards of Washington claims compensation for four persons.
1. Ann Grinful, aged 24, dark brown, 5 feet 4 inches tall, rather slender, but healthy. [Value $800]
2. Henry Grinful, aged seven, dark brown, 3 feet 8 inches tall, stout built and robust. [Value $200]
3. Julia Ann Marshall, aged 11, light brown, 4 feet 4 inches tall, healthy and likely. [Value $525]
4. Henry Green, aged about 17, 5 feet 2 inches tall. He has eight years remaining on his term before he is manumitted. [Value $275]

Richards' wife, Sarah A. M. Richards, inherited Ann, Henry and Julia Ann from her mother, Susanna Richards of Charles County, Md., by will. A copy of an excerpt from the will shows that at that time Ann was 20, Henry, aged three and Julia about nine [sic]. Richards states that he purchased Henry Green for a term of years from Green's father, Henry Green, Sr., and the bill of sale was filed by Alfred Richards.

[Commissioners paid Richards $1,051.20: Ann Grinful, $438; Henry Grinful, $262.80; Julia Ann Marshall, $175.20; Henry Green, $175.20.]

The 1860 Census for D.C., Vol. 2, p. 529, lists Henry Green, aged 18, as a house servant in Thomas and Sarah Richards' house. The census, of course, is supposed to list only free persons, not slaves.

No. 251, Petition of James S. Harvey   Filed May 16, 1862

James S. Harvey of Washington claims compensation for three persons.
1. Ann Taylor, about 35 years old, dark brown, 5 feet 6 inches tall. She is healthy, active and industrious. [Value $500]
2. Eliza Taylor, aged 13, dark brown, 4 feet 9 inches tall. She is able-bodied, active and healthy. [Value $300]
3. Moses Carter, aged 20, dark brown, 5 feet 6 inches tall. He is remarkably stout, healthy, well-disposed and affectionate. [Value $1,000]

Harvey acquired Ann Taylor in the division of the goods of his father, Thomas Harvey, who died in Prince George's County, Md., in 1846. Eliza Taylor is Ann's daughter and was born after Harvey became owner of Ann. Moses Carter was obtained through an exchange of slaves. He had been given to Harvey's wife by her grandfather.

[Commissioners paid Harvey $1,314: Ann Taylor, $438; Eliza Taylor, $306.60; Moses Carter, $569.40.]

No. 252, Petition of George W. Barkley   Filed May 16, 1862

George W. Barkley of Washington claims compensation for Maria Queen. Queen is about 50 years old, dark color, about five feet high with wooly hair. She is a excellent servant, in good health, intelligent and of excellent character. [Value $250]

Barkley inherited her from the estate of his father, Samuel Barkley of Charles County, Md., in 1852.
[Commissioners paid Barkley nothing as Queen was not produced and the claim was not allowed.]

No. 253, Petition of William C. Greenleaf   Filed May 16, 1862

William C. Greenleaf of Washington City claims compensation for two persons.

1. Dinah Patrick, aged 84, mulatto, 5 feet 4 inches tall. She is crippled from rheumatism and old age. [no value]
2. John Patrick, aged 44, mulatto, 5 feet 5 inches tall. His hair is dark and thick and his voice is husky. He is a valuable servant and for several years has been hired by Kennedy & Pugh, grocers, on 7th street. Patrick is "not what might be called a strong man", but has no disease that Greenleaf knows of and has lost very little time by sickness of any kind. [Value $1,000]

Greenleaf acquired his claim by marriage in 1847 to the daughter of Col. Washington Owen of Montgomery County, Md.

[Commissioners paid Greenleaf $372.30 for John Patrick.]

No. 254, Petition of William P. Trowbridge   Filed May 16, 1862

William P. Trowbridge of Washington City, temporarily in New York on business, claims compensation for Frank Ingersoll. Ingersoll is 14 years old, brown in color, not very large for his age but very bright and active. He had exclusive charge of Trowbridge's dining room and is an excellent dining room servant and waiter. [Value $900]

Trowbridge acquired title by his marriage with Lucy Parkman of the state of Georgia in 1857. She acquired her title by inheritance. Ingersoll's family, including his mother and grandparents belonged to his wife's family from the time of their birth. Frank was brought by Trowbridge to Washington in 1858 (?)

[Commissioners paid "Towbridge", by Richard H. Clarke, attorney, $306.60.]

The printed report of the Commissioners spells William's surname as "Towbridge", but that is incorrect.

No. 255, Petition of Francis & Robert P. Dodge, executors and trustees   Filed May 16, 1862
and Emily Dodge and Mary Thompson

Francis Dodge, Jr., Robert P. Dodge, executors and trustees, Emily Dodge and Mary Thompson of Georgetown claim compensation for five persons.

1. Ann Magruder is aged 52, dark, 5 feet 6 inches tall and thin. She has a cast (?) in her eyes. She is a cook and dairy maid. [Value $600]
2. Maria Warren, aged 40, is light mulatto and 5 feet 4 inches tall. She is a pastry cook and house servant. She is very capable and useful but, at times, has rheumatism. [Value $300]
3. Emeline Magruder, aged 24, is dark in color, stout and 5 feet 5 inches tall. She is a chambermaid. [Value 800]
4. John Magruder, 22, is dark and six feet tall. He has a small head. He is a waiter and gardener. [Value $1,000]
5. Nelly Warren, aged 42, is light mulatto and 5 feet 3 inches tall. She is a cook and house servant. [Value $600]

They are all reliable, trustworthy and have been family servants for the last twenty years.

They were purchased by Francis Dodge, Sr., deceased, of Georgetown. By his will, admitted to probate Oct. 11, 1851, they came into the possession of F. Dodge and R. P. Dodge, his sons and executors of the will, and trustees of Miss Emily Dodge, a daughter of the testator, and Miss Mary Thomson, his sister-in-law, each of whom enjoys a life estate in the servants.

[Commissioners paid $1,883.40: Ann Magruder, $197.10; Maria Warren, $287.70; Emeline Magruder, $438; John Magruder, $657; Nelly Warren, $306.60.]

No. 256, Petition of Ann Harbaugh   Filed May 16, 1862

Mrs. Ann Harbaugh of Washington City claims compensation for Susan Taylor. Taylor is 38, dark brown, about 5 feet 3 inches tall and slim. She is in delicate health, but not in any dangerous condition. She is a good house servant and has no infirmities except mentioned above. Harbaugh believes that her delicate health is not from any "settled disease" and cannot impair her value very much. [$Value $500]

Harbaugh acquired title by inheritance from her father about 24 years ago. She states that she is now a destitute widow and that her late husband, John Randolph Harbaugh, was a loyal citizen of the United States. He died in December, 1860.

[Commissioners paid Harbaugh $306.60.]

No. 257, Petition of Elizabeth Brown   Filed May 16, 1862

Elizabeth Brown of Washington County, D.C., claims compensation for Emma Mills, aged 28 years. Mills has a dark complexion, is about five feet tall, and weighs about 120 pounds. She has a strong and vigorous frame and very prepossessing in appearance. She is quite polite and affable in deportment. [Value $1,200]

Brown's title comes by a bill of sale from Thomas Parker of Washington.

[Commissioners paid Brown, by A. Thomas Smith, attorney, $416.10]

No. 258, Petition of Robert M. Coombs   Filed May 16, 1862

Robert W. Coombs of Washington City claims compensation for four persons.

1. Ann Jackson is aged 46, dark color with dark eyes and black hair and 5 feet 6 inches tall. She has what is called a "milk leg" that was present when he purchased her. It has seldom interfered with her duty as a servant and with cooking and washing. [Value $200]

2. Julia Carroll is aged 18, dark color with dark eyes and black hair and 5 feet 4 inches tall. [Value $1,000]

3. Ann Carrol is aged 11, dark color, with dark eyes and black hair, 4 feet 11 (?) inches tall. [Value $400]

4. William Carroll is aged seven, dark color, dark eyes and black hair, 3 feet 8 inches tall. [Value $300]

All of the above are healthy and sound, and good in their conduct, with the exception noted above.

Coombs purchased Ann Jackson and child from Dr. George M. Dove of Washington for between $300 and $400 about 1846. Ann and William Carroll were born after the purchase of Ann Jackson, who is their mother.

[Commissioners paid Coombs $1,095: Ann Jackson, $219; Julia Carroll, $459.90; Ann Carroll, $284.70; William Carroll, $131.40.]

No. 259, Petition of Sarah Ann Greeves   Filed May 16, 1862

Sarah A. Greeves of Washington City claims compensation for 11 persons.

1. Edward Bowen is aged 60, dark mulatto and about six feet tall. He is a fine farm hand and has had sole charge for the last nine years of Greeves' farm of some 80 acres in D.C. He is active, intelligent and very trustworthy.

2. Sallie Bowen, aged 50, is of medium height and black. He is a fine cook, washer and ironer.

3. Nelson Jones, aged 24, is black and about six feet tall. He is a valuable servant, first-rate coachmen and dining room servant. He is active and intelligent.

4. Morganna Greenleaf, female, aged 27, about five feet tall, stout and black. She is held to service until she reaches age 35. She is a good house servant, washer and ironer.

5. James Edward, child of Morganna Greenleaf, is aged seven and held to service until age 35. He is healthy and has every indication of becoming a valuable servant.

6. Infant female child of Morganna is aged one-and-a-half years. She is held to service until age 35. She was born lame. [No value]

7. Winna Ann Cecelia Greenleaf is aged 24 and about five feet tall, black. She is held to labor until age 35. She is a good house servant, but is now in delicate health and probably has consumption.

8. Mary J. Homes [Holmes], aged 27, is over five feet tall, black and is held to service until age 35. She is a good active house servant, good washer and ironer. She is slightly lame, but not enough to impair her value.

9. Nancy Catharine Rustin, aged 23, mulatto, about five feet tall is held to service until age 35. She is an excellent cook, nurse and dining room servant.

10. Amanda Young, aged 22, black, over five feet tall is held to service until age 35. She is a good dining room servant and chambermaid.

11. Filmore Young, aged six, black is held to labor until age 35. He is a remarkably intelligent and active boy and is very useful.

Greeves got title to Winna Ann Cecelia and Nancy Catharine by the will of her son, John Greeves, made July 21, 1853, and recorded in D.C. Morganna and Mary were purchased from Mary Lawrence by a bill of sale recorded in D.C. Liber W.B. No. 73, folio 328. She holds title to Amanda by a bill of sale from Mary Lawrence recorded in D.C. Liber W.B. No. 96, folio 297. Filmore is the son of Amanda and was born after her purchase. Edward and Sallie Bowen were conveyed to her by Henry Hurley, Jun. 17, 1853, for $800. Nelson Jones was purchased for $1,000 from Caroline Cromwell, Nov. 28, 1855. The children of Morganna belong to Greeves because they were born after she has purchased Morganna.

Morganna, Mary and Amanda were conveyed to Greeves as slaves for life, but were manumitted by her in January, 1854, when they reach 35 years old. This is recorded in Manumission Record No. 4, folio 681.

Greeves says the six of the above persons are assessed on the tax books of the Corporation of Washington at $3,600. She claims their total value to be $5,000.

[Commissioners paid Greeves, by T. F. Herbert, her attorney, $1,565.85: Edward Bowen, $43.80; Sallie Bowen, $43.80; Nelson Jones, $613.20; Morganna Greenleaf, $153.29; James Edward, $43.80; Infant child, no value; Winna A.C. Greenleaf, no value; Mary J. Holmes, $98.55; Nancy Catharine Rustin, $219; Amanda Young, $219; Filmore Young, $131.40.]

No. 260, Petition of Jedediah Gittings   Filed May 16, 1862

Jedediah Gittings of Washington City claims compensation for five persons.

1. Margaret E. Taylor is aged 23, black or dark brown and about 5 feet 2 inches tall. She is a good cook, washer, ironer and household servant and to replace her would cost about $8 or $9 a month. [Value $1,200]

2. Fanny Taylor is about six weeks old. She is the child Margaret and is a bright mulatto color.

3. Annie Taylor, child of Margaret, is aged five, about 3 feet 5 inches tall and of a dark mulatto color. She is a sprightly and smart child and is very useful about the house. [Value $200 or $300]

4. Hezekiah Smith is aged 38, black or dark brown, about six feet tall, strong and well-built. He has been hired out for the last four years as a cartman, about three years with Dr. Hagner (?) at $20 a month, and one year with J[ohn] B. Warder at $5 a week. Gitting paid $690 for him in 1858. [Value $1,400]

5. Louisa M. Whitaker is aged 17, black or dark brown and about 5 feet 2 inches tall. She has a scar on her neck (?) caused by a burn. She is a servant and chambermaid in the Gittings family. He purchased her in 1848 when she was about three years old for $80 (?) To replace her would cost about $6 or $8 a month. [Value $1,200]

Margaret Taylor belonged to Gittings' father, Thomas Gittings, deceased, and was given to him. Anne and Fanny were born after their mother belonged to Jedediah. Hezekiah Smith and Louise Whitaker were also held by Thomas Gittings and after his death in 1858 were purchased by Jedediah.

These persons have always been in Gittings family and that of his father. They are healthy, industrious, honest, and very capable servants.

[Commissioners paid "Gettings" $1,401.60: Margaret E. Taylor, $416.10; Fanny Taylor, $21.90; Annie Taylor, $131.40; Hezekiah Smith, $394.20; Louisa M. Whitaker, $438.]

Gittings's statement contains a contradiction regarding the purchase of Whitaker. In one place he says he bought her when she was three years old in 1848; later he says the purchase was after his father's death at the beginning of 1858. The Commissioners printed report spells the surname as "Gettings" but the original documents and other sources always spell it as "Gittings".

No. 261, Petition of Mary J. Rice   Filed May 16, 1862

Mary J. Rice of Georgetown claims compensation for Jane Ella Mahoney. Mahoney is aged about 50, black, tall, healthy, active and capable. [Value $600]

When she was very young, Rice was given Mahoney by her grandfather. After her husband died, Jane Ella was sold as part of his estate and Rice purchased her.

[Commissioners paid Rice, by R. R. Crawford, her attorney, $219.]

No. 262, Petition of Charles Hume, trustee, and Anna M. Hume   Filed May 16, 1862

Charles Hume of the city of Washington claims compensation for six persons.

1. Louisa Ware is bright copper colored and of medium size. She was raised in the family of J. M. Hume and has always lived in the family. She is Hume's main household servant and is capable, honest and healthy. [Value $1,500]

2. Juliet Ware, daughter of Louisa, is bright copper colored. She was born and raised in the Hume family. She is sound and healthy. [Value $1,200]

3. Richard Ware, son of Louisa, has a lighter complexion than Louisa and Juliet, and was born and raised in the family. He is sound and smart and active. [Value $800]

4. Jane Fauntleroy is aged 33, dark colored and of a large size. She is hired out to John C. Rives (?) and he pays $10 a month in wages. [Value $1,500]

5. Sarah Williams, niece of Jane Fauntleroy, is copper colored and was raised in the Hume family in Culpeper County, Va. She is sound and healthy. [Value $1,200]

6. Cynthia Williams, niece of Jane, is copper colored and was raised in the Hume family in Culpeper County, Va. She is sound and healthy. [Value $1,200]

Hume states that the claim comes from the will of Mary Sandriegle (?) to Mrs. Hume when she was a small girl. The will was filed somewhere about 1835 in Spottsylvania County, Va. Richard and Juliet are Louisa's children. The title to Jane Fauntleroy and Sarah and Cynthia Williams was acquired by deed from Hume's deceased brother,

Francis Hume of Washington, about 1859.

Anna M. Hume of Washington, in a petition filed July 14, 1862, asserts that Jane Fauntleroy, Sarah Williams and Cynthia Williams are hers by virtue of being the administratrix of the estate of the late Francis Hume, her husband.

1. Jane or Jennie Fauntleroy is about 30 years old, dark copper colored, stout and about 5 feet 2 inches tall. She is a first-class cook, washer and ironer.

2. Sarah Williams is about 19, of a dark color and about 4 feet 10 inches tall. She is as good as Jennie.

3. Cynthia William is 13 years old, mulatto and 4 feet 9 inches tall. She is a very good house servant.

She claims $3,000 for the three servants.

Anna M. Hume claims that the above persons were left to her husband, Francis, by his grandfather, with a dower interest to Francis's mother. This interest was purchased in full by Francis by funds that Anna M. had inherited from the estate of her father, John A. Donohoo.

There is attached to the petition a deed of gift dated July 19, 1859, by which Francis Hume gave to his brother, Charles, certain slaves who are to be held for Charles's six children, Mary Ann, Fannie Ella, Virginia Rawlings, Eliza Priscilla, Ida May and Suse Ellen Hume.

Also attached is a sworn statement made in Baltimore, Md., by Matilda Zimmerman dated July 12, 1862, saying that on Oct. 1, 1861, she went to Washington for three weeks and while there frequently visited the home of Mr. Charles Hume and that on Oct. 18 and 19, Charles's brother was lying dead in his house. She also saw there a lady who represented herself as the wife of the deceased. Zimmerman says during all that time the subject of secession was never spoken of and that she has never heard Mr. C. Hume express sentiments that would lead one to believe he was not a loyal citizen of the United States. There was but one daughter at home, a child about four years old. Four daughters were at the house of their grandmother in Virginia. The sixth child was visiting in Maryland at the house of Mr. Isaacs and returned the morning of the funeral.

Anna M. Hume disputes the deed of gift submitted by Charles Hume and says it was fraudulently obtained from her husband while he was laboring under "aberation of mind, and deep depression [to his] system caused by bad habits and indulgences (?), under which influence he was duped into the execution of the alleged bill or transfer of said servants."

[Commissions paid a total of $2,036.70: "Charles Hume, for $788.40. Apr 6, 1863. Charles Hume for $1,248.30, heretofore retained, as before stated, and now paid to me, no action having been taken by the contestant." The allotments were: Louisa Ware, $219; Juliet Ware, $394.20; Richard Ware, $175.20; Jane Fauntleroy, $350.40; Sarah Williams, $503.70; Cynthia Williams, $394.20.]

No. 263, Petition of Susanna Hughes   Filed May 16, 1862

Susanna Hughes of the District of Columbia claims compensation for her servant woman Anna Fisher. Fisher is nearly 22 years old (having been born July 8, 1840), and is a bright mulatto and of good appearance. She is held to service until she is 35 years old. Anna is of good moral and religious character and a member of St. John's Episcopal Church. She is able to read and write and was "brought up from earliest infancy with most scrupulous attention to morals and to household duties befitting her age."

Hughes estimates Anna's value at about $936. She figures that Anna could earn about $6 a month, or $72 a year. She is due to serve for 13 years, hence the $936 value.

Hughes's claim comes from the bequest of her aunt, Margaret Waters, of Anne Arundel County, Md., who left Anna's mother and her increase to Hughes. That will provided that the slaves be free at age 35.

[Commissioners paid Hughes $197.10.]

No. 264, Petition of William T. Duvall and   Filed May 16, 1862
Robert L. Adamson, trustees of John Smith, deceased.

William T. Duvall of Washington, D.C., and Robert L. Adamson of Montgomery County, Md., trustees of John Smith, deceased, of Washington City, claim compensation for three persons.

1. Margaret Tyler is 33 years old, bright mulatto, about 5 feet 2 inches tall and tolerably healthy. She is a good washer and ironer. [Value $800]

2. Mary E. Tyler is about nine and mulatto. [Value $400]

3. Sarah A. M. Tyler is about three and mulatto. [Value $200]

John Smith purchased Margaret for $450 on Oct. 12, 1847, from C. C. Hyatt of Bladensburg, Prince George's County, Md. Mary E. and Sarah A. M., were born in Smith's family after he had acquired title to Margaret. Another child of Margaret's, Berry [Tyler], was born since the death of Smith.

[Commissioners paid Duvall and Adamson, as trustees of Smith, $569.40: Margaret Tyler, $284.70; Mary E. Tyler, $197.10; Sarah A. M. Tyler, $87.60.]

No. 265, Petition of Benjamin H. Hall
Filed May 16, 1862

Benjamin H. Hall of Baltimore, Md., claims compensation for Isaac Boston. Isaac is 12 years old, mulatto and 4 feet 3 inches tall. He is good-looking, has small features and is in good health. He has resided with Daniel Boston, colored, on Capitol Hill, since last October. Hall says he believes he could have gotten $500 for Isaac a few months ago, but he had no desire to sell him. [Value $500]

Hall obtained title from his mother who died in September of 1861, although he knows of no written evidence of his title. Hall submits a statement from C[harles] W. Utermaehle and James Lynch stating that Isaac Boston resides with Daniel Boston, who drives an express and lives on Capitol Hill near Kenty's (?) cottage. They assert that the boy belonged to Margaret Hall.

Also included is a copy of Hall's letters of administration for the estate of Margaret Hall who died July 19, 1862, in Baltimore.

[Commissioners paid Hall $262.80.]

Boyd's Directory for 1860, p. 43, shows Daniel Boston, express driver, as residing on B St., north (now Constitution Ave.).

No. 266, Petition of William H. Birch
Filed May 16, 1862

William H. Birch of Montgomery County, Md., claims compensation for David Hawkins. Hawkins is 25 years old, black and about 5 feet 8 or 9 inches tall. He is honest, faithful, intelligent and healthy. He is employed as a coachman and ostler at Conklin's Livery Stable near Willard's Hotel and Birch receives $24 a month for his services. [Value $1,500]

Birch purchased him from Mr. Warren of Prince George's County, Md., ten years ago.

[Commissioners paid Birch $569.40.]

No. 267, Petition of Anna Le Compte
Filed May 16, 1862

Anna Lecompte of Washington claims compensation for Josephine Fisher. She is about 26 years old, very light mulatto and about 5 feet 2 inches tall. She is a fine cook, washer, ironer and house servant. She is honest, intelligent and likely and has no defects. [Value $1,000]

She purchased Josephine's mother from Mr. B. Raux of Norfolk, Va., and Josephine was born after that time. The attached receipt is dated Norfolk, Aug. 8, 1833, and shows that Anna Werckmuller paid $500 to purchase a mulatto woman named Maria and her male child.

[Commissioners paid "Anne Le Compte" $350.40.]

Boyd's Directory for 1860 lists "Anna Le Compte" as the widow of James L.

No. 268, Petition of Mary A. Paine
Filed May 16, 1862

Mary A. Paine of Washington claims compensation for six persons.

1. Ariana Turley is aged 45, mulatto and about 5 feet 2 inches tall. She is an excellent cook, washer and ironer and is honest and trustworthy. [Value $800]

2. Amelia Lyles is aged 37, brown and about 5 feet 5 inches tall. She is an excellent cook, washer and ironer. [Value $900]

3. Emma E. Freeman is aged 26, brown and about 5 feet 1 inch tall. She is an elegant house servant, washer and ironer. [Value $800]

4. John Turley is aged 23, mulatto and about 5 feet 6 inches tall. He is an accomplished house servant and waiter who is temperate, obedient and honest. [Value $1,200]

5. William H. Turley is aged 18, mulatto and about 5 feet 4 inches tall. He is a first-rate house servant and is polite and respectful. [Value $1,000]

6. Lewis A. Freeman is aged seven, brown, and about 4 feet 6 inches tall. He is a fine boy who runs errands and does other things. [Value $800]

Paine states that her father gave her Ariana Turley at the time of her marriage and subsequently confirmed this by the terms of his will. She believes, however, that his will was destroyed by the troops in Fairfax, Va. John, William and Emma are her children born after Ariana became Paine's property. Lewis Freeman is the son of Emma and the grandson of Ariana. Amelia was purchased by Paine's late husband from her late father.

[Commissioners paid Paine $1,971: Ariana Turley, $197.10; Amelia Lyles $438; Emma E. Freeman, $262.80; John Turley, $569.40; William H. Turley, $372.30; Lewis A. Freeman, $131.40.]

No. 269, Petition of Nicholas Callan   Filed May 16, 1862

Nicholas Callan of Washington claims compensation of Milley Anderson. She is about 52 years old, has a dark complexion and is about 5 feet 3 inches tall. She was Callan's cook and did all the house work of his family, including washing and ironing. Milly is peaceable, quiet and orderly and honest and faithful. She is healthy and has no defects except a slight impediment in her speech. [Value $500]

Callan purchased her about 15 years ago from Mrs. Jane E. Dunscomb, now of Georgetown and formerly of Washington City.

[Commissioners paid Nicholas Callan, by Nicholas Callan, Jr., his attorney, $87.60.]

The printed report of the Commissioners erroneously gives Anderson's name as "Metley."

No. 270, Petition of William A. T. Maddox   Filed May 16, 1862

Capt.. William A. T. Maddox of the District of Columbia, now temporarily of Philadelphia, Pa., claims compensation for two persons.

1. Jerry Mitchell is aged 22, yellow complexion and about six feet tall. He was Maddox's coachman and was also an excellent dining room servant and farm hand. He was active and intelligent.

2. Phillis is aged 40, black and of medium size. She was an excellent cook and house servant as well as a good washerwoman and ironer. She is intelligent, honest, faithful and moral.

Maddox values the two at $2,100.

He obtained title by marriage with Sarah E. Maughon (?) of Jones County, Ga.

[Commissioners paid Maddox $963.60: "Jesse" Mitchell, $657; Phillis, $306.60.]

The printed report of the Commissioners incorrectly gives Mitchell's first name as "Jesse." It is clearly "Jerry" in the original petition.

No. 271, Petition of Matthew McLeod   Filed May 16, 1862

Matthew McLeod of Georgetown claims compensation for Ellen Cole. Cole is 51 or 52 years old, of a light brown complexion and of the usual health for one her age. He acquired title from the will of his mother-in-law, Mrs. Mary Manning of St. Mary's County, Md., and later the will of his deceased wife. [Value $600]

[Commissioners paid McLeod $175.20]

No. 272, Petition of Anthony Thompson   Filed May 16, 1862

Anthony Thompson of Washington City claims compensation for Maria Dodson. She is 45 years old, about 4 feet 6 inches tall and of a dark copper color. She is good-looking and healthy. At the time of the act of Congress freeing slaves in D.C., she was hired out at $5 a month. [Value $600]

Dodson was given to his mother by her mother, Ann V. Soper of Prince George's County, Md. Thompson inherited Dodson when his mother died about eight months ago. Thompson's brother, Thomas Thompson, and his sister, Ann E. Thompson, are both minors.

[Commissioners paid Thompson $65.70.]

No. 273, Petition of Ann Scott   Filed May 16, 1862

Ann Scott of Washington City claims compensation for three persons.

1. Martha Ann Bird, aged 28, copper colored, 5 feet 6 inches tall is good-looking and healthy.
2. Sarah Maria Bailey is aged 12, four feet tall, bright mulatto and healthy. She has a defect in her eyes.
3. John Bird is about one year old, copper colored, and healthy.

Scott values them at $1,400. Martha Ann with her child is hiring regularly for $5 a month. Sarah Maria was living with Scott prior to passage of the manumission act and when she left was receiving $3 a month. They were both obedient servants until they were free.

Martha Ann was given to Scott by her mother, Ann V. Soper, in Prince George's County, Md., about 12 years ago. Since that time Martha Ann has lived in Washington and Sarah Maria and John are her offspring.

[Commissioners paid Ann Scott, her x mark, $613.20: Martha Ann Bird, $394.20; Sarah Maria Barley [*sic*], $175.20; John Bird, $43.80.]

No. 274, Petition of Thomas A. Newman Filed May 16, 1862

Thomas A. Newman of Georgetown claims the services of two persons.

1. William Mills is aged 24, black, about 5 feet 11 inches tall and weighs 175 pounds. He is a superior farm hand. Newman states that he was offered $1,500 for him 18 months ago.

2. Harriet Davis, aged 40, black, is moderately stout and weighs 160 (?) pounds. She is a first-class kitchen servant, cook, washer and ironer.

They are both obedient and pleasant spoken, healthy and free of any defects that would impair their value in the Southern market. He values them at $2,400.

Mills came to Mrs. Newman upon the death of her brother, Thomas Van Resnick, in 1858. Davis was purchased in 1855 from Dr. Hardy of Prince George's County, Md.

[Commissioners paid Newman $876: William Mills, $613.20; Harriet Davis, $262.80.]

Newman married Louisa J. VanRiswick on Feb. 20, 1844. See Pippenger, D.C. Marriage Licenses, 1811-1858, p. 441.

No. 275, Petition of Susan B. Sheriff Filed May 19, 1862

Susan B. Sheriff of Washington claims compensation for ten persons.

1. Frederick Jackson is aged 55, light brown and about 5 feet 4 inches tall. He is a good gardener and field hand and market man. [Value $1,000]

2. Dolly Jackson, Frederick's wife, is aged 54, light brown, about 5 feet 6 inches tall and stout and healthy. She is a good cook, washer and ironer. [Value $1,000]

3. Michael Jacks is aged 30, black, about 5 feet 10 inches tall and very healthy. He is a good gardener and field hand. [Value $1,400]

4. Polly Jackson, aged 25, light brown, about 5 feet 6 inches tall. She is a first-class house servant and good cook. [Value $1,400]

5. Charlotte Jackson, aged 22, light brown, about 5 feet 2 inches tall, very healthy. She is a first-class house servant and cook. [Value $1,400]

6. Bettie Crawford, aged 24, black, about 5 feet 2 inches tall, healthy. She is a first-class house servant. [Value $1,400]

7. Frederick Jackson, Jr., is aged 21, light brown, about 5 feet 10 inches tall and very healthy. He is a good gardener and farm hand. [Value $1.500]

8. Ellen Thomas, aged 15, about 5 feet 2 inches tall. She is a good nurse and house servant. [Value $1,200]

9. William James, aged 14, bright mulatto, well-grown and very healthy. He is a good gardener and farm hand. [Value $1,200]

10. Wesley Jackson, aged six, bright mulatto, sprightly, well-grown and healthy. [Value $500]

Sheriff acquired them from the estate of her aunt, Susan Beall of Washington County, D.C. By her marriage to Samuel Sheriff, deceased, of Prince George's County, Md., she acquired title to Bettie and when her husband died in August of 1843 she moved to the District of Columbia.

[Commissioners paid Sheriff $3,394.50: Frederick Jackson, $131.40; Dolly Jackson, $109.50; Michael Jacks, $525.60; Polly Jackson, $481.80; Charlotte Jackson, $350.40; Bettie Crawford, $481.80; Frederick Jackson, Jr., $525.60; Ellen Thomas, $394.20; William Jackson, $262.80; Wesley Jackson, $131.40.]

Susan B. Young married Samuel Sheriff on Sept. 4, 1836. See Pippenger, D.C. Marriage Licenses, 1811-1858, p. 535.

No. 276, Petition of Ann Maria S. Forrest Filed May 19, 1862

Ann M. Forrest of Rockville, Montgomery County, Md., claims compensation for Frederick Hepburn. Hepburn is 43 years old, dark mulatto in color, 5 feet 2 inches tall and about medium size. She has received $125 hire per annum for Hepburn for the last ten or 12 years. He has no infirmities or defects. [Value $800]

Hepburn was a gift from her mother when she married in 1823. To her knowledge, there is no record of this.

[Commissioners paid Forrest $306.60, by her attorney John W. Wilson.]

The Commissioners printed report gives Forrest's name as "Anna A. S.", but it is "Ann Marie S." in the original documents.

No. 277, Petition of Margaret Gormley Filed May 19, 1862

Margaret Gormley of Georgetown claims compensation for Mary Helena Payne. Payne is about 25 years old, black, short, stout and very healthy. She was purchased many years ago by Gormley's husband and was taken by her when she administered her husband's estate. (Signed Margaret her x mark Gormley)

[Commissioners paid Gormley $350.40.]

Margaret O'Reily married Philip Gormley on Jun. 28, 1830. See Pippenger, D.C. Marriage Licenses, 1811-1858, p. 238.

No. 278, Petition of Michael Shanks   Filed May 19, 1862

Michael Shanks of Washington claims compensation for Lethe Wood. Wood is about 45 years and eight months old, dark mulatto, about 5 feet 5 inches tall, healthy and strong.. She is stout and squarely built with masculine features. She is a first-rate servant and does all the household work. Shanks says he has refused $1,000 for her. [Value $1,000]

Shanks purchased her for $800 on May 2, 1859, from John Strider, the administrator of late Eleanor West.
[Commissioners paid Shanks $219.]

No. 279, Petition of Patience W. Peck   Filed May 19, 1862

Patience W. Peck of Georgetown claims compensation for three persons.

1. David Nokes is aged 61, of a very dark color and nearly six feet tall. He is strongly built but not fleshy and rather slow but very steady in his movements. He is generally healthy. He is a blacksmith and was hired for the years 1860-1861 at $20 a month which makes his annual hire $240. [Value $300]

2. Maria Nokes, David's wife, is aged 51, dark in color and rather below medium size and height. She is slenderly formed and bent forward when she walks. Her general health is not very good and she has a week constitution and is afflicted with rheumatism. She has been a cook and washerwoman in Peck's family of six and when released readily obtained employment at $1 a week with her board. [Value $200]

3. Ann Watson, aged 14, is not as dark as the others and is well-grown for her age. She is quick and active in her movements and free from infirmities. Her "moral character is as good probably as that of most negro girls her age." [Value $500]

David Nokes was purchased by Peck's late husband, Asa Peck of Loudoun County, Va., in February of 1834 for $625 from Joseph H. Washington, Esq., of Fairfax County, Va., who had given David the choice of moving with him to Kentucky or choosing a home in Virginia. If there is a record of this title it may be found at the Loudoun County Clerk's Office in Leesburg. Maria Nokes was owned by Mrs. Peck from birth as she was a child of a woman bequeathed to Peck in her father's will. Ann Watson has also belonged to Peck from her birth because her grandmother and mother were held under a like claim.

[Commissioners paid Peck, by Clement A. Peck, her attorney, $876: David Nokes, $262.80; Maria Nokes, $175.20; Ann Watson, $438,]

No. 280, Petition of Bridget Taylor   Filed May 19,1862

Bridget Taylor of Washington claims compensation for four persons.

1. Abigail Montgomery is aged 50, chestnut colored and five feet tall. [Value $250]
2. Isaac Montgomery, child of Abigail, is aged 25 and dark colored. [Value $1,000]
3. Georgiana Montgomery, child of Abigail, is aged 18 and dark colored. [Value $800]
4. Elizabeth Montgomery, child of Abigail, is aged seven and mulatto. [Value $400]

They are all excellent servants who are honest, trustworthy and healthy.

About 1814 or 1815 Taylor's father, the late Thomas Bailey of Somerset County, Va., willed Abigail to her. The three children were born after she acquired title.

A supplementary document signed Nov. 20, 1862, was filed and provided that Taylor assigned $348.52 to William R. Riley. (Signed Bridget her x mark Taylor)
[Commissioners paid William R. Riley, $348.52, and Bridget Taylor, per T[homas] E. Lloyd, her attorney, $1,009.28: "Abigal" Montgomery, $131.40; Isaac Montgomery, $569.40; Georgiana Montgomery, $481.80; Elizabeth Montgomery, $175.20.]

No. 281, Petition of William H. Edes   Filed May 19, 1862

William H. Edes of Georgetown claims compensation for Charlotte Gustus. Gustus is 26 years old, dark black, about 5 feet 7 inches tall and free of defects or infirmities. [Value $625]

Edes purchased her from Charles R. Belt of Washington County, D.C., for $625 on Oct. 19, 1858. She was at that

time living in Edes's household. Edes states that he intended to free Gustus when she repaid her purchase price out of her wages. She has been employed by Edes as a cook. He has kept a true account of her wages and she has paid about $300 towards purchasing herself. He, therefore, only claims the balance.
[Commissioners paid $547.50 to Edes.]

No. 282, Petition of Morris Adler　　　　　　　　　　　　　　　　　　　　　　　　　　　　Filed May 19, 1862

Morris Adler of Georgetown claims compensation for three persons.

1. John Smallwood is aged 28 and dark colored. An attached bill of sale dated Oct. 21, 1853, shows that he purchased Smallwood for $1,250 from George Mattingly and the executors of the estate of Charles E. Eckel. [Value $1,250]

2. Susan Norris is aged 35 and dark colored. The bill of sale dated Jun. 27, 1828, shows that Christopher Burckhardt (?) for $1,050, sold to Adler a Negro woman named Gracy and her daughter, Susanna. [Value $800]

3. Ann Bowie is aged 22 and dark colored. The attached bill of sale shows that he purchased Bowie on Sept. 15, 1859, from Charles R. Belt of Washington County, D.C., for $800. [Value $600]

[Commissioners paid Adler $1,445.40: John Smallwood, $569.40; Ann Bowie, $569.40; Susan Norris, $306.60,]

The acquisition of Smallwood was a complicated legal transaction and the reader is urged to consult the original petition and its attachments for additional information.

No. 283, Petition of William H. Dougal　　　　　　　　　　　　　　　　　　　　　　　　　Filed May 19, 1862

William H. Dougal of Washington County, D.C., claims compensation for two persons.

1. Catharine Mudd is 31, dark coloed, of medium height and stout. [Value $900]

2. Clara (Clarissa) Bowie is aged 20, dark mulatto, tall and good-looking. [Value $1,000]

They are sound in mind and body and are capable and accomplished servants.

He purchased Catharine Mudd for $1,000 by a bill of sale dated Oct. 10, 1857, from Joseph Bruin. He bought Clarissa Bowie for $850 from Charles R. Belt of the County of Washington on Feb. 23, 1860.

[Commissioners paid Dougal $1,007.40: Catharine Mudd, $394.20; Clara Bowie, $613.20.]

No. 284, Petition of Anne Blanchard　　　　　　　　　　　　　　　　　　　　　　　　　　Filed May 19, 1862

Ann Blanchard of Washington claims compensation for two persons.

1. Rachel Jackson is aged about 60. She is of "unmixed African blood", but her complexion is not very dark. She is a good house servant and is healthy. [Value $300]

2. William Henry Taylor is 28 years old, yellow colored and 5 feet 10 inches tall. He has been in charge of a steam engine in a printing office for many years and is healthy. [Value $1,000]

Blanchard states that her late husband purchased Jackson from Seth Hyatt of Washington about 1821. Taylor was born of a slave woman owned by Anne in the year 1835.

[Commissioners paid Blanchard $744.60: Rachel Jackson, $87.60; William Henry Taylor, $657.

No. 285, Petition of Joseph F. Brown　　　　　　　　　　　　　　　　　　　　　　　　　　Filed May 19, 1862

Joseph F. Brown of Washington claims compensation for Mary Jane Butler. Butler is 20 years old, of a light copper color, has regular features and is large and full-grown. She reads and writes correctly and rapidly, is very intelligent and altogether of a fine personal appearance. There is not a more valuable slave woman in the District. She is an excellent seamstress, house servant, cook, washer, ironer, marketer and nurse. She is neat, industrious and is a rigid Catholic. She is unmarried. He refused an offer of $1,400 for her in 1860.

He purchased her for $800 from Stanislaus Murray, agent for Dr. P. H. Hamilton of Maryland on Mar. 6, 1858.

[Commissioners paid Brown $569.40.]

No. 286, Petition of Catharine Palmer　　　　　　　　　　　　　　　　　　　　　　　　　Filed May 19, 1862

Catharine Palmer of New York, but now residing in Washington, claims compensation for Elizabeth Jackson. Jackson is 15 years old, light mulatto, with black hair and black eyes. She is 5 feet 2 inches tall and is stout and healthy. She is an excellent domestic servant and Palmer refused a check for $1,000 for her 18 months ago. Her value is much enhanced by her having been brought up in Palmer's family. [Value $1,000]

Palmer acquired her as a gift in May 1855 from her husband, General J. N. Palmer, who is now with General McClellan's army. Her husband purchased Jackson for $150 at St. Louis, Mo., Sept. 23, 1852, from George Stevenson.

[Commissioners paid Palmer, by John A. Smith, her attorney, $481.80.]

No. 287, Petition of William Emmert   Filed May 19, 1862

William Emmert of Washington County, D.C., claims compensation for four servants.

1. Ned is aged 60 and dark colored. He has lost one of his toes, but otherwise is healthy. [Value $150]
2. Charles is aged 21, mulatto and the son of Emeline. He is strong and healthy. [Value $1,000]
3. Emeline is aged 39, black and healthy. [Value $500]
4. Mary is aged 60 and black. She is "subject to complaints after such as many females, otherwise she is a good worker and strong." [Value $100]

He purchased Ned from a person named Rosenthal (?), deceased, about four years ago for $175. He bought Emeline and Charles about 15 years ago for $700 from a man named Martin from Georgetown. He purchased Mary from Mr. Moxley (?) of Georgetown for $100 about three years ago.

[Commissioners paid Emmert $591.30: Ned, $21.90; Charles $350.40; Emeline, $175.20; Mary, $43.80.]

No. 288, Petition of George W. Talburtt   Filed May 19, 1862

George W. Talburtt claims compensation for 16 persons.

1. John Mathews is aged 50, dark copper colored and 5 feet 6 inches tall. He is a first-rate farm hand, teamster and coachman. [Value $700]
2. Teresa Mathews, 40, light mulatto is 5 feet 6 inches. She is first-rate seamstress, washer and ironer. [Value $620]
3. Susan Jones, 20, bright mulatto, 4 feet 4 inches. She is a superior house servant and fair cook. [Value $1,000]
4. Charles Lee, 18, black, five feet tall. He is a first-rate farm hand and driver. [Value $1,000]
5. William Datcher, 32, black, is 5 feet 4 inches tall. He is a gardener and attended market as a salesman. He has been ruptured. [Value $700]
6. Henrietta Brown, 25, is 5 feet 4 inches tall. She is a superior cook, washer, ironer and house servant. {Value $1,000]
7. Rose Diggs, 23, dark mulatto, 5 feet 4 inches tall. She is a first-rate washer, ironer, house servant and plain cook. [Value $1,000]
8. Samuel Brown, 13, black, is 4 feet 6 inches tall. He is a stable hand and ploughman. [Value $800]
9. Robert Watkins, 30, is black and 5 feet 5 inches tall. He is a house servant and market man and farm hand. [Value $1,000]
10. Milley Mathews, aged 16 is black and 5 feet 6 inches tall. She is a house servant and field hand and is tall and fine looking. [Value $1,200]
11. Teresa Brown, 11, black, 4 feet 3 inches. She is a child's nurse. [Value $300]
12. Patsy Brown, 10, black, five feet tall. She is a child's nurse. [Value $300]
13. Augustus Brown, eight, black, 3 feet 2 inches tall and sprightly. [Value $200]
14. Alfred Mathews, 40, is black and 5 feet 8 inches tall. He is a ploughman and field hand. He has a defect in one arm (?) from it having been broken. [Value $300]
15. Joseph Brown, three, is light copper in color and 3 feet 1 inch tall. He is a likely boy, but slightly ruptured. [Value $100]
16. James Jackson, light mulatto, is 2 feet 4 inches tall. He is a likely boy. [Value $100]

John "Matthews" and Teresa "Matthews" were purchased in 1860 for $1,060 from F. H. Lancaster. He inherited the others with the death of his father and mother.

[Commissioners paid $5,234.10: John Mathews, $219; Teresa Mathews, $306.60; Susan Jones, $394.20; Charles Lee, $591.30; William Datcher, $219; Henrietta Brown, $525.60; Rose Diggs, $547.50; Samuel Brown, $438; Robert Watkins, $438; Milley Mathews, $569.40; Teresa Brown, $284.70; Patsy Brown, $219; Augustus Brown, $153.30; Alfred Mathews, $175.20; Joseph Brown, $87.60; James Jackson, $65.70.]

The surname "Mathews" is spelled with both one "t" and two in the original documents. Although the printed report gives the name of William "Dalcher", it is clearly "Datcher".

No. 289, Petition of Margaret Ann Smoot   Filed 19, 1862

The petition of Margaret A. Smoot, by Robert W. Smoot, her husband, both of Montgomery County, Md., states that Margaret had a slave named Frank Herbert whom she permitted to reside in the District of Columbia where he had a wife. Herbert is about 45 years old, black and about 5 feet 10 or 11 inches tall. He is healthy, well-made and erect, and honest, industrious, capable and faithful. He worked as a farm hand and she has hired him out as her slave and received his wages. [Value $1,500]

Margaret acquired title to Herbert in the distribution of the personal estate of Dr. Stephen N. C. White, late of Montgomery County. Her claim was prepared and filed about May 15 by Joseph H. Bradley of Washington on her behalf at the request of her brother, either Daniel or Benjamin White. This petition was mislaid and a new petition was submitted and signed July 17, 1862, by Robert W. Smoot. The Commissioners ordered that it be treated as filed on May 19th rather than July 18th.

[Commissioners granted Margaret Ann Smoot, by R. W. Smoot, her husband and attorney, $394.20.]

The 1860 Census for the District of Columbia, Vol. 1, p. 71, lists Frank Herbert, aged 45, black, a laborer, as residing in Georgetown with a woman named Rebecca, aged 49 (presumably his wife) and four children. Since the population census lists only free persons, Herbert and his family are living as free blacks and being counted as such by the census taker.

No. 290, Petition of Jacob Hines Filed May 19, 1862

Jacob Hines of Washington City claims compensation for five persons.

1. Alice Maria Robinson is aged 23, mulatto, about 5 feet 3 or 4 inches tall and well-built. She is due to be free at age 25. [Value $100]

2. James Henry Robinson is aged 15, dark, 5 feet 3 or 4 inches tall and stout built. He is to be free at age 28. [Value $300]

3. Alfred Curtis Robinson, aged 13, is dark, about five feet high and middle sized. He is to be free at age 28. [Value $300]

4. Eliza Jane Robinson is aged 17, dark color, 5 feet 3 or 4 inches tall and stout. She is to be free at age 25. [Value $250]

5. Sally Robinson is aged 11, dark,, about 4 feet 5 or 6 inches tall and slim. She is a slave for life. [Value $300]

From his late wife Himes acquired title to the mother of these five persons and about seven years ago he freed the mother. The retained children were subject to service for a set term of years.

[Commissioners paid Hines $667.95: Alice Maria Robinson, $32.85; James Henry Robinson, $219; Eliza Jane Robinson, $109.50; Alfred C. Robinson, $175.20; Sally Robinson, $131.40.]

No. 291, Petition of Ann Cosine, adm., Ann Weeden, and William B. Lacy, Filed May 19, 1862
heirs of John Cosine

Ann Weeden and W. B. Lacy, heirs at law of John Cosine, late of Alexandria County, Va., and Ann Cosine, administratrix of the estate, claim compensation for four persons.

1. Elizabeth is aged 31, a bright mulatto and about 5 feet 2 inches tall. She is a stout, healthy cook and has an excellent character. [Value $1,000]

2. Lucy is aged 15, a very bright mulatto and 4 feet 10 inches tall. She is a superior house servant and chambermaid. She is good, honest and intelligent. [Value $600]

3. Hanson is aged three and of a yellow complexion. He is a stout and healthy boy. [Value $400]

4. Eliza is aged 15, a very bright mulatto and about five feet tall. She has a mark on her left cheek caused by a burn when she was quite young. She is a stout, healthy girl and a reliable and honest house servant and chambermaid. [Value $700]

Elizabeth was bequeathed to Ann Cosine, Ann Weeden and W. B. Lacy by the will of the late John Cosine of Alexandria County, Va. Lucy and Hanson are Elizabeth's children born after Elizabeth came into the heirs' possession. Eliza is the daughter of Susan and was also acquired under the terms of the will. Attached is a copy the will of John "Cossens" signed Aug. 29, 1833.

[Commissioners paid Ann Cosine, by A. Weeden, her attorney, Ann M. Weeden, W. B. Lacy $1,116.90: Elizabeth, $350.40; Lucy, $328.50; Harrison [Hanson], $87.60; Eliza, $350.40.]

No. 292, Petition of William B. Lacy Filed May 19, 1862

William B. Lacy of Alexandria County, Va., claims compensation for John Ringold. He is aged about 40, dark and 5 feet 9 ½ inches tall. He is stout, well-made and healthy, and is a valuable servant, a first-rate garden and field hand and an excellent wagon man. He may be trusted with any duty connected with a farm or garden. [Value $1,000]

Lacy purchased Ringold from Benjamin F. Weeden, the former husband of his wife, Mary Jane, of Frisby Weeden, and others. The attached bill of sale filed May 11, 1839, shows that Benjamin F. Weeden, of Anne Arundel

County, Md., for $379 sold John Ringold, who had been previously purchased by him from Frisby Weedon, to Robert B. Moss. That sale stipulated that if Weeden repaid the $375 with interest before May 1, 1846, Ringold would be returned to him. The debt was repaid by means of $55 a year for the services of Ringold and $265.22 paid by Weeden on Apr. 24, 1843 and Ringold was released to Benjamin Weeden.

[Commissioners paid Lacy $350.40.]

No. 293, Petition of Eliza Ott   Filed May 19, 1862

Eliza Ott of Wheeling, Va., claims compensation for five persons.

1. Celia Coleman, aged 52, is 5 feet 8 inches tall and has a yellow complexion. She is an intelligent Christian woman and a good cook and well versed in all domestic services. Her health, however, is impaired. [Value $400]

2. Henry Coleman, aged 25, is 5 feet 8 inches tall and has a yellow complexion. He is healthy, able-bodied, honest, correct in his habits and is well-trained as a dining room and household servant. [Value $1,200]

3. Frances Coleman, aged 20, is 5 feet 5 inches tall and has a yellow complexion. She has a mark from a burn on her left breast and a small scar near her left eye. She is healthy, of a good character and trained in domestic service. [Value $800]

4. Ellen Coleman, aged 18, is 5 feet 9 inches tall and has a yellow complexion. She is healthy, of good character and trained in domestic service. [Value $800]

5. Anna Coleman, aged 13, is 5 feet 2 inches tall, with a yellow complexion. She is a very handsome servant. [Value $500]

Ott acquired them under the will of her father, Jacob Ott, of Woodstock, Va.

[Commissioners paid Ott, by John D. Ott, her attorney, $2,255.70: Celia Coleman, $262.80; Henry Coleman, $569.40; Frances Coleman, $481.80; Ellen Coleman, $547.50; Anna Coleman, $394.20.]

No. 294, Petition of John Eliason   Filed May 19, 1862

John Eliason of Georgetown claims compensation for four persons.

1. Linah Washington, aged about 36, is a bright color and 5 feet 4 ½ inches tall. [Value $1,000]
2. Daniel Washington is aged about 12, dark colored and 4 feet 5 1/3 inches tall. [Value $800]
3. Ida Mary Washington is aged nine, dark colored and 3 feet 11 inches tall. [Value $500]
4. Catherine J. Washington, five years old, is light colored and 3 feet 6 inches tall. [Value $300]

Eliason acquired title by his marriage to Mary Catherine Chume (?). The servants were recorded in 1858 in the D.C. Circuit Court Clerk's Office.

[Commissioners paid Eliason $941.70: Linah Washington, $262.80; Daniel Washington, $306.60; Ida Mary Washington, $240.90; Cath. J. Washington, $131.40.]

"Linah" Washington's first name may be "Sinah". The printed report gives it as "Linah" and the original petition could be read as either "Sinah" or "Linah".

No. 295, Petition of John S. Paxton   Filed May 19, 1862

John S. Paxton of Georgetown claims compensation for Henry. Henry is 15 years old, of a dark complexion, and is sound in body and limbs. Paxton states that he has been offered $1,000 for him. [Value $1,000]

He acquired title by marriage with Sarah A. Neill, who obtained the boy under the will of her former husband, George S. Neill, deceased.

[Commissioners paid Paxton $350.40.]

No. 296, Petition of James C. Pickett   Filed Jun. 13, 1862

James C. Pickett, now at the city of Washington, claims compensation for four persons.

1. Fanny is aged 34 and is "dark, but not very dark". Fanny is the mother of the three listed below. [Value $800]
2. Hannah, aged 14, is a good-looking mulatto. [Value $900]
3. Llewellen (or "Lewellen"), dark, is 11 years old. [Value $400]
4. George, mulatto, is nine years old. [Value $400]

Picket was given the mother of Fanny by his father-in-law 40 years ago in Kentucky. He knows of no written record of this and he has resided since 1829 outside of that state. His father-in-law has been dead more than 20 years so he cannot produce him as proof of the gift.

Pickett submits numerous letters and statements in support of his loyalty to the United States. Margaret A. Washington's sworn statement dated Jun. 11, 1862, says that to her knowledge Fanny and her three children have lived with her sister, Mary W. Johnson, in Washington City for more than 24 years. Mary W. Johnson swears on Jun. 10, 1862, that Fanny has resided with her continuously for more than 24 years and that her children were born in her house. Pickett also filed an additional statement dated Jun. 27 (?), 1862, in which he replies to a statement that Fanny made before the Board of Commissioners to the effect that Lewellen was unhealthy. Pickett says that he has not seen much of Lewellen since his birth and nothing of him for the three years and about ten months ended on last May 30. He still believes that all the persons were ordinarily healthy.

[Commissioners paid Pickett $1,182.60: Fanny, $394.20; Hannah, $394.20; Llewellen, $219; George, $175.20.]

No. 297, Petition of John C. Rives

John C. Rives of Washington claims compensation for three persons.

1. Louisa Jones, 35 years old, is a dark mulatto and about 4 feet 8 inches tall. She is an excellent servant and Rives intended to set her free. [Value $300]

2. Charles Sumner Jones, Louisa's son, is about six and a bright mulatto. He is very tall for his age. He is remarkably sprightly and intelligent and Rives intended to free him when he reached age 21.

3. James Jackson is about 36 years old.

Rives purchased Louisa for $300 about 19 years ago from William S. Colquhoun of Washington. Her son was born after that purchase. A supplementary statement by Rives dated May 19, 1862, claims ownership of James Jackson whom he purchased in 1848. James was then about 22 years old so now is 36. He is able-bodied and very healthy and Rives permitted him to hire himself out for the last six or seven years. Rives heard he hired himself to Mr. McCormick of D.C. for the last three years, but last winter he hired himself without Rives's permission to a man who lived in Maryland about 30 yards from the District line.

Rives states that he carried on his business in Washington, but considers himself a citizen of Maryland and his country residence is about 80 yards beyond the District line. Rives is not sure whether he is entitled to compensation or not.

[Commissioners paid Rives $1,182.60: Louisa Jones, $394.20; Charles Sumner Jones, $175.20; James Jackson, $481.80.]

John C. Rives is editor and proprietor of the Congressional Globe on Pennsylvania Ave.(the forerunner to the Congressional Record) and lives at Kildee Hill, Md.

No. 298, Petition of Daniel H. Tebbs and Martha Tebbs   Filed May 19, 1862

Daniel H. Tebbs and his wife, Martha Tebbs, of Washington City, claim compensation for Harriet Jones. Jones is 23 years old, of a black color, 5 feet 4 inches tall, with a "loss of the upper teeth broken out." She is intelligent, healthy, honest, industrious and free of defects. Martha acquired her from her mother, Caroline Stewart of Maryland, in September 1858. [Value $900]

[Commissioners paid Daniel and Martha Tebbs $438.]

No. 299, Petition of Samuel Shreve   Filed May 19, 1862

Samuel Shreve of Washington City claims compensation for three persons.

1. William Ceasor, aged 32, of a dark brown color, about 5 feet 7 inches tall and well-built. His wages at the time of the passage of the emancipation act were $1 a day.

2. Eveline Clark, aged 18, of a dark brown color, about 5 feet 4 inches tall and well-built. She is worth $8 a month with food and clothing.

3. Isabel Brook, she is worth $2 a month with food and clothing.

Shreve estimates their value at $2,400.

He bought them at the estate sale of his father, Samuel Shreve, of Montgomery County, Md., in November 1861.

[Commissioners paid Shreve $1,292.10: William Ceasor, $591.30; Eveline Clark, $481.80; Isabel Brook, $219.]

No. 300, Petition of Joseph Libby

Joseph Libby of Georgetown claims compensation for Rosa Payne. She is 50 years old, has tolerably dark skin and is about five feet tall. She has a remarkably youthful appearance for her age and is very active and sprightly. She is a first-class servant, an excellent cook and can do all kinds of housework. She has enjoyed excellent health. Libby acquired her by purchase from John James about 16 years ago. [Value $500.]

[Commissioners paid "Libbey" $175.20.]

No. 301, Petition of Joseph C. And Henry A. Willard　　　　　　　　　　　　　　　　　　　Filed May 19, 1862

　J. C. and H. A. Willard of Washington claim compensation for five persons.

　1. Mary Ann Thomas is aged about 50, light mulatto, short but generally hearty. She is the mother of William and John. [Value $1,000]

　2. William Thomas is aged about 22, light mulatto and about 5 feet 4 inches tall and stout. [Value $1,000]

　3. John Thomas is aged 21, light mulatto, about 5 feet 5 inches tall and stout. [Value $1,000]

　4. Jack Bowie, about 27 years old, black, is about 5 feet 6 inches tall. He is healthy but not so strong and stout as the others. [Value $1,000]

　5. James Montgomery, about 34 years old, is mulatto and about 5 feet 6 inches tall. He is sound and able-bodied and capable. [Value $800]

　An attached bill of sale shows that Philip Otterback of Washington, for $4,000 paid by J.C. and H.A. Willard, sell to them servant woman Mary Ann, aged about 47, and her three children, Celia, about 18, Henry [sic], about 15, and John about 19. They are not to be sold or taken to reside out of the District. (Signed Jun. 3, 1854)
The Willards state that Mary Ann, William and John Thomas were attached by the creditors of William Gadsby and were confined in the county jail for safekeeping. At the solicitation of some of the Negroes' friends, the Willards paid $1,000 each for the three, they being a mother and her children.

　A second bill of sale shows that John A. Keefe, Martha Ann Keefe, John T. Travers and Martha Ellen Travers of Washington, for $800 paid by J.C. and H.A. Willard, sell to them Negro man John [sic] Montgomery, aged 37 years. (Signed July 25, 1859)

　A third bill of sale shows that the executor of the estate of the late Roderick M. McGregor of Prince George's County, Md., for $1,000, sold to J.C. and H.A. Willard, Negro Jack. (Dated Feb. 2, 1858)

　[Commissioners paid the Willards $2,430.90: Mary Ann Thomas, $175.20; William Thomas, $569.40; John Thomas, $591.30; Jack Bowie, $547.50; James Montgomery, $547.50.]

　The Willards are the proprietors of Willard's Hotel on Pennsylvania Ave. There are some contradictions in regard to names, ages and number of persons between the petition statements and the copy of the bill of sale in the case of the Thomas family. Most importantly, Mary Ann's child, Celia, is named in the bill of sale but no where else.

No. 302, Petition of Elizabeth L. Young　　　　　　　　　　　　　　　　　　　　　　　　　　Filed May 19, 1862

　Elizabeth L. Young of Prince George's County, Md., claims compensation for five persons.

　1. Henry Hilleary is aged 30, mulatto and very healthy. He is a valuable servant, carpenter and carriage driver. [Value $1,500]

　2. Mary Bowman is from 23 to 26 years old and very black. She is a valuable servant. [Value $1,000]

　3. Matilda is aged about 23 (?) and is very black. She is a good cook and house keeper and a good field hand. [Value $800]

　4. William, aged about two, is black and healthy. [Value $200]

　5. Eliza, aged about six months, is black and hearty. [Value $100]

　Young acquired title by inheritance from her parents. The servants were born in her family and raised by her to their present age.

　[Commissioners paid Young by C. F. Perrie, attorney, $1,576.80: Henry Hilleary, $547.50; Mary Bowman, $481.80; Matilda, $438; William, $87.60; Eliza, $21.90.]

No. 303, Petition of Hester A. Wheeler　　　　　　　　　　　　　　　　　　　　　　　　　　Filed May 19, 1862

　Hester A. Wheeler of Georgetown claims compensation for Emily Herbert. Herbert is 52 (?) years old, light colored, with black hair and black eyes and is unusually stout. [Value $1,200]

　[Commissioners paid Wheeler $197.10]

　This petition is very faded and the author could not decipher much of it.

No. 304, Petition of William G. H. Newman　　　　　　　　　　　　　　　　　　　　　　　Filed May 19, 1862

　William G. H. Newman of Washington City claims compensation for two persons.

　1. Ann Bounds, about 47 years old is black and delicately built.

　2. Mary Bounds, child of Ann, is aged about 16, light black in color and well-built.

Newman estimates their total value as $1,500. They are well-instructed in their duties as house servants and are healthy and free of defects. Newman acquired them by gift from his wife's father, Charles Rider. The attached statements of gift are dated Somerset County, Md., Sept. 17, 1857, in the case of Ann Bounds, and Washington, May

24, 1852, in the case of Mary Bounds.
[Commissioners paid Newman: $525.60: Ann Bounds, $87.60; Mary Bounds, $438.]

No. 305, Petition of Elizabeth A. S. Bryan
Filed May 19, 1862

Elizabeth A. S. Bryant of Washington claims compensation for five persons.

1. Cecelia Coombs, 65, is black with dark eyes and black hair and is 5 feet 2 inches tall. She is a good cook and general servant. [Value $250]

2. Mary Coombs, aged 40, black with dark eyes and dark hair, 5 feet 2 inches tall. She is a first-rate cook and servant. [Value $750]

3. Maria Coombs, aged 35, copper colored, dark eyes and hair, about five feet tall. She is a first-rate cook and servant. [Value $750]

4. Eliza Coombs, aged 29, copper colored, dark eyes and hair, about 5 feet 10 inches tall. She is a first-rate cook, laundress and house servant. [Value $1,000]

5. Mary Coombs, aged 13, very light with light hair and dark eyes. She is a first-rate nurse. [Value $500]

Bryan acquired title by inheritance from Enoch Bryan, deceased.

[Commissioners paid Elizabeth A. S. Bryan, her x mark, $1,182.60: Cecelia Coombs, $21.90; Mary Coombs, $240.90; Maria Coombs, $131.40; Eliza Coombs, $394.20; Mary Coombs, $394.20.]

No. 306, Petition of William A. Nichols
Filed May 19, 1862

Lt. Col. William A. Nichols of the U.S. Army, claims compensation for Isabella Chisman. Chisman is about 43 years old, bright mulatto and about 5 feet 1 or 2 inches tall with black eyes. She has a pleasant expression of countenance and quiet and good manners. She is in good health, but sometimes complains of rheumatism. She is a first-rate cook, splendid laundress, good nurse and a "midwife of more than usual excellence for one of her class", and a first-class house servant. She has good morals and for many years has been a member of the Baptist church. [Value $1,000]

Nichols purchased her for $900 from Anna Gilliam of Hampton, Va., and for an additional $30 paid to Isabella, on Apr. 24, 1855. In addition to the bill of sale, Nichols attaches a letter from Dr. G. W. Semple dated Old Point, Apr. 30, 1855, informing Nichols that Isabella is now Nichols property and that he will see to her until he wants her. Nichols was in New York City at the time of this petition.

[Commissioners paid Nichols $328.50]

No. 307, Petition of Augusta McBlair
Filed May 19, 1862

Augusta McBlair of Washington claims compensation for six servants.

1. Henry King is aged 53, light brown, about 5 feet 8 inches tall, with black hair and eyes but rather bald. He is a good carpenter and bricklayer and a first-class waiter and marketman. He is sometimes rheumatic, but is generally healthy. [Value $1,000]

2. Maria King, wife of Henry, is 46, brown complexion, 5 feet 6 inches tall and has black hair and eyes. She is an excellent cook and laundress and commands $8 a month. [Value $800]

3. Maria Williams, aged 42, brown complexion, is about 5 feet 6 inches tall and has black hair and eyes. She is healthy but has a scarred face. She is a capital cook and laundress and commands $8 a month. [Value $800]

4. Nancy Syphax, is aged 53, yellow complexion, about 5 feet 2 inches tall, with black eyes and grayish-black hair. She is a good nurse, house servant and laundress. [Value $800]

5. George King is aged 19, brown colored, black hair and eyes and about 5 feet 9 inches tall. He is a first-class waiter and dining room servant. He would command $35 a month. [Value $1,500]

6. Martha King, aged 11, is about four feet tall, with a dark complexion and black hair and eyes. She is a smart child and a good waiter. [Value $500]

McBlair inherited these servants from her mother, Mrs. Provey Gadsby, in trust to Julia TenEyck

[Commissioners paid McBlair $1,489.20: Henry King, $175.20; Maria King, $175.20; Maria Williams, $175.20; Nancy Syphax, $87.60; George King, $613.20; Martha King, $262.80.]

See the will of John Gadsby, who died May 15, 1844. Provey Gadsby is his wife. Augusta Gadsby, who married J. Hollis McBlair in 1835, and Julia Gadsby, who married John C. TenEyck of Mt. Holly, N.J., were daughters of John and Provey. Pippenger, D.C. Probate Records, 1801-1852, p. 272 and 272n.

No. 308, Petition of Mary Augusta Gadsby
Filed May 19, 1862

Mary Augusta Gadsby claims compensation for James Williams. He is about 19 years old, black complexion, black hair and eyes, thick lips, gruff voice and about 5 feet 8 inches tall. He is a first-class waiter, superior cook and thorough house servant. He was willed to her by the late Mrs. Provey Gadsby.

[Commissioners paid Gadsby $525.60.]

See note accompanying No. 308. Mary Augusta Gadsby is John and Provey Gadsby's daughter-in-law.

No. 309, Petition of Benjamin C. Card   Filed May 19, 1862

Benjamin C. Card of Washington claims compensation for three servants.

1. Maria Walker, aged 32, black complexion and black hair and eyes, about 5 feet 4 inches tall. She is a very superior servant and a good cook and laundress, and faithful and honest. She resides in his family on I St. [Value $1,200]

2. Mary Walker, aged seven, is the daughter of Maria and has a black complexion with black hair and eyes. She is a sprightly child who waits on the table and goes to school. [Value $600]

3. Billy Walker, aged three, son of Maria, has a black complexion and black hair and eyes. He is a sound, bright boy. [Value $350]

Maria and Mary Walker were purchased from J. W. Vineyard of Platte Co., Mo., in 1857 for $1,255. Billy was born after that purchase.

[Commissioners paid Card $657: Maria Walker, $350.40; Mary Walker, $219; Billy Walker, $87.60.]

No. 310, Petition of Courtney Reeves   Filed May 19, 1862

Courtney Reeves of Washington City claims compensation for three persons.

1. George Champ is 23 years old, bright copper in color and about 5 feet 6 inches tall. He is well-set with a broad chest.

2. Andrew Champ is aged 18, bright copper complexion and about 5 feet 8 or 9 inches tall, well-built.

3. Mary Mildred Champ, aged 19, is bright copper colored and about 5 feet 5 inches tall. She is well-built and weighs about 150 pounds.

Reeves purchased them from Jane Peak, in Prince William County, Va., with their mother and one other daughter, who with the mother has since deceased, about the years 1839, 1841 and 1845. In 1846 he moved to Washington with the servants and recorded them with the clerk of court.

Attached is a copy of Reeves's "certificate of slaves" dated Nov. 18, 1846. He certifies that on Nov. 6, 1846, he moved from Prince William County, Va., into the District of Columbia, the following slaves: Mary, aged 38, Fanny Ann, aged nine, George, aged seven, Mary Mildred, aged three and Andrew, aged one year. They were residents of Virginia up until 1846 and are descendants of Virginia slaves that were resident before Apr. 21, 1793.

[Commissioners paid Reeves $1,752: George Champ, $547.50; Andrew Champ, $657; Mary Ann Champ, $547.50.]

No. 311, Petition of Mary Peter, adm. of Ann T. Washington   Filed May 19, 1862

Mary Peter, administratrix, of Georgetown, claims compensation for four persons.

1. Christina Dorsey is aged 35, dark complexion, medium size and healthy. She is the mother of the children listed below. She is a well-trained cook, washer and ironer and house servant. She is industrious and upright in character. [Value $800]

2. Mary Dorsey is aged six, dark colored and of ordinary size. [Value $300]

3. Levi Dorsey, aged four, has a dark complexion and is large for his age. [Value $400]

4. Osbourn Dorsey is aged eight months, dark colored and of ordinary size. [Value $50]

Mary Peter was granted on Mar. 16, 1861, letters of administration for the estate of Ann T. Washington. Washington received them under the terms of the will of her husband, George C. Washington. The children were born while their mother was still a slave.

[Commissioners paid Mary Peter, adm., $744.60: Christina Dorsey, $394.20; Mary Dorsey, $197.10; Levi Dorsey, $109.50; Osbourn Dorsey, $43.80.]

No. 312, Petition of Margaret W. Getty   Filed May 19, 1862

Margaret W. Getty of Georgetown claims compensation for two persons.

1. Eliza Bateman is aged 49, black, 5 feet 5 inches tall and is healthy and strong. She is a first-rate cook, washer and ironer. [Value $800]

2. William Bateman, dark mulatto, is about 5 feet 10 inches tall. He is a first-rate house servant and gardener and in the prime of life. He is strong, healthy and good-tempered. [Value $1,400]

She acquired title from her husband, Robert Getty, deceased, who purchased Eliza when she was six weeks old from Charles Jones. William was born of Eliza while she was a slave of her husband.

[Commissioners paid Getty $722.70: Eliza Bateman, $153.30; William Bateman, $569.40.]

No. 313, Petition of George Rhodes, Sr.   Filed May 19, 1862

George Rhodes of Loudon County, Va., claims compensation for four persons.

1. Frank Hutton, aged 55, is copper colored and about 5 feet 4 inches tall. He is lame in one leg and uses a crutch. He is a very reliable servant and able to do a great deal of light work about the house.

2. Eliza Hutton, wife of Frank, is aged 50, black in color and about five feet tall. She is a very good cook, washer and ironer and is in the family of his son.

3. Harriet Johnson, about 18, is copper colored and 5 feet 2 inches tall. She is a strong, hearty girl and a good cleaner, general house servant and dining room servant.

4. Eliza A. Johnson, daughter of Harriet, is about four months old and very light in color.

Frank and Eliza Hutton and Harriet Johnson work in the family of Rhodes's son who keeps a boarding house. Their estimated value is $2,000.

Rhodes purchased Eliza and Frank from his son, George Rhodes, Jr. Harriet Johnson and her infant were born of slave parents who were the property of Rhodes and he reared them. The slaves have been in the possession of his son, George Rhodes, Jr., for a number of years.

[Commissioners paid Rhodes, Sr., by his attorney J. Carter Marbury, $700.80: Frank Hutton, $43.80; Eliza Hutton, $87.60; Harriet Johnson, $547.50; Eliza A. Johnson, $21.90.]

No. 314, Petition of William James Stone, Sr.   Filed May 19, 1862

William J. Stone, Sr., of the city of Washington claims compensation for eight persons.

1. James Pleasants is aged about 45 and dark colored. He is a good ostler, carriage driver and gardener. He was purchased from J. C. Jones of Montgomery County, Md. [Value $1,000]

2. Fanny Brown, aged about 43, is a good cook and family servant. She was purchased from Robert Sewall of Prince George's County, Md. [Value $1,500]

3. Cornelius Diggs, aged about 23, mulatto, is a good house servant, waiter and driver. He was purchased from Robert Sewall of Prince George's County, Md. [Value $1,000]

4. Polly Pleasants, aged about 15, is black. [Value $1,000]

5. Susan Pleasants, aged about 14, is black. [Value $1,000]

6. Anne Pleasants, aged about 14, is black. [Value $1,000]

7. Ailcey Pleasants, aged about 13, is black. [Value $1,000]

Polly, Susan, Anne and Ailcey are chambermaids and house servants and were born and raised at Stone's place called Mount Pleasant near the city of Washington.

8. Tom Pleasants, aged about 13 is mulatto. He is useful in various ways about the house and farm. He also was born and trained at Mount Pleasant. [Value $1,000]

James Pleasant and Fanny Brown and Cornelius Diggs were purchased as specified above. Polly, Susan, Anne, Ailcey and Tom are the children of Minty and Henrietta and were born at his place and had been purchased from Robert Sewall.

Accompanying note from Stone states that he paid $6,000 for James and Samuel Pleasants on condition that he also took their father and mother, who were too old and infirm to be of any value but who had to be supported during their lifetime.

An attached bill of sale dated Clean Drinking, Montgomery County, Md., Aug. 22, 1842, shows that W.J. Stone paid $1,000 for four slaves named George Pleasants, aged about 65 and his wife, Polly, aged about 60, and James Pleasants, aged 25, and Samuel Pleasants, aged 23. Samuel has since died.

An additional bill of sale dated Washington, Aug. 2, 1842, shows William J. Stone, for $2,200 paid to Robert D. Sewall, purchased seven slaves: Fanny Brown, aged 22, Henrietta Clarke, aged 23 and her two-year-old son named Nealy; Henrietta Brown, aged 15, Minty Carrol, aged 21, John Johnson, aged 13 and Basil Lee aged eight.

In an additional note Stone refers to his sons, Dr. Robert King Stone and William James Stone, Jr., for additional information to identify the younger servants. He has not seen them for some time and he may not recognize them. He therefore names who has charge of them. Polly is with W. F. Mattingley; Susan is with Mrs. Eliza Watts, Annie and Ailcey are with Thomas Berry of Washington City; Thomas is with Charles Abert in Montgomery County, Olney, Md. Thomas wishes to remain with Abert and be bound as an apprentice.

[Commissioners paid Stone $3,394.50: James Pleasants, $350.40; Fanny Brown, $306.60; Cornelius Diggs, $613.20; Polly Pleasants, $525.60; Susan Pleasants, $459.90; Anne Pleasants, $459.90; Ailcey Pleasants, $394.20; Tom Pleasants, $284.70.]

No. 315, Petition of Sarah Tolson — Filed May 19, 1862

Sarah Tolson of Maryland claims compensation for George Tinney who is 35, copper colored and 5 feet 10 inches tall. He is rather slender, but is sound and healthy. He is a valuable cook and house servant. She raised him, having owned his mother from a child. [Value $1,500]

[Commissioners paid Tolson $438.]

The 1860 Census for D.C., Vol. 1, pp. 330-331 lists the following free household: George Tinney, aged 36, occupation, cook; Virginia Tinney, aged 30, black; John Tinney, aged three months, black; and Samuel Runnels, aged seven, black. Although George Tinney in the census is not listed as black, he probably is the same George Tinney that Tolson claims as a slave. As has been noted earlier, sometimes slaves who are living and acting as free are listed in the federal census as free persons. Boyd's Directory for 1864, p. 264, contains the following listing: Tinney, George (col'd), cook, h 16 K north.

No. 316, Petition of Washington Miller — Filed May 19, 1862

Washington Miller of the District of Columbia claims compensation for Susan Tyler. Tyler is 18 years old, a bright mulatto, 5 feet 4 inches tall, stout and healthy. She is an honest, faithful servant, a competent cook and seamstress, a beautiful washer and ironer, and the most valuable nurse to be found. She is amiable and devoted to his children. [Value $1,500]

He came into possession of Tyler on Nov. 22, 1855, by marriage. She was given to his wife by her father, Mr. Tolson, deceased, of Prince George's County, Md., when eight years old and she raised her from a child.

[Commissioners paid Miller $547.50.]

No. 317, Petition of John Manning — Filed May 19, 1862

John Manning of Prince George's County, Md., claims compensation for 15 persons.
1. Ann Bell is aged 50 and bright mulatto. [Value $500]
2. Joseph Bell, aged 22, dark brown. He is a first-rate field hand. [Value $1,200]
3. Jane, aged 20, brown. [Value $1,000]
4. Mary, aged five, bright mulatto. [Value $250]
5. John, 18 months old, bright mulatto. [Value $75]
6. Sandy, 17 years old, brown color. [Value $1,200]
7. Hannah, aged 43, mulatto. [Value $600]
8. Louisa, aged 45, mulatto. [Value $600]
9. Nelly Ann, aged 18, bright mulatto. [Value $1,200]
10. Harriet Ann, aged 12, bright mulatto. [Value $600]
11. Elizabeth, aged seven, bright mulatto. [Value $400]
12. Charlotte, aged 21, dark brown. [Value $1,000]
13. Agnes, 13 months old, dark brown. [Value $75]
14. Leathy, or Kitty, aged 25, mulatto. [Value $1,000]
15. Milley, nine years old, mulatto. [Value $500]

Those older than 12 years are excellent house servants and are sound, healthy and free infirmities.

Manning acquired them under the will of his father, Ignatius Manning. A copy of the will is attached and shows that Ignatius willed to his only son, John, the following Negroes now in the District of Columbia in the care of Dr. W. A. Manning: Harriet, Eliza, Alethe, Charlotte, Oscar, Sandy, William, Jacob, Jenny, Jane, John, Joe, William Jr., Hanson and Alfred and their increase. (Will proved May 17, 1852, in Prince George's County, Md.)

[Commissioners paid Manning $4,401.90: Ann Bell, $21.90; Joseph Bell, $613.20; Jane, $459.90; Mary, $109.50; John, $65.70; Sandy, $569.40; Hannah, $175.20; Louisa, $219; Nelly Ann, $569.40; Harriet Ann, $306.60; Elizabeth, $175.20; Agnes, $43.80; Charlotte, $481.80; Leathe, or Kitty, $459.90; Milley, $131.40.]

No. 318, Petition of Mary M. McIntire — Filed May 19, 1862

Mary M. McIntire of Washington claims compensation for three persons.

1. Susan West is aged 40, black and 5 feet 3 inches tall. She has a mild and kindly disposition, quite fun in conversation and is very valuable as a house servant and cook.

2. Mary Rebecca West, daughter of Susan, is aged 15 years, 5 feet 1 ½ inches tall and dark colored. She is very sprightly and a valuable servant.

3. Clement Alexander West, son of Susan, is seven years old and 3 feet 9 inches tall. He is exceedingly sprightly and intelligent and has a lively disposition. He "has been raised to his present age more as a child than as a slave and the family is much attached to him."

Their estimated value is $2,500.

The claim of Mary McIntire is contested by Stephen McDonald, William A., John E. and Laura E. McIntire. They claim that the servants were owned by Mary M. Ellis, who married Alexander McIntire, deceased, the father of the wife of Stephen McDonald, and the father of John A. and Laura E. McIntire and the grandfather of William A. McIntire. Mary M. McIntire, as administrator of the estate of late husband, has ignored the rights of claims of the others and thus they dispute her petition. They place the value of the three servants at $1,333. (Dated July 12, 1862, Stephen McDonald of La Porte County, Ind., and John E. and Laura E. and William C. McIntire of Washington, D.C.)

[The matter was settled Feb. 9, 1864, and the Commissioners paid Mary M. McIntire, by her attorney Peter Lammond, $1,007.40: Susan West, $350.40; Mary Rebecca West, $481.80; Clement Alexander West, $175.20.]

The printed report of the Commissioners gives the surname of the claimants as "McIntyre", but it is spelled "McIntire" in all the original documents. Mary Eliza McIntire married Stephen McDonald on Nov. 19, 1833. See Pippenger, D.C. Marriage Licenses, 1811-1858, p. 403.

No. 319, Petition of Sarah A. Landreth

Sarah A. Landreth of the District of Columbia claims compensation for four persons.

1. Maria Maddox, is aged 46, chestnut complexion and has a loose and full suit of hair. She speaks in a slow, drawling manner. She is the mother of Charles, Thomas and Elizabeth. She is an elegant washer and ironer and a good cook. About three years ago she was afflicted with slight lameness from rheumatism, but she is now recovered. [Value $400]

2. Charles [Maddox] is about 13, slender, very dark and has short and knotty hair. He has a dull, heavy countenance and lisps slightly. He is a good servant and has hired for $14 a month. [Value $500]

3. Thomas [Maddox] is aged about 10, chestnut colored, slender and has a thick suit of knotty hair. He is prompt and intelligent in speech. He is a good servant and is good at any domestic work. About six years ago his collar bone was injured by a fall, but all traces of that injury have now disappeared. [Value $300]

4. Elizabeth [Maddox] is aged about six-and-one-half years, of a chestnut color with short knotty hair. She has a bright countenance and a very diffident manner. She is a hearty, healthy, well-grown child and a promising servant. [Value $200]

Maria Maddox was inherited by Landreth from the will of her mother, Sarah Lamdreth of Somerset County, Va., about 1844. Maria was brought into D.C. about 1845 by Sarah A. Lambeth and she has remained there ever since. Maria's children were born while she was held to service by Sarah A.

Landreth says that Maria, with her consent, has tried to purchase her freedom, but has only paid from $35 to $40.

[Commissioners paid Landreth, by her attorney, T[homas] Scrivener, Jr., $876: Maria Maddox, $175.20; Charles, $306.60; Thomas, $219; Elizabeth, $175.20.]

No. 320, Petition of Jane E. Cochrell   Filed May 20, 1862

Jane E. Cochrell of Washington City claims compensation for Bettie Fairfax. Fairfax is 22 years old, very dark with "true African features" and about 5 feet 1 inch tall. She is rather thickly set and her teeth are decayed. Bettie is hearty, robust, and strong and "apt to learn". Cochrell says she has been offered $1,500 for her. [Value $1,500]

She acquired title to Bettie's mother and to Bettie by inheritance from her mother, Jane Davies, who died in Dumfries, Va., about 16 years ago. Bettie's mother died in Washington about 10 years ago. Bettie was about five years old when she and her mother came into Cochrell's possession.

[Commissioners paid Cochrell $525.60.]

No. 321, Petition of William Noell   Filed May 20, 1862

William Noell of Washington claims compensation for two persons.

1. Lewis Taylor is aged 25, black and 5 feet 8 ½ inches tall. He has club feet. He is a good mechanic and works with Noell in making blinds and upholstering. [Value $900]

2. Ellen Ashton, aged 18, is black, 5 feet 1 ½ inches tall, with a large mouth. She is a good house servant and excellent cook. [Value $1,000]

Lewis Taylor and Ellen Ashton were given to Mrs. Noell by her father, Isaac Wilkerson of King George County, Va., about six years ago.

No. 322, Petition of Joseph Bryan, trustee for Louisa Bryan — Filed May 20, 1862

Joseph Bryan, trustee for Louisa Bryan, of Washington City claims compensation for three persons.

1. Delia, aged 25, is dark in color and 4 feet 11 inches tall. She is stout and well-built. She is a honest and reliable house servant. Delia is mother of Robert and John. Bryan states that he pays Delia $8 a month for her hire and provides board for her and her children. He says he was offered $1,200 for her before her last child was born.

2. Robert, aged four, is a mulatto.

3. John, aged 18 months, is a mulatto.

Bryan claims a value of $1,200 for all three.

Delia and Robert were acquired by Louisa Bryan by purchase for $900 from James S. Holland, executor of Ann Holland, deceased, of Annapolis, by a bill of sale dated May 19, 1859. John was born after that purchase.

[Commissioners paid Joseph Bryan, trustee, $657: Delia, $481.80; Robert, $131.40; John, $43.80.]

No. 323, Petition of Joseph Bryan — Filed May 20, 1862

Joseph Bryan of Washington City claims compensation for Hampton Pool, aged 28, who is held for a term of seven years. Pool is a very dark color, nearly black, 5 feet 9 inches tall and well-built. Bryan says that he has always called Pool "Hamilton". Hampton is intelligent and honest and a valuable coachman and house servant. He pays him $10 a month for his services. [Value $500]

Bryan purchased Hamilton, or Hampton, when he was 17 years old and he was to serve until he reached age 35. The bill of sale is dated Dec. 30, 1850, and the sale was by Anne Barrett of Montgomery County, Md., for $250, to Joseph "Brien".

[Commissioners paid Bryan $131.40.]

No. 324, Petition of Melvina H. Bowie — Filed May 20, 1862

Mrs. Allen P. (?) Bowie of Washington claims compensation for seven persons.

1. William Ross, 56 years old, light brown in color, six feet tall, very stout.
2. James Skinner, aged 32, dark brown, 5 feet 7 inches tall, able-bodied.
3. Lemuel Perry, aged 25, black, 5 feet 6 inches tall, robust and stout.
4. Celia Ross, aged 55, dark brown, 5 feet 4 inches tall, stout and healthy.
5. Rachel Perry, aged 25, light colored, five feet tall, small frame but intelligent.
6. Nancy Ross, aged 14, mulatto, 5 feet 1 inch tall, likely and able-bodied.
7. Susan Perry, aged eight, dark brown, sprightly and likely.

Bowie claims a total value of $6,000. She says all of these persons have resided with her for a long time and have faithfully acquitted themselves.

She acquired them by the distribution of the estate of her late husband, Allen P. (?) Bowie.

[Commissioners paid Bowie $2,387.10: William Ross, $219; James Skinner, $438; Lemuel Perry $657; Celia Ross, $131.40; Rachel Perry, $262.80; Nancy Ross, $481.80; Susan Perry, $197.10.]

In this handwritten document it is difficult to distinguish between the capital letter "P" and the capital letter "T". Hence Lemuel "Perry" may be Lemuel "Terry" and Allen "P". Bowie may be Allen "T." Bowie. The printed report of the Commissioners gives the last name of "Perry" for Lemuel, Rachel and Susan.

No. 325, Petition of Henry S. Halley — Filed May 20, 1862

H. S. Halley of Washington claims compensation for four persons.

1. Sarah is aged 32, dark and of a medium build. She is a valuable washer and ironer. [Value $900]

2. Joseph is aged ten, copper colored and well-grown for his age. He is active and sprightly and can drive a cart and run errands. [Value $800]

3. Charles is aged six and copper colored. He is a very promising boy and is active and quick. [Value $500]

4. Eddy, mahogany color, is aged three and is stout for his age and healthy. [Value $300]

Halley says that he purchased Sarah and Joseph in Virginia about nine years ago. Charles and Eddy were born after that purchase.

[Commissioners paid Halley $832.20: Sarah, $394.20; Joseph, $219; Charles $131.40; Eddy, $87.60.]

No. 326, Petition of Leonard Storm   Filed May 20, 1862

Leonard Storm of the District of Columbia claims compensation for Susan Butler. Butler is 19 years old, copper colored and about five feet tall. She is a good and honest house servant and was raised with Storm's own children. She is the grandchild of Margaret who was purchased about 40 years ago from John Wilson. Margaret's child, Ann Maria, was raised by Storm from infancy and is the mother of Susan. [Value $800]

[Commissioners paid Storm, by Theodore Sheckels, attorney, $525.60.]

No. 327, Petition of Walter H. Marlow   Filed May 20, 1862

Walter H. Marlow of Washington City claims compensation for Henny Calvert who is aged about 45, dark colored and very stout and perfectly healthy. She is an excellent house servant, a good laundress and can make herself generally useful. [Value $800]

Marlow purchased her from the estate of Nancy Turner of Charles County, Md., about 1858.

[Commissioners paid Marlow $175.20.]

The Commissioners printed report gives Calvert's first name as "Henry", but that is erroneous.

No. 328, Petition of Peregrine W. Browning   Filed May 20, 1862

Peregrine W. Browning of Washington City claims compensation for Jane Simms (or Johnson), aged 38, dark brown and 5 feet 6 inches tall. She is an excellent house servant and a good cook. [Value $800]

Browning was given Simms over 20 years ago by his Aunt Holmes, widow of William Holmes, formerly a resident of Montgomery County, Md. Simms was born in the family of his aunt.

[Commissioners paid Browning $328.50 for Jane "Sims", or Johnson.]

No. 329, Petition of Joseph Bryan of Alabama   Filed May 20, 1862

Joseph Bryan (of Ala.), of Washington City claims compensation for two persons.

1. Jerry Blount, aged 39, is mulatto, about 5 feet 8 inches tall and 125 pounds. He looks delicate but has generally good health. He is a good cook and valuable house servant. [Value $700]

2. John Thomas Thornton, aged 30, is black, about 5 feet 7 inches tall and stout and compact in form. He is an excellent farm laborer as well as a skillful florist and horticulturalist and has been employed for many years by Mr. Henry Douglas. His only fault is a "slight tendency to indulge in drink." [Value $1,500]

Blount was purchased in 1848 from Hon. A. P. Bogby, Congressman from Alabama, for $700. Thornton was purchased Mar. 22, 1849, from Henry Douglas of Washington for $475. An attached receipt shows that Douglas had purchased Thornton on Feb. 27, 1849, from B[enjamin] O. Shekell for $475.

[Commissioners paid Bryan $744.60: Jesse Blount, $219; John Thomas Thornton, $525.60.]

Boyd's Directory for 1860, p. 66, lists Henry Douglas as a florist opposite the Treasury Dept. B.O. Shekell had inherited "servant man Jim" [possibly JohnThornton (?)] from his friend James P. Gannon in 1849. See Pippenger,D.C. Probate Records, 1801-1852, p. 361, for James Gannon's will.

No. 330, Petition of Mary E. Banning   Filed May 20, 1862

Mary E. Banning of Baltimore, Md., claims compensation for Ellen Gladden, aged 16. Gladden is about 5 feet 1 inch tall, dark chestnut, slender built and of a neat appearance. She has a good head of hair, a flat nose, thick lips and is quick spoken.

Banning claims title to Gladden through her mother, Eliza E. Banning, deceased.

[Commissioners paid Banning, by William G. Ridgley, attorney, $$481.80.]

No. 331, Petition of Noble Hurdle   Filed May 20, 1862

Noble Hurdle of Georgetown claims compensation for Maria, aged 33, chestnut colored and 5 feet 2 inches tall. She is an honest and industrious house servant and a good cook, ironer and washer. [Value $500]

Maria was purchased from Cornelius Barbour of Georgetown some 18 years ago.

[Commissioners paid Hurdle $372.30.]

No. 332, Petition Gabriel Coakley, colored Filed May 20, 1862

Gabriel Coakley of Washington claims compensation for eight persons.

1. Ann M. Coakley, is aged 39, of a brown complexion and about 5 feet 2 inches tall. She is an excellent nurse and chambermaid and at this time is hired by Dr. J. C. Riley at $38 a month in his family. She is a moral and well-behaved servant and is stout and healthy.

2. Mary Coakley, is aged 34, bright mulatto, about 5 feet 4 inches tall. She does all of Gabriel's cooking, washing and ironing together with his housework. She is moral, industrious and temperate.

3. Mary Ann Coakley, is aged 11 and has a yellow complexion. She is a good child's nurse and is employed in his family.

4. Sophia Coakley, aged about nine-and-one-half years, has a yellow complexion.

5. Veronica Coakley, aged about seven, has a yellow complexion.

6. Genova Coakley, aged about five-and-one-half years, has a yellow complexion.

7. Sarah Coakley, about three years old, has a yellow complexion.

8. Gertrude, about one-and-a-half years old, has a yellow complexion.

None of the above have any marks, except Mary Ann who has a scar on her chin caused by a fall and a scar on her right wrist caused by a knife cut.

All of the rest of the above named servants are living in his family.

He purchased Mary from Walter W.W. Bowie of Maryland before she was married to Coakley. Her name at the time was Mary Calloway. All the children were born since her marriage to Coakley. Ann M. Coakley was bought from Mr. John Larcombe. The accompanying bill of sale shows that Coakley, for the sum of $1, purchased "a negro girl" called Ann Mahala Coakley, the daughter of Nancy Coakley and Gabriel Stevens from Larcombe on June 12, 1857.

A second bill of sale shows that Walter W. W. Bowie of Prince George's County, Md., for $150 cash and a note for $350, sold to Southey S. Parker, W. E. Spalding and Gabriel "Cokely", all of Washington, a servant girl named Mary, who used to belong to Mary Weems, late of Prince George's County (Signed Mar. 1, 1850) A bill of sale dated Dec. 20, 1861, documents that Parker and Spalding assigned their title and interest in Mary to Gabriel Coakley.

[Commissioners paid Coakley, by Nicholas Callan, Jr., attorney, $1,489.20: Ann M. Coakley, $350.40; Mary Coakley, $306.60; Mary Ann Coakley, $284.70; Sophia Coakley, $197.10; Veronica Coakley, $109.50; Genora Coakley, $109.50; Sarah Coakley, $87.60; Gertrude Coakley, $43.80.]

Boyd's City Directory for 1860 (p. 55) lists "Gabriel Coakley (col'd), oysters, 214 H, north".

No. 333, Petition of Notley Moreland Filed May 20, 1862

Notley Moreland of Washington County claims compensation for the following six persons.

1. Caroline Bowie is aged 24, copper colored and about 5 feet 7 inches tall. She is an excellent cook and an elegant house servant, washer and ironer. [Value $1,200]

2. Jack Broom is aged 18, yellow complexion and about four feet tall. He is a good waiter and house servant. [Value $800]

3. Annie Broom is aged six, yellow complexion and about three feet high. [Value $500]

4. Mary Bowie, aged three, is copper colored and about 2 feet 6 inches tall. [Value $300]

5. Nace Johnson, aged 16 years, is black and about 4 feet 6 inches tall. He has a slight scar on his cheek caused by a scald. He is an excellent field hand and a fine boy. [Value $900]

6. Infant aged about four months. [Value $50]

Moreland acquired Caroline by marriage to his present wife. Jack, Annie, Mary and the baby are her children born while she was in the service of Moreland. Nace was purchased about 13 years ago from the estate of Richard Bowie.

[Commissioners paid Moreland $1,270.20: Caroline Bowie, $525.60; Jack Broom, $219; Annie Broom, $153.30; Mary Bowie, $131.40; Nace Johnson, $219; infant, $21.90.]

No. 334, Petition of Thomas H. Barron Filed May 20, 1862

Thomas H. Barron of Washington City claims compensation for two persons.

1. Sarah Harrison, aged 68, is dark colored, about 5 feet 2 inches tall, stout and in good health. [Value $150]

2. Maria Cole, aged 15, copper colored, is about 5 feet 3 inches tall, stout with bushy hair. She is a good house servant . She was held to service from birth, but was temporarily absent in Prince George's County on Apr. 16th, 1862, and returned soon after on her own accord and she is now enjoying her freedom. [Value $800]

Barron got Sarah Harrison by inheritance from his mother and Maria Cole by virtue of marriage.
[Commissioners paid Barron $503.70: Sarah Harrison, no value; Maria Cole, $503.70.]

No. 335, Petition of Judson Scott
Filed May 20, 1862

Judson Scott of Prince George's County, Md., claims compensation for Martha Dyer, aged 17, five feet tall and not very black. She is the daughter of Sophia Dyer. Martha has lived out in this city for the last six or seven years. She is industrious and active, has a very kind disposition and is an excellent house servant. [Value $1,400]

Scott came into the possession of her mother, Sophia Dyer, through his wife, and Martha was born on his farm in Prince George's County.

[Commissioners paid Scott, by William J. Miller, his attorney, $459.90.]

No. 336, Petition of Mary D. Lear
Filed May 20, 1862

Mary D. Lear of Washington claims compensation for Nelly Sutton, aged 52, copper colored and 5 feet 4 inches tall. She is a valuable house servant and useful at any employment given her. Lear bought Nelly from John C. Cook of Washington City, the said Cook having purchased her from William Whaley of Washington. [Value $400]

[Commissioners paid Lear $21.90, Mary D. Lear, her x mark.]

No. 337, Petition of Elizabeth C. Seybolt
Filed May 21, 1862

Elizabeth C. Seybolt of Washington City claims compensation for Thomas Coleman, aged 40, black and about 5 feet 9 inches tall. He is valuable in any capacity as a house servant, coachman or other duties. [Value $1,500] Coleman was purchased from her brother, John L. Dufief, for $1,365, in a bill of sale dated Apr. 7, 1857.

[Commissioners paid Seybolt, by Samuel Fowler, her attorney, $438.]

No. 338, Petition of William Peters
Filed May 21, 1862

William Peters of Georgetown claims compensation for Louisa Carter, aged 16, of a "dark brown color but not black although a real African", about five feet tall and healthy. She is an excellent house servant. He purchased her for $350 from Leonard Boarman of Charles County, Md., on Jun. 20, 1854, when she was about eight years old.

[Commissioners paid Peters $394.20.]

No. 339, Petition of John G. Stone
Filed May 21, 1862

John G. Stone of Georgetown claims compensation for William, aged about 16, light color and small for his age. He is a good and trusty house servant. Stone purchased William's mother for $450 about 30 years ago from the late John Bowles of Washington County, Md. The receipt is dated Apr. 7, 1840. [Value $600]

[Commissioners paid Stone $372.30.]

No. 340, Petition of Anna E. Stone
Filed May 21, 1862

Anna E. Stone of Georgetown claims compensation for Clara Adely, aged about 17, light color, medium stature, healthy and reliable. She is a good cook and washer. She was acquired as a gift to Stone about ten years ago by Stone's grandmother, Elizabeth Deitrich, late of Washington County, Md. [Value $600]

[Commissioners paid Stone $481.80.]

No. 341, Petition of Alfred R. Edelin
Filed May 21, 1862

Alfred R. Edelin of Washington City claims compensation for four persons.

1. Mary Loggins, 35, is copper colored and about 5 feet 5 inches tall. She hires with child, Margaret, at $5 a month.

2. Jane Loggins, aged 25, black, is about 5 feet 4 inches tall. She hires at $5 a month.

3. Alice Mealy is about 62, dark copper colored and about 5 feet 6 inches tall. She hires for $5 a month.

4. Margaret Loggins, aged eight, is light copper colored and about 3 feet 4 inches tall.

They are all healthy, good-looking and moral. Their value is $2,400.

About Dec. 30, 1859, William J. Edelin of Prince George's County, Md., died and Alfred became the administrator of his estate. Alice Mealy has been hired in this city about eight years; Mary and Margaret Loggins have been hired in this city about two years, and Jane Loggins about one year.

[Commissioners paid Edelin $941.70: Mary Loggins, $284.70; Jane Loggins, $438; Alice Mealy, $21.90; Margaret Loggins, $191.10.]

No. 342, Petition of Jonathan Ridenour
Filed May 21, 1862

Jonathan Ridenour of Washington County, Md., claims compensation for two slaves.

1. Harry Gillis, aged 24 this coming June, is mulatto and 5 feet 8 inches tall. He is a good and faithful servant. He has been in Washington with Mrs. J. W. Ridenour since May 25, 1860. [Value $1,000]

2. Kate Harrison, sister of Harry, will be 14 this coming September, is black, 4 feet 3 or 4 inches tall with a wooly head. She has a small scar on her forehead caused by a burn. She is a healthy and faithful servant. She has been in the city in the possession of Jonathan's son, Hugh H. Ridenour, for nearly nine years. [Value $600]

Ridenour purchased their mother, Mary Gillis, in 1824 from Henry Brewer of Washington County, Md., and she is still hiring (?) in the possession of Jonathan.

[Commissioners paid Ridenour, by his attorney, J. W. Ridenour, $941.70: Harry Gillis, $591.30; Kate Harrison, $350.40.]

No. 343, Petition of Mary Fenwick
Filed May 21, 1862

Mary Fenwick of Georgetown claims compensation for three persons.

1. Ann Shorter, aged 25, is black, 5 feet 2 inches tall, strong, healthy and handsome. She is intelligent and experienced as a cook.

2. Robert Shorter, aged six, is black and 3 feet 2 inches tall. He is handsome, healthy and intelligent.

3. Lucy Shorter will be two on July 31, 1862. She is light black in color, healthy and well-formed.

Ann and Robert Shorter were purchased for a term of years: Ann, to serve for 15 years starting on Sept. 1, 1858, and Robert for 25 years dating from Sept. 1, 1858. They were bought from Mrs. Margaret C. Barber of the county of Washington, D.C., about Sept. 1, 1858. Lucy was born after the purchase. They are valued by Fenwick at $1,800.

The attached copy of the bill of sale, which was recorded in D.C. Liber J.A.S. No. 154, folios 394-395, Sept. 13, 1858, shows that Fenwick paid $500 for Ann Shorter, aged 23, and her two children, Robert, born Sept. 18, 1855, and Harriet born July 18, 1855. Ann was to be free in 15 years. Her children were to serve Fenwick until they reached age 25, after which they were to be returned to Barber to serve five more years. (Signed Aug. 30, 1858)

[Commissioners paid Fenwick $328.50: Ann Shorter, $197.10; Robert Shorter, $87.60; Lucy Shorter, $43.80.]

The documents do not mention what may have happened to Harriet Shorter. The information about the ages of the persons differs between the petition and the bill of sale.

No. 344, Petition of Julia Fenwick
Filed May 21, 1862

Julia Fenwick of Georgetown claims compensation for Mary Hamilton, aged about 20, black, about five feet tall, straight, slender and of handsome appearance. She has a delicate constitution, but is very intelligent, amiable, truthful, honest and trustworthy. She has full charge of Fenwick's keys and of any valuables that Fenwick might possess. Fenwick purchased Hamilton for $150 from Notley Young of Prince George's County, Md., when she was six years old. [Value $800]

[Commissioners paid Fenwick $481.80.]

No. 345, Petition of George Washington Young
Filed May 21, 1862

George Washington Young of Washington City claims compensation for 68 [*sic*] persons.

1. Walter Bell is about 50 years old, black and about 5 feet 10 inches tall. He is a good field hand. [Value $600]

2. Beckie Bell, about 45, is black and about 5 feet 3 inches tall. [No Value]

3. Louisa Bell, about 25 years old, black, about 5 feet 1 inch tall, healthy. She is a first-rate house servant. [Value $1,000]

4. Nannie Bell, aged about 21, black, about 5 feet 3 inches tall, healthy, stout and strong. She is a good cook and washer and ironer. [Value $1,000]

5. Aloysius Bell, about 17, black, about 5 feet 5 inches tall, strong and healthy. He is a field hand. [Value $1,200]

6. Joanna Bell, about 15, black, about 5 feet 2 inches tall, strong and healthy. She is a field hand. [Value $900]

7. Crissina Bell, about 13, black, about 4 feet 2 (?)inches tall, strong and healthy. [Value $800]

8. Elizabeth Bell, about 11, black, about 4 feet 6 inches tall, healthy. [Value $$600]

9. Margaret Bell, about nine, black, healthy. [Value $500]

10. Francis Bell, male, about four, black, healthy. [Value $400]

11. Margery Sims is about 45, black and about 5 feet 3 inches tall. She is strong and a field hand. [Value $600]

12. William Sims, about 21, black, about 5 feet 8 inches tall, is strong and healthy. He is a carriage driver and

carter (?). [Value $1,200]

13. Clement Sims, about 19, black, about 5 feet 10 inches tall, strong and healthy. He is a field hand. [Value $1,200]
14. Sally Sims, about 17, of a dark color, about 5 feet 5 inches tall, healthy. She is a valuable house servant and cook. [Value $1,000]
15. Henrietta Sims, about 15, black, about 5 feet 2 inches tall, strong and healthy. She is a field hand. [Value $900]
16. Mary Sims, about 15, black, about 5 feet 1 inch tall, strong and healthy. She is a field hand. [Value $900]
17. Marion Sims, about 13, black, about five feet tall, healthy. She is a field hand. [Value $800]
18. Anna Maria Sims, about 11, black. She has scrofula. [Value $500]
19. Martha Sims, about nine, black, is supposed to be consumptive. [Value $200]
20. Charity Sims, about seven, black, healthy. [Value $400]
21. Joseph Sims, about five, black, healthy. [Value $400]
22. Mary Bruce, about 28, mulatto, about 5 feet 6 inches tall, healthy. She is a field hand. [Value $1,000]
23. Dick Bruce, aged about 12, dark color. [Value $700]
24. Sam Bruce, aged about four, mulatto color. [Value $400]
25. Betsy Bruce, aged about two, mulatto, healthy. [Value $200]
26. Sally Bruce, about three months old. [Value $50]
27. Annie Bruce, about 35 years old, black, about 5 feet 3 inches tall, strong and healthy. She is a field hand. [Value $700]
28. Jane Bruce, aged about 14, black, about 4 feet 2 inches tall, healthy. She is a field hand. [$500]
29. Rosier Bruce, about 10, black, healthy. [Value $800]
30. Lewis Bruce, about six, black, healthy. [Value $500]
31. Joseph Bruce, about three, black, healthy. [Value $200]
32. Mary Stuart is aged about 40, dark mulatto and about 5 feet 3 inches tall. She is a valuable nurse and house servant. [Value $600]
33. Julia Stuart is about 16, mulatto and about 5 feet 2 inches tall. She is hard of hearing. She is a field hand. [Value $800]
34. Anna Stuart, about 14, bright mulatto, about 4 feet 10 inches tall, healthy. She is a valuable nurse and house servant. [Value $800]
35. Margaret Stuart, aged about 12, bright mulatto, about 4 feet 1 inch tall, healthy. She is a valuable house maid. [Value $700]
36. Hamlet Stuart, about 10 years old, bright mulatto, healthy and smart. He is a valuable house boy. [Value $700]
37. Barney Covington, aged about 55, of a dark color, about 5 feet 7 inches tall, strong and healthy. He is a field hand. [Value $600]
38. Ellen Covington, aged about 50, black, about five feet tall, strong and healthy. She is a field hand. [Value $300]
39. John Covington, aged about 15, black. He is deformed. [No value]
40. Elias Covington, aged about 13, black, about 5 feet 2 inches tall, strong and healthy. He is a field hand. [Value $800]
41. Ellen Covington, aged about nine, black, healthy. [Value $500]
42. George Gordon, about 60, black, about 5 feet 6 inches tall. He is in delicate health. He is a field hand. [Value $100]
43. Lucy Gordon, about 48, black, about 5 feet 3 inches tall, stout, strong and healthy. She is a field hand. [Value $500]
44. Clement Gordon, about 12, black, about four feet tall, healthy. He is a field hand. [Value $700]
45. Vincent Gordon, about 10, black, healthy. [Value $600]
46. Jane Gordon, about eight, black, healthy. [Value $500]
47. Jerry Gordon, about seventy, black, about six feet tall. [Value $30]
48. Phil Dines, aged about 38, black, about 5 feet 8 inches tall, strong and healthy. He is a field hand. [Value $900]
49. Frank Stoddard, about 48, black, about 5 feet 6 inches tall, strong and healthy. He is a field hand. [Value $600]

50. Protus Sims, about 55, mulatto, about 5 feet 8 inches tall. His health is not very good. He is a field hand. [Value $300]
51. Charlotte Sims, about 52, black, about 5 feet 3 inches tall, healthy. She is a cook. [Value $300]
52. Elias Sims, about 15, black, about 5 feet 4 inches tall, strong and healthy. He is a field hand. [Value $900]
53. Daniel Sims, about 13, black, about 5 feet 2 inches tall, strong and healthy. He is a field hand. [Value $800]
54. Peter Graham, about 75, of a dark color, about 5 feet 8 inches tall, healthy. He is a blacksmith and a field hand. [Value $50]
55. Charity Graham, about 42, of a dark color, about 5 feet 3 inches tall, stout, strong and healthy. She is a field hand. [Value $600]
56. Joanna Graham, about 15, black, about five feet tall, strong and healthy. She is a field hand. [Value $900]
57. Robert Graham, about 11, black, healthy. He is a field boy. [Value $700]
58. Charley Graham, about nine, black, healthy. [Value $500]
59. Eliza Graham, about seven, black, healthy. [Value $400]
60. Beckie Graham is about five, dark colored and healthy. [Value $300]
61. Lucy Graham, about three, of a dark color, healthy. [Value $200]
62. Agnes Fletcher, about 36, mulatto, about 5 feet 6 inches tall, healthy. She is a field hand. [Value $700]
63. Henry Fletcher, about 15, about 5 feet 10 inches tall, healthy. He is a field hand. [Value $1,000]
64. Notley Fletcher, about 12, black. He has temporary scrofula in the leg. [Value $500]
65. Beckie Fletcher, about three, black, healthy. [Value $500]
66. Eliza Fletcher, about eight, black, healthy. [Value $400]
67. William Fletcher, about six, black, healthy. [Value $400]
68. Baby Fletcher (Mary Catharine), about eight months old, black, healthy. [Value $50]
69. Ann Virginia Fletcher, eight, child of Agnes Fletcher. [Omitted from original filing]

About 20 years ago, Young purchased Walter Bell from Notley Maddox of Prince George's County, Md; and Margery Sims from Barbara S. Young of Washington County, D.C.

Beckie Bell,, Lucy Gordon, Frank Stoddard, Protus Sims, Mary Stuart, Peter Graham and Charity Graham were inherited from Young's father, Nicholas Young.

Barney Covington, Ellen Covington, George Gordon, Jerry Gordon and Charlotte Sims were acquired by him in right of his wife, Henrietta Young.

Louisa Bell, Nannie Bell, Aloysius Bell, Joanna Bell, Crissina Bell, Elizabeth Bell, and Francis Bell are the children of Beckie Bell. William Sims, Clement Sims, Sally Sims, Henrietta Sims, Mary Sims, Marion Sims, Anna Maria Sims, Martha Sims, Charity Sims and Joseph Sims are the children of Margery Sims. John Covington, Elias Covington and Ellen Covington, the younger, are the children of Ellen Covington, the elder. Clement Gordon, Vincent Gordon, Jane Gordon and Jerry Gordon are the children of Lucy Gordon. Elias Sims, Daniel Sims are the children of Charlotte Sims. Joanna Graham, Robert Graham, Charley Graham, Eliza Graham, Beckie Graham, and Lucy Graham are the children of Peter and Charity Graham. Mary Bruce is the daughter of Ellen Covington, the elder. Dick Bruce, Jane Bruce, Betsey Bruce and Sally Bruce are the children of Mary Bruce. Annie Bruce is the daughter of Harriet Boarman, a person of African descent who was inherited by him from his father, but she has died. Jane Bruce, Rozier Bruce, Lewis Bruce and Joseph Bruce are the children of Annie Bruce. Julia Stuart, Anna Stuart, Margaret Stuart and Hamlet Stuart and the children of Mary Stuart. Phil Dines was born in Young's family of a mother whose name is not recollected but who was held to service or labor by Young. He was acquired by Young through right of his wife. Agnes Fletcher was acquired by right of his wife and Notley Fletcher, Beckie Fletcher, Eliza Fletcher, William Fletcher, and the infant Fletcher are the children of Agnes.

About last Mar. 18, William Sims, Aloysius Bell and Clement Sims ran away from Young, but he believes that they were in D.C. at the time of the Apr. 16th act of Congress and are still there.

[The Commissioners paid Young $17,771.85: Walter Bell, $197.10; Beckie Bell, no value; Louisa Bell, $438; Nannie Bell, $547.50; Aloysius Bell, $438; Joanna Bell, $481.80; Crissina Bell, $459.90; Elizabeth Bell, $328.50; Margaret Bell, $131.40; Francis Bell, $131.40; Margery Sims, $219; William Sims, $569.40; Clement Sims, $613.20; Sally Sims, $547.50; Henrietta Sims, $481.80; Mary Sims, $394.20; Marion Sims, $350.40; Ann Maria Sims, $175.20; Martha Sims, no value; Charity Sims, $175.20; Joseph Sims, $87.60; Mary Bruce, $350.40; Dick Bruce, $306.60; Sam Bruce, $131.40; Betsy Bruce, $87.60; Sally Bruce, $21.90; Annie Bruce, $328.50; Jane Bruce, $394.20; Rozier Bruce, $219; Lewis Bruce, $153.30; Joseph Bruce, $87.60; Mary "Stewart", $219; Julia "Stewart", $284.70; Anna "Stewart", $350.40; Margaret "Stewart", $372.30; Hamlet "Stewart", $284.70; Barney Covington, $197.10; Ellen Covington, $175.20; John Covington, no value; Elias Covington, $350.40; Ellen Covington, jr., $219;

George Gordon, $131.40; Lucy Gordon, $197.10; Clement Gordon, $328.50; Vincent Gordon, $328.50; Jane Gordon, $219; "Jerre" Gordon, $65.70; Phil. Dines, $503.70; Frank "Stoddart", $219; Protus Sims, $153.30; Charlotte Sims, $87.60; Elias Sims, $438; Daniel Sims, $350.40; Peter Graham, $87.60; Charity Graham, $175.20; Joanna Graham, $481.80; Robert Graham, $328.50; Charley Graham, $284.70; Eliza Graham, $219; Beckie Graham, $175.20; Lucy Graham, $87.60; Agnes Fletcher, $219; Henry Fletcher, $481.80; Notley Fletcher, $284.70; Beckie Fletcher, $87.60; Margaret Fletcher, $240.90; William Fletcher, $153.30; Ann Fletcher, $120.45; Infant Fletcher, $21.90

A supplementary letter from George W. Young, dated Jun. 11, 1862, says that he omitted one of Agnes Fletcher's children, named Ann Virginia, aged eight. Also that one child of Agnes Fletcher was erroneously called Elisa when her true name was Margaret; and Beckie Fletcher's age is three, not ten as originally written. The infant child of Agnes is named Mary Catharine.

No. 346, Petition of Elizabeth Brent   Filed May 21, 1862

Elizabeth Brent of Washington claims compensation for six persons.

1. Henry Lancaster is aged about 52, black and about 5 feet 9 inches tall. The middle finger on his right hand is stiff from the effects of a bone felon. He is a good waiter, house servant and gardener. He is handy with everything he does, but at times is subject to rheumatism attacks. [Value $500]

2. Susan Lancaster, child of Henry, unmarried, is aged about 30, chestnut colored and about 5 feet 7 inches tall. She is strong, active, intelligent and is a first-rate cook, washer, ironer and servant. She has been hired out for about a year at the reduced rate of $7 a month "in consequence of my desire to keep her in a good and safe employment". [Value $1,200]

3. Eliza or Lizzie Brown, child of Henry, is aged about 27. She is slightly lame in one of her feet but that does not interfere with her usefulness. She is strong and active and an excellent cook, washer and ironer and servant. [Value $1,000]

4. Sarah Jane, or Phebe Brown, is aged about nine and is the eldest daughter of Lizzie Brown. She is healthy and smart and is useful about the house as a waiter and chambermaid [Value $400]

5. Eliza Brown, child of Lizzie Brown, is aged about five. [Value $200]

6. Catharine Brown is aged about three. [Value $100]

Henry Lancaster, Susan Lancaster and Lizzie Brown were owned by her deceased husband, Col. William Brent. Actually, Henry was owned by her prior to her marriage and all six were born as slaves for life in her family.

[Commissioners paid Brent, by R. S. Chilton, attorney, $1,335.90: Henry Lancaster, $219; Susan Lancaster, $372.30; Eliza, or Lizzie, Brown, $350.40; Sarah Jane, or Phebe, $197.10; Eliza Brown, $131.40; Catharine Brown, $65.70.]

No. 347, Petition of Enoch F. Zell   Filed May 21, 1862

Enoch Zell of Washington claims compensation for Jane Turner Campbell, aged 12, of a dark copper color. She limps because of a shortness in her left leg, but that does not interfere with her housekeeping duties. She is an active, smart, obedient and honest house servant. [Value $500]

Campbell was given to his wife by Helen Brawner of Charles County, Md., and was raised with her mother in Mrs. Brawner family.

[Commissioners paid Zell $153.30.

No. 348, Petition of Ann Briscoe   Filed May 21, 1862

Ann Briscoe claims compensation for five persons.

1. Nelly Ann Easton, aged 31, is 5 feet 3 (?) inches tall, copper colored with large features and a thin face. She is a superior cook and is hired out at $10 a month. [Value $800]

2. Floreed Easton, aged 14, is 5 feet 2 inches tall, light mulatto with small black eyes. She has good features and a pleasing bright countenance. She is the daughter of Nelly. She is a very intelligent girl and waits on the table and does the marketing for a large boarding house [Value $600]

3. Mary Easton, daughter of Matilda, aged nine, is 4 feet 4 inches tall and very dark. She has small features, a good countenance and is of ordinary size for her age. She is very useful about the house.[Value $400]

4. Fanny Easton, daughter of Matilda, aged eight, is about four feet high, copper colored, good countenance and of ordinary size for one her age. She is very useful about the house. [Value $300]

5. Matilda Easton, aged 32, is 5 feet 6 inches tall, dark colored with large features and ordinary size. She is the

mother of Mary and Fanny Easton. She is a superior cook and she could be hired out for $10 a month. [Value $800]

Briscoe states that she inherited Louisa [Easton (?)], the mother of Nelly Ann and Matilda, from the estate of her father, Edward Briscoe of Charles County, Md., in 1815. Louisa died last winter.

[Commissioners paid Briscoe $1,226.40: Nelly Ann Easton, $262.80; Floreed Easton, $394.20; Mary Easton, $219; Fanny Easton, $153.30; Matilda Easton, $197.10.

Boyd's City Directory for 1860, p. 180, shows that Ann Briscoe keeps a boarding house on Pennsylvania Ave. In the printed report of the Commissioners the surname is spelled "Brisco", but "Briscoe" is used in the original documents.

No. 349, Petition of William B. Magruder   Filed May 21, 1862

William B. Magruder of Brookville, Montgomery County, Md., claims compensation for Mary Ellen Campbell, aged 18 years. She is of a dark brown color, 5 feet 3 inches tall, well-built, with a full face, thick lips and a pleasant countenance. She is intelligent, honest, industrious and very valuable either as a house servant or cook. He purchased her mother from Nathan Cook of Montgomery County and Cook's claim came from his wife who is Magruder's sister. [Value $1,000]

[Commissioners paid Magruder, by E.J. Hall, his attorney, $525.60.]

No. 350, Petition of Peter Wood, Sr.   Filed May 21, 1862

Peter Wood, Sr., of Charles County, Md., claims compensation for Benjamin Dorsey, aged 52, about 5 feet 9 inches tall and of a very black color. He has a "long thin visage, high features" and is pleasant looking. He believes that Benjamin is a good faithful, Christian man and is valuable as a farm hand and rough carpenter and superintendent of others. He has not seen him for four months and he was then ailing, but not seriously sick. [Value $500]

He inherited Benjamin from his father, John T. Wood of Prince George's County, Md., about 1821.

[Commissioners paid Wood $219.]

No. 351, Petition of M. Alice Shulze   Filed May 21, 1862

M. Alice Shulze of Washington City claims compensation for Orpheus Countee, aged about 29 years. He is about 5 feet 6 inches tall, black in color with a flat nose and large mouth. He has good teeth, but has had his leg and shoulder hurt. His employers, Kelleher and Pywell, at whose livery stable he has been hired for several years, say that he is now in sound condition and is a good, faithful man at business. They are paying him the highest class wages for such a man. Countee has yielded an income of over $150 a year clear of all expenses for several years. [Value $1,200]

She inherited Orpheus from the estate of her father and Orpheus is held in trust for her use. The trust was created by a marriage contract entered into before her marriage to Francis S. Shulze and this in recorded in the land records of Prince George's County, in Liber E.W.B. No. 1, folios 77-78, on Feb. 22, 1855.

[Commissioners paid M. Alice Shulze $569.40.]

No. 352, Petition of Nimrod Farr   Filed May 21, 1862

Nimrod Farr of Washington County, D.C., claims compensation for four persons.

1. Joseph Hill, aged 26, is light brown in color, about 5 feet 8 inches tall, stout and healthy. He is a first-class gardener and field hand. [Value $1,500]

2. Eliza Jane Hill, aged 22, black, is about 5 feet 6 inches tall, medium build and healthy. She is a good gardener and field hand. [Value $1,400]

3. James David Hill, black child of Eliza, is aged two, healthy and well-grown. [Value $300]

4. Mary Elen [sic] Hill, daughter of Eliza, is aged nine months, black, healthy, well-grown and sprightly. [Value $150]

Farr acquired title to Joseph Hill under the will of his mother, Elizabeth D. Farr of Washington County, D.C. He purchased Eliza Jane Hill and her child, William Henry, for $700 from his brother, Malachi B. Farr on Jan. 9, 1859. James David and Mary Elen were born after the purchase.

[Commissioners paid Farr $1,095: Joseph Hill, $481.80; Eliza Jane Hill, $481.80; James David Hill, $43.80; Mary "Ellen" Hill, $87.60.]

There is no information given about the fate of William Henry Hill.

No. 353, Petition of Alexander F. Bulley   Filed May 21, 1862

Alexander F. Bulley of Washington City claims compensation for two persons.
 1. Sarah Fairfax is aged 18, black and 5 feet 3 inches tall. She hires out with the incumbrance of her child at $5 a month.
 2. Allice Fairfax, Sarah's child, is aged two, mulatto and 2 feet 6 inches tall.
 Bulley estimates their value at $800.
 He purchased them for $900 from Nathan B. Masters of Prince George's County, Md., on Nov. 1, 1860.
 [Commissioners paid Bulley $547.50: Sarah Fairfax, $481.80; "Alice" Fairfax, $65.70.]

No. 354, Petition of John T. Sullivan   Filed May 21, 1862

John T. Sullivan of the city of Washington claims compensation for Margaret Brooks, aged about 24, dark brown complexion, 5 feet 2 inches tall, slender, with an open, bright and intelligent countenance. When she came into Sullivan's possession she was an inexperienced and untutored child of 11 and in delicate health. By care and attention and training she became healthy and skilled at sewing, cooking, washing, ironing and general housewifery. She has been taught to read. [Value $500]
 He purchased Brooks from Nicholas L. Queen of D.C. for $200 on Oct. 8, 1849, and she was bound to serve until she reached age 35.
 [Commissioners paid Sullivan $175.20.]

No. 355, Petition of Elizabeth Windsor   Filed May 21, 1862

Elizabeth Windsor of Washington City claims compensation for three persons.
 1. Jane Carr, aged 17, is black, stout, well-made and healthy. [Value $1,200]
 2. John Dodson, is aged 25, black and healthy. [Value $1,300]
 3. Mary Carr, 12 years old, is black and healthy. [Value $700]
 They are all valuable servants and are free of defects.
 Windsor inherited them from her late father, Richard Windsor, of Fairfax County, Va., about 12 or 13 years ago.
 [Commissioners paid Windsor $1,270.20: Jane Carr, $438; John Dodson, $547.50; Mary Carr, $284.70.]

No. 356, Petition of Baley Brown   Filed May 22, 1862

Baley Brown of the city of Washington claims compensation for four persons.
 1. Margaret Hanson, aged about 40, black, is about 5 feet one-half inch tall and weighs about 150 pounds. She is robust and healthy. [Value $1,000]
 2. Jane Rebecca Hanson, aged about 14, is dark copper colored and about five feet tall. She is stout and hearty. [Value $900]
 3. Milla Hanson is aged 12, copper colored and about 4 feet 8 inches tall. She is robust and healthy. [Value $800]
 4. John Hanson is aged ten, dark copper colored and 4 feet 6 inches tall. He is hale and hearty. [Value $600]
 He purchased Margaret Hanson from J.B. Bell of Prince George's County, Md. Jane, Milla and John were born after that purchase.
 [Commissioners paid Brown $1,379.70: Margaret Hanson, $350.40; Jane Rebecca Hanson, $438; Milla Hanson, $306.60; John Hanson, $284.70.]

No. 357, Petition of Bushrod W. Farr   Filed May 22, 1862

Bushrod W. Farr of Washington City claims compensation for five persons.
 1. Rebecca Hill, aged 45, very black, is about five feet tall and very robust and healthy. [Value $700]
 2. Daniel Hill is aged 15, very black, about five feet high, robust and healthy. [Value $800]
 3. Charles Hill is aged 13, dark copper colored, about 4 feet 10 inches tall, robust and healthy. [Value $600]
 4. Alice Hill is aged 11, dark copper colored, about 4 feet 10 inches tall, robust and healthy. [Value $500]
 5. John Hill is aged six, dark copper colored, about four feet high, robust and healthy. [Value $300]
 Farr inherited these slaves under the terms of the will of his mother.
 [Commissioners paid Farr $1,401.60: Rebecca Hill, $197.10; Daniel Hill, $481.80; Charles Hill, $306.60; Alice Hill, $262.80; John Hill, $153.30.]

No. 358, Petition of John C. Riley   Filed May 22, 1862

John C. Riley of Washington claims compensation for two persons.

1. Lamartine Shorter is aged 13 and dark mulatto. She is quick and active. She is a good dining room servant.

2. Margaret C. Shorter is aged about eight and dark mulatto. She was brought up in the family and is very useful in a general way about the house.

Their value is $1,800.

He got title through his wife, who inherited them from the estate of her father, Maj. Park G. Howell, who died in July 1857.

[Commissioners paid Riley $613.20: "Lamertine" Shorter, $394.20; Margaret C. Shorter, $219.]

No. 359, Petition of Henry M. Morris   Filed May 22, 1862

Henry M. Morris of New York City claims compensation for Bosquet Henry Shorter, aged about 10, dark mulatto and healthy. He is a good dining room servant. [Value $900]

He states that he acquired title through his wife, who was the daughter of Maj. P[ark] G. Howle who died in July 1857.

[Commissioners paid Morris, by John C. Riley his attorney, $306.60.]

No. 360, Petition of Henry Cost   Filed May 22, 1862

Henry Cost of Frederick County, Md., claims compensation for Fanny, aged 15 ½ years, mulatto, about 4 feet 4 inches tall and healthy. She is a good washer and general house servant. She is bound to service until she reaches age 35 and then to be freed. This was recorded with the Frederick County Court in 1857. Fanny was born a slave in his family and her parents were slaves of Cost before she was born. [Value $800]

[Commissioners paid Cost $284.70.]

No. 361, Petition of Reuben B. Clarke

Reuben B. Clarke of the city of Washington claims compensation for two persons.

1. Rebecca Plowden, aged 37, is a dark copper color, 5 feet 5 inches tall, with curly hair and dark eyes. She is intelligent and sprightly. She is a first-class housekeeper and has frequently been left for several weeks in charge of his house and family while he was absent.

2. Arthur Plowden, aged 14 years, is 4 feet 10 inches tall, dark copper color and has curly hair. He is very bright for his age, quick in speech and movement and remarkably intelligent. He makes himself generally useful about Clarke's store.

The corporation of Washington has assessed them at $1,300, which Clarke says is much below their real value. [Value $1,300]

He acquired title on Jan. 25, 1849, by his marriage with Margaret Thomas, who had inherited Rebecca through her brother from the estate of Joseph Johnson. Arthur was born after Clarke possessed his mother.

[Commissioners Clarke $700.80: Rebecca Plowden, $372.30; Arthur Plowden, $328.50.]

Boyd's 1860 City Directory, p.. 54, lists Reuben Clark as a grocer and also (Clark & Dunn), as a brick manufacturer.

No. 362, Petition of William H. Magruder   Filed May 22, 1862

William H. Magruder of Montgomery County, Md., claims compensation for two persons.

1. Mary Douglas is aged 26, black and healthy. She is a good house and farm hand. [Value $700]

2. Clara Douglas is aged two, black and healthy. [Value $100]

Magruder purchased Mary about 25 years ago and Clara was born in his family.

[Commissioners paid Magruder, $547.50: Mary Douglas, $481.80; Clara Douglas, $65.70.]

No. 363, Petition of Emily W. Farquhar   Filed May 22, 1862

Emily W. Farguhar of Georgetown claims compensation for three persons.

1. Fanny Brooks is aged about 24, dark colored, about 5 feet 4 inches tall, strong and healthy. She is a very capable cook, washer and ironer and house servant and is honest and faithful.

2. Frank Brooks, child of Fanny, aged five, mulatto, is very intelligent and about average size.

3. Melinda Brooks, child of Fanny, is aged three, mulatto.

Their value is $1,200. Both children are free from physical defects, "the latter being of a color and appearance that would always command a high price."

Farquhar states that she has owned Fanny since she was about eight years old and inherited her under the terms of the will of Anthony Smith, late of Washington County, D.C.

A copy of Smith's will, signed Feb. 21, 1859, shows that Anthony Smith, of Georgetown, bequeathed "his servant, Fanny and her issue to Emily W. Farguhar now living with me."

[Commissioners paid Farquhar $657: Fanny Brooks, $438; Frank, $131.40; Melinda, $87.60.]

No. 364, Petition of Anna C. Waters   Filed May 22, 1862

Anna C. Waters of Washington City claims compensation for Mary Ann Harris, aged about 28 years. She is a rather dark mulatto, large in body but not very tall. She has hired Mary Ann out in Washington to Benjamin E. Gittings for the last six years at a rate of $6 a month. She is an excellent servant and is healthy and well disposed. [Value $1,000]

Waters acquired title by gift from her brother-in-law, Nathan Waters, of Prince George's County, Md. Mary Ann has been living with Anna Waters since she was about nine years old and the gift was confirmed about 12 years ago on the distribution of the late Nathan Waters' estate.

[Commissioners paid Waters $438.]

No. 365, Petition of Susan Tyler   Filed May 22, 1862

Susan Tyler of Georgetown claims compensation for three persons.

1. Sarah Boyd, aged 40, is brown and of medium height. She is a good cook, washer, ironer and dairy maid.
2. Mary Boyd, aged 18, is brown and of medium height. She is a house maid and washer and ironer.
3. Maria Boyd is aged 16, bright yellow in color and of low statue. She is a good house maid and nurse to children.

Tyler estimates their value at $2,900. She obtained title under the terms of the will of Dr. J.W.L.W. Bowie, which was recorded at Rockville, Md., in Montgomery County, about 1853.

[Commissioners paid Tyler $1,226.40: Sarah Boyd, $262.80; Mary Boyd, $481.80; Maria Boyd, $481.80.]

No. 366, Petition of Margaret C. Barber   Filed May 22, 1862

Margaret C. Barber of Washington County, D.C., claims compensation for 34 persons.

1. Peter Jenkins is aged 65, black and 5 feet 8 ½ inches tall. He is number one farm hand and hires for $70 a year. [Value $250]
2. Mary Jenkins, aged 58, is black, 5 feet 2 inches tall and a number one cook. Her wages are $72 a year. [Value $200]
3. Ellen Jenkins, aged 60, black, is 5 feet 7 inches tall. She is a good cook and her wages are $82 a year. [Value $250]
4. Susan Carroll, aged 36, dark mulatto, is about 4 feet 11 7/8 inches tall. She is to serve until she is 44 years old. She is a seamstress and house servant and serves at home. She is delicate and cannot bear outdoor work and exposure.
5. Dennis Carroll, aged seven, is light mulatto. [Value $300]
6. Ann Maria Carroll is aged three. [Value $150]
7. William Carroll is aged two. [Value $100]
8. William Cyrass is aged 14.
9. Richard Williams, aged 25, is dark mulatto, 5 feet 10 inches tall. He is shoemaker, carpenter and a first-rate farm hand. He is at home. [Value $1,500]
10. Chapman Toyer, aged 45, is black, six feet tall. He is a good farm hand and his wages are $100 a year. [Value $1,000]
11. Sarah Toyer is aged 51, black, 5 feet 1 inch tall. She is a good laundress and her wages are $72 a year. [Value $600]
12. Mary Young, 59, black, about five feet tall. She is a good cook and her wages are $60 a year. [Value $400]
13. Kitty Silass, aged 37, is light mulatto, 5 feet 2 inches tall. She is a number one cook and laundress. She is at home. She is rather deaf. [Value $1,200]
14. Gilbert Silass, aged eight, is light mulatto, 4 feet 2 ½ inches tall. He is at home. [Value $300]
15. William Silass, aged five, is light mulatto, 3 feet 10 inches tall. He is at home. [Value $300]
16. Philip Silass, aged eight months, is light mulatto. He is at home. [Value $25]
17. Samuel Yates, aged 24, dark mulatto, is 5 feet 2 ½ inches tall. He is a house servant. He is deformed, having a curved spine. [Value $100]

18. Judah Yates, aged 31, dark mulatto, is 5 feet 3 ½ inches tall. She is a house servant at wages of $72. [Value $600]

19. John Thomas is aged 41, black, 5 feet 8 3/4 inches tall. He is a coachman at wages of $120 a year. He has had three fingers on his left hand injured by a corn sheller and has lost two joints of his little finger, one joint of his first finger, and his second finger is stiff. But he can drive the carriage and work as well as before. [Value $1,200]

20. Henry Toyer is aged 25, dark mulatto, 5 feet 10 ½ inches tall. He is a farm hand at $120 wages. [Value $1,400]

21. Joseph Toyer is aged 24, black, 5 feet 8 ½ inches tall. He is a farm hand at $120 wages. [Value $1,400]

22. Louisa Toyer is aged 23, 5 feet 7 inches tall. She is a good cook at wages of $72 a year. She was sickly about nine months ago, but is healthy now. [Value $1,200]

23. Daniel Toyer is aged four months. [Value $25]

24. Eliza Toyer is aged 18, dark mulatto, 5 feet 1 inch tall. She is a good house servant. Wages (?) [Value $1,000]

25. Jane Yates is aged 36, 5 feet 1 1/4 inches tall. She is a number one cook. [Value $1,200]

26. Mary Brown is aged 20, light mulatto, 5 feet 7 inches tall. She is a house servant and is at home. She is delicate and cannot bear outdoor work and exposure. [Value $800]

27. Betty Brisco is aged 16, dark mulatto, 5 feet 2 inches tall. She is a house servant. [Value $1,000]

28. Milly Brisco is aged 11, dark mulatto, 4 feet 6 inches tall. She is a house servant. [Value $400]

29. Margaret Brisco is aged two, black. [Value $100]

30. John Chapman is aged 34, black, about 5 feet 9 ½ inches tall. He is first rate farm hand and his wages are $120 a year. [Value $1,200]

31. Mortimer Brisco is aged 39, black, 5 feet 10 inches tall. He is a good farm hand and his wages are $120. He had one of his toes frost bitten, but is otherwise sound. [Value $1,000]

32. Townley Yates is aged 24, dark mulatto, six feet tall. He is a good farm hand and his wages are $120. [Value $1,400]

33. Rezin Yates is aged 33, dark mulatto, 5 feet 9 inches tall. He is a good hostler and farm hand at $120 in wages. [Value $1,200]

34. Andrew Yates is aged 20, dark mulatto, 5 feet 8 3/4 inches tall. He is a good currier.

Almost all of these free of moral or bodily defects. About nine years ago, Richard Williams, John Thomas, and Rezin Yates have on two occasions been caught taking some meat from the meat house and some chickens. Barber's rights come by inheritance from her parents and from her husband. Peter Jenkins, Mary Jenkins, Ellen Jenkins, Susan Carroll, Dennis Carroll, Ann Maria Carroll, William Carroll, Richard Williams she inherited from her father, Maj. John Adlum and her mother, Margaret Adlum, under their wills dated Feb. 29, 1836 and Aug. 14, 1850. The others were inherited from her husband, Cornelius Barber, by his will dated Aug. 23, 1853.

[Commissioners paid Barber $9,351.30: Peter Jenkins, $65.70; Mary Jenkins, $87.60; Ellen Jenkins, $65.70; Susan Carroll, $87.60; Dennis Carroll, $219; Ann Maria Carroll, $65.70; William Carroll, $43.80; William Cyrass, $372.30; Richard Williams, $591.30; Chapman Toyer, $131.40; Sarah Toyer, $109.50; Mary Young, $131.40; Kitty "Silas", $350.40; Gilbert, "Silas", $175.20; William"Silas", $87.60; Philip "Silas", $43.80; Samuel Yates, no value; Judah Yates, $262.80; John Thomas, $350.40; Henry Toyer, $613.20; Joseph Toyer, $613.20; Louisa Toyer, $438; Daniel Toyer, $21.90; Eliza Toyer, $438; Jane Yates, $284.70; Mary Brown, $394.20; Betty "Brisco", $503.70; Milly "Brisco", $306.60; Margaret "Brisco", $43.80; John Chapman, $481.80; Mortimer "Brisco", $394.20; Townley Yates, $525.60; Andrew Yates, $569.40.]

No. 367, Petition of Mary Ann Clarke   **Filed May 22, 1862**

Mary Ann Clark of Washington County, D.C., claims compensation for 16 persons.

1. Edmund Stewart, aged 47, is black and six feet tall. He is a hostler and teamster and his wages are $120 a year. He hires himself out and pays his wages to Clarke. [Value $1,000]

2. Nace Foster is aged 34, black, 5 feet 8 inches tall. He is a carpenter and his wages are $120 a year. He hires himself out and pays his wages to Clarke. [Value $1,200]

3. Susan Hutchins is aged 36, brown, 5 feet 6 inches tall. She is a good cook and is at home. [Value $900]

4. Lucy Clarke is aged 32, black, 5 feet 6 inches tall. She is a seamstress and lady's maid at $72 a year. [Value $900]

5. Clara Ridgley is aged 27, yellow, five feet tall. She is a house servant at wages of $60. [Value $900]

6. Mary Hutchins is aged 19, black, 5 feet 3 inches tall. She is a house servant at home. [Value $800]

7. Rachel Hutchins is aged 16, black, five feet tall. She is a house servant at wages of $36. She had her arm hurt by a cellar door falling on it and this has incapacitated her for heavy work such as washing. She is, however, quite able to attend to house work and hires out for that purpose.[Value $600]

8. David Hutchins is aged 15, black, 5 feet 4 inches tall. He is a house servant at wages of $48. [Value $800]

9. Tobias Hutchins is aged 13, black, five feet tall. He is a house servant at wages of $12. [Value $500]

10. George Hutchins is aged 12, brown. He is at home. [Value $400]

11. Eliza Hutchins is aged nine, brown. She is at home. [Value $300]

12. Louisa Hutchins is aged five, brown. She is at home. [Value $200]

13. Jack Clarke is aged seven, black. He is at home. [Value $200]

14. James H. Ridgley is aged seven, mulatto. He is at home. [Value $200]

15. William Ridgley is aged three, brown. He is at home. [Value $50]

16. Rachel Jackson is aged 65, brown. She is a good cook. [Value $200]

Clarke states that the wages derived from her servants have for many years been her only means of support. She is now 70 years old and unless renumerated for them, she would be entirely destitute.

Her title to these persons comes through the will of her father, David Clark formerly of Prince George's County, Md., dated May 3, 1792. Those claimed on the list above are the descendants of the slaves she obtained from her father. She has never purchased any and they have been brought up by her under her own eye and care. The woman Rachel Jackson is the mother and grandmother of all the rest, except Edmund Stewart.

[The commissioners paid Clarke $4,401.90: Edmund Stewart, $219; Nace Foster, $372.30; Susan Hutchins, $306.60; Lucy Clarke, $438; Clara Ridgley, $394.20; Mary Hutchins, $481.80; Rachel Hutchins, $350.40; David Hutchins, $481.80; Tobias Hutchins, $394.20; George Hutchins, $240.90; Eliza Hutchins, $197.10; Louisa Hutchins, $153.30; Jack Clarke, $109.50; James H. Ridgley, $131.40; William Ridgley, $109.50; Rachel Jackson, $21.90.]

No. 368, Petition of Benjamin E. Gittings   Filed May 22, 1862

Benjamin E. Gittings of the city of Washington claims compensation for two persons.

1. Darkey Ann Snowden, aged 39, mulatto.
2. Emma Snowden, aged 12, a bright mulatto.

Gittings values them at $1,500. The are both healthy, smart and orderly servants. He says he was offered $800 for Ann, but he did not sell "because opposed to doing so."

Darkey Ann was given to him by his father, Thomas Gittings, when she was about six or seven years old. Gittings' father has been dead some 12 years and his estate has been long since settled. Emma is Darkey's child and was born after she belonged to Benjamin. She [Emma (?)] has lived in his family ever since until about six weeks ago. They are both in the city now, and were at the time of the Apr. 16th act.

[Commissioners paid Gittings $547.50: Darkey Ann Snowden, $219; Emma Snowden, $328.50.]

No. 369, Petition of Matthew H. Stevens   Filed May 22, 1862

Matthew H. Stevens of the city of Washington claims compensation for two persons.

1. Hannah, aged 35, is of a "Plum colour", in good health and of a fine appearance, except that her upper front teeth are defective. She has a few white and gray hairs in the front of her head. [Value $1,000]

2. Jane, aged 28, is a plum color and full size (?). [Value $2,000]

They are both valuable servants and free of defects.

Stevens says he purchased Hannah from a trader "from what is termed his prison or pen," about four years ago in Alexandria, Va. An attached bill of sale shows that he purchased Jane from Charles A.C. Higgins of Montgomery County, Md., agent for Mary E. Gott, for $1,100, on Apr. 21, 1860.

[Commissioners paid Stevens $832.20: Hannah, $306.60; Jane, $525.60.]

No. 370, Petition of Nicholas Acker   Filed May 22, 1862

Nicholas Acker of Washington City claims compensation for Ann Maria Adams who is about 17 years old. She is 5 feet 3 inches tall and of a dark chestnut color. Her nose is slightly depressed. She is an excellent house servant and has a good disposition. Acker states that he has refused an offer of $1,100 for her. [Value $1,000]

Acker purchased her on Oct. 15, 1858, in Montgomery County, Md., for $650 from John E. Thompson, administrator of the late William Burford. The attached bill of sale states the Ann Maria had been sold to pay the debts of Burford.

[Commissioners paid Acker $569.40.]

No. 371, Petition of Robert P. Dunlop Filed May 22, 1862

Robert P. Dunlop of Montgomery County, Md., claims compensation for three persons.

1. Martha Wilson, about 40 or 45 years old, black, is about 5 feet 6 inches tall. She is a good house servant and has been hired to Mrs. Whitlock and to Mr. Beall in Georgetown. She was born Dunlop's slave.

2. Frank Wilson, son of Martha, is between seven and eight years old, about 4 feet 5 inches tall and of a dark complexion. He is very smart and is healthy and of good conduct.

Dunlop states that he used to reside in Georgetown, but about 20 years ago moved to Montgomery County. He hired Martha to Mrs. Whitlock of Georgetown for many years and after that to George W. Beall of Georgetown. She has lived with Beall as a domestic for seven or eight years. About four days before passage of the D.C. emancipation act, unknown to Mr. Beall, she and Frank returned home to Montgomery County and alleged that she was unwell and that the work assigned to her was too much for her to perform. Dunlop believes that Martha and her son would sell for about $1,000.

3. Lucy Wilson is Martha's sister and was born Dunlop's slave. About five years ago she was placed in the family of his niece Mrs. Lowry, wife of George Lowry, of Washington, where she is a domestic in their family. She is about 21 years old, about 5 feet 6 or 7 inches tall and has a very dark complexion. Dunlop believes that before the rebellion, she was worth from $800 to $1,000.

[Commissioners paid Dunlop $876: Martha Wilson, $153.30; Frank Wilson, $197.10; Lucy Wilson, $525.60.]

No. 372, Petition of Catharine A.M. Maddox Filed May 22, 1862

Catharine A.M. Maddox, who resides at the corner of N, 3d street east, in the 5th Ward of Washington, claims compensation for two persons.

1. Mary E. McKinsey, aged 27, mulatto, 5 feet 1 inch tall is very good-looking. She has a fine suit of hair and good teeth and figure. She is a valuable servant. She was claimed by Maddox in January 1838 from the estate of her father, William R. Maddox, late of Washington County, D.C., when she was three years old.

2. Charlotte K.E. McKinsey, was born Apr. 4, 1856, and is the daughter of Mary E.

Maddox states that she has been offered $1,500 for the mother and daughter.

[Commissioners paid Maddox $613.20: Mary E. McKinsey, $459.90; C.K.E. McKinsey, $153.30.]

No. 373, Petition of Elizabeth Jane Maddox Filed May 22, 1862

Elizabeth Jane Maddox, who resides at the corner of N 3rd street east, 5th Ward of Washington, claims compensation for Moses Smallwood, aged 42, black or brown skin, 5 feet 6 inches tall, with good hair and a good figure. He was acquired in January 1838 when he was 18 years old from the estate of her father, William R. Maddox, late of Washington County. Maddox states that he is worth $100 a year clear of all expenses. [Value $500]

[Commissioners paid Maddox $175.20]

There is apparently something wrong with Smallwood's hand, but exactly what is not stated. Maddox says that "he can do as good work as any other man his hand not preventing him from working."

No. 374, Petition of Lavinia Hall Filed May 22, 1862

Lavinia Hall of New York City claims compensation for Mary Jane Brooks who was residing in the District of Columbia on Apr. 16 when the emancipation act was passed. Brooks is about 23 years old, of a dark color, about 5 feet 5 inches high, of unblemished form and in good health. She is residing with Lavinia's brother in Washington. She is an excellent house servant and cook and is intelligent, honest and trustworthy. [Value $1,400]

Hall purchased her from James Gannon in Washington about 14 years ago, "said Mary Jane having been so purchased with the mother of the said Mary Jane."

[Commissioners paid Lavinia Hall, by Mary A. Hall, her attorney, $481.80.]

No. 375, Petition of Susan Ireland Filed May 22, 1862

Susan Ireland, residing on F St. between 6th & 7th, claims compensation for two persons.

1. Henry Hammond is aged 58, dark copper color, about 5 feet 7 inches high, slim made with a thin visage and healthy. He has a good hand for horses and is a tolerably good house servant. [Value $350]

2. Elizabeth Brent is aged about 20, dark copper color, about 5 feet 2 or 3 inches tall, stout, strong, able-bodied and in good health. She is a good cook, washer and ironer and a faithful family servant. [Value $1,000]

Ireland purchased Henry from Henry Burch in Washington in December 1851 and paid $650 for him. She purchased Elizabeth from John S. Dufief and paid $650 for her in January 1856.

[Commissioners paid Ireland $591.30: Henry Hammond, $131.40; Elizabeth Brent, $459.90.]

No. 376, Petition of Euridice F. Simms
Filed May 22, 1862

Euridice F. Simms of Washington claims compensation for four persons.
1. Julia Dodson is aged 35 and has a dark complexion.
2. Eliza Carter is aged 25 and has a light complexion.
3. John Carter, aged eight, has a light complexion.
4. Henry Dodson, aged two, has a dark complexion.

Simms states that there are "no more valuable women, who lately were slaves, in the City than Julia and Eliza". She has been offered $1,500 for one and $1,100 for the other. She estimates the value of the four at $3,500.

She purchased Julia Dodson from Mrs. Scott of Washington in 1854 for $700. Henry Dodson is her son. Her husband, Elexius Simms, now deceased, purchased the mother of Eliza Carter in 1835, and Eliza was born about two years after that and has lived in the family ever since. John Carter is her son.

[Commissioners paid Simms $1,138.80: Julia Dodson, $438; Eliza Carter, $438; John Carter, $197.10; Henry Dodson, $65.70.]

No. 377, Petition of Charles Bradley
Filed May 22, 1862

Charles Bradley of the District of Columbia claims compensation for two female persons.
1. Mary Hall is 20 years old and of medium stature. She is fleshy and has a rather pleasant countenance. Mary is serving a term that lasts until Nov. 12, 1865. She is healthy and intelligent and well-instructed in the duties of house servant and chambermaid.
2. Lydia Jackson is aged 28. She is in good condition. She has a sac on her right cheek, a mole on her left cheek and a pleasant face. She is an experienced house servant, nurse, seamstress and washerwoman. She is more than ordinarily intelligent and has collected and conducted a Sunday School for children of her color for the last three or four years and has about 40 pupils.

Together they are valued at $1,225.

Bradley inherited Lydia Jackson from the estate of his late father, Abraham Bradley, of the District. He purchased Mary Hall from William T. Eva on Nov. 12, 1857. Eva had purchased Mary to serve until she reached age 25 from Henry G. Watters of Harford County, Md., for $100 on Feb. 15, 1850. Mary at that time was part of the personal estate of the late Rowland Rogers and Watters was acting as administrator of that estate.

[Commissioners paid Bradley $453.33: Mary Hall, $59.13; Lydia Jackson, $394.20.]

No. 378, Petition of Martha D. Duncanson
Filed May 22, 1862

Martha D. Duncanson of Washington City claims compensation for Mary Caroline Lee, aged eight. She has a dark brown complexion, large full eyes and is 3 feet 9 inches tall. She is a good house servant and is intelligent, active and very likely. [Value $400]

Duncanson received Mary Caroline as a gift from her late husband, John A.M. Duncanson, at the time of Mary Caroline's birth.

[Commissioners paid Duncanson $175.20.]

No. 379, Petition of Reuben Collins
Filed May 22, 1862

Reuben Collins of Washington claims compensation for Harriet King, aged 48 years. She is 5 feet 5 inches tall, of a yellow color, medium sized and her hair is nearly straight. She is a good and trusty house servant and is strong and healthy. [Value $200]

Collins purchased her for $175 from Michael Duffy on Aug. 7, 1860.

[Commissioners paid Collins $175.20.]

No. 380, Petition of Jane E. Boone
Filed May 22, 1862

Jane E. Boone of Washington claims compensation for Rosanna Baker, aged nine. She is of a bright mulatto color, about four feet high and is likely and well formed. She is a valuable servant who does table setting and waiting, making beds and some cooking. She is intelligent, healthy and of a very genteel appearance.

Boone acquired her under the terms of the will of her late husband, John B. Boone, who had owned her mother when Rosanna was born. [Value $700]

[Commissioners paid Boone $262.80.]

No. 381, Petition of Rosalie Edelin Filed May 22, 1862

Rosalie Edelin of Maryland claims compensation for three persons.

1. Lizzie Young, about 20, is copper colored, about 5 feet 4 inches tall and of a fine appearance. She is an excellent house servant, washer and ironer and cook and is very genteel and likely. [Value $1,200]

2. Francis Young, son of Lizzie, is aged four and copper colored. He is a well-grown boy and intelligent and good-looking. [Value $300]

3. Sam Young, about 13, is black and well-grown. He is stout, healthy, intelligent and suitable for a field hand. [Value $1,000]

Edelin got title to Lizzie Young and Sam Young under the will of her relative, the late Mary Ann McPherson of Prince George's County, Md., about seven years ago. Francis was born to Lizzie after that time.

[Commissioners paid Edelin $985.50: Lizzie Young, $481.80; Francis Young, $109.50; Sam Young, $394.20.]

No. 382, Petition of Margaret A. Renshaw Filed May 22, 1862

Margaret A. Renshaw of Washington claims compensation for Mary Pipes, aged 24 years. She has a very black complexion, projecting teeth and gums, is about 5 feet 5 inches tall and is healthy. She is an excellent house servant, cook, washer, ironer and marketer. She is amiable and obedient and is unmarried. [Value $900]

Renshaw purchased Pipes for $300 from her father, James Duhamel of Baltimore, on Feb. 1, 1862.

[Commissioners paid Renshaw $350.40.]

No. 383, Petition of Henrietta J. Kennedy Filed May 22, 1862

Henrietta J. Kennedy of Washington claims compensation for Hanson Newton, aged 24. He is a dark mulatto, of medium size, who is thick set and muscular. He is an excellent workman and coachman. She acquired Hanson under the will of her sister, Miss Ann Hill, who died Jan. 18, 1862. That will is recorded in Marlboro in Prince George's County, Md. [Value $1,500]

[Commissioners paid Kennedy $350.40.]

No. 384, Petition of Ann L. Hamilton Filed May 22, 1862

Ann L. Hamilton of Washington claims compensation for the following slaves.

1. Nace Butler, aged 42, is near six feet high and mulatto. He is thick set and muscular. He is a valuable carpenter and house servant. [Value $1,500]

2. Margaret Tills, aged 41, is of a very dark color, about 5 feet 6 inches tall with a spare frame. She is good natured. She is a good cook and ironer and washer. [Value $800]

3. Sarah Tills, aged 20, very dark, is about 5 feet 5 or 6 inches tall with a stout frame. She is very good natured. She is an excellent house servant, cook, washer and ironer. [Value $1,000]

4. Henny Lee, is aged 18, very dark in color and 5 feet 4 or 5 inches tall. She has a good constitution and good countenance.

Nace was purchased by her late husband from Mr. Maxwell of Charles County, Md. Margaret Tills and Sarah Tills were always owned by her husband. They were left to Ann by her husband's will which is recorded in Port Tobacco, Md.

[Commissioners paid Hamilton $1,708.20: Nace Butler, $481.80; Margaret Lee [sic], $219; Sarah Lee [sic] $525.60; Henny Lee, $481.80.]

No information was given about the acquisition of Henny Lee. The printed report of the commissioners gives the surname of Margaret and Sarah as "Lee" when it is clearly "Tills" in the original petition.

No. 385, Petition of W. J. C. Duhamel Filed May 22, 1862

W.J.C. Duhamel of Washington claims compensation for Mary Ross, aged 32 or 34 years. She is of a very dark color, is thick set with a muscular frame, and is about 5 feet 5 inches tall. She is in excellent health and is an excellent housekeeper, cook, washer, ironer and marketer. She is unmarried and virtuous and a "rigid Catholic." She was raised under the same roof as Duhamel. She was purchased by Duhamel for a nominal sum from his father, James Duhamel, "as his father made a present to each of his children of a servant." The attached bill of sale shows that James Duhamel of Baltimore, for $300, sold Mary to his son on Jan. 14, 1857. [Value $1,100]

[Commissioners paid W.J.C. Duhamel, M.D., $438.]

No. 386, Petition of Smith Minor Filed May 22, 1862

Smith Minor of Washington claims compensation for seven persons.

1. Moses Bennett is about 49, of a dark copper color, stout and well made and 5 feet 8 or 9 inches tall. He is a good farm hand, wagoner and marketer. [Value $700]

2. Julia Branson, aged 52, black, is about 5 feet 2 inches tall. She is a fine servant, cook, washer and ironer. [Value $400]

3. William Branson, aged 25, is about six feet tall, very erect and straight and of a black color. He is a good wagoner, farm hand and marketer. He makes $1.25 a day on the average. [Value $1,200]

4. Mary Ann Branson is aged 19, of a copper color, about 5 feet 7 inches tall and good-looking. She is a fair cook and good washer and ironer. [Value $1,000]

5. Horace Branson is aged 17, black and about 5 feet 10 inches tall. He is a pretty good wagoner and fair farm hand. He makes $1.25 a day on the average. [Value $1,200]

6. James Branson, aged 13, black, is about 4 feet 10 inches tall. He is a fine, sprightly boy who earned $5 or $6 some months. [Value $800]

7. Frank Branson, aged about 11, is of a dark color and about 4 feet 3 inches tall. He is a sprightly and healthy boy. [Value $600]

Moses was given to Minor's wife by her father, the late Senior (?) Somers of Alexandria County, Va., when Moses was four years old. He bought Julia Branson about 1814 and William, Mary Ann, Horace, James and Frank are her children.

The Commissioners noted that at the start of the rebellion, Minor resided in Alexandria County and came into D.C. with his slaves in September 1861 because of the fighting that raged in his neighborhood, the waste of his farm and injury to his house by rebel armies. The Commissioners disallowed his claim because he voted for the Virginia ordinance of secession in May 1861. Minor and various witnesses attempted to explain this vote on the grounds that Minor didn't really understand what he was voting for and that he had been threatened with bodily harm, forfeiture of his property and other acts. The Commissioners were not convinced and denied his claim. See the printed report of the commissioners pages 5-7 as well as the statements of witnesses he attached to his petition.

No. 387, Petition of Edward H. Edelin   Filed May 22, 1862

Edward H. Edelin of Washington claims compensation for 14 persons.

1. Frank Lyles, about 28 years old, is very dark in color and of a large size. He is healthy except for a slight hernia which does not impair his usefulness. Edelin hires him at $15 a month.

2. Joseph Pinkney, about 14, bright mulatto, and is well-grown for his age.

3. George, about 12, is copper colored, tall and sparse and is intelligent and healthy.

4. Henry Ross, about 11, is a bright mulatto. He is not very well-grown and is rather delicate, but of good character.

5. Ananias, about nine, is a bright mulatto, a little under size, but sound and of excellent character.

6. Delozier, is about three, a bright mulatto and sound in mind and body.

7. Agnes, is aged about 58, dark color, under medium height. She is a good plain cook.

8. Rachel is aged about 44 and copper colored. She is an excellent cook, washer and ironer and is hired to Mrs. Spaulding at $9 a month.

9. Sophy, about 34, dark color, is under medium height. She is a good cook, washer and ironer. Her general health is not good and she has "rather loose morals." She is hired to Mrs. (?) at $6 a month.

10. Emily is about 22 years old, light copper color, under the medium height. She is very good-looking, though not a robust person, and is hired to Mrs. Coombs at $7 a month.

11. Barney, is about 14, light copper color, stout and healthy.

12. Sidney is aged about 15, bright mulatto, about usual height and very good-looking. She is a good plain cook, washer and ironer.

13. Jane is aged about 32, bright mulatto, quite tall. She is an excellent cook, washer and ironer and is a good pastry cook. She is hired to Mrs. Walker at $10 per month.

14. Male infant is about two months old and healthy.

He values them at $9,550. He acquired title by his marriage with Sidney Weightman, who inherited them from her mother, Sarah Lyles of Prince George's County, Md.

[Commissioners paid Edelin $3,963.90: Frank Lyles, $525.60; Joseph Pinkney, $416.10; George, $284.70; Henry Ross, $219; Ananias, $175.20; Delozier, $87.60; Agnes, $43.80; Rachel, $219; Sophy, $328.50; Emily, $481.80; Barney, $372.30; Sidney, $459.90; Jane, $328.50; infant boy, $21.90.]

No. 388, Petition of James M. Torbert   Filed May 22, 1862

James M. Torbert claims compensation for five persons.

1. Louisa Commodore is about 62, black, about medium height. She is a first-rate cook, washer and ironer.

2. Louisiana Commodore, daughter of Louisa, born Oct. 14, 1834, is of dark color and about medium height. She is an excellent cook, washer, ironer and seamstress. [Value $300]

3. Harriet Commodore, daughter of Louisa, born Nov. 1, 1841, is black and of medium height. She is an excellent house servant and nurse for young children. [Value $1,000]

4. Holdsworth Commodore, son of Louisiana, born June 22, 1857, mulatto, stout and healthy. [Value $300]

5. Virginia Commodore, born May 8, 1860, daughter of Louisiana, is mulatto and healthy. [Value $150]

Torbert obtained title through his marriage on Aug. 2, 1836, with Mary Elizabeth Peyton, daughter of Mrs. Eliza Peyton.

[Commissioners paid Torbert $1,138.80: Louisa Commodore, $87.60; Louisiana Commodore, $350.40; Harriet Commodore, $481.80; Holdsworth Commodore, $131.40; Virginia Commodore, $87.60.]

No. 389, Petition of Eliza Peyton   Filed May 22, 1862

Eliza Peyton claims compensation for five persons.

1. Lucinda Broom is about 39, dark color, about medium height, robust. She is an excellent cook, washer, ironer and pastry cook and confectioner. She has been hired to Mr. Kuchoffer (?) *[probably Christopher Kloeppinger who is a confectioner] for several years at $12 a month.* [Value $1,600]

2. Laura Broom is aged about 23, bright mulatto, medium height. She is a good cook, washer and nurse as well as an accomplished house servant. [Value $1,300]

3. Anne Eliza Broom is aged 19, twin sister to Maria and not unlike her except she has a scar on her neck from a burn. She is a good cook, washer and ironer and is hired to Mr. Leonard Anderson. [Value $1,300]

4. Maria Broom is aged about 19, twin sister to Anne Eliza, mulatto and rather small sized. She is a first-rate house servant and is hired to Maj. Andrews where she has lived for several years. [Value $1,300]

5. Lucy Broom, about 17 years old, is a very handsome mulatto of medium height and robust. She is an excellent cook, washer, ironer and a good house servant generally. [Value $1,300]

Lucinda was purchased in 1832 when she was about nine years old from Miss Mary Blake of Calvert County, Md. She is the mother of Laura, Anne Eliza, Maria and Lucy.

[Commissioners paid Peyton $2,321.40: Lucinda Broom, $394.20; Laura Broom, $525.60; Ann Eliza Broom, $438; Maria Broom, $438; Lucy Broom, $525.60.]

No. 390, Petition of Absalom Brown   Filed May 22, 1862

Absalom Brown of Washington claims compensation for Ned Howard, aged about 27. He is of a dark color, about 5 feet 8 inches tall and healthy. He commands the highest wages. [Value $1,500]

Brown's claim is based on his being executor of the will of his late father, William Brown of Savage, Howard County, Md., which was proved on Feb. 19, 1856. William Brown left his four slaves, one of whom was Ned, to his three daughters. Absalom was guardian to daughter Mary and she apparently inherited Ned. A copy of the full will is attached to the petition.

[Commissioners granted Brown $657.]

No. 391, Petition of Ellen Pumphrey   Filed May 22, 1862

Ellen Pumphrey of Washington claims compensation for Henny Brown, aged about 21. She is a brown color, about 5 feet 5 inches tall, with a very pleasant expression and is healthy. [Value $1,500]

She purchased Henny for $1,400 at a public sale of the personal estate of the late Levi Pumphrey.

[Commissioners paid Pumphrey, by Joseph Beasley, attorney, $547.50.]

Levi Pumphrey died Sept. 25, 1858. See Pippenger, District of Columbia Interments p. 290. The printed report of the commissioners gives the name of Brown as "Henry", but that is not correct.

No. 392, Petition of Joseph Beasley   Filed May 22, 1862

Joseph Beasley of Washington claims compensation for seven persons.

1. John Butler is about 57 years old, of a very dark color and about 5 feet 9 inches tall. He is an excellent hostler. [Value $500]

2. Harriet Butler is about 57 years old, very dark color, about 5 feet 4 inches tall. [Value $500]

3. Betty Ann Butler is about 16, black color, about 5 feet 4 inches tall. [Value $1,200]

4. Ned Thomas is about 34, black, about 5 feet 8 inches tall. He has a bent leg, but that does not effect his usefulness. [Value$700]

5. Sarah A. Tyler is aged about 33, a chestnut color, about 4 feet 10 inches tall. She is a good seamstress, washer and ironer. [Value $1,200]

6. Mary E. Tyler is about ten years old, about 4 feet 1 inch tall, dark color. [$600]

7. Dennis Brown is about 36 years old, dark color, about 6 feet 2 inches tall. He is an excellent gardener and is very intelligent. [$1,500]

Beasley purchased John Butler, Harriet Butler, Betty Ann Butler and Ned Thomas from Stanislaus Murray of Washington. He purchased Sarah A. Tyler, Mary Tyler and Dennis Brown from the estate of Mrs. Ann Talbot of the District.

[Commissioners paid Beasley $2,343.30: John Butler, $306.60; Harriet Butler, $131.40; Betty Ann Butler, $481.80; Ned Thomas, $175.20; Sarah A. Tyler, $438; Mary Tyler, $262.80; Dennis Brown, $547.50.]

No. 393, Petition of Richard B. and E.E. Lloyd   Filed May 22, 1862

Richard B. and his wife, E.E. Lloyd of Washington, claim compensation for William, a bright mulatto boy aged ten or 11 years. William's mother, Cynthia, is free under the terms of her purchase and has William with her. William is believed to be a sound and remarkably likely servant boy. [Value $300]

The mother, Cynthia, and slave were sold too H. M. Lloyd, trustee for E.E. Lloyd. H.M. Lloyd was the mother of R.B. Lloyd, and has been long since dead. The slaves were really purchased by R.B. Lloyd and made a present to his wife, E.E. Lloyd. The attached bill of sale, dated Mar. 17, 1852, shows that George Watterston, executor of the late Barbara Lowe of Washington, in consideration of $150 paid by H.M. Lloyd, trustee for E.E. Lloyd, sells to him mulatto woman, Cynthia, to serve until Oct. 20, 1858, and, for $20, her child William, as a slave for life.

[Commissioners did not allow this claim as the person was not produced.]

Barbara Lowe's will may be found in Pippenger, D.C. Probate Records, 1801-1852, p. 353. The will, recorded Nov. 4, 1851, provided that Cynthia was to serve seven years and then be free. Her will stipulated that the female children of her servants were to be freed at age 21, but did not say anything about their male children.

No. 394, Petition of widow and heirs of Henry Miller   Filed May 22, 1862

Henry Miller's widow, and heirs: Catzarina Miller, Thomas W. Miller, Francis Miller, George Miller, Henry Miller, Eliza Miller and J.H. Hood, claim compensation for six persons.

1. Thomas Rustin, aged 36 is black. He is a good field hand and hostler. [Value $1,000]

2. Charles Barton, aged 23, is light brown. He is a good dining room and house servant. [Value $1,200]

3. Elizabeth Barton, aged 21, is dark brown. She is a good cook and house servant. She is the mother of Mary. [Value $1,000]

4. William Barton, aged 19, is bright mulatto. He is a dining room servant and waiter. [Value $l,200]

5. Lewis Barton, aged 17, is dark brown. He is a dining room and house servant. [Value $1,000]

6. Mary Barton, aged four, is bright mulatto. She is the daughter of Elizabeth. [Value $200]

These persons were inherited from the late Henry Miller who purchased Thomas Rustin and his sister, Letty, the mother of Charles, Elizabeth, William and Lewis. Rustin was purchased about 25 years ago. The woman Letty was purchased about the same time for his son George Miller out of funds belonging to George Miller. George then sold to his father the children of Letty in 1858. The attached bill of sale signed Mar. 20, 1858, shows that George Miller, having received from his father, Henry Miller, certain property in Washington, sells to him six Negroes: Peter, Charles, Elizabeth, William, Lewis and Martha. (Recorded in D.C. Liber J.A.S. No. 150, folio 313) Another copy of a bill of sale, recorded in D.C. Liber W.B. No. 3, shows that on Oct. 31, 1821, Jesse M. Semms, for $125, sold to Mary Lydock, guardian for Catzarina Miller and Ellen Nevitt, a Negro girl named Mary, aged about seven.

[Commissioners paid Catzarina Miller, Thomas W. Miller, George Miller, Henry Miller, Eliza Miller, J.H. Hood, Francis Miller, by their attorney, Francis Miller, $2,606.10: Thomas Rustin, $350.40; Charles Barton, $613.20; Elizabeth Barton, $438; William Barton, $547.50; Lewis Barton, $525.60; Mary Barton, $131.40.]

Henry Miller and "Catzaliner" Nevitt were married Jan. 9, 1821. See Pippenger, D.C Marriage Licenses, 1811-1858, p. 414.

No. 395, Petition of William H. Stewart   Filed May 22, 1862

William H. Stewart of Baltimore claims compensation for Sally Johnson, aged about 22. Johnson is short, a bright mulatto and has a freckled face. She has for many years been a domestic in the family of James E. Stewart, William's brother, and has been living on K St. in Washington. She is a valuable cook and house servant.[Value $1,000]

William became entitled to her as heir to his deceased son, Archibald Kerr Stewart, to whom her mother had been given several years before by his grandfather, the late Archibald Kerr of Baltimore.

[Commissioners paid Stewart $438.]

No. 396, Petition of Walter M. Talbott   Filed May 23, 1862

Walter M. Talbott, near Rockville in Montgomery County, Md., claims compensation for Sophia Bateson, aged about 50. She is very black, about 5 feet 5 inches tall, of medium size with sharp features. She is fair looking, of a good disposition and a good cook and nurse. She has been hired in the family of Charles Sioussa on 18th St., west, between H and I Sts. From her birth one leg has been a little shorter than the other, but it does not appear to incommode her movements, except she has a slight limp. She is a first-rate family servant and commands good wages. [Value $500]

Talbott acquired Sophia by inheritance from his father about 16 years ago.

[Commissioners paid Talbott $43.80.]

No. 397, Petition of Elizabeth Ann Drane, guardian of Richard L. Jones

Elizabeth Ann Drane of Washington, as guardian of Richard L. Jones, claims compensation for Joseph Clark, aged about 47. He is a dark brown color, 5 feet 9 inches tall and well-built. He is a blacksmith and she has received wages of $25 a month for his services. Drane got title under the terms of the will of her former husband, Richard Isaac Jones of Washington, who died in August. [Value $1,000]

[Commissioners paid Drane, by J.W. Drane, her attorney, $350.40.]

No. 398, Petition of James Eslin   Filed May 23, 1862

James Eslin of the County of Washington, D.C., claims compensation for Jack Smith, aged 24, black, 5 feet 7 inches tall. Smith is intelligent, honest and free of any defects and Eslin has recently been offered $1,500 for him. Eslin attached a copy of a bill of sale by which he purchased Smith. [Value $1,500]

[Commissioners paid Eslin $613.20.]

The copy of the bill of sale is damaged and is unreadable.

No. 399, Petition of Alexander H. Mechlin, contested by Columbus Alexander

Alexander H. Mechlin of Washington claims compensation for Margaret Ann Maddox, who is bound to service until Jan. 1, 1868. She is now about 25, but was 12 years old when purchased by Mechlin. "She is a negress of pure african blood," below medium height, strong, healthy and active. She is a good tempered and well-disciplined house servant. She was brought up carefully in Mechlin's family and could be hired out for $7 a month, and has been hired for $8 a month. [Value $450]

A copy of a bill of sale is attached by which Sarah Ann Sasser of Farquier County, Va., in consideration of $150, sells to Alexander H. Mechlin a slave named Margaret Ann Maddox, to serve until she reaches the age of 30, which will be Jan. 1, 1868. See D.C. Liber J.A.S. No. 21, folios 138-139. (Signed Dec. 18, 1850)

On Dec. 13, 1862, Columbus Alexander filed a petition stating that on Jan. 16, 1860, the D.C. Circuit Court rendered a judgement in his favor against A.H. Mechlin for $100, with interest dating from May 27, 1858.

[The claim was settled and the Commissioners paid A.H. Mechlin, by Columbus Alexander, attorney, $98.55.]

No. 400, Petition of Florence Mechlin   Filed May 23, 1862

Florence Mechlin of Washington City claims compensation for John Maddox, aged about six. He was born in Washington and is a dark mulatto of usual size for a boy that age. He has a slight cast or cross in one of his eyes, but this does not impair his vision. He was raised and educated as a house servant and she intended to ultimately send him to Liberia should he wish to go there. [Value $350]

Attached is a copy of a bill of sale dated Jul. 12, 1858, by which Florence Mechlin purchased from A[lexander] H. Mechlin for $100, Negro slave John Maddox, the child of Margaret Ann Maddox, who is residing in A.H.'s family. Margaret Ann had been purchased by A.H. Mechlin by a bill of sale dated Dec. 18, 1850, recorded in D.C. Liber J.A.S. No. 21, folios 138-139.

[Commissioners paid Mechlin $131.40.]

No. 401, Petition of Ann G. Barker
Ann G. Barker, temporarily resident in Washington, claims compensation for Maria, aged about 40, mulatto, of a medium size. She is a valuable servant and cook, housekeeper, nurse and laundress who has lived in Barker's family for many years. She could have sold her for much more than she is claiming. [Value $1,200]

Barker purchased Maria and this was recorded in the city registrar's office about May or June 1859.

[Commissioners paid Ann G. Barker, by Sara R. Barker, her attorney, $218.70.]

No. 402, Petition of Maria Speiser   Filed May 23, 1862
Maria Speiser of Washington claims compensation for Eliza Jane Borman, aged 17. She is black, 5 feet 2 3/4 inches tall, very stout, with good teeth and is healthy. Speiser states that Borman has been in her family since infancy and it will cost about $75 or $80 a year to part with her "to say nothing of the anxiety and trouble I have experienced in protecting and raising her." [Value $1,000]

She inherited Borman from her late husband, Frederick Speiser, in August 1854

[Commissioners paid Speiser $525.60 for "Elizabeth J. Boarman".

No. 403, Petition of Judson Naylor   Filed May 23, 1862
Judson Naylor of Prince George's County, Md., claims compensation for six persons.
1. Henry Munroe is 36 years old, dark mulatto, five feet tall, stout, active in all his movements. [Value $1,400]
2. George Ward is aged 26, dark chestnut color, 5 feet 5 inches tall. [Value $1,400]
3. Ellen Ward is aged 26, black. She is a good house servant. [Value $800]
4. Sophia Ward is aged 27, black, about five feet tall, very stout. [Value $800]
5. Tom Ward is aged six, dark. He is a well-grown boy. [Value $300]
6. Alfred Ward is aged three, dark colored and well-grown for his age. [Value $150]

Naylor acquired title by his marriage with Sarah Willcoxen of Prince George's County and the slaves were raised by him. He states that he has hired out Henry Munroe and George Ward to Mr. Gardner in D.C. for several years past at $120 per year. Ellen and her child and Sophia and her child are hired out at $5 a month. These persons are good and competent farm hands and house servants and are honest, reliable and very healthy.

[Commissioners paid John T. Naylor, executor; Van Deusen Naylor, Lettice M. Brown, Henry Naylor, heirs and legatees of Judson Naylor, $2,058.60: Henry Munroe, $372.30; George Ward, $525.60; Ellen Ward, $459.90; Sophia Ward, $438; Tom Ward, $153.30; Alfred Ward, $109.50.]

No. 404, Petition of Verlinda Naylor   Filed May 23, 1862
Verlinda Naylor of the county of Washington claims compensation for John Beddo, aged 25 or 26 years. He is yellow in color, 5 feet 2 or 3 inches high, well-made, active and honest. He is a capable house servant and carriage driver. She has hired out Beddo for the last seven or eight years at the Washington Navy Yard at $10 a month. [Value $1,000]

She acquired Beddo's mother on Oct. 1, 1813, as a gift from her father, John L[awson] Naylor and this is recorded in D.C. Liber A.F. (?) No. 31, folios 297-298.

[Commissioners paid Naylor $569.40.]

No. 405, Petition of Anna Maria Stone   Filed May 23, 1862
Anna Maria Stone of Georgetown claims compensation for William [Waring (?)], aged about 18, dark colored, short for his age, healthy with a pleasant countenance. He is a good, efficient, able-bodied field hand. [Value $800]

She purchased his mother, Ruth [Waring], from Lawson Offutt, late of Montgomery County, Md., and William was born after that time. She says that Ruth was set free seven years ago with three of her youngest children, one of whom and herself have since died. The two free children are now living with Anna. The boy William she lent to her son in Maryland for use on his farm, but William is now in Georgetown.

[Commissioners paid Stone $569.40.]

Anna Maria recorded her manumission to Ruth and children in November 1855. The statement says that in consideration of $5, Ann Maria Stone frees her Negro woman Rutha Waring, who is about 35 years old, and her three children: Charles Stone, aged about eight; Mary Jane, about four, and Grafton Hanson, who is about five months old. See Provine, D.C. Free Negro Registers, Registration No. 2386.

No. 406, Petition of George M. Sothoron
Filed May 23, 1862

George M. Sothoron of Georgetown claims compensation for Basil Gross, aged about 39. He is a dark brown color, about 5 feet 5 inches tall and has a scar on his left wrist. Basil Gross had been owned by George's father, the late Dr. W. Sotheron and was inherited by him and his brother, John W. Sothoron. John W. subsequently conveyed his right to George. [Value $1,200]

[Commissioners paid Sothoron $350.40.]

No. 407, Petition of Catharine Pindell
Filed May 23, 1862

Catharine Pindle of Howard County, Md., claims compensation for two persons.

1. Priscilla Wallace is 34 years old, dark complexion, about 5 feet 4 inches tall and active and healthy. She is an excellent cook, washer and ironer and a good field hand. When hired out she commanded $8 a month. Pindell says she has been offered $1,000 for her. [Value $1,000]

2. Mary Wallace, daughter of Priscilla is aged four, black complexion, sprightly and healthy. [Value $250]

Pindell received Priscilla as a gift from her deceased husband, Renaldo Pindell of West River, Anne Arundel County, Md., and subsequently by his will filed in Annapolis, Md.

[Commissioners paid Pindell $416.10.]

No. 408, Petition of William Hickey
Filed May 23, 1862

William Hickey of the District of Columbia claims compensation for 16 persons.

1. John Massy is aged 37, black, 5 feet 8 inches tall, healthy, stout and strong. He is an excellent farm and garden hand, hostler and driver and is the head man working on the farm. [Value $1,500]

2. Rachael Fletcher is aged 45, black, 5 feet 4 7/10 inches tall. She is stout and strong and a good cook, washer, ironer and excellent dairy maid. [Value $700]

3. Henry Gantt is aged 23, black. 5 feet 11 1/8 inches tall. He is marked from smallpox. He is a strong farm and garden hand and can plough, axe, pick, spade and shovel, scythe and grain cradle. [Value $1,500]

4. Augustus Fletcher is aged 18, black, 5 feet 9 ½ inches tall. He is a good farm and garden hand and understands the care of horses and cattle and is a driver. [Value $1,500]

5. Andrew Fletcher is aged eight, black, 4 feet 3 inches tall. He is a healthy, robust boy. [Value $500]

6. John Fletcher is aged six, black, four feet tall. He is healthy and robust. [Value $300]

7. Charlotte Fletcher is aged nine months, black, healthy. [Value $50]

8. Sarah Dover is aged 39, "second shade of black color", 5 feet 2 8/10 inches tall. She is a healthy, stout, strong house servant and dairy maid and is well-qualified as a cook, washer, ironer, dining room servant, chambermaid, seamstress and parlor servant. She has gathered the produce of the dairy and market garden and sold it in the market and made correct and satisfactory returns. [Value $1,200]

9. Dick Massy, or Lee, is aged 21, "third shade in black color", 5 feet 9 inches tall. He is stout and strong and a good farm and garden hand and an excellent coachman and driver and is a complete manager of horses and cattle. He stutters in speaking. [Value $1,500]

10. Bettie Dover is aged 11, "second shade of black color", 4 feet 6 ½ inches high, robust and active. She is useful about the house and can sew and wait upon the table. [Value $500]

11. Mary Butler is aged 49, "second shade of black color", 5 feet 1/4 inch tall. She is a very fine house servant or maid in every respect and is an excellent cook, washer and ironer. [Value $800]

12. James Butler is aged 24, black, 5 feet 5 inches tall. He is healthy and strong and an excellent farm and garden hand, a good driver and understands the care and management of horses and cattle. [Value $1,500]

13. Bob Butler is aged 15, "second shade of black color", 5 feet 1 inch tall. He is smart and useful about the house, farm and garden. He understands the care of horses and cattle and drives carts, wagons and other vehicles. [Value $700]

14. Nelly Butler is aged 22, black, 5 feet one-half inch tall. She is a faithful housemaid and nurse for the children and is kind and amiable in disposition. She can wash and iron. [Value $800]

15. Mary Butler, Jr., is aged 20, black, 5 feet 1 3/8 inches tall. She is healthy and robust and a servant of particular merit and usefulness and is a kind nurse to children. [Value $1,200]

16. Maria Butler is aged 17, black, 5 feet 1/4 inch tall. She is an excellent seamstress, chambermaid, dining room servant and is healthy and intelligent. [Value $800]

Hickey says that the values he has given is $5,000 less than an offer from a gentleman from Texas that he declined "because it would separate married people, and remove the others forever from their relations and friends".

John Massy, Rachael Fletcher and Sarah Dover he acquired by his marriage and his wife got them as part of her father's estate. The off-spring of Rachel and Sarah were born after they came into his ownership. Rachael's children are Henry Gantt, Augustus, Andrew, John and Charlotte Fletcher. Sarah's children are Dick Massy, alias Lee, and Bettie Dover. Mary Butler was purchased by Hickey "to prevent her from being sold away from her husband, Jim Butler, who then belonged to Hickey, but who died some years ago. Her children are Jim, Bob, Nelly, Mary, Jr., and Maria Butler.

He states with regard to his loyalty, that he is in command of a brigade of the D.C. militia and that he took an oath to support the constitution and to perform the duties of a Brigadier General. In addition, on Aug. 26, 1861, he took the oath of allegiance as the Chief Clerk of the U.S. Senate.

[Commissioners paid Hickey $6,745.20: John Massi [sic], $525.60; Rachel Fletcher, $262.80; Henry Gantt, $657; Augustus Fletcher, $635.10; Andrew Fletcher, $219; John Fletcher, $175.20; Charlotte Fletcher, $43.80; Sarah Dover, $394.20; Dick Massi [sic], or Lee, $613.20; Betty Dover, $328.50; Mary Butler, $175.20; James Butler, $569.40; Bobb [sic] Butler, $525.60; Nelly Butler, $525.60; Mary Butler, Jr., $525.60; Maria Butler, $569.40.]

No. 409, Petition of Mary Darne
The whereabouts of the original petition is not known.
[Commissioners paid Darne $547.50: Cynthia Carter, $109.50; Ann Turner, $240.90; Charles H. Turner, $98.55; James Lewis Turner, $98.55.]

No. 410, Petition of Thomas Berry
The whereabouts of the original petition is not known.
[Commissioners paid Berry $525.60 for Francis Dorsey.]

No. 411, Petition of Aurelia H. Irwin   Filed May 23, 1862
Aurelia H. Irwin of Washington City claims compensation for Laura Jackson, aged 22 years. She is copper colored, 5 feet 5 inches tall and well-built with a fine figure. She is healthy and intelligent and very valuable as a cook, seamstress or lady's maid. [Value $1,000]

Irwin purchased her in 1847 from a man named Hunter in Virginia when she was about seven and she was brought into the District when Irwin moved there about nine years ago.

[Commissioners paid Irwin $525.60.]

No. 412, Petition of Susan T. Cruit, executrix of Robert Cruit   Filed May 23, 1862
Susan Cruit, executrix, of Washington claims compensation for four persons.

1. James is aged 55, black and about six feet high. He is a good farm hand and very faithful. He was purchased from the late Mr. Alexander of Georgetown in 1850 by Susan Cruit's late father, Robert Cruit. [Value $100]

2. Isaiah, or Isaac, Jones, about 32 is bright mulatto and about 5 feet 5 inches tall. He has had his fingers cut by a machine and has no front upper teeth because of being kicked by a horse. He is a stout and hearty farm hand and teamster. He was purchased from the late J. Henry Cramphin of Chester County, Pennsylvania, for $200 on Mar. 27, 1838, by her late father, Robert Cruit. [Value $1,200]

3. Humphrey Alfred Docket is 20 1/2 years old, black and about 5 feet 6 inches tall. He a good farm hand and very useful because of his "mechanical genius". He was born of a woman named Betsey Docket who was purchased by her late father from a "negro pen". Her master was Mr. Calvert of Maryland. [Value $900]

4. Priscilla Willis, nine years three months old, is black and about 3 feet 2 inches tall. She is a useful house servant. She was bought by Susan Cruit from Dr. [S.A.] Starrow of Washington in 1859. [Value $500]

[Commissioners paid Cruit $1,576.80: James, $284.70; Isaiah, $481.80; Humphrey Alfred, $569.40; Priscilla, $240.90.]

No. 413, Petition of Jane Turnbull   Filed May 23, 1862
Jane Turnbull of Washington City claims compensation for four persons.

1. Robert Young is aged 26, dark and about 5 feet 6 inches tall. He is a good house servant. [Value $1,000]

2. Henry Young is aged 15, dark colored and about five feet high. He is a good house servant and is hired out. [Value $1,000]

3. Kate Young is 13, dark and about 4 feet 6 inches tall. She is a house servant who is hired out. [Value $800]

4. Daniel Young is 12, dark colored and about four feet high. He is living in Turnbull's family. [Value $600]

Turnbull acquired them under the terms of her mother's will dated Apr. 1, 1813.

[Commissioners paid Turnbull $1,445.40: Robert Young, $569.40; Henry Young, $328.50; Kate Young, $306.60; Daniel Young, $240.90.]

No. 414, Petition of Joshua Riley
Filed May 23, 1862

Joshua Riley of Georgetown claims compensation for Mary Ann Marshall, aged 35. She is black, 5 feet 6 inches tall, well-proportioned and has good teeth. Her lower lip is "rather prominent and somewhat pendulous" and her cheek bones are prominent. Riley purchased her for $500 from Dr. H[ezekiah] Magruder in March 1851. Riley says that her master had been offered $800 for her by a trader, but rather than separate a family he was willing to sell her for less. [Value $500]

[Commissioners paid Riley $394.20.]

No. 415, Petition of Harriet Stanley and children
Filed May 23, 1862

Mrs. Harriet Stanley, of Washington City, for herself and her children, Charles A. Stanley, Henry C. Stanley, and Amelia Stanley, claims compensation for Jennie Chase, aged 14 years. Chase is a dark copper color, 4 feet 10 inches tall, of ordinary size, with a large mouth and eyes. She is good-looking, healthy and a valuable house servant with a kind and pleasant disposition. [Value $800]

She was purchased by Thomas Stanley for $500 from the estate of Samuel Hamilton of Prince George's County, Md., on Jun. 18, 1859. Jennie was conveyed by deed from Thomas Stanley to Harriet Stanley and her three children in a document filed Oct. 14, 1861.

[Commissioners paid Harriet Stanley, her x mark, $372.30.]

No. 416, Petition of Ulysses B. Ward
Filed May 23, 1862

Ulysses B. Ward of Washington claims compensation for Alice Jones and her three children.
1. Alice Jones is aged 38, dark in color and of medium height. She is an excellent house servant. [Value $1,200]
2. Jennie Jones is aged seven and is a sprightly girl. [Value $500]
3. John Jones is aged five and is an intelligent boy. [Value $500]
4. Mary Verlinda Jones is aged three and is a smart, healthy child. [Value $350]

Ward purchased them from his father, Ulysses Ward, Sr., who received them from his wife.

[Commissioners paid Ward $525.60: Alice Jones, $262.80; Jennie, $131.40; John, $87.60; Mary Verlinda, $43.80.]

No. 417, Petition of Thomas Jenkins, of Thomas
Filed May 26, 1862

Thomas Jenkins, of Thomas, of Washington claims compensation for three servants.
1. Jim Queen is aged 40, dark chestnut color, 5 feet 11 inches tall and is stout and well-made. He is a first-rate field hand. [Value $1,500]
2. Sam Bruce is aged 25, light chestnut color, about 5 feet 10 inches tall and is stout and well-made. He is a first-rate field hand. [Value $1,000]
3. Nora Bruce is aged 17, black and about five feet high. She is an excellent house servant. [Value $800]

He inherited Jim Queen from the estate of his father, Thomas Jenkins. Sam and Norah were born his property.

[Commissioners paid Thomas Jenkins, his x mark, $1,489.20: Jim Queen, $438; Sam Bruce, $569.40; Nora Bruce, $481.80.]

No. 418, Petition of William B. Todd
Filed May 26, 1862

William B. Todd of the city of Washington claims compensation for Jim Dashiel. Todd does not know Dashiel's age for certain, but when he was purchased about seven years ago he was said to be 48 years old. He is black, 5 feet 6 inches tall and has slightly gray hair. He has stooped shoulders and was ruptured when purchased by Todd, but this does not incapacitate him from labor. He is an excellent gardener, understands the care of horses and is an efficient servant. [Value $400]

He purchased Dashiel from a Miss Dashiel residing in Somerset County, Md., seven years ago.

[Commissioners paid Todd $87.60.]

No. 419, Petition of Darius T. Gladmon, trustee for Mrs. Ann Gladmon
Filed May 26, 1862

Darius T. Gladmon of Georgetown, trustee for Ann Gladmon, claims compensation for Lucy Brisco, aged about

52. She is a dark mulatto, about 5 feet 8 inches tall, strong and healthy, although she has an old ankle sprain. Brisco was born in Prince George's County, Md., in the service of Mrs. Hall. She has been in the service of Ann Gladmon for about eight years. [Value $300]

[Commissioners paid D.T. Gladman [sic] $43.80.]

No. 420, Petition of J. Frank Brown Filed May 26, 1862

J. Frank Brown of Baltimore claims compensation for Henrietta Johnson, aged 22 years. She is a bright mulatto and about 5 feet 6 inches tall. [Value $400]

She was purchased for $400 on Jan. 29, 1859, from Joseph S. Donovan for a term of years to end in 1870. Donovan states Henrietta was bequeathed to Mrs. F. M. Fuller by the will of Robert L. Hall dated Jan. 26, 1847, and recorded in Baltimore in Liber G.E.S. No. 21, folio 405.

[Commissioners paid Brown $153.30.]

No. 421, Petition of Frances J. Jones Filed May 26, 1862

Mrs. Frances J. Jones, widow of George H. Jones, of Washington claims compensation for three persons.

1. Susan Page is about 40, dark complexion, healthy. She has a pleasant countenance and address. She is the mother of James and Edward.

2. James Page aged 17, he was born in Petersburg, Va., on Nov. 6, 1846. He has a light brown complexion and is of a slight, straight figure, but is healthy and sound.

3. Edward Page, aged 12, a shade or more darker than his brother, is also a slender figure, but healthy. He was born in Washington City on Jun. 23, 1850.

Susan Page accompanied George H. Jones when he moved from Petersburg to Washington in 1846 and she brought her two oldest children. She has ever since remained a member of the household and is a valuable servant. The total value of the three is $2,100.

George H. Jones in December 1839 for $700 purchased from Benjamin H. Campland of Petersburg, Va., Susan Meredith, now Susan Page. Susan Meredith was in June 1842 married at the residence of George Jones to James Page, a slave owned by John Pollard of Petersburg. She had three children of whom two, James and Edward, are still living.

[Commissioners paid Jones $963.60: Susan Page, $219; James Page, $525.60; Edward Page, $219.]

No. 422, Petition of Robert C. Brooke Filed May 26, 1862

Robert C. Brooke of Washington claims compensation for five persons.

1. Sandy Diggs is aged 36, very black and 5 feet 6 inches high. He is a little lame in his left foot and has had only one eye from the age of three or four. He is a house servant and is very smart and active and honest. Sandy brought to Brooke some $200 a year. [Value $1,000]

2. Mary Diggs, wife of Sandy, is aged 45 and is 5 feet 6 inches high. She is a house servant and has been a servant and cook in Brooke's family for the last 15 years. [Value $1,000]

3. Sandy Diggs, alias Sandy Ryan, the son of Mary, is aged 18, very bright mulatto and 5 feet 8 inches tall. He is healthy and intelligent and an excellent house servant. He has brought to Brooke $60 a year since he was the age of ten. [Value $1,500]

4. Maria Diggs, alias Maria Ryan, daughter of Mary, is aged 20, very bright mulatto and 5 feet 4 or 5 inches high. She is a seamstress, house servant and nurse and is very smart and active. She was hired in Montgomery County, Md., for a term of years before the Apr. 16th act, but came into the District of her own voluntary accord without the consent of Brooke. She has brought in $72 a year. [Value $1,500]

5. Luke Gilbert is aged 45, black and 5 feet 8 inches high. He is intelligent, healthy and robust and a gardener or farmer. [Value $2,000]

Sandy Diggs was purchased by Brook at the public sale of the estate of the late Walter Z. Berry of Prince George's County, Md., some 26 years ago. Mary Diggs, Sandy Diggs, alias Ryan, and Maria Diggs, alias Ryan, who were Mary's children by a former husband, were purchased by Brooke from C.C. Magruder of Prince George's County. Luke Gilbert was purchased Mar. 22, 1858, for $1,015 from Richard H. Beall of Washington.

There is attached a statement of Maria Diggs that she has for many years been the property of Brooke and was in Washington on Apr. 16th, the date the emancipation act was passed. She has been hired out for a few years to Smith Thompson outside D.C., but often, with the consent of her owner and master, visited the city where her parents and friends reside. She asserts that she qualified to be free under the terms of the emancipation law. (Dated May 27,

1862, and signed by Maria Diggs as per her attorney, George E. H. Day.)

No. 423, Petition of Andrew Martine   Filed May 26, 1862
Andrew Martine of Washington claims compensation for six persons.
1. Maria Nelson, aged 45, bright mulatto color, about five feet tall, very freckled, stout built with short curly hair. [Value $1,000]
2. Flora Buchanan, aged 28, of a copper color, about five feet high, slight build with high cheek bones and curly hair. [Value $1,000]
3. John Brogden, aged 58, quite black in color, about five feet high, spare build, high cheek bones and short curly hair. He is a good carpenter and is quick spoken. [Value $800]
4. Daniel Buchanan, aged five, bright copper color, short curly hair with a scar over his left eye. He is a smart, active boy. [Value $400]
5. Charles Buchanan, aged three, bright mulatto color, straight black hair. [Value $250]
6. Catharine Buchanan, aged six months. [Value $50]
Martine's title to Maria Nelson came with his marriage to Elizabeth Ann Coolidge, widow of the late Edmund Coolidge, in 1854. Flora, John and Daniel were purchased for $1,550 about four years ago at the sale of the estate of the late Catharine Bowie at Upper Marlboro, Md. Charles and Catharine are the children of Flora Buchanan and were born after he purchased her.
[Commissioners paid Martine $1,084.05: Maria Nelson, $262.80; Flora Buchanan, $372.30; John Brogden, $153.30; Daniel Buchanan, $175.20; Charles Buchanan, $109.50; Catharine Buchanan, $10.95.]

No. 424, Petition of Horace White   Filed May 26, 1862
Horace White of Washington County, D.C., claims compensation for Florida, aged 18. She is dark brown in color, about five feet tall and a little pox marked. She is honest, intelligent and a valuable house servant and cook. He purchased Florida on Jun. 1, 1861, for $600 from Charles B. Melvin of Washington. [Value $600]
[Commissioners paid White $328.50.]

No. 425, Petition of Charles Miller   Filed May 26, 1862
Charles Miller of the city of Washington claims compensation for Milly Jordan, aged 35. She is a bright mulatto, about 5 feet 2 or 3 inches tall, with freckles and is well-made. He purchased Milly from Ninian Willett in Prince George's County, Md., for $95, when she was nine years old. He brought her home with him to Washington and she has resided there ever since.[Value $500]
[Commissioners paid $219 to Ellen Miller, administratrix, by George W. Miller, her attorney, George W. Miller, administrator of Charles Miller, deceased.]

No. 426, Petition of William H. Kurtz   Filed May 26, 1862
William H. Kurtz of Georgetown claims compensation for five persons.
1. Simon Brooks, aged about 60, mulatto, about 5 feet 5 inches tall. He has been ruptured. [Value $150]
2. Elizabeth Gibson, aged about 42, dark colored, about 4 feet 10 inches tall. [Value $600]
3. Henrietta Gibson, aged about 17, has a light complexion, is about 4 feet 4 inches tall. [Value $600]
4. Thomas Gibson, aged about 15, has a brown complexion, is about five feet tall. [Value $1,000]
5. George Gibson, aged about nine, has a light complexion. [Value $600]
They were the property of his wife long before they were married.
[Commissioners paid Kurtz $1,116.90: Simon Brooks, no value; Elizabeth Gibson, $197.10; Henrietta Gibson, $262.80; Thomas Gibson, $394.20; George Gibson, $262.80.]
William H. Kurtz married Susan R. Cartwright on Nov. 28, 1849. See Pippenger, D.C. Marriage Licenses, 1811-1858, p. 346.

No. 427, Petition of Mary A. Hewitt   Filed May 26, 1862
Mary A. Hewitt of Washington claims compensation for two persons.
1. Mary Jane Jones is aged 23, about five feet high, black, stout and square built. She is a first-rate domestic who is acquainted with all kinds of house work. [Value $1,000]
2. Cornelius Broker is aged 24, dark mulatto, about 5 feet 3 inches tall, stout and strong. He "has always stood high as a waiter in a hotel" and is intelligent, healthy and active. [Value $1,200]

Hewitt says that Mary Jane Jones was born her property and was the child of Rosetta [Jones (?)], who was Hewitt's slave. Broker was purchased on Sept. 14, 1840, from Ann E Bronaugh.

[Commissioners paid Hewitt $1,029.30: Mary Jane Jones, $459.90; Cornelius Broker, $569,40.]

No. 428, Petition of Susan A. Chapman   Filed May 26, 1862

Susan A. Chapman of Washington claims compensation for Mary Elizabeth Taylor, aged 15 years and eight months. She is a light brown, 4 feet 7 ½ inches tall, healthy and active. She has a small scar over her left temple. She is an excellent house servant. She was given Chapman by her father, John E. Dement, when she was about a year old. Taylor has been receiving $4 a month as a house servant and nurse. [Value $900]

[Commissioners paid Chapman $438.]

No. 429, Petition of Ann Maria Biscoe, Angelica Chew, Emma Biscoe   Filed May 26, 1862

Ann Maria Biscoe, Angelica Chew and Emma Biscoe claim compensation for 26 persons.
1. Ezekiel Biscoe, aged 65, mulatto. He is a whitewasher at $1.25 a day. [Value $500]
2. Samuel Wilson, aged 52, dark brown. He is a driver and makes $11 a month. [Value $800]
3. John Bealle, aged 32, chestnut colored. He is blind in one eye. He is a laborer at $8 a month. [Value $600]
4. Nancy Grey, aged 42, dark brown. She is a cook at $6 a month. [Value $800]
5. John Grey, aged 17, black, child of Nancy Grey. He works in a grocery store at $8 a month. [Value $800]
6. James Grey, aged 14, black, child of Nancy Grey. [Value $600]
7. Horace Grey, aged 12, child of Nancy Grey. He is a laborer. [Value $400]
8. Eliza A. Washington, aged 24, chestnut colored. She works as a cook for $6 a month. [Value $1,000]
9. Clara Washington, aged two, light brown, child of Eliza. [Value $100]
10. Ellen Warring, aged 23, black. She is a house servant at $6 a month. [Value $1,000]
11. Rebecca Herbert, aged 35, chestnut colored. She is a cook, washer, *etc.* [Value $1,000]
12. Levi Herbert, aged 12, black, child of Rebecca Herbert. [Value $400]
13. Margaret Coleman, aged 28, light brown. She is a cook at $6 a month. [Value $1,000]
14. Sally Coleman, aged 15, light brown, child of Margaret Coleman, she is a house servant. [Value $800]
15. Alice Coleman, aged 13, black, house servant, child of Margaret Coleman. [Value $500]
16. Laura Coleman, aged eight, light brown, child of Margaret Coleman. [Value $400]
17. Juliet Coleman, aged six, child of Margaret Coleman. [Value $300]
18. Martha Herbert is aged 16, light brown and is the child of Rebecca Herbert. She is a nurse and house servant. [Value $800]
19. Henry Herbert, aged 14, light brown, is the child of Rebecca Herbert. [Value $600]
20. Frederick Coleman, aged two, black, is the child of Margaret Coleman. [Value $150]
21. William Coleman, aged one month, brown, child of Margaret Coleman. [Value $25]
22. Maria Bealle, aged 32, light brown. She is a cook, *etc.* [Value $1,000]
23. Nicholas Bealle, child of Maria Bealle, aged nine, chestnut colored. [Value $400]
24. George Bealle, aged three, light brown, is the child of Maria Bealle. [Value $200]
25. Cecilia Bealle, aged 23, chestnut colored. She is a cook, *etc.* [Value $1,000]
26. Ida Beall, aged two, mulatto, is the child of Cecilia Bealle. [Value $100]

Briscoe states that she acquired title to the above persons from her late father, James Hopewell of St. Mary's County, Md., when his estate was distributed. Several of the original servants have died since then and, except the older ones listed, the others are the children and grandchildren of original servants. At the death of her late husband, General George Biscoe of Georgetown, by his will dated Jul. 19, 1859, his interest in the Negroes came to her for her lifetime and thereafter to his two daughters, Angelica Chew, widow, and Emma Biscoe.

All of the Negroes have always been in the possession and under the control of the family of her husband and her. She states she was advised after her husband's death, to rid herself of the trouble of attending to them and to sell them, but they had been brought up in her family and instructed and trained by her and she was averse to disposing of them in that manner. Since her husband's death, the wages derived from them has been the sole means of support for herself, now 63 years old, and her family. All the Negroes, except John Bealle who has lost one eye, are in good health and are well-behaved and orderly. John Bealle sometimes on holidays indulges and frolics, but not to excess or to the neglect of his work. The same with Ezekiel Biscoe as to drinking a little, but he is a faithful, diligent and useful servant. She knows of no other defects in any of them. Some have not been employed in her own family, but have been regularly hired out and have stayed a good while in their places.

[Commissioners paid Ann M. Biscoe, Angelica Chew, Emma Biscoe, $6,548.10: Ezekiel Biscoe, $175.20; Samuel Wilson, $153.30; John Bealle, $175.20; Nancy Grey, $109.50; John Grey, $481.80; James Grey, $306.60; Horace Grey, $219; Eliza A. Washington, $438; Clara Washington, $43.80; Ellen Warring, $262.80; Rebecca Herbert, $350.40; Levi Herbert, $306.60; Margaret Coleman, $372.30; Sally Coleman, $459.90; Alice Coleman, $262.80; Laura Coleman, $197.10; Juliet Coleman, $109.50; Martha Herbert, $481.80; Henry Herbert, $306.60; Frederick Coleman, $65.70; William Coleman, $21.90; Maria Beall [sic], $350.40; Nicholas Beall [sic], $262.80; George Beall [sic], $65.70; Cecilia Beall [sic], $525.60; Ida Beall [sic], $43.80.]

No. 430, Petition of Ann Maria Biscoe, trustee, Emma Biscoe   Filed May 26, 1862

Ann Maria Biscoe and Emma Biscoe of Georgetown claim compensation for six persons.

1. Mary Ayres is aged about 52, chestnut colored and of medium height. She has hired out as a cook, washer and ironer. [Value $600]

2. Caroline Jenifer, Mary Ayres's daughter, is aged about 32, light brown and is a house servant. Caroline is the mother of Charlotte, Richard, Louisa and Neenah Jenifer. [Value $1,000]

3. Charlotte Jenifer is aged ten and light brown. [Value $400]

4. Richard Jenifer is eight years old and light brown. [Value $400]

5. Louisa Jenifer is five years old, chestnut colored and twin to Neenah. [Value $300]

6. Neenah Jenifer is aged five, chestnut colored and twin sister of Louisa. [Value $300]

Ann Maria states that Mary Ayers came to her in the distribution of the estate of her late father, James Hopewell of St. Mary's County, Md. Caroline Jenifer is her daughter and Caroline and her four children were raised and instructed by Ann Maria. The will, dated Jul. 19, 1859, of Ann Maria's husband, General George Biscoe, late of Georgetown, devised the six Negroes to Ann Maria Biscoe in trust for the sole and separate use of Emma Biscoe, his daughter. The six Negroes have always been in the possession and under the control of the family.

[Commissioners paid Ann M. Biscoe and Emma Biscoe $832.20: Mary Ayres, $65.70; Caroline Jenifer, $219; Charlotte Jenifer, $175.20; Richard Jenifer, $175.20; Louisa Jenifer, $98.55; Neenah Jenifer, $98.55.]

No. 431, Petition of Angelica Chew   Filed May 26, 1862

Angelica Chew of Georgetown claims compensation for Sallie Coates, aged 35 years. She is of a chestnut color, medium height, stout and healthy. She is mainly a cook, but does house work generally, including washing and ironing, sewing. [Value $1,000]

Chew inherited Coates as part of the estate of her late husband, Frisby F. Chew, whose residence was in Mississippi at the time of his death about 12 years ago. After Frisby's death, she and her children moved to the house of her father, General George Biscoe, in Georgetown, and Coates came with her. [Value $1,000]

[Commissioners paid Chew $219.]

No. 432, Petition of Emma Biscoe   Filed May 26, 1862

Emma Biscoe of Georgetown claims compensation for Paralee Dockett, aged 21 years. Dockett is held to a term of three more years service as of April 1862. She is a light chestnut color, medium height and is a house servant. She would have brought in her hire $50 a year clear of all expenses. [Value $150]

Dockett was given to Biscoe by her aunt, Rebecca Hopewell, deceased, by her will recorded at Leonard Town in St. Mary's County, Md., and she was bound for a term of 20 years, of which 17 have expired.

[Commissioners paid Biscoe $54.75 for "Paralle Dochet".]

No. 433, Petition of Isaac Scaggs   Filed May 26, 1862

Isaac Scaggs of Prince George's County, Md., claims compensation for John Stewart, aged 46. Stewart is a black man, stout and well-built, 5 feet 8 or 10 inches tall. He is an active and industrious servant and a first-rate field hand. Isaac inherited John from his father, James Scaggs, who died over 30 years ago and whose will is recorded in Marlboro, Md. John has been hired to a person living in D.C. for the last four years. [Value $800]

[Commissioners paid Scaggs $306.60.]

No. 434, Petition of Clement Hill   Filed May 26, 1862

Clement Hill of Prince George's County, Md., claims compensation for five persons.

1. Nicholas is aged 61, black, stout and about 5 feet 7 inches tall. He is an "extra" [excellent (?)] carpenter and fair blacksmith. [Value $800]

2. William West, black, is 48 years old with a slight frame. He is an accomplished coachman and has been so employed for 22 years. [Value $2,000]

3. Susan West is aged 42, mulatto and about 5 feet 2 inches tall. She is an accomplished cook, ironer, washer and dairy woman. [Value $2,000.]

4. Peggy Herbert, mulatto, is 30 years old. She is the mother of Herbert. She is a first-rate lady's maid and house servant. [Value $2,000]

5. Child of Peggy Herbert, female, six weeks old. [Value $300]

The above, except for Nicholas, were inherited from the estate of Hill's father, William Hill of Maryland. Nicholas was purchased for $650 from Joseph Thornton of Montpelier, Orange County, Va., on May 18, 1854.

[Commissioners paid Hill $1,229.10: Nicholas, $21.90; William West, $394.20; Susan West, $350.40; Peggy Herbert, $525.60; Infant Herbert, not allowed.]

No. 435, Petition of John L. Kidwell   Filed May 26, 1862

John L. Kidwell of Georgetown claims compensation for three persons.

1. James Somerville is aged 24, mulatto and 5 feet 7 3/4 inches tall. He is a good gardener and florist and also a good cook. His main business is to have charge of Kidwell's extensive garden and greenhouse. He could have easily obtained $2,000 for Somerville a couple of years ago. [Value $1,500]

2. Mary Somerville is three and one-half years old, mulatto and about 2 ½ feet tall. [Value $150]

3. Sarah Brooks is aged 20, dark mulatto and 5 feet 5 inches tall. She is a good house servant and has been kept at home occupied with the duties of the family. He paid $850 for her and that is what she is worth. [Value $850]

He purchased James Somerville for $500 about ten or 12 years ago from Edward N. Roach, the late Register of Wills, and the next day was offered $1,000 for him by a trader. He says that Roach sold him at a low price because he was opposed to selling well-behaved Negroes from their homes. Mary Somerville, the "supposed child" of James, was purchased for $25 about three or four years ago when a baby from William Yerby of Georgetown. He purchased Sarah Brooks for $850 about 18 months ago from Isaac Barrett of Georgetown, who had previously purchased her from William Busey of the same place in whose family she had been raised in Montgomery County, Md.

[Commissioners paid Kidwell $1,182.60: James Somerville, $591.30; Mary Somerville, $65.70; Sarah Brooks, $525.60,]

No. 436, Petition of Emeline Sheriff   Filed May 26, 1862

Emeline Sheriff claims compensation for seven persons.

1. Harriet Watkins is 70 years old, 5 feet 8 inches tall, dark brown in color and healthy. She is a first-class cook. [Value $100]

2. James Allen is aged 50, son of Harriet, light yellow color and 5 feet 8 inches tall. He is a splendid farm hand and a number one teamster. [Value $1,000]

3. Ellen Norton, daughter of Harriet, is aged 27, dark chestnut color and about 5 feet 1 or 2 inches tall. She is a first-class cook, washer and ironer. [Value $1,200]

4. Benjamin Watkins, son of Harriet, is aged 25, brown and 5 feet 9 inches tall. He is a fine farm hand. [Value $1,500]

5. Martha Johnson is aged 19, dark brown and 5 feet 6 or 7 inches tall. She has no parents living. [Value $1,200]

6. Lewis Norton, son of Ellen Norton, is aged nine, dark brown and about 4 feet 1 or 2 inches tall. He is sprightly and healthy. [Value $600]

7. Charles H. Norton, son of Ellen Norton is aged seven, dark yellow and about four feet tall. He is in good health and is very sprightly. [Value $600]

Sheriff obtained them under the terms of the will of her father, the late Levi Sheriff of Washington County, D.C., about seven years ago.

[Commissioners paid Sheriff $2,146.20: Harriet Watkins, $21.90; James Allen, $219; Ellen Norton, $394.20; Benjamin Watkins, $569.40; Martha Johnson, $547.50; Lewis Norton, $197.10; Charles H. Norton, $197.10.]

No. 437, Petition of Margaret E. Lowrie   Filed May 26, 1862

Margaret E. Lowrie of Washington County, D.C., claims compensation for seven persons.

1. Mary Simmes is aged 40, bright yellow, 5 feet 8 inches tall, stout and healthy. She is a fine field hand and a good washerwoman. [Value $800]

2. Gabriel Clark, son of Mary Simmes, is aged 21, black, 5 feet 9 inches tall and well made. He is a first-class

field hand and teamster. [Value $1,500]

3. Frank Clark, son of Mary Simmes, is aged 15, dark yellow and about 5 feet 4 inches tall. He is a good field hand. [Value $1,200]

4. William Stewart, son of Mary Simmes, is aged 13, black, five feet tall and well-built. He is a first-class field hand. [Value $1,100]

5. Edward Stewart, son of Mary Simmes, is aged 11, dark brown and 4 feet 6 inches tall. He is a good house boy and also a fine waiter. [Value $700]

6. Laura Simmes, daughter of Mary Simmes, is aged five, 3 feet 2 or 3 inches tall, sprightly. [Value $500]

7. Kate Simmes, daughter of Mary Simmes, is aged three, three feet high, very sprightly. [Value $300]

Lowrie obtained them under the will of her father, the late Levi Sheriff of Washington County, D.C., about seven years ago.

[Commissioners paid Lowrie $2,124.30: Mary "Simms", $219; Gabriel Clarke, $569.40; William Stewart, $372.30; Edward Stewart, $284.70; Laura "Simms", $131.40; Kate "Simms", $87.60; Frank Clarke, $459.90.]

No. 438, Petition of Mary A. Smoot   Filed May 26, 1862

Mary A. Smoot of Georgetown claims compensation for two persons.

1. Henry Butler is aged 19 and dark in color. [Value $1,400]

2. Margaret Hall, aged 23, is copper colored. [Value $1,000]

Smoot's grandmother, the late Mrs. Mary B. Smoot, left these persons to her by a will that was recorded in D.C. in June 1857.

[Commissioners paid Mary A. Matthews, formerly M.A. Smoot, by her husband and attorney, W[illiam] S. Matthews $1,007.40: Henry Butler, $569.40; Margaret Hall, $438.]

No. 439, Petition of Francis M. Jarboe   Filed May 26, 1862

Francis M. Jarboe of Washington City claims compensation for six persons.

1. Susan Campbell is aged about 47 and has a dark complexion. She has a scar on her cheek from a burn. She is an experienced house servant. [Value $800]

2. Jane Campbell is aged about 24, dark mulatto and below medium height. She is well-educated and a skillful domestic servant. [Value $1,000]

3. Mille Campbell is aged about 22, dark complexion, tall and stout. She is an excellent house servant. [Value $800]

4. John Campbell is aged about 16, dark complexion and slim. He is an intelligent and useful house or office servant. [Value $800]

5. Joseph Campbell is aged about 14 and dark colored. He is intelligent and capable and useful as a house or office servant. [Value $800]

6. Mary Tyler, aged about 24, is dark and above medium height. She is an excellent house servant. [Value $800]

Jarboe's title to Susan Campbell, Jane Campbell, Mille Campbell and Mary Tyler is based on his marriage to Mary Marcelena Queen, who got her title from the will of her sister, Rosena Queen of Georgetown. Mary Marcelena inherited John and Joe Campbell under the will of her brother, Charles Richard Queen, which was probated in D.C. on Mar. 10, 1859. A copy of Rosena Queen's will, probated Feb. 15, 1847, shows that she left to her sister, Mary Marcelena, and her brothers, Charles Richard and Theodore Queen, her interest in six slaves: Sam, John, Robert, Ellen, Jane and Susan. Ann Queen, Rosena's mother, retained use of the slaves during her lifetime.

[Commissioners paid Jarboe $2,014.80: Susan Campbell, $109.50; Jane Campbell, $525.60; Mille Campbell, $503.70; John Campbell, $240.90; Joseph Campbell, $197.10; Mary Tyler, $438.]

No. 440, Petition of Martha E. Barnes   Filed May 26, 1862

Martha E. Barnes of Washington claims compensation for Jess Johnson, aged 67, light mulatto in color, about 5 feet 5 inches tall, stout and well-made. He is a good farm hand and excellent gardener. He is healthy except for being slightly ruptured. She obtained title from her late husband, James Barnes, who purchased Jess from Thomas Young about 22 years ago.

[Jesse Johnson was not produced and the claim was not allowed.]

No. 441, Petition of Robert Jones and Ellen C. Jones   Filed May 26, 1862

Robert Jones and Ellen C. Jones his wife of Washington claim compensation for two persons.

1. Amos Dean is aged about 28, quite black, 5 feet 6 inches tall, quite stout and strong. [Value $1,200]
2. Rachael, about 55 years old, is very black and about 5 feet 5 inches tall, healthy. [Value $200]

Ellen Jones acquired title to Amos from her late father, George Noble, of Loudoun County, Va. The woman Rachael was purchased in Fauquier (?) County, Va., for $150.

[Commissioners paid Robert Jones and Ellen C. Jones, his wife, by F. W. Jones, their attorney $657: Amos Dean, $569.40; "Rachel", $87.60.]

Ellen C. Noble married Robert Jones on Aug. 12, 1854. See Pippenger, <u>D.C. Marriage Licenses, 1811-1858</u>, p. 443.

No. 442, Petition of Robert Gunnell, colored   Filed May 26, 1862

Robert Gunnell of Fairfax County, Va., claims compensation for ten persons.
1. Pauline Booth, aged 24, is quite black. She is the wife of William Booth of Georgetown. [Value $1,000]
2. Sarah Fairfax, aged 26, is the widow of John Fairfax. She is brown colored and healthy. [Value $1,000]
3. Florida Gunnell, aged 17, is brown colored and healthy. [Value $900]
4. Anna Gunnell, is aged 12, brown colored, sound and healthy. [Value $800]
5. William Fairfax is aged eight, child of Sarah Fairfax, black, sound and healthy. [Value $500]
6. Frank Fairfax is aged four, child of Sarah, black, sound and healthy. [Value $250]
7. Thomas Fairfax is aged three, child of Sarah, black, sound and healthy. [Value $200]
8. Joseph Fairfax is aged one, child of Sarah, black, sound and healthy. [Value $100]
9. Sally Booth is aged one, child of Paulina Booth, brown in color. [Value $100.]
10. Charles Gunnell is aged four months, child of Florida, brown colored. [Value $50]

All of these persons have always lived in the District of Columbia. Gunnell purchased for $700 Paulina Booth from E.C. Morgan and his wife, Evelina on Sept. 20, 1858, and that is recorded in D.C. J.A.S. No. 161, folio 153. He purchased Sarah Fairfax and her child, William, and Florida and Anna for $600 from Maj. Richard B. Lee, then of the U.S. Army, in Washington in 1854. This bill of sale was in the possession of B[enjamin]F. Mackall, but he has since mislaid it. Frank, Thomas, Joseph, Sally and Charles were born of Paulina, Sarah and Florida since the purchase. (Signed Robert his x mark Gunnell)

[Commissioners paid Robert Gunnell, by F.W. Jones, his attorney, $2,168.10: Paulina Booth, $438; Sarah Fairfax, $438; Florida, $503.70; Anna, $284.70; William, $153.30; Frank, $131.40; Thomas, $109.50; Joseph, $43.80; Sally, $43.80; Charles, $21.90.]

No. 443, Petition of Harriet Donoho   Filed May 26, 1862

Harriet "Donohoo" of Washington claims compensation for Eliza, aged 44. She is black, about 5 feet 3 inches tall, stout, well-formed and sprightly. She is an excellent cook, washer and ironer. She purchased Eliza from William E. Hamilton for $406 on Mar. 26 [*no year given*]. The sum was comparatively low, because Hamilton was leaving the city and wanted to obtain a comfortable home for her.

[Commissioners paid Donoho $175.20.]

No. 444, Petition of John W. Wells   Filed May 26, 1862

John W. Wells of Washington claims compensation for Harriet Hawkins, aged 21 years. She is dark, about 5 feet 3 inches tall, straight and well-formed, short, curly hair, with regular features and a "mild expression". She is the cook for Wells's family and does the marketing herself and is invaluable to his family. Wells purchased her from Peter D. Posey of Tenallytown, near Georgetown, D.C., for $500 on Feb. 2, 1854, when Harriet was 13 years old. She had been living in Wells's family since she was eight and was a companion for his children. She is valued at $1,300. Attached are the receipts showing the series of payments to Posey from Wells.

[Commissioners paid Wells $525.60.]

No. 445, Petition of Henry Newman   Filed May 26, 1862

Henry Newman of the city of Washington claims compensation for three persons.
1. Mary is aged about 13, black, short for her age, but well-built and erect in her carriage. She is intelligent and likely. She is a tolerably good cook, and generally useful as a nurse or chambermaid. [Value $550]
2. Sally is aged about six, very bright mulatto, with long straight hair. She is spare in her build and tall for her age. She is useful about the house. [Value $250]
3. Frances is aged about four, bright mulatto, bushy hair, well-built, likely and intelligent. [Value $200]

He purchased their mother from Obadiah Stanford of Somerset County, Md., on May 20, 1822, when he paid $75 for two girls, Eliza, aged about four, now deceased, and Maria, aged about six.

[Commissioners paid Newman $525.60: Mary, $284.70; Sally, $153.30; Frances, $87.60.]

No. 446, Petition of William Nailor   Filed May 26, 1862

William Nailor of Washington City claims compensation for Sarah Johnson, aged 19. She is 5 feet 1 ½ inches tall, yellow in color, healthy. She is a good cook, washer and ironer and seamstress. [Value $2,000]

His title comes through his wife, who inherited Sarah from her mother, Elizabeth Thomas of Prince George's County, Md., about 15 years ago.

[Commissioners paid Nailor $525.60.]

No. 447, Petition of William McLain   Filed May 26, 1862

William McLain of Washington claims compensation for two persons.

1. Mary Louisa Jefferson, aged 19. She has a "full, black face and thick lips & African features generally". She is a capable servant. [Value $600]

2. Samuel Dorsey, aged 17, mulatto. He is short, smart and active. He has some education and is "a fine specimen of a boy" and a capable servant.[Value $900]

He obtained Mary Louisa from the estate of his wife's father, John G. Mosby, who died in 1856. Dorsey was born of Annie(?) Lee Dorsey, now deceased, whom he purchased from Mrs. Bland Lee of this city in 1846.

[Commissioners paid McLain $700.80: Mary Louisa Jefferson, $438; Samuel Dorsey, $262.80.]

No. 448, Petition of Roger Jones   Filed May 26, 1862

Roger Jones of Washington claims compensation for three persons.

1. George Gale, aged 55, dark mulatto, 5 feet 8 inches tall, gray hair, black eyes, compact build. He is a capital farm hand and can do much hard work. [Value $600]

2. Jane Gale, aged 45 black, about 5 feet 7 inches tall, hair mostly black and eyes black. [Value $200]

3. Eli Gale, son of George, aged 22, dark mulatto, 5 feet 9 inches tall, black woolly hair and black eyes. He is stout and compact in build. He is young and strong and well-trained to work on a farm. [Value $1,200]

Jones got title partly by inheritance from his father, the late General Roger Jones, who purchased them at public sale in Fairfax County, Va., from A. Moss in 1849, and partly by gift from the other heirs to the estate.

[Commissioners paid Jones, by W[illiam] Y. Fendall, attorney, $854.10: George Gale, $153.30; Jane Gale, $87.60; Eli Gale, $613.20.]

No. 449, Petition of William Orme   Filed May 26, 1862

William Orme of Washington claims compensation for two persons.

1. Judy Daines is aged 27, dark complexion, about 5 feet 5 inches tall. She is a good cook, washer and ironer, and is industrious, honest and obedient. [Value $800]

2. Henry Daines is five, light colored and about three feet tall. He is a hearty and healthy boy. [Value $400]

They were bequeathed to his wife by the will of her late mother, Mrs. Smith of Washington, which was recorded here about last November.

[Commissioners paid Orme $613.20: Judy Daines, $481.80; Henry Daines, $131.40.]

No. 450, Petition of Mary D.G. Ringgold   Filed May 26, 1862

Mary D.G. Ringgold of the District of Columbia claims compensation for two persons.

1. Louisa is aged about 40, bright mulatto, about five feet high, straight black hair with dark eyes and small regular features. She is an accomplished house servant, cook and seamstress.

2. Elizabeth, child of Louisa, is aged 18, light mulatto, slender. Her hair is shorter and "more African" in its character that her mother's. She is also an accomplished house servant, cook and seamstress.

They hire out for $14 a month, with Louisa bringing $8 and Elizabeth $6 a month. She values them at $2,000. Ringgold acquired their mother by gift about 1806 from Thomas S[im] Lee, the late governor [of Maryland].

[Commissioners paid J. Lee, attorney for Mary D.G. Ringgold, $810.30: Louisa, $284.70; Elizabeth, $525.60.]

No. 451, Petition of Hannah P. McCormick, Margaret L. McCormick,   Filed May 26, 1862
Sophia McCormick, Harriet P. McCormick and Mary E. McCormick

Hannah McCormick, Sophia McCormick, Margaret L. McCormick, Harriet P. McCormick and Mary E. McCormick, claim compensation for four persons:

1. Rachel Contee is aged about 37, about 4 (?) feet 1 inch tall and mulatto. She is a valuable servant and healthy, except she has had attacks of rheumatism. [Value $400]

2. Susan Contee is about 31, light mulatto and 5 feet 6 inches tall. She is a valuable servant. Sophia and Harriet McCormick gave her the chance to purchase herself, but she has not been able to pay more than her regular wages. She earns $7 a month. [Value $500]

3. Harriet Cox, aged 58, is about five feet tall. She was allowed to purchase herself, but has paid very little amounting to no more than her regular wages. [Value $200]

4. Abraham Cox, about 17, black, is about 5 feet 4 inches tall. He has always remained with his mother and your petitioner has never had any service from him.

The petitioners inherited the above from the estate of the late Rev. A. G. (?) McCormick. They were divided among his heirs: Hannah McCormick, widow, took Rachel Contee; Sophia and Harriet McCormick took Susan Contee; and the mother of Susan and Abraham Cox, Harriet Cox, are held as joint property among the heirs.

[The Commissioners paid Hannah McCormick, by Sophia McCormick, her attorney, $131.40 for Rachel Contee. The paid Sophia McCormick and Harriet McCormick $350.40 for Susan Contee; they paid Sophia McCormick, Hannah McCormick, Harriet McCormick, Mary E. McCormick, Margaret McCormick, by Sophia McCormick, their attorney, $635.10 for Harriet Cox, $109.50 and Abraham Cox, $525.60.]

No. 452, Petition of Stephen P. Franklin   Filed May 26, 1862

Stephen P. Franklin of Washington City claims compensation for five persons.

1. Washington Clements, aged 28, is very light in color, short in statue, but strong. [Value $1,200]
2. Lucinda Taylor, aged 30, tolerably light in color, short, but stout and strong. [Value $1,000]
3. Maria Parker, aged 35, tolerably light in color, medium height, strong and stout. [Value $1,000]
4. Lucy Brooks, aged 60, tolerably light in color. [Value $300]
5. Alfred Clarke, aged 35, tolerably light in color, medium height. He has absconded. [Value $1,200(?)]

He purchased Washington Clements from Dr. (?)_____ of Washington; he purchased Lucinda from James H. Birch; he purchased Maria from the estate of Philip Ennis; he purchased Lucy at an auction sale; he purchased Alfred from Mrs. Sarah Forrest.

[Commissioners paid Franklin $1,379.70: Washington Clements, $569.40; Lucinda Taylor, $438; Maria Parker, $350.40; Lucy Brooks, $21.90; Alfred Clarke, not allowed.]

No. 453, Petition of Lucy E. Mattingly, executrix   Filed May 26, 1862

Lucy E. Mattingly of Washington City, heir and executrix, claims compensation for eight persons.

1. Sophia, aged 37, brown complexion, black eyes, 5 feet 6 1/4 inches tall. Her "constitution is not so firm as the others", but her services have been equally valuable.[Value $1,200]
2. Charlotte, aged 31, brown complexion, black eyes, 4 feet 11 inches high. [with son Peter, Value $1,200]
3. Priscilla, aged 27, brown complexion, black eyes, 5 feet 6 inches tall. [Value $1,200]
4. Flora, aged 11, brown complexion, black eyes, 3 feet 11 inches tall. [Value $500]
5. Willie, aged seven, brown complexion, black eyes, 3 feet 8 ½ inches tall. [Value $500]
6. George, aged five, brown complexion, black eyes, 3 feet 5 inches tall. [Value $450]
7. Francis (Fanny), male, aged two, brown complexion, black eyes, 2 feet 8 inches high. [Value $250]
8. Peter, infant child of Charlotte, three months old.

All of the above are descendants of Mary, a slave who was purchased by Edward Mattingly (the father of Lucy E.) from Charles Knott of Charles County, Md., on Jan. 18, 1821. Edward Mattingly transferred them to his wife, who willed them to her daughter, Lucy.

[Commissioners paid Mattingly $1,795.80: Sophia, $394.20; Charlotte, $328.50; Peter, $21.90; Priscilla, $481.80; Flora, $197.10; Willis [sic], $153.30; George, $131.40; Francis, $87.60.]

No. 454, Petition of Lucy E. Mattingly   Filed May 26, 1862

Lucy E. Mattingly of Washington City claims compensation for Leonard, aged about 25 years. He is copper colored, 5 feet 6 inches tall and has black eyes. He was purchased at a public auction of the property of the late John Mattingly on Mar. 10, 1854, for $1,200. [Value $1,600]

[Commissioners paid Mattingly $547.50.]

No. 455, Petition of Ann Emeline Ward   Filed May 26, 1862

Ann Emeline Ward of Charles County, Md, claims compensation for Cecelia Thomas, aged 19 years. She is a dark copper color, about 5 feet 3 inches tall, with a "bushy head". She is stout and fleshy and square built. She inherited Cecelia from her father, John S. Ward who also owned Cecelia's mother. [Value $1,000]

[Commissioners paid Ann Amelia [sic] Ward, by F.T. Maddox, her attorney, $525.60]

No. 456, Petition of Ulysses Ward   Filed May 26, 1862

Ulysses Ward of Washington City claims compensation for two persons.
1. Rachel Cole, aged 29, dark color, of medium height. [Value $800]
2. Sibey Cole, aged 75, mother of Rachel, dark color, medium height. [Value $100]

Sibey Cole came to Ward from his wife and Rachel is Sibey's child.

[Commissioners paid Ward $350.40: Rachel Cole, $350.40; Sebra [sic] Cole, no value.]

No. 457, Petition of Anthony Addison   Filed May 26, 1862

Anthony Addison of the District of Columbia claims compensation for seven persons.
1. Samuel Mullikin, aged 14, dark with black hair, about five feet tall. He is scrofulous and is not very strong, but is useful as a house servant and waiter.
2. Elizabeth Bruce, aged ten, dark with black hair and eyes, about 4 feet 6 inches tall, strong and healthy.
3. Lizzie Lewis, aged 14, bright mulatto, dark hair and eyes, strong and healthy.
4. Marion Lewis, aged about ten, bright mulatto, 4 feet 2 or 3 inches tall, dark hair and eyes. He was delicate several years ago, but he is now in good health.
5. Mary Solomon, aged 36, very bright mulatto, about 5 feet 2 or 3 inches tall with black hair and eyes. She is an excellent, well-disposed woman and a good washer and ironer.
6. Thomas Solomon, aged 11, very bright mulatto, red hair and light eyes, about 4 feet 3 or 4 inches tall.
7. Julia Solomon, aged nine, very light mulatto, about 4 feet 3 or 4 inches tall.

Addison estimates their value at $2,000.

Mullikin was willed to Addison by Anthony Addison Callis about six years ago. He has one more year to serve from last March and five years to serve after he has learned a trade. Elizabeth Bruce was willed to him at the same time and has ten years to serve from last March. Lizzie and Marion Lewis are the children of Geraldine and Margaret Lewis, who were willed to him by an aunt about 27 years ago. Mary, Thomas and Julia Solomon were to serve Addison until a certain indebtedness was paid to him as administrator on the estate of the late S[arah] D. Hanson.

The attached will of Anthony Addison Callis of Prince George's County, Md., signed Oct. 4, 1852, and proved Nov. 9, 1854, provided that Negro boy Sam and Elizabeth were to serve Anthony Addison until aged 25, in the case of Sam, and 20 years old in the case of Elizabeth. Male children of the above were to be bound to some suitable trade at the age of 16 to serve until age 20, after which they would serve Addison an additional five years.

Also attached is a copy of the will of Sarah D. Hanson of Prince George's County, Md., which provided that her mulatto servant named Mary Solomon and all her children were to go to Anthony Addison for a term of six months, after which they were to be freed. (Will proved Feb. 3, 1857) Addison also attached a copy of his accounts as administrator of Hanson's will.

[Commissioners paid Addison $1,208.60: Samuel "Mulliken", $87.60; Elizabeth Bruce, $87.60; Lizzie Lewis, $306.60; Marion Lewis, $175.20; Mary Solomon, $306.60; Thomas Solomon, $219; Julia Solomon, $219. Of the amount allowed for Mary, Thomas and Julia Solomon, $744.60, only $551.60 was paid to the claimant, making the total $1,208.60.]

No. 458, Petition of Louisa G. Beall   Filed May 26, 1862

Louisa G. Beall of Georgetown claims compensation for two persons.
1. Betty Harris is about 57, mulatto, about 5 feet 6 inches tall and quite stout. She is a good cook, washer and ironer and is hired out for $8 a month. [Value $300]
2. Josephine Harris, child of Betty Harris, about 15, is "a shade or two darker than a full mulatto", 5 feet 2 or 3 inches tall and well-grown for her age. She is strong and healthy and an excellent house servant who is hired out for $6 per month.. [Value $900]

Betty Harris was a gift to Beall from her mother, Mrs. Elizabeth Darne, about the latter part of 1845 or the first part of 1846. Josephine is Betty's child and was born after Betty became Beall's property.

[Commissioners paid Beall, by Robert A. Lacy, her attorney, $569.40: Betty Harris, $87.60; Josephine Harris, $481.80.]

No. 459, Petition of Benjamin S. Bohrer   Filed May 26, 1862

Benjamin S. Bohrer of Georgetown claims compensation for thirteen persons.

1. Arabella Nash, aged about 38, dark mulatto, small in size. She is a first-rate cook and a reliable servant. [Value $900]

2. Martha Nash, aged about 21, bright mulatto, rather tall. She is trustworthy and capable in all respects. [Value $700]

3. Archy Nash, aged 18, bright mulatto. He is a first-rate dining room and house servant. [Value $800]

4. Horace Nash, aged 14, dark mulatto. He is an excellent carriage driver and does all kinds of house work. [Value $700]

5. Adelaide Nash, aged 17, very bright mulatto. She is capable, intelligent, a good washer and ironer and does all kinds of house work. [Value $700]

6. Son of Adelaide, three months old, of a bright complexion.

7. George Ruffin Nash, aged 19, bright mulatto, small size. He is smart and a first-rate gentleman's body servant and a good carriage driver. [Value $800]

8. James Nash, about 15, has a very bright complexion. He is very intelligent and well taught. [Value $800]

9. Selima Nash, aged ten, is bright mulatto girl who is well-grown. [Value $600]

10. George Green, aged 26, dark in color, tall and sprightly. He is a first-class servant. [Value $1,200]

11. Alexander Green, aged about 23, black, a good cook. [Value $800]

12. John Green, aged about 16, dark mulatto, well-grown. He is a useful house servant and carriage driver. [Value $700]

13. William Maize, aged about 25, bright mulatto. He is very capable as a farm hand and is also a good groom. [Value $800]

Alexander Green, George Ruffin Nash and Archy Nash, a few weeks prior to the passage of the D.C. emancipation act, were hired out to U.S. officers, with Bohrer's consent, and accompanied the officers to Fortress Monroe. Before the war James Nash was hired to a clergyman stationed in Virginia and he could not return to his home in the District. He is therefore unavoidably absent.

Bohrer says that all of the above persons were born in his family and raised by him and his wife. He had purchased the mother of a some of them over 40 years ago and others he acquired by his marriage in 1834.

[Commissioners paid George A. Bohrer, executor of Benjamin S. Bohrer, $5,781.60: Arabella Nash, $438; Martha Nash, $525.60; Archy Nash, $569.40; Horace Nash, $394.20; Adelaide Nash, $416.10; son of Adelaide, $21.90; George Ruffin Nash, $394.20; James Nash, $306.60; Selima Nash, $350.40; George Green $569.40; Alexander Green, $657; John Green, $569.40; William Maize, $569.40.]

No. 460, Petition of Betsy Roberson, colored   Filed May 26, 1862

Betsy Roberson of Washington City claims compensation for John Roberson, aged 26. He is of a dark color, 5 feet 8 inches tall, and "a polite well behaved man". Betsy Roberson says that John has supported her materially and she has never surrendered her claim to service or labor from him. A receipt dated Jul. 24, 1847, shows that Betsy, being then free, purchased a little boy of about ten years old for $150 from John Sharer of Hagerstown, Md. Attached is Sharer's statement that reads "any time within two years . . . a servant boy John, which I own . . . his mother to have him" by paying me $150. (Signed Jul. 24, 1847) Roberson values John at $1,000.

[Commissioners paid Betty [sic] Roberson, her x mark, $613.20.]

No. 461, Petition of Sarah E. King   Filed May 27, 1862

1. Mary Chase, about 64, mulatto, 4 feet 9 inches tall. [Value $150]

2. Rachel Coquire, aged about 28, mulatto, about five feet high. She broke her arm when a child and the value estimated for her is low considering the work she can do and the wages she has brought in. [Value $600]

3. Selina Coquire, aged 24, mulatto, about 5 feet 3 inches tall. [Value $1,000]

4. Mary Coquire, aged seven, mulatto, about four feet high. [Value $300]

5. John Coquire, aged five, bright mulatto, about three feet high. [Value $300]

6. Annette Coquire, aged two years five months, bright mulatto, about two feet tall. [Value $150]

King's title comes by purchase from the administrator of her father's estate.

[Commissioners paid King $1,467.30: Mary Chase, $65.70; Rachael Coquire, $438; Selina Coquire, $525.60; Mary Coquire, $219; John Coquire, $131.40; Annette Coquire, $87.60.]

No. 462, Petition of James M. Wright and Mary R. Wright   Filed May 27, 1862

James M. Wright and Mary R. Wright of Prince George's County, Md., claim compensation for two persons.

1. William Brown, aged 26, dark brown. He is a very valuable servant and has been working as a head waiter at Brown's Hotel. [Value $2,000]

2. Maria Brown, aged 33, dark brown, healthy. She is a valuable servant. [Value $1,400]

Mary R. Wright obtained them by inheritance from her uncle, Richard M. Foggett of Anne Arundel County, Md., about 23 years ago. James's title is based on his marriage to Mary.

[Commissioners paid James and Mary Wright $1,007.40: William Brown, $569.40; Maria Brown, $438.]

No. 463, Petition of Jane H.C. Scott   Filed May 17 [sic], 1862

Jane H.C. Scott of Washington City claims compensation for five slaves.

1. William Johnson, aged 24, very dark complexion, six feet high, stout built.
2. Charles Johnson, aged 28, very light complexion, 5 feet 9 inches high, stout built.
3. Susan Johnson, aged 52, very dark complexion, about 5 feet 6 inches tall, slender built.
4. Mary Clare Johnson, aged 21, light complexion, 5 feet 4 inches tall, stout built.
5. Mary Johnson, eight years old, very light complexion, about four feet high, stout built.

They are all healthy and valuable servants and she has received in this city as high as $30 a month wages for some of them. [Value $5,300]

She acquired title by inheritance from her late husband, John D. Scott, who died intestate in 1850.

[Commissioners paid Scott $1,817.70: William Johnson, $547.50; Charles Johnson, $569.40; Susan Johnson, $43.80; Mary Clare Johnson, $503.70; Mary Johnson, $153.30.]

No. 464, Petition of Susannah P. Bryan   Filed May 27, 1862

Susannah P. Bryan of Serrattsville, Prince George's County, Md., claims compensation for two persons.

1. Stephen Hagan, aged 52, black, six feet tall, missing two upper front teeth. He is a first-rate field hand and acted as foreman. He is a fugitive under the Fugitive Slave Act. [Value $500]

2. Caroline Henson, aged 53, dark copper color, about five feet tall. She is a good cook, washer and ironer. She is hired out in D.C. [Value $300]

Hagan came to Bryan by her dower rights as widow of William P. Bryan. She claims Henson by reason of her trusteeship over Richard Lanham, an insane man, whose title comes through the bequest of his mother, Julia Lanham, deceased.

[Commissioners paid Bryan by George Mattingly, her attorney, $372.30: Stephen Hagan, $240.90; Caroline Henson, $131.40.]

No. 465, Petition of Thompson Nailor   Filed May 27, 1862

Thompson Nailor of Washington City claims compensation for three persons.

1. Albert Hickman is aged 21, copper colored and 5 feet 11 inches tall. He is held to a term of service that expires May 23, 1870. [Value $500]

2. Ann Adams, 14, mulatto, 5 feet 1 ½ inches tall. [Value $1,000]

3. Maria Johnson, aged about four, black. [Value $200]

Nailor acquired Hickman for a term of years from William Marshall of Washington City on Aug. 29, 1859, he having purchased him from William H. Coyle of the same place on Sept. 23, 1852. With regard to Ann Adams, he purchased Negro Caroline, aged about 19, and her one-year-old child, for $145 from Gilbert L. Giberson of D.C. for $145 in March 1849. Caroline was to be freed on Nov. 3, 1855, and the child was sold as a slave for life. Caroline's term of service had been set by her mistress, Ann Camden, in Camden's sale to Newman B. Wilkerson on Nov. 23, 1847. Nailor received Maria Johnson in 1847 as "a gift of her mother by Notley Moulden" of D.C. to his daughter, who is Thompson's wife.

[Commissioners paid Nailor $722.70: Albert Hickman, $197.10; Ann Adams, $438; Maria Johnson, $87.60.]

Thompson Nailor married Sarah Ann "Molden" on May 15, 1847. See Pippenger, D.C. Marriages, 1811-1858, p. 437

No. 466, Petition of William Thomas Carroll
Filed May 27, 1862

William Thomas Carroll of Washington City claims compensation for three persons.

1. John Brooks, about 46 years old, about 5 feet 9 1/2 inches tall, dark brown color, slender, black hair slightly tinged with gray. He was the very best waiter and dining room servant Carroll ever saw. [Value $2000]

2. Ellen (or Nelly) Warren, about 27, about 5 feet 2 inches tall, dark brown complexion, with long glossy black hair. She was a valuable chambermaid and lady's dressing maid. [Value $750]

3. Henry Warren, aged about 23, 5 feet 8 inches tall, copper color, curly hair, full and stout. He is a very good waiter and house servant and marketman. [Value $50.]

John Brooks was given to his wife by her father in the spring of 1829. The mother of Ellen and Henry was purchased by Carroll in the summer of 1827 and thus they were born his slaves.

[Commissioners paid Carroll $1,182.60: John Brooks, $262.80; Ellen Warren, $438; Henry Warren, $481.80.]

No. 467, Petition of Thomas S. Mercer
Filed May 27, 1862

Thomas S. Mercer of Maryland, but for the past four months in Washington D.C., claims compensation for two persons.

1. Henrietta Warren, 25 years old, is about 5 feet 7 inches high, of a dark brown color, with a fine figure and long wavy hair. She has lost several of her front teeth and has a pleasant voice when spoken to. She was a child's nurse and a most elegant lady's maid. He states that he refused $1,500 for her 18 months ago. [Value $1,500]

2. Lucy Blackstone, aged about 16 years, is about 5 feet 3 inches tall, very dark in color with very bushy, curly hair. She has a good figure and appearance and a pleasant voice when spoken to. She is an excellent seamstress and lady's maid. [Value $1,000]

Henrietta was given to his wife by her father in the fall of 1856. Lucy Blacksmith was given to his wife by her grandmother in the spring of 1857.

[Commissioners paid Mercer $876: Henrietta Warren, $416.10; Lucy Blackstone, $459.90.]

No. 468, Petition of Jacob Ross, colored
Filed May 27, 1862

Jacob Ross of Georgetown claims compensation for two persons.

1. Keziah Ross, aged 46, about 5 feet 7 inches tall, brown complexion, about 190 pounds in weight.

2. Frances Ann Ross, daughter of Keziah, aged 25, 5 feet 2 or 3 inches tall, slender. Her complexion is a little darker than that of her mother.

Both persons are healthy and accustomed to labor at general house work. [Value $1,500]

Ross purchased Keziah from John M. Wilson of Lexington, Va., for $601 at a public sale on Jan. 19, 1856, and he purchased Frances Ann from J.D. Davidson also of Lexington on Dec. 24, 1859 for $700.

[Commissioners paid Ross $438 for Frances Ann Ross; the claim for "Kessiah" was withdrawn and not allowed.]

No. 469, Petition of Michael Green
Filed May 27, 1862

Michael Green of Washington City claims compensation for two persons.

1. Marian Adams, aged 17, bright mulatto, medium height, healthy. She is an excellent house servant. [Value $1,000]

2. Agnes Brooks, aged 14, copper color, healthy. She is a good servant. [Value $800]

Green inherited them from his wife, who got them from Gannon's estate from Owen Leddy of Washington, D.C.

[Commissioners paid Green $832.20: Marian Adams, $438; Agnes Brooks, $394.20.]

Michael Green married Mary Gannon on Jan. 28, 1852. It is probable that the Gannon mentioned above is Mary's father. See Pippenger, D.C. Marriage Licenses, 1811-1858, p. 222.

No. 470, Petition of Enos Ray
Filed May 27, 1862

Enos Ray of Washington County claims compensation for six persons.

1. Eliza Hinton, black complexion, about 5 feet 4 ½ inches tall. She is the mother of James, Emily, Hanson and George. [Value $350]

2. James H. Hinton, aged about 23, black complexion, about 5 feet 8 inches tall. [Value $1,200]

3. Emily J. Hinton, aged about 21, of a chestnut color, about 5 feet 6 ½ inches tall. [Value $1,200]

4. Hanson Hinton, about 18 years old, chestnut colored, about 5 feet 9 ½ inches tall. [Value $1,200]

5. George J. Hinton, aged 13 ½ years, chestnut colored, about 5 feet 3 inches tall. [Value $1,000]

6. Mary E. Dean, child of Emily J., aged about six, black complexion, about 3 feet 6 ½ inches tall. [Value $500]

Eliza and Emily are excellent house servants, first-rate cooks, washerwomen and ironers, as well as dairy maids. They lived in Ray's family. James, Hanson and George are excellent farm hands and familiar with the management of horses, cattle and hogs and are skilled in plowing, reaping and mowing.

Ray purchased Eliza Hinton and James Hinton from the estate of the late Thomas Crampton of Montgomery County, Md., about 21 or 22 years ago.

[Commissioners paid Ray $2,562.30: Eliza Hinton, $197.10; James H. Hinton, $569.40; Emily J. Hinton, $569.40; Hanson Hinton, $613.20; George J. Hinton, $438; Mary E. Dean, $175.20.]

An ink smudge has covered over the age of Eliza Hinton, and one can only make out a "5".

No. 471, Petition of Mary Ann Harvey   Filed May 27, 1862

Mary Ann Harvey of Washington City claims compensation for five persons.

1. Julia (or Juliet) Jefferson Cole, aged 40, light color, about five feet high. She is a first-rate house servant, excellent cook, washer and ironer and has lived in Harvey's family for the last 19 years. [Value $1,000]

2. Joseph Cole, aged 19, light complexion, about five feet high. He is a first-rate house servant and has been hired out for $8 a month. [Value $1,000]

3. Robert Cole, aged 16, dark complexion, about 4 feet 9 inches high. He has been hiring out since he was seven years old. [Value $800]

4. William Cole, aged 13, light complexion, about 4 feet 3 ½ inches tall. He has been hired out. [Value $600]

5. Albert Cole, aged 11, light complexion, about 4 feet 1 ½ inches tall. He has been hired out. [Value $400]

Harvey acquired them from her father the late Michael Sardo of Washington County, D.C. Attached is a bill of sale from Michael Sardo to Michael R. Coombs dated Aug. 15, 1844, and recorded in D.C. Liber W.B. No. 111, folios 162-163. That document states that Sardo, in consideration of the love and affection he has for his daughter, Mary Ann Harvey, wife of Henry Harvey, and for $1 paid by Michael R. Coombs, son of Mary Ann Harvey, sells to Coombs Juliet Jefferson, now Juliet Cole after her marriage, who was purchased by him on May 2, 1834, from John S. McWilliams as recorded in D.C. Liber W.B. No. 50, folio 144. He also sells to Coombs Juliet's child, Joseph, aged about 15 months. They and their increase are to be held for the sole use and benefit of his daughter, Mary Ann. (Signed Michael his x mark Sardo, Aug. 15, 1844)

[Commissioners paid Harvey $1,620.60: Julia Cole, $262.80; Joseph Cole, $481.80; Robert Cole, $350.40; William Cole, $284.70; Albert Cole, $240.90.]

No. 472, Petition of Ann M. Hill   Recorded May 27, 1862

Ann M. Hill of Washington City claims compensation for two persons.

1. Mary Fletcher, aged between 50 and 54, black, with black hair, 5 feet 1 inch tall. She is an excellent cook and house servant and a good washer and ironer. [Value $800]

2. Louisa Hawkins, aged 16, black with black hair, 5 feet one-half inch tall. She is a fine house maid. [Value $800]

Hill was given Mary Fletcher by her father before his death and she has been in Hill's possession for about 45 years. Hawkins was given to Hill by her brother and has been in her possession about eight years.

[Commissioners paid Hill $657: Mary Fletcher, $131.40; Louisa Hawkins, $525.60.]

No. 473, Petition of Juliana Barry   Filed May 27, 1862

Julianna Barry of Washington claims compensation for three persons.

1. James Sanders is aged 21, dark color, six feet high, healthy. [Value $1,200]

2. Rachel Sanders, aged 18, dark color, five feet high, healthy. [Value $1,100]

Nora Sanders, aged 16, dark color, four feet tall, healthy. [Value $1,000]

About 50 years ago Barry's husband purchased the grandmother of James, Rachel and Nora from Col. Naylor of Prince George's County, Md., and her daughter is the mother of the above.

[Commissioners paid Barry $1,620.60: James Sanders, $613.20; Rachel Sanders, $525.60; Nora Sanders, $481.80.]

No. 474, Petition of Barnet T. Swort   Filed May 27, 1862

Barnet T. Swort of Washington County, D.C., claims compensation for seven persons.

1. Colonel Johnson, aged 47, dark chestnut color, 5 feet 6 ½ inches tall, stout and healthy. [Value $1,000]

2. Emily Allen, aged 29, dark color, 5 feet 4 inches tall, healthy. [Value $1,000]

3. George Allen, aged ten, dark color, 4 feet 4 inches high, well made and sprightly. [Value $500]
4. Ellick Allen, aged five, dark color, 3 feet 4 inches high, lively and healthy. [Value $300]
5. Spencer Allen, aged four, dark color, 3 feet 6 inches high, smart and healthy. [Value $300]
6. Mary E. Allen, aged 16 months, dark color, 2 feet 6 inches high, healthy. [Value $200]
7. Charles Brown is bound for a term of years.

Colonel Johnson was purchased from F[rederick] A. Tschiffely and payment was completed by Jan. 1, 1859. Emily and her son, George, were purchased from Sarah Ross of Prince George's County, Md., for $800 on Sept. 2, 1856. A copy of that bill of sale gives Swort's name as "Bernard T. Swart" of Fauquier County, Va., and states that Ross had purchased the slaves from George W. Massey. Although Sarah Ross's name is the seller who is listed in the bill of sale, Swort in his petition says that his purchase of Emily and George Allen was from Sarah and Mary Ross.

[Commissioners paid Barret [sic] T. Swort, by his attorney Joseph Bryan, $1,095: Colonel Johnson, $175.20; Emily Allen, $438; George Allen, $219; Ellick Allen, $131.40; Spencer Allen, $87.60; Mary E. Allen, $43.80. Charles Brown, not allowed.]

No. 475, Petition of James L. Brawner   Filed May 27, 1862

James L. Brawner claims compensation for Mary Washington, aged about 30, copper colored, 5 feet 6 inches tall. She is an excellent domestic servant, a good cook, washer and ironer. He acquired title by marriage with A[manda] E.D. Alexander, who had acquired her title under the will of Catharine F. Alexander, probated Mar. 6 (?), 1855, in Alexandria County, Va. [Value $900]

[Commissioners paid Brawner $306.60.]

Amanda Alexander and James L. Brawner were married Sept. 27, 1836. See Pippenger, D.C. Marriage Licenses, 1811-1858, p.5.

No. 476, Petition of Catharine Golden   Filed May 27, 1862

Catherine Golden of Washington claims compensation for Mahilda Price, aged about 19, black, about 5 feet 6 inches tall, bushy hair, good-looking and lively. She is a first-rate house servant, cook, washer, waiter and ironer. She was hired out at the time of passage of the D.C. emancipation act for $ (?) a month to a friend, but she might have easily brought in $8 a month. [Value $1,000]

Golden received title from the distribution of the estate of her late husband, William P. Golden, of Charles County, Md., on Mar. 20, 1855.

[Commissioners paid Catharine Golden, by F. Golden, attorney, $306.60.]

No. 477, Petition of Catharine A. Golden   Filed May 27, 1862

Catherine A. Golden of Washington claims compensation for Austin Price, aged about 22. He is copper colored, six feet tall, wooly hair, straight, erect and active. He is a first-rate farm and field hand. Prior to Apr. 16th she hired him in Maryland for $70 a year, with his employer providing food, clothing and additional support.

She acquired Price under the distribution of the estate of her father, the late William P. Golden of Charles County, Md., on Mar. 20, 1855. [Value $1,400]

[Commissioners paid Golden, by F. Golden, attorney, $591.30.]

No. 478, Petition of George W. Riggs   Filed May 27, 1862

George W. Riggs of Washington claims compensation for two persons.

1. Anthony Bell, aged about 43, black, thin and rather tall. He stoops. He was a house servant, but now saws wood and works as a whitewasher. He is a honest and faithful servant, but because of attacks of asthma is not able to earn as much in wages as he otherwise would. [Value $500]

2. Mary Belt, aged about 25, black, of ordinary size with a pleasant expression. She is a house maid and a good servant in every respect. [Value $1,000]

Anthony was purchased about 12 years ago from the estate of Samuel H. Lofflin [or "Laughlin"]. Mary was bought with her mother in 1842 from John E. and Rebecca Dement of Maryland and was brought up in Riggs's house. He estimates that he paid about $100 for her.

Riggs states that if possible he wants any money from his claim to Anthony to be paid to Anthony.

[Commmissioners paid Riggs $788.40: Anthony Bell, $306.60; Mary Bell, $481.80.]

No. 479, Petition of William Marshall   Filed May 27, 1862

William Marshall of the city of Washington claims compensation for Mary Boyd, aged 11 years and nine months. She is a bright mulatto, 4 feet 8 inches tall, healthy. She is a fine nurse and chamber girl. She is held to service of eight years and three months. He purchased her when she was seven months old from the estate of Zachariah Hazle for $100.

[Commissioners paid Marshall $109.50.]

Zachariah Hazel's will may be found in Pippenger, D.C. Probate Records, 1801-1852, pp.354-355. Its terms provided that "negro girl Mary to serve her [Harriet Ann Hazel] until Mary attains age of 20 yrs. then free." The family name is spelled both "Hazel" and "Hazle" in various documents.

No. 480, Petition of William H. Moore   Filed May 27, 1862

William H. Moore of Washington claims compensation for two persons.
1. Winny Dines, aged about 60, dark complexion, healthy. [Value $400]
2. George Dines, aged 32, dark complexion. "He would be worth much more than $800 were he not in the habit of drinking spirituous liquor." [Value $800]

Moore's title is based on the will of his late mother, Verlinda Smith, dated Nov. 27, 1861.
[Commissioners paid Moore $700.80: "Winney" Dines, $175.20; George Dynes [*sic*], $525.60.]

No. 481, Petition of William B. Evans   Filed May 27, 1862

William B. Evans of Washington City claims compensation for Lewis, aged 15 years. He is about 5 feet 3 inches tall, has a black complexion with dark eyes and is stout and well-built. [Value $500]

He purchased Lewis Simms for $300 from John W. Pumphrey of Washington. (Bill of sale signed Mar. 4, 1862)
[Commissioners paid Evans $438]

The petition does not give Lewis's surname, but the bill of sale gives it as "Simms".

No. 482, Petition of William B. Kibbey, assignee of John Hoover   Filed May 27, 1862

John Hoover of Washington City (for the use of William B. Kibbey), claims compensation for seven persons.
1. Ben Taylor, aged 22, dark complexion, stout and strong. [Value $1,500]
2. John Taylor, aged 18, dark complexion, stout and strong. [Value $1,500]
3. Sam Reynolds, aged 52, yellow complexion, stout and strong. [Value $1,500]
4. Nancy, aged 19, yellow complexion, stout and healthy. [Value $1,000]
5. Bill, son of Nancy, aged four, yellow complexion. [Value $400]
6. Susan, daughter of Nancy, one and one-half years old. Black complexion. [Value $200]
7. Charley, aged 56, black, stout and strong. [Value $500]

Hoover purchased Ben Taylor and John Taylor from the estate of Robert Bowie of Prince George's County, Md. He purchased Sam Reynolds from John Young of Washington. He purchased Nancy from Mrs. Cross of Prince George's County. Susan and Bill were born after that purchase. He purchased Charley from John Brenton of Washington.

Hoover assigned to William B. Kibbey any payment he may receive from the commissioners.
[Commissioners paid Kibbey $2,036.70: Ben Taylor, $591.30; John Taylor, $569.40; Sam Reynolds, $262.80; Nancy, $438; Bill, $131.40; Susan, $43.80; Charles, no value.]

No. 483, Petition of Francis P. Blair   Filed May 27, 1862

Francis P. Blair of Silver Spring, Md., claims compensation for two persons.
1. Sarah Solomon, aged 13, dark brown complexion, healthy and intelligent.
2. Mary Simmes, aged eight, dark brown complexion, healthy and intelligent.
The value of the two is $600.

Sarah's mother was derived by Blair's son [Montgomery Blair] by his marriage with Caroline Buckner, whose father, Avis Buckner, gave her to him as part of the marriage portion. Montgomery [Blair] sells his rights [to Francis P. (?)]. Mary Simmes is the grandchild of Mary and was born while in Francis P.'s possession. *This section is very difficult to read and the transaction between father and son is not clear.*

[Commissioners awarded F.P. Blair, $525.60: Sarah Solomons [*sic*], $306.60; Mary Simms, $219. Of this $525.60, the amount of $50 was retained by the Treasury as paid on Sarah, leaving claimant the sum of $475.60.]

Francis Preston Blair (1791-1876) and his son Montgomery (1813-1883) were associated with antislavery politics and were major forces in the Republican Party. Indeed, Montgomery was Lincoln's Postmaster General.

No. 484, Petition of Alexander Elliott, Jr. Filed May 27, 1862

Alexander Elliot, Jr., of Washington claims compensation for Mary Beall, aged about 27 or 28 years. She is dark brown, mainly black, about 5 feet 1 or 2 inches high, quick spoken and intelligent. She is a first-class cook and house servant and, except for a slight enlargement of her left lower jaw produced by "quincy" or a similar affliction, is in good health. [Value $1,200]

She was bought by Elliott's wife, Mary L. Elliott, for $5 from her father, Selby B. Scaggs, on Mar. 1, 1862.
[Commissioners paid Elliott $350.40.]

No. 485, Petition of Louisa M. Wright Filed May 27, 1862

Louisa M. Wright of Washington claims compensation for four persons.

1. Polly Nelson, aged 50, brown complexion, black hair and eyes, 5 feet 6 inches tall. She is a good house servant, excellent cook, and good laundress and nurse. [Value $800]

2. Minnie Ann Nelson, aged between 18 and 19, brown complexion with black hair and eyes and 5 feet 4 inches high. She is a good house servant, tolerable cook, good dining room servant, laundress and nurse. [Value $1,000]

3. Nora Nelson is aged 15, brown complexion, black hair and eyes and 5 feet 3 inches high. She is a good house servant, seamstress and nurse. [Value $800]

4. Fanny Nelson, aged ten, brown complexion, black hair and eyes, about four feet tall. She is a good errand girl and good for waiting in the house. [Value $400]

Wright got title in the division in 1853 or 1854 of the estate of her father, Samuel R. Bradford, of Culpeper County, Va.

[Commissioners paid Wright $1,357.80: Polly Nelson, $153.30; Minnie Ann Nelson, $503.70; Nora Nelson, $481.80; Fanny Nelson, $219.]

No. 486, Petition of John Van Riswick Filed May 27, 1862

John Van Riswick of Washington City claims compensation for three persons.

1. George Barton, aged 48, mulatto, low in statue. He had his leg broken about ten or 12 years ago, but has not been much effected by it. [Value $300]

2. Harriet Clarke, aged 55, mulatto, large and fleshy. [Value $400]

3. Phoebe Ross, aged 14, mulatto, small in size. [Value $1,200]

Van Riswick inherited George Barton from his father. He purchased Harriet Clarke from Joseph Holliday about 12 years ago and he purchased Phoebe Ross from Wilfred A. Manning about six years ago.

[Commissioners paid Van Riswick $525.60: George Barton, $131.40; Harriet Clarke, $87.60; Phoebe Ross, $306.60.]

No. 487, Petition of Philip Fenwick Filed May 27, 1862

Philip Fenwick of Washington County, D.C., claims compensation for seven persons.

1. John Toogood, aged 32, black, of low statue. [Value $1,500]
2. Margaret Dorsey, aged 22, dark mulatto. [Value $1,200]
3. Louisa Thomas, aged 20, black., Value $1,500]
4. Henry Warren, aged 19, black. [Value $1,500]
5. Lewis Johnson, aged 17, black [Value $1,500]
6. Joseph Johnson, aged 15, black. [Value $1,500]
7. Lewis H. Didney, aged 20 months, dark mulatto. [Value $200]

John Toogood he purchased more than 20 years ago. All the rest have been purchased (?) by him or are the offspring of old servants.

[Commissioners paid Fenwick, by J. Van Riswick, his attorney, $3,197.40: John Toogood, $525.60; Margaret Dorsey, 459.90; Louisa Thomas, $525.60; Henry Warren, $569.40; Lewis Johnson, $525.60; Joseph Johnson, $525.60; Lewis H. Didney, $65.70.]

No. 488, Petition of Silas L. Loomis

This petition is missing.
[Commissioners paid Loomis $153.30 for Abraham Dent.]

No. 489, Petition of Alonza R. Fowler Filed May 27, 1862

Alonza R. Fowler of the city of Washington claims compensation for Lucy Washington, aged about 11 years. She has a black complexion, is about 4 feet 2 inches high, quite stout and strong. She is likely and intelligent. She is very useful as a chambermaid, nurse or housekeeper. Fowler got title from his wife, Hannah E. Fowler, the daughter of John Brady, who died about six or seven years ago and bequeathed Washington to his daughter. [Value $500]

[Commissioners paid Fowler, by his attorney A. Lloyd, $153.30.]

No. 490, Petition of Adelaide Wilson   Filed May 27, 1862

Adelaide Wilson of Washington claims compensation for two persons.

1. Charles Ferguson, aged 35, black, 5 feet 7 or 8 inches tall. He is working in the anchor shop at the Navy Yard for $1.50 a day. [Value $1,500]

2. Harriet Thomas, aged 16, black, 4 feet 5 inches tall. She is a house servant. [Value $500]

Charles Ferguson was willed to Wilson by her late husband, John H.A. Wilson, and the will was recorded in D.C. in 1858. Harriet Thomas was a gift about 12 years ago from Rezin Arnold, who purchased her mother, Susan Thomas, from Washington Young about 18 years ago.

[Commissioners paid Wilson $963.60: Charles Ferguson, $525.60; Harriet Thomas, $438.]

No. 491, Petition of Mary C. Dean   Filed May 27. 1862

Mary C. Dean of Washington County, D.C., claims compensation for six persons.

1. Robert Stewart is aged 45, very dark in color and 5 feet 9 inches high. He is a superior field hand and market man. [Value $1,000]

2. John Ambush is about 58, dark chestnut colored and 5 feet 10 inches tall. He is a good field hand and rough carpenter. [Value $250]

3. Albert Clark is aged 19, light yellow in color, 6 feet 1 or 2 inches tall. He is a superior field hand. [Value $1,600]

4. Jenny Johnson is aged 17, dark brown, 5 feet 4 inches tall. She is a good house woman. [Value $1,200]

5. Caroline Diggs is aged 44, light brown and 5 feet 6 inches tall. She is a superior cook, washer and ironer. [Value $900]

6. Philip Diggs, son of Caroline, is aged 15, light yellow in color and 5 feet 5 inches tall. He is a good waiter and house servant. [Value $1,200]

Dean says that she acquired four of the persons by inheritance from her father, Levi Sheriff, of Washington County, about seven years ago. She purchased two from J. Bruen of Alexandria, four or five years ago.

[Commissioners paid Dean $2,124.30: Robert Stewart, $262.80; John Ambush, $175.20; Albert Clarke, $613.20; Jenny Johnson, $438; Caroline Diggs, $153.30; Philip Diggs, $481.80.]

No. 492, Petition of William A. Linton   Filed May 27, 1862

William A. Linton claims compensation for two persons.

1. Fanny Stuart is aged about 40, dark copper colored and robust and healthy. She is a valuable servant and superior cook and has served him in that capacity for many years and, indeed, is still serving as his cook.

2. Robinson Crusoe Stuart, Fanny's son, is about 12. He is smart and active and a good house and dining room servant.

He values the two at $1,800. He purchased Fanny from his own son, John A. Linton, and paid something under $400 for her. Robinson was born after the purchase.

A document signed by Linton and dated Aug. 15, 1862, assigned his award for the two slaves to George William Philips of Boston, Mass.

[Commissioners paid George William Phillips, assignee of W.A. Linton, by Thomas Blagden, attorney, $525.60: Fanny Stewart [sic], $219; Robinson C. Stewart [sic] $306.60.]

No. 493, Petition of Israel Knode   Filed May 27, 1862

Israel Knode of the District of Columbia claims compensation for Rachel, aged 42. She has a black complexion, is about 5 feet 8 inches tall, is rather stout and has a front tooth out. She is an excellent cook and house servant. She was purchased from P.N. Leapley on Mar. 26, 1861. [Value $600]

[Commissioners paid Knode $87.60.]

No. 494, Petition of Pierce Shoemaker   Filed May 28, 1862

Pierce Shoemaker of Washington County, D.C., claims compensation for 20 persons.
1. George Dover, aged 45, mulatto. [Value $1,200]
2. Benjamin Lyles, aged 44, black, a mechanic. [Value $2,500]
3. Joseph Simms, mulatto aged 27. [Value $1,800]
4. Rachael Lyles, dark mulatto, aged 43 years. [Value $800]
5. Elizabeth Lyles, aged 26, dark. [Value $1,000]
6. Matilda Lyles, aged 24, dark. [Value $1,000]
7. Albert Lyles, aged two, dark. [Value $400]
8. Catharine Lyles, aged 22, dark [Value $1,100]
9. Leander Lyles, aged 18, dark. [Value $1,600]
10. Rebecca Lyles, aged 12, mulatto. [Value $800]
11. Osceola Lyles, aged nine, dark. [Value $800]
12. Mary Ann Foster, aged 36, dark [Value $1,000]
13. Margaret Foster, aged 18, mulatto. [Value $1,100]
14. Tobias Foster, aged 15, mulatto. [Value $1,000]
15. Benjamin Foster, aged 12, mulatto. [Value $1,000]
16. Annie Foster, aged eight, dark. [Value $800]
17. Cornelius Foster, aged six, dark. [Value $700]
18. Catharine Foster, aged four, dark. [Value $600]
19. Eugene Foster, aged three, mulatto. [Value $400]
20. Emma Lyles, aged three, mulatto. [Value $400]

He acquired them under the will of Abner Pierce and they were conveyed to him by his executor, Thomas Carbery. They are all in good health and are free of defects.

[Commissioners paid Peirce [sic] Shoemaker $5,803.50: George Dover, $284.70; Benjamin Lyles, $438; Joseph Simms, $394.20; Rachel Lyles, $219; Elizabeth Lyles, $438; Matilda Lyles, $481.80; Albert Lyles, $43.80; Catharine Lyles, $438; Leander Lyles, $569.40; Rebecca Lyles, $262.80; Osceola Lyles, $219; Mary Ann Foster, $284.70; Margaret Foster, $481.80; Tobias Foster, $328.50; Benjamin Foster, $284.70; Annie Foster, $197.10; Cornelius Foster, $153.30; Catharine Foster, $131.40; Eugine [sic] Foster, $65.70; Emma Lyles, $87.60.]

No. 495, Petition of Samuel Whitaker — Filed May 28, 1862

Samuel Whitaker of Harford County, Md., claims compensation for Charlotte Gover, aged 48. She is dark, nearly black, 5 feet 3 inches tall, stout with regular features. She is employed by Mrs. L. Russell at 495 7th St. She is an excellent cook, washer and ironer. She is the daughter of his slave Fanny who has since died. [Value $250]

[Commissioners disallowed the claim as Gover was not produced.]

No. 496, Petition of Isabella L. Turpin — Filed May 28, 1862

Isabella L. Turpin of Washington City claims compensation for Maria Watson, aged 35. Watson is a dark mulatto and 5 feet 2 inches tall. Maria "is very slightly Idiotic," but is a valuable house servant, nurse and is fond of the care of children. [Value $500]

Turpin acquired her in 1859 from the estate of Jane E. Swann of Alexandria, Va., as a gift.

[Commissioners paid Turpin $197.10.]

No. 497, Petition of Jane S. Burruss — Filed May 28, 1862

Jane S. Burruss of Washington City claims compensation for Charlotte Marshall, aged 55 years. She is mulatto, 5 feet 2 inches tall and is very marked with smallpox. She is an excellent cook, washer and ironer. Burruss acquired her as a gift from her brother, James Sutton, in 1827. [Value $500]

[Commissioners paid Burruss $87.60.]

No. 498, Petition of Andrew Hancock — Filed May 28, 1862

Andrew Hancock of Washington D.C., claims compensation for Ellen Johnson, aged 54 years. She is of a dark copper color and 5 feet 3 ½ inches tall. She was purchased for $300 on Dec. 27, 1856, from James Spinks. Johnson was a good house servant and was healthy, except she suffered occasionally from attacks of dyspepsia. [Value $200]

[Commissioners disallowed this claim as Johnson was not produced.]

No. 499, Petition of Benjamin F. Middleton Filed May 28, 1862

Benjamin F. Middleton of Washington claims compensation for three persons.
1. James Prather, aged 35, copper colored, 5 feet 10 or 11 inches high. [Value $1,100]
2. Moses Powell, aged 40, mulatto, 5 feet 5 inches high. [Value $1,000]
3. Amos Hoskins, aged 23, copper color, 5 feet 5 or 6 inches tall. [Value $1,000]

He acquired James and Moses by purchase from Benjamin Beall. Amos was born of a woman who was owned by Middleton.

[Commissioners paid Middleton, per Alpheus Middleton, his attorney, $1,511.10: James Prather, $547.50; Moses Powell, $438; Amos Hoskins, $525.60.]

No. 500, Petition of William Hamilton Williams Filed May 28, 1862

William Hamilton Williams of Charles County, Md., claims compensation for Fannie Smallwood, aged 21 years. She has a black complexion, is about 5 feet 8 inches tall, with a large build. She has one front tooth missing. She is a good cook, washer and ironer and general house servant. He acquired her by a deed of gift from Charles S. Williams, his father, who owned her from her birth. [Value $1,200]

[Commissioners paid Williams $481.80.]

No. 501, Petition of William Nottingham Filed May 28, 1862

William Nottingham of Washington claims compensation for two persons.
1. Cagy Ware, aged 50, mulatto. She is a good cook and house servant. [Value $400]
2. Charles H. Green, aged 15, copper color. He has lost his left forefinger which has been cut off at the joint. He was bound by his father to service until he reached age 21. [Value $300]

He purchased Ware from Luther L. Leland of Charles County, Md., for $225 on Oct. 20, 1858. The copy of the apprenticeship indenture that is attached shows that Charles H., at the age of 12 years and ten months, with the consent of his father, Henry Green, bound himself as an apprentice to Nottingham to learn the trade of carpenter. He was to be released on Sept. 16, 1867, when he reached age 21. (Signed July 15, 1859; Charles his x mark Green; Henry his x mark Green).

[Commissioners paid $87.60 for Ware. The claim for Green was not allowed.]

Apprentices are not slaves. Presumably Green remained an apprentice to Nottingham.

No. 502, Petition of Francis J. Fugitt Filed May 28, 1862

Francis J. Fugitt of Washington claims compensation for John Mitchell aged 18. He is of a dark color, very active and healthy. He is an excellent house servant and has been hired to great advantage in the summer season in the brick yard. Fugitt purchased him from Ignatius Millstead. [Value $1,000]

[Commissioners paid Fugitt $569.40.]

No. 503, Petition of Oliver H.P. Clark Filed May 28, 1862

Oliver H.P. Clark of Montgomery County, Md., claims compensation for Richard Proctor, aged 37. He is of a dark copper color, about 5 feet 11 inches tall, weighs about 180 pounds and has large whiskers. He has a smiling pleasant countenance and, except for prominent knuckles, has no marks or scars. He is a valuable farm hand and a good gardener and a skillful driver of a team. Clark has been getting $150 a year hiring out Proctor. He acquired title by purchase from Agnes Clark and Charles H. Clark in the division of the estate of Henson Clark. The attached copy of the bill of sale, dated Montgomery County, May 10, 1855, states that Oliver Clark paid $1,200 for certain personal property, of which Proctor was worth about $800. [Value $1,000]

[Commissioners paid Oliver H.P. "Clarke" $569.40.]

No. 504, Petition of Joseph W. Webb Filed May 28, 1862

Joseph W. Webb of Washington City claims compensation for William Harrod, aged 35. He has a dark brown complexion, is stout, about 5 feet 6 inches tall and medium sized. He is an excellent coachman and house servant. Harrod is held for a term of three years nine months dating from Jul. 23, 1860, and was worth $25 by the month. He purchased him for a term of time from Jane Trumbull of Washington and Mrs. Sophia Krumbhaar of Philadelphia to whom he belonged. The attached bill of sale shows that Webb paid $400 for Harrod's service for a term of three years and nine months, after which he was to be manumitted.

[Commissioners paid Webb $54.75.]

No. 505, Petition of Joseph W. Webb, guardian of Sarah G. Anderson   Filed May 28, 1862

Sarah G. Anderson, through her guardian, Joseph W. Webb, claims compensation for five persons.
1. Jeannette, aged 34, light mulatto. She is a good cook, washerwoman and general house servant. [Value $800]
2. Charles, aged 12, dark brown. He is a bright boy and a good servant. [Value $900]
3. Mary Jane, aged nine, very light mulatto. [Value $500]
4. Betty, aged four, very light mulatto. [Value $400]
5. Becky, aged two, very light mulatto. [Value $400]

The three female children are of a "tender age" but are bright. Anderson acquired them as a gift from her paternal grandmother.

[Commissioners paid Webb, guardian for Anderson, $635.10: Jeannette, $284.70; Mary Jane, $175.20; Charles, no value; Betty, $109.50; "Beckie", $65.70.]

No. 506, Petition of Jane C. Penn   Filed May 28, 1862

Jane C. Penn of Prince George's County, Md., claims compensation for two persons.
1. Elias Lee, aged 21, bright mulatto, 5 feet 6 inches high, intelligent. He is a farmer and coachman. [Value $1,500]
2. Julia Lee, sister of Elias, aged 12, bright mulatto, about five feet high. She is very intelligent and is a house servant. [Value $800]

She acquired the two from the estate of her late father, William Marbury, of Prince George's County and through the will of her late husband, Harrison Penn.

[Commissioners paid Penn, by William J. Miller, her attorney, $1,095: Elias Lee, $657; Julia Lee, $438.]

No. 507, Petition of Edward Hall   Filed May 28, 1862

Edward Hall of Washington City claims compensation for two persons.
1. Lloyd Jones is aged 30, dark brown, about 5 feet 9 ½ inches tall, medium sized. Jones is very intelligent and has been in the grocery business for the last 11 years. [Value $1,100]
2. William Henry Harrison, about 18, copper color, about 5 feet 7 ½ inches tall, strong build. He is very likely and a fine young man who has been with Hall in the grocery business for the last three years. [Value $1,400]

Hall says he purchased Jones for $675 about 15 years ago from Eliza Duval, his sister, of Prince George's County. He also purchased Harrison from Eliza Duval for $1,000 on Aug. 8, 1859.

[Commissioners paid Hall: $1,160.70: Lloyd Jones, $569.40; William H. Harrison, $591.30.]

No. 508, Petition of Elizabeth Crawford   Filed May 28, 1862

Elizabeth Crawford of the District of Columbia claims compensation for three persons.
1. Jane Lee, aged about 30, light mulatto, about 5 feet and one-half inch tall, quite thin with long curly hair and a pleasant face. She is one of the best servant women to be found, an elegant cook, washerwoman and ironer. She understands the dairy business, is a beautiful seamstress, and can do anything required of her. [Value $1,200]
2. Clinton Lee, about three, copper color, large for his age. He is the son of Jane Lee and is a fine hearty boy. [Value $150]
3. Martha Ann Johnson is aged 16, mulatto, very short and thick set with a long and full suit of hair. She is a fine house servant, nice chambermaid and nurse. [Value $800]

Crawford purchased Jane Lee from William Pinkney Brooke on Dec. 1, 1858. The attached bill of sale states that John H. Sansbury, agent for Elizabeth Crawford, presented a note of the late William Z. Beall for $2,000 which would pay in full for Negroes Jane and her daughter, Charlotte, and Wallace. Clinton Lee was born after that purchase. She purchased Johnson for $500 from D.R. Wall and Sarah J. Wall, his wife, of Prince George's County on Dec. 15, 1860.

[Commissioners paid Elizabeth her x mark Crawford $876: Jane Lee, $262.80; Clinton Lee, $131.40; Martha Johnson, $481.80.]

The fate of Charlotte and Wallace is not known.

No. 509, Petition of Martha T. Hall   Filed May 28, 1862

Martha T. Hall claims compensation for Cecelia Walker, aged about 20. She is of a copper color, about 5 feet 10 inches tall, stout, healthy, and unmarried. She is a good washerwoman and ironer. She is a young woman of "excellent habits" and very likely and finely made. Hall obtained Walker from the estate of her father, the late

Thomas Hall of Prince George's County, Md., who died about 1849.[Value $1,200]
[Commissioners paid Hall $525.60.]

No. 510, Petition of Eliza Duvall Filed May 28, 1862
Eliza Duvall claims compensation for three persons.
1. Amanda Augusta Harris, aged 16, dark brown, about 5 feet 2 inches tall, very stout and healthy. She is a fine chambermaid, house servant and dining room servant. [Value $1,000]
2. Charles Asbury Harris, aged 14, light brown, about four feet high, slim made and not very strong. He is a fine dining room servant and is very handy and useful. [Value $1,000]
3. Cornelius Hunt Harris, aged 12, light brown, four feet tall, stout and strong. He is too young to be useful now, but gives every indication of being a very valuable man. [Value $800]
Duvall says that she purchased Kitty Harris, the mother of the above, about 1832 from Hanson Clarke of Montgomery County, Md. The children were born after that purchase.
[Commissioners paid Duvall $1,051.20: Amanda Harris, $503.70; Charles A. Harris, $284.70; Cornelius H. Harris, $262.80.]

No. 511, Petition of Rinaldo J. Bowen Filed May 28, 1862
Rinaldo J. Bowen of Washington County, D.C., claims compensation for two persons.
1. Charlotte Mathews, aged 35, medium height, black, ordinary size. She has been hired as a house servant and cook at $6 a month. Bowen says that within the last two years he has been offered and refused $900 for such persons. [Value $900]
2. William Mathews, aged two, black, ordinary size. [Value $300]
Bowen gets title through his wife, Jane Bowen. Eleanor Adams's will, recorded Jun. 22, 1847, provided that her two daughters, Catharine Adams and Jane Bowen, have joint possession of Charlotte Mathews. Catharine Adams has since died, so Jane became sole owner.

Eleanor Adams's will may be found in Pippenger, D.C. Probate Records, 1801-1852, p. 311 and 311n.. It provided that Catharine Adams and Jane Bowen, her daughters, were to have equal rights to Negro woman Sucky, and Negro girl Sharlotte. Eleanor died in Georgetown May 1, 1847.

No. 512, Petition of John M. Belt Filed May 28, 1862
John M. Belt of Georgetown claims compensation for two persons.
1. Minty Clark, aged 42, dark complexion, about five feet tall, with a flat nose, high cheek bones. She is rather slow in movement but has a pleasant smile. [Value $800]
2. William Henry Thornton, aged 16, is a bright mulatto who is quick, sprightly and intelligent. He has nearly straight hair, dark eyes, good teeth and is about 4 feet 6 inches tall. He is held to service until age 21. [Value $200]
Belt acquired title from his mother, Mary G. Belt, 18 years ago. Mary G. had inherited her from her father, John McGill. William Thornton was bequeathed to him by the late Mary Ann Miller's will.
[Commissioners paid Belt $262.80: Minty "Clarke", $175.20; William H. Thornton, $87,60.]

No. 513, Petition of Thomas Pursell and Mary Ann Pursell Filed May 28, 1862
Thomas Pursell and Mary Ann Pursell of Washington City claim compensation for Minty Cross, aged about 53. She is black, 5 feet 6 or 7 inches tall, medium size, stout and healthy. Cross was purchased by Mary Ann Pursell on Apr. 8, 1857, for $225 from George F. Richards of Prince George's County, Md. [Value $500]
[Commissioners paid Thomas and Mary Ann Pursell $131.40.]

No. 514, Petition of Margaret A. Wood Filed May 28, 1862
Margaret A. Wood of the city of Washington claims compensation for five slaves.
1. Henrietta, aged about 57, mulatto, about 5 feet 4 inches tall. She is an excellent cook, washer, ironer and house keeper.
2. Susan, daughter of Henrietta, aged about 18, mulatto, about 5 feet 5 inches tall. She is a chambermaid, nurse and house servant.
3. Isabella, daughter of Susan, aged about 20 months, mulatto.
4. Fanny, daughter of Henrietta, mulatto, about 5 feet 4 inches tall. She is a chambermaid, nurse and house servant.

5. Infant son of Fanny, aged about four weeks, mulatto.

The value for them is estimated to be $2,600. She purchased Fanny from Anna Rolles of St. Augustine, Fla., for $900 on Jun. 8, 1857. She purchased Henrietta and her child, Susan, for $600 from Ann Rogers of St. Augustine, Fla., Jun. 18, 1851. In the two bills of sale attached, Wood is described as being of St. Augustine. She states that she registered the three eldest with the D.C. Circuit Court in the fall of 1858.

[Commissioners grant Wood $1,095: Henrietta, $109.50; Susan, $481.80; Isabella, $43.80; Fanny, $59.90; infant son, not allowed.]

No. 515, Petition of Christopher Grammer, executor of Gottlieb C. Grammer   Filed May 28, 1862

Christopher Grammer of Washington, executor of Gottlieb C. Grammar of the same place, who died Jan. 14, 1857, claims compensation for Lucretia Leonard, aged 58, mulatto, nearly 5 feet 1 inch tall. She has freckles and a wart or mole under her right eye and is "sedate, respectful & civil." She is a good cook and an experienced nurse and for the last two years has been hired out at wages of from $6 to $8 a month. [Value $400]

She was purchased by Gottlieb in 1839 from the estate of the late Joseph Kent, former governor of Maryland and U.S. Senator. Gottlieb Grammer's will appointed Christoper Grammer and his brother, Julius E. Grammer, now living in Columbia, Ohio, his executors.

[Commissioners paid Grammer $131.40.]

No. 516, Petition of Henderson Fowler   Filed May 28, 1862

Henderson Fowler, of 3rd St., east, between L & M St., south, claims compensation for two slaves.

1. Rosetta Davis, aged 39, dark color, about 5 feet 3 inches high, ordinary size. She is a good cook, washer, nurse and family servant. [Value $600]

2. Harriet Davis, aged four, daughter of Rosetta, of a dark color. She is a "fine fat and healthy child" and quite useful. [Value $300]

He purchased Rosetta from a trader named [John C.]Thompson about 12 [sic] years ago and paid $625 for her. Harriet was born since that purchase. The attached receipt for the purchase is dated May 9, 1853, and signed John C. Thompson.

[Commissioners paid Fowler $416.10: Rosetta Davis, $328.50; Harriet Davis, $87.60.]

No. 517, Petition of Rachel Harrison   Filed May 28, 1862

Rachel Harrison claims compensation for three persons.

1. Edward Welsh, aged about 45, dark color, about 5 feet 8 inches high, robust. He is a waiter at a public restaurant and makes $20 a month. [Value $500]

2. Mary Ellen Bowman, aged 25, about 5 feet 6 inches tall, dark color, of a delicate frame. She has been accustomed to wait on Harrison and would earn $7 a month. [Value $500]

3. Stanislaus Bowman, aged 25, dark color, about 5 feet 10 or 11 inches high, very stout and athletic. He is a first-rate waiter. She has hired him at $16 a month. [Value $1,200]

Edward Welsh and Mary Ellen Bowman were acquired from her father's estate. Stanislaus Bowman was born after the death of her father and was thus her property by birth.

[Commissioners paid Harrison, by Walter Helen, her attorney, $1073.10: Edward Welsh, $306.60; Mary Ellen Bowman, $197.10; Stanislaus Bowman, $569.40.]

Rachel Harrison is the sister-in-law of Benjamin Harrison of Washington, who died Feb. 23, 1835. His will left all his property to Harrison who was living with him. See Pippenger, D.C. Probate Records, 1801-1852, p.194. Harrison, however, clearly states in this petition that Harrison is her father. In addition, if Mary Ellen were alive at the time of Benjamin Harrison's death, she must be older than 25 years..

No. 518, Petition of Ann Pickrel   Filed May 28, 1862

Ann Pickrel claims compensation for seven persons.

1. Sarah Collins, aged 48, light brown, 5 feet 6 inches tall, with a freckled face. [Value $900]

2. Thomas Dorris, aged 45, light brown, 5 feet 11 inches tall, healthy and active. [Value $1,000]

3. Maria Dorris, aged 40, very light complexion, 5 feet 4 inches tall, slender. She sometimes complains of sickness yet never fails in her duties. [Value $700]

4. Samuel Collins, aged 23, bright brown, 6 feet 2 inches tall, very active and intelligent. [Value $1,000]

5. Amy Collins, aged 20, bright brown, 5 feet 7 inches tall, well-formed and exceedingly polite. [Value $800]

6. Louisa Collins, aged 17, bright brown in color, 5 feet 5 inches tall, healthy and active. [Value $600]

7. Frank Tyler, aged 30, dark brown, 5 feet 8 inches tall, polite and active. [Value $1,000]

These people were born in her family, and likewise their parents for several generations belonged to her ancestors. The one exception is Frank Tyler, who was purchased by Pickrel's husband about 25 years ago from Mrs. Queen, "to prevent his being sold for the Southern Market."

[Commissioners paid Ann "Pickrell" $2,321.40: Sarah Collins, $131.40; Thomas Doris [*sic*], $306.60; Maria Doris [*sic*] $43.80; Samuel Collins, $700.80; Amy Collins, $438; Louisa Collins, $438; Frank Tyler, $262.80.]

No. 519, Petition of Theodore Bailey   Filed May 28, 1862

Theodore Bailey of Washington claims compensation for Maria, aged 22. She has a light complexion, is about 5 feet 3 inches tall, with woolly hair and is missing a part of her front tooth which has broken. She is bound to service until she reaches age 35, and then to be free. She is a first-rate family servant, cooks and washes well. She was bound to serve 12 years, four months and 18 days according to the bill of sale from Lewis Bailey of Fairfax County, Va., dated Apr. 8, 1862, to Theodore Bailey for $220. Lewis Bailey had acquired her for that term on Apr. 8, 1852, for $250 by a bill of sale from Marietta S. Minor of Alexandria County, Va. [Value $220]

[Commissioners paid Bailey $175.20.]

No. 520, Petition of John H.C. Coffin   Filed May 28, 1862

John H.C. Coffin of Newport, R.I., claims compensation for seven persons.

1. Nancy Rustin, aged about 65, black. [Value $100]
2. Louisa Rustin, aged about 30, black. [Value $500]
3. Sarah Ann Rustin, aged about 28, black. [Value $600]
4. Joseph Cornelius Harrison, son of Louisa, aged about 13, black. He is sickly.
5. Infant child of Louisa, aged about one year.
6. Eliza, grandchild of Nancy, aged about 13. [Value $200]
7. Jane Rustin, aged about 40, black. [Value $500]

Coffin says he inherited the above persons from his wife, formerly Louisa Harrison, who got them from her sister, Ann Harrison, late of Charles County, Md. In 1849, with Ann Harrison's death, the slaves were removed from Charles County into Washington and they have resided there in Ward 1 on G St. in the neighborhood of 22nd St. west since that time.

Coffin amended his original petition by a statement dated July 3, 1862. He gave Cornelius's full name of Joseph Cornelius Harrison and added the name of Jane Rustin. He had supposed she was hired out in Maryland, but has since learned that she returned to Washington and was there on Apr. 16th.

[Commissioners granted Coffin, by J.S. Hubbard, his attorney, $1,719.15: Nancy Rustin, $43.80; Louisa Rustin, $394.20; Sarah Ann Rustin, $481.80; Cornelius, $87.60; Infant, $32.85; Eliza, $306.60; Jane Rustin, $372.30.]

No. 521, Petition of Ann Carroll   Filed May 28, 1862

Ann Carroll of Montgomery County, Md., claims compensation for two slaves.

1. Winnean Norton, aged 35, dark coffee colored, 5 feet 3 inches tall, stout and sprightly. She is polite when spoken to.

2. William Rosier, aged seven, quite dark, 4 feet 1 or 2 inches tall, well-built. He stands erect and speaks freely and cheerfully when spoken to.

They are valued at $1,500. Carroll says that they were born her slaves.

[Commissioners paid Josiah Harding, administrator ad collegendum of Ann Carroll, $547.50: Winnean Norton, $372.30; William Rosier, $175.20.]

No. 522, Petition of Josiah Harding   Filed May 28, 1862

Josiah Harding of Montgomery County, Md., claims compensation for Eliza Coquire, aged 34, light coffee colored, stout, 5 feet 3 inches tall, pleasing in address and sprightly in manner. He inherited Coquire from his father, Edward Harding, late of Montgomery County. [Value $1,200]

[Commissioners paid Harding $394.20.]

No. 523, Petition of Edward Owen   Filed May 28, 1862

Edward Owen of Washington, for himself and as trustee for Dr. J. Owen, claims compensation for three persons.

1. Harriet Hawkins, aged 40, mulatto, is the mother of Virginia and Lucinda.
2. Virginia Hawkins, aged 16, is mulatto.
3. Lucinda Hawkins, aged eight, is mulatto.

He values the three at $2,500. He acquired title by marriage with Virginia Barrell, who had inherited them from her father in Virginia about 1854.

[The Commissioners disallowed all three claims. As the stated in their printed report, Owen claimed compensation for himself and as trustee for Dr. J. Owen. A witness testified that he knew the servants to be owned by Dr. J. Owen and that he sold them to Edward Owen. However, Edward Owen admitted he had no title nor trusteeship and the Negroes belonged to Dr. Owen, who lives near Winchester, and who had written Edward Owen that he could do as he pleased with them. Edward Owen has "no shadow of claim" under the law.]

No. 524, Petition of William R. Riley — Filed May 24, [sic] 1862

William R. Riley of the city of Washington claims compensation for three persons.

1. Isaac Bailey, aged 60, black complexion, 5 feet 6 or 7 inches tall, tolerably stout. He is a little stiff in one leg. He is a good working hand. [Value $400]
2. Grace Fortune, aged about 65, black, medium height, rather stout. She is the sister of Isaac. She is a good cook and nurse and very useful at any kind of housework. She is very pious. [Value $300]
3. Adam Brown, aged about 42, black, medium height, stout, strong, likely and intelligent. He is an excellent teamster and commands good wages. [Value $1,000]

Riley inherited them from his father, Thomas R. Riley, who died in January 1846 (?) and whose will is filed in D.C.

[Commissioners paid Riley $284.70: Isaac Bailey, $43.80; Grace Fortune, $21.90; Adam Brown, $219.]

Thomas Robinson Riley, a native of Accomack County, Va., but a resident of Washington for the last 20 years, died Jan. 27, 1846. See Pippenger, D.C. Probate Records, 1801-1852, p. 295 and 295n.

No. 525, Petition of Thomas W. Riley — Filed May 28, 1862

Thomas W. Riley of Washington claims compensation for five persons.

1. Alexander Martin, aged about 60, black, tall and stout. He stoops a little and is "knocked kneed". He is a good working hand and a good hostler and teamster and can command good wages. [Value $400]
2. Rachel Martin, aged about 55, black, tall, is also a little knock-kneed. She is a good cook and housekeeper and can command good wages for her services.[Value $300]
3. Lucy Montgomery, aged about 22, black, medium size, very likely and intelligent. She is a good cook, chambermaid, housekeeper and can command good wages for her services. [Value $1,200]
4. Adelaide [Montgomery] daughter of Lucy, aged about two, black or copper colored, well formed and likely. [Value $300]
5. Sidney [Montgomery], daughter of Lucy, about one year old, black or copper colored, well-formed and likely. [Value $200]

Alexander was purchased from Benjamin McQuay about ten years ago for $100. Rachel was purchased for $100 about ten years ago from Mudd, now deceased. Lucy was purchased from B. (?) T. Hodges of Montgomery County, Md., for $900, about six years ago.

[Commissioners paid Riley $547.50: Alexander Martin, no value; Rachel Martin, no value; Lucy Montgomery, $459.90; Adelaide, $65.70; Sidney, $21.90.]

No. 526, Petition of Harriet White — Filed May 28, 1862

Harriet White of Washington County, D.C., claims compensation for 21 persons.

1. William Mathews, aged 45, bright yellow, about six feet and one-half inch tall. [Value $800]
2. Ary Herbert, aged 43, yellow, about 5 feet 6 inches tall. She has a scar on one of her arms caused by a burn. [Value $500]
3. John Mathews, aged 23, dark yellow, about 5 feet 6 inches tall. He has had the second finger of his right hand cut off. [Value $1,000]
4. Lucinda Mathews, aged 23, dark yellow, about 5 feet 6 inches high. [with her infant, value $1,400]
5. Infant, child of Lucinda, about ten months old, dark yellow color.
6. Edmund Herbert, aged 18, dark yellow, about 5 feet 10 inches tall. [Value $1,000]
7. Matilda Rigney, aged 50, very black, about 5 feet 1 ½ inches tall. [Value $300]

8. Mary Carrol, aged 35, dark complexion, about 5 feet 3 inches high. [Value $800]
9. Thomas Rigney, aged 32, dark color, 5 feet 6 inches tall. [Value $1,000]
10. Hester Rigney, aged 22, dark color, about 5 feet 2 inche high. [Value $1,200]
11. Archibald Rigney, aged 20 (?), dark complexion, about 5 feet 6 inches tall. [Value $1,200]
12. William Rigney, aged 17, dark complexion, about 5 feet 1 inch tall. [Value $1,200]
13. David Rigney, aged 14, dark complexion, about 4 feet 9 inches tall. [Value $1,000]
14. Louis Rigney, aged (?), very black, about 5 feet 3 inches high. [Value $1,200]
15. Georgiana Rigney, aged nine, dark color, about 5 feet 1 inch tall. [Value $1,200]
16. Margaret Carrol, aged 14, dark color, about 4 feet 9 inches high. [Value $1,000]
17. Matilda Carrol, aged 13, black, about 4 feet 6 inches tall. [Value $900]
18. Mary Carrol, Jr., aged nine (?), black color, about 4 feet 1 inch. [Value $600]
19. Charles Henry Rigney, aged 15, mulatto about 4 feet 6 inches tall. [Value $900]
20. Albert Rigney, aged 13 years, mulatto, about 4 feet 5 inches tall. He is bound to serve a period of two years. [Value $100]
21. Cornelius Rigney, aged eight, very black, about 3 feet 8 inches tall. [Value $600]

William Mathews, Tom, Lewis, Archey, Ned, William Rigney and David are field hands and generally labor on White's farm. The rest are good house servants and live in her family. All are slaves for life, except Albert, who is bound for a term.

White inherited them from her late husband, Capt. James White of Washington County, D.C. Matilda, Mary Rigney and Ary and William Mathews were taken by her at their appraised value. The rest were born since that time and in my family.

[Commissioners paid White $6,876.60: William Mathews, $306.60; Ary Herbert, $219; John Mathews, $219; Lucinda Mathews, $481.80; infant, $43.80; Edmund Herbert, $591.30; Matilda Rigney, $43.80; Mary "Carroll", $394.20; Thomas Rigney, $525.60; Hester Rigney, $481.80; Archibald Rigney, $569.40; William Rigney, $394.20; David Rigney, $306.60; "Louisa" [Louis] Rigney, $525.60; Georgeanna Rigney, $481.80; Margaret "Carroll", $350.40; Matilda "Carroll", $262.80; Mary " Carroll", Jr., $197.10; Charles Henry Rigney, $262.80; Albert Rigney, $21.90; Cornelius Rigney, $197.10.]

No. 527, Petition of Mary F.E. Purcell   Filed May 28, 1862

Mary F.E. Purcell of Washington claims compensation for Patsy Wheeler, aged about 29 years. She is copper colored and about 5 feet 6 inches tall. She is a good cook, house servant, washerwoman and ironer. About 18 months ago, Purcell was offered $1,400 for her. She holds title by deed of gift from grandmother, Margaret S. Wagener, late of Prince William County, Va., more than 20 years ago and Patsy was settled upon her by her husband, Hon. William F. Purcell, after their marriage. [Value $1,400]

[Commissioners paid Mary F.E. Purcell, by her husband and attorney, William F. Purcell, $481.80.]

No. 528, Petition of Samuel Byington   Filed May 28, 1862

Samuel Byington of the city of Washington claims compensation for Catharine, aged 32. She is about five feet tall, has a dark brown complexion, with regular features and good bodily proportion. She is a good cook, washer and ironer and housekeeper. She was purchased Oct. 24, 1849, from Ann Smoot of Washington for $500.

[Commissioners paid Byington $394.20.]

No. 529, Petition of William H. Champion   Filed May 28, 1862

William H. Champion of Washington claims compensation for Clara Bradley, aged 15 years. She is dark brown in color, five feet high, with woolly hair, flat nose "and having generally the distinguishing marks of the African." She was raised as a house servant and is intelligent and healthy. Champion holds title through his wife, Elizabeth J. Champion, who inherited Clara from the estate of Violetta Padgett of Prince George's County, Md. [Value $800]

[Commissioners paid Champion, by S.E. Arnold, his attorney, $428.]

No. 530, Petition of Sallie E. Pearce   Filed May 28, 1862

Sallie E. Pearce of Georgetown claims compensation for George Elzey, aged 22, mulatto, 5 feet 9 inches high, with black curly hair and dark eyes. Several years ago, she was offered $1,000 for him. She got Elzey as a gift in 1856 from her mother, now deceased, who owned both the mother and grandmother of Elzey. [Value $1,200]

[Commissioners paid Pearce, by Edmund Pearce, her attorney, $569.40.]

No. 531, Petition of Jeremiah Stevens   **Filed May 28, 1862**

Jeremiah Stevens of Washington claims compensation for Kate Warren, aged 11. She is a dark copper color and, naturally smart as a house servant. She has recently recovered from smallpox. His title comes from the fact that he owned Kate's mother and raised Kate from birth. She was registered as a slave in D.C. about November 1860. [Value $800]

[Commissioners paid Stevens $219.]

No. 532, Petition of James Selden for son, Albert Augustus Selden   **Filed May 28, 1862**

James Selden of Washington D.C. claims compensation for Henrietta Hanson, aged about 22 or 23. She has a dark complexion, is tall and well-formed. Because she is young and likely, she would readily command from $6 to $7 a month. His title comes through Margaret Selden, as trustee for her son, Albert Augustus Selden, a minor. Henrietta was conveyed to her by deed by her sister, Augusta A. Walker, for the benefit of the child. The mother of the Albert has since died and thus he, as the father, is the natural guardian. [Value $1,000]

[Commissioners paid Selden, trustee, $459.90.]

No. 533, Petition of James Selden   **Filed May 28, 1862**

James Selden of Washington claims compensation for Harriet Johnson, aged 55 [*sic*], with a dark complexion. She is short and stout. He only paid a nominal sum for her and he has hired her ever since at $6 a month or $72 per annun. He has refused an offer of $250 for her. He purchased her from Ann Scott of Washington County, D.C., for $75 on Dec. 15, 1860. [Value $500]

[Commissioners paid Selden $65.70.]

Johnson is described as being 55 years old in the bill of sale dated December 1860. She is therefore closer to 57 by May of 1862.

No. 534, Petition of Georgie Mechlin   **Filed May 28, 1862**

Georgie Mechlin of the city of Washington claims compensation for Minnie Haddox, aged about three. She is a very dark mulatto and is the "usual size and appearance of healthy colored children of her age." She acquired title by a gift from her father, A.H. Mechlin, shortly after Minnie was born. [Value $200]

[Commissioners paid Mechlin $87.60.]

No. 535, Petition of Helen L. Stewart   **Filed May 28, 1862**

Helen L. Stewart of Georgetown claims compensation for two persons.

1. Mary Lucy Brown, aged 17, 5 feet 3 ½ inches tall, bright complexion, healthy
2. Fanny Elizabeth Brown, aged 14, about five feet tall, bright complexion, healthy.

They are both valuable servants. The two were born of a slave woman named Louisa Annette Brown, whose mother and grandmother were owned by Stewart's mother. Louisa Annette has recently deceased and her two surviving children, Mary L. and Fanny E., were given to Helen. This was confirmed by the will of Margaret C. Stewart dated Jul. 23, 1853. She values them both at $1,500.

[Commissioners paid Stewart $1,007.40: Mary Lucy Brown, $525.60; Fanny Elizabeth Brown, $481.80.]

No. 536, Petition of Mary Jones   **Filed May 28, 1862**

Mary Jones of Georgetown claims compensation for Lewis Neale, aged 35, a dark mulatto. She got her title under the will of her relation, Mary Hopewell. [Value [$1,200]

[Commissioners paid Mary Jones, by James A. Reily, her attorney, $438.]

Mary Hopewell may be a free Negro. See Provine, D.C. Free Negro Registers, Registration No. 1,000 in which Mary Hopewell is granted a certificate of freedom on Nov. 5, 1831. In Registration No. 1609, recorded Aug. 2, 1838, Negro Mary of Georgetown is granted a certificate of freedom based on Mary Hopewell's will. Mary's age is given as 22. Sybilla Carbery, who is testifying for Mary, says that she lives in Georgetown and was at that time married to a free man named Henry Chamber. Hopewell's will is recorded in Pippenger, D.C. Probate Records, 1801-1852, p. 224. "My negro woman slave, now in St. Mary's Co., Md., and my negro woman Mary, now in George Town, D.C., I hereby manumit and set free at my death; also manumit and set free all the children which both or either of them may have after this time. . . .To my negro woman Mary, now in George Town with me, all my personal property other than the slaves aforesaid. (23 Oct 1837; 16 Jul 1838) The Mary Jones listed in the 1860 Census for Georgetown (Vol. 1, p. 170) as a free mulatto woman, aged 35, born in Maryland, may be the daughter of the Mary freed by Hopewell. She has living with her three children aged six, four, and six months. The same census for the Georgetown section of D.C. (Vol. 1, p. 184), lists: Louis Neal, aged 31, mulatto, laborer; Fannie Neal, aged 36, mulatto, born D.C., and three children aged three, two and 11 months.

No. 537, Petition of John W. Mankin   Filed May 28, 1862

John W. Mankin of Georgetown claims compensation for Emma Rebecca Netter. She is about five years and five months old, dark copper colored and 3 feet 5 inches tall. She is handsome and intelligent, but has a slight curve in the bones below the knees. This does not, however, affect her activity. On May 25, 1855, E.B. Mills of D.C., for $50, sold to Mankin a Negro woman named Ellen Netter, the mother of Emma, as a slave to serve three years from May 7, 1855. Emma was born on Nov. 25, 1856, before her mother's term had ended and thus Emma was a slave for life. [Value $300]

[Commissioners paid Mankin $153.30.]

No. 538, Petition of Robert L. McPherson   Filed May 28, 1862

Robert L. McPherson of Georgetown claims compensation for Dory Slaten, a male, aged about 18 years. He is about 5 feet 6 or 8 inches tall, quite black in color, and strong and healthy. Dory was born in the service of Mr. Marsh (?), who married the daughter of Ariana Lyles near Tennelytown in D.C. Slaten has been in McPherson's service for five years. [Value $1,000]

[Commissioners paid McPherson $569.40 for "Dorey Slatten."]

No. 539, Petition of Sarah B. Adams   Filed May 28, 1862

Sarah B. Adams of Georgetown claims compensation for Joanna Penn, aged 20. She is black in color, about five feet tall, healthy and strong. The little finger on one of her hands is crooked. She is capable of performing all kinds of house work and has an excellent disposition. Adams purchased Penn from the executor of the estate of Benedict J. Sanders of Baltimore on July 9, 1845. The accompanying bill of sale shows that $1,875 was paid for four slaves sold to Sarah B. Adams of Charles County, Md. [Value $1,000]

[Commissioners paid Adams, by R.R. Crawford, attorney, $525.60.]

No. 540, Petition of William L. Hoyle, (William R. Woodward, trustee,   Filed May 28, 1862
and John C. McKelden claim $166.17 of Mary)

William L. Hoyle of Washington claims compensation for three persons.

1. Mary Dyson, aged about 47, mulatto, of medium height, sound and healthy. She is a first-rate cook. [Value $1,000]

2. Margaret Dyson, about 17 years old, dark color, medium height, sound. She is a good house servant and child's nurse. [Value $1,200]

3. Matilda Dyson, aged about ten, dark color, sound and healthy. [Value $800]

Hoyle acquired his title by marriage with Susan A.J. Rollins of Prince George's County, Md., in 1848.

An accompanying document shows that William R. Woodward, trustee and John C. McKeldin laid claim to Mary Dyson based on the fact that Hoyle is indebted to McKelden for $132.94 by virtue of a note dated Jan. 9, 1858, payable in 30 days. On Jan. 27, 1858, Hoyle executed a deed conveying Mary Dyson to Woodward in trust to secure said debt. Woodward and McKelden therefore claim $132.94 and interest with regard to Mary Dyson.

[Commissioners paid Hoyle $722.79; and John C. McKelden for $131.40: Mary Dyson, $131.40; Margaret Dyson, $503.70; Matilda Dyson, $219.]

No. 541, Petition of Baker W. Johnson   Filed May 28, 1862

Baker W. Johnson of Washington City claims compensation for Elias Raymond, aged 17 years. He is about 5 feet 5 or 6 inches tall, coal black, with large eyes and a pleasing countenance. He is quick and active and healthy. Raymond's grandparents who were raised by Johnson's parents, his mother by Baker's father, and Elias by Baker. They have been family servants in his family for four generations. [Value $1,200]

[Commissioners paid Johnson $394.20]

No. 542, Petition of Mary E. Blake   Filed May 29, 1862

Mary E. Blake of Washington claims compensation for two persons.

1. Isabel Tolson, aged 28, bright mulatto. She is a good cook and house servant.

2. Ella Tolson, aged 15 months, bright mulatto, child of Isabel.

The woman Isabel was taxed by the Corporation for $800. Value for both is $1,000.

Mary, with her sister, purchased Isabel's mother about 1822 (?). In 1859, Blake purchased her sister's interest in Isabel, who had been born a slave.

[Commissioners paid Blake $525.60: Isabel Tolson, $481.80; Ella Tolson, $43.80.]

No. 543, Petition of Theodore Sheckels   Filed May 29, 1862

Theodore Sheckels of Washington City claims compensation for Henry Duvall, aged 57 years. He is black, about 5 feet 8 inches tall, well-formed and moderately stout. He is a valuable servant, a good farm hand and cook. He has been employed as a cook by the Government for the last eight months at $20 a month. He is healthy, but at times has slight attacks of rheumatism. Sheckels acquired title from his mother about ten years ago. Duvall had been in his mother's family for at least 40 years previous to that. [Value $400]

[Commissioners paid Sheckels $175.20.]

No. 544, Petition of Richard Southern   Filed May 29, 1862

Richard Southern of Alexandria County, Va., claims compensation for William Henry Speaks, aged 33. He is an able-bodied farm hand and gardener, is jet black, of medium size and has regular features. He has an unexpired term of one year, three months of service to Southern. Southern purchased him from Maj. William D. Nutt of Alexandria County for $464 to serve until he reached age 35, and then to be free. Nutt had purchased Speaks from the estate of Eliza Sommers and it was her will that provided that he be freed. The bill of sale to Southern is dated July 18, 1856, and Speaks was 28 years old as of Sept. 15, 1855. [Value $180]

[Commissioners paid Southern $17.52.]

No. 545, Petition of Mary Hasson, colored   Filed May 29, 1862

Mary Hasson of Washington claims compensation for Henry Hasson, aged 40, of a chestnut color, of medium height, healthy. He is a good carpenter and is steady and industrious. She purchased him from Artemesia Bean, administratrix, and recorded the bill of sale in the clerk's office in City Hall on Apr. 15, 1862.   [Value $600] (Mary her x mark Hasson)

[Commissioners paid Hasson $525.60.]

The 1860 Census for D.C., Ward 7 (Vol. 2, p. 904) contains the following entry for Mary "Haston", aged 40, black, cook on a boat, born in Virginia; William H. Haston, aged 20, laborer, born D.C.; Abel Haston, aged 13, born D.C., John Haston, aged 11, born D.C., and Anna Haston, aged nine, born D.C. Mary Ann "Hason" is registered as free in 1840. She is the daughter of Jane Day, who was born of free parents in Prince William County, Va. Jane's daughter, Mary Ann, aged 20, was born in Alexandria, Va. See Provine, <u>D.C. Free Negro Registers</u>, Registration No. 1818.

No. 546, Petition of Nancy Parker   Filed May 29, 1862

Nancy Parker of Georgetown claims compensation for two persons.

1. Louisa Rhodes, aged 14, bright color, 4 feet 9 inches tall. [Value $600]
2. Jane Rhodes, aged ten, bright color, 4 feet 4 inches tall. [Value $600]

Parker's title comes from the will of William Parker that is recorded in the D.C. Orphans' Court.

[Commissioners paid Parker, by her attorney, R.P. Jackson, $678.90: Louisa Rhodes, $372.30; Jane Rhodes, $306.60.]

No. 547, Petition of Catharine Thompson   Filed May 29, 1862

Catharine Thompson of Alexandria, Va., claims compensation for six persons.

1. Nancy King is aged 36, mulatto, stout and fine looking. She is the mother of William, John, James and Thompson and the grandmother of Lucien. [Value $1,000]
2. William King, aged 19, mulatto, tall and strong. [Value $1,000]
3. John King, aged 15, mulatto, tall and strong. [Value $800]
4. James King, aged 13, mulatto, tall and strong. [Value $600]
5. Thompson King, aged ten, bright mulatto, healthy. [Value $500]
6. Lucien King, aged four, is the grandson of Nancy. [Value $200.

Nancy King's mother was a slave owned by Catharine Thompson's mother, and she became Thompson's property after Thompson's mother died. Nancy's mother died several years ago. Nancy's children were born while she was a slave of Thompson.

[Commissioners paid Thompson, by Andrew Wylie, attorney in fact, $2,671.80: Nancy King, $350.40; William King, $657; John King, $569.40; James King, $525.60; Thompson King, $394.20; Lucien King, $175.20.]

No. 548, Petition of William Tucker   Filed May 29, 1862

William Tucker of Washington claims compensation for Ralph Carter, aged 55 [*sic*]. Carter has a black complexion and is 5 feet 8 inches high. His position is straight, his countenance is dull and his form is proportionate. He was purchased for $150 from Thomas B. Balch of Fauquier County, Va., on Mar. 10, 1852. [Value $150] According to the bill of sale, Ralph Carter was about 54 or 55 years old in 1852.

[Commissioners paid Tucker $131.40.]

No. 549, Petition of John A. Smith   Filed May 29, 1862

John A. Smith of Washington claims compensation for 14 persons.

1. Isaac Mason, aged 60, black, about 5 feet 8 inches tall. He is a valuable farm hand. [Value $500]
2. Charlotte, black, about 5 feet 2 inches tall, 55 years old. She is a good cook, ironer, washer and dairy woman. [Value $500]
3. Henry, child of Charlotte, aged 22, black, over six feet tall. He is a very good farm hand. [Value $1,000]
4. Aldezina, child of Charlotte, aged 13, black. She is a smart, active girl. [Value $500]
5. Frank, son of Betty, aged six, dark chestnut colored. He is smart and active. [Value $400]
6. Mary, child of Betty, aged three, black. She is strong and healthy. [Value $200]
7. Ellen Clark, mulatto, about 42, 5 feet 6 inches tall. She is stout and strong and a good cook, washer and dairy woman. [Value $800]
8. Jane [Clark], child of Ellen, aged 18, mulatto, about 5 feet 1 or 2 inches tall. She is a good house servant and nurse. [Value $800]
9. Leonard is aged 17, dark mulatto and 5 feet 8 inches tall. He is a good farm hand and house servant. [Value $1,000]
10. Caroline, child of Ellen, aged 14, mulatto. She is a healthy house servant. [Value $600]
11. Emily [Clark], child of Ellen, is aged nine and mulatto. She is smart and active. [Value $500]
12. Bill Woodley, black, 20 years old, about 5 feet 7 inches tall. He is a strong farm hand. [Value $1,000]
13. Betty, child of Charlotte, aged 27, chestnut colored, about 5 feet 3 or 4 inches tall. She is a good house servant, nurse and cook. She is slight in figure but strong and healthy. [Value $800]
14. Anthony, child of Charlotte, 21 years old, black, nearly six feet tall. He is a good, strong farm hand. [Value $1,000]

Isaac Mason was purchased from Thomas Peter of Georgetown about 1830. Charlotte was bought from Mr. Duvall of Prince George's County, Md., about 24 years ago. Betty, Henry, Anthony and Aldezina are her children. Frank and Mary are the children of Betty. Ellen Clark was a gift from Smith's sister, the late Mary Smith, to his family 17 years ago. Bill Woodley was bought about six years ago from Mrs. Duvall of Washington County, D.C. He states that Ellen's children have been considered to belong to his children, Rebecca, Samuel and Mary. This petition is also signed by R[ebecca] M. Phenix (?), Samuel P. Smith, and M[ary] C. Smith.

[Commissioners paid Smith $5,146.50: Isaac Mason, $109.50; Charlotte, $109.50; Henry, $657; "Aldezena", $328.50; Frank, $153.30; "Mary or Margaret Drusilla" $65.70; Ellen "Clarke", $175.20; Jane, $547.50; Leonard, $591.30; Caroline, $438; Emily, $262.80; Bill Woodley, $613.20; Betty, $438; Anthony, $657.]

No. 550, Petition of Alfred H. Boucher   Filed May 29, 1862

Alfred H. Boucher of Georgetown claims compensation for Lucien Jones, aged 35, light brown color, about 5 feet 10 inches high, very straight and able-bodied. He purchased Jones from Mrs. Saunders of Georgetown in 1851, but he has mislaid the bill of sale. [Value $1,400]

[Commissioners awarded Boucher $438. Of this amount, only $110 was paid to the claimant and the residue remained in the Treasury.]

No. 551, Petition of James T. Boiseau   Filed May 29, 1862

James T. Boiseau of Washington claims compensation for Maria Shorter, aged 17, black, five feet tall, very stout. She is healthy and honest and a good servant who has been in his family many years. Shorter was willed to Boiseau by his aunt, Mrs. Susan Evans, about three years ago. [Value $1,200]

[Commissioners paid Boiseau $547.50.]

No. 552, Petition of George F. Harbin, Julia A. Harbin, Sarah P. Harbin, and Catharine A. Harbin
Filed May 29, 1862

George F. Harbin, Julia A. Harbin, Catharine A. Harbin and Sarah P. Harbin of Washington claim compensation for Harriet Miles, aged 36. She is a dark copper color, 5 feet 5 inches tall and has very large eyes. She is a good servant who has been in the family 14 years. Miles was inherited from their father, Walter Harbin, about nine years ago. [Value $800]

[Commissioners paid the Harbins, by their attorney, R.F. Boiseau, $219.]

No. 553, Petition of Lois E. Offutt
Filed May 29, 1862

Lois E. Offutt of Montgomery County, Md., claims compensation for Nancy Scott, aged 15 years. She is black, about 4 feet 8 inches tall. She is a good house servant who is presently in the employ of R.W. Burr of Washington, from whom she receives good wages. She received title to Scott under the terms of the will of her mother, Sarah B. Offutt. [Value $500]

[Commissioners paid Offutt, by her attorney, B.B. Burr, $306.60.]

No. 554, Petition of Henry P.C. Wilson
Filed May 29, 1862

Henry P.C. Wilson of Washington City claims compensation for six slaves.

1. Harriet, aged 61, mulatto, about 5 feet 6 inches tall. She is a first-rate cook and can get $8 a month pay. [Value $150]

2. Severn, male, aged 57, black, about 5 feet 5 inches tall. He has had his own time and has earned $1 a day as a wood sawyer. Wilson says he has found him his house, room and fuel for which Severn has paid $2 a week. [Value $400]

3. Comfort, female, aged 59, black, 5 feet 3 inches tall. She is a good washer and ironer and can get $7 a month. [Value $150]

4. Irving, aged 24, black, 5 feet 8 inches tall. He is an excellent house servant and has been hired at $15 a month. [Value $1,300]

5. Cooper, 22, chestnut colored, 5 feet 8 inches tall. He is the twin of Ede. He is an excellent house servant and has been hired at $15 a month. [Value $1,300]

6. Ede, aged 22, chestnut colored, 5 feet 5 inches tall. She is the twin of Cooper. She has been hired at $7 a month as a house servant. [Value $700]

He purchased Harriet about 1835 from Dr. Samuel K. Handy in Princess Anne, Eastern Shore, Md. Severn and Comfort he acquired by marriage. Severn and Harriet are man and wife and the parents of Irving, Cooper and Ede, who were born in Wilson's family.

[Commissioners paid Wilson $1,992.90: Harriet, $65.70; Severn, $175.20; Comfort, $153.30; Irving, $569.40; Cooper, $547.50; Ede, $481.80.]

No. 555, Petition of Matilda Coyle

Matilda Coyle of Washington claims compensation for five slaves.

1. Henny Dant, aged 32, mulatto, 4 feet 11 inches tall. [Value $800]
2. Elizabeth Dant, aged 16, mulatto, 4 feet 9 inches tall. [Value $800]
3. Eliza Dant, aged 28, mulatto, 4 feet 11 inches tall. [Value $800]
4. William Dant, aged eight, mulatto. [Value $500]
5. Rachel Dant, aged six, mulatto. [Value $400]

The first three are valuable house servants and the last two are smart, active children. Coyle states that her title is based on inheritance.

[Commissioners paid Coyle $1,314: Henny Dant, $262.80; Elizabeth Dant, $438; Eliza Dant, $350.40; William Dant, $131.40; Rachel Dant, $131.40.]

No. 556, Petition of Mary C. Krafft
Filed May 29, 1862

Mary C. Krafft of Washington City claims compensation fo James Beander, aged 24. He is dark brown, 5 feet 3 inches tall, with dark eyes and a flat nose. He is employed by Mr. Fassell at the corner of F St. north and 12th St.

west. Her title is based on inheritance from her father. [Value $1,000]

[Commissioners paid Krafft $569.40.]

Boyd's Directory for 1864, p. 106, lists Beander as a hackdriver who boards at 337 12th, west.

No. 557, Petition of Fanny P.T. Bronaugh — Filed May 29, 1862

F.P.T. Bronaugh of Georgetown claims compensation for Maria Montgomery, aged about 65. She is a bright mulatto of average height and is stout. Montgomery is an old family servant and was raised by Bronaugh's grandmother. Maria has lost the use of the third finger on her right hand. She received Montgomery as a gift from her sister, M.M. Bronaugh to Robert Ould, as trustee, dated Mar. 8, 1859. This is recorded in D.C. Liber A.L. No. 170, folios 315-317. [Value $200]

[Commissioners paid Bronaugh $43.80.]

No. 558, Petition of Sophia Ridgely — Filed May 29, 1862

Soiphia Ridgely of Georgetown, administrator of the estate of the late William G. Ridgely, claims compensation for two persons.

1. Hester Gibson is aged 21, black, about five feet tall, strong, well-built and active. [Value $1,000]

2. Eliza Gibson, aged 19, black, about the same height, is healthy, strong and active. [Value $1,000]

They are both carefully trained servants and were assessed by the corporation of Georgetown two years ago at $800 each. She purchased them on July 14, 1848, from Dr. William Plater of Georgetown. They were the children of a woman named Susan [Gibson (?)]. The accompanying bill of sale shows that William G. Ridgely paid $775 to Plater for Negro woman Susan and her four children, William, Hester, Eliza and Thomas.

[Commissioners paid Ridgely, by William G. "Ridgley", attorney, $876; Hester Gibson, $394.20; Eliza Gibson, $481.80.]

No. 559, Petition of Anne M. Hurley — Filed May 29, 1862

Ann [sic] M. Hurley of Washington City claims compensation for Eliza Macoy, aged 18, copper colored, about medium size. She is healthy, but recently took the smallpox and is now nearly recovered. Anne's son, William Hurley, purchased Eliza in Norfolk, Va., when she was about seven years old and took her to Richmond where Anne resided. In 1859 he gave Eliza to Anne and a little over a year ago Anne moved to Washington bringing Eliza with her. Ann describes herself as "a subject of the English crown." [Value $600]

[Commissioners paid Hurley $350.41.]

No. 560, Petition of George M. Moore — Filed May 29, 1862

George M. Moore of Washington County, D.C., claims compensation for two persons.

1. Eliza Clark, aged 30, black, about 5 feet 6 inches tall. She is an excellent cook, washer and ironer and a good house keeper. [Value $700]

2. Margaret Clark, aged seven, black, about four feet high, hale and sound. [Value $400]

Moore inherited them from the late Mrs. Mary Scaggs, the mother of his wife, who died at her home in Prince George's County, Md., about five years ago.

[Commissioners paid Moore $481.80: Eliza "Clarke", $306.60; Margaret "Clarke", $175.20.]

No. 561, Petition of Maria Clark — Filed May 29, 1862

Maria Clark of Montgomery County, Md., claims compensation for Jacob Stephens, aged about 45, dark complexion, about 5 feet 3 or 4 inches tall, rather stout and well-made. He is a competent servant and is now the principal means of support of Clark. Her title comes from settlement of her father's estate, between Baley L. Clark and Mason E. Clark. The property acquired by Maria was conveyed to Hanson Clark in trust for her. All of these people have since died. Clark also includes a deed of manumission dated Apr. 20, 1862, by which Clark frees Stephens upon her death. [Value $600]

[Commissioners paid Clark $306.60.]

No. 562, Petition of Violet A. Abell, executrix of William H. Williams — Filed May 29, 1862

Violet A. Abell, executor of William H. Williams, of Baltimore, claims compensation for five persons.

1. John Brent, aged 24, mulatto, about 5 feet 9 inches tall, healthy. He is an excellent servant and coachman. [Value $1,800]

2. Adam Bell, aged 20, mulatto, about 5 feet 9 inches tall, medium sized, healthy. He is a good blacksmith. [Value $2,000]

3. Joseph Davis, aged 17, dark copper color, about 5 feet 5 inches tall, stout. He is a valuable house servant. [Value $1,400]

4. John Jackson, aged "14 less 6 months", dark color, about 5 feet 2 or 3 inches tall. He is healthy, active and a good house servant. [Value $1,300]

5. Maria Douglass, dark color, aged 40, medium size. She is now pregnant and expects to be confined shortly. She is a good cook. [Value $1,000]

All of the above have been a source of good revenue by their hire. Abell says she was appointed executrix of her late husband, W.H. Williams, by the Orphans' Court of D.C. in April of 1858.

[Commissioners paid "Violette A. Abel" $2,387.10: John Brent, $613.20; Adam Bell, $569.40; Joseph Davis, $547.50; John Jackson, $394.20; Maria "Douglas", $262.80.]

No. 563, Petition of Henry M. Dellinger — Filed May 29, 1862

H. M. Dellinger of Washington claims compensation for Benjamin Belt, aged 23. He is black, rather spare in frame, 5 feet 6 inches tall. He has been hired out as a servant at $15 a month for some time past. He was purchased from the estate of his father, Jacob Dellinger of Maryland, about 1859, by his mother, Sarah Dellinger, and afterwards sold by her to Henry. [Value $1,000]

[Commissioners paid Dellinger $591.30.]

No. 564, Petition of Sarah T. Simpson — Filed May 29, 1862

Sarah T. Simpson of 59 Congress St., Georgetown, claims compensation for Ellen Worthy, aged about 40. Worthy is a bright chestnut color, about 5 feet 6 inches high, well-proportioned and healthy except for a slight tumor in her side. She has extraordinary abilities as a house servant. Worthy was purchased from Thomas Bayne of Washington for $350 on May 20, 1853, by her late husband, Richard Gibson. Worthy is now held under a marriage contract in trust for Simpson by William B. Todd and William H. Ward, trustees. [Value $500]

[Commissioners paid Simpson $284.70.]

Sarah Gibson married James A. Simpson on Jul. 9, 1858. See Pippenger, D.C. Marriage Licenses, 1811-1858, p. 230.

No. 565, Petition of Annie E. Taylor — Filed May 29, 1862

Annie E. Taylor of Georgetown claims compensation for Sally Jones, aged between 15 and 16 years. Jones is black, healthy and about four feet high. She is held to service until she reaches age 28, which will be in June of 1874. Taylor purchased Jones from the estate of her late husband, Vincent J. Taylor, of Georgetown. An accompanying bill of sale shows that George Rhodes, of Loudon County, Va., for $300, sold Sally Jones to Vincent J. Taylor of Georgetown to serve until she reaches age 28. Jones was 12 years old in June, 1858. Any children that Jones had were to be free at age 28. (Signed Feb. 24, 1858.) [Value $800]

[Commissioners paid Taylor, by Joshua T. Taylor, her attorney, $219.]

No. 566, Petition of Elenora Knott — Filed Jun. 2, 1862

Ellenora Knott, late of Georgetown but now of Baltimore, claims compensation for Betsey Wood, aged about 30. She is a dark mulatto, about 4 feet 5 inches tall, healthy and stout. She is a valuable house servant. Knott purchased Wood from George W. Biscoe of Georgetown on Oct. 9, 1858, for $750. She then determined that when she was repaid that purchase price, Wood should be freed. Wood has paid $176. [Value $574]

[Commissioners paid "Elenora" Knott $438.]

No. 567, Petition of Charles S. Middleton — Filed Jun. 2, 1862

Charles S. Middleton of Prince George's County, Md., claims compensation for Sam Noble, aged 35. Noble is a dark copper color, about 5 feet 8 or 9 inches tall and stout. He acquired Charles from the estate of his father, Theodore Middleton, in 1843 in Prince George's County. Middleton has hired Noble in Washington for $240 a year. [Value $1,500]

[Commissioners paid Middleton $262.80.]

No. 568, Petition of Nancy Allnutt — Filed Jun. 2, 1862

Nancy Allnutt of Montgomery County, Md., claims compensation for Aquilla Butler, aged 47. He is a dark copper color, 5 feet 9 inches tall, well-built and healthy. She has hired him in Washington to great advantage. Her title comes from distribution of the estate of her father, John Allnutt, who died Oct. 11, 1836, in Montgomery County. [Value $800]

[Commissioners paid Allnut, by William Bryan, her attorney, $372.30.]

No. 569, Petition of the Sisters of the Visitation of Georgetown, D.C.   Filed Jun. 2, 1862

The Sisters of the Visitation in Georgetown claim compensation for 12 persons.

1. Ignatius Tighlman, aged 40, dark mulatto, 5 feet 2 inches tall. [Value $1,200]
2. Mary Elizabeth Tighlman, wife of Ignatius, aged 41, black, five feet tall. She is intelligent, stout and active. The seven children below are Ignatius's and Mary Elizabeth's children.
3. Mary Tighlman, aged 17, mulatto, 4 feet 8 inches tall, strong and healthy. [Value $700]
4. Charles Tighlman, aged 15, mulatto, 4 feet 6 inches tall, active and healthy. [Value $600]
5. Ignatius Tighlman, Jr., 13, mulatto, 4 feet 5 (?) inches tall, healthy and active. He is now with the Federal army at Yorktown. [Value $450]
6. Jane Tighlman, aged ten, four feet tall, mulatto. [Value $300]
7. Cecilia Tighlman, four years old, mulatto, about three feet high. [Value $200]
8. Josephine Tighlman, aged two, mulatto, healthy. [Value $100]
9. Rosalie Tighlman, six months old, mulatto. [Value $50]
10. Benjamin Mahoney, aged 25, bright mulatto, 5 feet 6 inches tall, strong and healthy. [Value $1800]
11. Thomas Weldon, 28 years old, about 5 feet 4 inches tall, strong and healthy. He understands gardening. [Value $1,200]
12. Joseph Dixon, aged 21, black, about 5 feet 3 inches tall. He is healthy but "rather sulky and has a bad countenance." He ran away after the Battle of Manassas and is now with the Federal army. [Value $1,000]

The Sisters acquired title to the services of Ignatius and Mary Elizabeth Tighlman, Benjamin Mahoney and Thomas Weldon from Notley Young who gave them to his daughter, Sister Mary Ellen, a member of the order, in 1841, with the distribution of Young's estate. Sister Mary Ellen gave them to the Sisters of the Visitation. The children of Ignatius and Mary Elizabeth were born later. Joseph Dixon was a gift from John Neal to his daughter, Margaret (Sister Regina), about 1842, and she gave them to the Sisters. (Signed by Sister Mary Angela Harrison, Superior of the Sisters of the Visitation.)

Attached to the petition is a petition from Ignatius Tighlman stating that on July 7, 1856, he reached agreement with the Sisters that on payment of $500 he, his wife, and five children would be freed. He has paid $298.75. One of the children, John, has died. Tighlman wants the amount he has paid to the Sisters to be paid to him and also the value of the children born since the agreement. The Sisters of the Visitation protested Tighlman's claims for compensation.

[Commissioners paid $4,073.40 to the Sisters of Visitation, of which $298.75 was deducted and withheld as having been paid by Ignatius Tighlman for himself and his family. Thus $3,774.65 was paid the Sisters by their attorney, Richard H. Laskey. Ignatius Tighlman, $438. Mary E. Tighlman, $350.40; Mary, $438; Charles, $416.10; Ignatius, Jr., $306.60; Jane, $219; Cecilia, $131.40; Josephine, $65.70; Rosalie, $21.90; Benjamin Mahoney, $547.50; Thomas Weldon, $613.20; Joseph Dixon, $525.60.]

No. 570, Petition of Lyde Griffith   Filed Jun. 2, 1862

Lyde Griffith of Montgomery County, Md., claims compensation for two persons.

1. Mary Washington, aged 55, of a dark copper color, rather stout and fleshy and healthy. [Value $100]
2. Romulus Washington, aged about 13, dark copper color, about medium size. He is very intelligent, obedient and industrious. [Value $800]

He purchased Mary Washington from George Mearing of Carroll County, Md., on Apr. 11, 1844, for $190. Mearing had purchased Mary for $200 from Abraham Crabster of Frederick County, Md., on Mar. 25, 1842. Griffith says that he purchased Mary at the request of her husband. Romulus is her son born about five years after his purchase.

[Commissioners paid $438 to Griffith: Mary Washington, $131.40; Romulus Washington, $306.60.]

No. 571, Petition of George W. Hopkins and John S. Hopkins,   Filed Jun. 2, 1862
executors and trustees of John Hopkins

The trustees and executors of John Hopkins, deceased, being George W. Hopkin and John S. Hopkins of the District of Columbia, claim compensation for ten persons.

1. Gathy Handy, aged 52, dark copper color. She is a cook. [Value $600]
2. Joe Handy, aged 30, dark copper color. He has a defect in one eye. He is a dray man doing duties for $1 a day. [Value $1,200]
3. Dennis Handy, aged 26, dark copper colored. He performs similar duty, but is a more valuable boy. [Value $1,300]
4. Hannah Handy, aged 22, dark copper colored. She is a seamstress and chambermaid who is hired for $8 a month. [Value $1,300]
5. Rachel Lourge, aged 17, black in color. She is a cook hired at $6 a month. [Value $1,000]
6. Leah Tyler, aged 31, dark copper color. She is a house servant, laundress and cook for whom $7 a month can be obtained. [Value $1,200]
7. Frank Tyler, aged 13, dark copper colored. He is a dining room servant and general workman who would hire for $6 a month. [Value $800]
8. Eliza Tyler, aged 11, dark copper colored. She is a house servant worth $4 a month. [Value $700]
9. Robert Tyler, aged five, dark copper colored. [Value $300]
10. Dennis Ellsworth Tyler is six months old and dark copper colored. [Value $50]

These persons were bequeathed by the will of John Hopkins of the District and were to be held by the petitioners until about May 1, 1864, when the division of them was to have been made. Hopkins's will was admitted to probate on Dec. 4, 1858.

[Commissioners paid $2,912.70 to George and John S. Hopkins, trustees: Gathy Handy, $65.70; Joe Handy, $350.40; Dennis Handy, $525.60; Hannah Handy, $481.80; Rachel Lourye [sic], $481.80; Leah Tyler, $262.80; Frank Tyler, $306.60; Eliza Tyler, $306.60; Robert Tyler, $109.50; Dennis E. Tyler, $21.90.]

No. 572, Petition of James C. McGuire   Filed Jun. 2, 1862

James C. McGuire of Washington claims compensation for five persons.

1. Henson Mackall is a stout healthy man formerly employed as a bricklayer and hod carrier.
2. Louis Lee is a small man, very dark and employed in McGuire's house as a waiter and house servant.
3. Jennie (or Jenny) Powers is a smart and likely girl and an excellent cook. She is employed in McGuire's house.
4. Jennet Powers is a child of Jenny Powers.
5. Jack Powers is a child of Jenny Powers.

McGuire claims $3,500 for all of the above. Henson Mackall he purchased from Gerald Cochran for $800 on Oct. 17, 1854. Louis Lee he purchased from J.B.H. Smith, trustee of Col. Bramford about 13 years ago for $400. At the time, Louis was only 13 years old. Jenny Powers he purchased from Edward C. Dyer about 1849 for $400. Jennet and Jack were born after the purchase of Jenny.

[Commissioners paid McGuire $1,533: Henson Mackall, $438; Louis Lee, $438; "Jenette" Powers, $109.50; "Jenne" Powers, $481.80; Jack Powers, $65.70.]

No. 573, Petition of Philip Mackey   Filed Jun. 2, 1862

Philip Mackey of Washington claims compensation for six persons.

1. Nancy Holmes, aged 25, copper colored, five feet high. She is an excellent nurse and cook. [Value $1,000]
2. Irene Holmes, aged 23, copper colored, five feet high. She is an excellent cook. [Value $1,000]
3. Thomas Holmes, aged six, copper color, three feet high. He is a smart, intelligent boy. [Value $500]
4. Wesley Holmes, aged 21, dark copper color, 5 feet 6 inches tall. He is marked by smallpox. He is an industrious servant. At the time of the passage of the act, he was hired temporarily in Montgomery County, Md., but D.C. has been his home and he is now here. [Value $1,200]
5. Jefferson Holmes, aged two, bright mulatto, two feet high. He is a bright, healthy child. [Value $300]
6. Stephen Holmes, aged two, bright mulatto, two feet high. He is a bright, healthy child. [Value $300]

Nancy, Irene and Wesley are the children of Harriet and Henry Holmes who were Mackey's slaves willed to him about 25 years ago by his mother, Mary Mackey. That will is recorded in Easton, Talbot County, Md. Thomas, Jefferson and Stephen are children of Nancy and of Irene.

Columbus Alexander of Washington challenges the above petition and states that Mackay [sic] has no interest or claim to the above slaves, but that they belong to him.

[The Commissioners rejected Mackey's claim as the servants were not allowed or produced by him. They were claimed, produced and allowed to Columbus Alexander. See No. 893.]

No. 574, Petition of Richard W. Carter
Filed Jun. 2, 1862

Richard W. Carter of Washington claims compensation for Henry Lee, aged 22, light mulatto, 5 feet 9 inches tall. He is intelligent, gentlemanly and courteous. He works behind the counter in Carter's dry goods store and is a salesman who waits on, among others, his colored friends. He is paid about $250 a year. He purchased Lee from William Burnes in Howard County, Mo., when Henry was only five months old. [Value $1,500]

[Commissioners paid Carter $569.40.]

No. 575, Petition of William S. Colquhoun
Filed Jun. 2, 1862

William S. Colquhoun of Washington City claims compensation for James Dyson, aged 20. He is black, 5 feet 4 inches high. His left hand and arm are paralyzed from birth, but he uses it in aid to his right hand. Otherwise, he is healthy and strong. Dyson's mother was Colquhoun's property so he was born a slave. Dyson's mother has since died. [Value $200]

[Commissioners stated that Dyson was of no value.]

No. 576, Petition of John Robinson
Filed Jun. 2, 1862

John Robinson of Washington City claims compensation for Nancy Robinson, aged 50. She is a black woman who is free of defects and "her morals as good as those of persons of color generally." He purchased Nancy on Apr. 10, 1852, for $300 from Allison Nailor of Washington.

[Commissioners paid Robinson $87.60.]

No. 577, Petition of Robert S. Patterson
Filed Jun. 2, 1862

Robert S. Patterson of Washington City claims compensation for John Barnes Johnson, aged 24, light mulatto, about 5 feet 8 or 9 inches high. He is a first-class dining room and family servant and is active and intelligent. He received Johnson as a gift from his mother, the late Margaret Patterson of Georgetown. [Value $1,200]

[Commissioners paid Patterson $525.60.]

No. 578, Petition of Charles H. Mann
Filed Jun. 2, 1862

Charles H. Mann of Baltimore claims compensation for Louisa Coates who is 23 years old. She is a light colored woman with wavy black hair and a mole on her face. She is 5 feet 3 inches tall with "rather sunken eyes and tolerably good teeth." She is bound to service for a term of two years and six months from Jun. 1, 1862. Mann is the proprietor of a hotel and has employed Louisa as his chief cook, there being none better in the county. He has had to employ two servants at the rate of $8 a month to take her place and he would greatly prefer Louisa to these two.

He purchased Coates on May 14, 1860, from Asbury McKendree Boyd of Baltimore for a term of three years from Jun. 1, 1860, for $125. On account of her being then in delicate health and subsequently on account of her running away, on Feb. 12, 1862, her time was extended for 18 months beyond the original term by the Orphans' Court in Baltimore City. The order from the Orphans' Court reads that "said Negress has been in the habit of absconding and thus subjecting said Petitioner to much expense and trouble" and thus the court extends her service for 18 months.

[Commissioners paid Mann $65.70.]

No. 579, Petition of Seth Hyatt
Filed Jun. 2, 1862

Seth Hyatt of Washington claims compensation for four persons.
1. Ann Maria Dodson, aged 22, dark copper color, 5 feet 6 inches tall. [Value $1,000]
2. Francis Ann Dodson, aged 20, dark copper color, 5 feet 6 inches tall. [Value $1,000]
3. Charlotte [Dodson], aged eight, dark copper color, four feet high. She is the child of Ann Maria. [Value $300]
4. Elmer [Dodson], aged eight months, is the child of Ann Maria. [Value $100]

They are all first-class servants. Hyatt says they were born his slaves.

[Commissioners paid Hyatt $1,138.80: Ann Maria Dodson, $481.80; Francis Ann Dodson, $438; Charlotte, $175.20; Elmer, $43.80.]

No. 580, Petition of Henry Warrington
Filed Jun. 2, 1862

Henry Warrington of Washington claims compensation for Margaret [Perry], about 18 years old, dark mulatto, about 5 feet 4 or 5 inches tall. She is an excellent chambermaid, having been raised in the family of his late father, Commodore Warrington, U.S.N. Henry purchased her from Charles St. John Chubb of Washington for $800 on Sept.8, 1859. Margaret Perry had been willed by Commodore Lewis Warrington to his daughter, Mrs. Charles St. John Chubb. [Value $1,000]

[Commissioners paid Warrington $503.70.]

No. 581, Petition of Benjamin B. Hodges   Filed Jun. 2, 1862

Benjamin B. Hodges of Montgomery County, Md., claims compensation for two persons.

1. Esau Brent, aged 34, copper color, large whiskers, weights 230 to 250 pounds, six feet tall, with a pleasant countenance. He is a powerfully strong man and an excellent mower, cradler, wood cutter and farm hand. [Value $1,500]

2. James K. Polk, aged 18, dark complexion, high forehead, 5 feet 6 inches tall. He is rather delicate. He is a most gentlemanly Negro, a fine house servant and an admirable carriage driver. [Value $1,500]

He purchased Esau at a public sale of the estate of Polador E. Scott of Prince George's County, Md., about four years ago for about $1,000. James K. Polk was born his slave, being the son of Henry and Matilda Hall both of whom were owned by Hodges.

[Commissioners paid Hodges $1,007.40: Esau Brent, $438; James K. Polk, $569.40.]

No. 582, Petition of Mary A.B. Cummin   Filed Jun. 2, 1862

Mary A.B. Cummin of the District of Columbia claims compensation for Arthur Frisby, aged 17, mulatto, 5 feet 4 inches high. He has lost some of his front teeth but is healthy and intelligent. Frisby is bound to serve until he reaches age 35. She inherited Frisby's mother from the estate of her father Col. John Bordley of Kent County, Md., and Frisby was thus born her slave. She executed a deed of manumission dated Apr. 29, 1854, and recorded in D.C., by which he would become free at age 35. [Value $600]

[Commissioners granted Cummin $306.60.]

No. 583, Petition of Elizabeth J. Fowler

The original petition is missing.

[Commissioners granted Fowler $1,007.40, of which $97.34, as paid on account of Ellen and child, Eliza, was deducted: Ellen Lee, $219; Mary Lee, $438; Eliza Lee, $175.20; Margaret Lee, $109.50; William Lee, $65.70.]

No. 584, Petition of Lydia S. English

The original petition is missing.

[Commissioners paid English $2,518.50: Nelly Carpenter, $131.40; Clara Carpenter, $481.80; George Carpenter, $591.30; Catharine Carpenter, $547.50; Jenny Carpenter, $43.80; Sarah Phenix, $175.20; Mary Ellen Phenix, $547.50.]

No. 585, Petition of James George Naylor   Filed Jun. 2, 1862

James George Naylor of Washington claims compensation for Fanny Ross, aged 38. Ross is of a dark chestnut color, 5 feet 5 inches tall, well-formed and very genteel in her personal appearance. She is a first-rate servant and house keeper. She was confined in the jail here as a runaway, the property of Mrs. Mary Chichester of Montgomery County, Md., who wanted to sell her south. Naylor purchased her from Chichester for $700 on Sept. 14, 1857. [Value $1,000]

[Commissioners paid $284.70.]

No. 586, Petition of Margaret J. Beall   Filed Jun 2, 1862

Margaret J. Beall of Rockville, Md., claims compensation for five persons.

1. Lucy Moore, aged 33, mulatto, is about 5 feet 5 inches tall. She is the mother of the children listed below. She is an excellent house servant, first-rate cook, ironer and washer. [Value $1,000]

2. William H. Moore, six years old, is a mulatto boy. He is not very strong due to a fall some time back, but otherwise is healthy. [Value $300]

3. Richard Moore is a mulatto boy aged five years. He is strong and healthy. [Value $300]

4. John Louis Moore is a mulatto boy aged three years. He is strong and healthy. [Value $200]

5. George Moore is a mulatto boy ten months old. He is strong and healthy. [Value $1,000]

Lucy Moore was a gift from Margaret's mother, Mrs. Jane M. Beall of Rockville, when Lucy was a child. Her four children were born after that time.

[Commissioners paid Margaaret J. Beall, by Jane E. Beall, her attorney, $667.95: Lucy Moore, $350.40; William H. Moore, $87.60; Richard Moore, $109.50; John Lewis Moore, $87.60; George Moore, $32.85.]

No. 587, Petition of Elsey Curtis   Filed Jun. 2, 1862

Elsey Curtis claims compensation for Madaline Curtis, aged about five, dark brown color, stout and well-made and healthy. Mary Curtis, the wife of Elsey and the mother is Madaline, was the slave of Henry C. Matthews, now deceased, of Georgetown. Elsey purchased Madaline from Matthews on Jul. 9, 1860, for $125. Elsey has paid Matthews a total of $109.12 in a series of payments: $50 on July 9, 1860, $37.87 on Sept. 1, 1860; $10 on Aug. 19, 1861, and in work a total of $11.25. (Signed Elsey his x mark Curtis.)

[The Commissioners did not allow this claim from Elzey [sic] Curtis for "Madeline" Curtis.]

No. 588, Petition of Fielder R. Dorsett   **Filed Jun. 2, 1862**

Fielder R. Dorsett, Sr., of the District of Columbia, claims compensation for two persons.

1. Silas Dobson, aged 16, chestnut colored, about 5 feet 6 inches high. He is hired out at $10 a month. [Value $600]

2. California, aged about 11, a bright mulatto about 4 feet 10 inches tall. She is in service in Dorsett's family. [Value $600]

Both are held to service until the arrive at age 21.

Dorsett says they were given to him by their mother, Judy Dobson, ,who is now dead, and were afterwards bound to him by the Orphans' Court about five years ago.

[The Commissioners did not allow this claim.]

No. 589, Petition of Jacob G. Smoot   **Filed Jun. 2, 1862**

Jacob G. Smoot of Fairfax County, Va., near Langley, claims compensation for eight persons.

1. Eliza Ann, aged about 26 or 27, dark, 5 feet 2 inches high, healthy. She is a good cook and first-rate house or field servant. Her four children are listed directly below.

2. Alexander is aged 11, dark brown and of usual size.

3. Julia Rouselle, aged eight, nearly black, usual size.

4. John Calvert, aged four, nearly black, usual size.

5. George Washington, aged from 20 to 24 months, dark copper color.

6. Winny Ann, aged 23, copper color, about five feet high, compactly made.

7. Infant child of Winny Ann, four months old, of a light color and healthy.

8. Nelly, aged 50 to 55 years, black, 5 feet 3 or 4 inches tall, well-made. She is a good cook, washer and ironer. [Value $500]

He values Eliza Ann and her four children at $2,500 and Winny Ann and her infant at $1,000. Smoot states that he purchased Eliza Ann from his brother, J.H. Smoot, about 11 years ago for less than their value "because he did not wish to sell beyond his friends." He only paid $500 for her and her infant. Winny Ann and her infant were acquired by Smoot's marriage. Nelly he purchased from Richard Simmons of Maryland.

Smoot further states that he has been compelled by "our Army" to leave his farm in Fairfax County last October and come to Georgetown with his slaves for a temporary residence. He is not sure that the above slaves should be included under the terms of the emancipation act or whether they may be classed as fugitives and still be retained by him. He leaves this for a legal decision.

[The Commissioners denied Smoot's claim based on the issue of his loyalty. Mr. Smoot voted for the Virginia ordinance of secession in May, 1861. Smoot admitted that was true but stated that he voted for secession "because I thought it would lead to a settlement; I had no idea of breaking up the Union and government."]

No. 590, Petition of Mary Key Wallace   **Filed Jun. 2, 1862**

Mary Key Wallace of Washington claims compensation for two persons.

1. Catharine A. Herbert, aged 34, copper color, 5 feet 1 inch tall. She was brought up by Wallace with care from childhood as a house and kitchen servant.

2. Charles Henry Herbert, aged 11, 4 feet 7 inches tall. He is a very sprightly and intelligent house servant.

The value of the two is $1,600.

Wallace's husband, Robert Wallace, purchased Milly Herbert and her infant child, Catharine A., at Rockville, Montgomery County, Md., at a sale of the estate of Charles Young. Charles Henry is Catharine's son. Robert immediately brought them to Washington City in 1838 when he moved there to live and he held them until his death in December 1846. Catharine was allotted to Mary Key as part of her dower interest.

Attached to the petition is a statement from the Register's Office in D.C. dated Jul. 5, 1862, certifying that on May 25, 1838, Robert Wallace registered in his office six slaves, one of whom was named Kitty.

[Commissioners paid Wallace $591.30: Catharine A. Herbert, $284.70; Charles Henry Herbert, $306.60.]

No. 591, Petition of Susanna G. Henshaw   Filed Jun. 2, 1862

Susannah G. Henshaw of Washington City claims compensation for three persons.

1. Leonard Taylor, aged 70, dark copper color, 5 feet 11 inches tall. He is quite infirm and has asthma.
2. Alexander Taylor, aged 50, light copper color, 5 feet 10 inches tall. He is of intemperate habits.
3. Leonard Taylor, Jr., aged 29, light copper color, about 5 feet 10 inches tall. He is a very valuable servant and has no moral, mental or bodily infirmities.

The value of the three is $2,000.

Henshaw inherited them from her mother, Mrs. Dorothy Wailer [*possibly "Wailes"*], who died in 1846.

[Commissioners paid Henshaw, by J.L. Henshaw, her attorney, $788.40: Leonard Taylor, no value; Alexander Taylor, $219; Leonard Taylor, Jr., $569.40.]

No. 592, Petition of Adam G. Herold, for daughter, Alice King Herold   Filed Jun. 2, 1862

Adam G. Herold, for his daughter, Alice King Herold who is ten years old, of Washington, claims compensation for Charlotte Cambell, aged about nine. Cambell is a dark copper color, 4 feet 4 ½ inches tall, with regular features and a pleasant and intelligent countenance. She is useful for light family duties and is worth $2.50 to $3 a month for her services. She was a gift from Peter King, who owned Charlotte's mother, to Adam's daughter.
[Value $450]

[Commissioners paid A.G. Herold for his daughter $262.80.]

No. 593, Petition of Hope Thomas   Filed Jun. 2, 1862

Hope Thomas of the city of Washington claims compensation for Ann Smoot, aged 45, very dark brown, about 5 feet 5 inches tall. She is quite stout and has lost her front upper teeth. She is a first-rate servant and has not been sick a day since Thomas owned her. [Value $400]

Thomas purchased her on Aug. 31, 1858, for $512 from Reuben Collins of Washington.

[Commissioners paid Thomas $240.90]

No. 594, Petition of Alfred Y. Robinson   Filed Jun. 2, 1862

Alfred Y. Robinson of Prince George's County, Md., claims compensation for Edward Humphreys, aged 35 or 40. He is mulatto, about 5 feet 8 inches tall, of a delicate make but healthy. He is a good house and hotel servant and has resided in D.C. for 15 years. Robinson inherited Humphreys from his mother, Elizabeth Robinson of Prince George's County, and he has held Edward for over 30 years. [Value $800]

[Commissioners paid Robinson $328.50.]

No. 595, Petition of Walter Godey   Filed Jun. 2, 1862

Walter Godey, corner of Green and Dumbarton St. in Georgetown, claims compensation for Minty Clark, a mulatto woman aged about 50, about 5 (?) feet 2 inches tall. His wife tells him that Minty has been troubled with dropsy in her leg, but that should not impair her value more than $50. [Value $400]

He purchased "Minta" from Captain John W. Bronaugh, trustee for Mildred M. Bronaugh, of Georgetown, for $150 on May 5, 1859.

[Commissioners paid Godey $131.40.]

No. 596, Petition of Laura Virginia Tayman, Mary Angelica Cooksey   Filed Jun. 2, 1862
and Sarah Ann Amelia Cooksey

Laura V. Tayman of Washington claims compensation for Steven Queen, aged 14, light brown in color, five feet high, well-formed and intelligent. He is a valuable servant and she has refused to sell him for $1,000. [Value $1,000]

She acquired Queen by inheritance from her father, William W. Cooksey, and he was brought from Maryland to D.C. in 1858 and registered in the Office of the Register. Attached is a copy of the will of Marcus S.S. Waring of Prince George's County in which he leaves his three granddaughters, one of whom is Laura Virginia Cooksey, certain slaves "to share and share alike." The will was admitted to probate Oct. 17, 1843. Laura Virginia, Mary Angelica and Sarah Ann Amelia are the daughters of Eleanor and William Cooksey.

[Commissioners paid Laura V. Tayman, Mary A. Cooksey, by Laura V. Tayman, per attorney, Sarah A.A. Cooksey, $372.30.]

No. 597, Petition of Margaret Taylor   Filed Jun. 2, 1862

Margaret Taylor of Georgetown claims compensation for Hester Solomon. She is about 60 years old, dark copper color, 5 feet 2 inches tall. Taylor says she has been in her household nearly 50 years and has nursed nearly all her children. She is intelligent, active and religious and is worth as much as two servants. [Value $600]

Solomon was purchased by Vincent Taylor for $400 from Benjamin M. Brooke of Fairfax County, Va., on Apr. 1, 1812. At that time, she was about 15 years old.

[Commissiones paid Taylor, by Eliza Daly, per attorney, $87.60.]

No. 598, Petition of Eliza Kolp   Filed Jun. 2, 1862

Eliza Kolp of Washington County, D.C., temporarily in Frederick City, Md., where she has been detained by sickness, claims compensation for Ned Selby. Selby is 27 years old, of a dark complexion, is 6 feet 2 inches tall and is strong and powerful. He is an excellent farm hand and is good at all kinds of work. He could have been sold to a dealer for $1,500, but "being averse to selling negroes from their homes, she kept him here." [Value $1,500]

She inherited Selby under the will of Margaret Adlum of Washington County, D.C., who died about 1851.

[Commissioners paid Kolp, by W. Redin, her attorney, $525.60.]

No. 599, Petition of Christian Gittings   Filed Jun. 2, 1862

Christian Gittings of Washington City claims compensation for Otha Bell, aged 48. He is about 5 feet 8 inches tall, black and has dark hair and dark eyes that have a reddish appearance. He has been hired out as a laborer for wages of from fifty cents to $1.25 per day. She figures that he brings in about $200 a year. Bell was the property of her late husband, Thomas Gittings, who died in the latter part of 1847. At the sale of his property in 1848 she purchased Bell for $630. [Value $1,000] (Signed Christian her x mark Gittings)

[Commissioners paid Jedediah Gittings, legatee of Christiana [sic] Gittings, $328.80, for Otho [sic] Bell.]

No. 600, Petition of Anna Cecil   Filed Jun. 2, 1862

Ann Cecil of Washington City claims compensation for nine persons.

1. Mary Bryant is aged about 42. She is the mother of the next five persons and the grandmother of the three Harley children.
2. Mary Lloyd is aged 23.
3. Sarah Lloyd is aged 20.
4. Edward Lloyd is aged 18.
5. Anthony Lloyd is aged 15.
6. Henry Lloyd is aged 13.
7. John Harley is aged seven.
8. Susan Harley is aged five.
9. James Moore is aged four.

All of the above are of a dark brown color and have no distinguishing marks.

She acquired Mary Bryant and her three oldest children by inheritance from her father, Henry Bryant. Anthony and Henry were born after that acquisition. Mary Lloyd is the mother of John and Susan. James Moore is the child of Sarah Lloyd.

The value of these slaves is at least $6,200. Mary and Sarah Lloyd were apprenticed and taught mantua making and tailoring trade. Edward Lloyd is an engineer working steam engines. Anthony is a barber.

[The Commissioners rejected Anna Cecil's petition. It was filed by J.H. Peters, now deceased. Neither Cecil nor the two witnesses to the petition come forward to establish the claim. The claim, therefore, was regarded as abandoned, "if it ever had any foundation in fact."]

The names given in the printed report of the commissioners differ from the names given in the petition. Mary

Bryant, the elder, is given the name "Margaret Byant"; James Moore is given the name "James Harley."

No. 601, Petition of Ann Blake

Ann Blake of Washington claims compensation for Hannah Horden, aged 40, black and 5 feet 6 inches tall. She purchased Hannah from Elizabeth Horden for $700 in 1846 in South Carolina, but she has lost the receipt. [Value $500]

[Commissioners did not allow Blake's claim. This claim, as No. 600, was filed by J.H. Powers, deceased. Neither Blake nor her witness came forward, thus nothing was been allowed.]

No. 602, Petition of Andrew Wylie, trustee

Andrew Wylie of Washington, trustee, claims compensation for Leanna Diggs. Diggs is about 21 years old, dark mulatto, and is tall and well-formed. She is a first-rate, competent servant and is now employed by Mr. Kiekoffer (?) [*probably Christopher Kloeppinger, a confectioner*] at $8 a month in wages. He acquired title by a deed of trust dated May 31, 1862, from Judson Diggs, which is filed in the clerk's office of D.C. He does not doubt that Diggs was the owner of Leanna at the time of the passage of the emancipation act. [Value $1,000]

[Commissioners paid Wylie $394.20.]

Judson Diggs is a free Negro. See Registration No. 2221 in Provine, <u>Free Negro Registers</u>. That document states that Elisha D. Owen, in consideration of $100 paid by Judson Diggs, manumits him. Diggs was then 45 years old. The note accompanying that registration says that Judson Diggs is supposed to be the informer who betrayed the fugitives aboard the <u>Pearl</u>. In 1848, 77 slaves from D.C. attempted to escape to freedom on board Capt. Daniel Drayton's schooner, <u>Pearl</u>. The escape failed and the fugitives were captured when the ship was forced to put in at Cornfield Harbor. Diggs was roughed up a bit for his role in the affair, but continued to live in Washington until the late 1860s. For additional information, see John H. Paynter, <u>Fugitives of the Pearl</u> (Washington, 1930.) The 1860 Census for Ward 2 (Vol. 1, p. 634) lists in the "Degges" family: Judson, aged 50, a waiter; Mary, aged 50, washerwoman; Delia, aged 18, washerwoman; Lena, aged 16, washerwoman, Lewis aged 14.

No. 603, Petition of Patrick J. Torney

Patrick J. Torney of 558 Pa. Ave., between 1st and 2nd west, claims compensation for two persons.

1. Millie Jackson, or Turner, (she is married to a man named Turner), aged between 28 and 29, about 4 feet 11 ½ inches tall, has a "complexion darker than a mullatto [*sic*], but lighter than a pure Ethiopian." She has a scar on one foot from a cut. She is a valuable house servant. She is due her freedom upon reaching age 35. [Value $500]

2. Edward, son of Millie, is aged nine months, light complexion, robust and healthy. [Value $150]

Torney acquired them through his marriage. The will of George Peacock, filed at Baltimore about 1837, left Millie to Torney's wife. Her child was born since that time.

[Commissioners paid Torney $131.40: Millie Jackson, or Tuney [*sic*], $109.50; Edward, $21.90.]

No. 604, Petition of Leonard O. Cook   Filed Jun. 2, 1862

Leonard O. Cook of the city of Washington claims compensation for eight persons.

1. Hannah Harper, aged 55, is about 5 feet 7 inches tall and black. She has been afflicted with a hip disease which has made her a little lame.
2. Maria Harper, aged 26, about 5 feet 5 inches tall, black.
3. Julia Frances Harper, aged 24, about 5 feet 6 inches tall, black.
4. Susannah Harper, aged 20, about 5 feet 8 inches tall, bright.
5. Chrisa Harper, aged three months, black.
6. Margetta Harper, aged four years, bright.
7. Harvey Harper, aged seven months, bright.
8. Levinia Harper, aged five months, bright.

All of the adults are first-rate servants and the children are likely and promising. [Value $4,000]

He purchased Hannah and her child Maria for $190 from Albert G. Tidwell (?) on Dec. 19, 1837. The others are children or grandchildren of Hannah.

[Commissioners paid Cook $1,642.50: Hannah Harper, $21.90; Maria Harper, $481.80; Julia Francis [*sic*] Harper, $459.90; Susanna [*sic*] Harper, $525.60; Chissa [*sic*] Harper, $21.90; Margella [*sic*] Harper, $87.60; Henry [*sic*] Harper, $21.90; Levinia Harper, $21.90.]

No. 605, Petition of Samuel R. Carr
The original petition is missing.
[Commissioners paid Carr $876: Ammy [*sic*] Lancaster, $262.80; William Dorsey, $613.20.]

No. 606, Petition of Edward Craycroft   **Filed Jan. 2, 1862**
Edward Craycroft of Montgomery County, Md., claims compensation for John Clark, aged ten, a bright mulatto. Clark is held to service until he reaches age 25. He is a likely and promising boy and is free of infirmities. [Value $400]

He acquired his title by marriage with Ann Amelia Holland, who received the same by inheritance. Attached is a copy of the will of Amelia Holland of Montgomery County, which names her daughter, Ann Amelia, as one of her heirs. Also attached is the 1828 will of Amelia Holland's sister, Deborah Ray, which left her three Negro females, Jinny, Eliza, and Sally, who were to be freed at age 25. Their children were also to be freed at age 25.

[Commissioners paid Craycroft $87.60.]

No. 607, Petition of George W. Wren and Catharine Ann Wren   **Filed Jun. 2, 1862**
George W. Wren and his wife, Catharine A. Wren, of Washington, claim compensation for nine persons.
1. Alice Lewis, aged 42, 5 feet 1 inch tall, dark color. The joint of the little finger on her right hand is off.
2. Oscar Lewis, son of Alice, aged 29, 5 feet 8 inches high, dark color. He has a scar under his chin.
3. Helen Lewis daughter of Alice, aged 24, 5 feet 1 inch high, copper color. She has a scar on her right wrist.
4. Mashack Lewis, aged four, bright mulatto.
5. Cora Lewis, aged two, bright mulatto.
6. Sarah Curtis, aged 32, 5 feet 3 inches high, copper color. She has a scar in her forehead.
7. Wallis Curtis, aged 11, copper color.
8. Henry Curtis, aged six months, copper color.
9. George Cane, aged 42, 5 feet 8 inches tall, black in color.

The adults are all first-rate servants and are the children are promising and likely. [Value $5,000]

The will of Sarah S. Wren, the mother-in-law of Catherine Ann, proved on May 15, 1843, conveyed George Cane to Catherine Ann Wren. The will of Sinah E. Lee, who was Catherine Ann's mother, made in 1851, devised Alice, Oscar, and Helen Lewis, and Sarah Curtis to Catherine Ann. The others were children of the above. These wills are filed in the Fairfax County, Va., Courthouse. George Wren was in debt to both his mother and his mother-in-law and in both cases their wills conveyed the slaves to his wife for her sole and separate estate.

[Commissioners paid George W. and Catharine Wren $2,146.20: Alice Lewis, $175.20; Oscar Lewis, $613.20; Helen Lewis, $438; Marshack [*sic*] Lewis, $109.50; Cora Lewis, $43.80; Sarah Curtis, $219; Wallis Curtis, $197.10; Henry Curtis, $43.80; George Cane, $306.60.]

No. 608, Petition of A. Ross Ray and Albert Ray   **Filed Jun. 2, 1862**
A. Ross Ray and his brother, Albert Ray, of Georgetown, claim compensation for Aaron Hall, aged about 60, mulatto, about six feet tall. He is an honest and industrious servant and a good miller. [Value $500]

They purchased Hall from Mr. V.J. Taylor of Georgetown about seven or ten years ago.

[Commissioners paid A. Ross and Albert Ray $175.20.]

No. 609, Petition of James S. Morsell   **Filed Jun. 2, 1862**
James S. Morsell of Georgetown claims compensation for Priscilla Quad. Quad is aged from 23 to 25 years old, is five feet high with black skin, good features, and is well-proportioned. She is invaluable and was brought up in Morsell's house as a domestic servant and can do any and all duties. [Value $500]

She was born in Morsell's house of a slave whom he had inherited from his father.

[Commissioners paid Morsell $481.80.]

No. 610, Petition of John P. Wheeler   **Filed Jun. 2, 1862**
John P. Wheeler of Washington claims compensation for three persons.
1. Sarah Offutt, aged 47, rather dark, medium statue, good countenance and pleasant when spoken to. She is a good cook, ironer and washer.
2. Robert Offutt, son of Sarah, aged 16, very dark color, good features, well-grown for his age.
3. James Wesley Offutt, son of Sarah, aged seven, very dark, well-featured.

Wheeler purchased at a public sale Sarah Offutt for about $400 ("to retain her in the family") from the administrator of the estate of Thomas F.W. Vinson, late of Montgomery County, Md., who died in 1843. Robert and Wesley were born after that purchase. He estimates their value at $1,500.

[Commissioners paid Wheeler $876: Sarah Ann Offutt, $175.20; Robert, $569.40; James Wesley, $131.40.]

No. 611, Petition of Samuel B. Anderson   Filed Jun. 2, 1862

Samuel B. Anderson of Montgomery County, Md., claims compensation for two persons.

1. Chloe Marshall, aged 50, has a copper colored complexion, is about 5 feet 10 ½ inches tall and of medium size. She is a fine cook, washer and ironer and house servant. She now hires herself as a house servant at the rate of $10 a month. [Value $800]

2. William Smith, aged 52, is black, six feet tall and stout. He is a first-rate farm hand and can plow, sow wheat and corn, ditch, cut wood and do fence work. He is a mild, pleasant man and is healthy except for a slight rupture. [Value $800]

He purchased Chloe from Thomas W. Clagett of Prince George's County, Md., in 1850. He purchased William from E.G.W. Hall of Prince George's County in 1855.

[Commissioners paid Anderson $394.20: Chloe Marshal [sic], $87.60; William, $306.60.]

No. 612, Petition of William P. Clark   Filed Jun. 2, 1862

William P. Clark of the District of Columbia claims compensation for two persons.

1. George Jenkins, aged 26, dark brown, is about 5 feet 8 ½ or 9 inches tall, well-proportioned with an intelligent countenance.

2. Elizabeth Moore, aged 41, is very dark, about 5 feet 4 ½ or 5 inches tall, very erect in statue and sprightly.

Clark values them at $800.

He purchased Moore from A.H. Morehead of Washington for $250 on Feb. 10, 1862. He purchased Jenkins from Morehead for $700 on the same date.

[Commissioners paid Clarke [sic] $832.20: Jenkins, $613.20; Moore, $219.]

No. 613, Petition of Randolph Birch   Filed Jun. 3, 1862

Randolph Birch of Georgetown claims compensation for four persons.

1. Elizabeth Walker, aged 26, dark color, 5 feet 7 inches high. [Value $1,500]
2. Lewis Walker, aged 12, bright mulatto, 4 feet 6 inches high. [Value $1,000]
3. Andrew Walker, aged nine, bright mulatto. [Value $800]
4. Simon Walker, aged 22, dark color, about 5 feet 6 inches tall, stout. He is a good and obedient servant, but has a slight defect in one leg which is stiff. [Value $600]

The first three are all first-class servants and are free of infirmities.

Birch, on Jan. 1, 1860, inherited them from the estate of his father, John Birch of Alexandria, County, Va.

[Commissioners paid Birch $876; Elizabeth Walker, $438; Lewis, $219; Andrew, $131.40; Simon, $87.60.]

No. 614, Petition of John M. Caldwell
The original petition is missing.

[Commissioners paid Caldwell, by William R. Woodward, his attorney, $591.30: Lucy Whiting, $350.40; Cornelia Harris, $240.90.]

No. 615, Petition of Amelia Tilghman, colored.

Amelia Tilghman of Washington claims compensation for Fanny Lee. Lee is about 56 years old, "hardly five feet high," quite black, with bad teeth and very gray hair. She is a first-rate pastry and French cook and was hired in that capacity to Dr. [Hezekiah] Magruder at $5 a month from Tilghman's purchase of her in 1856 to Apr. 16, 1862. Except for her age and infirm health she would have been worth a large sum of money. Tilghman purchased her for $40 from William Thomas Carroll in July of 1856. Carroll, in turn, had purchased Lee from William S. Nichols of Georgetown. [Value $200] (Signed Amelia her x mark Tilghman)

[Commissioners paid $43.80 to John Tilghman, his x mark, husband of Amelia Tilghman, deceased.]

John Tilghman, Amelia's husband, registered his free status in D.C. in 1839. He was freed by the will of Henry Lowe Hall, rector of St. John's Episcopal Church, in Prince George's County, Md. The D.C. 1860 Census (Vol. 1, p. 244) lists John Tilman's [sic] family: John, aged 38, a whitewasher; Amelia, aged 37, Elizabeth, aged 19, Mary, aged 17, Ann, aged 13, James, aged 12, William, aged 11, Sarah aged eight, Rosah, aged seven, and Amelia, aged eight months. See Registration 1654 and accompanying note in Provine, D.C. Free Negro Registers.

No. 616, Petition of Caroline E. Sanders   **Filed Jun. 3, 1862**

    Caroline E. Sanders of the District of Columbia claims compensation for 17 slaves.
1. John Dodson, aged 37, 5 feet 8 inches tall, wagoner. [Value $1,200]
2. William Snowden, aged 36, five feet 6 inches tall, carriage driver. [Value $1,300]
3. Sylvester Brooks, aged 24, 5 feet 11 ½ inches tall, gardener. [Value $1,500]
4. Edward Hepburn Howard, aged 22, 5 feet 3 ½ inches high is an ostler. [Value $1,400]
5. Henry, aged 19, 5 feet 1 ½ inches tall, field hand. He is not bright. [Value $600]
6. Marie, aged 33, 5 feet 2 inches tall, cook. [Value $1,000]
7. Sallie Wallis, aged 33, 5 feet 4 inches tall, seamstress. [Value $1,000]
8. Henny Howard, aged 20, 5 feet 1 1/4 inches tall, nurse and chambermaid. [Value $1,200]
9. Nelly Arnold, aged 50, cook. [Value $350]
10. Jim Dodson, aged 12, 4 feet 4 ½ inches tall, waiter. [Value $700]
11. George Dodson aged ten, 4 feet 3 inches tall, errand boy. [Value $600]
12. Frank Hepburn, aged 11, waiter and errand boy. [Value $650]
13. Louis Adams, aged 11, 4 feet 4 inches, waiter. [Value $650]
14. Tom Adams, aged nine, 3 feet 10 inches tall, waiter. [Value $550]
15. Jenny Hepburn, aged nine, four feet tall, waiter. [Value $550]
16. Fanny Wallis, aged three, three feet tall. [Value $250]
17. Kate Wallis, aged two, 2 feet 4 inches tall. [Value $200]

    She inherited some of the slaves, she purchased others, and still others were reared by her from infancy. She attaches several bills of sale, but not all of them because they are filed in Maryland and various places. One bill of sale dated Nov. 1, 1846, shows that she, purchased from Ann L. Contee for $400 Negro boy Sylvester; another dated Jan. 7, 1856, and signed by John Contee shows she purchased Negro boy Henry from the administrator's sale of the estate of Thomas Duckett on Dec. 23, 1855; a third shows she paid $800 for William Snowden to Richard Nicols Snowden of Anne Arundel County, Md. The second item, regarding the purchase of Negro Henry, refers to her as "Caroline E. Fairfax."

    [Commissioners paid Sanders $4,949.40: John Dodson, $438; William Snowden, $438; Sylvester Brooks, $657; Edward Howard $547.50; Henry, no value; Maud [*sic*], $350.40; Sallie, $350.40; Henry [*sic*] Howard, $525.60; Nelly Arnold, $65.70; Jim Dodson, $262.80; George, $219; Frank Hepburn, $306.60; Louis Adams, $240.90; Tom, $197.10; Jenny Hepburn, $197.10; Fanny Wallace [*sic*] $98.55; Kate, $54.75.]

    Caroline E. Fairfax married William G. Sanders on Mar. 1, 1838. See Pippenger, D.C. Marriage Licenses, 1811-1858, *p. 196.*

No. 617, Petition of Thomas McGuire   **Filed Jun. 3, 1862**

    Thomas McGuire of Washington claims compensation for two persons.
1. Eliza Ann Jones, aged 18, light colored, 5 feet 1 or 3 inches high. [Value $1,300]
2. Thomas Edward Berry, aged 12, mulatto, about 4 feet 8 or 9 inches tall. [Value $1,000]

    They are both excellent house servants. He repurchased Eliza Ann on May 8, 1857, from John C. Cook for $700. He had originally purchased her from Nicholas Queen, but then sold her to Cook. He purchased Thomas on Oct. 11, 1859, for $500, from Price Birch (?) Lee (?). (Signed Thomas his x mark McGuire)

    [Commissioners paid $635.10 to McGuire: Eliza Ann Jones, $394.20; Thomas Edward Berry, $240.90.]

No. 618, Petition of Lieut. Egbert Thompson   **Filed Jun. 3, 1862**

    This petition was filed July 11, 1862, by permission of the commissioners in lieu of and substitution for that filed Jun. 3, 1862, by attorney of the petitioner.

    Lieut. Egbert Thompson, citizen of Washington, but now lieutenant commander of the U.S. gunboat Pittsburgh on the Mississippi River, claims compensation for five persons.

1. Betsy Greenfield, about 35 or 36 years old, of a yellow or copper color, about 5 feet 5 inches tall, and "of full habit." She is healthy, but suffers from attacks of sick or nervous headache which sometimes causes temporary "flightiness." She is a first-rate cook, a good washer and ironer, and generally useful as a servant. She has had entire control of all the family stores for years. Her former owner had been offered $1,200 for her. Betsy is the mother of

Louisa, Alice and George. [Value $800]

2. Louisa Greenfield, about 14, of a dark brown color, ordinary height. She has a blink in her right eye and her sight is bad in that eye. In addition, she has an "usually slow and shuffling gait." She is a fair nurse for children and familiar with ordinary housework. [Value $400]

3. Alice Greenfield, about ten years old, yellow or copper color, well-grown and very quick and active. She is left-handed. She is very handy and useful. [Value $400]

4. George Greenfield, about eight, of a very dark complexion, nearly black, of good size, well-built and has a pleasant expression. He is handy and useful. [Value $400]

5. Rachel Greenfield, aged about six, bright copper color, well-grown for her age, quick and intelligent. She is very bowlegged. [Value $250]

He is half owner with his wife, Emily B. Thompson, formerly Mudd, of the first four persons. His wife inherited them from her mother by a will admitted to probate in August 1861. With regard to Rachel, his wife was half owner with her brother, J.H. Clay Mudd, but he transferred his interest to her on May 10, 1862.

Attached is a copy of the will of Mary Mudd whereby she leaves to her daughter servant woman Betsy and her three children, Louisa, Alice and George. Also attached is a statement by J.H. Clay Mudd that for consideration of $150 paid by Egbert Thompson, he sells his one-half interest in Rachel Greenfield.

No. 619, Petition of Judith C. Bayne   Filed Jun. 3, 1862

Judith C. Bayne of Prince George's County, Md., claims compensation for three persons.

1. Lawrence Hensley, aged 50, dark brown, of medium size. He is very intelligent and reads and writes. For many years he has been employed in Boteler's Auction Rooms in an important position. He is an excellent salesman. [Value $800]

2. Sophia Hensley, aged about 28 or 30, dark brown and quite tall. She is a good cook and washerwoman and ironer. [Value $1,500]

3. Eliza Hall, aged 18, black and quite tall. She is a good cook, washer and ironer. [Value $1,500]

These persons came to her from the estate of her late husband, William Bayne of Prince George's County. Sophy and Elizabeth were born and raised as slaves in her family and were children of a slave belonging to Bayne.

[Commissioners paid William B. Bayne, executor of Judith C. Bayne, $985.50: Lawrence Hensley, $131.40; Sophia Hensley, $306.60; Eliza Hall, $547.50.]

No. 620, Petition of Aloysius Graham

The original petition is missing.

[Commissioners paid Aloysius Graham, by Thomas A. Scott, attorney, $3,219.30: Rachel Clarke, $306.60; James H. Clarke, $613.20; Robert Clarke, $547.50; Maria Clarke, $481.80; Caroline Clarke, $350.40; Margaret Clarke, $394.20; William F. Clarke, $240.90; Charles Clarke, $153.30; Martha Clarke, $87.60; Louisa Clarke, $43.80.]

No. 621, Petition of Ann C. Carroll and Maria Fitzhugh, executors &c.,
of Daniel Carroll

The original petition is missing.

[Commissioners paid Ann C. Carroll and Maria Fitzhugh, executors of Daniel Carroll, by Richard H. Clarke, their attorney, $569.40: Beckey Rawlings, $394.20; Louis Brown, $175.20.]

No. 622, Petition of Thomas J.S. Perry and Louis F. Perry   Filed Jun. 4, 1862

Thomas J.S. Perry and Louis F. Perry of the District of Columbia claim compensation for three persons.

1. Robert Brooks, aged 15, bright mulatto, black hair and eyes, medium size, with a pleasant countenance. He is about 4 feet 7 inches tall. He is a fine dining room servant. [Value $1,000]

2. Charles Carter, aged nine, bright mulatto, with brown hair and black eyes, medium size, stout built. He is about four feet high. He is a very bright boy and gives every indication of making a useful man. [Value $800]

3. Zora Carter, aged five, bright mulatto, black hair and eyes, large for her age. She is about 3 feet 7 ½ inches tall. She is a fine looking girl who is well-proportioned and healthy. [Value $600]

He purchased them from Rachel Beall of Washington. The accompanying memorandum of agreement dated Mar. 31, 1856, provided that in consideration of certain sums of money advanced for the support of Rachel Beall and an agreement to furnish additional money from time to time as she may need, plus $100 in cash, that Thomas J.S. and

Louis F. Perry and Thomas A. Lazenby shall have title to several slaves: Martha Carter, aged about 29, to be freed at age 35; Robert Brooks, aged nine and Charles Carter, aged about three. (Signed Rachel her x mark Beall)   Thomas A. Lazenby sold his interest to Thomas J.S. Perry for $300 on Jan. 29, 1859.

The Perrys add a note that Charles Carter, because of his youth, was sent to Montgomery County, Md., to live and has been boarded there at the rate of $20 at the home of Ruth Ann Perry. He was returned to Washington on May 18, 1862.

[Commissioners paid Thomas and Louis Perry $416.10: Robert Brooks, $153.30; Charles Carter, $175.20; Zora Carter, $87.60.]

No. 623, Petition of George W. Cochran   Filed Jun. 4, 1862

George W. Cochran of Washington claims compensation for two persons.

1. Nora Coquia, aged 37, dark mulatto. She is a delicate woman but has never been laid up with sickness since she came into his possession.

2. Adele Francis Coquia, daughter of Nora, aged 15, very stout with tolerably straight hair.

They are both valuable servants and worth $1,500.

He purchased them for $1,000 on Mar. 19, 1858, from Sarah A.J. Burch and John H. Burch.

[Commissioners paid Cochran $722.70: Nora "Coquire", $262.80; "Adela Francis Coquire", $459.90.]

No. 624, Petition of Ann E. and William H. West

The original petition is missing.

[Commissioners paid Ann E. and William H. West $438 for Emma Bowen.]

No. 625, Petition of William Brenton Boggs

The original petition is missing.

[Commissioners paid William B. Boggs, by W. Redin, his attorney, $219 for Laura Jackson.]

No. 626, Petition of Georgiana Monroe   Filed Jun. 5, 1862

Georgiana Monroe of Washington City claims compensation for Hannah Lee. Lee is aged 15, black with black eyes and black hair, and about medium size. She is an excellent cook and nurse. She was acquired from the estate of the late Lawrence Monroe of Fairfax, Va., in the settlement of that estate and the papers are filed at the Fairfax Courthouse.

[Commissioners awarded Munroe [*sic*] $459.90.]

No. 627, Petition of Mary Queen and Elizabeth Queen   Filed Jun. 5, 1862

Mary Queen and Elizabeth Queen claim compensation for 24 persons.

1. Fendall (or Fendell) Taylor, aged 47, black, 5 feet 6 inches high, hump shoulders. [Value $800]

2. Charlotte Taylor, wife of Fendall, aged 40, 5 feet 2 inches high, black, corpulent. She had scrofula when young, but is now in good health and is an excellent cook, washer and ironer. The eight persons listed below are Fendall and Charlotte's children. [Value $500]

3. Frances Taylor, aged 21, a black woman, 5 feet 3 inches tall. [Value $800]

4. Louis Taylor, aged 19, black, six feet high. [Value $1,200]

5. Rachel Taylor, aged 17, black, 5 feet 4 inches high, stout. [Value $800]

6. Gabriel Taylor, aged 16, black, 5 feet 8 inches high, stout. [Value $1,000]

7. Catharine Taylor, aged 13, black, 4 feet 11 inches high. [Value $700]

8. Lloyd Taylor is aged ten, black and 4 feet 5 inches tall. [Value $600]

9. Olivia Taylor, aged seven, black, about four feet tall. [Value $300]

10. Mary Abbey Taylor, aged five, brown, 3 feet 7 inches tall. [Value $300]

11. Andrew Price, aged 33, black, 5 feet 10 1/4 inches tall, fine personal appearance.[Value $1,200]

12. Eveline Gutridge, aged 45, chestnut colored, 4 feet 11 inches high. [Value $800]

13. Henry Gutridge, aged 23, copper color, 5 feet 6 inches high, genteel looking. [Value $1,200]

14. Sally Gutridge, aged 21, copper colored, 5 feet 1 inch tall, stout. [Value $800]

15. Virginia Gutridge, aged 19, copper colored, five feet high, fine appearance. [Value $800]

16. Henrietta Gutridge, aged 17, copper colored, 4 feet 10 inches tall, large eyes. [Value $800]

17. Charles Gutridge, aged 15, copper color, 5 feet 5 inches high. [Value $1,000]

18. Albert Gutridge, aged 13, copper color, 4 feet 10 inches tall. [Value $1,000]
19. Francis Gutridge, aged 11, copper colored boy, 4 feet 7 inches tall. [Value $800]
20. Basil Gutridge, aged five, copper colored, 3 feet 4 inches tall. [Value $400]
21. Albert Bodely, aged 27, brown, 5 feet 7 inches tall, held to service until age 35. [Value $900]
22. Edward Bodely, aged 21, copper color, 5 feet 2 inches tall, held to service until age 35. [Value $900]
23. George Bodely, aged 19, copper color, 5 feet 6 inches tall, held to service until age 35. [Value $900]
24. Louisa Brooks, aged 21, 5 feet 1 ½ inches tall, held to service until age 35. [Value $500]

All of the above are sound and healthy and strictly moral and honest, some of them practical members of the church, and generally intelligent and capable. They were acquired by a bill of sale from Nicholas L. Queen, their father. The bill of sale, signed Oct. 1, 1857, provided that for $5 Nicholas Queen conveyed to his daughters, Mary and Elizabeth, certain slaves. The bill of sale names several slaves who are not on the list: Lavenia Brooks, aged about 14; Sally Price, aged about 60, and William Jones, aged about 19.

[Commissioners paid Mary and Elizabeth Queen $8,256.30: Fendal [sic] Taylor, $175.20; Charlotte Taylor, $197.10; Frances Taylor, $481.80; Louis Taylor, $591.30; Rachel Taylor, $525.60; Gabriel Taylor, $569.40; Catharine Taylor, $372.30; Lloyd Taylor, $284.70; Olivia Taylor, $153.30; Mary Abby Taylor, $131.40; Andrew Price, $569.40; Eveline Gutridge, $197.10; Henry Gutridge, $481.80; Sally Gutridge, $525.60; Virginia Gutridge, $372.30; Henrietta Gutridge, $438; Charles Gutridge, $525.60; Albert Gutridge, $394.20; Francis Gutridge, $306.60; Basil Gutridge, $131.40; Albert Bodely, $153.30; Edward Bodely, $219; George Bodely, $240.90; Louisa Brooks, $219.]

The petition also refers to the will of John M. Wightt recorded Sept. 2, 1819. That will contained a provision that stated: "To mother Cary Wightt, and Nelly G. Queen, jointly during their lives, tract of land on which I reside called "Inclosure," with improvements, which was devised to me by my father, at their deaths to Henry, Mary, Ann and Elizabeth Queen, children of Nicholas L. Queen." See Pippenger, D.C. Probate Records, 1801-1852, p. 91.

No. 628, Petition of Eliza Jenkins   Filed Jun. 5, 1862

Eliza Jenkins of the District of Columbia claims compensation for six persons.

1. Susan, aged 35, dark copper colored, about 5 feet 2 inches tall. She is a valuable house servant, good cook, ironer and washer. The next five persons are her children. [Value $600]
2. Alice, aged 12, dark copper color, 4 feet 7 inches tall. She was raised as a house servant. [Value $500]
3. Mary, aged eight, about 5 feet 1 inch tall. She is strong and healthy. [Value $400]
4. Laura, aged seven, dark copper colored, 3 feet 8 inches tall, strong and healthy. [Value $300]
5. Susanna, aged five, about 3 feet 2 inches tall, strong and healthy. [Value $200]
6. James, aged two, about 2 feet 6 inches tall, strong and healthy. [Value $200]

Jenkins purchased Susan July 10, 1843, for $250 from Caesar Gantt of Prince George's County, Md., as per bill of sale recorded in D.C. Liber W.B. No. 3, folio 239. The other five are Susan's children born while she was owned by Jenkins.

[Commissioners paid Eliza Jenkins, her x mark, $1,182.60: Susan, $306.60; Alice, $306.60; Mary, $219; Laura, $175.20; Susanna, $109.50; James, $65.70.]

No. 629, Petition of Joseph T. Jenkins   Filed Jun. 5, 1862

Joseph T. Jenkins of the District of Columbia claims compensation for three persons.

1. Maria, aged 15, dark copper colored, about 4 feet 10 inches tall. She is a very good house servant and is strong and healthy. [Value $600]
2. Kitty, black, about 13 years old, about 4 feet 10 inches tall. She is strong and healthy and was raised as a house servant. [Value $500]
3. John, aged 11, black, about 4 feet 10 inches tall. He is strong and healthy. [Value $500]

Jenkins purchased Hannah, the mother of these three persons, from the estate of George Kirby of Prince George's County, Md. Hannah has since died. The bill of sale is dated Dec. 31, 1849, and shows that Jenkins paid $500 for Hannah and her two youngest children.

[Commissioners paid Jenkins $1,292.10: Maria, $438; Kitty, $525.60; John, $328.50.]

No. 630. Petition of Jackson Beall   Filed Jun. 5, 1862

Jackson Beall of Georgetown claims compensation for Ann Johnson, aged 16 or 17 years, light in color, about 5 feet 1 inches tall, healthy. She is a good house servant and nurse. Beall paid $400 for her to his father's estate when she was not more than nine years old. She was allotted to him as a portion of his share of the estate of his father, Ninean Beall. [Value $800]

[Commissioners paid Beall $481.80.]

No. 631. Petition of George W. Beall   Filed Jun. 5, 1862

George W. Beall of Georgetown claims compensation for Ella Johnson, aged about 11 years. She is a mulatto, about 4 feet 6 or 7 inches tall. She can read and is now of the age when she is likely to be useful. He paid $200 for her in the settlement of his father's estate when she was an infant. She was born to a slave mother owned by his father, Ninean Beall, and she was allotted to him in the division of his father's estate. [Value $600]

[Commissioners paid Beall $284.70.]

No. 632, Petition of Barbara Williams   Filed Jun. 5, 1862

Barbara Williams of Georgetown claims compensation for Lucy Jamison. She is about 15 years old, about 4 feet 9 inches tall, mulatto, strong and healthy. She is a capable servant good for housework. She was born in her family of a slave mother and was raised by Williams from a child. [Value $700]

[Commissioners paid Williams, by J.C. Marbury, attorney, $481.80.]

No. 633, Petition of Sarah T. Hughes   Filed Jun. 5, 1862

Sarah T. Hughes of Washington claims compensation for three persons.

1. Catharine Butler, aged about 36, mulatto, good-looking, 5 feet 4 inches tall. Her two children are listed below. She is a first-rate house servant, cook, washer and ironer.[Value $1,000]

2. Jane Butler, aged about six, mulatto, well-grown for her age. She is very useful about the house as a maid &c. [Value $300]

3. Mary Butler, about three, of a dark mahogany color. [Value $150]

Hughes owned Catharine before her marriage and was devised her by the last will of her husband which is recorded in D.C. The two children were born in her family and raised by her.

[Commissioners paid Hughes, by John T. Cheever her attorney, $657: Catharine Butler, $438; Jane, $153.30; Mary, 56.70.]

Sarah was the wife of Thomas Hughes who died Apr. 27, 1837. His will may be found in Pippenger, D.C. Probate Records, 1801-1852, p. 212.

No. 634, Petition of John Hinsley   Filed Jun. 5, 1862

John Hinsley of Washington, claims compensation for three persons.

1. Cornelius Delavan, aged 14 (?), about 4 feet 10 inches tall, of a chestnut color, healthy. He would hire for $6 a week. [Value $600]

2. Henry Hopkins, 20, about 5 feet 10 inches tall, mulatto. He would hire for $6 a week. [Value $1,000]

3. William Mansfield, aged about 22, copper colored, 5 feet 9 inches tall. He is cut in the face, but is sound and healthy. He would hire for $6 a week. [Value $1,150]

He purchased Cornelius Delavan in April 1861 from William F. Berry of Prince George's County, Md. He bought Henry Hopkins in May 1860 from W. Luckett of Baltimore. He bought Mansfield from John Clow of Queen Anne County, Md.

[Commissioners paid Hinsley $1,270.20: Cornelius Delavan, $438; Henry Hopkins, $306.60; William Mansfield, $525.60.]

No. 635, Petition of J. Madison Cutts   Filed Jun. 5, 1862

J. Madison Cutts of Washington claims compensation for seven persons.

1. Louisa Adams, aged about 30, copper complexion, 5 feet 4 ½ inches tall. She is an excellent house servant, excellent cook, very good plain seamstress and perfect washer and ironer. She is the mother of the six children listed below. [Value $800]

2. Molly Adams, aged 14, very bright mulatto, about 4 feet 5 inches tall. She is an excellent dining room servant, chambermaid and house servant. [Value $600]

3. John Adams, aged 13, black, about four feet high. He is a useful house servant and errand boy. [Value $500]

4. Nancy Adams, aged 12, of a copper complexion, about 3 feet 6 inches tall. She is generally useful. [Value $450]

5. Florence Adams, aged 11, copper complexion, about 3 feet 6 inches high. She is generally useful. [Value $400]

6. Aaron Adams, about ten, of a copper complexion, about three feet high. He is generally useful. [Value $350]

7. Gertrude Adams, about eight, of a copper complexion, about 2 feet 10 inches high. She is generally useful. [Value $300]

Cutts says that Louisa was given to his wife by her uncle, John Hamilton of Maryland, about 28 years ago. The children were all born since Louisa came into his possession.

[Commissioners paid Cutts $1,423.50: Louisa Adams, $306.60; Molly Adams, $306.60; John Adams, $240.90; Nancy Adams, $175.20; Florence Adams, $153.30; Aaron Adams, $131.40; Gertrude Adams, $109.50.]

No. 636, Petition of Allen Dodge
Filed Jun. 5, 1862

Allen Dodge of the District of Columbia, claims compensation for seven persons.

1. Anthony Washington, aged 40, dark color, full height. He does farming and planting work.
2. Wesley Snowden, aged 24, mulatto, tall. He does farming and planting also and is an excellent ostler.
3. Rosa Brown, aged 45, light brown, short. She is an excellent cook, washer &c. She is the mother of the four sons listed below.
4. Thomas Brown, aged 23, brown, stout, full height. He does farming and planting and is a first-rate teamster.
5. Robert Brown, aged 19, brown, very stout, short. He does farming and planting and is a good ox driver.
6. Frank Brown, aged 16, dark brown, stout. He does farm work, chops wood, and works in the garden.
7. Wesley Brown, aged 13, light brown, very active. He is an excellent house servant.

He values the seven at $8,000. He purchased Washington from the estate of Elizabeth Ann Chew of Prince George's County, Md., Sept. 1, 1857, for $900. He purchased Wesley Snowden from William C. Ogle of Maryland on Mar. 20, 1854, for $800. He purchased Rosa Brown and her four sons from Theodore Mosher on Mar. 25, 1854, for $2,800.

[Commissioners paid Dodge $3,175.50: Anthony Washington, $306.60; Wesley Snowden, $635.10; Rosa Brown, $175.20; Thomas Brown, $613.20; Robert Brown, $591.30; Frank Brown, $569.40; Wesley Brown, $284.70.]

No. 637, Petition of Mary Walker
Filed Jun. 5, 1862

Mary Walker of Washington County, D.C., claims compensation for four persons.

1. Amanda Hanson, aged 38, dark mulatto, 5 feet 4 inches tall, slender, with decayed teeth. She is a good cook and house servant. [Value $1,000]
2. Sophia Hanson, aged 12, copper colored, 4 feet 6 inches tall, with large eyes. She is a good house servant and waitress. [Value $600]
3. Clara Hanson, aged eight, four feet high, copper colored. She is a bright and active, child. [Value $300]
4. Edward Hanson, aged five, 3 feet 5 inches high, copper colored. He is an active, smart boy. [Value $200]

Amanda Hanson was purchased by Mary's husband, Maj. George W. Walker. Sophia, Clara and Edward are her children born since that purchase. Upon Walker's death, the property was left to Mary. Attached is a note dated Washington City, 1846, showing Walker's purchase for $450 of Negro woman Amanda from Susan D. Shepherd. Also attached is a copy of the will of George Walker, Capt. In the U.S. Marine Corps, and in the city of Brooklyn, N.Y., by which he left his possession to his wife, Mary. (Signed May 6, 1836)

Walker died about 1852. See Pippenger, D.C. Probate Records, 1801-1852, p. 441.

[Commissioners paid Walker $919.80: Amanda Hanson, $219; Sophia Hanson, $350.40; Clara Hanson, $219; Edward Hanson, $131.40.]

No. 638, Petition of William D. Shepherd
Filed Jun. 6, 1862

William D. Shepherd of the city of Washington claims compensation for Harriet Hatton. Hatton is dark brown, stout, well-made, active. She is a reliable servant and is a cook, washer and ironer and housekeeper. He purchased Hatton from George Horseman about four years ago "to prevent her being sold south." [Value $1,000]

[Commissioners paid Shepherd $219.]

No. 639, Petition of Jane E. Beall, Matilda B.L. Beall and Margaret J. Beall

Jane E. Beall, Matilda B.L. Beall and Margaret J. Beall of Montgomery County, Md., claim compensation for 17 persons.

1. Cicily Talbott, aged about 70, black, 5 feet 2 or 3 inches tall, active and healthy. She is very active and healthy for her age and is a good cook. [Value $50]

2. Charlotte Plowden is a black woman about 5 feet 5 or 6 inches tall and stout. She is a first-rate cook, ironer and washer. [Value $800]

3. Charles Plowden, black is nine years of age. He is a smart and likely boy. [Value $500]

4. Lotty Plowden, black girl, is aged seven. She is stout and healthy. [Value $350]

5. Teresa Tyler is 40 years old, black, very tall. She is an excellent nurse, first-rate cook, ironer and washer. [Value $800]

6. Henry Tyler, about 44 years old, is black and about 5 feet 8 inches tall. He is strong and healthy and a house servant. [Value $1,000]

7. Sophia Clements, 41 years old, black, is 5 feet 3 or 4 inches tall. She is a house servant, a good cook, ironer and washer. [Value $800]

8. Harriet Smith, mulatto, 30 years old, is 5 feet 3 inches tall. She is a very capable house servant and an excellent cook, ironer and washer. [Value $900]

9. Jennie Smith, bright mulatto, is nine years old. She is a smart and intelligent child. [Value $500]

10. Bell Smith, bright mulatto girl, is four years old. She is a bright child. [Value $300]

11. Margery Smith, bright mulatto girl, is one year old, healthy. [Value $100]

12. Louisa Smith, black, is 28 years old. She is a good cook, ironer and washer. [Value $900]

13. Billy Smith, copper colored, is 11 years old. He has been raised as a house servant. [Value $600]

14. Mary Jane Smith, mulatto, is nine years old. She is strong, healthy and very smart. [Value $500]

15. Charles Smith, black, is six years old. He is strong and healthy. [Value $300]

16. Maurice, mulatto, is 29 years old. He is lame from having had his leg broken. He has been a first-class field hand and house servant, but at present is unable to do anything because of his leg. [Value $500]

17. Ann Maria Tyler, mulatto, is nine years old and very smart. She is strong and active. [Value $500]

Cicily Talbott, Henry Tyler, Charlotte Plowden, Teresa Tyler, Sophia Clements, Harriet Smith, Louisa Smith, Lucy Moore [sic] and Maurice were inherited from their mother, Mrs. Jane M. Beall of Montgomery County. The others were children of the above born while they were owned by the petitioners.

A statement dated July 11, 1862, is attached to the petition. The Misses Bealls, residing in Montgomery County, Md., about eight or ten miles from D.C., have for the last 12 or 15 years hired their slaves in D.C. When the emancipation act was passed, only a portion were in the District and the others were in Montgomery County waiting to be hired in D.C. This statement is designed to amend the original petition to include those slaves temporarily absent from the District on Apr. 16th.

[Commissioners paid Jane E. Beall and Matilda B.L. Beall, Margaret J. Beall, by Jane E. Beall, their attorney $3,810.60: "Cecily" Talbott, $87.60; Charlotte Plowden, $350.40; Charles Plowden, $219; Lotty Plowden, $175.20; Teresa Tyler, $262.80; Henry Tyler, $350.40; Ann Maria Tyler, $219; Sophia Clements, $262.80; Harriet Smith, $394.20; Jennie Smith, $219; Bell Smith, $87.60; Margery Smith, $43.80; Louisa Smith, $350.40; Billy Smith, $262.80; Mary Jane Smith, $175.20; Charles Smith, $219; Maurice Smith [sic], $219.]

No. 640, Petition of Mary R. Stewart and Mary R. Patterson — Filed Jun. 6, 1862

Mary R. Patterson and Mary R. Stewart of the District of Columbia claim compensation for Lucy Whitney. Whitney is 20 years old, of dark chestnut complexion, stout and well-built, with a full suit of rather straight hair. She has a pleasant and intelligent countenance. She is useful at any kind of housework. [Value $800]

Lucy Whitney was conveyed to Mary R. Stewart by Robert Patterson of Somerset County, Md., which granted to Mary the services of Whitney until she reached age 30. The attached bill of sale, dated Apr. 13, 1855, provided that Rebecca Stewart, widow of the late Charles W. Stewart of Washington, pay $300, for the services of Lucy. Then Patterson, in a document dated Oct. 15, 1860, sold to his daughter Mary, for $300, his Negro girl Lucy, aged 18 years and five months, subject to the prior clause regarding Lucy's service to end when she reaches age 30.

[Commissioners paid Mary R. Stewart and Mary R. Patterson, by their attorney, T[homas] Scrivener, Jr., $481.80.]

No. 641, Petition of William G.W. White — Filed June 6, 1862

William G.W. White of the District of Columbia claims compensation for three persons.

1. James Anderson, aged about 35, nearly six feet tall, dark complexion. He is very likely and has a genteel address. Anderson is now at large. [Value $1,200]

2. Eliza Butler, aged about 45, dark complexion, 4 feet 11 inches tall. She is a valuable family servant. [Value $1,000]

3. Fanny Brown, about 20 years old, light complexion, very likely. She is slightly lame in her right leg. She is a desirable house servant. [Value $1,000]

White notes that his claim is subject to a deed of trust to James M. Carlisle in favor of James R. Smith, dated Jul. 12, 1856.

He purchased James Anderson from R.L. Ogle of Prince George's County, Md., for $750. He purchased Eliza Butler when she was a child from John Thompson of Alexandria (then a part of D.C.). Fanny Brown was born of a slave owned by him, but she died while Fanny was a child.

[The Commissioners paid White $503.70: Eliza Butler, $240.90; Fanny Brown, $262.80. The claim for Anderson was not allowed as he was not produced.]

No. 642, Petition of Robert Read   Filed Jun. 6, 1862

Robert Read of Georgetown claims compensation for Ariana Dorsey, aged about 25. Dorsey is very dark colored and about 5 feet 2 or 3 inches tall. She is a first-rate house servant, good seamstress and fully capable of doing all kinds of work. [Value $800]

Dorsey was born a slave in the family of Mrs. R.D. Cook of Montgomery County, Md., whose daughter married J.D. Read, the son of Robert Read, who died in May 1855.

[Commissioners paid R. Read $525.60.]

No. 643, Petition of George D. Ramsey   Filed Jun. 6, 1862

George D. Ramsey of the District of Columbia claims compensation for a mulatto woman named Kitty. Kitty is between 47 and 50 years old, 5 feet 5 inches tall, well-formed and stout. She is invaluable to his family. He purchased her from John C. Robertson of Henrico County, Va., on Jul. 17, 1852, for $425 at her request. She had lived in his family but was taken by her master to Richmond to be sold. Ramsey said he felt he had an "obligation to keep her from want as long as she may live."

[Commissioners paid Ramsey $262.80.]

No. 644, Petition of Sarah Forrest   Filed Jun. 6, 1862

Sarah Forrest of Washington City claims compensation for four persons.

1. George Gantt, aged about 28, tall, black, capable and valuable in all aspects. [Value $1,000]

2. Charles Hopp, about 45, very black, well-behaved, competent as a house servant and coachman. [Value $500]

3. Rachel Hopp, aged 60, very dark, an excellent cook, washer and ironer. [Value $300]

4. Richard Marshall, aged about 35, very bright mulatto. He is lame in one foot so he does only light work such as blacking boots, cleaning knives, and the like. [Value $300]

George Gantt and Charles Hopp were inherited by Forrest. Rachel Hopp she purchased from her brother, David M. Forrest. Marshall she purchased from the estate of her uncle, Col. Crawford.

[Commissioners paid Forrest $722.70: George Gault [sic], $372.30; Charles Hopp, $262.80; Rachel Hopp, $87.60; Richard Marshal [sic], no value.]

No. 645, Petition of Rebecca Sears   Filed Jun. 7, 1862

Rebecca Sears of Washington County, D.C., claims compensation for eight persons.

1. Jane Addison, aged 37, light complexion, hearty. She is a good cook, washerwoman, ironer and house servant. [Value $1,000]

2. Nace Diggs, aged 19, black, strong. He has "one leg knock-kneed." He is a good house servant and an excellent dining room servant. [Value $800]

3. Louisa Addison, aged 13, black, well-developed and healthy. She is a good chambermaid and house servant. [Value $800]

4. Charity Diggs, aged 12, black, well-developed and healthy. She is a good chambermaid and house servant. [Value $800]

5. Ellen Addison, aged 11 years six months, light complexion, healthy and well-developed. She is a bright and intelligent girl. [Value $700]

6. Harriet Addison, aged eight, dark complexion, well-developed for her age. She is bright and intelligent. [Value $700]

7. Alfred Addison, aged five, light complexion. [Value $400]

8. Henry Addison, aged two years and six months, dark complexion. [Value $300]

She inherited them under the will of her late husband, James W. Sears, that was admitted to probate on Aug. 1, 1853, in Alexandria, Va. The younger ones were born as her slaves.

In addition to a copy of Sears's will, there is an inventory of his personal property dated Feb. 26, 1859, that was recorded in the Orphans' Court of D.C. That inventory lists ten slaves, several of whom were sold or were not listed above: Bettsey Marshall, aged 20, sold; Charles Marshall, aged 18, sold; Margaret Diggs, aged one, sold. In the inventory, the surnames of Louise, Ellen, Harriet and Alfred are given as "Solomon," not "Addison".

[Commissioners paid Sears $1,883.40: Jane Addison, $306.60; Nace Diggs, $350.40; Louisa Addison, $306.60; Charity Diggs, $262.80; Ellen Addison, $262.80; Harriet Addison, $197.10; Alfred Addison, $131.40; Henry Addison, $65.70.]

No. 646, Petition of Thomas W. Williams   Filed Jun. 7, 1862

Thomas W. Williams of Washington City claims compensation for Henrietta Young, aged 44, dark complexion, 5 feet 2 inches tall, active and sprightly. He purchased Young from John C. Cook on Apr. 23, 1860, for $500. Young is an excellent house servant, good cook, and attentive and obedient. [Value $1,000]

[Commissioners paid Williams $109.50.]

No. 647, Petition of John B. Blake   Filed Jun. 7, 1862

Dr. John B. Blake of Washington City claims compensation for Henry Peterson. He is about 36 years old, of a light black complexion, 5 feet 10 inches tall, with a sprightly countenance and stout frame. Blake purchased him Nov. 27, 1852, for $1,050 from Mr. Campbell of Baltimore. Blake says that he purchased him to enable him to use the proceeds from his labor to buy his freedom by repaying his purchase price. Peterson has paid all but $290.66 of the $1,050.

[Commissioners valued Peterson at $525.60, of which $290 was paid to Blake.]

No. 648, Petition of Ellen M. Brooke   Filed Jun. 10, 1862

Ellen M. Brooke of Washington claims compensation for three persons.

1. Eliza Shorter, aged about 35, copper colored, 5 feet 4 inches tall, stout and erect in her carriage. She is an accomplished house servant, cook, washerwoman and ironer. [Value $1,200]

2. Hannah Shorter, daughter of Eliza, aged nine, copper colored, well-grown and likely. She is very useful and handy and a good chambermaid and house servant. [Value $500]

3. Anna Shorter, aged six, copper colored, well-grown and likely. She is smart, active and useful. [Value $400]

Eliza Shorter was inherited by Brooke from her mother and she was born in her family. She has been in Brooke's service for the last thirty years. Her children were born as slaves.

[Commissioners paid Brooke by Stephen Thayer, her attorney, $657: Eliza Shorter, $350.40; Hannah Shorter, $175.20; Anna Shorter, $131.40.]

No. 649, Petition of Charles H. James, trustee of Matilda S. Holmead   Filed Jun. 10, 1862

Charles H. James, as trustee, of the city of Washington, claims compensation for three persons.

1. Priscilla Mason, aged about 31, 5 feet 5 or 6 inches tall, of a high brown color. She is a capable house servant. [Value $1,000]

2. Rachel Mason, about 28, about 5 feet 6 inches tall, dark brown color. She is a fine cook, washer and ironer and a good house servant. [Value $1,000]

3. Lucinda Mason, aged about 22, about 5 feet 4 inches tall, dark brown color. She is a highly gifted house servant. [Value $1,000]

Attached is a bill of sale dated Oct. 13, 1840, by which Sarah Holmead, for $5, conveys to Charles H. James the following slaves: Lucy, about 35, Frances, about 14, Louisa, about 12, Priscilla, about ten, Rachel, about eight, and Lucinda, about three months old. James is to hold them in trust on behalf of Sarah Holmead and, after Sarah's death, on behalf of Matilda S. Holmead, free from the control or management of any future husband.

[Commissioners paid Matilda S. Holmead, her trustee, C.H. James being deceased, pending trust, $1,270.20: Priscilla Mason, $438; Rachel Mason, $306.60; Lucinda Mason, $525.60.]

No. 650, Petition of Elizabeth Windsor   Filed Jun. 10, 1862

Elizabeth Windsor of Washington claims compensation for Lucy Ann Jones. Jones is 19 or 20 years old, chestnut colored, 5 feet 3 or 4 inches in height. She is an industrious servant, a good cook, ironer and washer. Lucy's mother belonged to Windsor and Windsor raised Lucy from a child. [Value $1,200]

[Commissions did not allow the claim as Jones was not produced.]

No. 651, Petition of Charles J. Stewart — Filed Jun. 11, 1862

Charles J. Stewart claims compensation for ten persons.

1. Samuel, aged 27, brown color, quite tall. He is a first-rate gardener and farm hand. He has refused $1,500 for him. [Value $1,500]
2. Violetta, aged 29, brown. She is an excellent house servant. [Value $1,000]
3. Eliza, aged 12, brown, she is exceedingly smart and active. [Value $700]
4. Alfred, nine. He is very smart and active. [Value $600]
5. Maria, aged 25, black. She is a first class house servant and he was offered $1,100 for her two years ago. [Value $1,100]
6. Susan, aged 15. She is an excellent servant. [Value $800]
7. Rachel, aged 13, black, smart. [Value $600]
8. Eliza, aged eight, very light color, smart and healthy. [Value $400]
9. Priscilla, six months old, very light, healthy. [Value $200]
10. Sarah, 60 years old, an excellent nurse and housekeeper. [Value $150]

Stewart's title comes from the will of his uncle, William Stewart of Anne Arundel County, Md., who left the mother of these persons to Charles and they have been raised by him from their childhood.

[Commissioners paid Stewart $2,671.80: Samuel, $635.10; Violetta, $284.70; Eliza, $284.70; Alfred, $219; Maria, $372.30; Susan, $372.30; Rachel, $284.70; Eliza, $197.10; Priscilla, $21.90, Sarah, no value.]

No. 652, Petition of John A. Peake — Filed Jun. 11, 1862

John A. Peake claims compensation for three persons.

1. Teresa Clarke, aged 18, dark color, 5 feet 1 inch high, stout and well-built. She is a good cook and valuable house servant. He has been offered $1,350 for her. [Value $1,200]
2. Harriet Clarke, aged 12, dark color, 4 feet 6 ½ inches tall, stout and well-built. She is an excellent nurse. [Value $800]
3. Thomas Clarke, aged 16, dark, 4 feet 11 inches tall. He has a sore (?) on the calf of his legs from unknown causes, but he is otherwise healthy. Peake has received for several years $8 a month for his hire. [Value $500]

[Commissioners paid Peake $1,182.60: Teresa Clarke, $503.70; Harriet Clarke, $306.60; Thomas Clarke, $372.30.]

No. 653, Petition of Emanuel D. Etchison — Filed Jun. 11, 1862

Emanuel D. Etchison of Washington claims compensation for two persons.

1. Frank Mason, aged 17, dark copper color, five feet high. He has a high forehead, snow white teeth, full chest, and heavy suit of hair. He has a good open countenance and is free and polite in conversation. He is a valuable and experienced hotel servant. [Value $1,000]
2. Joseph Mason, aged 15, very black, about 4 feet 5 inches high, stoutly built, healthy. He has a rather grim countenance when spoken to. He is a trusty office servant. [Value $1,000]

He purchased Frank from J. Hill of Baltimore on Mar. 30, 1861, for $750. He purchased Joseph from R.H. Harrison of Baltimore on Apr. 9, 1861, for $825.

[Commissioners paid Etchison $876: Frank Mason, $481.80; Joseph Mason, $394.20.]

No. 654, Petition of Lucretia R. Higgins — Filed Jun. 11, 1862

Lucretia R. Higgins of Washington claims compensation for William Johnson, aged 29. He is about 5 feet 9 or 10 inches high, of a dark brown color, and stout and well made. Thomas L.F. Higgins, Lucretia's husband, on Nov. 1, 1847, purchased "Negro Boy Bill" to serve 19 years from July 17, 1847, for $310, from the administrator of the estate of R.S. Anderson.

[Commissioners paid Higgins, $109.50.]

No. 655, Petition of Emily Beale — Filed Jun. 11, 1862

Emily Beale of the District of Columbia near Washington City claims compensation for 15 persons.
1. Delilah Johnson, aged 56, black, servant.
2. Smith Ingram, aged 75, black, servant.
3. Phillis Ingram, aged 56, light colored, servant.
4. Martha Gains, aged 35, light colored, servant.
5. Ann Gains, aged six, child of Martha.
6. Phillis Gains, aged four, child of Martha.
7. Eveline Gains, aged two, child of Martha.
8. Infant Gains, aged three weeks.
9. Rachel Ross, aged 31, dark.
10. Smith Ross, aged three, child of Rachel.
11. Anna Maria, aged one year, child of Rachel.
12. Susan Chase, aged 30, dark.
13. Robert Chase, aged ten months, con of Susan.
14. William Ingram, aged 15, light colored.
15. Isaac Jones, servant, dark, aged 60.

She purchased Delilah "Johnston" from Mr. Richards; she purchased Isaac Jones from Mr. Nicholas Queen near Washington, D.C.; she bought Smith Ingram from Mr. Hyatt in Washington. Phillis was raised in her family and all of these servants are her children and grandchildren "except the three first." [Value of all: $7,725]

[Commissioners paid Beale $2,606.10: Delilah Johnson $65.70; Smith Ingram, $21.90; Philis [sic] Ingram, $153.30; Martha Gains, $328.50; Ann, $175.20; Phillis, $131.40; Eveline, $87.60; Infant, $21.90; Rachel Ross, $459.90; Smith, $109.50; Ann Maria, $43.80; Susan Chase, $481.80; Robert Chase, $43.80; William Ingram, $438; Isaac Jones, $43.80.]

No. 656, Petition of Mary M. Manning   Filed Jun. 11, 1862

Mary M. Manning of Washington County, D.C., claims compensation for two persons.
1. Harriet Gasaway, aged 52, five feet high, chestnut color, well-built and strong. [Value $500]
2. Nancy Gasaway, child of Harriet, aged 15, medium size, intelligent and healthy. [Value $1,000]

Both are excellent house servants. They were conveyed to her by her husband, F. Manning, on Feb. 18, 1859, in consideration of $1 payment.

[Commissioners paid Manning $569.40: Harriet "Gassaway", $87.60; Nancy "Gassaway", $481.80.]

No. 657, Petition of James E. Morgan   Filed Jun. 11, 1862

Dr. James E. Morgan of the District of Columbia claims compensation for three persons.
1. Columbus Warren, aged 13 or 14, mulatto, likely, sprightly and intelligent. He drives Morgan's carriage and is his house waiter and sometimes attends to the horses and carriages. "I brought him up to my liking and he therefore to me was invaluable." [Value $800]
2. Louisa Warren, aged 42 or 43, mulatto. She is tall and rather athletic. She is an excellent cook, washer and ironer. She is sound in body "but is subject at times to depression of spirits this, as a Physician, I consider as not of the least importance." [Value $600]
3. John Warren, aged six or seven, mulatto, thick set and rather dark. He is a likely and intelligent boy and would be very useful in a year or two. [Value $500]

He purchased all three from N[icholas] Callan and Lieut. Somerville Nicholson, U.S.N., administrators of the property of the late A.A. Nicholson.

[Commissioners paid Morgan $700.80: Columbus Warren, $306.60; John Warren, $175.20; Louisa Warren, $219.]

No. 658, Petition of Daniel B. Clarke

David B. Clarke of Washington claims compensation for two persons.
1. Caroline Key, aged about 49, brown in color, medium height. She is a good cook, house servant and nurse. She is sometimes rheumatic. [Value $700]
2. Ellen Key, is aged about 39, brown, of medium height. She is a good cook, washer and ironer. [Value $800]

He inherited them. He got Caroline from the estate of his deceased father, Walter Clarke of Washington; and Ellen from the will of his deceased brother, Walter M. Clarke (who had inherited Ellen from his father).

[Commissioners paid Clarke $394.20: Caroline Key, $153.30; Ellen Key, $240.90.]

No. 659, Petition of Myra M. Alexander   Filed Jun. 12, 1862

Myra M. Alexander of Missouri, but now living with her son-in-law, F[rancis] P[reston] Blair, Jr., in Washington County, D.C., claims compensation for Florida Scott, aged 16. She is a mulatto, about 4 feet 10 inches or five feet tall, fleshy, active and free of infirmities. Her mother was owned by Alexander in Kentucky and during that time Florida was born. She was a valuable servant and attentive to Alexander's wishes and "mentally and morally compared favorably with those of her class in life." [Value $700]

[Commissioners paid Mira [sic] Alexander, by James T. Hallowell, dis. clerk P.O., acting for M[ontgomery] Blair, her attorney, $459.90.]

Montgomery Blair is Postmaster General.

No. 660, Petition of James W. Pumphrey   Filed Jun. 12, 1862

James W. Pumphrey of the District of Columbia claims compensation for two persons.

1. Gusty Jenifer, aged about 38, of a copper color, about 5 feet 8 or 9 inches tall, strong and able-bodied.
2. Bill Coates, aged about 28, about 5 feet 6 or 7 inches high, of a dark copper color, strong and able-bodied.

They were both brought up to do stable work and are known in the city as having superior qualities as ostlers. It would be difficult to replace them. They are valued at $3,000.

He purchased Gusty for $1,000 sometimes in 1858 from Joseph Beasley and William H. Thomas, administrators of the estate of the late Levi Pumphrey. He bought Bill Coates for $800 on Apr. 16, 1861, from William H. Thomas.

[Commissioners paid Pumphrey $963.60: Gusty Jenefer [sic], $438; Bill Coates, $525.60.]

Boyd's Directory for 1864, p. 232, shows that James W. Pumphrey had a livery stable on C St., north, near 6th St., west.

No. 661, Petition of John R. Ashby and Ellen G. Ashby, his wife   Filed Jun. 12, 1862

John R. and Ellen G. Ashby of the District of Columbia claim compensation for Alice Harris, aged 17. She is of a chestnut or deep copper color, about 5 feet 4 inches high, and has a large nose and thick lips. She speaks slowly when interrogated. She is an excellent nurse and house servant. [Value $800]

Alice Harris and her mother, Lucy, were in 1851 the property of John R. Ashby, who had inherited them from his father. On Mar. 10, 1851, he sold them for $350 to his brother, Samuel T. Ashby of Fauquier County, Va. On Sept. 20, 1854, for $350, Ellen G. Ashby, purchased Alice from Samuel T. Ashby. Ellen Ashby holds Alice in her own right by virtue of the articles of agreement entered into with John Ashby prior to their marriage in 1848.

[Commissioners paid John R. Ashby, Ellen G. Ashby, $525.60.]

No. 662, Petition of Joseph Prather   Filed Jun. 12, 1862

Joseph Prather of Washington City claims compensation for Fanny Smith, aged 45 years. Smith is about 5 feet 8 inches tall, copper colored, and walks very erect. He purchased her Dec. 19, 1854, from John Smith Suite for $500. (Signed John S. his x mark Suite) [Value $500]

[Commissioners paid Prather $219.]

No. 663, Petition of Terence Drury

Terence Drury of Washington City claims compensation for Nelly Semmes, aged 52. She has a very light complexion, is about 5 feet 7 inches high and is slender. She is a very desirable servant and good cook. He acquired her from Henry Ould and wife when he purchased a farm with all its crops, stock, chattels and personal effects. This was recorded May 27, 1848, in D.C. Liber W.B. No. 143, folios 313-317. [Value $800]

[Commissioners paid Drury $131.40.]

No. 664, Petition of Benjamin Ogle Tayloe   Filed Jun. 12, 1862

Benjamin Ogle Tayloe of the city of Washington claims compensation for two persons.

1. Catherine Lawson, aged 22.
2. Melinda Lawson, aged 18.

They are two light colored mulatto girls (Malinda rather lighter in color as well as size), of a pleasing appearance. They are both accomplished and valuable and worth more than $1,000 cash. The one is his cook; the other a good seamstress and his wife's maid servant. They were both educated in the family. Tayloe inherited them from his father, the late Col. John Tayloe, who inherited their ancestors from his father, who is believed in like manner to have inherited their ancestors.

[Commissioners paid Tayloe $1,095: Catharine Lawson, $547.50; Melinda Lawson, $547.50.]

No. 665, Petition of Eliza B. Mills Filed Jun. 12, 1862

Eliza B. Mills of the city of Washington claims compensation for Eliza Waters. Waters is about 62 years old, somewhat darker than the ordinary mulatto, with short hair and of a middle stature. She acquired her services by purchase from Dr. John McHenry of Baltimore about 46 years ago for $300 when Eliza Waters was about 16 years old. That purchase was made by Mills's late husband, Robert Mills, but the bill of sale, if there ever was one, has been lost or mislaid. [Value $300]

[Commissioners paid Ann M. Cosby, "executor in her own wrong", $87.60]

Robert Mills (1781-1855) was an architect and engineer who, among other things, designed the Washington Monument.

No. 666, Petition of Robert Beale Filed Jun. 12, 1862

Robert Beale of Washington claims compensation for two persons.

1. Isaac Gross, aged 35, dark but not black skin, about 5 feet 7 inches tall, rather stout with a high forehead and intelligent countenance. He is a good driver and house servant as well as a good carpenter. [Value $2,000]

2. Harriet Mason, aged 60, about 5 feet 7 inches high, dark skin, with a "projecting under lip." She stands very straight and is very heavy for her age. She is an excellent cook. [Value $300]

He purchased Isaac about ten or 11 years ago from James J. Forbes of Maryland and Harriet from George Ascom (?) about 20 years ago.

[Commissioners paid Beale $525.60: Isaac Gross, $481.80; Harriet Mason, $43.80.]

No. 667, Petition of Theodore Wheeler Filed Jun. 12, 1862

Theodore Wheeler of Washington claims compensation for three persons.

1. Elizabeth Smith, aged nine, dark brown, medium size, healthy. [Value $250]

2. Lucy Smith, aged seven, dark mulatto, good size for her age, healthy. [Value $200]

3. Martha Smith, aged two, dark brown, well-grown for her age, healthy. [Value $50]

They are children of Maria Ann Smith. Maria Ann and her infant male child were purchased on Mar. 19, 1844, by Wheeler from Thomas Burch, late of the city of Washington but now of Prince George's County, Md. At that time, Maria was aged about 18 and she, as well as of her children, were to serve until they reached age 35. (Recorded in D.C. Liber W.B. No. 107, p. 122)

[Commissioners did not allow this claim as the persons were not produced.]

No. 668, Petition of John Gibson Filed Jun. 12, 1862

John Gibson of Washington claims compensation for Jane Brooks, aged 30 or 31. She is a dark chestnut color, about 5 feet 5 inches high, stout and well-formed. She is erect in her carriage, likely and intelligent. He purchased her on Nov. 25, 1858, for $975, from Owen Sheckell, acting as agent for C.M. Price. Jane is an excellent cook and housekeeper and can command good wages for her services. [Value $1,000]

[Commissioners paid Gibson, by A. Lloyd, his attorney, $438.]

No. 669, Petition of Lucy B. Walker

Lucy B. Walker of the County of Washington, D.C., claims compensation for 13 persons.

1. Sillah West, about 56 years old, black, about 5 feet 6 inches high, a good farm hand. [Value $300]

2. Zilphia Hall, mulatto, about 42, 5 feet 6 inches high. She is a good house servant, washer and ironer, and first-rate cook. [Value $1,000]

3. Thomas Hall, black, about 37 years old, 5 feet 10 inches tall. He is a good farm hand, carriage driver, and house servant. [Value $1,200]

4. John Hall, black, about 33, about 5 feet 10 inches high. He is a good farm hand, carriage driver and house servant. [Value $1,200]

5. Hilleary Speaks, dark about 29 years old, about 5 feet 8 inches tall, a good farm hand, carriage driver and house servant. [Value $1,200]

6. Sophia Ross, dark, about 29, about 5 feet 6 inches tall. She is a first-class house servant. [Value $1,000]

7. Philip Bruce, black, about 22 years old, 5 feet 7 inches high. He is a good farm hand, carriage driver and house servant. [Value $1,200]

8. Anna Brown, mulatto, about 21 years old, 5 feet 6 inches tall. She is a good house servant, washer and ironer. [Value $1,000]

9. Benjamin Brown, mulatto, about 18, about 5 feet 7 inches high. He is a good farm hand, first-rate carriage driver, and house servant. [Value $1,200]

10. Cassy Mullican, copper colored, about 12, about 4 feet 4 inches high. She is a good house girl, very neat and tidy in her appearance. [Value $700]

11. George Ross, mulatto, about 10, about four feet high. He is a good house boy and is very active and sprightly. [Value $600]

12. Hannibal Hall, copper color, about four, about three feet high, good-looking. [Value $200]

13. Aisey Brown, mulatto about two, about 2 feet 6 inches high, good-looking. [Value $100]

The above are very valuable servants and command fine prices as hired hands (?), the men getting $20 (?) a month and the women from $6 to $8 a month.

She inherited them under the terms of the will of her late husband, Zachariah Walker, which was admitted to probate Sept. 26, 1857. That will provided that Lucy inherit all the slaves with the exception of Milly, Harriet and Mary, whom he set free and gave a portion of his farm for their use, and asked that Milly be paid $30 a year.

[Commissioners paid Walker, by Samuel Cox, attorney, $5,168.40: Sillah West, $131.40; Zilphia Hall, $306.60; Thomas Hall, $481.80; John Hall, $657; Hilleary Speaks, $657; Sophia Ross, $525.60; Philip Bruce, $613.20; Anna Brown, $481.80; Benjamin Brown, $613.20; Cassy Mullican, $306.60; George Ross, $219; Hannibal Hall, $87.60; Aisey Brown, $87.60.]

Lucy B. Cox married Zachariah Walker on Jan. 27, 1825. See Pippenger, <u>D.C. Marriage Licenses, 1811-1858</u>, p. 616.

No. 670, Petition of Mary Eleanor Tolson

Mary Eleanor Tolson of Washington County, D.C., claims compensation for Henry MacKenny, aged 11 years. He is very black, 4 feet 1 ½ inches tall, well-made and healthy. She acquired him by purchase or gift from John Tolson and George Semmes of Henry's grandmother's mother, Polly, the mother of Sally, who was the mother of Henry. Attached is a copy of the bill of sale dated 1823 by which Tolson and Semmes of Prince George's County, Md., for $500, sell to Mary E. Tolson, slaves Polly and her three children, Crissey, Henry and George. [Value $500 or $600]

[Commissioners paid Mary Ellen [sic] Tolson $240.90 for Henry "McKenny".]

No. 671, Petition of George W. Haller   Filed Jun. 12, 1862

George W. Haller of Cumberland, Md., claims compensation for Joseph Woodland. Woodland, aged about 67, is a resident of the District of Columbia, about six feet high, stout, dark colored. He is a brickmaker. Haller purchased him in 1833 with a brickyard from Joseph Libbey of Georgetown for $1,500 for both. [Value $500]

[Commissioners paid Haller, by L. Kemp Sengstack, his attorney, $65.70.]

The 1860 Census for Georgetown (Vol. 1, p. 82) lists Joseph Woodland as a free black man, aged 64 and gives his occupation as brick moulder.

No. 672, Petition of Samuel C. Crawford   Filed Jun. 12, 1862

Samuel C. Crawford of Prince George's County, Md., claims compensation for two persons.

1. Jane West, aged 35, bright copper color, five feet high, large eyes and mouth. She is a good cook, washer and ironer and servant. [Value $800]

2. Amelia Cross, aged 19, copper colored, five feet high with very long hair. She is a good cook, washer and ironer. She has been in the family of Mr. McElfresh for 11 years and has "has given entire satisfaction." [Value $1,200]

At the time of the passage of the D.C. emancipation act, they were both hired in the District of Columbia and had been for the past eleven years. He acquired them by marriage about 15 years ago. Jane West had been willed to his wife about 25 years ago; Amelia Cross was the child of Lucy Cross, who had been willed to his wife by Thomas R. Cross about 32 years ago. These wills are recorded in Annapolis, Md.

[Commissioners paid Crawford $810.30; Jane West, $262.80; Amelia Cross, $547.50.]

No. 673, Petition of Conrad Schwarz　　　　　　　　　　　　　　　　　　　　　　　　　　　Filed Jun. 12, 1862

Conrad Schwartz of Georgetown claims compensation for seven persons.

1. Ellen Amelie Thomas, aged 39, dark complexion, 5 feet 5 ½ inches tall. She is the mother of the six persons listed below. She is a cook. [Value $1,000]
2. Ann Eliza Thomas, aged 17, dark, 5 feet 2 inches tall, general house servant. [Value $800]
3. Francis Elizabeth Thomas, aged 16, brown, 5 feet 2 inches tall, general house servant. [Value $600]
4. Caroline Isabella Thomas, aged 14, brown, 4 feet 11 inches tall, chambermaid. [Value $400]
5. Louisa Alley Thomas, aged nine, brown, four feet tall, chambermaid. [Value $200]
6. Susan Virginia Thomas, aged seven, 3 feet 10 inches tall, brown. [Value $100]
7. Sarah Baker Thomas, aged five, brown, 3 feet 5 inches tall. [Value $100]

He purchased Ellen Amelia Thomas from Septimus Davis on Jan. 30, 1844. The others are her children.

[Commissioners paid J.M. Snyder, M.D., executor of Conrad Schwarz, $2,168.10: Ellen Amelia Thomas, $219; Ann Eliza Thomas, $481; Francis E. Thomas, $503.70; Caroline I. Thomas, $372.30; Louisa Alley Thomas, $284.70; Susan Virginia Thomas, $175.20; Sarah Baker Thomas, $131.40.]

No. 674, Petition of Rachael E. White　　　　　　　　　　　　　　　　　　　　　　　　　　　Filed Jun. 13, 1862

Rachael E. White of the District of Columbia claims compensation for two persons.

1. Martha Nelson, aged about 39, dark complexion, medium size, rather stout frame. She is a first-rate cook and valuable house servant. [Value $1,200]
2. Mary Jane Nelson, Martha's daughter, aged nine, light complexion. She is a bright, promising girl. [Value $800]

She purchased Martha in Alexandria, Va., from a trader named Martin about 1852 and paid $800 for her. Mary Jane was born since that purchase.

[Commissioners paid White, by W.G.W. White, her attorney, $569.40: Martha Nelson, $328.50; Mary Jane Nelson, $240.90.]

No. 675, Petition of John Wilson　　　　　　　　　　　　　　　　　　　　　　　　　　　　　Filed Jun. 14, 1862

John Wilson of the city of Washington claims compensation for Catharine Francis. Francis is aged 37, about 5 feet 5 inches tall, dark in color with black eyes and black hair. She is an industrious and valuable servant. He purchased her from John P. Hilton for $350 "to prevent her from being sent south." [Value $800]

[Commissioners paid Wilson $262.80.]

No. 676, Petition of Henry M. Harman, executor of Susanna Lowe　　　　　　　　　　　　　Filed Jun. 14, 1862

On Jun. 3, 1862, Henry M. Harman of Baltimore was granted letters of administration for the estate of Susanna Lowe, late of Washington City, D.C. He claims compensation for Maria Smith, aged 20 years and three or four months, of a dark color, about five feet high, healthy. She is a good house servant and resides with Wallace Eliot at the corner of F and 12th. Lowe purchased Smith when she was about two years old to serve until she reached age 21, which will be Dec. 20, 1862. He claims $48 on the basis of her hire of $6 a month.

[Commissioners paid Harmon [sic], executor of Susanna Lowe, $17.52.]

No. 677, Petition of Benjamin Beall　　　　　　　　　　　　　　　　　　　　　　　　　　　Filed Jun. 14, 1862

Benjamin Beall of Prince George's County, Md., claims compensation for four persons.

1. Maria Ross, aged 36, dark brown color, 5 feet 5 inches tall, stout and healthy. [Value $600]
2. George Ross, aged 26, dark brown color, 5 feet 8 inches high, well-built and healthy. [Value $800]
3. William Ross, aged 24, dark brown, 5 feet 8 inches tall, medium size. [Value $800]
4. Francis Jenifer, aged 18, mulatto, 5 feet 7 inches high, healthy and strong. [Value $900]

These persons have been a source of considerable revenue to him for a long time. He acquired title with the division of the estate of his mother, Mrs. Margaret Beall, who died in Prince George's County. (Signed Benjamin his x mark Beall)

[Commissioners paid Beall $2,124.30: Maria Ross, $240.90; George Ross, $613.20; William Ross, $635.10; Francis Jenifer, $635.10.]

No. 678, Petition of Lettisha Harshman　　　　　　　　　　　　　　　　　　　　　　　　　Filed Jun. 16, 1862

Lettisha Harshman of the District of Columbia claims compensation for William Edward Smilo, aged 27 years.

He is a black man, 5 feet 9 inches tall, stout and well-made. He is an industrious servant and a good field hand and is now engaged by Mr. Arnold at his mill at the Navy Yard Bridge. [Value $1,200]

[Commissioners paid "Letisha" her x mark Harshman, $657.]

The "Mr. Arnold" named above is probably William H. Arnold who had steam flour mills at 11th east, corner O south. See Boyd's Directory for 1864, p. 101.

No. 679, Petition of John McGinnis   Filed Jun. 16, 1862

John McGinnis of Carlisle, Tenn., claims compensation for Edward Hammond. He is about 46 years old, 5 feet 9 or 10 inches high, stout and healthy. He is a good waiter, carriage driver and whitewasher. His wife, Elizabeth McGinnis, inherited him from her father, Jeremiah Berry, who died in Prince George's County, Md.

[Commissioners paid McGinnis, by Robert C. Brooke, attorney, $262.80.]

Edward Hammond is probably the same Edward Hammond listed as a free Negro in the 1860 Census, Ward 4, (Vol. II, p. 335): Edward Hammond, aged 48, black, waiter, born in Maryland; Debora Hammond, 47, mulatto, waiter, born in Maryland; Susan Hammond, aged 19, black, waiter, born in Maryland; Robert, aged 8, black, born D.C. There is some discrepancy in the ages, but that is not at all unusual. In fact, it is probable that petitioners listed ages as younger than reality hoping to gain a higher compensation.

No. 680, Petition of Peter G. Washington   Filed Jun. 16, 1862

Peter G. Washington of Washington City claims compensation for five persons.

1. Lucinda Black, aged about 62, mulatto, of medium complexion and delicate figure. She is uncommonly smart and a good cook, washer. [Value $100]

2. Louisa Gantt, aged about 30, mulatto, of a light complexion and delicate figure. She is not of perfect health and has been reduced in flesh by nursing her infant and, probably, by overwork, and her condition not is not free from danger. She is the mother of the three children listed below. [Value $600]

3. Georgiana Gantt, aged eight, mulatto, of a dark complexion. [Value $400]

4. Lucinda Gantt, aged six, mulatto, of a dark complexion. [Value $300]

5. Sophia Gantt, aged seven months, mulatto of dark complexion. [Value $100]

Lucinda was purchased Sept. 12, 1829, from Philip Holbrook Nicklin of Philadelphia, by Margaret Washington, Peter's wife, and John Macpherson Berrien and held in trust by Berrien for Margaret. Berrien, on July 6, 1839, with Margaret's permission, assigned interest in the slaves to Peter G. Washington. Louisa Gantt is the child of Lucinda.

[Commissioners paid Washington $700.80: Lucinda Black, $43.80; Louisa Gantt, $350.40; Georgiana Gantt, $153.30; Lucinda Gantt, $131.40; Sophia Gantt, $21.90.]

The documents attached to explain the title to Lucinda are difficult to read because notations have been written on top of the originals. It appears that Margaret Washington had certain property in Philadelphia, including land and tenements and slaves, held in trust for her use and benefit, and that Lucinda Black was one of those slaves.

No. 681, Petition of Olivia C. Wootton   Filed Jun. 16, 1862

Olivia C. Wootton of Montgomery County, Md., claims compensation for Sophia Stewart. Stewart is 52 years old, dark chestnut colored and about 5 feet 1 or 2 inches tall. She is a first-rate cook and has been hired out in D.C. for many years at $6 a month. About five or six years ago she had smallpox, and since then her health has been delicate, but she has been able to perform her duties.

She was born a slave in the family of James Hopewell of St. Mary's County, Md., who is Olivia's father. His will bequeathed Sophia to her and, after her marriage to Dr. Turner Wootten, to him. Her husband's will left her in sole ownership of Sophia.

[Commissioners paid Wootton $153.30.]

No. 682, Petition of Alexander A. Greer   Filed Jun. 16, 1862

Alexander A. Greer of Washington claims compensation for two persons.

1. Ann Brooks, aged 45, 5 feet 1 or 2 inches tall, healthy and able-bodied. [Value $500]

2. Jerry Simms, son of Ann, aged 18, 5 feet (?) inches tall, sound and healthy. [Value $1,000]

They are both good house servants and are intelligent and industrious. His title comes from his wife, Mary E. Greer, who inherited Ann from the estate of her grandmother, Mrs. B. Webster, of Prince George's County, Md. Jerry was born after Ann became his property.

[Commissioners paid Greer $635.10: Ann Brooks, $109.50; "Jerre" Simms, $525.60.]

No. 683, Petition of William McKnew   Filed Jun. 16, 1862

William McKnew of Prince George's County, Md., claims compensation for four persons.

1. Maria Walker, aged about 30, dark brown or copper colored, medium size, likely. She is a first-rate house servant and excellent cook, washer and ironer and always commanded high wages. [Value $800]
2. Mary Walker, aged about eight, of a dark brown or copper color and fine-looking. [Value $500]
3. Nelly, aged about 45, black and large. She is somewhat afflicted with rheumatism, but still performs her work well. [Value $300]
4. Isaac Walker, aged five or six, dark brown or copper color, fine-looking. [Value $400]

Maria Walker was born his slave. Mary Walker and Isaac Walker were children of Maria. Nelly was allotted to his wife, Mary McKnew, in the distribution of the estate of her father, John C. Prather, whose will was filed in Prince George's County in the spring of 1861.

[Commissioners paid McKnew $700.80: Maria Walker, $284.70; Mary Walker, $219; Nelly, $87.60; Isaac Walker, $109.50.]

No. 684, Petition of Penelope Tyler   Filed Jun. 16, 1862

Penelope Tyler of Washington City claims compensation for Andrew Smith. Smith is aged 15, rather light in color, of medium size. He was a gift from Penelope's aunt, Elizabeth Tyler, in July of 1858. [Value $1,000]

[Commissioners paid Tyler $394.20.]

No. 685, Petition of Josiah Dent, adm. of William S. Nicholls   Filed Jun. 16, 1862

Josiah Dent, administrator of William S. Nicholls, claims compensation for Mary Brown, aged 62. She is a dark mulatto of full size and is a first-rate family cook. She belonged to Nicholls, late of Georgetown, at the time of his death. [Value $200]

[Commissioners paid Dent $131.40.]

No. 686, Petition of Mary Throckmorton and Josiah Dent, her trustee

The original petition is missing.

[Commissioners paid Throckmorton, by Josiah Dent, trustee $700.80. Of the amount, the sum of $440, with interest from Apr. 1, 1862, is allowed to claimants.: George Smith: not produced and not allowed; Martha, $438; Blanche, $131.40; Isaac, $87.60; Robert, $43.80; George Hays, not allowed.]

The printed report of the commissioners, p. 4, contains a discussion of Throckmorton's claim for compensation for six slaves. They were the property of John A. Throckmorton, her husband, who, in May, 1861, joined the Confederate military and went to Virginia, leaving the slaves with Mary and of their son, Charles Throckmorton. On Apr. 1, 1860, John had conveyed five of the slaves to Edward C. Carrington in trust to secure for Charles Miller the payment of a promissory note for $440. That note was repaid by Mary Throckmorton and Miller assigned the deed of trust to Josiah Dent in trust for the use of Mary. The commissioners decided that the claim by Mrs. Throckmorton as the wife of a man in rebel service could not be allowed. Mrs. Throckmorton, however, is a loyal citizen as is her son who is an officer in U.S. military service. She is thus entitled to be paid $440, the amount of the note she repaid.

No. 687, Petition of Virginia Nicholls

Virginia Nicholls of Georgetown claims compensation for two female slaves.

1. Penelope, aged 20, very dark.
2. Lavinia, aged 25, very dark.

They are both healthy and are able to perform the ordinary domestic servicing required in a family. [Value $1,000]

She got them by transfer from her brother-in-law, Robert Bowling of Fauquier County, Va., in 1856 and they have been in the District ever since.

[Commissioners paid Nicholls $1,029.30: Penelope, $525.60; Lavinia, $503.70.]

No. 688, Petition of Mary E. Reintzell and Margaret Reintzell

Mary E. Reintzell and Margaret Reintzell of Georgetown claim compensation for two slaves.

1. Charles Stewart, aged 38, a dark mulatto.
2. Walter Stewart, aged 34, a dark mulatto.

They are both sound and earn an average of $20 a month each. [Value $2,000]

They hold title by descent from Henry Reintzell, who is the husband of Mary and the father of Margaret.

[Commissioners paid Mary E. Reintzell; Margaret Reintzell, by Mary E. Reintzell, her attorney, $963.60: Charles Stewart, $438; Walter Stewart, $525.60.]

No. 689, Petition of James H. Shreve   Filed Jun. 16, 1862

James H. Shreve of Washington claims compensation for nine persons.

1. Henry Clark is aged about 24 (?), black and yellow in color, about 5 feet 9 inches tall and very likely. [Value $1,000]
2. Sandy Clark, aged about 18, black, 5 feet 9 inches high, very likely. [Value $1,000]
3. Ann, black, about 19, medium height, very likely. Value $800]
4. Henny West, black, about 33 or 34 years old, 5 feet 3 inches tall. [Value $700]
5. Julius West, about ten years old, black, medium height. [Value $700]
6. John West, about four years old, very black, likely [Value $300]
7. Laura West, about two, dark color, stout and likely. [Value $200]
8. Jubah Jones, about 57 or 58 years old, black, medium height, a little lame. [Value $200]
9. Jack Fenwick, about 63 or 64 years old, black, medium height. [Value $150]

He purchased Jubah Jones from H.G.S. Key of St. Mary's County, Md., on Sept. 12, 1858, for $525 and two pairs of mules. Negro Juba is now run away, but if Key cannot deliver him within three months, Key will pay $175 for the mules. He purchased servant woman Ann from Peter Williams of Charles County, Md., for $175 on May 7, 1856. He purchased servant woman Henny and her two boys, Julius and John on Feb. 20, 1860, from Horatio Beall of Prince George's County, Md., for $1,400. He purchased Jack Fenwick from Francis Diggs (?) of Charles County, Md. He purchased for Sandy and Henry Clark from his brother Caleb Shreve, deceased (?). They were originally the property of the late Samuel Shreve of Montgomery County, Md. Laura West is the daughter of Henny West.

[Commissioners paid Shreve $2,474.70: Henry "Clarke", $657; Sandy "Clarke", $547.50; Ann, $438; Henny West, $284.70; Julius West, $240.90; John West, $87.60; Laura West, $43.80; Jubah Jones, $87.60; Jack Fenwick, $87.60.]

No. 690, Petition of Charles Lyons

Charles Lyons of Washington City claims compensation for Jacob Cole, aged 23. Cole is of a light complexion and about 5 feet 10 inches tall. He has had the two first fingers of his left hand cut off by a hay cutting machine about four years ago. Lyons says he purchased Jacob from Mr. Sheckell of Washington, a Negro dealer, about the year 1854, as will be shown by the annexed bill of sale. Ann attached receipt dated Aug. 11, 1854, shows that B[enjamin] O. Shekell paid $700 for Jacob Cole to T.H. Barron. An attached bill of sale dated Aug. 14, 1854, shows that Thomas H. Barron and Catharine his wife, of Washington, in consideration of $900, sold to Charles Lyons three slaves: Milly Cole, of a copper color, aged about 32, to serve six years; Negro boy, Jacob Cole, aged about 15; and Negro Rosa Cole, aged about two. Rosa and Jacob are the children of Milly and are sold as slaves for life.

Jacob is a very good mechanic and has been working in Lyons's carpenter shop. [Value $1,500]

[Commissioners paid $657 to Jacob E. Lyons, administrator of Charles Lyons, deceased, by William Q. Force, his attorney, and administrator of Charles Lyons.]

No. 691, Petition of Thomas R. Brightwell

Thomas R. Brightwell of Washington claims compensation for five persons.

1. George Hawkins, aged 60, dark yellow color, about 5 feet 8 inches tall. He is a good garden and farm hand. [Value $350]
2. Margaret Fletcher, aged 40, dark mulatto, about 5 feet 4 inches high, stout. She is a first-class cook, washer and ironer and seamstress. [Value $1,200]
3. Washington Johnson, aged 33, black, about 5 feet 8 inches tall, medium build. He is a first-class garden and field hand. [Value $1,400]
4. Addel Davis, aged 21, about 5 feet 4 inches tall, black. She is a first class gardener and field hand and a good house servant. [Value $1,400]
5. Charles Fletcher, aged 11, son of Margaret, is light brown. He is sprightly and well-grown. [Value $800]

He acquired all but Margaret and Charles Fletcher, by the terms of the will of his father, John L. Brightwell, in 1846. He got Margaret from his father's estate by his sister, Ann Naylor, by an exchange by which he gave one of his servants to her for Margaret. Charles Fletcher was born of Margaret after she came into Brightwell's possession.

[Commissioners paid Brightwell $1,664.40: George Hawkins, $131.40; Margaret Fletcher, $306.60; Washington Johnson, $481.80; "Adel" Davis, $481.80; Charles Fletcher, $262.80.]

No. 692, Petition of Newton James Cox

Newton James Cox of Washington City claims compensation for Eliza Jackson. Jackson is about 53 years old, dark mulatto, about 5 feet 3 inches tall. She is an excellent domestic and makes herself useful in all ways. Cox was given Jackson by his mother, Elizabeth Pollett, in February 1858. [Value $500]

[Commissioners paid Cox $65.70.]

No. 693, Petition of James L. Cassin   Filed Jun. 17, 1862

James L. Cassin of Baltimore claims compensation for two persons.
1. Harriet Ann Thomas, aged 21, dark colored, medium size, robust and healthy.
2. Catharine Jane Thomas, aged 16 years 11 months at Apr. 16th, dark colored, medium size, healthy.

Cassin values them at $600, being one-third of the value of $900 each.

They were owned by Tabitha M. Cassin, James's mother, and were the children of Hessey Thomas who was owned by Tabitha as a slave for life. Tabitha died in April 1861, intestate, leaving James and two other sons as her only heirs. This petition pertains to James's one-third portion.

[Commissioners valued Harriet Thomas at $350.40 and Catharine Thomas at $525.60: total $876. James L. Cassin received $292. The other two interests were held by persons not claiming.]

No. 694, Petition of Barbara Ann Allnutt   Filed Jun. 17, 1862

Barbara Ann Allnutt of Montgomery County, Md., claims compensation for George Johnson. Johnson is 43 years old, copper colored, about 5 feet 9 or 10 inches tall and medium size. He is skilled in agricultural labor and has been employed in the quarries near Georgetown and at Senica. He has much experience and skill in that business. [Value $600]

She acquired title from the estate of her husband, James N. Allnutt, late of Montgomery County.

[Commissioners paid Allnutt, by J.H. Allnutt, her attorney, $350.40.]

No. 695, Petition of Francis Mohun   Filed Jun. 17, 1862

Francis Mohun of Washington claims compensation for Mary Marlow. She is 27 years old, dark mulatto, about 5 feet 3 inches tall, medium size with a pleasant, open countenance. She is quite intelligent and reads and writes tolerably well. She is a good cook, washer and ironer and seamstress. Mohun purchased her by a series of notes totaling $400 on Mar. 13, 1848, at her request, from David Barry when he was about to sell her, as he did others of his slaves, to the South. At the time of her purchase she was called Lydia, but since then has changed her name to Mary. [Value $1,000]

[Commissioners paid Mohun $438.]

No. 696, Petition of Jourdan W. Maury   Filed Jun. 17, 1862

Jourdan W. Maury of Wilmington, Del., claims compensation for three persons.
1. Maria, aged about 23, very black, very short, weighs above 110 pounds. She is the mother of John and George. Maria is a good cook and nurse and is efficient in every branch of house work.
2. John, mulatto, about eight.
3. George, between two and three years, mulatto.

[Value for the three, $2,000]

He purchased Maria and John about seven years ago from his brother-in-law, Thomas (?) S. McNeir.

[Commissioners paid Maury, by A. Thomas Bradley, his attorney, $613.20: Maria, $372.30; John, $153.30; George, $87.60.]

Maury married Sally Maria McNeir on Nov. 9, 1846. See Pippenger, D.C. Marriage Licenses, 1811-1858, p. 391.

No. 697, Petition of Harriet R. Marshall   Filed Jun. 17, 1862

Harriet R. Marshall of Prince George's County, Md., claims compensation for two persons.
1. Rezin Gantt, aged about 52, very black, 5 feet 9 inches high. He has a pleasant face, but is slow of speech. He is a good farm hand.

2. Nancy Gantt, wife of Rezin, about 50, copper colored, with a very thin face and long and rather straight hair. She is an excellent nurse, but last July she was struck with paralysis which greatly diminished her value.

She values the two at $550.

She acquired them under the terms of the will of her mother, the late Eleanor A.H. Marshall of D.C. Attached is a copy of the will by which Eleanor bequeathed to Harriet, when she reached age 18, the servants Rezin, Nancy, Hannah, Isreal, Frank, Mariah and Easter. The will was proved Nov. 20, 1852.

[Commissioners paid Marshall, by A. Thomas Bradley, her attorney, $153.30: "Resin" Gantt, $153.30; Nancy Gantt, no value.]

No. 698, Petition of Leonard Harbaugh — Filed Jun. 17, 1862

Leonard Harbaugh of Washington City claims compensation for four persons.

1. Henry Diggs, about 24 or 25 years old, dark brown, about 5 feet 8 inches tall, well-built and strong. He has a scar on his face caused by a burn when he was a child. He is a capable house servant.

2. Sarah Prout, about 30, a little lighter in color than Henry, same height, rather slender. She is a good cook.

3. Juliana Prout, child of Sarah, between five and six years old, mulatto, thin. She is very promising.

4. Rose Prout, child of Sarah, about two years old, mulatto, thin. She is very promising.

He obtained Henry and Sarah in right of his wife. Juliana and Rose were born while their mother was in servitude. He values them at $2,700.

[Commissioners paid Harbaugh, by D. Harbaugh, his attorney, $1,182.60: Henry Diggs, $591.30; Sarah Prout, $416.10; Juliana, $131.40; Rose, $43.80.]

Leonard Harbaugh married Winifred Sophia Page on Feb. 5, 1839. See Pippenger, D.C. Marriage Licenses, 1811-1858, p. 260.

No. 699, Petition of George S. Krafft — Filed Jun. 17, 1862

George S. Krafft of the District of Columbia claims compensation for Linda Wood. Wood is about 50 years old, dark copper color, about 5 feet 2 inches tall. She has a pleasant face and hesitates in speech when spoken to. She is a valuable cook. She was purchased Linda from Abraham F. Kimmell of Washington about 185-, for $125, to prevent her from being sold and separated from her husband who resided in Washington. [Value $300]

[Commissioners paid Krafft $87.60 for Lucinda or Linda Wood.]

No. 700, Petition of Joseph C. Fearson — Filed Jul. 17, 1862

Joseph C. Fearson of Washington City claims compensation for two persons.

1. Emily Clarke, about 28 or 29 years old, black, about 5 feet high, stout and well-built. She is a valuable general house servant. She is good-tempered and can read and write.

2. Jenny Clarke, Emily's child, aged about five, dark copper color, 3 feet 6 inches tall, very sprightly. She is a promising child for her age.

He values both at $1,200. He purchased them from William A. Brown of Washington on Jul. 8, 1858, for $1,000.

[Commissioners paid Fearson $613.20: Emily Clarke, $481.80; Jenny Clarke, $131.40.]

No. 701, Petition of Verlinda W. Wells by her husband, John Wells

Verlinda M. Wells, by her husband, John Wells, of Prince George's County, Md., claims compensation for two persons.

1. William Henry Harrison, aged 34, dark brown or black in color, 5 feet 6 inches high, smooth face.

2. Isaac Keppler, William Henry's brother, aged 29, very much like his brother in color and size. He has a scar on one of his ears.

He estimates the value of both at $2,400.

Wells states that he received them from his daughter, Elizabeth Susannah Wells, late of Washington City. He was her next of kin. He also states there is a deed by which John Wells, administrator of Elizabeth Wells, transfers title to Washington Hilleary "in trust in consideration of natural love & affection."

[Commissioners paid $1,007.40 to Verlinda M. Wells, by C. O. Lewis, her attorney: William H. Hanson [sic], $438; Isaac Kepler [sic], $569.40.]

No. 702, Petition of William R. Birch — Filed Jun. 17, 1862

William R. Birch of Alexandria County, Va., claims compensation for Lucy Honesty. Honesty is ten years old, a very dark person with regular features. She is held to service until she reaches age 28, after which she is to be free. She has been well-raised and trained in all the purposes of housekeeping and has just come of an age to be very serviceable. [Value $900]

She was given to his wife by her mother, Mrs. Barbary Shreves, about eight years ago. Mrs. Shreves acquired Lucy from the will of her sister, Solony Swinks (?), who formerly owned Lucy's mother.

[Commissioners paid Birch $131.40.]

No. 703, Petition of James H. Shreve, administrator of Samuel Shreve

This original petition is missing.

[Commissioners paid Shreve $657: Caroline Grayson, $481.80; George W. Grayson, $43.80; Leannan Smith, $131.40.]

No. 704, Petition of Woodford Stone

Woodford Stone of Washington City claims compensation for two persons.

1. Barney Clark, aged 31, light mulatto, about 5 feet 7 or 8 inches tall, strong and well-built. He is capable of all kinds of work, especially such as relates to saw mills and boats.

2. George Clark, aged about 14, copper colored. He is a good house servant and stable boy.

He purchased Barney about ten years ago in Virginia. He inherited George from his father.

[Commissions paid Stone $810.30: Barney "Clarke", $481.80; George "Clarke", $328.50.]

No. 705, Petition of Henry Naylor — Filed Jun. 17, 1862

Henry Naylor of the County of Washington, D.C., claims compensation for 18 persons.

1. Charles Young, aged about 67, dark chestnut color, about 5 feet 10 inches tall. He is a good farm hand. [Value $200]

2. James Dixon, about 57, dark color, about 5 feet 3 inches high. He is a good farm hand and gardener. [Value $500]

3. William Taney, about 38, black, about 5 feet 8 inches high. He is a good farm hand, carriage driver, grain and grass mower and a good plain cook. [Value $1,500]

4. Bill Wood, about 28, dark, about 5 feet 9 inches high. He is a good farm hand, carriage driver, corn planter, gardener, and the like. [Value $1,200]

5. Clara Norris, about 55, dark, about 5 feet 3 inches tall. She is a good house servant, washer and ironer and a first-rate cook. [Value $400]

6. Frank Williams, aged about 19, dark mulatto, 5 feet 3 inches tall. He is a good farm hand, and pretty good house servant. [Value $1,200]

7. Tom Williams, aged about 15, black, about 5 feet 1 inch tall. He is a very active, smart boy about the farm and house. [Value $1,000]

8. Dick Williams, about 14, dark, about 4 feet 8 or 9 inches tall. He is quick and sprightly and handy about the house. [Value $800]

9. John Williams, about eight years old. He is a very good boy. [Value $400]

10. Chloe Dixon, about 38 or 39, about 5 feet 4 inches tall, dark chestnut color. She is a good washer and ironer. [Value $1,000]

11. Mary Jane Diggs, about 23, bright mulatto, 5 feet 2 inches tall. She is a very capable house servant, good cook, washer and ironer. [Value $1,200]

12. Stephen Dixon, about 21 or 22, black, 5 feet 6 inches tall. He is a good farm hand. [Value $1,500]

13. Sarah Dixon, about 17, dark, five feet high. She is a good house servant, washer and ironer. $1,200]

14. Ellen Dixon, about 13, dark, 4 feet 9 inches high. She is accustomed to house duties. [Value $1,100]

15. Winney Dixon, about ten, dark, very stout. She is stout and well-maid. [Value $700]

16. Maria Ann Dixon, about six, dark, very stout. She is sprightly and active. [Value $500]

17. Joseph Dixon, about 14 months, dark. He is a fine, healthy child. [Value $150]

18. Kitty West, about seven years, dark mulatto, very stout. She is going to make a very smart woman. She is the daughter of Mary Jane Diggs. [Value $500]

Numbers 11 through 17 are the children of Chloe Dixon.

Naylor states that Chloe Dixon and her children and grandchildren are his by right of survivorship as joint tenant with his late brother, George Naylor. He wishes the award for these to be separate and distinct from his other claims as he intends that the kin of his brother should have equal share in amount awarded.

Charles Young he purchased from Mrs. R[osa] O. Gantt. James Dixon he purchased from Thomas Williams. William Taney he purchased from Dennis Sweeny. Bill Wood he purchased from Sarah Holmead and others. Clara Norris he purchased from the marshal of the District; Frank Williams, Tom Williams and John Williams are the children of Ann Williams, and Dick Williams is the child of Clara Williams. Both Ann and Clara were purchased by Naylor for a term of years and their children were born during this period.

[Commissioners paid Naylor $5,518.80: Charles Young, $21.90; James Dixon, $131.40; William Taney, $525.60; Bill Wood, $284.70; Clara Norris, $219; Frank Williams, $481.80; Tom Williams, $394.20; Dick Williams, $306.60; John Williams, $175.20; Chloe Dixon, $394.20; Mary Jane Diggs, $525.60; Stephen Dixon, $613.20; Sarah Dixon, $481.80; Ellen Dixon, $372.30; Winney Dixon, $219; Maria Ann Dixon, $131.40; Joseph Dixon, $43.80; Kitty West, $197.10.]

No. 706, Petition of Henry Naylor, Administrator of George Naylor   Filed Jun. 17, 1862

Henry Naylor, administrator of George Naylor of the County of Washington, D.C., claims compensation for five persons.
1. Susan Vigel, about 44 (?) years old, dark, 5 feet 3 or 4 inches high. She is a good family servant.
2. Jane Vigel, about 18, dark, 5 feet 1 inch tall. She is a good house girl.
3. Sally Washington, about 13 (?) years old, black, 4 feet 9 inches tall. She is a good house girl.
4. Aline Washington, about 10, dark, 4 feet 7 inches high.
5. John Washington, about seven, dark, three feet high.

Jane, Sally, Aline, and John are the children of Susan Vigel.

Henry states that he is the administrator of the personal estate of his brother, George, and that Susan "Vigil" was a part of that estate. The other servants are the children of Susan and were born since the death of George. George's children were quite small when he died and Henry has had general charge and management of his family and estate, which has never been settled or distributed.

[Commissioners paid Naylor $1,379.70: Susan "Vigell", $350.40; Jane "Vigell", $175.20; Sally Washington, $372.30; Aline Washington, $284.70; John Washington, $197.10.]

No. 707, Petition of Martha A. Linton   Filed Jun. 17, 1862

Martha A. Linton of Washington claims compensation for eight persons.
1. Charlotte Mudd, aged 52, dark color, 5 feet 3 inches tall. [Value $450]
2. Henny Geary, aged 49, dark color, 5 feet 6 inches tall. [Value $700]
3. Camilia Jones, aged 40, dark color, 5 feet 3 inches tall. [Value $800]
4. George P. Mudd, aged 25, dark color, 5 feet 6 inches tall. [Value $1,250]
5. Cornelia Jones, aged 26, dark color, 5 feet 7 inches tall. [Value $1,050]
6. George Jones, aged 12, light color, medium size. [Value $600]
7. Frances Geary, aged nine, dark, medium size. [Value $425]
8. Allice Jones, aged four, light color, medium size. [Value $225]

Linton inherited them. They were deeded by her father, James H. Birch, to his wife, Sarah B. Birch, and at Sarah's death, were held for the benefit of her children. Martha is the only living child of Sarah. Her trustee, William E. Posey, when last heard from was living in Alabama.

[Commissioners paid Linton $2,430.90: Charlotte Mudd, $131.40; Henry [sic] Geary, $219; Camilia Jones, $284.70; George P. Mudd, $613.20; Cornelia Jones, $569.40; George Jones, $284.70; "Francis" Geary, $219; "Alice" Jones, $109.50.]

No. 708, Petition of Leonora M. Williams

Leonora M. Williams of Washington claims compensation for three persons.
1. Charlotte Jones, aged 66, black, an excellent cook and servant.
2. Nancy Carter aged about 30, above 5 feet 5 inches tall, of a copper color.
3. John Hawkins, about nine. He is a useful house servant.

They were assessed for taxes at a valuation of $1,400. She values them now at $1,800.

They belonged to her husband, John Williams, before they were married, and by a deed recorded in D.C. Liber J.A.S. No. 211, folio 154, they were conveyed to Frederick W. Jones, in trust, for the sole use of Leonora.

[Commissioners paid Williams $810.30: Charlotte Jones, $65.70; Nancy Carter, $525.60; John Hawkins, $219.]

No. 709, Petition of James F. Essex Filed Jun. 17, 1862

James F. Essex of Georgetown claims compensation for three persons.
1. Abraham Gibson, aged 55, black, 5 feet 10 inches tall. He is a hostler.
2. Sarah Ward, aged 50, light mulatto, 5 feet 6 inches high. She is a cook, washer and ironer.
3. John Morsell Ward, aged 13, dark mulatto, 4 feet 6 inches tall. He attends to Essex's stable.
The value of the three is $1,300.

He bought Abraham for $600 at public sale of the property of John W. Bronaugh about ten yeas ago. Sarah was bought out of jail 12 years ago for $800. John was born his property.

[Commissioners paid Essex $503.70: Abraham Gibson, $65.70; Sarah Ward, $109.50; John Morsell Ward, $328.50.]

No. 710, Petition of William Basil Robertson Filed Jun. 17, 1862

William B. Robertson of Prince George's County, Md., claims compensation for Lewis Cammel, aged 23. He is of a dark color, about six feet high, straight, stout and well-made. He works in the anchor shop at the Navy Yard in Washington and Robertson receives for his hire $300 a year. He inherited Cammel under the terms of the will of his late father, John Robinson of Prince George's County. Attached is an except from John Robinson's will by which he bequeaths to his son, William Basil Robertson, Negro man William and Negro man Lewis. The will was admitted to probate on Sept. 7, 1848. [Value $1,500]

[Commissioners paid Robertson $788.40.]

No. 711, Petition of William Swann, administrator of Meekey Lanham Filed Jun. 18, 1862

William Swann of Prince George's County, Md., as administrator of the late Meekey Lanham of the same county, claims compensation for Negro Eliza. Eliza is 40 years old, dark color, about 4 feet 11 inches tall, stout. She is a good house servant, cook, washer and ironer. Meekey Lanham held title by inheritance from his father, the late Hezekeiah Lanham of Prince George's County. Eliza is held by Swann for the benefit of the heirs of the late Meekey Lanham: William Swann, Richard Swann, Ellen Ball, Charlotte Ann Sheriff, Mary Atchison, Sarah Ann Talbott, Caroline Talbott, Rachael Talbott and Charlotte Osborne. Swann was granted his letters of administration on Apr. 11, 1862. [Value $1,000]

[Commissioners paid Swann $219.]

No. 712, Petition of Thomas Orme Filed Jun. 18, 1862

Thomas Orme of Georgetown claims compensation for Kitty Lucas. Lucas is 59 years old, a dark mulatto, about 5 feet 5 inches tall. She is a good cook, washer and ironer. He purchased Lucas on Oct. 6, 1858, for $175 from Elizabeth E. Hunton. [Value $175]

[Commissioners paid Orme $87.60.]

No. 713, Petition of Mary H. Murray, widow and admin. of Stanislaus Murray Filed Jun. 18, 1862

Mary H. Murray, widow and administrator of the late Stanislaus Murray, claims compensation for three persons.
1. John Butler, aged about 25 or 26, about 5 feet 10 or 11 inches high, of a light yellow complexion. He has few superiors as a dining room and house servant.
2. Charlotte Butler, aged about 22 or 23, very light complexion, about five feet high. She is a good cook, washer and ironer and general house servant.
3. Margaret Marlow, aged 16, about 4 feet 7 or 8 inches high, of a brown complexion. She is a good house servant and is active and smart.

The value of the three is $3,000. John Butler was bought from Charles S. Williams of Charles County, Md., in the spring of 1855 for $800; Charlotte Butler was bought from Williams in the fall of 1853 for $750; Kitty belonged to the late Mary C. Hamilton and came to Stanislaus Murray through his wife to whom she had been devised by Hamilton.

[Commissioners paid Murray $1,511.10: John Butler, $569.40; Charlotte Butler, $547.50; Margaret Marlow, $394.20.]

Stanislaus Murray married Mary H. Hamilton on Mar. 19, 1839. See Pippenger, D.C. Marriage Licenses, 1811-1858, p. 435.

No. 714, Petition of John Marbury, Jr., Judson Mitchell   **Filed Jun. 18, 1862**
   Charles A. Buckey, trustees for Mrs. Ann Ogle

John Marbury, Jr., Judson Mitchell and Charles A. Buckey, of Georgetown, trustees for Mrs. Ann Ogle, claim compensation for three persons.

   1. George W. Butler, aged two years and six months, chestnut colored. He is of the usual size for one his age. He is near the age to be useful. [Value $400]

   2. John Summerfield Butler, aged three years six months, a little darker color than George, of the usual size for children his age. [Value $300]

George and John were owned by William Nelson, deceased, and at the distribution of his estate was allotted to his daughter, Mrs. Ann Ogle. On Jul. 3, 1855, Ann Ogle and her husband, Benjamin Ogle, entered into a deed by which they settled all the property of the wife upon the trustees for the benefit of Ann Ogle. The two children are the offspring of the woman named in that deed of trust. This is recorded in D.C. Liber J.A.S. No. 107, folio 132.

   [Commissioners paid the trustees $284.70: John S. Butler, $197.10; George W. Butler, $87.60.]

   Benjamin R. Ogle married Anna V[irginia] Nelson Jun. 9, 1849. See Pippenger, D.C. Marriage Licenses, 1811-1858, p. 453.

No. 715, Petition of Bladen Forrest, trustee for Mary Helen Forrest   **Filed Jun. 18, 1862**

Bladen Forrest of Georgetown, trustee of Mary Helen Forrest, claims compensation for eight persons.

   1. George Carter, aged 40, dark complexion, about 5 feet 10 inches tall. He has a scar on one cheek. He is a first-class teamster and farm hand. He has for several months been employed by the government at $25 a month. [Value $1,200]

   2. Theodore Butler, aged 19, dark complexion, 5 feet 6 inches tall. He is very stout with round shoulders, large eyes and a serious countenance except when spoken to. He is a first-class carriage driver and house servant. [Value $1,300]

   3. Ann Carter, aged 43, dark complexion, about 5 feet 6 inches tall. She has bad upper teeth and a rather pleasant expression. She is an excellent cook, washer and ironer and chamber maid. [Value $1,000]

   4. Mary Carter, aged 16, dark complexion, about 5 feet 6 inches tall. She has short hair, sound teeth, a pleasant countenance and is well-proportioned. She is a good nurse and chambermaid. [Value $1,100]

   5. Adelaide Carter, aged nine, dark complexion, about 4 feet 3 inches tall. She "shows her teeth very much when she smiles." She is very smart for her age. [Value $750]

   6. John Carter, aged five, dark complexion, supposed to be three feet tall. He is a healthy boy. [Value (?)]

   7. Sally Carter, aged 14, dark complexion, about 5 feet 4 inches tall. She is quite large for her age. She is a good bread maker, nurse and chamber servant. [Value $1,000]

   8. Susan Mason, aged about 90, mulatto. She is very much bent with a low statue and is about four feet high. She is old and infirm. [no value]

George Carter was acquired by inheritance. Theodore Butler, Ann Carter, Mary Carter and Sally Carter were purchased from the estate of Charles King in 184 (?) with funds he held as executor of the estate of his father-in-law, James Keith. The investment was made for the sole benefit of his family. Adelaide and John are the children of Ann Carter. Susan Mason was given to him by his aunt, Catherine Forrest, so that "she might be property cared for being at the time old & unable to support herself."

   [Commissioners paid Forrest $2,628: George Carter, $525.60; Theodore Butler, $547.50; Ann Carter, $284.70; Mary Carter, $481.80; Adelaide Carter, $219; John Carter, $131.40; Sally Carter, $438; Susan Mason, no value.]

   Bladen Forrest married Mary Helen Keith on Oct. 8, 1840. See Pippenger, D.C. Marriage Licenses, 1811-1858, p. 210.

No. 716, Petition of Andrew Mercer of R.   **Filed Jun. 18, 1862**

Andrew Mercer, of R., of Lisbon, Howard County, Md., claims compensation for Thomas Oren, aged about 23. He is mulatto, about 5 feet 8 inches high with thick hair and is healthy and strong. He is held for a term to end in November 1869, but he has been a fugitive from service since March 1861 and that will add to his term. Mercer believes him to be residing in Georgetown, but has no proof. He has requested the clerk of the court that when Thomas applies for his free papers, that the clerk require him to call upon the Commissioners and identify himself. He purchased Thomas about nine years ago from William Norris, administrator of John McElfresh of Frederick County, Md., for $350, to serve a term of years. [Value $400]

   [Commissioners did not allow the claim as Orem was not produced.]

No. 717, Petition of Lewis Carusi   Filed Jun. 20, 1862

Lewis Carusi of Washington City claims compensation for the following three persons.

1. Harry Whiting, aged about 47, copper colored, about 4 feet 8 ½ inches tall. He is an uncommonly intelligent servant. [Value $1,200]

2. Kitty Whiting, aged about 44, black, rather stout, medium height. She is an excellent cook and washer and ironer. She is "apt to indulge in the use of intoxicating drinks to excess." [Value $900]

3. Peter Whiting, aged about 20, black, about 5 feet 9 ½ inches high. He is an intelligent servant and store hand and understands the care of horses. [Value $1,500]

He purchased Harry and Kitty Whiting upwards of 20 years ago. Pete was born since that purchase.

[Commissioners paid Lewis Carusi, by E[ugene] Carusi, his attorney, $1,095: Henry Whiting, $328.50; Kitty Whiting, $175.20; Peter Whiting, $591.30.]

No. 718, Petition of Zachariah Duvall   Filed Jun. 20, 1862

Zachariah Duvall of Washington City claims compensation for six persons.

1. Mary Harwood, about 30 years old, dark copper color, below medium height. She is a good cook and house servant. She is a little lame in one foot.

2. Tom [Harwood}, child of Mary, three or four years old.

3. Martha Johnson, 21 or 22 years old, copper colored, about 5 feet 4 (?) inches tall. She is a good nurse, laundress, seamstress and a first-rate servant.

4. Frank [Johnson], child of Martha, rather lighter in color than his mother, three or four years old.

5. Hester Wright, aged about 19 or 20, light copper colored, about 5 feet 8 inches high. She is a good nurse, laundress, seamstress and a first-rate servant.

6. Mary [Wright], Hester's daughter, about 19 months old, of a light copper color.

The children are all healthy and very promising. Value of the total: $3,600.

Mary was purchased from Mr. Thomas (?) Pumphrey of Anne Arundel County, Md., about 12 years ago. Martha and Hester were given to his wife by her father, John Ridout, of Pleasant Plains, Anne Arundel County, Md., on Jun. 18, 1852.

[Commissioners paid Duvall $1,642.50: Mary Harwood, $394.20; Tom, her son, $109.50; Martha Johnson, $481.80; Frank, her son, $87.60; Hester Wright, $525.60; Hester [sic], her infant, $43.80.]

In the original petition, the name of Hester's child is given in one place as "Hester" and at another as "Mary". The commissioners gave her name as "Hester."

No. 719, Petition of Edward M. Linthicum   Filed Jun. 20, 1862

Edward M. Linthicum of Georgetown claims compensation for four slaves.

1. Elizabeth, aged 39, dark mulatto.

2. Martha, light mulatto, aged 32.

3. Jenny, very dark, aged 26.

4. Peggy, dark mulatto, aged 19.

All of the above are of full size and good appearance and healthy. They are valuable household servants who have been well-trained by himself and his wife. He values them at $2,500.

His right is based on that of his wife, Mary Linthicum, to whom they descended from her parents in Maryland.

[Commissioners paid Linthicum $1,730.10: Elizabeth, $372.30; Martha, $438; Jenny, $438, Peggy, $481.80.]

No. 720, Petition of William P. Drury   Filed Jun. 20, 1862

William P. Drury of Washington City claims compensation for Priscilla McPhearson. She is 60 years old, dark in color, 4 feet 8 inches tall and "quick in expression." She is an honest, faithful servant. He obtained his title by marriage to Mary Elizabeth Lenman in 1845, who acquired her title by inheritance from her parents who had purchased Priscilla in Alexandria. [Value $300]

[Commissioners paid Drury $87.60 for Priscilla "McPherson".]

No. 721, Petition of Andrew J. Harding, executor of John Harding   Filed Jun. 20, 1862

Andrew J. Harding of Maryland, executor, claims compensation for George Brooks. Brooks is 28 years old, mulatto, about six feet high. He is an "A. No. 1 farm hand" and can direct and supervise all the work on a farm. Brooks belonged to Andrew's father, John Harding, who resided in Montgomery County, Md., and he is his father's heir and the executor of his will. John Harding died last August. [Value $1,500]

[Commissioners paid Andrew his x mark Harding, $591.30.]

No. 722, Petition of John M. Roberts   Filed Jun. 20, 1862

John M. Roberts of Washington City claims compensation for Eliza Jordan. Jordan is between seven and eight years old, black, 4 feet 10 inches tall. She has two scars caused by burns, one on her right forehead and the other on the back of one of her hands. She is quick and active and promising in every way. He purchased Eliza from a man named Thomas Sheriff in Prince George's County, Md., about three or four years ago. That purchase included Eliza's mother and her four children and was made to prevent their being sold out of the country. Within the past few months, the mother and three of the children have absconded. [Value $500]

[Commissioners paid Roberts $175.20.]

No. 723, Petition of Ann Roberts   Filed Jun. 30, 1862

Ann Roberts of Washington City claims compensation for four persons.

1. Harriet Gordon, aged about 46, dark mulatto, about 5 feet 3 inches tall. She is a first-rate cook, washer and ironer.

2. David [Gordon], Harriet's son, aged 12, dark mulatto, about 5 feet 8 inches high. He is very promising and is very useful as a stable boy and servant.

3. Lilly Tibbles, aged 43, black, about 5 feet 6 inches high. She is a first-rate nurse, cook, washer and ironer.

4. Lucinda [Tibbles], aged 18, bright mulatto, about 5 feet 6 inches tall. She is a valuable house servant, chambermaid, washer and ironer.

She values them at $3,600.

She purchased Harriet from her brother, Thomas Loker about 20 years ago. Lilly's mother was inherited by Roberts from her father. David and Lucinda were born after their mothers were held to servitude by Roberts.

[Commissioners paid Ann Roberts, by John W. Roberts, attorney, $1,160.70: Harry [sic] Gordon, $131.40; David, her son, $350.40; Lilley Tibbes [sic], $153.30; Lucinda, her child, $525.60.]

No. 724, Petition of Erasmus J. Middleton, trustee for Mary Jane Perry   Filed Jun. 20, 1862

Erasmus J. Middleton of the County of Washington, trustee for Jane Perry of the city of Washington, claims compensation for three persons.

1. Caroline Shaw, aged 30, mulatto, about 5 feet 5 inches high, medium size. She is a hypochondriac and but for that would be a most excellent servant. She is a good cook, washer and ironer. [Value $300]

2. Anna Maria Smith, aged 23, brown colored, 5 feet 3 inches high, rather stout. She is a good cook, washer and ironer, and a good house servant. [Value $1,000]

3. Maria Louisa Dorsey, aged 15, copper colored, 4 feet 11 inches high, of ordinary size. She is a very good house servant and an excellent nurse. [Value $750]

The above named are the descendants of old family servants. His title comes by right of his wife by Augustus E. Perry, on a division of the estate of her father, Richard Ross of Montgomery County, Md. Anna Maria Smith also comes to him by right of his wife by Augustus E. Perry on a division of the estate of her mother, Mrs. Elizabeth Ross, who died in Washington in 1848.

[Commissioners paid E.J. Middleton $1,095: Caroline Shaw, $175.20; Ann Maria Smith, $481.80; Maria Louisa Dorsey, $438.]

Elizabeth Ross's will may be found in Pippenger, D.C. Probate Records, 1801-1852, p. 322. Erasmus J. Middleton was Elizabeth's son-in-law and was named trustee of Mary Jane Perry, her daughter and the wife of Augustus E. Perry. Erasmus is probably the husband of Ellen Ross Middleton. See directly below.

No. 725, Petition of Augustus E. Perry, trustee for Ellen R. Middleton   Filed Jun. 20, 1862

Augustus E. Perry, trustee for Ellen R. Middleton, claims compensation for six persons.

1. Lucy Shaw, aged 58, brown colored, 5 feet 5 inches tall. She has a scar over her left eye. She is a good cook, washer and ironer. [Value $700]

2. Gusty Shaw, aged 27, brown colored, six feet high, stout, straight and well-made. He is an excellent farmer, gardener and marketer. He manages the farm and garden of Mr. [Erasmus J.] Middleton. [Value $1,800]

3. Dawson Shaw, aged 22, black, 5 feet 7 ½ inches high, straight and well-made, of ordinary size. He is a first-rate house servant and coachman. [Value $1,400]

4. Sidney Shaw, son of Lucy Shaw, aged 18, dark mulatto, 5 feet 9 inches tall. He is a good farm hand. [Value $1,300]

5. Sally Price, aged seven, dark brown, 3 feet 11 inches tall, sprightly with a pleasant countenance. She is a promising girl. [Value $300]

6. Gusty Jones, aged 27, black man, 5 feet 6 inches high, straight and well-made. He has lost the nail of his right thumb. He is a good farm hand, house servant, hostler and coachman. [Value $1,200]

Lucy, Gusty and Dawson Shaw come by right of E[rasmus] J. Middleton, in right of his wife, on division of the estate of her father, the late Richard Ross of Montgomery County, Md. Sidney is the son of Lucy and was born in the family of Middleton. Sally was also born in Middleton's family but her mother died about a year ago. The claim to her service was acquired of Mr. Middleton in right of his wife, on the division of the estate of her mother, Elizabeth Ross who died in 1848. Augustus (Gusty) Jones was purchased by Perry, as trustee, on May 7, 1857, from the agent for Nicholas L. Queen for $!,100.

[Commissioners paid Perry $2,759.40: Lucy Shaw, $109.50; Gusty Shaw, $700.80; Dawson Shaw, $613.20; Sidney Shaw, $591.30; Sally Price, $197.10; Gusty Jones, $547.50.]

See No. 724 directly above. Augustus E. Perry is the son-in-law of Elizabeth Ross and the trustee for her daughter, Ellen Middleton. Augustus Perry married Mary Jane Ross on Dec. 26, 1844. See Pippenger, D.C. Marriage Licenses, 1811-1858, p. 469.

No. 726, Petition of John D. Hammack   Filed Jun. 20, 1862

John D. Hammack of Washington City claims compensation for two persons.

1. Rachel Meekins, about 40 years old, copper colored, about five feet tall. She has a slight defect in her foot from her birth. She is a fine housekeeper, an excellent cook and has superintended his restaurant for the last three years. [Value $700]

2. Charlotte, aged about 40, copper colored, about 5 feet 3 inches tall. She has been used as a dishwasher and general help in the kitchen. She is also a good chambermaid. [Value $300]

He purchased "Sharlotte" from Thompson Nailor of Washington on Oct. 14, 1861, for $300. He purchased Rachel for $500 from Allison Nailor of Washington on Mar. 15, 1860. [Value $700]

[Commissioners disallowed this claim as the persons were not produced.]

Hammack had a restaurant on Pennsylvania Avenue in Washington. See Boyd's Directory for 1860.

No. 727, Petition of Emily Lang   Filed Jun. 20, 1862

Emily Lang of Washington City claims compensation for Lin. Lin is aged 45, black, 5 feet 5 inches tall. She is a valuable house servant, cook, washer and ironer. Lang purchased her from the estate of her father, Samuel Shreve, late of Montgomery County, Md. [Value $300] (Signed Emily her mark Lang)

[Commissioners paid Lang $131.40.]

Emily Ann Shreve married Robert Lang on Dec. 6, 1842. See Pippenger, D.C. Marriage Licenses, 1811-1858, p. 350.

No. 728, Petition of Robert R. Aylmer   Filed Jun. 20, 1862

Robert R. Aylmer of Washington City claims compensation for Margaret Watkins, aged 20 years. Watkins has a copper colored complexion, is about five feet high and has a very pleasing countenance. She was raised in his family from infancy and is very intelligent. She has been taught to spell and read quite well and "every advantage, indulgence and comfort given to her, the same as rendered to my own family." She is a valuable servant and child's nurse, and an excellent washer and ironer and a good seamstress. His title comes from inheritance. [Value $1,500]

[Commissioners paid Aylmer $525.60.]

No. 729, Petition of Henry Naylor, trustee of George Marbury   Filed Jun. 20, 1862

Henry Naylor, trustee for the late George Marbury, claims compensation for James William, aged about 63 years. He is a dark mulatto, 5 feet 4 inches tall, and is stout and well-made. Naylor is now paying him $8 a month for his services. George Marbury was declared insolvent and Naylor was appointed his trustee. As such, he came into possession of Negro man Jim, who has been in Naylor's possession ever since, excepting a portion of the time when he was serving the brother of George Marbury, John Marbury.

[Commissioners paid Naylor, trustee, $131.40.]

No. 730, Petition of Martina Maguire Filed Jun. 20, 1862

Martina Maguire of Washington claims compensation for two persons.

1. Letty Ford, aged about 28, of a dark complexion, about 5 feet 4 inches high. She is an experienced washer and ironer and an excellent cook. She has yielded $70 a year, clear of all expenses.

2. Mary Young, about one year old, yellow complexion, healthy. [Value $200]

Maguire acquired Letty as a gift from her father, James Maguire, upwards of two years ago. Mary was born since that date.

[Commissioners paid Maguire, by James Maguire, her attorney, $525.60: Letty Ford, $481.80; Mary Young, $43.80.]

No. 731, Petition of Elizabeth Minor Filed Jun 20, 1862

Elizabeth Minor of Washington claims compensation for two persons.

1. Mary Ellen Jackson, aged 18, light brown, about 5 feet high, healthy. She is a good cook. [Value $1,200]

2. Fanny Jackson, aged 14, light brown, about 5 feet 1 inch tall, healthy. She is a useful house servant. [Value $1,000]

Minor inherited them under the terms of the will of her mother, Ann M. Minor, who bequeathed them and their mother, Eliza [Jackson (?)], to her. Minor's will was admitted to probate Mar. 9, 1860.

[Commissioners paid Minor $936.60: Mary Ellen Jackson, $481.80; Fanny Jackson, $481.80,]

No. 732, Petition of Ammon Green Filed Jun. 20, 1862

Ammon Green of the District of Columbia claims compensation for two persons.

1. Charles Mahoney, aged between 50 and 60, bright mulatto, about 5 feet 8 inches high. He drives a furniture car, acts as bell ringer at auction sales and attends to the delivery of goods sold from the auction store. He is slightly ruptured. [Value $400]

2. Friday Hurburt (or "Herbert"), aged about 65, black, about 4 feet 11 ½ inches tall. She is a good cook, washer and ironer. [Value $100]

He purchased Charles for $475 in Washington between four or five years ago at a public sale of the estate of the late Mr. Bowie. He purchased Friday for $40 about 12 years ago in Montgomery County, Md., at a public sale of the estate of Thomas Geddings, deceased. The price was low because Geddings' family publicly said they wished him to buy her and other persons at the sale thus did not bid against him.

[Commissioners paid Green $175.20: Charles Mahoney, $131.40; Friday "Herbert": $43.80.]

No. 733, Petition of Nancy W. Balmain

Nancy W. Balmain of Washington claims compensation for four persons.

1. Mary Jane Turley is aged about 32, black, about five feet high and slender and erect in her carriage. She is a good plain cook, washer and ironer and house servant. [Value $900]

2. Fanny Turley, daughter of Mary Jane, is aged about 14, light mulatto and about 4 feet one-half inch tall. She sews and does general house work.

3. Martha Turley, daughter of Mary Jane, is aged about 12, with the same complexion as Fanny and near her height. She does the same work as her sister.

4. Charlotte Erving, is about 50, about six feet tall, black color, of a spare figure and erect carriage. She is a good cook and excellent washerwoman and ironer.

Balmain claims $2,000 for the four persons.

Balmain inherited Mary Jane Turley from the division of the estate of her father, the late Andrew Balmain of Virginia, and has been in possession of her for the last 30 years. Her children were born slaves. Erving was purchased from the late Major W[illiam] B. Scott of this city and John Cryer in about 1842.

[Commissioners paid Balmain, by H.W. Balmain, her attorney, $1,292.10: Mary Jane Turley, $306.60; Fanny Turley, $438; Martha Turley, $372.30; Charlotte Erving, $175.20.]

No. 734, Petition of Richard L. Ross Filed Jun. 20, 1862

Richard L. Ross of Washington claims compensation for 19 persons.

1. Leonard Smith, aged 60, dark brown in color, medium height. He is a good farm hand and Ross was getting $6 a month and his board for him. He sometimes suffers from rheumatism. [Value $400]

2. Henrietta Smith, aged 53, dark brown, medium height. She is a good cook and house servant and has

considerable experience in monthly nursing. [Value $500]

 3. Lewis Smith, aged 33, dark brown, medium height. He is an excellent farm hand and wagoner and Ross was receiving $10 a month and his board for him. [Value $1,400]

 4. Alfred Smith, aged 27, dark brown, about 5 feet 9 inches high. He is an excellent farm hand and Ross was receiving $10 a month and his board for him. [Value $1,500]

 5. George Smith, aged 23, dark brown, about 5 feet 7 inches high. He has a scar on one hand. He is a good farm hand, house servant and rough carpenter and Ross was receiving $12 a month and his board for him. [Value $1,500]

 6. Julia Smith, aged 22, dark brown, about 5 feet 3 or 4 inches tall. She is a good cook, washer and ironer and house servant. [Value $1,300]

 7. Thomas Smith, aged 20, dark brown, medium height, stout and well-built. He is a good farm hand and wagoner and Ross was receiving $10 a month and his board for him. [Value $1,500]

 8. Henry Smith, aged 14, dark brown, medium height. He is a good farm hand and manager of horses. [Value $1,000]

 9. Caroline Smith, aged 13, dark brown, medium height. She is a good cook and house servant. [Value $800]

 10. Rosina Smith, aged 11, dark brown, medium height. She is a good house servant. [Value $700]

 11. Andrew Smith, child of Julia Smith, aged three, light brown, about three feet high. He is sprightly and healthy. [Value $250]

 12. Sarah Hopkins, aged 42, dark mulatto, about 5 feet 5 inches tall. She is an excellent cook, washer and ironer and house servant. [Value $1,000]

 13. Eliza Hopkins, aged 18, dark brown, about 5 feet 3 inches tall. She is a good cook, washer and ironer and house servant. [Value $1,200]

 14. Hellen Hopkins, aged 17, dark brown about 5 feet 3 inches tall. She is a good house servant, washer and ironer. [Value $1,200]

 15. Charles Hopkins, aged 13, dark brown, about 4 feet 6 or 7 inches high. [Value $900]

 16. Edgar Hopkins, aged 11, dark brown, about 4 feet 4 inches high. [Value $800]

 17. Sallie (Sarah) Hopkins, aged six, dark brown, about three feet high. She has had a scrofulous affliction of the eyes and face. [Value $100]

 18. William Hopkins, aged eight months, dark brown. [Value $50]

 19. John Addison, aged 39, black, about six feet high, stout and well-built. He is a good farm hand and gardener. [Value $1,000]

At the time of passage of the D.C. emancipation act, Leonard, Lewis, Alfred, George, Thomas, and Henry Smith were temporarily hired out of D.C. in Montgomery County, Md., although they were held to service in D.C. as Ross is a resident of this city.

Ross acquired Leonard, Henrietta, Lewis, Alfred, George, Julia and Thomas Smith, Sarah Hopkins and John Addison in the division of the estate of his father, the late Richard Ross of Montgomery County, Md. Henry, Caroline and Rosina Smith are the children of Leonard and Henrietta Smith. Andrew Smith is the child of Julia Smith. Eliza, Hellen, Charles, Edgar, Sarah and William Hopkins are the children of Sarah Hopkins and were born in the family of Ross.

Attached is a statement signed by Richard L. Ross assigning $209.11 of any compensation he might receive to William R. Riley.

[Commissioners paid a total of $6,307.20, of which $209.11 went to William R. Riley and the rest to Ross: Leonard Smith, $109.50; Henrietta Smith, $109.50; Lewis Smith, $525.60; Alfred Smith, $613.20; George Smith, $547.50; Julia Smith, $503.70; Thomas Smith, $613.20; Henry Smith, $372.30; Caroline Smith, $328.50; Rosina Smith, $284.70; Andrew Smith, $65.70; Sarah Hopkins, $262.80; Eliza Hopkins, $525.60; "Helen" Hopkins, $481.80; Charles Hopkins, $306.60; Edgar Hopkins, $262.80; Sallie Hopkins, no value; William Hopkins, $43.80; John Addison, $350.40.]

No. 735, Petition of Isabella Morton   Filed Jun. 20, 1862

 Isabella Morton of Georgetown claims compensation for Sophia Hurd, aged 28 years. She is black, about 4 feet 8 inches tall and rather fleshy. She is an excellent cook, washer and ironer. She was acquired by gift from Ann Waring when a child and has been owned ever since by Morton. [Value $1,500]

 [Commissioners paid Morton $438.]

No. 736, Petition of Mary M. Dufief
Filed Jun. 20, 1862

Mary M. Dufief of Washington claims compensation for Maria, aged 56. She is black, of medium height, very stout and has slightly gray hair. She is gruff when spoken to. She is a valuable servant, a first-class cook, washer and ironer and is healthy and strong. Dufief purchased her Sept. 7, 1852, from John L. Dufief, her son, for $375.

[Commissioners paid Mary M. Dufieff [sic] by D.S. Walker, her attorney, $394.20.]

No. 737, Petition of Amos Denham, trustee of Mrs. A. E. Balmain
Filed Jun. 20, 1862

Amos Denham, trustee for Mrs. A.E. Balmain, claims compensation for six persons.

1. Eliza Ann Lee is aged 36, bright mulatto. [Value $1,000]
2. Mary Eliza Lee is aged 15, bright mulatto. [Value $1,000]
3. Alfred Lee is aged 13, bright mulatto. [Value $1,000]
4. Edmonia Lee is aged 11, dark mulatto. [Value $850]
5. Leslie Lee is aged eight, light mulatto. [Value $650]
6. Lettie [Lee] is aged three and bright mulatto. [Value $450]

They are all healthy, sound and likely and good servants. He holds them in trust from Andrew Balmaine of Washington for the benefit of his wife, A. E. Balmaine, by deed of trust dated Aug. 28, 1858. Andrew Balmaine obtained them through his wife, who obtained them from the estate of Amos Denham of Loudon County, Va., about 20 years ago. See D.C. Liber J.A.S. No. 206, folio 16.

[Commissioners paid Denham, trustee of A.E. Balmain, Annie E. Balmain; A. Balmain, $1,489.20: Eliza Ann Lee, $284.70; Mary Eliza Lee, $394.20; Alfred Lee, $306.60; Edmonia Lee, $240.90; Leslie Lee, $175.20; Lettie Lee, $87.60.]

The surname is spelled both "Balmain" and "Balmaine" in these documents. The petition states that the trusteeship agreement is dated Aug. 28, but the attached copy of that document is dated Aug. 21.

No. 738, Petition of Matilda W. Emory
Filed Jun. 20, 1862

Matilda W. Emory of the city of Washington claims compensation for Mary Johnson, aged about 35. Johnson is about 5 feet 7 inches tall, stout, but not corpulent, dark brown, with a "face of the usual African type". She is a first-rate cook, washer and ironer and has no bad habits. She received Johnson as a gift from her father-in-law, the late General Thomas Emory of Queen Anne's County, Md., in 1838. [Value $1,200]

[Commissioners paid Emory, by D.S. Walker, her attorney, $394.20.]

No. 739, Petition of Mary Eliza Read
Filed Jun. 20, 1862

Mary Eliza Read of Montgomery County, Md., claims compensation for Julius Cesar Skinner, aged about 50 years. He is about 5 feet 5 inches high, has a very black complexion, with black eyes and a broad nose and short, woolly hair. She was getting $120 a year for his hire at the U.S. Lunatic Asylum [Saint Elizabeths Hospital] near Washington where he had been employed as a servant. She also received the same wages for his services prior to that at the U.S. Navy Yard. He was purchased for $400 by her mother, Emily Beale, living near Washington, from J[ohn] D. Hammack of Washington. Read purchased Skinner from her mother for the same amount on May 14, 1854. Accompanying documents show that Hammack had purchased Cesar from Allison Naylor who, in turn, had bought "Caesar" on May 3, 1853, for $200 from Dewitt Kent.

[Commissioners paid Read $175.20 for Julius Caesar Skinner.]

No. 740, Petition of Philip T. Berry
Filed Jun. 20, 1862

Philip T. Berry of Georgetown claims compensation for 13 persons.

1. Nelly Beall, aged about 66 or 67, black, stout and thick set. She is a good cook, but often has rheumatism and is not very healthy.

2. Sandy Beall, aged 48 or 50, dark copper color, 5 feet 6 inches tall. He is a good driver and valuable farm hand.

3. Grandison Beall, aged 46 or 47, dark copper color, 5 feet 4 inches high. He is a valuable driver and carer of horses and generally good for town purposes.

4. Sophy Beall, aged 48 to 50 years, dark copper color, tall and very stout and large. She is a first-rate cook, but occasionally has rheumatism in one knee.

5. Susan Beall, aged 22 or 23, dark copper color, five feet high. She is a first-rate servant, cook, washer, ironer and seamstress.

6. Margaret Beall, aged 19 or 20, copper colored, 5 feet 2 or 3 inches tall. She is a valuable house servant.

7. Kitty Beall, aged 18, black, stout and thick set. She is a good cook, washer and ironer and a first-rate nurse.

8. Robert Beall, aged 14 or 15, copper colored. He is well-grown for his age.

9. Alexander Beall, aged 11 or 12, black, stout and well-formed.

10. Mary Beall, aged 26, bright copper color, 5 feet 3 or 4 inches high with a long, full suit of hair. She is a good cook, washer and ironer and a valuable house servant.

11. Henry Thomas, aged 40, dark mulatto, 5 feet 4 or 5 inches high. He is a valuable house servant, teamster and tender of horses. He is now employed in soap making.

12. Ann Thomas, aged 37, dark mulatto. She is a valuable servant and "the best I know of any where". Her health is delicate.

13. Infant female child of four months who is the daughter of Susan Beall.

He values the above at $11,000.

Nelly, Sandy, Grandison, Sophy and her five children (Susan, Margaret, Kitty, Robert and Alexander) he received from the distribution of his father's estate in Prince George's County, Md., in 1840. Mary Beall he purchased from his brother, A.M. Berry of Maryland in 1850 for $500. Henry and Ann Thomas he purchased from the estate of Jane Walls in 1829 when they were six and ten years old.

[Commissioners paid Berry $3,723: Nelly Beall, $21.90; Sandy Beall, $219; Grandison Beall, $306.60; Sophia Beall, $131.40; Susan, $438; infant of Susan, $21.90; Margaret, $481.80; Kitty, $525.60; Robert, $438; Alexander, $262.80; Mary Beall, $372.30; Henry Thomas, $175.20; Ann Thomas, $328.50.]

Boyd's City Directory for 1860, p. 162, shows that Alexander E. Beall & Co. manufactured soap and candles on Greene St. in Georgetown and it is possible that Henry Thomas worked there.

No. 741, Petition of Clark Mills   **Filed Jun. 20, 1862**

Clark Mills claims compensation for 11 persons.

1. Lettie Howard, aged 33, black, short and thick set. She is the mother of Tilly, Tom, Elick, Jackson, George and Emily. [Value $700]

2. Tilly [Howard] is aged ten and black. [Value $500]

3. Tom [Howard] is aged eight and black. [Value $500]

4. Ellick [Howard] is aged six-and one-half years and black. [Value $400]

5. Jackson [Howard] is aged five and black. [Value $250]

6. George [Howard] is aged three and black. [Value $150]

7. Emily [Howard] is aged three months and is black. [Value $50]

8. Levi Thomas, aged 59, is black and over six feet tall. He has a large leg that is rather stiff but he is in good health. [Value $300]

9. Rachel Thomas, Levi's wife, is aged 49 and mulatto. She is very large and weighs about 200 pounds. [Value $400]

10. Ann Ross, aged 48, is mulatto, about 5 feet 7 inches tall and rather slim. [Value $600]

11. Philip Reid, is aged 42, mulatto, short in statue, not prepossessing in appearance, but smart. He is a good workman in a foundry where he has been employed by the government at $1.25 a day. [Value $1,500]

Lettie Howard and her child, Tilly, was bought from Peter Havenner some eight or nine years ago. Her five other children have been born since then. Levi and his wife Rachel he purchased in Baltimore about the same time and paid $950 for them. Philip Reid he purchased in Charleston, S.C., many years ago when he was a youth. He bought him for $1,200 because of his evident talent for the foundry business in which Mills was engaged.

[Commissioners paid Mills $1,916.25: Letty Howard, $372.30, and her children: Tilly, $175.20; Tom, $197.10; Ellick, $131.40; Jackson, $98.55; George, $87.60; Emily, $21.90; Levi Thomas, $87.60; Ann Ross, $219; Philip Reed [sic], $350.40; Rachel Thomas, $175.20.]

Clark Mills was an early American sculptor who designed and cast several famous statues in the capital. His most famous is the equestrian statue Andrew Jackson that is in Lafayette Square, but he also did the equestrian statue of George Washington that stands in the middle of Washington Circle, and many other projects. His foundry on Bladensburg Road did the casting of the statue of Freedom that is atop the Capitol dome and Philip Reid worked on that project and supervised the placement of the statue in 1863. There is a video available about Reid that is based on a lecture by Capitol Historian William C. Allen. See http://www.philipreid.org/essay2.html.

No. 742, Petition of Ann Maria Summers   **Filed Jun. 21, 1862**

Ann Mariah Summers of Prince George's County, Md., claims compensation for Lucy Gray, or Jackson, aged 18 or 19 years. She is ginger colored, good-looking, hearty and able to labor. She is a good servant. Ann Mariah inherited Lucy from her father, Nathaniel Summers of Prince George's County, and has held her from her infancy. [Value $1,000]

[Commissioners paid Summers $394.20.]

In the original petition, Summers' first name is spelled both "Maria" and "Mariah".

No. 743, Petition of Lemuel Clements, committee for Anna M. Warring   Filed Jun. 21, 1862

Lemuel Clements, committee for Anna M. Warring of Montgomery County, Md., claims compensation for Gabriel, aged about 50. Gabriel is rather light or copper colored, about 5 feet 5 inches high, and "of a light and active form." He was born a slave of slave parents who were held by Anna's father, Henry Warring of Montgomery County, and became Anna's property under her father's will. Gabriel is healthy and strong and has been employed for the last ten years by Joshua Pierce [Peirce] of D.C. to work in his nursery and fruit garden. [Value $700]

Attached is a copy of the document from the Montgomery County Court dated Nov. 12, 1851, that appointed Clements committee for Anna M. Warring.

[Commissioners paid Clements, committee for A.M. Warring, $262.80.]

No. 744, Petition of John Little   Filed Jun. 21, 1862

John Little of Washington County, D.C., claims compensation for 12 persons.

1. Delilah Prout, aged 63, black, well-built, weighs over 180 pounds. She is an old woman of good appearance and a first-rate cook. [Value $100]
2. Leander [Prout] child of Delilah, aged 28, black. He is a butcher by trade and a first-rate hand. He could easily bring $25 or $30 a month. [Value $3,000]
3. Tabitha [Prout] Rigney, child of Delilah, aged 25, copper colored. She has a good appearance but complains considerably. She is a first-rate house servant. [Value $1,000]
4. Celeste [Prout] aged 23, child of Delilah, black. She is a healthy and industrious house servant. [Value $1,500]
5. Hortense [Prout] aged 21, child of Delilah, black. She is a healthy and industrious house servant. [Value $1,500]
6. Kalisti Prout, child of Delilah, aged 20, black. She is a healthy and industrious house servant. [Value $1,500]
7. Narcissa Rigney, aged seven, daughter of Tabitha, mulatto. She is healthy and promising. [Value $300]
8. Fermore (?) Worthington, aged five, child of Tabitha, mulatto. He is healthy and promising. [Value $300]
9. Matilda Rigney, aged six months, child of Tabitha, mulatto. She is healthy and promising. [Value $50]
10. Elsie Grey, daughter of Kalisti, aged five, black. She is healthy and promising. [Value $300]
11. Benjamin Purnell, aged 26, black. He is a butcher by trade and a first-rate hand and could easily bring $25 or $30 a month. [Value $3,000]
12. Geoffrey McKenzie, aged 50, black. He is a very good farm hand. [Value $300]

He purchased Delilah and her two children, Leander and Tabitha, from B[enjamin] O. Shekell and W.H. Williams in January 1839, while they were on their way South. Celeste, Hortense, Kalisti, Narcissa, Fermore, Elsie and Matilda were born while their mother was held by the Little. He purchased Ben from Mr. Darnell about 18 years ago and he purchased Geoffrey from J.B.H. Smith, the executor of the estate of George Bomford, about 15 years ago.

[Commissioners paid Little $3,635.40: Delilah Prout, $65.70; Leander, $613.20; Tabitha Rigney, $350.40; Celeste, $438; "Hortensi", $525.60; Kaliski Prout, $481.80; Narcissa Rigney, $175.20; "Fermour" Worthington, $87.60; Ann Matilda, $21.90; "Elisie" Gray, $43.80; Benjamin Purnell, $613.20; "Geoffray" McKenzie, $219.]

No. 745, Petition of John Little, guardian of John O. Little   Filed Jun. 21, 1862

John Little, guardian of John O. Little, of Washington County, D.C., claims compensation for William Crown, aged 33 years. He is a mulatto, about 5 feet 8 inches tall, very stout and weighs at least 200 pounds. He is very strong and active and is a butcher by trade. He hires for $25 a month. He was purchased by John Little and Samuel J. Little jointly at a public sale of some Negroes belonging to the estate of one Hilliary in Prince George's County, Md., in 1834. Some years ago in the settlement of their affairs, William was assigned to Samuel J. Little, father of John O. Little, and in the division of his estate was given to John O. Little. [Value $2,000]

[Commissioners paid John Little $569.40.]

No. 746, Petition of John Little, guardian of Julia A. Little   Filed Jun. 21, 1862

John Little, guardian of Julia A. Little of Washington County, D.C., claims compensation for four persons.

1. Lucy Simms, about 24 years old, bright mulatto, tall and good-looking. She is the mother of Willie and Lillie and is an industrious house servant.
2. Willie Simms, aged three, bright mulatto, is very promising.
3. Lillie Simms, about five months old, is very promising.
4. John Hamilton, aged 22, is black, stout and very strong. He is a first-class farm hand.

About twenty years ago Samuel J. Little, the father of the petitioner's ward, Julia A. Little, purchased Lucy from Mr. Perry of Montgomery County, Md.. He bought John from Mrs. Hamilton of this city about eight years ago. Little values the above persons at $3,200.

[Commissioners paid Little $1,138.80: Lucy Simms, $459.90; Willie, $65.70; Lillie, no value; John Hamilton, $613.20.]

No. 747, Petition of Thomas B. Entwisle   Filed Jun. 21, 1862

Thomas B. Entwisle claims compensation for Margaret Hammond, who is a good cook and excellent house servant. Entwisle states he has refused $250 for her and now estimates her value at $300. His wife, M[ary] M. Entwisle, acquired title by purchase on Nov. 10, 1855, from Samuel Crown, for $100. At that time, Margaret was described as being black in color and about 55 years old.

[Commissioners paid Entwisle $21.90.]

Thomas Entwisle married Mary M. Dove Sept. 26, 1843. See Pippenger, D.C. Marriage Licenses, 1811-1858, p. 191.

No. 748, Petition of Joshua A. Ritchie and his wife Mary S.,   Filed Jun. 21, 1862
Joseph F. Carbery, and Pierce Shoemaker and Martha, his wife.

Joshua A. Ritchie, acting administrator of Lewis Carbery, Joshua A. and Mary S. Ritchie, his wife (late Carbery), and Joseph F. Carbery, and Pierce Shoemaker and Martha L. Shoemaker, his wife (late Carbery) all of Washington County, D.C., claim compensation for two persons.

1. John Simms, aged about 18, black, about 5 feet 2 inches tall, stout and able-bodied. He is a good hostler and house servant. [Value $1,000]
2. Mary Simms, aged about 20, black, 5 feet 6 inches tall, stout and large. She is a good cook and general house servant. [Value $1,200]

The late Lewis Carbery acquied title to the mother of John and Mary from his brother, Thomas Carbery. They were family servants and raised in Lewis's family. When Lewis died, they came to Joshua Ritchie and James L. Carbery as his administrators. James L. is now absent so Ritchie is the acting administrator. Mary S. Ritchie, Joseph F. Carbery, Martha L. Shoemaker, and James L. Carbery are the children of Lewis Carbery.

[Commissioners paid J.A. Ritchie, Mary S. Ritchie, J.F. Carbery by J.A. Ritchie, attorney, Pierce Shoemaker, Martha L. Shoemaker, $1,138.80: John Simms, $569.40; Mary Simms, $569.40. Of the total three-fourths, $854.10, was paid to the claimants; the other fourth, $284.70, being the interest of one not claiming.]

No. 749, Petition of Virginia S. Wood   Filed Jun. 21, 1862

Miss Virginia S. Wood of Washington County, D.C., claims compensation for Sarah Jones, aged 45. She is a dark brown woman, 5 feet 6 inches tall. She has several scars on her right shoulder from biles. She is a good cook, washer and ironer and has been in the family since she was purchased. Jones was purchased for her by her father, the late Robert S. Wood, for $500 from Joseph S. Donovan of Baltimore on Oct. 7, 1851. [Value $500]

[Commissioners paid Wood, by E[rasmus] J. Middleton, her attorney, $197.10.]

No. 750, Petition of Ellen Scott   Filed Jun. 23, 1862

Ellen Scott claims compensation for five persons.

1. Thomas Johnson, about 23, six feet tall, dark brown in color. [Value $1,500]
2. Harriet Crawford, aged about 40, 5 feet 2 or 3 inches tall, of a dark brown color. She is a faithful and good servant. [Value $1,000]
3. Hannah Johnson, 25 years old. She is a first-rate servant. [Value $1,000]
4. Jesse Wheeler, aged six, dark brown, sprightly. [Value $300]
5. Henry Waters, 12 months old, light brown. [Value $100]

They were inherited from her sister, Elizabeth C. Scott, whose will is recorded in D.C. All of the above are to be free at the time of Ellen Scott's death.

[Commissioners paid Benjamin S. Bayly, administrator of Ellen Scott, $56.94: Thomas Johnson, $26.28; Harriet Crawford, $13.14; Hannah Johnson, $17.52; Jesse Wheeler, no value; Henry Waters, no value.]

No. 751, Petition of Grace Dulaney   Filed Jun. 23, 1862

Grace Dulaney of Washington City claims compensation for William Dulaney. He is 21 years old, dark copper colored, about 5 feet 10 inches high and slender. He has a scar on his forehead from a fall when he was a child. He is a first-rate house servant and cook and has brought to the petitioner wages ranging from $8 to $16 per month. For the past year he has been employed in waiting and in cooking for some of the officers in the army and is at this time with the army. Grace acquired title by deed from Mrs. Sarah Ann Duvall dated Aug. 5, 1852, which is recorded in D.C. Liber J.A.S. No. 41, folio 403.

[Commissioners paid Grace her x mark Dulaney $350.40.]

William is probably Grace Dulaney's son. The 1860 Census for D.C., Vol. 1, p. 255, contains an entry for the following household: Thomas Abbott, aged 50, white, clerk; Grace Dulaney, aged 45, black, born in Maryland; William Dulaney, aged 19, black, waiter, born in Maryland.

No. 752, Petition of Margaret Ann Miller   Filed Jun. 23, 1862

Margaret Ann Miller of Howard County, Md., claims compensation for two persons.

1. Charlotte, about 45, stout, 5 feet 5 or 6 inches high. She is a first-rate cook, but is lame and that detracts from her value.

2. Brice Martin, about 23 years old, about 5 feet 8 inches tall, medium size. He is a first-rate waiter and Miller has been offered $1,600 for him. Charlotte and Brice were both residing in Washington at the time of the passage of the emancipation act.

She values the two at $2,200. She acquired them under the terms of the will of her mother, Mrs. Ann Jenkins, which is filed in the District of Columbia.

[Commissioners paid Miller $700.80: Charlotte, $131.40; Price [sic] Martin, $569.40.]

No. 753, Petition of Caroline McAlister   Filed Jun. 23, 1862

Caroline McAlister of Washington City claims compensation for Rachael Edmonston. Edmonston is 38 years old, about five feet tall, has a dark complexion and is stout built. She is an able-bodied servant and, except for stiffness in one left finger caused by a burn, she has no physical defects. McAlister inherited Edmonston from her father who had raised her from childhood. He purchased her from the estate of Mrs. Nancy Middleton of Montgomery County, Md..

[Commissioners paid McAlister $153.30.]

No. 754, Petition of Baruch Hall, for daughter, Rosa E.   Filed Jun. 23, 1862

Baruch Hall, the father and guardian of Rosa E. Hall, a minor aged 12, of Washington City, claims compensation for Mary Ann Sprigg. Mary Ann is about eight years old, dark brown with black curly hair and black eyes. She is healthy and of medium size for her age. She is remarkably intelligent and he values her at $500. Rosa E. Hall inherited her from her uncle, Jacob Hall of Prince George's County, Md., who died in the fall of 1858.

[Commissioners paid Baruch Hall, guardian for R.E. Hall, $197.10.]

No. 755, Petition of Baruch Hall, for son, Harry W.   Filed Jun. 23, 1862

Baruch Hall, the father and guardian of Harry W. Hall, a minor aged 16, of Washington City, claims compensation for Thomas Sprigg. Sprigg is about 13 years old, has a dark brown complexion, black curly hair, black eyes and is of medium size for his age. He has a quick and sprightly mind and is capable of doing anything anyone of his age can perform. Sprigg's brother, "who is an inferior boy in every respect" to Thomas, was sold when 12 years old for $900. He values Thomas at $1,000. Harry Hall inherited Sprigg from his uncle, Jacob Hall of Prince George's County, who died in the fall of 1858.

[Commissioners paid Baruch Hall, guardian for H.W. Hall, $262.80.]

No. 756, Petition of Helen L. Joy   Filed Jun. 23, 1862

Helen L. Joy of Washington City claims compensation for two persons.

1. Lucinda Sewell is aged 36, light mulatto, stout and of medium size. Her hands are very deformed. She is strong and can do a great deal of work such as washing, scrubbing and can make (?) their supper herself. She leaves her child with Helen when she hires out at fifty cents a day.

2. Mary Sewell is aged 14 months, child of Lucinda, very light, almost white, in complexion. She is a promising child.

Helen was given Lucinds by her father some seven or eight years ago.

[Commissioners paid Joy $43.80: Lucinda Sewall, no value; Mary Sewall, $43.80.]

No. 757, Petition of Edward Hall, trustee for Baruch Hall and Absalom A. Hall   Filed Jun. 23, 1862

Edward Hall of Washington D.C. claims compensation for Fillis (or Phillis) Howard, aged about 40 years. She is very dark with black curly hair and black eyes. She is healthy and well-developed. She is a valuable house servant, admirable cook and fine washerwoman and ironer. On Mar. 1, 1856, Baruch Hall signed a deed of trust recorded in D.C. Liber J.A.S. No. 112, folio 26, conveying Fillis Howard to Edward Hall to secure payment of a debt due by Baruch Hall to Absalom A. Hall. That Baruch Hall and Absalom Hall have agreed that Edward Hall shall receive whatever compensation is given for Fillis. Baruch Hall obtained Fillis from the estate of his father, Thomas Hall of Prince George's County, Md., who died about 1849.

[Commissioners paid Ed. Hall $328.50.]

No. 758, Petition of Elisha J. Hall   Filed Jun. 23, 1862

Elisha J. Hall of Montgomery County, Md., claims compensation for George Tyler, aged 19. Tyler is a bright mulatto about 5 feet 6 inches high. He is a valuable coachman and waiter and is worth $1,200. Hall purchased him from Allen Bowman when he was two years old.

[Commissioners paid Hall $547.50.]

No. 759, Petition of Thomas Young   Filed Jun. 23, 1862

Thomas Young of Washington City claims compensation for eight persons.

1. Louisa Forrest is a bright mulatto of short statue. She is a good cook, washer and ironer and can cut and make men's or women's clothing. [Value $1,500]

2. Joseph Forrest is a dark copper color and short. He is a fine cook and a fine dining room and general house servant.

3. Jane Rosetta Forrest is a bright mulatto.

4. Martha Ann Forrest is dark copper colored and short.

5. John Wesley Forrest is a bright mulatto.

6. Adelaide Clinton Forrest is a bright mulatto.

7. Arthur Forrest is very bright mulatto in color. Young says he has refused $1,000 for Arthur.

8. Annie Forrest is copper colored.

They are together valued at $9,700. They are all healthy and of good moral character.

Maria Forrest and Louisa Forrest in 1836 were given by the will of James A. Crane of St. Mary's County, Md., to his daughter Mary, whom Young married. Louisa and the first named five persons are the children of Maria Forrest; Arthur and Annie Forrest are the children of Louisa.

[Commissioners paid Young $3,285: Louisa Forrest, $481.80; Joseph Forrest, $547.50; Jane Rosetta Forrest, $547.50; Martha Ann Forrest, $438; John Wesley Forrest, $547.50; Adelaide Clinton Forrest, $438; Arthur Forrest, $175.20; "Anna" Forrest, $109.50.]

No. 760, Petition of Jane E. Johns   Filed Jun. 23, 1862

Jane E. Johns of the state of Maryland claims compensation for six slaves.

1. James is aged 25 and dark in color. He is a field and garden hand.

2. Nancy is aged 23 and copper colored. She is a good house servant, cook, washer and ironer.

3. Alice is aged one and the same color as above.

4. Henry is aged 60 and the same color as above. He is a good field and garden hand.

5. Harriet is aged 55 and the same color. She is a good field and garden hand.

6. Joanna is aged 22 and mulatto. She is a good house servant, cook, washer and ironer.

She values them at $4,000. James, Nancy, Alice, Henry and Harriet were inherited by Johns from her parents and brother of Charles County, Md. Joanna was the property of her late husband, Dr. Berryman of Charles County.

[Commissioners paid Johns, by J. Dent, attorney, $1,095: James Smith, $569.40; Nancy, $350.40; Alice, $43.80; Henry, $87.60; Harriet, $43.80; "Johanna", not allowed and the claim was withdrawn.]

The printed report of the commissioners gives James's last name as "Smith", but no surname is given in the original documents.

No. 761, Petition of Lemuel J. Middleton   Filed Jun. 23, 1862

Lemuel J. Middleton of Washington City claims compensation for two persons.

1. Virginia Bowie is aged about 20, bright mulatto, 4 feet 10 ½ inches tall and rather stout. She has a full suit of long black hair. She is a good servant and is perfectly honest and reliable. [Value $900]

2. Sarah Bowie, aged about 13, is a bright mulatto girl about 4 feet 11 ½ inches tall and has a full suit of black hair. She is a promising girl. [Value $600]

Middleton purchased their mother, Saulina Bowie from Sarah Talbot, administratrix of Benjamin Talbot, about Oct. 20, 1841.

[Commissioners paid Middleton $788.40: Virginia Bowie, $438; Sarah Bowie, $350.40.]

No. 762, Petition of Daniel W. Middleton   Filed Jun. 23, 1862

Daniel W. Middleton of Washington City claims compensation for six persons.

1. Eliza Jane Berry is aged 33, bright mulatto, 4 feet 11 inches high, of ordinary size. She has a full suit of long black hair and her upper front teeth are defective. She is a good cook, washer and ironer and servant. [Value $1,000]

2. James [Berry], son of Eliza Jane, aged about three years and six months, bright mulatto, with a full suit of black hair. [Value $200]

3. John [Berry], son of Eliza Jane, is aged about two years six months, bright mulatto, with a full suit of straight black hair. [Value $100]

4. Mary Ann [Berry], daughter of Eliza Jane, aged one year, is a bright mulatto. [Value $50]

5. Clara Thomas is aged about 30, bright mulatto, 4 feet 11 ½ inches high, of ordinary size. She has a mole on her under lip and a full suit of long black hair. She is a first-rate house servant. [Value $1,000]

6. Helen [Thomas], child of Clara, aged about three, is a bright mulatto with a full suit of black hair. [Value $150]

Middleton purchased them from John P. Ingle, executor of the late Edward Ingle, about July 1840. The others were born while living in his family.

[Commissioners paid Middleton $1,204.50: Eliza Jane Berry, $394.20; James, $109.50; John, $87.60; Mary Ann, $43.80; "Clary" Thomas, $481.80; Helen, $87.60.]

No. 763, Petition of Susan Worthington   Filed Jun. 23, 1862

Miss Susan Worthington claims compensation for two persons.

1. Betsey Jokey is aged 24, black and about 5 feet 9 inches tall. She is straight and well-formed and is an excellent cook and house servant. [Value $1,000]

2. John Jokey, Betsey's son, is a bright mulatto boy about three years old. He is very likely and promising. [Value $200]

Susan acquired Betsey under the will of her late father, James Worthington of Frederick County, Md. John has been born since that time.

[Commissioners paid Worthington $438: "Betsy" Jokey, $350.40; John, her child, $87.60.]

No. 764, Petition of Nancy W. Davis   Filed Jun. 23, 1862

Nancy W. Davis of the District of Columbia claims compensation for four persons.

1. Ann Lowry, aged 45, is black and quite small with a long head. She is a good cook and house servant.

2. Steptoe Lowry, aged 25, is black and about 5 feet 10 inches high. He is a good farm hand.

3. George Lowry, aged 20, is black and about 5 feet 6 inches high. He is a good farm hand and can do anything assigned to him either as house servant, buying and selling or other work.

4. Simon Moore, aged 55, is black and about 5 feet 10 inches high. He is a capable and faithful servant.

She values them at $3,800. Ann Lowry was given to her by her father, Leonard Y. Davis of Jefferson County, Va., when Ann was a small child and she was raised by Nancy. Steptoe and George are Ann's children born during her servitude. Simon was purchased by Davis's father for her at a sale of the property of the estate of Eben Taylor, late of Clark County, Va., about 1831 or 1832.

[Commissioners paid Davis $1,445.40: Ann Lowry, $175.20; Steptoe Lowrie [sic], $657; George Lowrie [sic], $569.40; Simon Moore, $43.80.]

No. 765, Petition of Mary Jane Turner and Rebecca H. Turner   Filed Jun. 23, 1862
Mary Jane Turner and Rebecca H. Turner of Frederick County, Md., claim compensation for three persons.

1. James Thomas, aged 55, is black and about 5 feet 10 inches high. He hires himself out at $14 a month. He is sometimes affected with rheumatism but that does not impair his value.

2. Rachel Johnson, aged 30, is a dark mulatto, about 5 feet 5 or 6 inches tall. She is now married but the name of her husband is not known.

3. Lucinda Johnson, aged 15, a dark mulatto, is about 4 feet 6 inches high.

Mary Jane and Rebecca acquired one-third by purchase from their brother, the late Thomas Turner, and two-thirds by inheritance from their father, Thomas Turner of D.C.

[Commissioners disallowed the claim because the persons were not produced.]

No. 766, Petition of Henry A. Willard, trustee for Caroline M. Willard   Filed Jun. 23, 1862
Henry A. Willard of Washington City, as trustee for Mrs. Caroline M. Willard, claims compensation for two persons.

1. Celia Radcliffe, aged about 25, is a very bright mulatto of about medium height. She is a very good lady's maid and is well bred and educated.

2. Caroline [Ratcliffe], daughter of Celia, is only a few months old.

He values them at $1,200. Radcliffe was purchased by Joseph C. Willard, Henry's brother, for $1,000 seven or eight years ago, and she has increased in value since then. His brother on last March 6 conveyed her to Henry upon certain trusts for Joseph's wife, Caroline M. Willard.

[Commissioners paid $525.60 to H.A. Willard, trustee for C.M.W., J.B. Freeman, attorney for Mrs. C.M. Willard, present and receiving money: Celia Radcliffe: $4181.80; Caroline, $43.80.]

No. 767, Petition of Mary E. Watts   Filed Jun. 23, 1862
Mary E. Watts of St. Mary's County, Md., claims compensation for Margaret Statesman. Stateman is 47 (?) years old, black and about 5 feet 4 inches tall. She is a good house servant and hires out at $6 to $8 a month. Watts values her at $700. Mary's father, Richard H. Watts of St. Mary's County, gave her to Mary and she has been hired in Washington City for many years.

[Commissioners paid Watts, by Thomas Young, her attorney, $219.]

No. 768, Petition of Sarah Crane   Filed Jun. 23, 1862
Sarah Crame of Washington, D.C., claims compensation for Betsey Thomas. Thomas is 46 years old and of a very dark color. She is a good house servant and cook and has been hired at from $6 to $8 a month. For the past year she has been in the employ of Randolph Coyle and continues there now. Her health has not very robust the past three years, but she has been constant in her duties during that time. She inherited Thomas under the will of her late father, James A. Crane of St. Mary's County, Md.

[Commissioners paid Crane $197.10 for "Betsy" Thomas.]

No. 769, Petition of Catharine S. Lyons   Filed Jun. 23, 1862
Catharine S. Lyons of Washington City claims compensation for four persons.

1. Lucretia Bembrage, aged 35, is black in color and about 5 feet 7 inches tall. [Value $1,000]

2. Isaac Bembrage, aged ten, is mulatto. [Value $800]

3. Maria Bembrage, aged eight, is a bright mulatto color. [Value $600]

4. Charles Bembrage, aged five, is bright mulatto color. [Value $400]

She got them as a gift from her aunt, Miss Serena Simmons of Frederick County, Md., in March 1851. Attached is a statement dated Jul. 21, 1862, from Miss Simmons stating that prior to March 1860 she made a gift to her niece, Catharine S. Lyons of the city of Washington, of slave Lucretia and her three children.

[Commissioners paid Joseph Lyons and Catharine S. Lyons $876: Lucretia Bembrage, $262.80; Isaac Bembrage, $306.60; Maria Bembrage, $175.20; Charles Bembrage, $131.40.]

No. 770, Petition of Frederick Cudlipp   Filed Jun. 23, 1862

Frederick Cudlipp of Washington claims compensation for Thomas Henson. Henson is 42 years old, black, 5 feet 4 inches high, stout and able-bodied. He has been used by Cudlipp as a house servant and is healthy and vigorous. Cudlipp purchased him on Jan. 17, 1850, for $500 from Francis P. Blair. [Value $500]

[Commissioners paid Cudlipp $350.40.]

No. 771, Petition of Sarah J. Summervill   Filed Jun. 23, 1862

Sarah J. "Sommervill" of Washington claims compensation for four persons.

1. Dinah Dorsey, aged about 51, is a dark copper color and about 5 feet 3 inches tall. She is a good cook and house servant as well as a good seamstress and washer and ironer. [Value $800]

2. Stephen Dorsey, son of Dinah, aged 14, is a dark copper color and about 4 feet 11 inches tall. He is very smart and is a good house servant, dining room servant and driver of a horse carriage. [Value $1,000]

3. Priscilla Wilson, about 23 years old, is quite dark in color and about five feet high. She is smart, a good house servant and a number one cook, washer and ironer and a first rate nurse. [Value $1,200]

4. Alice Sifas, about 15 or 16 years old, is dark in color and about five feet tall. She is a good dining room servant and chambermaid. She frequently does the marketing for the family. Sommervill states she refused $800 for her a year or so ago. [Value $1,000]

Sommervill purchased them at different times and has had them in her possession as her servants for a number of years.

[Commissioners paid "Somervill" $1,423.50: Dinah Dorsey, $109.50; Stephen Dorsey, $328.50; Priscilla Wilson, $525.60; Alice Sifas, $459.90.]

No. 772, Petition of Jane C. Boone   Filed Jun. 28, 1862

Jane C. Boone of Maryland claims compensation for Harriet Queen. Queen is 24 or 25 years old, chestnut colored, well-made and of good size. She is a very good cook, washer and ironer and is good at housework of any kind. Boone says she was offered $1,200 for her in 1860. She acquired title by inheritance from her deceased father, Edward Boone of Charles County, Md.. She was given title to Queen's mother about 40 years ago and Harriet was born her slave. She claims $1,200 for her.

[Commissioners paid Boone $481.80.]

No. 773, Petition of John Chandler Smith

John Chandler Smith of Baltimore County, Md., claims compensation for Sarah Ellen Brown. Sarah Ellen is 12 years old, brown colored and rather slight in frame. Smith owned Sarah's mother when Sarah was born. Sarah is healthy and has been raised as a house servant. He values her at $500.

[Commissioners paid Smith $219.]

No. 774, Petition of Joshua Peirce   Filed Jun. 28, 1862

Joshua Peirce claims compensation for ten persons.

1. Jeremiah Gibson, is 48 years old, black and about 5 feet 7 inches tall. [Value $1,200]

2. Nancy Carroll is about 45 years old, black and 5 feet 4 inches high. She has lived in Peirce's family for 26 years and is his housekeeper. She is an excellent cook and has charge of the keys and the whole management of his house. [Value $800]

3. William H. Beckett is about 29 years old, light yellow complexion and about 5 feet 7 inches tall. He has a scar on his cheek from a burn he received as a child when he fell on a stove. He has acted as foreman in Peirce's garden and greenhouses and nurseries. He can read and write and is a good coachman. He is now employed by Secretary of State W[illiam] H. Seward for $20 a month as a coachman. [Value $2,000]

4. Thomas Rhodes, is about 24 years old, black and about 6 feet 3/4 inches tall. He is a first-rate coachmann and skilled in the management of horses. He is also an excellent farm hand. [Value $1,600]

5. Anna Maria Rustin is about 23 years old, mulatto and about 5 feet 1 inch tall. She is an excellent house servant and knows cooking, washing and ironing and plain sewing. [Value $1,200]

6. Ellen Beckett is about 23 years old, dark mulatto and about 5 feet 6 3/4 inches tall. She is an excellent house servant and has been taught cooking, washing and ironing and plain sewing. [Value $1,200]

7. Charlotte R. Carroll is about 17, black and about 5 feet 4 inches high. She is an excellent house servant and has been taught cooking, washing and ironing and plain sewing. [Value $1,200]

8. Anthony J. Carroll is about 14 years old, black and about 5 feet 4 inches high. He is smart and promises to be

an excellent servant and useful man. [Value $1,200]

9. Charles J. Carroll is about nine months old and has a bright yellow complexion. He is bright and healthy. [Value $100]

10. William Nicholas Rustin is about three months old and has a bright yellow complexion. He is bright and healthy. [Value $100]

Gibson was bought by Peirce from the estate of Thomas B. Offutt of Montgomery County, Md., about 1821. Nancy Carroll was bought from John P. Ingle of Washington about 26 years ago. All the others were born in the possession of Peirce.

[Commissioners paid Peirce $3,635.40: Jeremiah Gibson, $306.60; Nancy Carroll, $175.20; William H. Beckett, $569.40; Thomas Rhodes, $613.20; Anna M. Rustin, $438; Ellen Beckett, $525.60; Charlotte R. Carroll, $481.80; Anthony J. Carroll, $459.90; Charles J. Carroll, $43.80; William Nicholas Rustin, $21.90.]

No. 775, Petition of William Gunton, administrator of William A. Gunton   Filed Jun. 28, 1862

William Gunton, administrator of William A. Gunton, of Washington, claims compensation for two persons.

1. Joshua is 26 years old, dark mulatto in color and about 5 feet 10 inches tall. Joshua left William Gunton's farm in Prince George's County, Md., last March and it is believed that he was detained in one of the camps within D.C. that is near the farm. Gunton says that Joshua has "always conducted himself with great propriety [and] I feel confident he would not remain from his father, mother, brother and sister unless prevented from returning." [Value $1,100]

2. Hennie, aged 22 on May 14, 1862, is dark mulatto in color and about 5 feet 4 inches tall. [Value $900]

The late William A. Gunton purchased Joshua from William Tolson. Hennie was a gift from John B. Mullihin of Prince George's County to his daughter upon her marriage to his son, William A. Gunton, on Jun. 20, 1848.

[Commissioners paid Gunton $1,095: Joshua, $569.40; Henrie [*sic*], $525.60.]

No. 776, Petition of Rachel Piles   Filed Jun. 28, 1862

Rachel Piles of Montgomery County, Md., claims compensation for Sophia Sewal[l]. Sophia is about 58 years old, of a copper complexion and about 5 feet 8 inches tall. She is an excellent cook, washer and ironer and a good housekeeper. She was purchased when a baby with her mother by Piles's late husband from Stephey Caywood of Prince George's County, Md. (Signed Rachel her x mark Piles) [Value $400]

[Commissioners paid W.H. Piles, administrator of Rachel, $131.40 for Sophia "Sewall".]

No. 777, Petition of Peter C. Howle, administrator of Parke G. Howle   Filed Jun. 28, 1862

Peter C. Howle, administrator of the estate of his late father, Maj. Parke G. Howle, claims compensation for three persons.

1. William Shorter, aged about 40 or 42 years is dark brown in color. He was purchased Mar. 14, 1850, for $750 by Peter's father from the late Edward Fenwick of D.C. by whom William was raised. William is a valuable servant and a good carriage driver and hostler. Up to the time of his purchase, he worked on a farm and understands farming and gardening. He also has had some experience within the last 12 years as a house servant. [Value $1,000]

2. Ann Shorter, wife of William, is about the same age as William and is of a dark brown color. She was brought up as a family servant and is a very superior cook and understands all things about being a house servant. She was raised by Peter's father and has had seven children. She occasionally is troubled by rheumatism. [Value $900]

3. Rebecca Shorter, daughter of William and Ann, is five and of a dark brown color. [Value $550]

Howle submitted a supplement to the petition dated Jul. 12, 1862, in which he states that he filed the petition as administrator of his father's estate for the benefit of his brother, Augustine N.Y. Howle, who has been absent for the last four or five years and he has had no word from him. When last heard from, he was in California.

[Commissioners paid P.C. Howle $678.90: William Shorter, $306.60; Ann Shorter, $262.80; Rebecca Shorter, $109.50.]

Parke G. Howle, marine officer, died Jul. 16, 1857. See Pippenger, D.C. Interments, 1855-1874, p. 173.

No. 778, Petition of James White

James White of the District of Columbia claims compensation for Henry White, who is six years old. Henry is a bright mulatto and is intelligent and a very promising servant. He has a scar on his arm from a burn. He acquired title to Henry by purchase for $100 of Amanda White, Henry's mother, from Sarah Ann Sasser of Washington on

May 9, 1849. Amanda was then ten years old and was to serve until she was 30. Henry was born about 1856 and Amanda died about the same year. He estimates Henry's value at $200. (James his x mark White)

[Commissioners paid James White, by Thomas Scrivener, Jr., his attorney, $175.20.]

No. 779, Petition of Mary S. Yerby

The original petition is missing.

[Commissioners paid Mary S. Yerby, by Alexander R. Shepherd, her attorney, $394.20, in compensation for Ann Booth.]

No. 780, Petition of Ann Green   Filed Jun. 28, 1862

Ann Green claims compensation for ten persons.

1. Mary Jane Dorsey, aged 38, is a bright mulatto of medium stature. She is a first-rate cook and faithful servant. [Value $1,000]
2. Henry Dorsey, aged 21, is a bright mulatto and a valuable servant. [Value $1,500]
3. Charles Dorsey, aged 19, is of a very bright color, short in stature, and is a first-rate farm hand and valuable house servant. [Value $1,300]
4. Susanna Dorsey, aged 16, is of a dark color. She is a first-rate nurse. [Value $1,100]
5. Francis Dorsey, aged 14, is of a dark color with a quick, bright countenance and is very capable and reliable. [Value $1,200]
6. Gustavus Dorsey, aged ten, is black in color with a open, bright countenance. He is a remarkable child and is good and capable. [Value $1,200]
7. Thomas Waters, aged 30, is black, rather tall and straight. He is upright and capable. [Value $300 for his unexpired term]
8. Aaron Edmonson, aged 27, is tall, black, rather straight, active and capable. [Value $500 for his unexpired term]
9. Vachel Henry Edmonson, aged 20, is rather tall, black, athletic and is a first-rate servant. [Value $800 for his unexpired term.]
10. Phebe Edmonson, aged 22, is very tall for a woman, black, robust and capable of great indurance and determination. [Value $500 for her unexpired term.]

Green states that the mother of the Dorsey family was purchased in 1815 and the children were born and raised in her family. The others were inherited from her mother, Mrs. Rebecca Forrest. Thomas Waters, Aaron and Vachel Edmonson were to be freed at age 35; Phebe at age 30.

[Commissioners paid Green $3,066: Mary Jane Dorsey, $240.90; Henry Dorsey, $525.60; Charles Dorsey, $525.60; Susanna Dorsey, $503.70; Francis Dorsey, $459.90; John Gustavus Dorsey, $284.70; Thomas Waters, $87.60; Aaron "Edmonston", $109.50; Vachel Henry "Edmonston", $219; Phebe "Edmonston", $109.50.]

The will of Rebecca Forrest, the widow of Gen. Uriah Forrest, who died in 1843, is recorded in Pippenger, D.C. Probate Records, 1801-1852, pp. 270-271. The will left to her daughter, Ann Green wife of John Green, the estate known as Rosedale, and various slaves. The will, signed in 1840, provided that "Negro woman Caroline shall be free; negro boy William (now about 14 yrs. old) to dau. Ann Green, to serve until he is 35 yrs. old, then free; negro boys Tom and Aaron, to son George P. Forrest, to serve until they are 35 yrs. old, then free, Tom is now about 9 yrs. old and Aaron is about 7 yrs. old; negro girl, the dau. of Caroline, now about 2 yrs. old, to son George P. Forrest, to serve until she is 20 yrs. old, then free, that increase of girl to serve until they are 21 yrs. old then free". Codicil 2, dated Aug. 14, 1843, provided that "servant boys William, Tom, Aaron, Vatch and any others born during the period of Caroline's bondage, I leave to use of dau. Anne Green, until they arrive at age 35 yrs., then to be free; Phebe I now leave to Maria Green until she is 30 yrs. of age."

No. 781, Petition of George W. Hatton   Filed Jun. 28, 1862

George W. Hatton of Washington City claims compensation for two persons.

1. Lethee Bowie is aged 45, black, 5 feet 7 inches tall. She has a scar on her right foot below the instep caused by the cut of an axe and a scar on her left wrist caused by a cut. She is a good and faithful servant and has never lost a day from sickness except the usual time at the birth of John.
2. John Bowie, son of Lethee, is three years old, mulatto and 2 feet 7 inches tall.

Hatton bought "Letha" and her child from B[enjamin] O. Sheckell for $650 on Sept. 25, 1856. The child purchased from Sheckell is not John Bowie, but another child who is living in Maryland. He values them at $500.

[Commissioners paid $350.40 to Hatton: "Lethe" Bowie, $306.60; John, $43.80.]

No. 782, Petition of Charles H. Leiberman   Filed Jun. 28, 1862

Charles H. "Libermann" of Washington, D.C., claims compensation for Daniel Jones. Jones is aged 25 years nine months, is about 5 feet 4 inches high, has a black complexion and a stout build. He has a considerable and distinct scar under his right eye. Jones was purchased from Ann Payne of D.C. for $200 on Jul. 6, 1849, to serve a term of 15 years, which would end when Jones reaches age 28. Ann Payne, the widow of Jacob Payne, had inherited Jones from her husband. Payne's sale to Liberman provided that Lieberman could not sell Jones's services at a greater distance than 15 miles from D.C. Liberman claims $225 for Jones.

[Commissioners paid Leiberman $65.70.]

Charles's last name is spelled variously: "Leiberman", "Libermann", "Liberman","Lieberman".

No. 783, Petition of Leah L[yttleton] G[ale] Wilson   Filed Jun. 28, 1862

Leah L.G. Wilson of Washington claims compensation for nine persons.

1. James, aged 40, is brown, tall and robust. He is a good laborer though formerly intemperate. His wages since his emancipation are $1.25 per day. [Value $1,200]

2. Lowder, aged 33 or 34, is dark, of medium height and robust. He is an excellent laborer and his wages are $1.25 a day. [Value $1,500]

3. Daniel, aged about 31 or 32, is very dark and tall. He is a good laborer and his wages are $20 per month. [Value $1,500]

4. William Henry, aged near six, is of a brown color. [Value $250]

5. Preston Brown, is supposed to be aged about 70, and is black and tall. He is infirm and diseased in his leg, but is still useful. [Value $80]

6. Ibbey, aged 23, is a very bright mulatto, tall, large, well-formed and good-looking. [Value $1,000]

7. Rachel, is about 34 or 35 years old, dark, of medium height. [Value $550]

8. Sabra, aged two years and nine months, is brown in color. [Value $100]

9. Sarah, aged 14 months, is brown in color. [Value $80 (?)]

In addition, Leah owns jointly with her sister, Mary G. Wilson, the services of Horace, Mady and Littleton. Horace is aged about 38, dark, tall and slender and has a bend in one leg. Mady is aged about 62, mulatto, tall and large. Littleton is about 62 and square built.

James, Daniel, Preston Brown and Rachel were willed to her by her mother. William Henry, Sabra and Sarah are hers by birth. Ibbey and Lowden are hers by virtue of her sister Margaret's will. Half ownership of Horace comes from her mother's and sister's wills and partly by purchase from her brother. Her half ownership of Mady is based on her sister's will. Attached is a copy of Margaret Eleanor Gale Wilson's will that provides that her estate go to her two sisters. (Will signed Jan. 25, 1841 and admitted to probate on Oct. 1, 1844)

[Commissioners paid Wilson $2,671.80: James, $569.40; Lowder, $481.80; Daniel, $481.80; William Henry, $131.40; Preston Brown, $43.80; Ibbey, $525.60; Rachel, $306.60; Sabra, $87.60; Sarah, $43.80.]

Leah L. Wilson, formerly of Somerset County, Md., died in Washington on Dec. 5, 1837. Her will is recorded in Pippenger, <u>D.C. Probate Records, 1801-1852</u>, pp. 216-17. In addition to her daughters, Leah Lyttleton Gale, Mary Gale and Margaret "Elenor" Gale, she had a son named Samuel Lyttleton Wilson.

No. 783 and 784, Petition of Leah L[yttleton]G[ale] Wilson and Mary G[ale] Wilson   Filed Jun. 28, 1862

Leah L.G. Wilson and Mary G. Wilson jointly own:

1. Horace, aged about 38, dark, tall and slender. He has a bend in one leg near his knee. [Value $1,000]

2. Mady is about 62 years old, mulatto, tall and large. She is rheumatic and infirm but is a nice pastry cook. [Value $50]

3. Littleton, aged about 62, is square in build and of medium height. He is intemperate and left his employer in December, but has been seen in the neighborhood. [Value $50]

[Commissions granted Leah Wilson and Mary G. Wilson $525.60: Horace, $438; Maddy [*sic*], $43.80; Middleton [*sic*], $43.80.]

Mary G. Wilson claims compensation for two slaves totally owned by her.

1. Samuel is aged 19 years seven months, brown in color, tall and well-formed. His wages last month were $1 a day. [Value $1,400]

2. John is aged about 35 and mulatto. He is paralyzed and helpless.

She acquired Samuel and John under the terms of the will of her late sister, Margaret Eleanor Gale Wilson. [Commissioners paid Wilson $613.20: Samuel, $613.20; John, no value.]

No. 785, Petition of Joshua Morsell   Filed Jun. 28, 1862

Joshua Morsell of Washington claims compensation for three persons.

1. Elizabeth Hays, aged 38, dark brown in color. She is a good cook and washerwoman.
2. Lewis Preston Hays, child of Elizabeth, aged 12, light brown in color. He is a good house servant.
3. Davy Hays, child of Elizabeth, aged seven, very dark in color. He is a healthy child and likely.

He values the three at $1,600.

His title derives through his wife, Jane Gray Morsell, who inherited Elizabeth and Lewis Preston, under the will of her mother, Jane Chesley. Davy was born after Chesley's death. The attached copy of an extract from Chesley's will provides that her daughter get Betsey and her two daughters, Sally Ann and Eliza Jane, with their future increase, and Betsey's two sons, John and Lewis Preston. She also bequeathed to Jane a boy named William, who was Dinah's son. (The will is recorded in will book Liber BGG No. 1, folio 268, of the records of Anne Arundel County, Md.)

[Commissioners paid Morsell $613.20: Elizabeth "Hayes", $262.80; Lewis Preston "Hayes", $219; Davy "Hayes", $131.40.]

No. 786, Petition of Henry Weaver   Filed Jun. 28, 1862

Henry Weaver of Georgetown, D.C., claims compensation for Jane who is 34 years old and black in color. She is a first-rate cook and general house servant. He purchased her. Weaver values her at $1,000.

[Commissioners paid Weaver $438.]

No. 787, Petition of Henry Weaver for self and as guardian of   Filed Jun. 28, 1862
Henry S., Angeline and Theodore Barnes

Henry Weaver of Georgetown claims compensation for three persons in whom he holds one-third interest. The other two-thirds is held as guardian to Henry S. Barnes, Angeline Barnes and Theodore Barnes.

1. Cato, is 34 years old, black, 5 feet 9 or 10 inches tall. He is a first-rate butcher. [Value $1,400]
2. Sarah, aged 17, is black in color. She is a fine house servant. [Value $1,200]
3. Dennis, aged 51 (?) years, is black in color. He is a fine hand. [Value $500]

His individual one-third interest comes to him by marriage. The other two-thirds results from his appointment as guardian for Henry S., Angeline, and Theodore Barnes.

[Commissioners paid Weaver, for self and as guardian, $1,029.30: Cato, $569.40; Sarah, $394.20; Dennis, $65.70.]

The 1860 D.C. Census for Georgetown (Vol. 1, p. 168), lists Henry Weaver as a master butcher. Living in Weaver's household are Angeline Barnes, aged 24, Henry Barnes, a master butcher, aged 22, and Theodore Barnes, aged 16.

No. 788, Petition of Samuel Riggs of R.   Filed Jun. 28, 1862

Samuel Riggs of R. of Montgomery County, Md., claims compensation for two persons.

1. Eliza Hall is about 45 years old, a bright mulatto, medium sized. She is a first-rate cook, house servant, washer and ironer, and was hired at $8 a month. [Value $600]
2. John Litch is aged about 21, black, six feet tall and stout built. He is a first-rate farm hand. [Value $1,400]

The title to Eliza Hall comes through his wife's inheritance from her father, the lateLyde (?) Griffith of Montgomery County who died about 1839. He owned the father and mother of John Litch and raised him.

[Commissioners disallowed both claims as the persons were not produced.]

The printed report spells John's name as "Fletcher", but this is clearly wrong. It appears to be Litch or Leitch in the original petition.

No. 789, Petition of Stephen Gough and Georgianna Gough   Filed Jun. 28, 1862

Stephen Gough and Georgiana Gouch of Georgetown claim compensation for six persons.

1. Emily Greenwell, aged 57, is a bright yellow color with regular features, medium height and good address. [Value $400]
2. Charlotte Greenwell, aged 29, has a dark complexion with irregular features. She is of medium height and has a good figure and demeanor. [Value $800]

3. Martha Greenwell, aged 25, is bright yellow with good features. She is below medium height has a slight figure and amiable address. [Value $800]

4. Betty Greenwell, aged 19 years four months, has a dark complexion and irregular features. She has a slight figure and is of medium height. [Value $800]

5. Emily 2nd is aged 17 years nine months. She is bright yellow, has irregular features, a slight figure and is of medium height. [Value $600]

6. Louisa Jane Greenwell is aged 14 years three months. She has a bright complexion, good features, slight figure, but is well-grown for a girl her age. [Value $400]

The estimated values given above are based on the assessments made of them by the corporation of Georgetown two years ago. They estimate that Emily 2nd and Louisa Jane have increased in value $200 each since that assessment. They request a total of $4,200.

They inherited the slaves as the children of Stephen and Elizabeth Gough, late of Saint Mary's County, Md., who died intestate.

[Commissioners paid William G. Ridgley, administrator of Stephen Gough and Georgiana Gough, by W.G. Ridgley, her attorney, $2,277.60; Emily Greenwell, $131.40; Charlotte Greenwell, $481.80; Martha Greenwell, $350.40; Betty Greenwell, $481.80; Emily Greenwell, $438; Louisa Jane Greenwell, $394.20.]

Gough's first name is spelled both "Georgianna" and "Georgiana".

No. 790, Petition of Rebecca Williams   Filed Jun. 28, 1862

Rebecca Williams of Georgetown claims compensation for eight persons.

1. Sarah Mason, aged about 48, is over five feet tall, has dark skin and is healthy. She is a good housekeeper and cook and has been hired out as such some years. She has brought in her monthly returns and has yielded $60 a year over and above the $5 a month that belongs to herself. [Value $1,000]

2. Sophia Mason, 30 years old, is over five feet tall, has dark skin and is healthy. She is the child of Sarah and has been brought up in Rebecca's services and has cooked and washed for her family for several years. [Value $1,400]

3. Sarah Mason, aged 12, is about five feet tall with dark skin and is healthy. The daughter of Sophia is a good servant and able to do the work an ordinary woman. [Value $1,000]

4. William Mason, aged seven is about four and one-half feet tall, has dark skin and is healthy. He acts as a waiter and runs errands. [Value $500]

5. Charity Ambush, aged 45, is over five feet, has not very dark skin and is in good health. She is a good housekeeper and a very fine cook. For some years she has been prompt in her monthly returns and yields $60 a year over and above the $5 a month she is allowed for herself. [Value $1,000]

6. Samuel Stevenson, aged 30, is about six feet tall, has not very dark skin and is a strong and able-bodied. He has been hired out for several seasons at from $1.25 to $1.50 a day as a bricklayer and farm laborer. He pays Williams a dollar a day and keeps the remainder of his wages. During the winter he hired at the National Hotel and at Willard's Hotel at $15 a month, of which he gave Williams $12. He has been headwaiter at the National Hotel and an assistant cook for a season or more at Willard's. After that he hired to one of the companies of the 7th Regiment. of the New York Volunteers when they encamped opposite Columbian College on 14th St. in Washington and transferred to the 8th Regiment when the 7th returned to New York. [Value $2,000]

7. Henry Ambush, aged 23, is about six feet tall, has not very dark skin and is healthy. He is a first-class waiter and house servant. He has been hired at Willard's Hotel for $15 a month, of which he pays Williams $12. [Value $1,800]

8. John Thomas, aged 21, is about six feet tall, has not very dark skin and is healthy. He is a first-class waiter and house servant. At present he is hired at the Kirkwood Hotel as a waiter. [Value $1,800]

Sarah Mason was purchased about 1833 and her children were born since that time. Charity Ambush was purchased about 1826. Samuel Stevenson, Henry Ambush and John Thomas are her children.

[Commissioners paid Williams $2,890.80: Sarah Mason, $153.30; Sophia Mason, $306.60; William Mason, $219; Charity Ambush, $219; Samuel Stevenson, $569.40; Henry Ambush, $525.60; John Thomas, $547.50; Sarah Mason, $350.40.]

No. 791, Petition of Thomas Knowles   Filed Jun. 28, 1862

Thomas Knowles of Georgetown claims compensation for three persons.

1. Joe Trusty, aged 16, is very black. He has large feet for a boy, has a fine set of white teeth with a pleasing

smile when spoken to. He is a house servant. [Value $800]

    2. Andew Trusty, aged 15, is very black with a large head and short, curly hair. He is in excellent health and has a pleasing expression in his countenance. He is a house servant. [Value $800]

    3. Anna Trusty, aged 13, is very black with short, curly hair. Her face has a rather pleasing expression. She has thick lips and might be considered small for her age. She has learned to read. Anna is a house servant. [Value $400]

    Knowles purchased their mother, Henny Trusty, who has since died, and her son, Joe, from Susan Elizabeth Smith of Georgetown on Oct 1, 1847, for $475. See D.C. Liber W.B. No. 137, folio 226.

    [Commissioners paid Knowles $897.90: Joe Trusty, $350.40; Andrew Trusty, $306.60; Anna Trusty, $240.90.]

No. 792, Petition of Mary R. Bibb   Filed Jun. 28, 1862

    Mary R. Bibb of Georgetown claims compensation for Harriet Williams, aged 28. Williams is light in color, 5 feet 3 inches high and sound in body. Her value is $1,000. She was purchased in Kentucky many years ago.

    [Commissioners paid Bibb $372.30.]

No. 793, Petition of Capt. James E. Harrison   Filed Jun. 28, 1862

    Capt. James E. Harrison of Washington City claims compensation for Emily. Emily is about 16 years old, 5 feet 4 inches tall with a medium dark complexion. She is a body servant. She was the property of his wife before they were married. He values her at $900. At the time of this petition, Harrison with in the 5th Cavalry of the Army in camp near Richmond, Va.

    [Commissioners paid Harrison $525.60.]

No. 794, Petition of Verlinda Shaw   Filed Jun. 28, 1862

    Verlinda Shaw of Prince George's County, Md., claims compensation for ten persons:

    1. George Lee, aged 23, has a dark complexion. [Value $1,000]

    2. Virginia Brogden, aged 35, has a dark complexion. [Value $800]

    3. Eliza Waters, aged 33, has a dark complexion. [Value $800]

    4. Mary Lee, aged 20, has a dark complexion. [Value $800]

    5. Ellen Lee, aged 15, has a dark complexion. [Value $800]

    6. Julia Waters, aged six, has a dark complexion. [Value $300]

    7. James Waters, aged three, is black in color. [Value $300]

    8. Harriet Ann Brogden, aged eight months, has a dark complexion. [Value $100]

    9. Ellen Brogden, aged seven, has a dark complexion. [Value $100]

    10. Caroline or Catharine, aged 13, has a dark complexion. [Value (?)]

    She claims a total of $5,250. They are good servants and are free of defects of any kind. (Signed Verlinda her x mark Shaw)

    [Commissioners orginally awarded Shaw $3,044.10: Virginia Bragden [sic], $394.20; George Lee, $591.30; Eliza Waters, $416.10; Mary Lee, $503.70; Ellen Lee, $284.70; Julia Waters, $197.10; James Waters, $87.60; Harriet Ann Bragden [sic], $43.80; Ellen Bragden [sic], $175.20; Caroline, $350.40. The printed report contains a note that states that $700.80 was paid to George B. Scaggs, Shaw's attorney, on Mar. 21, 1863, as per order of the Secretary of the Treasury on Mar. 19, 1863.]

No. 795, Petition of Charles E. Sherman, William Lee, conflicting claimant   Filed Jun. 28, 1862
as to servants Henry, Ann, Rose and Lou

    Charles E. Sherman of Washington claims compensation for nine persons.

    1. Henny Mockabee, aged 45, is dark brown in color, large, strong and healthy. She is a first-rate cook and a good washer and ironer and a good house servant.

    2. Mary Mockabee, the daughter of Henny, aged 28, is light brown in color. She is an experienced and first-rate house servant and also a very good cook, washer and ironer. She is of medium size, strong and healthy.

    3. Rose Mockabee, daughter of Henny, aged 21, darker in color than her mother, a little above medium height, strong and healthy. She is a first-rate house servant and a good cook, washer and ironer

    4. Ann Mockabee, daughter of Henny, aged 19, about the same color as her mother. She is full-sized, strong and healthy. She is an experienced house servant and also a good outdoor and farm servant.

    5. Louisa Mockabee, daughter of Henny, aged 17, is the same color as her mother and is medium sized, strong and healthy. She is a good nurse and house servant and a fair seamstress.

6. Frank Mockabee, son of Mary, is aged between eight and nine, light mulatto, very likely and intelligent. He is a good dining room servant. He can read, write and cypher and has an unusual capacity for business.

7. Sarah Mockabee, daughter of Mary, is between three and four years old, very bright mulatto in color and is exceedingly likely.

8. Henry Mockabee, son of Rose, is aged three, mulatto. He is a large, intelligent and healthy boy.

9. Walter Garner is about 47 years old, dark in color, over six feet tall, strong and healthy. He is a good cook, servant, carriage driver and field hand. He had paid in part for his freedom and thus Sherman's claims only a portion of his value.

He claims a total of $8,000 for the slaves. He acquied Henny, Mary, Rose and Ann by purchase from Samuel T. Stonestreet of Rockville, Montgomery County, Md., trustee, on Jun. 7, 1844. The other persons, except Garner, are children of Henny, Mary and Rose born since that purchase. Garner he bought from Philip King of Prince George's County, Md.

Attached is a statement dated Oct. 3, 1862, by William Lee that he holds a note against William Sherman, dated Nov. 22, 1854, for $4,100 secured by slaves Henny, Ann, Rose and Lou as described in another and subsequent deed of trust to William S. Holliday dated Feb. 20, 1858. See D.C. Liber J.A.S. No. 89, folios 375-378.

[Commissioners valued the slaves at $2,825.10: Henry [sic] Mockabee, $219; Mary Mockabee, $328.50; Frank Mockabee, $219; Sarah Mockabee, $109.50; Rose Mochabee [sic], $481.80; Henry, her son, $87.60; Ann Mochabee [sic], $503.70; Louisa Mochabee [sic], $438; Walter Garner, $438. The Commissioners paid Sherman $1,182.60 on May 9, 1863. The sum of $1,642.50 (for Henry [sic], Ann, Rose and Lou) was contested by Lee.]

Not only does the printed report of the commissioners gives Henny's name as "Henry", but it lists Frank and Sarah as Mary's children. If you only read the report, you would assume that "Henry" and Mary were man and wife rather than mother and daughter.

No. 796, Petition of Rachel M.A. Tolson, John E. Turton, executors of William H. Turton, Jr.
Filed Jun. 28, 1862

Rachel M.A. Tolson (formerly Turton and a resident of the District of Columbia) and John E. Turton, executors of the will of William H. Turton, Jr., late of Prince George's County, Md., claim compensation for the following 16 persons.

1. Ellen Green, aged 38 or 39, is about 5 feet 2 inches high and black. She is a good cook, washer and ironer.
2. William Green, aged 16, black, 5 feet 1 inch tall, is a good farm hand.
3. Nancy Green, aged 14, black, 4 feet 11 inches high, is a good house servant.
4. Gassaway Green, aged 12, black, 4 feet 6 inches high, is a good house servant.
5. Leona Green, aged three, black, is 2 feet 10 inches high.
6. John Ludlow, aged about 51, black, about 5 feet 6 inches high, is a good farm hand although subject to occasional attacks of rheumatism.
7. Eliza Gray, about 37 years old, mulatto, about 5 feet 6 inches tall, is a good house or field hand.
8. Henny Gray, aged 13, mulatto, about 4 feet 11 (?) inches tall, is a good house servant.
9. Grace Gray, aged 11, black, 4 feet 6 inches tall, is a good house servant.
10. Orlando Gray, aged nine, black, 4 feet 2 inches tall, is a good house servant.
11. Walter Gray is aged seven, dark mulatto, about 3 feet 10 inches tall.
12. Reverdy Gray is aged three, dark mulatto, three feet high.
13. John Asbury Gray is aged two, dark mulatto.
14. Caroline Gray, aged 17, bright mulatto, 5 feet 2 inches tall, is a good house servant.
15. Charles Gray is about eight months old and a very bright mulatto.
16. Isaac Taylor, aged 19, black, 5 feet 5 inches tall, is a good farm hand.

The petitioners claim $9,000. Their title is based on the will of William H. Turton, Jr. A copy of the will, proved Sept. 3, 1855, is attached. Rachel was William Turton's wife.

[Commissioners paid Rachel M.A. Tolson, by John E. Turton, her attorney, and John E. Turton, executors, $4,139.10: Eliza Gray, $306.60; Henry [sic] Gray, $306.60; Grace Gray, 4284.70; Orlando Gray, $197.10; Walter Gray, $153.30; Reverdy Gray, $87.60; John Asbury Gray, $43.80; Caroline Gray, $459.90; Charles Gray, $43.80; Isaac Gray [sic], $569.40.]

No. 797, Petition of Henry Kengla
Filed Jun. 28, 1862

Henry Kengla of Georgetown, claims compensation for nine persons.

1. Peter Warring, aged 47, is 5 feet 10 inches tall, quite black and a butcher by trade. [Value $800]
2. Nathan Brooks, aged 38, is 5 feet 8 inches tall, black and a butcher by trade. [Value $800]
3. Rebecca Brisco, aged 35, is 5 feet 6 inches tall. She is an excellent cook, washer and ironer. She is also a midwife and is constantly and frequently employed in this. [Value $600]
4. Mary Brisco, aged 16, is 5 feet 4 inches tall. She is an excellent cook and house servant. [Value $1,000]
5. Henry Brisco, aged 14, is 4 feet 10 inches tall, black, and assists in butchering. [Value $800]
6. Joseph Brisco, aged 12, is 4 feet 6 inches tall, black, and assists in butchering. [Value $700]
7. Washington Brisco, aged ten, is 4 feet 2 inches tall. He is young, strong and handy. [Value $500]
8. Martha Brisco, aged seven, is 3 feet 10 inches tall. [Value $400]
9. Fanny Brisco, aged five, is 3 feet 4 inches tall. [Value $300]

He purchased Warring from Mr. West in about 1855; he purchased Brooks from Peter G. Posey about 1849; he purchased Rebecca Brisco with Mary about 1847 from Mrs. Clement Smith of Georgetown. Henry, Joseph, Washington, Martha and Fanny are Rebecca's children born since she was bought.

[The Commissioners did not allow Kengla's claim as the persons were not produced.]

Boyd's 1860 Directory, p. 168, shows that Kengla was a butcher at the Georgetown Market.

No. 798, Petition of William F. Dickinson   Filed Jun. 30, 1862

William F. Dickinson of the District of Columbia claims compensation for two persons.

1. Harriet Winston, aged 50, is dark in color, five feet three-fourths inches high, straight and spare. She is pleasing and intelligent in expression and polite and respectful when addressed. She is an excellent house servant and is healthy, except for corns on her feet. [Value $400]
2. Robert Winston, aged 15, is dark, 4 feet 10 inches tall, very likely with regular features and an intelligent expression. He is respectful and polite when addressed. [Value $800]

Dickinson's title is based on a decree of the court of Caroline County, Va., for the division of the estate of F. Dickinson in 1849.

[Commissioners paid $591.30: Harriet Winston, $175.20; Robert Winston, $416.10.]

No. 799, Petition of Lucinda S. Matthews, executrix of Henry C. Matthews   Filed Jun. 30, 1862

Lucinda S. Matthews of Georgetown, executor of the will of her late husband, Henry C. Matthews, claims compensation for seven persons.

1. Dennis Berry, aged 54, very black, stout made, is of medium height. He is a fine, number one field hand and has been the foreman of H.C. Matthews's farm in Maryland. At the time of emancipation he was hired as a cook at the Washington Navy Yard for $120. [Value $1,000]
2. William Sybolt, 21 years old, copper colored, well-made, is of medium height. He is a fine house servant and hostler and was hired at the Washington Navy Yard as a house servant at $120 per year. [Value $1,400]
3. Lucinda Ross, aged 51, well-made, of a dark copper color, is of medium size. She is a first-class cook and washerwoman, and has been hired at $6 a month. [Value $700]
4. Eliza Jane Somers, aged 22, is very stout and of medium height. She is a first-class cook and washerwomann and has been hired for $6 a month. [Value $1,200]
5. Mary Jackson Curtis, aged 39, is of a dark color, and of medium height. She is a fine house servant and splendid washerwoman and has been the petitioner's house servant. Her usual rate of hire is $6 a month. [Value $1,000]
6. Madeline Curtis is Mary's child, aged five years, and is very black and of ordinary height. [Value $200]
7. Agnes Curtis, aged two, is black and of usual size. She has died since the filing..

Her husband acquired Dennis Berry, the mother of William Sybolt, Lucinda Ross and Eliza Jane Somers, under the will of Alexander Matthews dated Apr. 15, 1842, and admitted to probate in Charles County, Md., about two years later. William Sybolt was born of a woman while she was owned by Henry C. Matthews. Mary Jackson Curtis was born of Susan Jackson while Susan was owned by H.C. Matthews. Madeline and Agnes were born after their mother was owned by Matthews. Lucinda's title comes under the terms of the will of her husband, H.C. Mathews, admitted to probate in D.C. on May 10, 1862.

[Commissioners awarded Matthews $2,058.60, but paid only $27.13 of the sum of $109.50 allowed for Madeline, thus making a payment of $1,960.73 [*sic*].The amounts awarded were as follows: Dennis Berry, $262.80; William Sybolt, $591.30; Lucinda Ross, $153.30; Elizabeth J. Somers, $525.60; Mary Curtis, $372.30; Madaline [*sic*] Curtis, $109.50; Agnes Curtis, $43.80.]

The printed report gives incorrect amounts paid. If they only paid $27.13 instead of $109.50 for Madeline, then the total paid would have been $1,976.23. Clearly the fact that Agnes died before the payout affected the total. The surname of H.C. and Lucinda is spelled both "Matthews" and "Mathews" in the original documents.

No. 800, Petition of Lucinda S. Matthews   Filed Jun. 30, 1862

Lucinda S. Mathews of Washington County, D.C., claims compensation for four persons.

1. Susan Jackson, aged 70, tall and stout, is of a dark color. She has been Lucinda's cook for the past 40 years although she is somewhat affected by age.

2. Ann Jackson, aged 21, is small, stout and a bright mulatto. She is a good washerwoman, house servant and cook.

3. Matilda Miller, aged about 50, is tall and a bright mulatto. She has been the nurse to all of Lucinda's children and is now her house servant and seamstress.

4. Frederick Adkinson, aged 28, is well-made, very black, and of ordinary height. He is a gardener, hostler and general attendant about Lucinda's premises.

Matthews values them at $3,400. Susan Jackson was given to her late husband, Henry C. Mathews, in 1821, by John S. Haw. Ann Jackson is the daughter of Susan's daughter, Mary Jackson, born while Mary was owned by H.C. Mathews. Miller was purchased by her husband from the estate of Henry H. Chapman, late of D.C,. on Sept. 18, 1822, for $276. Atkinson was willed to her husband by Alexander Mathews, late of Charles County, Md., by his will dated Apr. 15, 1842. Lucinda is the heir under the will of Henry C. that was admitted to probate May 10, 1862.

Attached is a copy of the bill of sale from Mary Chapman of Georgetown, administrator of Henry H. Chapman, by which on Sept. 18, 1822, she sells Matilda to H.C. Mathews. (Signed and filed Oct. 3, 1828)

[Commissioners paid Matthews $1,182.60: Susan Jackson, no value; Ann Jackson, $438; Matilda Miller, $153.30; Frederick Atkinson, $591.30.]

See No. 799 directly above. The surname is spelled both Matthews and Mathews.

No. 801, Petition of John F. Bridgett   Filed Jun. 30, 1862

John F. Bridgett of Washington claims compensation for Laura Diggs. Laura is about eight years old, a dark mulatto, and is held to service until she reaches age 16, which will be in 1870. She is very handy about the house and he values her at $300. His title comes by a bill of sale from Sarah Ann Duvall of Washington. A copy of the bill of sale is attached and shows that Bridget paid $90 for Sylvia, aged about 34, to serve a term of six years (until Aug. 20, 1861), and Sylvia's daughter, Laura, aged about one, to serve until age 16, after which they were to be free. (Bill of sale recorded in D.C. Liber J.A.S. No. 103, folios 214-215)

[Commissioners paid Bridgett $65.70.]

John's surname is spelled both "Bridget" and "Bridgett" in these documents.

No. 802, Petition of Thomas Blagden

Thomas Blagden of Washington County, D.C., claims compensation for three persons.

1. Charles Bell is aged about 50 years, black and about 5 feet 10 inches high. In December 1851 Bell and Blagden agreed that he might purchase his time for $500 and he has paid all but $50 of that sum. Since his purchase he has been allowed to be at large and work for himself. [Value $180]

2. Walter Boyd is aged about 16 and is held to service until age 25. He is a dining room servant. [Value $450]

3. John Boyd is aged about 16 and is held to service until age 25. He is a field hand. [Value $450]

Blagden purchased Bell about 1828 or 1829 from W. Loker. The terms of service of Walter and John were purchased from the estate of Zachariah Hazle of Washington.

[Commissioners paid Blagden $481.80: Charles Bell, $219; Walter Boyd, $131.40; John Boyd, $131.40.]

The will of Zachariah "Hazel", filed in 1851, provided that Horatio Maryman, his son-in-law, hold certain slaves in trust for his children: slave Mary [Ann Boyd] to serve five years; Sarah [Boyd], to serve seven years, John and Walter [Boyd] to serve until they reached age 25. The profit from the labor of the Negroes was to be used for the education and maintenance of Hazel's grandchildren. The slaves were to be freed at the end of their terms of service. See Registration No. 2851 in Provine, <u>Free Negro Registers, 1821-1861</u>. See also Pippenger, <u>D.C. Probate Records, 1801-1852</u>, pp. 354-355.

No. 803, Petition of Presley W. Dorsey   Filed Jun.. 30, 1862

Presley W. Dorsey of Washington City claims compensation for four persons.

1. Dolley Bell, about 35 (?) years old, is a dark mulatto about 5 feet 10 inches tall, straight and well-formed. She is an excellent cook and house servant. [Value $1,500 (?)]

2. Wesley Bell, son of Dolley, aged about 20, is a dark mulatto, about 5 feet 8 inches tall, and "of quite unusual size." He is a good house servant and could cook, wash and be generally useful. [Value $500]

3. Ann Brotten, aged 28, is about 5 feet 7 inches tall, a bright mulatto, and quite good-looking. She is an excellent cook and house servant. [Value $1,500]

4. James Brotten, son of Ann, is aged five, a bright mulatto who is good-looking. [Value $300]

In 1834 Dolley was given to Dorsey's wife by her late father and Wesley was born to Dolley. Ann was given to him by his father many years ago and James was born to Ann.

[Commissioners paid Dorsey $1,007.40: "Dolly" Bell, $372.30; Wesley Bell, $21.90; Ann Brotten, $481.80; John Boyd, $131.40.]

Something is wrong with Wesley Bell to be valued by the commissioners at only $21.90. This is not explained in the petition, except by the use of the phrase "of unusual size."

No. 804, Petition of Sarah Dorsey   Filed Jun. 30, 1862

Sarah Dorsey of Frederick County, Md., claims compensation for Maria Snoden. Maria is 45 years old, quite black, about 5 feet 9 or 10 inches tall, straight and well-formed. She is an excellent cook and house servant. She has an enlargement of one ankle, but that does not impair her value. Dorsey inherited Snowden by the terms of the will of her late father, James Worthington, late of Frederick County, who died about eight or ten years ago. [Value $800]

[Commissioners paid P[resley] W. Dorsey, Sarah Dorsey's attorney, $240.90 for Maria "Snowden."

In the petition, Maria's name is given as "Snoden", but it was probably more often spelled "Snowden".

No. 805, Petition of Ann Macdaniel of Queensboro Chapel   Filed Jun. 30, 1862

Ann Macdaniel of Queensboro and of Washington, D.C., claims compensation for six persons.

1. George Allen, aged 26, is dark in color and about 5 feet 6 inches tall. He is a fine restaurant cook and market gardener and is handy with all tools. [Value $1,125]

2. Thomas Turner, aged 44, is of a dark color and is 5 feet 6 inches high. He is brick moulder and waiter. He is unsound in body and of immoral habits. When last heard from he was in the army waiting on the colonel and mess of one of the Ohio regiments. [Value $500]

3. Armstead Turner, aged 23, is of a light color and about 5 feet 8 inches tall. He is a good house carpenter, market gardener and waiter. [Value $1,500]

4. Lucy Turner is aged 30, dark in color, about 5 feet 4 inches high. She is a first-rate cook, washer and ironer, and a fine seamstress and mantua maker. [Value $1,000]

5. Elizabeth Turner, aged 15, is light colored and about 5 feet 6 inches tall. She is a good cook, washer and ironer and chambermaid. [Value $1,200]

6. Cecilia Turner, aged 14, is light colored and about 5 feet 4 inches high. [Value $1,000]

Macdaniel purchased George Allen for $1,125 on Aug. 23, 1850, from J.A. Williams. She owned the parents of Thomas, Armstead, Lucy, Elizabeth and Cecilia Turner.

[Commissioners paid Macdaniel $2,452.80: George Allen, $459.90; Armistead [sic] Turner, $613.20; Thomas Turner, $131.40; Lucy Turner, $328.50; Elizabeth Turner, $481.80; Cecilia Turner, $438.]

No. 806, Petition of Joseph Ingle   Filed Jun. 30, 1862

Joseph Ingle of Washington City claims compensation of Maria [Bell], who is held to service until she reaches age 25. Maria, aged five, mulatto, is 3 feet 9 inches tall and is smart and healthy. He purchased Maria's mother, Ann Bell, from Catharine E. Coyle of Washington for $150 on May 11[sic], 1853. The attached copy of the bill of sale shows that Ann Bell was then aged about 18, a mulatto, and had been bequeathed to Catharine by the will of her mother, the late Catharine Coyle, that was executed May 10, 1848. Ann Bell was to be manumitted on Oct. 1, 1860, and any children she might have were to be freed at age 25. In addition neither Ann Bell nor any of her children should be sold out of the District of Columbia. (Signed May 10, 1853) [Value $500]

[Commissioners paid Ingle $87.60.]

The petition also has attached a copy of the will of "Catherine" Coyle. The will provided that Coyle's servant woman Maria be freed at her death; that Maria's daughter Ann go to her daughter "Catherine", and that Maria's other three children be freed at age 30. For additional terms of the will, consult the original petition and its attachments.

No. 807, Petition of Esau Pickrell Filed Jun. 30, 1862

Esau Pickrell of Georgetown claims compensation for six persons.
1. Bill Green, aged 62, black. [Value $300]
2. Anna Green, Bill's wife, aged 61, black. [Value $300]
3. Eliza Green, child of Bill and Anna, aged 24, black. [Value $850]
4. Florence Green, daughter of Eliza, aged three, black. [Value $150]
5. Eliza Green, daughter of Eliza, aged 18 months. [Value $100]
6. George, aged 51, black. [Value $550]

They are all first-rate servants. Attached is a bill of sale whereby under the terms of an indenture dated Feb. 12, 1840, between William B. Thompson and his wife of the first part, and Farmers and Mechanics Bank of Georgetown of the second part and Clement Cox and John Kurtz, trustees, of the third part, Bill Green, Anna his wife and their three children, Eliza, Nelly and Florence, are sold for $535 to Esau Pickrell. (Bill of sale dated Jan. 18, 1847) He purchased George on Feb. 1, 1861, from John F. Pickrell of Baltimore for $700.

[Commissioners paid Pickrell $788.40: Bell [*sic*] Green, $87.60; Anna Green, $87.60; Eliza Green, $481.80; Florence, $87.60; Eliza, $43.80; George, not produced and not allowed.]

There is no information about Bill and Anna's children named Nelly and Florence.

No. 808, Petition of John McKenney Filed Jun. 30, 1862

John McKenney of Washington claims compensation for Harriet Bond. Bond is 35 or 36 years old, brown in color, of medium height, with rather sharp features and quick movements. She is slightly lame because of an accident in childhood, but this does not impair her efficiency as a servant. She is a first-class plain cook, washer and ironer. For years past she has had entire control and management of his kitchen and stores and she is trusted in all things. He "knows of no woman white or coloured for whose services I would exchange" her. Harriet's mother was a slave of McKenney's father, John McKenney of Harford County, Md. He inherited the mother and her children at the death of the elder McKenney about 1835. He manumitted Harriet's mother and about 1847 or 1848 he moved Harriet Bond to Washington and she has remained in his family ever since. [Value $1,200]

[Commissioners paid McKenney $262.80.]

No. 809, Petition of Fitzhugh Coyle Filed Jun. 30, 1862

Fitzhugh Coyle of the District of Columbia claims compensation for Len Calvert. Calvert is 44 years old, of a light color and about 5 feet 8 inches tall. He is healthy and robust and has an excellent character. He purchased Calvert about six years ago from Mr. Brooks for $1,000 in gold and thus seeks compensation of $1,000.

[Commissioners paid Coyle $306.60.]

No. 810, Petition of Phineas F. Wood, Mary Eliza Wood, Filed Jun. 30, 1862
Elizabeth M. Clements, and Asbury Lloyd, trustee

Phineas F. Wood and Mary E[liza] Wood, his wife, Elizabeth M. Clements, and Asbury Lloyd, trustee, claim compensation for Sarah F[rances] Mason. Mason is about 17[*sic*] years old, a dark mulatto of medium height, who is stout, strong and intelligent. She is a useful housekeeper, cook and chambermaid. She was purchased by Mary E. Wood, formerly Clements, from the estate of Columbus Alexander. There is a deed of trust from Mary E. Wood, prior to her marriage, to Asbury Lloyd in trust for the benefit of Elizabeth M. Clements. They value Mason at $1,000. Attached is a copy of a deed dated Jan. 29, 1861, by which Mary Eliza Clements, in consideration of $5, sells to Asbury Lloyd certain furniture and effects as well as a girl named Sarah Frances Mason, aged about 13 [*sic*], to hold in trust for Elizabeth M. Clements, Mary Eliza's sister.

[Commissioners paid $503.70 to Phinneas [*sic*] Ward, Mary E. Wood, Elizabeth N.[*sic*] Clements, by Asbury Lloyd, their attorney; Asbury Lloyd, trustee.]

No. 811, Petition of John S. Johns and Lucy M. Johns, Filed Jun. 30, 1862
William S. Darrell and Virginia E. Darrell

John S. Johns, Lucy M. Johns, William S. Darrell (in his own right and as guardian of Virginia E. Darrell) of Washington, D.C., claim compensation for four persons.

1. Susan, aged about 27, is a dark mulatto of medium height who is quite stout, likely and intelligent. She is a good cook and housekeeper and can command good wages. [Value $1,200]

2. Marion, daughter of Susan, is about 12 and is a dark mulatto girl who is stout, likely and intelligent. She is a

useful girl about the house as a chambermaid or nurse. [Value $700]

3. Martha, daughter of Susan, about seven years old, is a dark mulatto who is strong and stout, likely and intelligent. She is useful about the house. [Value $500]

4. William Henry, son of Susan, is about 14 months old, a dark mulatto who is well-formed and likely. [Value $200]

The title to the above persons comes through Sarah V[irginia] Darrell, formerly Brooke, deceased, the late wife of William Darrell. Benjamin E. Brooke, who died testate, left his interests in the slaves to Lucy M. Johns (formerly Darrell) the wife of John S. Johns, William Darrell and Lucy Ann Brooke, who died testate, leaving her interest to the children of William Darrell, viz., Lucy M. Johns, Virginia E. Darrell, Mary Darrell, William Brooke Darrell, Benjamin V. Darrell and Florence E., now the wife of H. Howard Young. Mary, William Brooke and Benjamin V. are minors and William S. Darrell is their guardian. The children are considerably in debt to William S. Darrell.

[Commissioners paid $876 to John S. Johns; Lucy M. Johns, William S. Darrell, Virginia E. Darrell, by their attorney, John S. Johns: Susan, $394.20; Marion, $262.80; Martha, $175.20; William Henry, $43.80.]

That part of the petition explaining the petitioners' title is hard to read and confusing. William S. Darrell married Sarah Virginia Brooke on Aug. 31, 1835. See Pippenger, D.C. Marriage Licenses, 1811-1858, p. 67.

No. 812, Petition of Cornelia Munson   Filed Jun. 30, 1862

Cornelia Munson of Washington City claims compensation for Dolly Munson, aged three years and nearly one month. She is of a mulatto color, nearly white, and is a smart bright child who is healthy and sound. Munson claims $200 for Dolly, which is the amount she refused for her two years ago. Dolly "was a pet in the family, and no price would be taken for her." Cornelia's title comes by a bill of sale dated Aug. 27, 1858, by which her husband, Dr. Owen Munson, for $1,000, sold to her his servant woman, Sarah, the mother of Dolly. The bill of sale shows that Cornelia paid the $1,000 out of her own separate property which she realized by giving a mortgage on certain property in New York State.

[Commissioners paid $87.60 to Cornelia Munson, O. Munson.]

No. 813, Petition of Charles H. Wiltberger   Filed Jun. 30, 1862

Charles H. Wiltberger of the District of Columbia claims compensation for four persons.

1. William Hawkins, aged 29 years and two months. He is of a dark chestnut color and about 5 feet 10 inches tall. Hawkins is held for a term of years and has 22 months left on his time (until Feb. 14, 1864). He is hired out at $28 a month. [Value $440]

2. Margaret Guttridge, aged 15 years seven months, is a bright mulatto girl with thick lips and straight hair. She is a cook who took the place of one hired at $7 per month and for whom $1,200 in cash was offered in March of 1860. [Value $700]

3. Cornelius Guttridge, aged ten years one month, is a sprightly boy who has dark skin, wooly hair and bright eyes. He is a house servant. [Value $400]

4. Sarah Frances Guttridge, aged eight years and eight months, has yellow skin, curly hair and large bright eyes. [Value $250]

Wiltberger inherited Hawkins under the will of Rebecca Burch. The terms of that will provided that her slave boy William go to Charles H. Wiltberger to serve until aged 31 or during the natural life of slave woman Sally, if longer than that time, and then he shall be manumitted. Wiltberger was charged with seeing that Sally be comfortably provided for whether as a free woman or as a slave. Wiltberger apparently purchased the Guttridges as slaves for life from the estate of S.O. Hilleary.

[Commissioners paid Wiltberger $1,040.25: William Hawkins, $54.75; Margaret Guttridge, $481.80; Cornelius Guttridge, $284.70; Sarah Frances Guttridge, $219.]

Rebecca Burch, wife of the late Capt. Benjamin Burch, died Jan. 31, 1848. Her will provided that slave woman Sally be free and that her son-in-law, Charles H. Wiltberger, get slave boy William until he is 31 years of age or during the natural life of Sally. See Pippenger, D.C. Probate Records, 1801-1852, pp. 321-322. Charles Wiltberger married Verlinda Mary Burch on Jul. 9, 1821. See Pippenger, D.C. Marriage Licenses, 1811-1858, p. 649.

No. 814, Petition of Frederick Bates   Filed Jun. 30, 1862

Frederick Bates of Washington claims compensation for two persons.

1. Jemima Johnson, aged 50, is of medium height, very black and of a delicate make. [Value $100]

2. Jane Johnson, daughter of Jemima, is aged 15, above five feet tall and very black. [Value $800]

They are both good house servants. Jemima "enjoys indifferent health" but Jane is very healthy. He values Jemima at $100 and Jane at $800, for a total of $800 [*sic*]. Bates purchased "Mymy" and youngest child, "Toby", then aged about four years six months, on May 6, 1852, for $425 from E.F. Barnard and Rachael B. Barnard.

[Commissioners paid Bates $525.60: Jemima Johnson, $87.60; Jane Johnson, $438.]

No. 815, Petition of William Jones — Filed Jul. 1, 1862

William Jones of Washington claims compensation for three persons.

1. Richard H. Jefferson, aged about 21 or 22, dark in color and about 5 feet 6 inches tall. He is sprightly and intelligent but is too fond of drink. [Value $800]

2. Susan Hill is aged about 44, mulatto, of medium height. She is an excellent house servant. [Value $700]

3. Annie Hill, the daughter of Susan, is six years old and dark in color. [Value $200]

Richard Jefferson is the son of Ellen Demar (?) who belonged to Jones's mother of Montgomery County, Md. Ellen was left to him when she was about 35 years old upon division of his mother's estate and Richard was born while she was in Jones's service. Susan Hill was purchased from Guilder (?) Darnall of Montgomery County, Md., in 1852 and Annie Hill is her daughter.

[Commissioners paid Jones $1,007.40: Richard H. Jefferson, $569.40; Susan Hill, $262.80; Annie Hill, $175.20.]

No. 816, Petition of J. Fenwick Young — Filed Jul. 1, 1862

J. Fenwick Young of the District of Columbia claims compensation for 14 persons.

1. Anthony Lewis is aged 25, black and about 5 feet 10 inches tall. He is a first-rate farm hand and carriage driver and is Young's foreman on the farm. [Value $1,600]

2. Belinda Lewis is aged 23, black and about 5 feet 2 inches tall. She is a prime field hand and a good cook. [Value $1,300]

3. Maria Lewis is about five, black and three feet tall. [Value $400]

4. Harriet Lewis is about three, black and about 2 feet 8 inches tall. [Value $300]

5. Kitty Lewis is aged six months and black. [Value $50]

6. Charlotte Covington is aged 29, mulatto and about 5 feet 3 inches tall. She is a good cook and house servant. She is pregnant at this time. [Value $1,000]

7. Samuel Covington is aged ten, mulatto and about 4 feet 5 inches tall. He is rather delicate but is a good waiter and house boy. [Value $600]

8. Margaret Covington is aged 10, copper colored and about 4 feet 3 inches tall. She is a good child's nurse. [Value $500]

9. William H. Covington, aged eight, copper colored, is about four feet tall. [Value $500]

10. Henny Covington is aged five, copper colored, about 3 feet 8 inches tall. [Value $350]

11. Daniel Dines is 12 (?) years old, black, about 4 feet 4 ½ inches tall. He is one of the quickest and handiest boys in D.C. [Value $1,000]

12. Joseph Dines is aged ten, mulatto, about 4 feet 4 inches tall. He is quick and active either in the house or on the farm. [Value $900]

13. Eliza Dines is aged eight, mulatto, about 3 feet 10 inches tall. She is a good girl about the house. [Value $500]

14. Philip Dines, aged four, is black and about 2 feet 8 inches tall. He is "from a good family as the others of his name". [Value $400]

He purchased Anthony Lewis from Thomas Marshall of Prince George's County, Md., in 1852. He purchased Charles Diggs and Belinda Lewis from George W. Young of D.C. in 1857. He raised Maria, Harriet and Kitty Lewis. He purchased Charlotte, Samuel. Margaret, William H. and Henny Covington from his mother, Mrs. Barbara S. Young of D.C., in February, 1860. His mother gave him Daniel, Joseph, Eliza and Philip Dines at the time of their birth and he raised them.

[Commissioners paid Young $3,219.30: Anthony Lewis, $657; Belinda Lewis, $438; Maria Lewis, $175.20; Harriet Lewis, $87.60; Kitty Lewis, $21.90; Charlotte Covington, $372.30; Samuel Covington, $240.90; Margaret Covington, $219; William H. Covington, $109.50; Henry [*sic*] Covington, $109.50; Daniel Dines, $262.80; Joseph Dines, $219; Eliza Dines, $153.30; Philip Dines, $87.60.]

No. 817, Petition of Mary C. Young — Filed Jul. 1, 1862

Mary C. Young of the District of Columbia claims compensation for Fanny Dines. Dines is 14 years old, copper colored and about 5 feet 5 inches tall. She is a good child's nurse and house girl. Mary Young's mother, Barbara S. Young, gave Fanny to her. She values her at $1,000.

[Commissioners paid Mary C. Young, by J.F[enwick] Young, attorney, $459.90.]

No. 818, Petition of Clementina S. Young   Filed Jul. 1, 1862

Clementina S. Young of the District of Columbia claims compensation for two persons.

1. Susan Dines, aged 16, is black in color and about 5 feet 3 inches high. She is a good cook and house girl and field hand. [Value $1,200]

2. Barbara Dines is aged six and is copper colored and 3 feet 8 inches tall. She is strong and healthy. [Value $500]

Clementina received them as a gift from her mother, Barbara S. Young of D.C.

[Commissioners paid Clementina S. Young, by J.F[enwick] Young, attorney, $657: Susan Dines, $525.60; Barbara Dines, $131.40.]

No. 819, Petition of Benjamin H. Clements   Filed Jul. 1, 1862

Benjamin H. Clements of Washington claims compensation for Josephine "Furgeson". Josephine is aged 15, dark chestnut in color, 5 feet 2 inches high and very likely. She is a first-rate house servant. Clements owned her mother and thus she was born his property. He values her at $800.

[Commissioners paid Clements $525.60 for Josephine "Ferguson".]

No. 820, Petition of William Pressy   Filed Jun. [sic] 1, 1862

William "Pressey" of Washington claims compensation for five persons.

1. Eliza Ann is 23 years old and dark mulatto. She is somewhat lame. She is an industrious servant and a good cook, ironer and washer. [Value $1,000]

2. John Thomas, aged 20, dark colored, and about 5 feet 8 or 9 inches tall. He is a first-rate servant and has been hired out as a driver of a cart at a wood yard for $20 a month. [Value $1,500]

3. George Albert is 12 years old and very black. He is strong and smart and has been raised as a house servant. [Value $700]

4. Laura Ann Virginia is nearly six years old and is a dark mulatto. [Value $300]

5. James Thomas, aged about six months, is a bright mulatto boy. [Value $100]

He acquired the mother of the first three by marriage. Laura and James are the children of Eliza Ann. (Signed William his x mark Pressey)

[Commissioners paid "Pressy" $1,357.80: Eliza Ann, $284.70; John Thomas, $591.30; George Albert, $328.50; Laura Ann Coquire [sic], $131.40; James Thomas $21.90.]

No. 821, Petition of Samuel Higgins   Filed Jul. 1, 1862

Samuel Higgins of Montgomery County, Md., claims compensation for two persons.

1. Lucy, aged about 48, dark in color, about 5 feet 6 inches high and thick set. She has performed service as a domestic in several households in Georgetown during the five years she has been hired there. [Value $600]

2. Lucinda, daughter of Lucy, aged about eight, of a light color, and about 3 feet 6 inches tall. [Value $400]

He acquired Lucy and Lucinda in 1855 from John T. Vincent of Montgomery County, Md.

[Commissioners paid Higgins $394.20: Lucy, $240.90; Lucinda, $153.30.]

No. 822, Petition of Thomas C. Cox for self and Francis V. Robinson   Filed Jul. 1, 1862
and Walter W.H. Robinson

Thomas C. Cox, in right of his wife, Margaret Cox, formerly Robinson, and as guardian of Francis V. Robinson and Walter W.H. Robinson, who are under the age of 21, claims compensation for six persons.

1. Nancy West is 60 years old, mulatto and 5 feet 2 inches tall. She is lame. [Value $200]

2. Margaret West, aged 42, is copper colored and 4 feet 11 inches tall. [Value $500]

3. Loulie Briscoe, aged 17, is copper colored and 5 feet one-half inch tall. [Value $1,000]

4. Ellen G. West, aged three, is a bright mulatto color and 2 feet 9 inches tall. [Value $300]

5. Delilah Henson, aged 15, is a bright mulatto and 5 feet 3 ½ inches tall. [Value $1,000]

6. Charles Carter, aged 60, is black and 5 feet 9 inches tall. He is addicted to drink. [Value $200]

They were held as slaves by Mrs. Frances H.P. Robinson, late of Georgetown, and Margaret, Francis and Walter H. are three of the six children who were her heirs.

[Commissioners awarded Cox, for self and others, $1,160.70: Nancy West. $43.80; Margaret West, $175.20; Loulie Briscoe, $438; Ellen G. West, $87.60; Delilah Henson, $372.30; Charles Carter, $43.80. Of the total, only one-half ($580.35) was paid to Cox with the other half held in the interest of persons not claiming.]

Frances H.P. Turner married William Robinson on Aug. 4, 1829. See Pippenger, D.C. Marriage Licenses, 1811-1858, p. 508.

No. 823, Petition of Martha Isherwood   Filed Jul. 1, 1862

Martha Isherwood of the city of Washington claims compensation for three persons.

1. Richard Ross, aged about 26 or 27, is black, healthy and able-bodied. He is a farm hand, takes care of horses, drives carriages and wagons and is a good house servant.

2. Caddy Foreman, aged 24 or 25, is black. She has been afflicted with rheumatism in her hands and legs. When she is healthy, she can cook very well but cannot wash or iron.

3. Samuel Brooks is about 11 or 12, black, good sized and active. He can wait in the house very well and do almost any thing a boy of his age can do.

She values the servants at $2,000. She got title to Richard Ross and Caddy Foreman by the will of Robert Isherwood, her late husband. Samuel Brooks was a gift from her father, Aden Darby, of Montgomery County, Md., when he was an infant. Attached is a copy of a bill of sale by which Aden Darby of Montgomery County, Md., on Aug. 27, 1851, for $1, sold Johnson Brooks, aged four, and Samuel Brooks, about eight months old, to Martha Isherwood. Also attached is a copy of the will of Robert Isherwood.

Robert Isherwood died Jun. 1, 1849. See Pippenger, D.C. Probate Records,1801-1852, p. 327n.

No. 824, Petition of Rebecca R. Darby, for self and   Filed Jul. 1, 1862
Ruth E. and James A. Darby

Rebecca R. Darby, Ruth E. Darby and James A. Darby of Montgomery County, Md., claim compensation for Rachel Chambers. Chambers is about 26 or 27 years old, black, above average height and in good health. She is a good cook, can wash and iron well, is a good nurse and a first-rate chambermaid and house servant. She is also a good dairy woman and manages the planting and tending of a kitchen garden. She is superior in every way, is trusted with the keys and has access to all their valuables. She values Chambers at $1,000

Chambers was a gift from Aden Darby of Montgomery County, Md., about 1851 or 1852. Rebecca is the oldest of two sisters and a brother and she files this claim for herself and her siblings. James Darby is crippled and confined to his bed. Attached is a copy of the bill of sale dated May 6, 1852, whereby Aden Darby, for $50, conveys to his daughters, Rebecca and Ruth, and his son, James, several slaves of whom Rachel is one.

[Commissioners paid Rebecca R. Darby, for self and Ruth E. and J.A. Darby, $481.80.]

No. 825, Petition of Maria Watterston   Filed Jul. 1, 1862

Maria Watterson of Washington City claims compensation for Virginia Clark and her five children.

1. Virginia Clark, aged 27, is mulatto, about 5 feet 6 inches tall with a large frame and spare figure. She is a valuable house servant, washes and irons well and is a good cook. She "is honest, industrious and faithful and to your petitioner as a nurse & friend cannot be replaced by another." [Value $1,200]

2. Charles Clark, aged nine, is light mulatto and short and round. [Value $500]

3. Edmond Clark, aged eight, is mulatto. [Value $300]

4. Jannet Clark, aged five, is light mulatto. [Value $300]

5. Alexander Clark, aged four, is mulatto. [Value $300]

6. Washington Clark, aged one, is a dark mulatto. [Value $100]

Virginia Clark's mother was purchased from the estate of Louisa Magruder of Prince George's County, Md., prior to Virginia's birth.

[Commissioners paid Watterston $810.30: Virginia Clarke [sic], $394.20; Charles, $131.40; Edmund [sic], $131.40; Jannett [sic], $87.60; Alexander, $43.80; Washington, $21.90.]

No. 826, Petition of David A. Watterston   Filed Jul. 1, 1862

David A. Watterston of Washington claims compensation for Dudley Nelson. Nelson is 22 years old, mulatto, about 5 feet 8 inches tall and "spare made" with a "thin visage." He is a valuable house servant and was a gift from

his mother, Maria Watterston, and such is recorded in D.C.Liber J.A.S., folio 253. He values Nelson at $1,500.
[Commissioners paid Watterston $459.90.]

No. 827, Petition of Mary Johnston
Filed Jul. 1, 1862

Mary Johnston of Fairfax County, Va., claims compensation for Addison Jones. Jones is 32 years old, about 5 feet 7 inches tall, dark mulatto in color and stout built. She inherited Jones upon the death of her father, Dennis Johnston. She values Jones at $1,400.
[Commissioners did not pay Johnston as Jones was not produced.]

No. 828, Petition of William S. Johnston
Filed Jul 1., 1862

William S. Johnston of Fairfax County, Va., claims compensation for two persons.
1. Henson Nokes is about 40 years old, bright, 5 feet 8 inches tall and slender. He is supposed to be living with his wife on Capitol Hill in Washington. [Value $800]
2. Frederick Smith is about 38 years old, very black and stout made. He has been employed for several months in driving a government wagon. [Value $1,400]
Johnston states that he inherited the two slaves about seven years ago from his father, Dennis Johnson.
[Commissioners did not allow the claim as Smith and Nokes were not produced.]

No. 829, Petition of William S. Johnston
Filed Jul. 1, 1862

William S. Johnston of Fairfax County, Va., claims compensation for George Carmichael. Carmichael is 38 years old, very black, about 5 feet 10 inches tall and stout. He states that he inherited Carmichael from his father, Dennis Johnston. He values Carmichael at $1,500.
[Commissioners did not allow the claim because Carmichael was not produced.]

No. 830, Petition of Jane Johnston
Filed Jul. 1, 1862

Jane Johnston of Fairfax County, Va., claims compensation for three persons.
1. Mary Ellen, aged 22, is small and dark. She is the mother of Milly and the infant child listed below.
2. Milly, aged three, is the daughter of Mary Ellen.
3. Infant child of Mary Ellen is aged six months.
Johnston acquired title by inheritance from her father, Dennis Johnston. She values the three at $1,400.
[Commissioners did not allow the claim because the persons were not produced.]

No. 831, Petition of John A. Ruff
Filed Jul. 1, 1862

John A. Ruff of Washington City claims compensation for Teresa Pool. Pool is 17 years and six months old, dark in color, 5 feet 4 inches high and heavy in form. She is held to service until she reaches age 35. Ruff purchased her time from Lewis Barrett of Montgomery County, Md. Pool is a valuable house servant and children's nurse. He values her at $950.
[Commissioners paid Ruff $219.]

No. 832, Petition of Rebecca S. Harrison
Filed Jul. 1, 1862

Rebecca S. Harrison of Washington City claims compensation for Maria Foreman. Foreman is about 20 years old, bright mulatto in color and about 5 feet 8 inches tall. She is stout, robust, erect and has a pleasing personal appearance and manner. She acquired Foreman about 1851 as a gift from Thomas M. Foreman of Georgia to whom she belonged since her birth. Harrison states she raised and educated Maria in all the duties of a first-rate family and house servant. Foreman is intelligent, faithful, docile and is a first-rate house servant, nurse, washer and ironer and cook. Within the last five or six years persons have offered to pay as high as $1,400 for Foreman.
[Commissioners paid Harrison $569.40.]

No. 833, Petition of Isabel Maury
Filed Jul. 1, 1862

Isabel Maury of Washington claims compensation for Eliza Dyson and her five children.
1. Eliza Dyson is about 35 years old, nearly black, about 5 feet 6 inches tall and has a scar on her face.
2. Joseph [Dyson] is aged 15, and a mulatto.
3. Daniel [Dyson] is aged 11 and is of a dark copper, nearly black, color.
4. Mary Caroline [Dyson] is aged eight and is a dark copper, nearly black, color.

5. Stella [Dyson] is six years old and is of the same color as Mary Caroline.

6. Archy [Dyson] is four and is a little lighter in color than the others.

Eliza is a good house servant and Joe is a good dining room servant. Daniel is very quick, well-grown and a good servant. The other children are very promising. The values them all at $4,200.

Maury inherited the above upon the death of her husband, John W. Maury.

[Commissioners paid Maury $1,182.60, as follows: Isabel Dyson, $262.80; Joseph, $262.80; Daniel, $240.90; Mary Caroline, $175.20; Stella, $153.30; Archy, $87.60.]

John W. Maury was mayor of Washington, 1852-1854.

No. 834, Petition of James W. McDaniel, colored   Filed Jul. 1, 1862

James W. McDaniel of Washington claims compensation for two persons.

1. Jemima McDaniel is 27 years old, has a brown complexion and is about 4 feet 6 inches high.

2. Lucy Ellen McDaniel is eight years old, has a light complexion and is about three feet high.

McDaniel purchased them at a private sale "from a negro trade[r] in Alexandria, Virginia."

Jemima is a good cook, excellent washer and ironer, and washes and prepares ladies' laces, *etc.*. She is strong and healthy. [Value $1,000]

Lucy is strong and healthy. [Value $200]

Attached are receipts showing 4 payments to Peter Trisler of Alexandria made between Oct. 1, 1857, and May 9, 1859, by McDaniel totalling $900 for his wife, Jemima, and her child. Also attached is a copy of a letter written to Benjamin Hallowell at McDaniel's request to vouch for McDaniel. The writer states that during the approximately two years that James McDaniel worked at the Woolen (?) Factory in the Goose Creek neighborhood he lived with him for most of that time. McDaniel worked in the dyeing and finishing department and was steady, industrious and gave attention to business. He did not use liquor. He was "circumspect in his language" and was regarded by all as trustworthy. (Letter dated Prarie House, Nov. (?) 15, 1857.)

[Commissioners paid McDaniel $613.20: Jemima, $438; Lucy, $175.20. (Signed James W. McDaniel, his x mark).]

Banjamin Hallowell was a well-known Quaker educator in Alexandria. The author cannot read the name of Hallowell's correspondent. The printed report of the commissioners fails to give the surname of Jemima and Lucy, but it is clearly given in the original petition..]

No. 835, Petition of Thomas Lyddane   Filed Jul. 1, 1862

Thomas Lyddane of Montgomery County, Md., claims compensation for Aloysius. Aloysius is a dark mulatto and about four feet high. He purchased Aloysius from his brother, Edmund Lyddane.

Aloysius, with the consent of Lyddane, has lived with his mother in Washington from infancy as his services were not of use on Lyddane's farm. Lyddane has full confidence his Aloysius's mother and intended to bring Aloysius home when he was needed. He claims $700 for Aloysius.

[Commissioners paid Lyddane $197.10.]

No. 836, Petition of Joseph Holt   Filed Jul. 1, 1862

Joseph Holt of the District of Columbia claims compensation for Alfred Allen. Allen was 34 years old last March. He is black in complexion, about 5 feet 8 or 10 inches tall and has a sound constitution. Holt acquired him by means of a trade in the spring of 1857 with his mother and brother, Thomas. Joseph Holt traded his slave Richard (whose wife was owned by Holt's mother and brother), for Allen, which enabled Richard to live with his wife when Holt moved to D.C. in 1857.

Allen is a coachman and gardner and resides with Holt in D.C.

[Commissioners paid Holt $569.40.]

No. 837, Petition of James W. Fling   Filed Jul. 2, 1862

James W. Fling of Montgomery County, Md., claims compensation for Mary Bell. Bell is 22 years old, dark copper in color, medium sized, and healthy and active. She is a useful house servant. He acquired Bell by the terms of the will of his father, James Fling, who died about May 12, 1836. He values her at $1,000.

[Commissioners paid Fling $525.60.]

No. 838, Petition of Dorothy Williams   Filed Jul. 2, 1862

Dorothy Williams of Montgomery County, Md., claims compensation for Lucy J. Butler. Butler is 41 years old, light brown in color and of medium height. She is an excellent cook, washer and ironer and house servant. She hires out at $8 a month with board. She bought Butler from the estate of her late husband, Walter Williams. [Value $800]

[Commissioners paid Williams, by James Williams, her attorney, $306.60.]

No. 839, Petition of Mahlon Falconer   Filed Jul. 2, 1862

Mahlon Falconer, residing at M St., between 6th & 7th west in Washington, claims compensation for Ann Anderson. Anderson is 22 years old, about 5 feet 6 inches high, medium size, chestnut color and good-looking. She is a good cook and valuable house servant. Anderson is held for a term of years which is to expire on Dec. 31, 1866.

Falconer's wife, the daughter of Walter Brown of Howard County, Md., was given Anderson as a gift in 1842. Falconer and his wife, Jane D., issued a deed of manumission to Anderson that provided that she be freed on or before Jan. 1, 1867, and that any issue she may have been freed when they were aged 27 years. (Dated Anne Arundel County, Jun. 9, 1851) [Value $500]

[Commissioners paid Falconer $87.60.]

No. 840, Petition of Thomas C. Bowie   Filed Jul. 3, 1862

Thomas C. Bowie of Prince George's County, Md., claims compensation for Sophia Coolidge. She is 45 years old, bright mulatto and 5 feet 7 inches tall. She is a valuable seamstress and house servant. He acquired title to Coolidge under the will of his grandmother, Mary Weems of Prince George's County. [Value $500]

[Commissioners paid Bowie, by his attorney, Rob. Bowie, $306.60.]

No. 841, Petition of Henry Naylor, trustee under the will of John L. Brightwell   Filed Jul. 3, 1862

Henry Naylor, trustee under the will of John E. Brightwell, claims compensation for six persons.
1. Ann Handy is about 65 years old, very stout and black. She is a good washer and ironer.
2. Lettie Davis is black, 45 years old and about 5 feet 4 inches high.
3. Margaret Davis is 17 years old, black and about five feet high.
4. Matilda Davis is 16 years old, black and five feet high.
5. James Davis is 14, black and 5 feet 9 inches high.
6. John H[enry] Johnson is 21 years old, black and 5 feet 5 inches high.

He values them at $6,500

A copy of Brightwell's will, dated Oct. 4, 1846, is attached. Brightwell's slaves were divided among his three children, Thomas R. Brightwell, Eliza Bestor and Ann Naylor. Ann Naylor, the wife of Francis Y. Naylor, inherited "Anny, Margaret, John Henry, and Letty and her daughter named Margaret."

[Commissioners paid Naylor, trustee, $1,839.60: Ann Handy, $21.90; Lettie Davis, $240.90; Margaret Davis, $394.20; Matilda Davis, $394.20; James Davis, $350.40; John H. Johnson, $438.]

Ann E. Brightwell married Francis Y. Naylor on Dec. 4, 1837; Eliza Brightwell married Owen H. Bestor on Sept. 20, 1836. See Pippenger, Marriage Licenses, 1811-1858, p. 85. John Brightwell died Oct. 27, 1846. See Pippenger, Probate Records, 1801-1852, p. 294 and 294n.

No. 842, Petition of William Christian

William Christian claims compensation for six persons.
1. Amelia Jane Lee
2. Thornton Lee
3. Alexander Lee
4. Rosie Lee
5. Susan Lee
6. William Arthur Lee

Christian, in a letter dated Georgetown, Aug. 12, 1862, withdrew his petition.

[Commissioners did not allow the claim as the petition was withdrawn.]

No. 843, Petition of Robert Smyth Chilton   Filed Jul. 5, 1862

Robert Smyth Chilton of Washington claims compensation for Joe Brown. Brown is about 28 years old, dark brown in color, about 5 feet 4 or 5 inches tall and stout. He has the partial loss of two fingers on his right hand, which defect was present at the time Chilton purchased him.

Chilton states he bought Brown "solely for his own benefit & with the view of his being made free," in October of 1855 for $600 from Mrs. Elizabeth Brent. Since that time, Brown has paid $350 to Chilton. Chilton claims about $250 for him.

[Commissioners paid Chilton $350.40.]

No. 844, Petition of James L. Barbour, administrator of Horace Edelin   Filed Jul. 5, 1862

James L. Barbour of D.C., administrator of Horace Edelin, deceased, claims compensation for Alfred. Alfred is 13 years old, well-formed and likely. He is an active, healthy boy of good disposition. Alfred was purchased from Dr. Alfred Edelin of Prince George's County, Md., for $250 in April, 1859. [Value $1,000.]

[Commissioners paid Barbour $240.90.]

No. 845, Petition of William Brown   Filed Jul. 5, 1862

William Brown of Washington City claims compensation for Maria Cook, who is held to service for a term of 20 years. Cook is 18 years old, has a light complexion, is of medium height and has a pleasant countenance. She is a superior servant and is proficient at any household work. He acquired her by an assignment and manumission from Ann E. Newton dated Dec. 7, 1854, and recorded in D.C. Liber [J.A.S.] No. 94, folios 280-281. [Value $700].

[Commissioners paid Brown $175.20.]

No. 846, Petition of Eleanor H. Callis   Filed Jul. 5, 1862

Eleanor H. Callis of Prince George's County, Md., claims compensation for four persons.

1. Margaret A. Hamilton, aged 17, is copper colored, short and has black eyes and hair.
2. Levinia Weeks, aged 15, is bright colored, spare and has red hair and light, or dark eyes.
3. Nellie Janifer, aged 12, is bright colored and has black hair and eyes.
4. Lewis Hanson, aged 37, is of a dark color with black hair and eyes. He is a little lame. Hanson works at the anchor shop at the Navy Yard in Washington and she receives for him a dollar a day besides what is allotted to him. Callis obtained title by the will of her husband, Henry A. Callis. She values the slaves at $3,800.

A copy of Callis's will is attached whereby he leaves to his wife slaves Gerard, Chloe and her children, Louisa and her children (all of whom he acquired with his marriage to Eleanor) and Sophia, Mariah, William Hanson and Lewis Hanson. (Will recorded in Prince George's County and proved Mar. 20, 1855.)

[Commissioners paid Callis, by her attorney William B. Bayne, $1,445.40: Margaret A. Hamilton, $459.90; Levinia Weeks, $438; Nellie "Jennie", $284.70; Lewis "Harrison", $262.80.]

No. 847, Petition of Lorenzo Thomas   Filed Jul. 7, 1862

Lorenzo Thomas of Washington City claims compensation for three persons.

1. Lucy Berry is 43 years old, copper colored and 5 feet 3 inches high. She is a cook, washer and ironer and a good servant. George and Lorenzo are her children.[Value $800]
2. George Berry is three years old and is delicate. [Value $100]
3. Lorenzo Berry is one year old and is very healthy. [Value $100]

Thomas purchased Lucy from Eleanor Robertson of Maryland on Jan. 4, 1853.

[Commissioners paid Thomas $262.80: Lucy Berry, $219; George Berry, no value; Lorenzo Berry, $43.80.]

No. 848, Petition of Simeon M. Johnson   Filed Jul. 7, 1862

Simeon M. Johnson of the city of Washington claims compensation for two persons.

1. Susan Mathews is 21 years old, has a dark chestnut complexion, about 4 feet 10 ½ inches tall and is "of compact solid figure." She is a good-natured, willing and valuable house servant. Susan was born the property of Mrs. Winifred A. Roche in Charles County, Md., and Mrs. Roche brought her to this city about 15 years ago. She gave Susan to her daughter, Mrs. Ellen T. Reily, and Johnson married Mrs. Reily on July 11, 1861.
2. Lucy Ross, aged 30, is about 5 feet 2 ½ inches tall. She is a valuable housekeeper and seamstress.

Johnson values the two at $1,000.

[Commissioners paid Johnson, by W.D. Davidge, his attorney, $438 for Susan Matthews. The claim for Ross was not allowed as she was not produced.]

No. 849, Petition of George and Thomas Parker   Filed Jul. 7, 1862

George and Thomas Parker of Washington claim compensation for Horace Sprigg. Sprigg is 50 years old, mulatto and of medium height. He is subject to slight attacks of asthma, but is otherwise sound. He is a good servant and has been employed as a porter in and about the store and warehouse. He was born their property. [Value $600]

[Commissioners paid George and Thomas Parker $109.50.]

No. 850, Petition of Christopher S. O'Hare
Filed Jul. 7, 1862

Christopher S. O'Hare of Washington claims compensation for four persons.

1. Louisa Brook is about 26 years old, mulatto and about five feet high. She is a first-class washer and ironer and understands plain cooking. She was raised as a field hand and is in perfect health. {Value $1,200]

2. Washington Brook is about eight years old, bright mulatto and about four feet high. He is useful for making fires and bringing in water and similar work. [Value $700]

3. Caroline Brook is about four years old, mulatto and about three feet high. She is likely and intelligent. [Value $450]

4. George Brook, about 20 months old, is mulatto and about 2 feet 6 inches high. He is likely and intelligent. [Value $200]

He purchased them from the estate of his father-in-law, the late Samuel Shreve, Sr. They were delivered to the petitioner and have been in his possession in the District since Nov. 21, 1861.

[Commissioners paid $832.20 to O'Hare: Louisa Brook, $438; Washington Brook, $197.10; Caroline Brook, $131.40; George Brook, $65.70.]

No. 851, Petition of James H. Fowler
Filed Jul. 7, 1862

James H. Fowler of Prince George's County, Md., claims compensation for George Banks. Banks is 17 years old, copper colored, quite stout and well-made. He is a strong and healthy servant and has been employed as a field hand. He is useful at anything. Fowler received Banks as a gift from his grandfather, Joseph Fowler, now deceased, of Prince George's County. [Value $l,200]

[Commissioners paid Fowler $525.60.]

No. 852, Petition of Ellen J. King
Filed Jul. 7, 1862

Ellen J. King of Washington County, D.C., claims compensation for four persons.

1. Betsy is aged about 54 years, is a dark color, about 5 feet 8 inches high and rather thin. [Value $200]

2. Nace is about 49 years old and is Betsy's brother. He is also dark in color, between 5 feet 10 and six feet high and robust. [Value $1,800]

3. Hezekiah is about 37 years old, dark, "moderate development of person" and about 5 feet 10 inches tall. [Value $2,000]

4. Charles Montgomery is 17 or 18 years old, light brown in color, about 5 feet 10 inches high and is robust. He is held as a slave for 26 years from Jan. 3, 1853. [Value $1,000]

King holds title by the terms of the will of her late husband, John H. King of Washington County.

[Commissioners paid King $1,182.60: Betsy, $43.80; Nace, $306.60; Hezekiah, $350.40; Charles Montgomery, $481.80.]

No. 853, Petition of Susan M. Burche
Filed Jul. 7, 1862

Susan M. Burche of Washington City claims compensation for three persons.

1. Verlinda Silvey, aged 35, black, slender and about 5 feet 3 or 4 inches high. She is a good cook, washer and ironer. She is the mother of the two children listed below.

2. Anna Patterson, aged 14 (?), is very black, about five feet tall and is well-made.

3. Maria Edmonia Silvey is four years old, dark copper color, about three feet high and very sprightly.

She purchased Verlinda and Anna from Sheckels and Company, "called Negro traders." Maria was born after that purchase. She values them at $1,000.

[Commissioners paid Susan Burche, by Raymond W. Burche, her attorney, $832.20: Verlinda Silvey, $262.80; Anna Patterson, $438; Maria Silvey, $131.40.]

No. 854, Petition of William E. Howard
Filed Jul. 7, 1862

William E. Howard of Washington City claims compensation for three slaves.

1. Ann Sophia Thomas is 31 years old and about medium sized. She is the mother of Alice and Susan. She is a good cook, washer and ironer and a fine servant. [Value $1,000]

2. Alice Thomas is 13 years old and is a well-grown child for her age. She is a useful girl and a good servant. [Value $500]

3. Susan Thomas is eight years old is also well-grown. She is beginning to be useful. [Value $100]

Ann Sophia's mother was a slave for life of his father and Ann Sophia came to him by descent. Her children were born Howard's slaves.

[Commissioners paid Howard $744.60: Ann Sophia Thomas, $372.30; Alice Thomas, $240.90; Susan Thomas, $131.40.]

No. 855, Petition of Abel G. Davis   Filed Jul. 7, 1862

Abel G. Davis of Washington, D.C., claims compensation for Billy. He is nearly 12 years old, black, about 4 feet 6 inches high and of fine physical development. Davis inherited Billy from his late sister, Mrs. Caroline Coote of Hampton, Va., and he was delivered to Abel by Dr. Charles W. Davis, administrator of the estate, in 1858.

Davis states that he has been offered $500 for Billy several times.

[Commissioners paid Davis $328.50.]

No. 856, Petition of Horace Sprigg   Filed Jul. 8, 1862

Horace Sprigg of Washington City claims compensation for Martha Ann Sprigg, aged 15 years. She is a dark brown color, 5 feet 2 or 3 inches high and healthy. He purchased her from John Parker of Prince George's County, Md. He values her at $600. (Horace his x mark Sprigg)

[The Commissioners did not allow the claim.]

No. 857, Petition of Charles Homiller   Filed Jul. 8, 1862

Charles Homiller of the District of Columbia claims compensation for 12 persons.

1. Mary Etchison is aged 38, dark brown color, 5 feet 3 inches high with a pleasant face. She is a capable cook and house servant. She is mother to the next five persons.

2. Kingsley Etchison, aged 22, is dark brown, 6 feet 1 inches tall and good in appearance. He is a skillful butcher.

3. Dallas Etchison, aged 20, light brown, 5 feet 6 inches tall, of good appearance. He is a skillful butcher.

4. Adelaide Etchison, aged 11, light brown, 3 feet 11 inches high, good appearance. She is a quick, sprightly servant.

5. Laura Etchison, aged six, light brown, 3 feet 5 inches tall, good appearance. She is able and handy.

6. Banks Etchison, aged two and a half, 2 feet 10 inches tall, good appearance.

7. Mary Ann Hawkins, aged 26, dark brown, five feet tall, pleasant face. She is the mother of Virginia, George and Abraham Lincoln. She is a good house servant.

8. Virginia Hawkins, aged ten, light brown, 4 feet 2 inches, pleasant face. She promises to be a good servant.

9. George Hawkins, aged three and a half, light brown, 3 feet 1 inch, pleasant face.

10. Abraham Lincoln Hawkins, aged 18 months, light brown, 2 feet 2 inches tall, pleasant face.

11. Fanny Hawkins, aged 45, dark brown, 5 feet 4 inches tall, pleasant face. She is still a useful and efficient servant.

12. Catherine (Kate) Jackson, aged 17, dark brown, 4 feet 9 inches high, pleasant face and intelligent. She is a superior house servant.

They are all healthy and sound and free of defects. He values them at $8,350.

About ten or 12 years ago, he purchased Mary Etchison and her children Kingsley and Dallas from Mr. (?). Adelaide and her other children were born since that purchase. He purchased Mary Ann Hawkins from John Hensley about 22 or 23 years ago and Ann, Virginia, George and Abe were born since that purchase. He purchased Fanny from Mr. Donohue of Georgetown about five years ago and he purchased Kate from Jacob Smoot of Georgetown about 15 years ago.

[Commissioners paid Homiller $3,263.10: Mary Etchison, $219; "Kinsley" Etchison, $657; Dallas Etchison, $613.20; Adelaide Etchison, $219; Laura Etchison, $131.40; Banks Etchison, $87.60; Mary Ann Hawkins, $394.20; Virginia Hawkins, $262.80; George Hawkins, $87.60; Abraham Lincoln Hawkins, $43.80; Fanny Hawkins, $87.60; Kate Jackson, $459.90.]

Charles Homiller was a butcher and had a shop in Centre Market. He is listed as living in Georgetown. See Boyd's City Directory for 1860, p. 88.

No. 858, Petition of William V.H. Brown   Filed Jun. 8 [*sic*] 1862

William V.H. Brown of the city of Washington claims compensation for two persons.

1. Martha Vandrey is about 37 years old, of a brown complexion, 5 feet 4 or 5 inches high, well-formed with a "genteel personal appearance." She can read and is quite intelligent. She is the mother of William.

2. William Vandrey, aged 19, light mulatto, 5 feet 4 ½ inches tall, compact and well-built. He has a handsome, full suit of black hair and is sprightly and intelligent. He can read and write very well and "is quite prepossessing in his personal appearance."

He purchased Martha and her son in July, 1847, at Martha's request to prevent their being sold South from a widow lady named Preuss (?), then a resident of D.C. He bought them in the name of his father, Rev. O[badiah] B. Brown who was at the time out of the city. When his father died in May 1852 he inherited the two slaves.

Martha Vandrey is an excellent cook and house servant and commands the highest wages. He had refused $800 for her before "our present political difficulties." He has also been offered $1,500 for William, who is a first-class servant boy.

[Commissioners paid $876 to Adelaide J. Brown, administratrix of William V.H. Brown: Martha Vandrey, $306.60; William Vandry, $569.40.]

No. 859, Petition of William B. Jones   Filed Jul. 8, 1862

William B. Jones of Washington D.C., at the U.S. Arsenal, claims compensation for two persons.

1. Virginia Williams, aged 18, is of a dark color and is healthy. [Value $700]

2. Margaret Williams, aged 16, bright mulatto and healthy. [Value $800]

They are held as slaves until they reach age 30. They and their mother were purchased by William's late father, Thomas Jones, from the estate of Baptist Kirby and were inherited by William after the death of Thomas. Kirby's will had provided that his slaves be freed when they arrived at 30 years of age.

Both Virginia and Margaret are useful, healthy and industrious.

[Commissioners paid Jones $372.30: Virginia Williams, $175.20; Margaret Williams, $197.10.]

No. 860, Petition of John H. Smoot   Filed Jul. 8, 1862

John H. Smoot of Georgetown claims compensation for four persons.

1. Sophy Hawkins, aged about 40, is a dark mulatto, about 5 feet 6 inches high. She is a good cook and washer, but is sometimes troubled with rheumatism.

2. Dick [Hawkins], aged four and a half, is the son of Sophy. He is a light mulatto and is very smart.

3. Rebecca McPherson is aged 18, dark colored and about 5 feet 2 inches tall.

4. Charles [McPherson] is the son of Rebecca.

He acquired Sophy as a result of his marriage and Dick was born since that time. He purchased McPherson four years ago from Mr. Belt's estate of Montgomery County, Md., for $650, which he says is much less that she would have brought if sold to go South. He values Sophy and Dick at $1,000; Rebecca and Charles at $1,200.]

Attached is the copy of a bill of sale dated Rockville, Md., Nov. 16, 1857, by which Smoot purchased Rebecca, aged about 14, for $650

[Commissioners paid Smoot $832.20: Sophy Hawkins, $175.20; Dick, her son, $131.40; Rebecca McPherson, $481.80; Charles, her son, $43.80.]

No. 861, Petition of Sarah E. Sollers   Filed Jul. 8, 1862

Sarah E. Sollers of Washington, D.C., claims compensation for Sarah Woodley. Woodley is 18 years old, dark chestnut color and 5 feet 4 inches tall. She is an excellent cook and house servant. She received Woodley as a gift about June of 1860 from her grand uncle, Henry S. Mudd, who lived in Charles County, Md. [Value $1,000]

Attached is a statement from Mudd dated Jun. 30, 1862, by which he certifies that he gave his niece title to Sarah Wood [*sic*] "who remained in the service of Mr. H.A. Clarke for several years."

[Commissioners paid Sollers $525.60.]

No. 862, Petition of George J. Johnson   Filed Jul. 8, 1862

George J. Johnson of the city of Washington claims compensation for two slaves.

1. Adaline Smith, aged about 25 years, is dark colored, short and stout with short hair. She is a good house servant. She is the mother of Mary Smith.

2. Mary Smith, aged about two, is a mulatto with nearly straight hair.

He got title to Adaline by division of his father's estate in 1835 or 1836. Mary was born after that time. He values them at $1,500.

[Commissioners paid Johnson $525.60: "Adeline" Smith, $459.90; Mary Smith, $65.70.]

863, Petition of Robert M. Sutton   Filed Jul. 8, 1862

Robert M. Sutton of Washington City claims compensation for two persons.

1. Lishy Lewis, aged about 18, is of a light color and medium height.

2. Elizabeth Lewis, aged about 13, is light colored and sprightly. She is the sister of Lishy.

He acquired Elizabeth in the regular division of his father's estate on Dec. 25, 1860. He got Lishy by exchange with his brother, Frederic, in January, 1861. He values them at $1,800.

[Commissioners paid Sutton $810.30: "Lishey" Lewis, $525.60; Elizabeth Lewis, $262.80.]

No. 864, Petition of Alison Nailor, Jr.   Filed Jul. 9, 1862

Alison Nailor, Jr., claims compensation for two persons.

1. John Bundy, is 22 years old, dark mulatto, stout and about five feet tall. He is a first-rate hostler both regarding driving and taking care of horses. He is also a fair painter and blacksmith and can shoe horses. He is a good cook, dining room servant, farm hand and ploughman. He is quick to learn any mechanical trade.

2. Sally Ferguson, aged 11, is dark brown, four feet high and has a pleasing countenance. She is a good dining room servant and can cook well. She washes her own clothes and is advanced beyond her age. His wife has taken special pains to teach her and they are always together.

He acquired title by gift from his father several years ago. He values them at $3,000.

[Commissioners paid Nailor $919.80: John Bundy, $657; Sally Ferguson, $262.80.]

No. 865, Petition of Lizzie R. Nailor   Filed Jul. 9, 1862

Lizzie R Nailor of Washington claims compensation for Mary Columbia Meekins. Meekins is 18 years old, dark brown or copper colored, about 5 feet 6 inches high and has a pleasing countenance. She is a good cook and nurse and a first-rate chambermaid. She was given to Lizzie by her father, Allison Nailor of Washington, some years ago. [Value $1,500]

[Commissioners paid Nailor $525.60.]

No. 866, Petition of Elizabeth Williams   Filed Jul. 9, 1862

Elizabeth Williams of the District of Columbia claims compensation for seven persons.

1. Mary Carter is 45 years old and of a bright color. She is the mother of the persons listed below She is a first-rate cook.

2. Lewis Carter, aged 25, is of a very light color. He is a good ostler and waiter.

3. Andrew Green, aged 18, is copper colored. He is a first-class dining room and house servant.

4. Georgianna Carter, aged ten, is very light in color. She is a promising child.

5. Jane Johnson, aged 20, is of a light copper color. She is the mother of William and John listed below. She is a good house servant.

6. William [Johnson], aged two, is very light.

7. John [Johnson], aged about eight months, is very light.

She values them at $5,000.

Mary Carter was willed to Williams by the late Thomas Cramphin of Montgomery County when Mary was about ten or 12 years old. Her children were born since that bequest.

[Commissioners paid Williams $2,168.10: Mary Carter, $262.80; Lewis Carter, $438; Andrew Green, $657; Georgianna Carter, $262.80; Jane Johnson, $459.90; William, $65.70; John, $21.90.]

No. 867, Petition of Arianna J. Lyles   Filed Jul. 9, 1862

Arianna J. Lyles of the District of Columbia claims compensation for 13 persons.

1. Randell Ford is 57 years old, dark copper colored and about 5 feet 7 inches tall.

2. Andrew Contee is 32 years old, dark copper colored, about 5 feet 10 inches tall.

3. David Oliver is 24 years old, dark copper colored, about 5 feet 9 inches tall.

4. John Oliver is 20 (?) years old, dark copper colored, and 5 feet 8 inches tall.

5. Henry Rosier, aged eight, dark copper colored, four feet high.

6. Hannibal Rosier, aged six, dark copper colored, three feet high.
7. Sophia Ford, aged 70, dark copper color, 5 feet 5 inches high.
8. Chiah Bowman, aged 62, dark copper color, five feet high.
9. Eliza Rosier, aged 31, dark copper color, about five feet high.
10. Maria Brown, aged 26, dark copper color, about 5 feet 4 inches tall.
11. Caroline Oliver, aged 16, is lighter in complexion and of a yellow color. She is five feet high.
12. Sallie Rosier, aged 4, is a dark copper color and about 30 inches high.
13. Anthony [*no description is given.*]

Lyles purchased Chiah from the estate of Hanson Marshall, late of Charles County, Md. All the rest she acquired under the will of her late husband, Dennis M. Lyles, of Prince George's County, Md.

The above are good and honest farm hands and servants. The children are promising and all are healthy. She sets their value at $13,790.

[Commissioners paid Lyles $3,679.20: Randell Ford, $131.40; Andrew Contee, $547.50; David Oliver, $438; Henry Rosier, $153.30; Hannibal Rosier, $197.10; Sophia Ford, no value; "Chia" Bowman, $43.80; Eliza Rosier, $350.40; Maria Brown, $525.60; Caroline Oliver, $481.80; Sallie Rosier, $87.60; John Oliver, $591.30; Anthony, $131.40.]

No. 868, Petition of Elisha Jones, executor   Filed Jul. 9, 1862

Elisha Jones, executor of the will of his father, Edward Jones of Charles County, Md., claims compensation for the following six persons.

1. Henry Dade, Sr., aged 57, is quite black, about 5 feet 7 inches high and has lost the end of his right forefinger.
2. George Ward, aged 47, is black, about 4 feet 10 or 11 inches high and has a rocking gait when he walks.
3. Henry Dade, Jr., aged 25, is a dark copper color, about 5 feet 8 or 9 inches high, rather stout and has lost the end of three of his fingers.
4. Lewis Dade, aged 22, is quite black, more than six feet tall and rather slender. He had his hand burned about seven months ago, but whether it will leave a scar or not is not known.
5. Richard Dade, aged 21, dark copper colored, is about 5 feet 8 inches tall and has heavy lips.
6. Washington Dade, aged 18, is about 5 feet 6 inches tall, light copper colored and has a small knot on the side of each of his little fingers. He has a pleasant look when spoken to.

He values the men at a total of $8,000.

The will of Edward Jones is filed at Port Tobacco, Md., and Elisha Jones holds the slaves for the benefit of the heirs, i.e., himself and his unmarried sisters Caroline, Lucretia, Rosina and Rosanna.

[Commissioners paid $2,715.60 to Caroline Jones, executrix of Elisha Jones, Lucretia Jones, Roseeany'r [*sic*] Jones, Rozanna [*sic*] Jones, by Thomas H. Taylor, their attorney: Henry Dade, $525.60; George Ward, $131.40; Henry Dade, Jr., $262.80; Lewis Dade, $569.20; Richard Dade, $613.20; Washington Dade, $613.20.]

No. 869, Petition of James L. Addison   Filed Jul. 9, 1862

James L. Addison of Prince George's County, Md., claims compensation for three persons.

1. Charles Hall, aged about 35, is about 5 feet 10 inches high, dark brown, with a full suit of black hair. He has a fine countenance and is ordinary in size. He has a slight hernia, but is otherwise in perfect health. [Value $1,200]
2. Jane Hall, aged about 32, is about 5 feet 6 inches high, brown in complexion, with a delicate figure and good countenance. She is of delicate health but has a excellent character. [Value $400]
3. Betty Ann Humphreys, aged about 32, has a dark complexion, is about 3 [*sic*] feet 5 inches tall and of medium size. She is a first class cook and is hired out by the month. [Value $1,000]

Addison says he purchased Suckey Hall, the mother of Charles and Jane, from his father, John Addison, Sr., of Prince George's County, before her children were born. Betty Ann Humphreys belonged to his wife, who was the daughter of the late William Bayne of Prince George's County, Md.

[Commissioners paid Addison $963.60: Charles Hall, $262.80; Jane Hall, $306.60; Betty Ann Hampton [*sic*], $394.20.]

No. 870, Petition of Elizabeth Goszler   Filed Jul. 9, 1862

Elizabeth Goszler of Georgetown claims compensation for Ann Maria Montgomery, who is 16 years old. She acquired title to Ann Maria by descent and values her at $1,000.

[Commissioners paid Goszler, by her attorney, R.P. Jackson, $438.]

No. 871, Petition of Catharine Chisholm Filed Jul. 9, 1862

Catharine Chisholm of the District of Columbia claims compensation for two persons.

1. Caroline Scott, is about 48 years old, copper colored and about 5 feet 2 inches high. She is capable and well-instructed in cooking, washing and ironing and housework.

2. Elizabeth Scott, aged ten, the daughter of Caroline, is a light copper color and about 4 feet 3 ½ inches tall. She is intelligent and apt for her age.

Chisholm received them as a gift some years ago from her sister, the late Mary Gibbs of Anne Arundel County, Md. She values them at $1,000.

Attached is a statement signed by the two daughters of Mary Gibbs, widow of A. Chisolm Gibbs, by which they acknowledge the gift of the two slaves to Catharine Chisolm.

[Commissioners paid Chisholm $481.80: Caroline Scott, $219; Elizabeth Scott, $262.80.]

No. 872, Petition of Joseph Weaver and Thomas Weaver Filed Jul. 9, 1862

Joseph Weaver and Thomas Weaver of Georgetown claim compensation for seven persons.

1. John Cepas, aged 60, black, about 5 feet 10 or 11 inches high. [Value $1,000]

2. Margaret Cepas, wife of John, aged 43, black, about five feet tall. John and Margaret are the parents of those listed below. [Value $800]

3. Emily Cepas is 15 years old, black and about 5 feet 4 inches tall. [Value $1,000]

4. Mary Cepas, aged 13, is black and about 4 feet 6 inches tall. [Value $900]

5. George Washington Cepas, aged seven, black, is about 3 feet 6 inches tall. [Value $700]

6. Jeremiah Cepas, aged five, is black and about three feet tall. [Value $500]

7. Alexander Cepas is about one year old, black and about two feet tall. Value $100]

John is an invaluable manager on the Weaver's farm such "as is rarely found"; Margaret is a field hand as are their children.

They were purchased Jun. 9, 1858, from John H. Sommerville and Sarah J. Sommerville, with the exception of Alexander who was born after the purchase. This is recorded in the clerk's office in the Circuit Court of Washington County, D.C.

[Commissioners paid the Weavers $1,511.10: John "Sepas", $153.30; Margaret "Sepas", $262.80; Emily, $481.80; Mary, $306.60; George Washington, $153.30; Jeremiah, $109.50; Alexander, $43.80.]

No. 873, Petition of Joseph Weaver Filed Jul. 9, 1862

Joseph Weaver of Georgetown claims compensation for three persons.

1. Mariah, aged 27, dark brown in color and about 5 feet 4 inches tall. She is the mother of John and George Washington. Mariah is a first-rate house servant, cook and washer and ironer. [Value $1,000]

2. John, aged five, is about 3 feet 6 inches in height. [Value $500]

3. George Washington, aged six months, is about 2 feet 3 inches in height. [Value $100]

He purchased Mariah and John from Benedict Milburn, trustee, on Jul. 15, 1857, and such is recorded in the records of the Circuit Court of Washington County, D.C. George Washington was born after that purchase.

[Commissioners paid Joseph Weaver $613.20: "Maria", $459.90; John, $131.40; George Washington, $21.90.]

No. 874, Petition of Rebecca S. Weaver Filed Jul. 9, 1862

Rebecca S. Weaver of Georgetown claims compensation for Catharine Louisa. Catharine is seven years old, dark brown in color and about 3 feet 10 inches in height. She purchased Catharine from Joseph Weaver on Jul. 29, 1857, and such is recorded in the D.C. clerk's office.

[Commissioners paid Weaver $175.20.]

No. 875, Petition of Erastus M. Chapin Filed Jul. 9, 1862

Erastus M. Chapin of Washington City claims compensation for Mary Lewis. Lewis is 14 years and two months old, bright mulatto, about 4 feet 11 inches high and very likely and neat. He purchased her from Luther R. Smoot in 1855. She is a very competent house servant and he values her at $1,000.

An attached bill of sale dated Jan. 4, 1855, shows that Chapin paid $850 to L.R. Smoot for Negro Jane [Lewis (?)], aged about 30, and her child, Mary, aged about six.

[Commissioners paid Chapin $394.20.]

No. 876, Petition of William J. Williams Filed Jul. 9, 1862

William J. Williams of Washington, D.C., claims compensation for Leah Keffert. Keffert is 18 years old, black, 5 feet 3 inches high, and stout and well-made. She is a first-class house servant and he values her at $1,400. A copy of a bill of sale dated May 15, 1860, shows that Williams purchased her from Jemima Hurst. (Signed Jemima x Hurst, recorded in D.C. Liber J.A.S. No. 198, folio 199). The bill of sale states that Hurst's brother, Robert Gunnell, had given "Kerfut" to her.

[Commissioners paid Williams $547.50.]

No. 877, Petition of Arian Tweedy Filed Jul. 9, 1862

Arian Tweedy of Washington, D.C., claims compensation for Frank Marshal. Marshal is about 20 years old, bright mulatto, medium sized, erect in his carriage and likely and intelligent. Marshall is primarily a waiter and commands good wages for his services. She inherited Frank under the will of her late husband, Robert Tweedy, who died about 15 or 16 years ago. [Value $1,200]

[Commissioners paid Tweedy, by Asbury Lloyd, her attorney, $525.60.]

No. 878, Petition of Alexander McD. Davis and Martha A. Davis Filed Jul. 9, 1862

Alexander McD. Davis and his wife, Martha A. Davis, claim compensation for four persons.

1. Harriet Louisa McLain is 25 years old, black, about 5 feet 1 or 2 inches high, strong and compact. Julia, Eugene and Fanny are her children. She is a first-class servant.

2. Julia [McLain] is ten, bright yellow, about 4 feet 6 or 7 inches high and in good health.

3. Eugene [McLean] is seven, bright yellow, about 3 feet 10 or 11 inches high and in perfect health.

4. Fanny [McLean] is five years old, very black, about 3 feet 1 or 2 inches tall and healthy. She is somewhat knockkneed, but this can be remedied.

He values them at $3,000.

When Harriet was born, her mother was a slave to Mrs. Davis's father. He subsequently gave Harriet to her and Harriet's children have been born since that time.

[Commissioners paid A. McD. Davis and Martha A. Davis $876: Harriet L. McLain, $394.20; Julia, $219; Eugene, $153.30; Fanny, $109.50.]

No. 879, Petition of Eleanor B.M. Hilleary Filed Jul. 11, 1862

Eleanor B.M. Hilleary of Maryland claims compensation for four persons.

1. William West is about 42 years old, black, about 5 feet 10 inches high, stout and well-made. He has lost the end of his middle finger. He is "not accessible at this time" and may be in the employ of the government. [Value $1,200]

2. George Allen is about 24 years old, about 5 feet 4 inches tall and brown or copper in color. [Value $1,200]

3. Isaac Hamilton is about 23 years old, about 5 feet 7 inches tall and has a brown or copper complexion. [Value $1,200]

4. Spencer Snowden is about 18, about five feet high and has a dark brown complexion. [Value $1,000]

West, Allen and Hamilton are first-rate farm hands and good for all kinds of work, especially being teamsters and drivers. Snowden is equally valuable, but is younger than the others. The first three have been hired out for $10 to $12 a month and William has been hired out for eight years and George and Isaac for four. Spender has been hired for $5 a month.

William West and the mother of Isaac and Spencer came to Hilleary by the will of her grandmother, Elleanor M----- (?) of Prince George's County more than 30 years ago. Allen was willed to her by her grandfather, Tilghman Hilleary.

[Commissioners paid E.B.M. Hilleary, by Will. H. Tuck, her attorney, $2,124.30: William West, $372.30; George Allen, $569.40; Isaac Hamilton, $613.20; Spencer Snowden, $569.40.]

No. 880, Eleanor B.M. Hilleary and William H. Tuck, adm. of Clement T. Hilleary Filed Jul. 11, 1862

Eleanor B.M. Hilleary and William H. Tuck, administrator of Clement T. Hilleary of Prince George's County, Md., claim compensation for four persons.

1. Charles West is about 40 years old, black and about 5 feet 9 inches high. [Value $1,200]

2. Robert Allen is about 21 years old, has a dark brown complexion and is about 5 feet 4 inches tall. [Value $1,200]

3. Juliet Coates is about 31 years old, brown or copper colored and about five feet high. [Value $1,200, with her child]

4. William Coates, son of Juliet, is about six years old with a brown complexion. He is well-grown but has lost the tips of three fingers on his left hand.

Charles and Robert are first-rate farm hands and excellent teamsters. For the last eight years Charles has been hired for $12 a month and for the last four years Robert has been hired at the same rate. Juliet is a valuable servant and a good seamstress and chambermaid and laundress. She hired for $5 a month before her child was born and afterwards with her child at $3 a month.

Charles, Robert and Juliet belonged to Ann T. Hilleary who died in April 1852. Title then passed to her father, Clement T. Hilleary, and after Clement died in 1859, title passed to his daughter, Eleanor Hilleary. William was born while Juliet belonged to Clement.

[Commissioners paid E.B.M. Hilleary, by William H. Tuck, her attorney, and Tuck, adm. of C.T. Hilleary, $1,533: Charles West, $438; Robert Allen, $613.20; Julia Coates, $350.40; William Coates, $131.40.]

No. 881, Petition of Anna M. Hamilton   Filed Jul. 11, 1862

Anna M. Hamilton of Illinois claims compensation for Harriet Chase. Chase is about 40 years old, about 5 feet 5 inches tall and has a bright complexion. She has earned $5 a month as a cook, house servant and chambermaid for the last few years. Chase's health has not been very good, but Hamilton does not know the cause. Anna M. is the widow of the late Samuel Hamilton of Prince George's County and she inherited his estate about five years ago. [Value $700]

[Commissioners paid Hamilton, by W[illiam] H. Tuck, her attorney, $87.60.]

No. 882, Petition of Harriet E. Muncaster   Filed Jul. 11, 1862

Harriet E. Muncaster, by her friend, Julian Magruder of Montgomery County, Md., claims compensation for Samuel Martin. Martin is about 43 years old, black, about 5 feet 8 or 9 inches high and is strong and healthy. He is capable of any farm work and for roughly ten years past has been driving a cart or dray. At the time of the passage of the act, he was getting $5 a week in wages and boarding himself. She values him at $1,700 and states that she could have gotten that amount for him in the fall of 1860.

She acquired Martin upon the distribution of the estate of her father, Zadock Magruder, late of Montgomery County. Harriet is the wife of Otto Z. Muncaster of Montgomery County.

[Commissioners paid Muncaster, by O.Z. Muncaster, her husband and attorney, $481.80.]

No. 883, Petition of George W. Hopkins   Filed Jul. 11, 1862

George W. Hopkins of Washington City claims compensation for two persons.

1. Solomon Lowndes is 11 years old, black and well-grown for his age.
2. Samuel Lowndes is nine, black and well-grown for his age.

He purchased their mother, who is now dead, about 14 years ago. He values them at $1,500.

[Commissioners paid Hopkins $678.90: Solomon Lowndes, $372.30; Samuel Lowndes, $306.60.]

No. 884, Petition of John B. Semmes   Filed Jul. 11, 1862

John B. Semmes of D.C. claims compensation for four persons.

1. Jane Young is about 28 years old and has a dark complexion. She is a good house servant, cook washer and ironer.

2. Joe King is bout 28 years old, dark copper colored, nearly six feet high and stout. He is employed as a blacksmith at the Washington Navy Yard at $480 a year.

3. Ned King, or Campbell, is about 19 or 20, nearly six feet high, black complexion and well-built. He is a good driver and capable of general work.

4. Hilleary Davis is about 32 (?), light yellow in color, thick-set and of medium height. He is employed as a porter and drayman.

He values them at $6,500. Jane, Joe and Ned were the property of Semmes's wife at the time of their marriage, and they had been left to her by the will of Mary Ann McPherson of Prince George's County, Md. Hilleary Davis became his property under the will of his grandmother, Henrietta Semmes.

[Commissioners paid Semmes $2,080.50: Jane Young, $350.40; Joe King, $613.20; Ned King, or Campbell, $591.30; Hilleary "Dan" [Davis], $525.60.]

Henrietta Semmes of Georgetown had her will filed in 1833. It provided that her infant sons, which included John B., inherit servant woman Prudence and her three children, Lidia, Hillery and Clement. See Pippenger, District of Columbia Probate Records, 1801-1852, p. 184.

No. 885, Petition of Eliza M. Mosher   Filed Jul. 11, 1862

Eliza M. Mosher of Georgetown claims compensation for three persons.
1. Frank Mockabee is about 44, dark brown and 5 feet 7 inches tall. [Value $800]
2. Martha Snowden is about 27, dark brown and 5 feet 4 inches tall. [Value $1,200]
3. Mary Davis is about 21, dark brown and 5 feet 5 inches in height. [Value $1,200]

They are all well-trained servants, but Mary's hearing is slightly defective.

Mosher is the heir of Dr. Ninian Magruder of D.C. and under his will she inherited Nancy Williams, the mother of Martha and Mary. She acquired Frank from the estate of John Braddock of Rockville, Montgomery County, Md., about the month of May 1846 for $550.

[Commissioners paid "Moshier" $1,204.50: Frank Mockabee, $306.60; Martha Snowden, $481.80; Mary Davis, $416.10.]

The printed report of the commissioners gives Eliza's surname as "Mosier," but the original documents clearly spell it "Mosher."

No. 886, Petition of Theodore Mosher   Filed Jul. 11, 1862

Theodore Mosher of Washington County, D.C., claims compensation for two persons.
1. Anthony Lee is about 50 years old, dark brown and 5 feet 10 inches tall. [Value $1,000]
2. Joseph Bruce is about 40 years old, dark brown and about 5 feet 5 inches tall. [Value $700]

He purchased Lee for $700 from the estate of Robert Y. Brent of Montgomery County, Md., in June 1857. He purchased Bruce for $350 from Rezin Arnold of D.C. about August 1849.

[Commissioners paid "Moshier" [Mosher] $569.40: Anthony Lee, $262.80; Joseph Bruce, $306.60.]

The petitioner's surname is "Mosher", not "Moshier", the spelling given in the printed report of the commissioners.

No. 887, Petition of Cornelius G. Wildman, guardian   Filed Jul. 11, 1862

Cornelius G. Wildman, as guardian of his seven children, of Washington, D.C. claims compensation for four persons.
1. Cely Hill is 55 years old, black in color and about 5 feet 6 inches tall. She is a good cook, washer and ironer and servant. She has been working for $10 a month. [Value $600]
2. Eliza Brown is 20, black in complexion and about 5 feet 4 inches tall. She is a good nurse and house servant and washer and ironer. [Value $1,500]
3. Annie [Brown], daughter of Eliza, is one and a half years old and black in color. [Value $200]
4. Thomas Scifas or Cephas is about 11 years old, black, and about 4 feet 3 inches high. He is a house servant and is used for general purposes. [Value $1,000]

Cely Hill has been held by Wildman since 1834. Eliza Brown was purchased from Bruce Hill in 1848 for Mrs. Wildman $425. Scifas was in 1856 conveyed to Wildman by Dr. P.H. Heiskell of Prince George's County and was brought to D.C.

[Commissioners paid Wildman $941.70: Cely Hill, $109.50; Eliza Brown, $525.60; Anna Brown, $43.80; Thomas Scifas or Cephas, $262.80]

No. 888, Petition of Eliza Bestor   Filed Jul. 11, 1862

Eliza Bestor of Washington City claims compensation for William Alexander Johnson. Johnson is 22 years old, dark mulatto, about 5 feet 8 inches tall and stout with straight hair. She says that when he was only 15, she was offered $1,500 for him and he is now worth $2,000. He is a skillful mechanic (?).

She was willed Johnson by her father, John Lawson Brightwell of Washington County D.C., in about 1847.

[Commissioners paid Bestor $657.]

Brightwell's will is recorded in Pippenger, District of Columbia Probate Records, 1801-1852, p. 294. William Alexander was the son of Negro Eliza.

No. 889, Petition of Ignatius F. Young, trustee for Mrs. James Anna Brent   Filed Jul. 11, 1862

Ignatius F. Young, trutee for Mrs. James Anna Brent, both of D.C., claims compensation for four persons.
1. Henny Bowie is a mulatto woman aged about 50. She is the mother of the persons below. [Value $700]
2. Rezin Bowie is a black boy aged about 18. [Value $900]
3. Hank Bowie is a copper colored boy aged about 15. [Value $700]
4. Mary Louisa Bowie is a bright mulatto girl aged about 13. [Value $800]
Mrs. James Anna Brent inherited the above from her grandmother.
[Commissioners paid Young, as trustee of Mrs. James Anna Brent, $1,357.80: Henry [Henny] Bowie, $175.20; Rezin Bowie, $481.80; Hank Bowie, $372.30; Mary Louisa Bowie, $328.50.]

No. 890, Petition of Joseph S. Wilson   Filed Jul. 11, 1862

Joseph S. Wilson of Washington City claims compensation for Mary Harrison. Harrison is about 18 years old, dark in color and of ordinary height. She is sound and vigorous, although a member of his family says there is a defect in one of her eyes. [Value $750]
He purchased Harrison for $350 from William H. Hager of Hagerstown, Md., on Oct. 4, 1855.
[Commissioners paid Wilson $416.10.]

No. 891, Petition of Thomas C. Magruder   Filed Jul. 11, 1862

Thomas C. Magruder of the District of Columbia claims compensation for two persons.
1. Olivia Anderson is aged about 43, black and about 4 feet 10 inches high. She is a little deaf. Anderson is a first-rate cook, washer and ironer.
2. Emanuel Pinkwood, about 14 years old, is copper colored with a full face. He is a good waiter and carriage driver.
He values them at $900.
He purchased Anderson from Mr. Kearns of Charles County, Md., about four or five years ago. He purchased Pinkwood from Mr. Jamieson of Alexandria, Va., about 13 years ago.
[Commissioners paid Magruder $328.50: Olivia Anderson, $109.50; Emanuel Pinkwood, $219.]

No. 892, Petition of Thomas H. Nelson   Filed Jul. 11, 1862

Thomas H. Nelson of Virginia claims compensation for Hannah Davis, or Bradley. She is 50 years old, dark in color and 5 feet 6 inches tall. He purchased her. [Value $500]
[Commissioners paid Nelson, by Richard P. Jackson, attorney, $65.70.]

No. 893, Petition of Columbus Alexander   Filed Jul. 11, 1862

Columbus Alexander of Washington claims compensation for 15 persons.
1. Beverly Davis, a male, is about 25 years old, black, medium sized and about 5 feet 8 inches tall. He is an elegant dining room servant and a good carriage driver and host. He can cook, serve and scrub. He was purchased on Jul. 29, 1858, from Lewis Warrington for $800. [Value $2,000]
2. Nancy Holmes is about 25, copper colored and about five feet high. She, with Thomas her child, was purchased from Philip Mackey for $1,200. [Value $1,200]
3. Thomas Holmes, son of Nancy, is about six, copper colored and about three feet high. [Value $600]
4. Arena Holmes, female, is about 23 years old, copper colored and about five feet high. She can cook, wash and iron. She was purchased for $926 (?) from John Waters on Sept. 12, 1857. [Value $1,200]
5. Jefferson D. Holmes, son of Arena Holmes, is about one year old, copper colored or mulatto and about two feet high. [Value $300]
6. Maria Bowman is about 18, brown, and about 4 feet 9 inches tall. She is an excellent housekeeper and good cook and washer and ironer. She was purchased from Dr. Johnson Elliot on Feb. 14, 1855, for $300. [Value $1,200]
7. Josephine Bowman, daughter of Maria, is about two years old, bright mulatto and about 2 feet 7 inches tall. She is sprightly and healthy. [Value $350]
8. Frank Digges is about 21 years old, black, medium sized and about 5 feet 9 inches tall. He is a good engineer and has been accustomed to run a steam engine in Alexander's printing establishment. He also a good field hand, hostler and can cook. He was purchased for $500 on Apr. 9, 1852, from William T. Duvall. [Value $1,800]
9. George Singleton is about 25 years old, black and has thick lips. He is medium sized and about 5 feet 8 inches high. He is an excellent field hand and a good hostler and wagoner. He also cooks. Singleton was purchased Feb. 23, 1836, for $600 from late Major William B. Scott and his wife.[Value $1,500]

10. John Wesley Holmes is about 21 years old, dark copper colored and about 5 feet 6 inches high. He has marks from smallpox. He drives a cart. He was purchased Apr. 8, 1858, for $825 from Jacob F. King and Philip Mackey. [Value $1,200]

11. Stephen Holmes, son of Nancy Holmes, is a year old and is bright mulatto in color. [Value $300]

12. Betty Hopp is about 70 years old, black in color and of low statue. She has defective eyesight but can care for young children. She was purchased for $80 on Mar. 1, 1844, from William Ginnell. [Value $100].

13. Eliza Jones is about 35, black and about 4 feet 9 inches tall. She is valuable house help and an excellent cook and irons well. She was purchased for $600 some 12 or 15 years ago from the estate of a deceased relative. [Value $1,200]

14. Lucy Jones, daughter of Eliza Jones, is about six years old and has a black complexion. She is healthy and sprightly. [Value $600]

15. John Jones, son of Eliza Jones, is about one year old and of a dark copper color. He is sprightly and healthy. [Value $300]

[Commissioners paid Alexander $4,818: Beverly Davis, $657; Nancy Holmes, $503.70; Thomas Holmes, $131.40; Arena Holmes, $481.80; Jefferson D. Holmes, $43.80; Maria Bowman, $503.70; Josephine Bowman, $65.70; Frank Digges, $744.60; George Singleton, $613.20; John Wesley Holmes, $525.60; Stephen Holmes, $21.90; Betty Hopp, no value; Eliza Jones, $328.50; Lucy Jones, $153.30; John Jones, $43.80.]

No. 894, Petition of John W. Clarke   Filed Jul. 11, 1862

John W. Clarke of Washington claims compensation for Caroline who is about 27 years old, bright mulatto, medium sized and likely and intelligent. She is a good housekeeper and washes and irons well. He purchased her for $800 on Dec. 27, 1855, from John B. Catlett, Harriet T. Catlett and Anna E. Catlett. [Value $1,000]

[The claim was withdrawn and thus not allowed.]

No. 895, Petition of Martha E. Nixon   Filed Jul. 11, 1862

Martha E. Nixon claims compensation for Isaiah Carter, aged three, dark brown and about three feet high. She claims his services until he is 21 years old.. Nixon states that Carter's mother, Eliza Carter, was "an indolent trifling character [who] abandoned her son" when he was six months old at Nixon's house. She subsequently bound her son by indenture to Nixon. [Value $700]

[The Commissioners did not allow the claim.]

No. 896, Petition of Charles E. Mix   Filed Jul. 11, 1862

Charles E. Mix of Georgetown claims compensation for nine persons.

1. Matilda Jones, 45 years old, dark, 5 feet 6 inches tall. She was purchased for $800 from Young. Bill Hamilton is her son. [Value $1,200]

2. Henson or Henderson Perry, aged 45, dark, 5 feet 9 inches tall. He was purchased for $600 by agreement with C.M. Watkins of Montgomery County, Md., on Jun. 2, 1860. Perry requested this transaction and was to serve four years from 1 February 1860. Attached is a note from Mix stating that Perry asked for his intervention because he had a wife and children residing in Georgetown. His master had given him a chance to purchase himself and he had paid all but $600 of that price. Mix therefore advanced Perry's master $600 and agreed to pay Perry $150 a year for his labor, exclusive of clothing and food. [Value $338.13]

3. Charles Edward Wilson, aged 24, dark, 5 feet 10 inches tall. He was purchased for $870 from the administrators of the estate of Sarah M. Worthington late of Nottingham, Md. He was previously employed by Mix to provide a horse and carriage, which Charles had charge of, for his afflicted daughter. [Value $1,800]

4. Susan Contee, aged 19, mulatto, 5 feet 3 inches tall. [Value $1,200]

5. Alice Contee, aged 16, mulatto, five feet tall. [Value $1,000]

6. Lizzie Contee, aged 14, mulatto, 4 feet 10 inches tall. [Value $800]

7. George Washington Davis, aged ten, dark, 3 feet 11 inches tall. [Value $400]

8. Bill Hamilton Jones, son of Matilda Jones, aged four, dark, 2 feet 8 inches tall. [Value $150]

9. Maria Myers, three months old, mulatto. She died Jun. 1, 1862, and her burial expenses were $20.

At the sale of the estate of Mix's wife's parents, she bought in as part of her interest Maria Contee and her two children, Susan and Alice. Maria had issue in his family of Lizzie Contee and George Washington Davis. Susan had issue of Maria Myers.

[Commissioners paid Mix $2,715.60: Matilda Jones, $262.80; Henson or Henderson Perry, $175.20; Charles

Edward Wilson, $613.20; Susan Contee, $481.80; Lizzie Contee, $394.20; George W. Davis, $219; Bill Hamilton Jones, $131.40; Alice Contee, $438; Maria Myers, claim denied.]

No. 897, Petition of Landon W. Worthington   Filed Jul. 12, 1862

Landon W. Worthington of Washington City claims compensation for Jennie Carter, who is bound to service until Dec. 31, 1867. Carter is 15 years old, about 5 feet 4 inches tall, "tolerable fleshy and large", chestnut colored and good-looking. She can read and write and is a fair cook and house servant. About 12 years ago when Worthington was a resident of Loudoun County, Va., Jennie Carter and her mother and a sister were manumittted when they reached the age of 21 years. Her grandfather, Ellick Carter, gave them to Worthington to serve their terms. At the time, the mother had two years to serve and she is now free. Jennie was then about 15 months old. The youngest sister, who was about three months old, has since died. [Value $400]

[Commissioners paid Worthington $105.12.]

No. 898, Petition of Thomas Brown   Filed Jul. 12, 1862

Thomas Brown of Washington County claims compensation for three persons.

1. Richard Johnson, aged 25, is black and about six feet high. He was purchased for $1,000 in 1857 from Edward Shoemaker of Montgomery County, Md. [Value $1,500]

2. Charles A. Dorsey is eight, dark copper colored and about four feet high. [Value $500]

3. Ann Dorsey is 16 months old, black and healthy. [Value $100]

Charles and Ann Dorsey are held to service until they are 25 years old. They are the children of Rosetta , who was held as a slave by Brown for a term of years as per agreement with Samuel Shreve. The attached agreement with Shreve is dated July 2, 1851, and shows that Brown paid Shreve $200 for Rosetta, who would be 15 years old in December 1851. She was to serve until Dec. 1861 and if she had children, they were to serve until they were 25.

[Commissioners paid Brown $919.80: Richard Johnson, $657; Charles A. Dorsey, $208.05; Ann Dorsey, $54.75.]

No. 899, Petition of Mary A. Holmead   Filed Jul. 12, 1862

Mary A. Holmead of Washington County claims compensation for two persons.

1. Mary Garner, aged 48, dark in color, about five feet high. She is blind in her left eye but is otherwise healthy. [Value $500]

2. William Garner, aged 12, is dark in color and about 4 feet 6 ½ inches tall. [Value $800]

She acquired the two as a gift from her father, James Eslin, in the last of 1858 or early in 1859.

[Commissioners paid Holmead $459.90: Mary Garner, $131.40; William Garner, $328.50.]

No. 900, Petition of Thomas Murphy   Filed Jul. 12, 1862

Thomas Murphy of Washington County claims compensation for Lewis Ferguson. Lewis, aged about 55, is copper colored and about 5 feet 7 inches high. He was a drunkard when bought by Murphy, but has since reformed. He was purchased from William H. Williams of Washington City for $390 on Jan. 24, 1850. [Value $600]

[Commissioners paid Murphy $197.10.]

No. 901, Petition of Mary A. Edmonston   Filed Jul. 12, 1862

Mary A. Edmonston of Washington City claims compensation for two persons.

1. Caroline Parker aged 20, is dark brown and about five feet tall. She is a house servant. [Value $800]

2. Marandy Parker is a female servant aged 16, nearly black and about 5 feet 2 inches tall. [Value $600]

They are the children of a slave woman who was given to her in her father's will about 30 years ago.

[Commissioners paid Mary Edmonston, by her attorney, Charles Edmonston, $1,007.40: Caroline Parker, $525.60; Maranda [sic] Parker, $481.80.]

No. 902, Petition of Abraham F. Kimmell and A. Thomas Bradley, trustee   Filed Jul. 12, 1862

Abraham F. Kimmell of the city of Washington claims compensation for five persons.

1. Darkey Jackson is about 45 or 50 years old, copper colored and of medium size. She is a first-rate cook and house servant. She was bought at a jail in Rockville, Md., about ten years ago.

2. Rose Cartwright, is about 27 years old and black. She is the mother of Violet, Daisy and the infant. She is a first-rate house servant and nurse. His title comes from his wife, who inherited from her father, William Lambell of Washington.

3. Violet Cartwright is aged ten and a yellow copper color.
4. Daisy Cartwright is aged four and a yellow copper color.
5. Infant Cartwright, aged three months, is a yellow copper color.
He values them at $3,000.

[Commissioners paid A. Thomas Bradley, trustee, $1,029.30: Darkey Jackson, $131.40; Rose Cartwright, $481.80; Violet, $240.90; Daisey [*sic*], $153.30; infant, $21.90.]

No. 903, Petition of Caroline Lashley, Matilda Lloyd, Samuel E. Douglas, Elizabeth E. Wheeler   Filed Jul. 12, 1862

The petitioners, residents of the city of Washington, claim compensation for four persons.
1. Terry Carter is 42 years old, black and about 5 feet 4 inches tall. [Value $500]
2. Mary Carter is 21, light colored and about 5 feet 2 inches tall. [Value $1,000]
3. James Carter is about 18, black and five feet high. He is "slightly diseased in the mind." [Value $500]
4. George Carter is 15, black and six feet tall. [Value $1,000]

Terry Carter was part of the estate of Edward Douglas who died in 1824. Mary, James and George are the children of Terry. They are excellent house servants.

[Commssioners paid Caroline Lashley, Matilda Lloyd, E.E. Wheeler, by S.E. Douglas, their attorney; Samuel E. Douglas, $1,620.60. Terry Carter, $262.80; Mary Carter, $525.60; James Carter, $262.80; George Carter, $569.40.]

Caroline Ashley's oath was taken in Wayne County, Ind., and she may be a resident of that place.

No. 904, Petition of Samuel Cooper   Filed Jul. 12, 1862

Samuel Cooper of Boston, Mass., claims compensation for Rachel Crawled. She is 65 years old, very black and tall. He purchased her about 1852 from William G. Hardy of Prince George's County, Md.

[Commissioners paid Cooper, by John Potts, attorney, $87.60.]

No. 905, Petition of Anne R. O'Neale for self and as executrix   Filed Jul. 12, 1862

Anne R. O'Neale of Georgetown, for herself and as executrix of Timothy O'Neale, her deceased husband, claims compensation for three persons.
1. Lloyd Mason is 45 years old and is dark brown in color. He is a quarry hand. [Value $700]
2. Hillary Young is 40 years old and is dark brown in color. He is a stone quarry hand and is somewhat affected with rheumatism. [Value $350]
3. George Phenix is about 20 and is dark brown in color. He is a good house servant and cook. [Value $700]

She claims title by virtue of being the executrix of her husband's estate.

[Commissioners paid O'Neale $766.50: Lloyd Mason, $219; "Hilleary" Young, $219; George Phenix, $328.50.]

No. 906, Petition of William Cammack   Filed Jul. 12, 1862

William Cammack of Washington County, D.C., claims compensation for Elizabeth Simms. Simms is 33 years old, light brown and 4 feet 10 inches tall. She is an excellent cook and house servant. He purchased her on Apr. 5, 1860, for $875 from L.W.B. Hutchins. [Value $1,000]

Attached is a document dated Apr. 3, 1860, showing that Cammack bought Simms from Wall & Barnard, General Auctioneers and Commission Merchants, located on the south side of Penn. Ave. at the corner of 9th.

No. 907, Petition of Edward C. Fitzhugh and Cora, his wife   Filed Jul. 12, 1862

Robert Bowie, "next friend" of Edward and Cora Fitzhugh, claims compensation for six persons.
1. Ellen, aged about 35, is mulatto and of ordinary height. She is the mother of John, Ruth, Josephine and Lewis. She is healthy, but "requires more than ordinary attention against exposure to wet weather to avoid taking cold." She is an excellent cook and has been employed at that since she was 19 years old.
2. John, aged 11, is a mulatto, but having taken a cold this spring was "attacked with rheumatism" which caused the loss of vision in his left eye. This may be temporary or permanent. He is otherwise healthy and strong.
3. Ruth, aged between nine and ten, is a dark mulatto, very erect in form and has a bright, intelligent face.
4. Josephine, aged two years and nine months, is mulatto in color.
5. Lewis, aged nine months, is a mulatto.
6. Annie, aged 13 years, is black, robust and healthy.

Cora Fitzhugh, who before her marriage was Cora Bowie, inherited the services of the above by the will of her grandmother, Mary Weems of Prince George's County, Md. The value of the persons is estimated at $3,150.

The attached oath signed by E.C. and Cora Fitzhugh was executed at Olympia, Territory of Washington.

[Commissioners paid E.C. Fitzhugh, in his own right and as surviving husband of Cora Fitzhugh, $1,138.80: Ellen, $262.80; John, $153.30; Ruth, $197.10; Josephine, $87.60; Lewis, $43.80; Annie, $394.20.]

No. 908, Petition of Eleanor H. Brawner   Filed Jul. 12, 1862

Eleanor H. Brawner of Washington City claims compensation for three persons.

1. James Thompson, aged 27, is mulatto and of medium height. He is a good ostler and has been employed for several years as a porter and has had but two employers in the last 15 years. [Value $1,500]

2. Jefferson Thompson, aged 20, is black and of medium height. He is a good ostler and has been employed for a number of years driving a cart and working in a brick yard. He has worked for one person for the last eight years. [Value $1,500]

3. William Warner, aged 18, is black, of medium height and very well-built. He is an excellent house servant and has never been employed by anyone but Eleanor herself. [Value $1,500]

Brawner owned their mother and the children were born in her house.

[Commissioners paid "Elleanor" Brawner $1,730.10: James Thompson, $525.60; Jefferson Thompson, $613.20; William Warren, $591.30.]

No. 909, Petition of James Selden, trustee for George L. Selden   Filed Jul. 12, 1862

James L. Selden, trustee for George L. Selden, claims compensation for nine persons.

1. Jim, aged about 57, is "the ordinary color of negroes", very stout and of low statue. He is a superior farming hand. He is married to Anne. [Value $500]

2. George, about 27 years old, is the same color as Jim, tall and stout. He is a fine house servant and carriage driver. He has "lately gone away to parts unknown and can not be produced." [Value $1,500]

3. Charlotte, aged about 60, is low of statue. She is a good cook, washerwoman and nurse. [Value $250]

4. Anne, about 42 years old, is dark in color and well-formed and strong. She is a good cook, chambermaid and nurse. She and her husband, Jim, are the parents of Louisa, Jim and John Lincoln. [Value $500]

5. Louisa is about eight and is a superior child. [Value $400]

6. Jim is about four years old. [Jim and John Lincoln together are valued at $350]

7. John Lincoln was born a few days before the emancipation act.

8. Eliza Carter, the wife of Robert Carter, is about 57 years old. She is a superior cook and nurse. [Value $400]

9. Susan, aged about 40, is mulatto. [Value $600]

About 10 years ago, Col. William Selden of Washington borrowed $7,000 from Lt. George L. Selden, now in the U.S. Navy. To secure the loan, on Mar. 24, 1855, he gave George S.'s trustees, of whom James Selden is one, a deed of trust upon the persons described above. By some neglect, the name of Susan was omitted, but she should have been included. An attached statement by William Selden states that to be true and that Susan was purchased from Mrs. Anne Safford of Wood County, Va., who, in turn, got Susan from the estate of her brother, Maj. General Alexander Hunter.

[Commissioners paid James Selden, trustee, $1,883.40: Jim, $262.80; George, $569.40; Charlotte, $65.70; Anne, $131.40; Jim, $87.60; John Lincoln, $153.30; Eliza Carter, $109.50; Louisa, $197.10; Susan, $306.60.]

No. 910, Petition of Nancy Woodland   Filed Jul. 12, 1862

Nancy Woodland of Washington, D.C., claims compensation for Mary Ann Williams. Williams is 36 years old, dark and five feet high. She is an excellent servant. Woodland purchased her about five years ago from Mary Massey of Alexandria, Va., for $500. [Value $800] (Signed Nancy Woodland x her mark)

[Commissioners paid Woodland $284.70.]

No. 911, Petition of Sophia Baker   Filed Jul. 12, 1862

Sophia Baker of Montgomery County, Md., claims compensation for two persons.

1. Rebecca Johnson, aged 22, is black and about 5 feet 3 or 4 inches high. She has thick lips, a flat nose and is good-looking. She is a good cook and chambermaid. [Value $1,000]

2. Louisa Johnson, aged 14, is dark brown and about 5 feet 4 or 5 inches tall. She has a flat nose, low forehead and large eyes. She is a good chambermaid and house servant. [Value $1,000]

Baker purchased the mother of Rebecca and Louisa from John Baker's estate about 30 years ago. (Signed Sophia x her mark Baker)

[Commissioners paid Baker, by Cephas T. Willett, her attorney, $963.60: Rebecca Johnson, $459.90; Louisa Johnson, $503.70.]

No. 912, Petition of Susan W. Harris   Filed Jul. 12, 1862

Susan W. Harris of Philadelphia claims compensation for four persons.

1. Georgiana Ringold is 21 years old, a bright mulatto and about 5 feet 1 or 2 inches high. She is a valuable house servant but "has been subject to fits for the last three years." [Value $300]

2. Mary Ann Ringold, is 17 years old, a dark mulatto and about 5 feet 1 or 2 inches high. She is a good house servant and ladies' maid. [Value $900]

3. Amelia Wells is ten years old, a dark mulatto and four feet high. [Value $600]

4. William Wells is five years old, a dark mulatto and 3 feet 6 inches high. [Value $400]

The mother of these persons was purchased by Susan's husband, Arnold Harris, about the month of October in 1840.

[Commissioners disallowed this claim. In the printed report, they explained that a witness stated that Arnold Harris, the real owner, had southern sympathies and went south after the start of the war.]

No. 913, Petition of William A. Marks   Filed Jul. 12, 1862

William A. Marks of Washington claims compensation for Emma Clark. Clark is about 12 years old, bright mulatto complexion, 4 feet 2 ½ inches high, full suit of black, slightly curly hair and is well-formed. She is "very gentle and prepossessing in her appearance." She is an excellent and dining room servant and sews and washes beautifully for her age. He acquired her as a wedding present from his father, Samuel H. Marks, about Feb. 1, 1859. [Value $900]

[Commissioners paid Marks $438.]

No. 914, Petition of Robert Bowie   Filed Jul. 12, 1862

Robert Bowie of Prince George's County, Md., claims compensation for Sidney Coolidge. Coolidge is 55 years old, copper colored and about 5 feet 9 or 10 inches high. He is valuable for his thorough knowledge of horticulture and as an accomplished body servant. He inherited him under the will of his mother, Mary M. Bowie. Bowie states that Sidney's wife, Sophy, was residing in D.C. at the time of the emancipation act and both lived there several years prior to the act. He temporarily removed Sidney from Washington in March 1860. He has been marketing in Washington ever since and remained near the city with his wife. He spent nearly half his time in Washington.

[Commissioners paid Bowie $175.20.]

No. 915, Petition of Sarah Ann Stone   Filed Jul. 12, 1862

Sarah A. Stone of Maryland claims compensation for four persons.

1. Thomas Payne, aged 38, is copper colored and about 5 feet 8 inches tall. He is a good field hand and wagon driver. [Value $1,000]

2. Eliza Stewart, aged 22, is black and about five feet tall. She is a good house servant, cook, washer and ironer. [Value $1,200]

3. Alice Payne, aged 15, is a light mulatto girl about five feet tall. She is a house servant. [Value $1,000]

4. Harriet Tenny, aged 13 or 14, is dark colored. She is a house servant. [Value $800]

She inherited them under the will of her late husband, John M. Brown, of Marlboro, Md.

A complete copy of Brown's will is attached. Also attached is a note stating that a deed in trust is recorded in D.C. Liber J.A.S. No. 209, folio 256, that conveys Sarah's property to William H. Dietz for her benefit, "she then about to marry her present husband, John H. Stone." Dietz is now in a federal regiment in Kentucky and his address is not known.

[Commissioners paid Stone $1,773.90: Thomas Payne, $481.80; Eliza Stewart, $525.60; Alice Payne, $459.90; Harriet "Tenney": $306.60.]

No. 916, Petition of Josiah Burgess, colored   Filed Jul. 14, 1862

Josiah Burgess, colored, of the city of Washington, residing in an alley between Mass. Ave. and H and 4th and 5th streets, claims compensation for William Thompson. Thompson is about 21 years old, dark brown and about 5 feet 6 or 7 inches tall. He is strong and healthy and he values him at $500. Burgess says he has no papers to prove ownership, but that about 17 years ago William's master, George Parker, who thought William unhealthy, refused to pay his board and told the colored woman who boarded the boy that anyone who paid the board could have him. Burgess paid the board and has owned and supported the boy ever since. (Signed Josiah his x mark Burgess)

[Commissioners paid Burgess $547.50.]

No. 917, Petition of Judson Richardson

Judson Richardson claims compensation for two persons.

1. Reny Ann is about 29 years old, dark and of medium height. She is a first-rate cook, washer and ironer. [Value $1,400]

2. Johanna is the daughter of Reny and is about 13 years old, dark and well-grown. She is a good house servant. [Value $900]

[Commissioners paid Richardson $832.20: Reny Ann, $438; Johanna, $394.20.]

No. 918, Petition of Harrison Wallis   Filed Jul. 14, 1862

Harrison Wallis of Maryland claims compensation for Letha Coleman. Coleman is about ten years old and a very dark mulatto. She serves as a nurse for children. He purchased her and her brother and sister for $350 from W.W. Hall of Prince George's County, Md., in December 1856. He values her at $450.

The attached bill of sale is dated Dec. 4, 1856, and states that Wallis paid William W. Hall $350 for James Jefferson, Sarah Sophia and Letha, the children of Linda Coleman.

[Commissioners paid Wallis $175.20 for "Lethe".]

No. 919, Petition of Henry E. Marks, administrator of Marion M. Taylor   Filed Jul. 14, 1862

Henry E. Marks of the city of Washington, administrator of Marion M. Taylor, deceased, claims compensation for two persons.

1. Henry Carroll, aged 50, is very dark and about 5 feet 4 inches tall. He has a scar under his right eye. [Value $400]

2. Lotty Bell, aged 45, is very dark and 5 feet 1 inch tall. She is a house servant, cook and washer. [Value $300] Marion Taylor had purchased the slaves from the estate of his wife's father, George B. Scott.

[Commissioners paid Marks $394.20: Henry Carroll, $175.20; Lotty Bell, $219.)

No. 920, Petition of Charlotte Maria Dawes   Filed Jul. 14, 1862

Charlotte Maria Dawes of Washington, D.C., claims compensation for Catherine Baltimore. Baltimore is 32 or 33 years old, dark colored and about 5 feet 3 inches tall. She is a first-rate house servant and understands all parts of housekeeping. She is likely, intelligent and healthy. Charlotte was given to her husband, the late Dr. Frederick Dawes, about 30 years ago. [Value $1,000]

[Commissioners paid Dawes $372.30.]

No. 921, Petition of Catharine Bates   Filed Jul. 14, 1862

Catharine Bates of Washington County, D.C., claims compensation for Mary A.E. Mathews. Mary is about 40 years old, bright mulatto, rather stout and about 5 feet 2 inches tall. She is "decidedly prepossessing in manners and appearance" and is an excellent house servant. Bates's husband, the late Thomas Bates, purchased her in 1855 from Mrs. Queen of Washington. [Value $1,000]

[Commissioners paid Bates $328.50.]

No. 922, Petition of Eliza Dashiell   Filed Jul. 14, 1862

Eliza Dashiell of Washington City claims compensation for two persons.

1. John Brent is 17 years old, bright mulatto and marked by smallpox. He is a promising boy and brings about $12 a month in wages. He is Leah's son.

2. Leah Lounds is 45 years old and chestnut colored. She is a first-rate cook and washer and ironer. She commands $10 a month in wages.

Leah was acquired by Eliza's husband about 40 years ago from the estate of his deceased father. John was born after the acquisition.

She values them at $2,000.

[Commissioners paid Dashiell $635.10: John Brent, $438; Leah Lounds, $197.10.]

No. 923, Petition of Charles Edmonston
Filed Jul. 14, 1862

Charles Edmonston of Washington City claims compensation for David Green. Green is 30 years old, copper colored and 5 feet 8 inches high. He is a valuable assistant to Edmonston in his business as a carpenter. He purchased Green for $800 about eight years ago from Robert Edmonston, executor of Archibald Edmonston. He values him now at $3,000.

[Commissioners paid Edmonston $547.50.]

No. 924, Petition of Rachel Brown
Filed Jul. 14, 1862

Rachel Brown of Washington claims compensation for Caroline Crumwell. Crumwell is 18 years old, dark brown and about 5 feet 5 inches high. She is a first-rate servant who was born her property. Brown says she has refused $1,500 for Crumwell and values her now at $1,200.

[Commissioners paid Brown $525.60.]

No. 925, Petition of Henry Tolson, administrator of George H. Marriott
Filed Jul. 14, 1862

Henry Tolson, administrator of George H. Marriott of Prince George's County, claims compensation for four persons.
1. Kitty Mead is about 76 years old and a mulatto. [No market value]
2. Hannah Butler is about 62 years old and dark copper colored. She is an excellent house servant. [Value $150]
3. Harriet Boone is about 65 years old and black. She is a good house servant. [Value $100]
4. Charlotte Brooks is about 80 years old and black. [No market value]

Tolson makes this claim as administrator of the late George W. Marriott of Prince George's County, as per order of the Orphans' Court to recover the value of Marriott's Negroes residing in the District of Columbia. He was appointed administrator on Jan. 27, 1862.

[Commissioners paid Tolson, administrator of Marriott, $120.45: Kitty Mead, $10.95; Hannah Butler, $87.60; Harriet Boone, $21.90; Charlotte Brooks, no value.]

No. 926, Petition of Greenberry M. Watkins
Filed Jul. 14, 1862

Greenberry M. Watkins of Montgomery County, Md., claims compensation for two persons.
1. James Edwards is about 21 years old, copper colored and about 5 feet 8 or 9 inches high. He is lame in one leg. He is a good house servant and carriage driver and his lameness does not materially affect his value. He readily brought in $84 a year with board and clothing.
2. Elizabeth Jenkins is about 21 years old, yellow and well-built. She is a good house servant and nurse.

Edwards was born while Watkins owned his mother. Jenkins he acquired by right of his wife, who inherited her from the estate of the late Zachariah Gaither (?) of Montgomery County.

He values them at $1,800.

[Commissioners paid Watkins $657: James Edwards, $175.20; Elizabeth Jenkins, $481.80.]

No. 927, Petition of Alanson Morehouse
Filed Jul. 14, 1862

Alanson Morehouse of Washington, D.C., claims compensation for two persons.
1. Mary, aged 16, is copper colored. [Value $1,000]
2. Richard Thomas, Mary's brother, is 17 years old and copper colored. [Value $900]

Morehouse purchased their mother in 1839 or 1840 in Mississippi and they were born in his house in Kentucky.

[Commissioners paid Morehouse $1,095: Mary, $525.60; Richard Thomas, $569.40.]

No. 928, Petition of Catharine McKnight
Filed Jul. 14, 1862

Catharine McKnight of Washington City claims compensation for Mary Murray. Murray is 65 years old, dark brown and about 5 feet 2 or 3 inches tall. She has lost the first joint of one of her forefingers. She is a good cook and is active and healthy. She purchased her and her son, Charles, who was afflicted with scrofula, in the latter part of 1837 from John A. Wilson for $300. [Value $300]

[Commissioners paid McKnight, by John Bartlett, attorney, $10.95.]

No. 929, Petition of Joshua Peirce
Filed Jul. 14, 1862

This is a supplemental petition from Joshua Peirce of Washington County, D.C. claiming compensation for James Becket. Becket is about 20 years old and dark olive or mulatto in complexion. He purchased Mary Becket, James's mother, from Thomas Addison and James was born in his household. [Value $1,200]

[The claim was withdrawn and not allowed.]

See No. 774 for the earlier claim by Peirce for ten slaves.

No. 930, Petition of Truman Lynch   Filed Jul. 14, 1862

Truman Lynch of Georgetown claims compensation for William Lynch. William is 22 years old, dark mulatto in color and about 5 feet 1 inch tall. He is a first-rate day laborer and garden worker. He purchased William from his mistress when he was about a year old for $100. [Value $1,500]

[This claim was abandoned and withdrawn. William Lynch had been bound for a period of time, which time had expired before passage of the Act of Oct. 17, 1862.]

The Georgetown portion of the D.C. Census for 1860 (Vol. 1, p. 90) shows that Truman Lynch was a 65-year-old mulatto who was a sexton. Living with him was William Mathews, aged 21, mulatto. William Lynch and William Mathews are probably the same person. See Registration No. 2767 in Provine, <u>District of Columbia Free Negro Registers, 1821-1860,</u> by which Truman "Linch" received his certificate of freedom. He was manumitted by Joseph Libbey of Georgetown on Aug. 6, 1836. Truman's will names William Lynch as his adopted son.

No. 931, Petition of Sarah M. Holcomb, guardian of Florence Holcomb   Filed Jul. 14, 1862

Florence Holcomb, by her guardian, Sarah M. Holcomb of Washington City, claims compensation for Henrietta Bruce. Bruce is 20 years old, black, 5 feet 2 or 3 inches tall, stout and good-looking. She is an excellent house servant. Eleanor Magruder willed Bruce to Florence Holcomb about 1848 and this is recorded in Prince George's County, Md. [Value $1,000]

[Commissioners paid Sarah M. Holcomb, guardian, $525.60.]

No. 932, Petition of Caroline R. Dulaney, for herself and as guardian for   Filed Jul. 14, 1862
Phoebe P. Dulaney and Rosa R. Dulaney

Phoebe R. Dulaney and Rosa R. Dulaney, by their guardian and mother, Caroline R. Dulaney, claim compensation for six persons. Phoebe and Rosa are under the age of 13 years.

1. Fanny Brown is 32 years old, mulatto and about 5 feet 4 inches tall. She is a good cook and washer and ironer. [Value $500]

2. Mary Brown is 17 years old, dark mulatto and about 5 feet 2 inches tall. She is a house servant. [Value $600]

3. Sarah Brown is 14 years old, dark mulatto and about 4 feet 6 inches tall. [Value $300]

4. Louisa Brown is ten years old, dark mulatto and about 4 feet 2 inches tall. [Value $200]

5. Lucy Brown is eight, dark mulatto and about four feet tall. [Value $200]

6. Winnefred Nead is 17 years old, black and about 5 feet 4 inches tall. She is a house servant. [Value $325]

The petitioners acquired title under the will of their late father, Capt. Bladen Dulaney. That will, made November 1856, is recorded in Fauquier County, Va. Caroline held them to service during her lifetime, after which they went to her daughters.

[Commissioners paid Caroline Dulaney, guardian, $1,730.10: Fanny Brown, $372.30; Mary Brown, $481.80; Sarah Brown, claim withdrawn and not allowed; Louisa Brown, $262.80; Lucy Brown, $153.30; Winnefred Nead, $459.90.] *See directly below for two children of Fanny's born since 1856.*

No. 933, Petition of Caroline R. Dulaney   Filed Jul. 14, 1862

Caroline R. Dulaney of the County of Washington claims compensation for two persons born to Fanny Brown after the death of her husband, Capt. Bladen Dulaney.

1. Walter Brown, aged four, is dark mulatto and about four feet high. [Value $250]

2. Rose Brown, aged two, is mulatto and three feet tall. [Value $150]

Walter and Rose Brown were born to Fanny Brown while Fanny belonged to Caroline R. Dulaney. She therefore holds absolute title to them. After her husband's death, she moved to the District of Columbia.

[Commissioners granted Dulaney $219; Walter Brown, $131.40; Rose Brown, $87.60.]

See No. 932 for Fanny Brown and her other children.

No. 934, Petition of Luther O. Sullivan   Filed Jul. 15, 1862
Samuel S. Williams, trustee, contestant as to all;
John E. Kendall and John A. Rowland, contestants as to the two first

Luther O. Sullivan of Washington, D.C., claims compensation for three persons.

1. Barney Grimsly Briant is about 17 years old, copper colored, about 5 feet 7 or 8 inches high and has fine teeth. He is a valuable body and dining room servant and cook. His title is based on the will of his mother which is recorded in Fauquier County, Va. [Value $1,500]

2. Charlotte Hudley is about 15, about 4 feet 8 inches high, black and has fine teeth. She is a valuable lady's maid, first-rate seamstress and knows all about housekeeping. She came to him by a deed from his brother (?), J.B. Sullivan, and it is recorded in Fauquier County, Va. [Value $1,500]

3. Rose Lee is 13 years old, black, about 4 feet 4 inches high and is thick set. She is a good nurse, chambermaid and general house servant. She was born his slave by a woman acquired by his marriage 15 years ago. [Value $500]

Samuel S. Williams, trustee, of Washington City claims compensation for the above three persons by reason of a deed of trust for payment of $2,000 executed by L.O. Sullivan.

John E. Kendell and John A. Rowland of Washington City claim that Luther Sullivan on Apr. 6, 1859, conveyed to Charles Wallack a Negro boy named Grimsly and a Negro girl named Lotty as collateral for a loan of $2,000. Kendell and Rowland say they are now the holders of the two notes which are past due and unpaid.

[The claims were settled Mar. 32, 1863, and the Commissioners paid Sullivan, $195.40; S.S. Williams, trustee, $700; Kendall and Rowland, $550.10: Barney G. Brant [sic], $569.40; Charlotte Hudley, $481.80; Rose Lee, $394.20.

No. 935, Petition of Thomas P. Trott   Filed Jul. 15, 1862

Thomas P. Trott of Washington, D.C., claims compensation for Daniel Hickman. Hickman is about 17 years old, a dark copper color and about 5 feet 9 inches tall. He has become expert in a manufacturing business in which Trott is engaged. He purchased him from Catherine Coyle, to whom Hickman's service had been willed by her mother until he reached age 30. [Value $1,000]

[Commissioners paid Trott $219.]

In Boyd's Washington directory for 1860, Trott's occupation is listed as a clerk in the Post Office.

No. 936, Petition of Virginia Scott   Filed Jul. 15, 1862

Virginia Scott of Fairfax County, Va., claims compensation for Catherine Johnston. Johnston is 20 years old, dark mulatto, medium build and 4 feet 11 3/4 inches tall. She has a bone felon on the end of her right first finger which shortens the first joint to about half its natural length. She acquired title under the will of Richard M. Scott of Fairfax County, Va, recorded Dec. 4, 1856.

[Commissioners paid Scott, by Leon C. Gunnell, attorney, $525.60.]

No. 937, Petition of Martha E. Harris   Filed Jul. 15, 1862

Martha E. Harris of Washington County, New York (?), claims compensation for Mary Ann. Mary Ann is 30 years old, bright mulatto and about five feet high. She is a good cook, house servant and washer,. She was given to Harris by her mother in November 1860.

[This claim was abandoned and not allowed.]

No. 938, Petition of Dennis Johnston for self and other heirs   Filed Jul. 15, 1862
of Francis Johnston, Sr.

Dennis Johnston for himself and other heirs of Francis Johnston, Sr., deceased, claims compensation for two persons.

1. George Quander is 39 years old, brown, heavy made and about 5 feet 8 inches high. [Value $1,400]

2. Ned Quander is 37 years old, brown, short and delicate in appearance. [Value $1,400]

George and Ned had been owned for more than 30 years by Francis Johnston and the petitioners acquired their title with the death of Francis.

[This claim was abandoned and not allowed.]

No. 939, Petition of William Noyes   Filed Jul. 15, 1862

William Noyes of Georgetown claims compensation for Binah Reynolds. Reynolds is 62 years old, dark mulatto and about five feet tall. She is a good cook and washer and ironer. Since her freedom she has gone from the District, having been hired by some gentleman. [Value $500]

[Commissioners paid Noyes, by H.C. Noyes, his agent and attorney, $87.60.]

No. 940, Petition of Philip R. Fendall Filed Jul. 15, 1862

Philip R. Fendall of Washington City claims compensation for Henry Tate. Tate is about 53 years old, dark brown and about 5 feet 10 inches tall. He is a good cook and dining room servant. He sometimes suffers from rheumatism, but this doesn't stop him from attending to his duties. He was born in Fendall's family and is the son of Mary Tate a slave woman. Fendall inherited him. [Value $400]

[Commissioners paid Fendall $153.30.]

No. 941, Petition of Joseph H. Bradley Filed Jul. 15, 1862

Joseph H. Bradley of the city of Washington claims compensation for Louisa Carter, aged 13 this July, who is held for a term of service. She is of medium height, bright mulatto in color and remarkably grown for her age. He purchased her from Elizabeth Williams for a term of service due to expire on Sept. 1, 1874. She has been trained as a lady's maid, chambermaid and seamstress and can wait the table. [Value $1,000]

The bill of sale is included and was signed Jun. 8, 1854, and recorded in D.C. Liber J.A.S. No. 81, folios 2-3.)

[Commissioners paid Bradley $219.]

No. 942, Petition of A. Thomas Bradley, trustee for Eliza M. Bradley Filed Jul. 15, 1862

A. Thomas Bradley of Washington City, trustee of infant Eliza M. Bradley, claims compensation for Ginnie Dorsey. Dorsey is about 21 years old, a dark chestnut color and 5 feet 2 inches tall. A. Thomas acquired title by a bill of sale executed by his brother, Joseph H. Bradley, Jr., on Apr. 1, 1862. She is a good nurse and generally healthy, although she sometimes complains of rheumatism. [Value $800]

[Commissioners paid Bradley, as trustee, $525.60.]

No. 943, Petition of Mary A. Smith, administratrix of Thomas Smith Filed Jul. 15, 1862

Mary A. Smith of the city of Washington claims compensation for four persons.

1. Emmeline Jackson is about 40 years old, a light mulatto. She is a first-rate cook.
2. "Boker" is about 45 years old and very dark brown. He is healthy and industrious.
3. James Brown is about 43 years old and is black in color. He is a first-rate blacksmith.
4. Thomas Carter is about 14 years old and is black in color. He is healthy and very promising.

This claims was originally filed by her husband, Thomas Smith, but he died on Jul. 14, 1862, and she is entitled to be administrator of his estate. Emmeline was purchased from A. Balmain; "Booker" from Robert Clarke; James from Mrs. Barrett; and Thomas from Sarah Cravens (?). She values them at $3,500.

An attached page lists the names and ages of Smiths who are probably children of Mary and Thomas and thus heirs to their father's estate.

[Commissioners paid M.A. Smith, administrator of Thomas, $744.60: "Emeline" Jackson, $262.80; Boker [*sic*], $350.40; James Brown, no value; Thomas Carter, $131.40.]

No. 944, Petition of Charles Lenman Filed Jul. 15, 1862

Charles Lenman of Washington, D.C., claims compensation for two persons.

1. Anna Peck is 42 years old, copper colored, medium sized and strong and healthy.
2. Elenora Peck is Anna's daughter and is 23 years old, dark in color, healthy and strong.

They are both excellent house servants and he values them at $1,500.

He acquired title under the will of James W. Fling of Montgomery County, Md., who died in 1844, and gave the mother of Anna, who has since died, to the petitioner.

[Commissioners paid Lenman $635.10: "Army" Peck, $197.10; Elnora Peck, $438.]

No. 945, Petition of Thomas T. Barnes Filed Jul. 15, 1862

Thomas T. Barnes of Washington City claims compensation for two persons.

1. Ellen Middleton is about 26, dark, medium sized. She is a first-rate cook, washer and ironer. [Value $500]
2. Henry Allen is about 22 years old, dark mulatto and about 5 feet 7 inches high. He is intelligent and industrious. [Value $800]

They are held for a term of years which is to expire when they are 30 years old.

He purchased them and their mother, Lethe, from the estate of Ann Orm[e] of Washington and thinks he paid about $400. He says that the mother was to serve until age 35 [*sic*] and he "presumes the said Ellen and Henry also to be free when they arrived at that age."

[Commissioners paid Barnes $229.95; Ellen Middleton, $76.65; Henry Allen, $153.30.]

There is clearly a conflict over how long Middleton and Allen had to serve. The commissioners apparently thought the age of 30 was correct and their awards reflect that.

Ann Orme's will, filed in 1839, provided that her daughter, Caroline D. Orme, be loaned Negroes Lethe and her two children and Anna. See Pippenger, District of Columbia Probate Records, 1801-1852, p. 235.

No. 946, Petition of Thomas T. Barnes, trustee of George A. Barnes's heirs — Filed Jul. 15, 1862
William C. Tuck, Ruth A. Tuck and Elizabeth Barnes

Thomas T. Barnes as trustee for the heirs of George A. Barnes, claims compensation for Cesar Butler. Butler is about 60 years old, dark and about 5 feet 9 inches high. He is a first-rate ostler and very intelligent and industrious. He was left to Barnes in trust for the use and benefit of George Barnes's heirs. [Value $500]

[Commissioners paid Barnes, trustee, $219.]

No. 947, Petition of Robert Dick — Filed Jul. 15, 1862

Robert Dick, a citizen of Maryland but presently residing in Georgetown, claims compensation for three persons.

1. Tom is 35 years old, dark and about 5 feet 10 inches high. [Value $1,500]
2. Mary is 17, dark, 5 feet 3 or 4 inches high and rather stout. [Value $800]
3. Barbara is about 15, of a light color, five feet high and of neat appearance. [Value $1,000]

They were born his slaves on his farm in Montgomery County, Md., of parents who were his slaves. All of the above are healthy, strong and active and are valuable house servants.

[Commissioners paid Dick $1,489.20: Tom, $481.80; Mary, $525.60; Barbara $481.80.]

No. 948, Petition of Susan Keene — Filed Jul. 15, 1862

Susan Keene, through her agent and attorney, Benjamin R. Keene, claims compensation for Adam Lee. Lee is about 27 years old, medium colored mulatto, about 5 feet 8 inches high, of medium stoutness and has rather long woolley hair. He is neat and careful in his appearance. He is a first-class cook and waiter and has for many years commanded high wages. He had "charge of the dining room in the most fashionable restaurant and eating saloon in this city at the time of his discharge." He is very intelligent and can read and write. He has been a slave of Susan Keene for about ten years and she acquired him by inheritance from her mother. [Value $1,500]

[Commissioners paid Keene, by her attorney, $569.40.]

No. 949, Petition of Eugenia Sweeny — Filed Jul. 15, 1862

Eugenia Sweeny of Washington City claims compensation for two persons.

1. Rose West is about 33 years old, very bright mulatto and about 4 feet 8 inches high. She is a good cook, washer and ironer and a competent house servant. [Value $1,600]
2. William Henry West, the son of Rose, is about six years old, bright mulatto, active and intelligent. He is capable of becoming a valuable house servant. [Value $400]

Sweeny was bequeathed Rose under her father's will. William Henry was born subsequent to that.

[Commissioners paid Sweeny $525.60: Rose West, $350.40; William Henry West, $175.20.]

No. 950, Petition of Andrew P. Hoover — Filed Jul. 15, 1862

Andrew P. Hoover of Washington, D.C., claims compensation for two persons.

1. Margaret Allen is 32 years old, copper colored and 4 feet 10 inches tall. [Value $1,000]
2. Addison Allen is 14 years old, dark in color and 4 feet 4 inches tall. He has a scar on his forehead from a burn. [Value $700]

Hoover purchased them from B[enjamin] O. Shekell in Alexandria, Va., on Sept. 5, 1856, for $1,450 ($1,000 for Margaret and $450 for Addison).

[Commissioners paid Hoover $788.40: Margaret Allen, $394.20; Addison Allen, $394.20.]

No. 951, Petition of WilliamWilson — Filed Jul. 15, 1862

William Wilson of the city of Washington claims compensation for two persons.

1. Elcy Diggs is 52 years old and about five feet high. [Value $600]
2. Nancy Diggs, Elcy's daughter, is 19 years old, black and five feet high. [Value $900]

They have lived with Wilson for over 15 years and had charge and management of his house. They are honest,

industrious and valuable servants. He purchased Elcy and her child from John Pettibone for $350 on Mar. 15, 1847.
[Commissioners paid Wilson $569.40: Elcy Diggs, $65.70; Nancy Diggs, $503.70.]

No. 952, Petition of Ann M. Washington   Filed Jul. 15, 1862
Ann M. Washington of the city of Washington claims compensation for two persons.
1. Eliza Tippins, aged 11, is mulatto and 4 feet 6 inches tall. She acquired Eliza by gift from Cornelia Macrae of Fauquier County, Va., about two years ago. She is a waiter and chambermaid.
2. Ludwell Gunnell, aged 21, is dark mulatto and 5 feet 8 inches tall. She acquired Gunnell by gift from Richard B. Lee, formerly of Washington, about ten years ago. He is a good dining room and house servant.
She values them at $2,000.
[Commissioners paid Washington $897.90: Eliza Tippins, $284.70; Ludwell Gunnell, $613.20.]

No. 953, Petition of Virginia Bell, Esther Ellen Bell and Virginia Caroline Bell   Filed Jul. 15, 1862
Virginia Bell, Esther E. Bell and Virginia C. Bell of the city of Washington claim compensation for four persons.
1. Winney is 47 years old, bright mulatto in color and large. She is a good nurse.
2. Susan is 37 years old, bright mulatto and very likely. She is a cook and nurse.
3. Ottoway is 35 years old and of a bright mulatto color. He is a coachman.
4. Sally is 18 years old, rather darker than the others, very tall and fine looking. She is a seamstress.
They are valued at $4,700.
Their title is based on a conveyance dated May 28, 1859, from the late Alexander Bell, husband of Virginia Bell and the father of Esther Ellen and Virginia Caroline.
[Commissioners paid Virginia Bell $1,795.80: Winney, $262.80; Susan, $438; Ottoway, $547.50; Sally, $547.50.]

No. 954, Petition of Elizabeth Bohrer   Filed Jul. 15, 1862
Elizabeth Bohrer of Montgomery County, Md., claims compensation for the following persons.
1. Maria Book is a mulatto woman about 52 years old, short and thick set and marked from smallpox. She acquired title from the will of her husband, Jacob Bohrer of Montgomery County.
2. Sandy Book is 22 years old, about 5 feet 6 inches tall, and has a scar on the left side of his head. He is timid when spoken to. Bohrer did not file her claim to Sandy until Aug. 9, 1862, because she did not know where he was. Sandy, however, appeared before the Commissioners and said he was residing in D.C. at the time of the passage of the emancipation act. [Value $1,200]
[Commissioners paid Bohrer, by C[harles] H. Wiltberger, her attorney, $700.80: Maria, $87.60; Sandy, $613.20.]

No. 955, Petition of Ann E. Jones   Filed Jul. 15, 1862
Ann E. Jones of Montgomery County, Md., claims compensation for Magdelane. She is about 12 years old, mulatto, about 4 feet 6 inches tall and has a scar over her right eye caused by a fall. She is a good house servant. [Value $700]
Magdelane's mother was given to Ann Jones by her father, John Jones of Montgomery County. Magdelane was born after that time.
[Commissioners paid Jones $306.60.]

No. 956, Petition of Nathan Prather   Filed Jul. 15, 1862
Nathan Prather of Maryland claims compensation for three persons.
1. William McCubbins is about 60 years old, black, short and bow-legged. He sometimes suffers from rheumatism. He is an excellent hand with stock. [Value $200]
2. Harriet Stewart is about 35 and is dark copper colored. She is a good house servant, cook, washer and ironer. [Value $500]
3. Nathan Lang is about 20 years old and jet black in color. He is an excellent farm hand. [Value $1,200]
Prather acquired title by inheritance from his father, John C. Prather of Prince George's County, Md.
[Commissioners paid William McKnew, adminstrator of Nathan Prather, $919.80: William McCubbins, $109.50; Harriet Stewart, $240.90; Nathan Lang, $569.40.]

No. 957, Petition of Ann Sheehy   Filed Jul. 15, 1862
Ann Sheehy of Washington, D.C., claims compensation for Harriet Jackson. Jackson is about 45 years old, a dark

copper color, 5 feet 8 inches high and stout. She is a good cook and house servant. She was purchased by Ann's late husband about 30 years ago in Fairfax County, Va., from Mr. Dulaney. [Value $800]

[Commissioners paid Sheehy $197.10.]

No. 958, Petition of Joseph T. Mitchell   Filed Jul. 15, 1862

Joseph T. Mitchell of Washington, D.C., claims compensation for Anna Simms. Simms is 60 years old, 4 feet 10 inches tall, very stout and a dark copper color. She is a good and trusty servant. He purchased her for $45 ("she being sold in the family for that sum") from the estate of the late Mrs. Ann Smoot about 10 years ago. [Value $100]

[Commissioners asserted Simms was of no value.]

No. 959, Petition of Allison Nailor   Filed Jul. 15, 1862

Allison Nailor of Washington, D.C., claims compensation for six persons.

1. William Johnson is 15 years old, mulatto and about 5 feet 2 inches high. He is a good plough boy and is handy with horses. He purchased William from William's mother to serve until age 21.

2. Joseph Johnson is 10 years old, mulatto and 4 feet 3 inches high. He is a good house boy. He purchased him from Joseph's mother to serve until age 21.

3. Sallie Butler is 19 years old, dark mulatto and five feet high. She was born of a slave owned by Nailor.

4. Martha Wharton is 38 years old, mulatto and 5 feet 4 inches high. She is a first-rate cook, washer and ironer. Nailor purchased her from Col. Smoot.

5. Phillis is 35 years old, black and 4 feet 6 inches high. She is a first-rate cook, washer and ironer. Nailor purchased her.

6. Lewis is 24 years old, black and 5 feet 10 inches high. He is a first-rate coach painter and plays the violin and is the leader of a band. He purchased him from Mrs. Thomas.

He values them at $5,400.

[Commissioners paid Nailor $1,620.60: William Johnson is free born and the claim disallowed; Joseph Johnson is free born and the claim disallowed; Sallie Butler, $438; Martha Wharton, $284.70; Phillis, $284.70; Lewis, $613.20.]

No. 960, Petition of Ellen J. Abbot   Filed Jul. 15, 1862

Ellen J. Abbott of Georgetown, by George D. Abbot her next of kin, claims compensation for Jennie Young. Young is about 50 years old and dark brown in color. She came from the estate of her father, Samuel B. Harris, late of Loudoun County, Va. [Value $400]

[Commissioners did not allow the claim because the owner was in the South.]

No. 961, Petition of Delilah Clark   Filed Jul. 15, 1862

Delilah Clark of Washington, D.C., claims compensation for seven persons.

1. Benjamin Marler is 70 years old, black and 5 feet 8 ½ inches tall. He is blind in one eye.

2. Sarah Dickerson is 54, black and 5 feet 5 inches tall.

3. William Butler is 32, copper colored and 5 feet 9 inches tall. According to the will of his former owner, he is to be free at age 35.

4. Frank Joyce is 30, black and 5 feet 7 ½ inches tall.

5. Mary Johnson is 21, mulatto and 5 feet 3 inches tall. She is the mother of Robert and Joe Johnson.

6. Robert Johnson is three years old and three feet high.

7. Joe Johnson is aged a year and a half.

She values them at $3,700.

Clark's late husband, William Clark, died on Jul. 7, 1855, and he owned the persons listed above, except Robert and Joe Johnson who were born after his death.

Attached are bills of sale that show that William Clark purchased Frank Joyce for $250 on Oct. 14, 1846, from Ellen Wilcoxen and this is recorded in D.C. Liber J.A.S. No. 6, folio 456. He purchased Sarah Dickerson for $225 from John H. Calrroe (?) of Prince George's County on Jun. 27, 1849. He purchased on Feb. 20, 1855, two-thirds interest in Negro girl Mary ($416.66) and Bill Butler ($266.66) from J.C.S. Keich, the guardian of George W. Kerby and J. Owen Kerby of Prince George's County. Butler was sold to serve only for a term of years.

[Commissioners paid "Clarke" $1,434.45: Benjamin Marler, $43.80; Sarah Dickinson [sic], $109.50; William Butler, $54.75; Frank Joyce, $569.40; Mary Johnson, $503.70; Robert Johnson, $109.50; Joe Johnson, $43.80.]

No. 962, Petition of Albert B. Berry Filed Jul. 15, 1862
Albert B. Berry of Maryland claims compensation for three persons.
1. Maria Lee is about 27 and light copper colored. She is a good cook, washer and ironer. [Value $1,200]
2. Alice Lee, Maria's child, is copper colored and seven years old. She is strong and healthy. [Value $400]
3. Sandy Bowie is about 14 years old and black in color. He is hired out in D.C. [Value $800]
He purchased Maria from Charles Eversfield of Maryland and her child was born after that purchase. Sandy's mother was owned by Berry when Sandy was born.
[Commissioners paid Samuel Berry, by John E. Berry, Jr., his attorney, adminstrators of Albert B. Berry, $1,095: Maria Lee, $438; Alice Lee, $65.70; Frank [*sic*] Bowie, $591.30.]
The printed report of the commissioners gives Maria's child's name as "Alice." The original petition gives no name for the child.

No. 963, Petition of Matilda Hamilton Filed Jul. 15, 1862
Matilda Hamilton of Washington City claims compensation for Susan Blackstone. Blackstone is 50 or 51 years old and copper colored. She is a cook, washer and ironer. She purchased her from her son, John C.C. Hamilton. [Value $800]
[Commissioners paid Hamilton $219.]

No. 964, Petition of John Frederick May Filed Jul. 15, 1862
John F. May of Washington, D.C., claims compensation for Kitty Wilson. Wilson is about 50 years old, light mulatto, tall and slender. She is an excellent cook and a good servant. After living with May for six or seven years, she started complaining of rhuematism, but she is otherwise healthy. He purchased her from the estate of Sallie Worthington. [Value $200]
[Commissioners paid May $131.40.]

No. 965, Petition of Edwin Wallace, Elizabeth B. Wallace, Mary E. Wallace, Filed Jul. 15, 1862
William A. Wallace, Roberta A. Robinson and Emma B. Williams
Edwin Wallace, Elizabeth Wallace, Mary Wallace, William Wallace, Roberta A. Robinson and Emma Williams claim compensation for Juliet Brooks. Brooks is 54, copper colored and medium sized. She belonged to their mother, Harriet Wallace, who died in May 1862 without a will. The property was amicably divided. [Value $500]
[Commissioners paid Edwin Wallace, Elizabeth B. Wallace, Mary E. Wallace, William A. Wallace, Rebecca A. Robertson [*sic*], Emma B. Williams, by Edwin Wallace, their attorney, $153.30.]

No. 966, Petition of Cornelia Baldwin Filed Jul. 15, 1862
Cornelia Baldwin of Prince George's County, Md., claims compensation for Milly Naughton. Naughton is 40, yellow in color and very tall. She is a good house and field servant. Cornelia inherited her from her aunt, Sarah Baldwin of Prince George's County, about 13 years ago. [Value $1,000] (Signed Cornelia her x mark Baldwin)
[Commissioners did not allow the claim as the slave was not produced.]

APPENDIX A

List of Servants to whom certificates have been granted under the supplemental act of July 12, 1862, and names of alleged owners

Names of Servants	Names of Alleged Owners
Addison, Ellenor, and child, and Henrietta	Sarah Ann Keller, Washington City
Allen, Jane, and son, William Henry	Dr. A.Y.P Garnett, late of Washington City, now of Virginia
Allen, Sarah, and three children, William H., Sarah and Anna	J. Pottinger McGill, Maryland
Barber, Mary, and child, Henry	Charles Wilson, Georgetown
Barber, William	Eliza Dent, Maryland
Barker, Orange and Helen	Thomas Green, Washington City
Bayley, Martha E.	James Gregg, Alexandria, Va.
Bayley, Henry A.	Martha A. Scott, Maryland
Beall, Mary	James Fling, Montgomery County, Md.
Beckett, Sarah Ann	Benjamin Lowndes, Prince George's County, Md.
Beckett, Charlotte, and four children, George, Zara, Mary A., and Bohemia[1]	Mary R. Bibb, late of Georgetown
Beckett, Francis	Fletcher R. Veitch, Maryland
Beckett, Sarah Ann	Benjamin Lowndes, Prince George's County, Md.
Bell, Mary	J. Thomas Davis, Georgetown
Belt, Harriet F.	William F. Bayley, Washington City
Billings, Julia A. And John	Dr. James J. Coombes, Washington City
Bird, Hector and Rachel A. Boston	Dr. James J. Warring, late of Washington City
Blackeston, Mary, and child, Lucy	James S. Holland, Washington City
Booker, Lucy	William J. Bronaugh, Washington City
Bowyer, Lois	R.M. Harrison, Maryland
Brown, Charlotte [2]	Robert Marshal, Prince George's County, Md.
Butler, Jane	Matilda Harrington, Westmoreland County, Va.
Calvert, Ophelia	Thomas J. Galt, Washington City
Campbell, Lila, and children, George, Albert, and Mary	Samuel Pumphey, Washington City
Carroll, Sarah, and children, William and Mary	Nathaniel M. McGregor, Washington City
Chambers Richard	Harry W. Blunt, District of Columbia
Chapman, Rachel	Teresa Burgess's estate
Childs, Washington	Thomas A. Withers, Stafford County, Va.
Chism, Jesse	Francis B. Gibson, Prince William County, Va.
Chism, John F.	Francis B. Gibson, Prince William County, Va.
Chism, Mary E.	John Henry Smith, Maryland
Clarke, Sally	John Knoxville, Stafford County, Va.
Cole, Kate	Charles Lyons or Thomas H. Barron, Washington
Collins, Eliza	Abraham Williams

---

[1] Bibb asserted that she had no notice of the application and that her servants were fugitives. The Commissioners heard the complaint, but did not alter their decision to issue a certificate.

[2] Marshal stated that he had not received notice of the application and denied that she was here with his consent. Mrs. Miller, however, stated that Brown had lived with her about a year and six months and that she had paid her. The Commissioners upheld their original decision to issue Brown a certificate on Aug. 8, 1862.

Cox, Ellen	Judge William M. Merrick, Washington City
Dodson, Charles and Ann	Dr. William Palmer, Washington City
Domer, Philip	William F. Chick, Fredericksburg, Va.
Duckett, Ann	George Buirns, deceased, Washington City
Gardiner, Nelly	Amelia T. Young, now of Georgia
Getter, Elizabeth	Elizabeth Gunnell, Fairfax Court-House, Va.
Ghentt, Rozetta[3]	Sarah Webster, California
Gray, Cornelia, and son, Julius A. McClelland	Louisa Hunter, Alexandria County, Va.
Harrison, Ellen, and son, William H.	John L. Trook, Washington City
Harrison, Martha	Mary Antonette Carrington, Washington City
Herbert, Frank	Benjamin L. Jackson, Washington City
Howard, Lewis	Bushrod W. Hunter, Virginia
Hubbard or Herbert, Elizabeth	Sarah B. Bronaugh, Washington City
Jackson, Ariana	S.D. Lynn, Georgetown
Jackson, John	Henry Cheatham, Alexandria, Va.
Jennefer, Jacob	Joseph Turner, Prince George's County, Md.
Johnson, Eliza	Caroline Noland, Montgomery County, Md.
Johnson, John	Maria Mills, Washington City
Jones, Sophia Caroline	Hannah Ward
Key, Ann	Thompson, L. Hayden
King, Henry, and Cecilia or Celia King	Julia Ten Eyck, New Jersey
Lee, Amelia and son, Jacob	Francis Boyle, Washington City
Lee, George	Nancy Talbott, Maryland
Lee, Samuel	Jonathan B.H. Smith, Washington City
Lee, Trecey	Matilda Simms, now of Virginia
Lewis, Caroline	Thomas Marshall, Maryland
Lineless, Harriet, and son, George W.	Amelia Gray, Maryland
Loudon, Jane	Orcelius Harry, Washington City
Mackall, Samuel	Mathew Duvall, Maryland
Mann, Emeline	George Selkman, Virginia
Mars, Anna	Mary Marlow, Georgetown
Martin, Ellen	Thomas Green, Washington City
Meredith, Philip	Gen. Robert E. Lee, late of Arlington Heights
Miller, Fatina	Jesse D. Bright, Indiana
Neale, Harriet	Lewis Henry Phillips, Washington City
Nichols, John	Lucy J. Tidball, Winchester, Va.
Ogle, Jackson Pymon, son of Sarah Pymon	Benjamin O. Sheckells, Washington City
Page, Annanias	Lucy J. Tidball, Winchester, Va.
Parker, Amanda	Alexander W. Russell, Washington City
Patterson, Caroline and Caroline E.	Warring Grimes, Prince George's County, Md.
Reintzell, Caroline	Charles Slemmer, late of Georgetown now of Pa.
Rideout, Mary	Eliza Powers
Riley, Anthony[4]	Ariana J. Lyles, Washington County
Robertson, George	Margaret Wise, Virginia
Robinson, Caroline	Judge William M. Merrick, Washington City
Ross, James	Dr. Septimus Cook, Prince George's County, Md.
Rustin, Jane[5]	John H.C. Coffin, Naval School, Rhode Island

---

[3] The Commissioners later paid Webster $306.60.

[4] See Petition No. 867.

[5] See Petition No. 520.

Sanders, Henry	Samuel Pumphrey, Washington City
Smith, Charlotte, and Mary Catharine and Amelia	Benjamin L. Jackson, Washington City
Smith, Lina	Giles Fitzhugh, Fauquier County, Va.
Smith, Stephen	Nathaniel McGregor, Washington City
Snowden, Hariet A.	Ann Riley, Washington City
Snowden, Margaret, Emily Jane, Lucinda, George, Ellen, Henrietta, Samuel	Dr. Septimus Cook, Prince George's County, Md.
Spriggs, Julia	Harriet Williams's heirs, Georgetown
Stevenson, Maria	Caroline Noland, Montgomery County, Md.
Thomas, Alice V.	Alexander McCormick, Washington County
Thomas, Dennis	Flavilla Turner, Maryland
Thomas, Mary	Alexander McCormick, Washington County
Thomas, Mary and daughter, Catharine	John F. Boone, Washington City
Upsher, Henry	Elizabeth Upsher, late of Washington City, but now of Richmond, Va.
Vaughan, Margaret	Mrs. Alvert V. (Rebecca B.) Scott, Alabama
Warren, Charity	Jesse B. Wilson, Washington City
Warren, Maria	John Warren, Washington City
Waters, Henrietta, Charles, Jane, George	Voltaire Willett, Washington City
Watkins, Louisa	Margaret Baden, Washington City
Wedge, Emeline, and children, Martha A., George W.	Alexander McCormick, Washington County
Williams, Arthur A.	Abraham Williams
Williams, Lucy	Julia Ten Eyck, New Jersey
Worthington, Mary, and William Williams	Benjamin L. Jackson, Washington City
Wright, Mary, and Margaret L. Wallace	Maria De Ford, now of Richmond, Va.

APPENDIX B

List of persons from whom certificates have been withheld on their applications under the supplementary act of July 12, 1862, with the names of alleged owners

Names of Servants	Names of Alleged Owners
Anderson, Mary Jane	Maria Morton, Maryland
Blair, Eliza Ann	James Johnson, Alexandria, Va.
Blaney, Matilda	Daphney Brody, Maryland
Bell, Johnson	John Manning, Prince George's County, Md.
Hollis, Martha A. and Lina E.	Daniel Fitzhugh, Fairfax Court-House, Va.
Hall, William	Eliza V. Griffith, Maryland
Jackson, Alice	Jaqueline Smith, Virginia
Johnson, Elizabeth	Caroline Noland, Montgomery County, Md.
Johnson, Emily	Solomon Stover, Washington City
Jordan, Patsy	Francis B. Gibson, Prince William County, Va.
Mason, John W. and Eliza	Sarah Forrest, Prince George's County, Md.
Pearson, Linah E.	Daniel Fitzhugh, Fairfax Court-House, Va.
Pynion, George N.	Gill Fur, Virginia
Prather, Mary A., and child, Arthur L.	Dr. Septimus J. Cook, Prince George's County, Md.
Scott, Ann	James H. McVeigh, Alexandria, Va.
Smith, Coleman	Edward Ford, Fairfax County, Va.
Thomas, Henrietta	Samuel Pumphrey, Washington City
Upsher, Leah	Susan Ringold, now of Virginia
Watts, Celia	D.B. Blacklock, Alexandria, Va.
Webster, Addison	Francis B. Gibson, Prince George's County, Md.
Wilson, Lucretia	Daniel Fitzhugh, Fairfax Court-House, Va.

APPENDIX C

Disposition of Late Claims[6]

	Petitioner	Servant	Value	Total	To whom paid
No. 1	Kate A. Gaither	Minty Mathews		$438.00	Kate A. Gaither
No. 2	John C. Brashears	George Johnson		$438.00	John C. Brashers
No. 3	Sarah Webster	Rozetta Ghent		$306.60	Sarah Webster, by James E. Morgan, attorney
No. 4	Hugh McCormick	Ann Baxter	$175.20		
		Louisa Bell	$328.50		
		Mary Bell	$219.00		
		George Bell	$175.20		
			$897.90		Hugh McCormick
No. 5	Lloyd Brooke	Kitty Barber		$481.80	Lloyd Brooke, by E.H. Brooke, attorney
No. 6	Ann H. Cunningham	Ann Blow	$240.90		
		Anthony Blow	Denied		
			$240.90		Ann H. Cunningham, by W.B. Webb, her attorney
No. 7	Teresa Ann Saffell, for self and children, viz: Richard Saffell, Ann M. Young, (wife of William H. Young), John T. Saffell, James L. Saffell, Mary C. Saffell	Alice Addison	$131.40		
		Rachel Addison	$481.80		
		Mary Ann Addison	$394.20		
		Alice Addison, Jr.	$ 87.60		
		George Addison	$197.10		
		James Addison	$ 21.90		
				$1,314.00	Teresa Ann Saffell, Rich'd, Saffell, Ann M. Young and Wm. H. Young, John T. Sheffell, James T. Saffell, Mary C. Saffell, by Richard H. Clarke, their attorney
No. 8	Thomas J. Perry and Mary A., his wife	Adam Johnson	$569.40		Thos. J. Perry, by Mary Perry (her x mark) his wife and agent
No. 9	Richard Younger	Washington Johnson	not produced		
No. 10	John A. Dorsey	Nelson Douglas	$569.40		
		Luther Watkins	$569.40		
				$1,038.80	John A. Dorsey
No. 11	Mary Stevenson	Thomas Page	$613.20		
		Polly Taylor	$481.80		
		Edward	$ 21.90		
		Lucy Carey	$197.10		
				$1,314.00	Mary Stevenson
No. 12	George White, colored	Louisa White	$525.60		
		Thomas White	$ 87.60		George White, by Richard H. Clarke, his attorney
No. 13	Moses Kelly, administrator of W.W. Russell, U.S.M.	Alice	$350.40		
		George Rose	109.50		
				$459.90	Moses Kelly, adm.
Total paid				$7,212.50	

---

[6] The Commissioners, in a letter dated Jan. 13, 1863, recommended that Congress grant the above claims for compensation and stated that had the petitions been filed in due time, they would have been granted. In some instances the parties were in Oregon or California and in other cases, petitioners' claims were not filed by their attorneys.

INDEX TO NAMES

The numbers after the entries refer to petition numbers, not to page numbers. Those entries in boldface indicate that the individual is one of the petitioners submitting a claim to the commissioners. This index is to Petitions 1 - 966. It does not include the introduction or the appendixes.

Abbot, Ellen J.	960
Abbot, George D.	239, 960
Abbot, Henry L. (Lt.)	73
Abbott, Charles	179
Abbott, Elizabeth	239
Abbott, John	239
Abbott, Sarah A.	179
Abbott, Thomas	751n
Abell, Violet A.	562
Abert, Charles	314
Acker, Nicholas	370
Adams, Aaron	635
Adams, Ann	465
Adams, Ann Maria	370
Adams, Catharine	511
Adams, Eleanor	511
Adams, Florence	635
Adams, Gertrude	635
Adams, Green	127
Adams, John	14, 635
Adams, Kate	177
Adams, Louis	616
Adams, Louisa	635
Adams, Marian	469
Adams, Molly	635
Adams, Nancy	635
Adams, Randolph	127
Adams, Sarah B.	539
Adams, Tom	616
Adamson, Robert L.	264
Addison, Alfred	645
Addison, Anthony	457
Addison, Ellen	645
Addison, Harriet	645
Addison, Henry	645
Addison, James L.	869
Addison, Jane	645
Addison, John	734
Addison, John, Sr.	869
Addison, Louisa	645
Addison, Thomas	929
Addison, Watkins	23
Adely, Clara	340
Adkinson, Frederick	800
Adler, Morris	282
Adlum, John (Maj.)	366
Adlum, Margaret	366, 598
Ailer, George	234
Albert, Joshua	35
Alexander (Mr.)	412
Alexander, Amanda E.D.	475
Alexander, Catharine F.	475
Alexander, Columbus	399, 573, 810, 893
Alexander E. Beall & Co.	740
Alexander, Lucy	180
Alexander, Myra M.	659
Alexander, T. L. (Col.)	129
Allen, Addison	950
Allen, Alfred	836
Allen, Ellick	474
Allen, Emily	474
Allen, George	474, 805, 879
Allen, Henry	945
Allen, James	436
Allen, Louisa	137
Allen, Margaret	137, 950
Allen, Mary E.	474
Allen, Robert	880
Allen, Spencer	474
Allen, William	133
Allnutt, Barbara Ann	694
Allnutt, J.H.	694
Allnutt, James N.	694
Allnutt, John	568
Allnutt, Nancy	568
Ambush, Charity	790
Ambush, Charles Henry	239
Ambush?, Harriet	239
Ambush, Henry	790
Ambush, John	491
Anderson, Ann	839
Anderson, James	641
Anderson, Milley/Milly	269
Anderson, Olivia	891
Anderson, R.S.	654
Anderson, Samuel B.	611
Anderson, Sarah G.	505
Andrews (Maj.)	389
Ann Robertson	48
Armstead, Susannah	13
Arnold, Nelly	616
Arnold, Rezin	140, 490, 886
Arnold, S.E.	529
Arnold, Willilam H.	678
Ascom?, George	666
Ashby, Ellen G.	661
Ashby, John R.	661
Ashby, Samuel T.	661
Ashton, Ellen	321
Atchison, Mary	711
Austin, John	203
Austin, John (Dr.)	179
Aylmer, Robert R.	728
Ayres, Mary	430
Bacon, Georgiana	214
Bacon?, Maria	214
Bailey, Isaac	524
Bailey, Lewis	519
Bailey, Sarah Maria	273
Bailey, Theodore	519
Bailey, Thomas	280
Baily, Elizabeth	194
Baird, William	218
Baker, John	911
Baker, Rosanna	380
Baker, Sophia	911
Balch, Thomas B.	548
Baldwin, Cornelia	966
Baldwin, Sarah	966
Ball, Ellen	711
Ball, James N.	58
Balmain, A.	943
Balmain, A.E. (Mrs.)	737
Balmain, Andrew	733, 737
Balmain, Annie E.	737
Balmain, H.W.	733
Balmain, Nancy W.	733
Balmaine. *See Balmain.*	
Baltimore, Catherine	920
Banks, George	851
Banning, Eliza E.	330
Banning, Mary E.	330
Barber, Cornelius	366
Barber, Margaret C.	343, 366
Barbour, Angeline	82
Barbour, Cornelius	331
Barbour, James L.	844
Barbour, Thomas (Col.)	183
Barker, Ann G.	401
Barker, Casper	238
Barker, Harry, Jr.	238
Barker, Henry	238
Barker, John H.	238
Barker, Mary Ellen	238
Barker, Quintin	244
Barker, Rachel	238
Barker, Sara R.	401
Barker, Sarah Ellen	238
Barkley, George W.	252
Barkley, Samuel	252
Barnard, E.F.	814
Barnard, Rachael B.	814
Barnes, Angeline	787
Barnes, Elizabeth	946
Barnes, George A.	946
Barnes, Henry S.	787
Barnes, Henry T.	249
Barnes, James	440
Barnes, James S.	249
Barnes, Martha E.	440
Barnes, Sophia	249
Barnes, Theodore	787
Barnes, Thomas T.	945, 946
Barrett (Mrs.)	943
Barrett, Anne	323
Barrett, Isaac	435
Barrett, Lewis	831
Barron, Catharine	690
Barron, Thomas H.	334, 690
Barry, Davis	695
Barry, Juliana/Julianna	473

Barry, Juliana/Julianna	473	Bean, Thomas	11	Berry, Jane	204
Barton, Charles	394	Beander, James	556	Berry, Jeremiah	679
Barton, Elizabeth	394	**Beasley, Joseph**	391, 392, 660	Berry, John	762
Barton, George	486	Beck, Susannah	192	Berry, John E., Jr.	962
Barton, Letty	394	Becket, James	929	Berry, Lorenzo	847
Barton, Lewis	394	Becket, Mary	929	Berry, Lucy	847
Barton, Mary	394	Beckett, Ellen	774	Berry, Mary	131, 189
Barton, William	394	Beckett, William	2	Berry, Mary Ann	762
Bass, Mary	241	Beckett, William H.	774	**Berry, Philip T.**	740
Bassett (Mrs.)	120	Beckham, Fontane	241	Berry, Samuel	962
Bateman, Eliza	312	Beddo, John	404	**Berry, Thomas**	314, 410
Bateman, William	312	Bell, Adam	562	Berry, Thomas Edward	617
Bates, Catharine	921	Bell, Alexander	953	Berry, Walter Z.	422
Bates, Edgar H.	9	Bell, Aloysius	345	Berry, William F.	634
Bates, Edward	9	Bell, Ann	317, 806	Berryman (Dr.)	760
Bates, Frederick	814	Bell, Anthony	478	Beson, Hannah	240
Bates, John E.	7, 9	Bell, Beckie	345	Beson, Mary Lucy	240
Bates, Thomas	921	Bell, Caroline	13, 79	**Bestor, Eliza**	841, 888
Bateson, Sophia	396	Bell, Charles	802	Bestor, Owen H.	841n
Bawner, Helen	347	Bell, Crissina	345	Beverly, Affrays	31
Bayley, Benjamin	210	Bell, Dolley/Dolly	803	**Bibb, Mary R.**	792
Bayly, Benjamin S.	750	Bell, Elizabeth	345	Billingslee, Joseph Clinton	229
Bayne, Elsworth	61	Bell, Ellen Nora	13	Birch, James A.	452
Bayne, John	136	Bell, Ellenora	13	Birch, James H.	707
Bayne, Judith C.	619	**Bell, Esther Ellen**	953	Birch, John	613
Bayne, Thomas	564	Bell, Francis	345	**Birch, Randolph**	613
Bayne, William	619, 869	Bell, J.B.	356	Birch, Sarah B.	707
Bayne, William B.	619, 846	Bell, Jane Maria	81	**Birch, William H.**	266
Beale, Emily	655, 739	Bell, Joanna	345	**Birch, William R.**	702
Beale, Robert	666	Bell, Joseph	317	**Birckhead, Elizabeth**	242
Beall, Alexander	740	Bell, Lewis	238	Birckhead, Oliver H.	242
Beall, Ann E.	6	Bell, Lotty	919	Bird, John	273
Beall, Benjamin	217. 218, 499, 677	Bell, Louisa	345	Bird, Martha Ann	273
Beall, George W.	371, 631	Bell, Margaaret	345	**Bird, Thomas R.**	120
Beall, Grandison	740	Bell, Maria	806	Biscoe, Angelica	429, 431
Beall, Horatio	689	Bell, Mary	837	**Biscoe, Ann**	165, 166, 429
Beall, infant	740	Bell, Nannie	345	**Biscoe, Ann Maria**	430
Beall, Jackson	630	Bell, Otha/Otho	599	Biscoe, Bennett	165
Beall, Jane E.	586, 639	**Bell, Virginia**	953	**Biscoe, Emma**	429, 430, 432
Beall, Jane M.	639	**Bell, Virginia Caroline**	953	Biscoe, Ezekiel	429
Beall, Jeffrey/Jeffry	173	Bell, Walter	345	Biscoe, George (Gen.)	429, 430, 431
Beall, Kitty	740	Bell, Wesley	803	Biscoe, George W.	566
Beall, Louisa G.	458	Belt (Mr.)	860	Bissell, S. (Com.)	173
Beall, Margaret	677, 740	Belt, Benjamin	563	Black, Lucinda	680
Beall, Margaret J.	586, 639	**Belt, Charles R.**	223, 281, 283	Blackstone, Lucy	467
Beall, Mary	484, 740	**Belt, John M.**	512	Blackstone, Susan	963
Beall, Matilda B.L.	639	Belt, Mary	478	**Blagden, Thomas**	492, 802
Beall, Nelly	740	Belt, Mary G.	512	Blair, Francis P.	770
Beall, Ninean	630, 631	Bembrage, Charles	769	**Blair, Francis Preston**	483
Beall, Rachel	622	Bembrage, Isaac	769	Blair, Francis Preston, Jr.	659
Beall, Richard H.	422	Bembrage, Lucretia	769	Blair, Montgomery	483, 659
Beall, Robert	740	Bembrage, Maria	769	**Blake, Ann**	601
Beall, Sandy	740	Bender, Betty	117	**Blake, John B. (Dr.)**	647
Beall, Sarah Ann	57	Bender, George	27	Blake, Mary	389
Beall, Sophy	740	Bennett, Agnes	43	**Blake, Mary E.**	542
Beall, Susan	275, 740	Bennett, Anne	43	Blake, Milly	178
Beall, William Z.	508	Bennett, Moses	386	**Blanchard, Anne**	284
Bealle, Cecilia	429	Berkley, John	130	Blaxton, Eliza	65
Bealle, George	429	Berrien, John Macpherson	680	Blaxton, Joe	65
Bealle, Ida	429	**Berry, Albert B.**	962	Blaxton, Martha Ann	65
Bealle, John	429	**Berry, Benjamin**	63	Blount, Jerry	329
Bealle, Maria	429	Berry, Dennis	799	Boarman, Eliza	166
Bealle, Nicholas	429	Berry, Eliza Jane	762	Boarman, Elizabeth J.	402
Bean, Artimesia	92, 545	Berry, Emma L.	37	Boarman, George (Dr.)	176
Bean, Benjamin	92	Berry, George	847	Boarman, Leonard	338
Bean, George	188	Berry, James	762	Boarman, Ralph H. (Capt.)	44

Name	Page
Boarman, Sarah	16
Boarman, Susanna	176, 177
Boarman, Sylvester B.	176
Bodely, Albert	627
Bodely, Edward	627
Bodely, George	627
Boggs, William Brenton	235, 625
Bohrer, Benjamin S.	459
Bohrer, Elizabeth	954
Bohrer, George A.	459
Bohrer, Jacob	954
Boiseau, James T.	551
Boiseau, R.F.	552
Bond, Harriet	808
Book, Maria	954
Book, Sandy	954
Boone, Edward	772
Boone, Harriet	925
Boone, Jane C.	772
Boone, Jane E.	380
Boone, John B.	380
Booth, Ann	779
Booth, Pauline	442
Booth, Sally	442
Booth, William	442
Boothe, Thomas	124
Bordley, John (Col.)	582
Borman, Eliza Jane	402
Boston, Daniel	265
Boston, Isaac	265
Boucher, Alfred H.	550
Bounds, Ann	304
Bounds, Mary	304
Bowen, Edward	259
Bowen, Emma	624
Bowen, Jane	511
Bowen, Rinaldo J.	511
Bowen, Sallie	259
Bowie (Mr.)	732
Bowie, Allen P.?	324
Bowie, Allen P.? (Mrs.)	324
Bowie, Andrew	223
Bowie, Ann	282
Bowie, Caroline	333
Bowie, Catharine	423
Bowie, Clara/Clarissa	283
Bowie, Cora	907
Bowie, J.W.L.W. (Dr.)	365
Bowie, Eliza	71, 223
Bowie, George	223
Bowie, Hamilton	223
Bowie, Hank	889
Bowie, Hannah	223
Bowie, Harriet	223
Bowie, Henny	889
Bowie, Henry Augustus	223
Bowie, Jack	301
Bowie, John	781
Bowie, Lethe/Lethee	781
Bowie, Lethea	223
Bowie, Mary	333
Bowie, Mary Louisa	889
Bowie, Mary M.	914
Bowie, Melvina H.	324
Bowie, Nicholas	71
Bowie, Rezin	889
Bowie, Richard	333
Bowie, Robert	482, 907, 914
Bowie, Sandy	962
Bowie, Sarah	761
Bowie, Saulina	761
Bowie, Thomas C.	840
Bowie, Thomas J.	206
Bowie, Virginia	761
Bowie, Walter W.W.	332
Bowles, John	339
Bowles, Lucy	240
Bowling, Robert	687
Bowman, Allen	758
Bowman, Chiah	867
Bowman, Fanny Isabella	200
Bowman, Josephine	893
Bowman, Maria	893
Bowman, Martha	59
Bowman, Mary	302
Bowman, Mary Ellen	517
Bowman, Stanislaus	517
Boyd, Asbury McKendree	578
Boyd, Harriet	41
Boyd, John	802
Boyd, Maria	365
Boyd, Mary	365, 479
Boyd, Mary Ann	802
Boyd, Sarah	365, 802
Boyd, Walter	802
Boyd, William Thomas Clinton	41
Braddock, John	885
Bradford, Samuel R.	485
Bradley, A. Thomas	696, 697, 902, 942
Bradley, Abraham	377
Bradley, Anna	77
Bradley, Charles	377
Bradley, Clara	529
Bradley, Eliza M.	942
Bradley, Hannah	892
Bradley, Joseph H.	289, 941
Bradley, Joseph H., Jr.	942
Bradley, Phinious	77
Brady, John	489
Brady, Nathaniel	198
Bramford (Col.)	572
Brannon, Amelia S.	132
Branson, Frank	386
Branson, Henry	241
Branson, Horace	386
Branson, James	386
Branson, Julia	386
Branson, Mary Ann	386
Branson, William	386
Brawner, Eleanor H.	908
Brawner, James L.	475
Breckinborough (Mrs.)	208
Brent, Elizabeth	346, 375, 843
Brent, Esau	581
Brent, James Anna	889
Brent, John	562, 922
Brent, John Carroll	15
Brent, Robert Y.	886
Brent, William (Col.)	15, 346
Brenton, John	482
Brewer, Henry	342
Briant, Barney Grimsly	934
Bridgett, John A.	801
Brien, Mary	155
Brightwell, Ann E.	841
Brightwell, Eliza	841
Brightwell, John L.	691, 841
Brightwell, John Lawson	888
Brightwell, Thomas R.	691, 841
Brisco, Betty	366
Brisco, Margaret	366
Brisco, Milly	366
Brisco, Mortimer	366
Brisco, Fanny	797
Brisco, Henry	797
Brisco, Joseph	797
Brisco, Lucy	419
Brisco, Martha	797
Brisco, Mary	797
Brisco, Rebecca	797
Brisco, Washington	797
Briscoe, Ann	27, 348
Briscoe, Betty	366
Briscoe, Edward	348
Briscoe, Loulie	822
Briscoe, Margaret	366
Briscoe, Milly	366
Briscoe, Mortimer	366
Briscoe, Richard S.	27
Briscoe, Wilson	193
Brocchus, Perry E.	77
Brogden, Ellen	794
Brogden, Harriet Ann	794
Brogden, John	423
Brogden, Virginia	794
Broker, Cornelius	427
Bronaugh, Ann E.	427
Bronaugh, Emily	126
Bronaugh, Fanny P.T.	557
Bronaugh, John W.	709
Bronaugh, John W. (Capt.)	595
Bronaugh, M.M.	557
Bronaugh, Mary	126
Bronaugh, Mildred M.	595
Brook, Caroline	850
Brook, George	850
Brook, Isabel	299
Brook, Louisa	850
Brook, Washington	850
Brooke, Benjamin E.	811
Brooke, Benjamin M.	597
Brooke, Ellen M.	154, 648
Brooke, Lucy Ann	811
Brooke, Robert C.	422
Brooke, Sarah Virginia	811
Brooke, Willliam Pinkney	508
Brooks (Mr.)	809
Brooks, Agnes	469
Brooks, Ann	682
Brooks, Charlotte	925
Brooks, Fanny	363
Brooks, Frank	363
Brooks, George	721
Brooks, Jane	668
Brooks, John	122, 466
Brooks, Johnson	823
Brooks, Juliet	965
Brooks, Lavenia	627

Brooks, Lewis 85	Brown, Louisa Annette 535	Bryant, Mary 600
Brooks, Louisa 627	Brown, Lucy 248, 932	Buchanan, Catharine 423
Brooks, Lucy 452	Brown, Maria 462, 867	Buchanan, Charles 423
Brooks, Margaret 354	**Brown, Marshall** 68	Buchanan, Daniel 423
Brooks, Mary 100	Brown, Mary 366, 390, 685, 932	Buchanan, Flora 423
Brooks, Mary Jane 374	Brown, Mary A. 132	**Buchignani, Margaret** 208
Brooks, Melinda 363	Brown, Mary Catharine/Catherine 159	**Buckey, Charles A.** 714
Brooks, Nathan 797	Brown, Mary Lucy 535	Buckner, Avis 483
Brooks, Robert 622	Brown, Mary Sophia 76	Buckner, Caroline 483
Brooks, Samuel 823	Brown, Obadiah B. (Rev.) 858	**Buell, Martin** 121
Brooks, Sarah 435	Brown, Patsy 288	**Bulley, Alexander F.** 353
Brooks, Simon 426	Brown, Patty 209	Bundy, John 864
Brooks, Sylvester 616	Brown, Phebe/Phoebe 346	Burch, Banjamin (Capt.) 813
Broom, Ann/Anne Eliza 389	Brown, Preston 783	Burch, Henry 375
Broom, Annie 333	Brown, Rachael/Rachel 118	Burch, John H. 623
Broom, Jack 333	**Brown, Rachel** 924	Burch, Rebecca 813
Broom, Laura 389	Brown, Reuben 58	Burch, Sarah A.J. 623
Broom, Lucinda 389	Brown, Richard 132	Burch, Thomas 667
Broom, Lucy 389	Brown, Robert 636	Burch, Verlinda Mary 813
Broom, Maria 389	Brown, Rosa 636	Burche, Raymond W. 853
Brotten, Ann 803	Brown, Rose 933	**Burche, Susan M.** 853
Brotten, James 803	Brown, Sally A. 160	Burckhardt?, Christopher 282
Brown, Absalom 390	Brown, Samuel 288	Burford, William 370
Brown, Adam 524	Brown, Sarah 118, 932	Burgess, Alice 169
Brown, Adelaide J. 858	Brown, Sarah Ellen 773	Burgess, Cynthia 169
Brown, Aisey 669	Brown, Sarah Jane 346	Burgess, George 169
Brown, Ann 160	Brown, Susan 60	Burgess, Henry 47
Brown, Ann J. 12	Brown, Susanna 212	Burgess, Jane 169
Brown, Anna 669	Brown, Teresa 288	**Burgess, Josiah** 916
Brown, Anne 2	**Brown, Thomas** 636, 898	Burgess, Julia 169
Brown, Annie 887	Brown, Walter 839, 933	Burgess, Margaret 169
Brown, Augustus 288	Brown, Wesley 636	Burgess, Mille 169
Brown, B. H. 81	**Brown, William** 12, 390, 462, 845	Burgess, Sarah 169
Brown, B. Peyton (Rev.) 214	Brown, William A. 700	Burgess, Susan 169
Brown, Baley 356	**Brown, William V.H.** 858	Burgess, Tempe 169
Brown, Benjamin 669	**Browning, Peregrine W.** 328	Burley, Alexander 80
Brown, Caroline 76	Brown's Hotel 105, 462	Burley, Margaret 80
Brown, Caroline V. 81	Bruce, Annie 345	Burley, Maria 80
Brown, Catharine 159, 346	Bruce, Betsy 345	Burnes, William 574
Brown, Cecelia 159	Bruce, Dick 345	Burnet/Burnett, Joseph 163
Brown, Charles 76, 159, 474	Bruce, Elizabeth 457	**Burr, Benjamin B.** 96
Brown, Charles E. 160	Bruce, Henrietta 931	Burr, David A. 73
Brown, Daniel 115	Bruce, Jane 345	Burr, R.W. 553
Brown, Dennis 392	Bruce, Joseph 345, 886	Burrell, George 112
Brown, Eliza/Lizzie 346, 887	Bruce, Lewis 345	Burrell, William 157
Brown, Elizabeth 257	Bruce, Mary 345	**Burruss, Jane S.** 497
Brown, Eugene 159	Bruce, Nora 417	Busey, William 435
Brown, Fanny 314, 641, 932	Bruce, Philip 669	Butler?, Ann Maria 326
Brown, Fanny Elizabeth 535	Bruce, Rosier 345	Butler, Anthony 162
Brown, Frank 636	Bruce, Sally 345	Butler, Aquilla 568
Brown, George 212	Bruce, Sam 345, 417	Butler, Betty Ann 392
Brown, Henny 391	Bruen, J. 491	Butler, Bob 408
Brown, Henrietta 288, 314	Bruin, Joseph 283	Butler, Cassy Ann 162
Brown, Isaac 46	Brumley, Mary 210	Butler, Catharine 633
Brown, J. Frank 420	**Bryan, Daniel** 183	Butler, Cesar 946
Brown, James 943	**Bryan, Elizabeth A.S.** 305	Butler, Charlotte 713
Brown, James Albert 159	Bryan, Enoch 305	Butler, Eliza 114, 641
Brown, Jane D. 839	**Bryan, Joseph** 322, 323, 474	Butler, Eliza Ann 1
Brown, Jemima 115	**Bryan, Joseph** (of Ala.) 329	Butler, Fanny 114
Brown, Jesse 68	**Bryan, Julia A.** 20	Butler, George W. 714
Brown, Joe 843	**Bryan, Louisa** 322	Butler, Grace 1
Brown, John M. 212, 915	Bryan, Mary 39	Butler, Hannah 162, 925
Brown, Joseph F. 285	**Bryan, Susannah P.** 464	Butler, Harriet 392
Brown, Lettice M. 403	Bryan, William P. 464	Butler, Henry 438
Brown, Louis 621	Bryant, Henry 600	Butler, James 114, 408
Brown, Louisa 932	Bryant, Margaret 600n	Butler, Jane 146, 633

244

Butler, Jenny	163	Carpenter, Catharine	584	Cartwright, infant	902
Butler, John	392, 713	Carpenter, Clara	584	Cartwright, Rose	902
Butler, John Summerfield	714	Carpenter, George	584	Cartwright, Susan R.	426
Butler, Lucy J.	838	Carpenter, Nelly	584	Cartwright, Violet	902
Butler, Margaret Ellen	160	Carper, Philip	149	Carusi, Eugene	717
Butler, Maria	155, 408	**Carper, Thomas J.**	149	**Carusi, Lewis**	717
Butler, Martha	1	Carr, Jane	355	Casey, Maria	130
Butler, Mary	408, 633	Carr, Mary	355	Cass, Lewis	242
Butler, Mary Jane	285	**Carr, Samuel R.**	605	**Cassell, Elizabeth E.**	105
Butler, Nace	384	Carrington, Edward C.	686	Cassell, John A.	105
Butler, Nelly	408	Carrol, Margaret	526	**Cassin, James L.**	693
Butler, Sallie	959	Carrol, Mary	526	Cassin, Tabitha M.	693
Butler, Sam	155	Carrol, Minty	314	Catlett, Anna E.	894
Butler, Susan	326	Carroll?, Anachy?	230	Catlett, Harriet T.	894
Butler, Theodore	715	**Carroll, Ann**	258, 521	Catlett, John B.	894
Butler, Walter	1	**Carroll, Ann C.**	621	**Cawood, Philip A.**	200
Butler, William	163, 962	Carroll, Ann Maria	366	**Cawood, Sarah E.**	200
Butler, Winney	49	Carroll, Anthony J.	774	Caywood, Stephey	776
Butt, Richard	147	Carroll, Charles J.	774	Ceasor, William	299
Butts, Caroline R.	231	Carroll, Charlotte R.	774	**Cecil, Anna**	600
Byington, Samuel	528	Carroll, Daniel	621	Cepas, Alexander	872
Caldwell, A. M.	130	Carroll, Dennis	366	Cepas, Emily	872
Caldwell, John H.	130	Carroll, Eliza	22	Cepas, George Washington	872
Caldwell, John M.	614	Carroll, Hanson	230	Cepas, Jeremiah	872
Caldwell, Mary L.	130	Carroll, Henry	919	Cepas, John	872
Caldwell, Sarah	130	Carroll, James	230	Cepas, Margaret	872
Caldwell, William S.	130	Carroll, Julia	258	Cepas, Mary	872
Callan, Nicholas	657	Carroll, Margaret	526	Cephas, Thomas	887
Callan, Nicholas, Jr.	269, 332	Carroll, Mary	161, 526	Cesil, Z.	93
Callan, Nicholas, Sr.	269	Carroll, Matilda	526	Chamber, Henry	536
Callis, Anthony Addison	457	Carroll, Nancy	774	Chambers, Rachel	824
Callis, Eleanor H.	846	Carroll, Susan	366	Champ, Andrew	310
Callis, Henry A.	846	Carroll, William	161, 258, 366	Champ, George	310
Calloway, Mary	332	**Carroll, William Thomas**	466, 615	Champ, Mary Mildred	310
Calrroe?, John H.	962	Carroll?, Anachy?	230	Champion, Elizabeth J.	529
Calvert (Mr.)	412	Carter, Adelaide	715	**Champion, William H.**	529
Calvert, Amanda F.	198	Carter, Andrew	52	Chandler, Sarah Ann	69
Calvert, Henny	327	Carter, Ann	715	**Chapin, Erastus**	875
Calvert, Len	809	Carter, Charles	622, 822	**Chapman, Edward**	103
Cambell, Charlotte	592	Carter, Cynthia	409	Chapman, Henry H.	800
Camden, Ann	465	Carter, Eliza	376, 895, 909	Chapman, John	366
Cammack, Christopher	112	Carter, Ellick	897	Chapman, Mary	800
Cammack, William	906	Carter, Flora	114	**Chapman, Susan A.**	428
Cammel, Lewis	710	Carter, George	715, 903	Chase, Basil	145
Campbell (Mr.)	647	Carter, Georgianna	866	Chase, Harriet	881
Campbell, Jane	439	Carter, Isaiah	895	Chase, Jennie	415
Campbell, Jane Turner	347	Carter, James	903	Chase, Lucy	145
Campbell, John	439	Carter, Jennie	897	Chase, Mary	461
Campbell, Joseph	439	Carter, John	52, 376, 715	Chase, Robert	655
Campbell, Mary Ellen	349	**Carter, John E.**	49	Chase, Sophronia	32
Campbell, Mille	439	Carter, Letty	15	Chase, Susan	655
Campbell, Ned	884	Carter, Lewis	866	Cheever, John T.	633
Campbell, Susan	439	Carter, Louisa	338, 941	Chesley, Jane	785
Campland, Benjamin H.	421	Carter, Martha	622	**Chew, Angelica**	429, 431
Cane, George	607	Carter, Mary	715, 866, 903	Chew, Elizabeth Ann	636
Carbery, James	22	Carter, Moses	251	Chew, Frisby F.	431
Carbery, James L.	748	Carter, Nancy	708	**Chew, Walter B.**	159
Carbery, Joseph F.	748	Carter, Ralph	548	Chichester, Mary	585
Carbery, Lewis	748	**Carter, Richard W.**	574	Chilton, R.S.	346
Carbery, Sybilla	536n	Carter, Robert	52, 909	**Chilton, Robert Smyth**	843
Carbery, Thomas	39, 44, 494, 748	Carter, Sally	715	**Chisholm, Catharine**	871
Card, Benjamin C.	309	Carter, Terry	903	Chisman, Isabella	306
Carlisle, James M.	641	Carter, Thomas	943	**Christian, William**	842
Carlton, Guy	209	Carter, William	52	Chubb, Charles St. John (Mrs.)	580
Carmichael, George	829	Carter, Zora	622	Chume?, Mary Catherine	294
Carol, Matilda	526	Cartwright, Daisy	902	**Cissel, George W.**	67

Cissel, Isabella	93	Clarke, Lucy	367	Coleman, Frances	293
Cissell, George W.	67	Clarke, Margaret	620	Coleman, Frederick	429
Cissell, Thomas	67	Clarke, Maria	620	Coleman, Henry	293
Clagett, Martha	1	Clarke, Martha	620	Coleman, James Jefferson	918
Clagett, Thomas W.	611	**Clarke, Mary Ann**	367	Coleman, Juliet	429
Clark & Dunn	361	**Clarke, Reuben B.**	361	Coleman, Laura	429
Clark, Agnes	503	Clarke, Nealy	314	Coleman, Letha/Lethe	918
Clark, Alexander	825	Clarke, Rachel	620	Coleman, Margaret	429
Clark, Alfred	152	Clarke, Richard H.	100, 254, 621	Coleman, Mary Ann	213
Clark, Baley L.	561	Clarke, Robert	620, 943	Coleman, Sally	429
Clark, Barney	704	Clarke, Teresa	652	Coleman, Sarah Sophia	918
Clark, Charles	825	Clarke, Thomas	652	Coleman, Thomas	337
Clark, Charles H.	503	Clarke, Walter	658	Coleman, William	429
Clark, David	367	Clarke, Walter M.	658	Collins, Amy	518
Clark, Delilah	961	Clarke, William F.	620	Collins, Louisa	518
Clark, Edmond	825	Claxton, Nace	50	**Collins, Reuben**	379, 592
Clark, Eliza	560	**Clements, Benjamin H.**	819	Collins, Sallie	37
Clark, Eliza Ann	152	**Clements, Elizabeth M.**	810	Collins, Samuel	518
Clark, Ellen	549	**Clements, Lemuel**	743	Collins, Sarah	518
Clark, Emily	549	Clements, Mary Eliza	810	**Colquhoun, William S.**	297, 575
Clark, Emma	913	Clements, Sophia	639	**Colton, Edwin**	75
Clark, Eveline	299	Clements, Washington	452	Commodore, Harriet	388
Clark, Frank	152, 437	Clow, John	634	Commodore, Holdsworth	388
Clark, Gabriel	437	Coakley, Ann M.	332	Commodore, Louisa	388
Clark, George	704	Coakley, Ann Mahala	332	Commodore, Louisiana	388
Clark, Hanson	561	**Coakley, Gabriel**	332	Commodore, Virginia	388
Clark, Henry	152, 689	Coakley, Genova	332	Compton, Clarence	110
Clark, Henson	503	Coakley, Gertrude	332	Compton, Eugene	110
Clark, Isaac	48	Coakley, Mary	332	Compton, Henry	110
Clark, Jack	367	Coakley, Mary Ann	332	Compton, Jane	235
Clark, Jane	549	Coakley, Nancy	332	Compton, Lizzie	110
Clark, Jannet	825	Coakley, Sarah	332	Compton, Maria	110
Clark, John	606	Coakley, Sophia	332	Compton, William	110
Clark, Joseph	397	Coakley, Veronica	332	Coney, Jane	1
Clark, Lizzie	152	Coates, Bill	660	Conklin's Livery Stable	266
Clark, Margaret	560	Coates, Juliet	880	**Connell, Lucy A. M.**	66
Clark, Maria	561	Coates, Louisa	578	Connell, William G.	66
Clark, Maria L.	152	Coates, Sallie	431	Conrad, Eliza	240
Clark, Mary Jane	152	Coates, William	880	Conrad?, Martha A.	240
Clark, Mary Ann	367	Coates, Winny	103	Conrad, Mary L.	240
Clark, Mason E.	561	**Cochran, George W.**	623	**Conrad, Nelson**	240
Clark, Minty/Minta	512, 595	Cochran, Gerald	572	Contee, Alice	896
Clark, Oliver H.P.	503	**Cochrell, Jane E.**	320	Contee, Andrew	867
Clark, Reuben B.	361	Cockrell, George H.	221	Contee, Ann L.	616
Clark, Sandy	689	**Coffin, John H.C.**	520	Contee, John	616
Clark, Virginia	825	Cokely, *see Coakley*		Contee, Lizzie	896
Clark, Washington	825	Colbert, Minty	59	Contee, Rachel	451
Clark, William	962	Cole, Albert	471	Contee, Susan	451, 896
Clark, William Henry	152	Cole, Ellen	271	Cook, J. C.	75
Clark, William P.	612	Cole, Jacob	690	Cook, John C.	336, 617, 646
Clarke, Albert	491	Cole, James Henry	196	**Cook, Leonard O.**	604
Clarke, Alfred	452	Cole, Joanna	73	Cook, Louisa	148
Clarke, Caroline	620	Cole, Joseph	471	Cook, Maria	845
Clarke, Charles	620	Cole, Julia/Juliet Jefferson	471	Cook, Nathan	349
Clarke, Daniel B.	658	Cole, Maria	334	Cook, R.D. (Mrs.)	642
Clarke, David	367	Cole, Milly	690	Cook, Sarah	158
Clarke, Emily	700	Cole, Rachel	456	Cook, William	158
Clarke, H.A.	861	Cole, Robert	471	Cooksey, Eleanor	596
Clarke, Hanson	510	Cole, Rosa	690	**Cooksey, Mary Angelica**	596
Clarke, Harriet	486, 652	Cole, Seth L.	245	**Cooksey, Sarah Ann Amelia**	596
Clarke, Henrietta	314	Cole, Sibey	456	Cooksey, William W.	596
Clarke, Jack	367	Cole, William	471	Coolidge, Edmund	423
Clarke, James H.	620	Coleman, Alice	429	Coolidge, Elizabeth Ann	423
Clarke, Jenny	700	Coleman, Anna	293	Coolidge, Sidney	914
Clarke, John W.	894	Coleman, Celia	293	Coolidge, Sophia	840
Clarke, Louisa	620	Coleman, Ellen	293	Coolidge, Sophy	914

Coombs (Mrs.)	387	Crawford (Mr.)	168	Dant, Rachel	555
Coombs, Cecelia	305	Crawford, Bettie	275	Dant, William	555
Coombs, Eliza	305	**Crawford, Elizabeth**	508	Darby, Aden	823, 824
Coombs, Maria	305	Crawford, Harriet	750	**Darby, James A.**	824
Coombs, Mary	305	Crawford, Mary	168	**Darby, Rebecca R.**	824
Coombs, Michael R.	196, 471	Crawford, R.R.	261, 539	**Darby, Ruth E.**	824
Coombs, Robert M.	258	**Crawford, Samuel C.**	672	Darnall, Guilder?	815
Cooper, Eliza	119	Crawley, Rachel	904	Darne, Elizabeth	458
Cooper, Kate Luck	119	**Craycroft, Edward**	606	**Darne, Mary**	409
Cooper, Mary Ellen	119	Cripps?, William McL.	86	Darrell, Benjamin V.	811
Cooper, Samuel	904	Cromwell, Caroline	259	Darrell, Florence E.	811
Coquia, Adele Francis	623	Cross (Mrs.)	482	Darrell, Lucy M.	811
Coquia, Nora	623	Cross, Amelia	672	Darrell, Mary	811
Coquire, Annette	461	Cross, Harriet	180	**Darrell, Virginia E.**	811
Coquire, Eliza	522	Cross, Howerton	180	Darrell, William Brooke	811
Coquire, John	461	Cross, Lucy	180, 672	**Darrell, William S.**	811
Coquire, Laura Ann	820	Cross, M. Louisa	150	Dashiel, ,Jim	418
Coquire, Mary	461	Cross, Minty	513	Dashiel (Miss)	418
Coquire, Rachel	461	Cross, Osborn	150	**Dashiell, Eliza**	922
Coquire, Selina	461	Cross, Thomas H.	180	Datcher, William	288
Coquire. *See Coquia.*		Cross, Thomas R.	672	Davidson, J.D.	468
Cosby, Ann M.	665	Crown, Samuel	747	Davidson, James	85
Cosine, Ann	291	Crown, William	745	**Davidson, John**	52
Cosine, John	291	Crowner, George	140	Davies, Jane	320
Cossens, John	291	**Cruit, Robert**	412	**Davis, Abel G.**	856
Cost, Henry	360	**Cruit, Susan T.**	412	Davis, Addel	691
Counselman, Lucy A. M.	66	Crumwell, Caroline	924	Davis, Adel Frances	239
Counselman, Samuel	66	Crusey, Anna	1	**Davis, Alexander McD.**	878
Countee, James	94	Crusey, Eveline	1	Davis, Beverly	893
Countee, Orpheus	351	Crusey, Frank	1	Davis, Catharine Ann	239
Covington, Barney	345	Crusey, Henrietta	1	Davis, Cora	239
Covington, Charlotte	816	Crusey, James	1	Davis, George Washington	896
Covington, Elias	345	Crusey, John Lewis	1	Davis, Hannah	202, 892
Covington, Ellen	345	Crusey, Julius	1	Davis, Harriet	274, 516
Covington, Henny	816	Crusey, Lydia	1	Davis, Hilleary	884
Covington, Margaret	816	Crusey, Martha	1	Davis, Indiana	239
Covington, Samuel	816	Crusey, William	1	Davis, James	841
Covington, William H.	816	**Cudlipp, Frederick**	770	Davis, John	116
Cox, Abraham	451	**Cummin, Mary A.B.**	582	Davis, Joseph	239, 562
Cox, Clement	807	Curtis, Agnes	799	Davis, Leonard Y.	764
Cox, Cornelius	181	**Curtis, Elsey/Elzey**	587	Davis, Lettie/Letty	841
Cox, Harriet	451	Curtis, Elsie	165	Davis, Margaret	841
Cox, John (Col.)	23	Curtis, Francis	25	**Davis, Martha A.**	878
Cox, Lucy B.	669	Curtis, George	25, 166	Davis, Mary	885
Cox, Margaret	822	Curtis, Henry	607	Davis, Matilda	841
Cox, Newton James	692	Curtis, Louisa	25	**Davis, Nancy W.**	764
Cox, Richard S.	23	Curtis, Madaline/Madeline	587, 799	Davis, Rosetta	516
Cox, Samuel	669	Curtis, Marion	165	**Davis, Sarah of Abel**	116
Cox, Thomas C.	822	Curtis, Mary	25, 587	Davis, Septimus	673
Cox, Walter S.	23	Curtis, Mary Jackson	799	Davis, Sophia	221
Coyle, Catharine/Catherine	806, 935	Curtis, Sarah	607	**Davis, Thomas J.**	222
Coyle, Catharine/Catherine E.	806	Curtis, Wallis	607	**Dawes, Charlotte Maria**	920
Coyle, Fitzhugh	809	**Cutts, J. Madison**	635	Dawes, Frederick (Dr.)	920
Coyle, Matilda	555	Cyrass, William	366	Dawson, Elizabeth	53
Coyle, Randolph	768	Dade, Henry, Jr.	868	**Dawson, Thomas B.**	53
Coyle, William H.	465	Dade, Henry, Sr.	868	Day, Benjamin (Dr.)	224
Crabster, Abraham	570	Dade, Lewis	868	Day, George E.H.	422
Cramphin, J. Henry	412	Dade, Richard	868	Day, Jane	545
Cramphin, Thomas	866	Dade, Washington	868	Day, Rachael	74
Crampton, Elias	238	Daines, Henry	449	Dean, Amos	441
Crampton, James	22	Daines, Judy	449	**Dean, Mary C.**	491
Crampton, Thomas	470	Daly, Eliza	597	Dean, Mary E.	470
Crane, James A.	759, 768	Dangerfield, James	163	**Deeble, Edward**	26
Crane, Sarah	768	Dant, Eliza	555	Degges. *See Diggs.*	
Cravens?, Sarah	943	Dant, Elizabeth	555	Deitrich, Elizabeth	340
Crawford (Col.)	644	Dant, Henny	555	Delaney, Louisa	199

Delaney, Margaret	199	Dixon, Winney	705	Dorsey, Susanna	780
Delavan, Cornelius	634	**Dobbyn, James**	194	Dorsey, William	605
Dellinger, Henry M.	563	Dobson, Judy	587	**Dougal, William H.**	283
Dellinger, Jacob	563	Dobson, Silas	588	Douglas, Clara	362
Dellinger, Sarah	563	Dochet, Paralle	432	Douglas Maria	562
Demar, Charles H.	224	Docket, Betsey	412	Douglas, Edward	903
Demar?, Ellen	815	Docket, Humphrey Alfred	412	Douglas, Henry	329
Dement, John E.	428, 478	Dockett, Paralee	432	Douglas, Mary	362
Dement, Rebecca	478	**Dodge, Allen**	636	**Douglas, Samuel E.**	903
Denham, Amos	737	**Dodge, Emily**	255	Douglass, Maria	562
Dent, Abraham	488	Dodge, F. J. (Mrs.)	103	Dove, George M. (Dr.)	258
Dent, J.	760	Dodge, Francis	103	Dove, Mary M.	747
Dent, Josiah	685, 686	**Dodge, Francis, Jr.**	255	Dover, Bettie	408
Dick, Robert	947	Dodge, Francis, Sr.	255	Dover, George	163, 494
Dickerson, Sarah	962	**Dodge, Robert P.**	135, 255	Dover, Maria	162
Dickinson, F.	798	Dodson, Ann Maria	579	Dover, Sarah	408
Dickinson, William F.	798	Dodson, Charlotte	579	**Downes, John**	118
Dickson, John	23	Dodson, Elmer	579	**Downing, Joseph**	122
Didney, Lewis H.	487	Dodson, Francis Ann	579	Downs, Zachariah	118
Dietz, William H.	915	Dodson, George	616	**Drane, Elizabeth Ann**	397
Digges, Charles	145	Dodson, Henry	376	Drane, J.W.	397
Digges, Frank	893	Dodson, Jim	616	Drayton, Daniel (Capt.)	602
Digges, Grace	52	Dodson, John	355, 616	Drummond, Matilda	47
Digges, Wesley	52	Dodson, Julia	376	**Drury, Samuel**	17
Diggs, Caroline	491	Dodson, Maria	272	**Drury, Terence**	663
Diggs, Charity	645	Dodson, Vanduden	237	**Drury, William P.**	720
Diggs, Cornelius	314	Dodson, William	5	Duckett, Frances	142
Diggs, Delia	602n	Doniphan, Catherine P.	64	Duckett, Thomas	616
Diggs, Elcy	951	**Doniphan, William T.**	64	Duffin, William	103
Diggs?, Francis	689	**Donoho/Donohoo, Harriet**	443	Duffy, Michael	379
Diggs, Henry	71, 698	**Donoho, Thomas**	35	Dufief, John A.	375
Diggs, Judson	602, 602	Donohoo, John A.	262	Dufief, John L.	337, 736
Diggs, Laura	801	Donohue (Mr.)	857	**Dufief, Mary M.**	736
Diggs, Leanna	602	Donovan, Joseph S.	420, 749	Duglas, Sarah	185
Diggs, Lena	602n	Doris/Dorris, Maria	518	Duhamel, James	382, 385
Diggs, Lewis	64, 602	Doris/Dorris, Thomas	518	**Duhamel, W.J.C.**	139, 385
Diggs, Margaret	645	Dorman, Leah	179	Dulaney (Mr.)	957
Diggs, Maria	422	**Dorsett, Fielder R.**	588	Dulaney, Bladen (Capt.)	932, 933
Diggs, Mary	422, 602	**Dorsey, Achsey**	214	**Dulaney, Caroline R.**	932, 933
Diggs, Mary Jane	705	Dorsey, Ann	898	**Dulaney, Grace**	751
Diggs, Nace	645	Dorsey, Annie? Lee	447	**Dulaney, Phoebe P.**	932
Diggs, Nancy	951	Dorsey, Ariana	642	**Dulaney, Rosa R.**	932
Diggs, Philip	491	Dorsey, Benjamin	350	Dulaney, William	751
Diggs, Rose	288	Dorsey, Charles	780	Duncanson, John A.M.	378
Diggs, Sandy	422	Dorsey, Charles A.	898	**Duncanson, Martha D.**	378
Diggs, Sylvia	801	Dorsey, Christina	311	**Dunlop, Robert P.**	371
Dines, Barbara	818	Dorsey, Dinah	771	Dunscomb, Jane E.	269
Dines, Daniel	816	Dorsey, Francis	410, 780	Duskin, Valinda Ann	92
Dines, Eliza	816	Dorsey, Ginnie	942	Duval, Eliza	507
Dines, Fanny	817	Dorsey, Gustavus	780	Duvall (Mr.)	549
Dines, George	480	Dorsey, Henry	124, 780	Duvall (Mrs.)	549
Dines, Joseph	816	Dorsey, James	105	Duvall, Caroline Mackall	110
Dines, Phil	345	Dorsey, Joseph Cornelius	111	**Duvall, Eliza**	510
Dines, Philip	816	Dorsey, Levi	311	Duvall, Henry	543
Dines, Susan	818	Dorsey, Margaret	487	Duvall, Jesse	128
Dines, Winny/Winney	480	Dorsey, Maria Louisa	724	Duvall, M. Louisa	150
Dison. *See Dyson.*		Dorsey, Mary	311	Duvall, Matthew E.	110
Dixon, Chloe	705	Dorsey, Mary E.	98	Duvall, Sarah Ann	751, 801
Dixon, Ellen	705	Dorsey, Mary Jane	780	**Duvall, William T.**	264, 893
Dixon, Henry T.	154	Dorsey, Osbourn	311	**Duvall, Zachariah**	718
Dixon, James	705	**Dorsey, Presley W.**	803, 804	Duviel, Elizabeth	189
Dixon, Joseph	569	Dorsey, Rose	98	Duviell, Susan	247
Dixon, Maria Ann	705	Dorsey, Rosetta/Rozetta	139, 898	Dyer, Edward C.	572
Dixon, Mary Ann	705	Dorsey, Samuel	447	Dyer, George	152
Dixon, Sarah	705	**Dorsey, Sarah**	804	Dyer, John	246
Dixon, Stephen	705	Dorsey, Stephen	771	Dyer, Julia	27

Dyer, Martha	335	Entwisle, Mary M.	747	Fisher, Josephine	267
Dyer, Mary	152	**Entwisle, Thomas B.**	747	**Fister, John**	249
Dyer, Melinda	27	Erving, Charlotte	733	**Fitzhugh, Cora**	907
Dyer, Rose	27	**Eslin, James**	398, 899	**Fitzhugh, Edward**	907
Dyer, Sophia	335	Essex, Debra?	152	**Fitzhugh, John W.**	182
Dynes, George	480	Essex, James F.	152	**Fitzhugh, Maria**	621
Dyson, Ann	102	**Essex, James F.**	709	Fletcher, Agnes	345
Dyson, Archy	833	Etchison, Adelaide	857	Fletcher, Andrew	408
Dyson, Benjamin	102	Etchison, Banks	857	Fletcher, Ann Virginia	345
Dyson, Daniel	833	Etchison, Dallas	857	Fletcher, Augustus	408
Dyson, Delilah	102	**Etchison, Emanuel E.**	653	Fletcher, Beckie	345
Dyson, Eliza	833	Etchison, Kingsley	857	Fletcher, Charles	691
Dyson, Emily	102	Etchison, Mary	857	Fletcher, Charlotte	408
Dyson, James	575	Eva, William T.	377	Fletcher, Daniel	146
Dyson, Joseph	833	Evans, Alexander	54	Fletcher, Eliza	345
Dyson, Margaret	540	Evans, Eliza	54	Fletcher, Henry	191, 345
Dyson, Mary	540	Evans, Henrietta	207	Fletcher, John	408
Dyson, Mary Caroline	833	Evans, Robert	55	Fletcher, Margaret	691
Dyson, Matilda	540	Evans, Sally	54	Fletcher, Mary	472
Dyson, Sarah	42	Evans, Susan	551	Fletcher, Mary Catharine	345
Dyson, Stella	833	**Evans, William B.**	481	Fletcher, Notley	345
Dyson, Thomas	102	Evelin, J. B. (Dr.)	170	Fletcher, Rachael	408
Earl/Earle, Robert	245	Everett, Jane H.	156	Fletcher, William	345
Easton, Fanny	348	**Everett, Thomas T.**	156	Fling, James	837
Easton, Floreed	348	Eversfield, Charles	962	**Fling, James W.**	837, 944
Easton, Louisa	348	**Ewell, Fanny B.**	25	Foggett, Richard M.	462
Easton, Mary	348	Ewell, Jesse	24, 25	**Follansbee/Follansby, Joseph**	41
Easton, Matilda	348	Ewell, Mildred	24, 25	Forbes, James J.	666
Easton, Nelly Ann	348	**Ewell, Mildred E.**	24	Force, William Q.	690
Eckel, Charles E.	282	Fairfax, Alice/Allice	353	Ford, Joseph	18
Edelin, Alfred R.	341	Fairfax, Bettie	320	Ford, Letty	730
Edelin, Edward H.	387	Fairfax, Caroline E.	616	Ford, Randell	867
Edelin, Horace	844	Fairfax, Frank	442	Ford, Solomon	18
Edelin, James (Lt. Col.)	100	Fairfax, Joseph	442	Ford, Sophia	867
Edelin, Rosalie	381	Fairfax, Sarah	353	Ford, Winney	18
Edelin, William J.	341	Fairfax, Thomas	442	Foreman, Caddy	823
Edes, William H.	281	Fairfax, William	442	Foreman, Maria	832
Edlin, Alfred (Dr.)	844	Falconer, Jane D.	839	Foreman, Thomas M.	832
Edmonds, Ruthey	143	**Falconer, Mahlon**	839	Forrest, Adelaide Clinton	759
Edmonson, Aaron	780	**Farquhar, Emily E.**	363	**Forrest, Ann Maria S.**	276
Edmonson, Phebe	780	**Farr, Bushrod W.**	357	Forrest, Anna M.L.	229
Edmonson, Vachel Henry	780	Farr, Elizabeth D.	352	Forrest, Annie	759
Edmonston, Archibald	923	Farr, Malachi B.	352	Forrest, Arthur	759
Edmonston, Charles	901	**Farr, Nimrod**	352	**Forrest, Bladen**	715
Edmonston, Charles	923	Fassell (Mr).	556	Forrest, Catherine	715
Edmonston, Mary A.	901	Fauntleroy, Jane (Jennie)	262	Forrest, Clarissa	242
Edmonston, Rachael	753	Fearson, Joseph	185	Forrest, David M.	644
Edmonston, Robert	923	**Fearson, Joseph C.**	700	Forrest, Elizabeth	242
Edward, James	259	**Fearson, Joseph N.**	186, 185	Forrest, George P.	780
Edwards, James	926	Fearson, Samuel	186	Forrest, Jane Rosetta	759
Ehrmantrout, Joseph	202	Fearson, Samuel S.	185, 186	Forrest, John Wesley	759
Eliason, John	294	**Fendall, Philip R.**	940	Forrest, Joseph	759
Eliot, Wallace	676	Fendall, William Y.	448	Forrest, Louisa	759
Eliot, Johnson (Dr.)	893	**Fenwick, Benjamin J.**	56	Forrest, Maria	759
Elliott, Alexander, Jr.	484	Fenwick, Edward	777	Forrest, Martha Ann	759
Elliott, Mary L.	484	Fenwick, Jack	689	Forrest, Mary	165
Elliott, Seth A.	3	**Fenwick, Julia**	344	**Forrest, Mary Helen**	715
Ellis, Mary M.	318	**Fenwick, Mary**	343	Forrest, Rebecca	780
Elwood, Isaac T.	4	**Fenwick, Mary C.**	146	**Forrest, Sarah**	242, 452, 644
Elzey, George	530	**Fenwick, Philip**	487	Forrest, Uriah (Gen.)	780
Emmert, William	287	Ferguson, Charles	490	Fortune, Grace	524
Emory, Matilda W.	738	Ferguson, Josephine	819	Foster, Annie	494
Emory, Thomas (Gen.)	738	Ferguson, Lewis	900	Foster, Benjamin	494
English, Lydia S.	584	Ferguson, Sally	864	Foster, Catharine	494
Ennis, Gregory	231	Finnick, Mary	7	Foster, Cornelius	494
Ennis, Philip	452	Fisher, Anna	263	Foster, Eugene	494

Name	Page
Foster, Margaret	494
Foster, Mary Ann	494
Foster, Nace	367
Foster, Tobias	494
Fowler, Alonza R.	489
Fowler, Elizabeth J.	583
Fowler, Hannah E.	489
Fowler, Henderson	516
Fowler, James H.	851
Fowler, Joseph	851
Fowler, Samuel	337
Francis, Catharine	675
Franklin, Stephen P.	452
Freeman, Emma E.	268
Freeman, J.B.	766
Freeman, Lewis A.	268
French, William F.	151
Frisby, Arthur	582
Fugitt, Francis J.	502
Fuller, F.M. (Mrs.)	420
Furgeson, Josephine	819
Gadsby, Augusta	307
Gadsby, John	307, 308
Gadsby, Julia	307
Gadsby, Mary Augusta	308
Gadsby, Provey	307, 308
Gadsby, William	301
Gains, Eveline	655
Gains, infant	655
Gains, Martha	655
Gains, Phillis	655
Gaither?, Zachariah	926
Gale, Eli	448
Gale, George	448
Gale, Jane	448
Gale, Margaret Eleanor Gale	783
Gallaher, Eliza A.	180
Gallaher, Eliza A.	180
Gallaher, John S., Jr.	180
Gannon, James	374
Gannon, James P.	181, 329
Gannon, Mary	469
Gantt, Caesar	628
Gantt, Ceasa A.	172
Gantt, George	644
Gantt, Georgiana	680
Gantt, Henry	408
Gantt, Louisa	680
Gantt, Lucinda	680
Gantt, Nancy	697
Gantt?, R.? O. (Mrs.)	705
Gantt, Rezin	697
Gantt, Rosa O.	172, 705
Gantt, Sophia	680
Gantt, Thomas T.	46
Gantt, Thomas T. (Mrs.)	46
Gardiner, Francis Ignatius	97
Gardner (Mr.)	403
Gardner, Charles T.	219
Gardner, Francis Ignatius	97
Gardner, Julia	219
Gardner, Juliet	219
Gardner, R.C.	219
Gardner, Rachel	77
Gardner, Thomas J.	219
Garner, Mary	899
Garner, Walter	795
Garner, William	899
Garrett, Milton	130
Garrick, Henry	109
Gasaway, Harriet	656
Gasaway, Nancy	656
Gassaway. See Gasaway.	
Geary, Frances/Francis	707
Geary, Henny	707
Geddings, Thomas	732
Getty, Margaret W.	312
Getty, Robert	312
Gibbons, John L. (Dr.)	177
Gibbs, A. Chisolm	871
Gibbs, Mary	871
Giberson, Gilbert L.	465
Gibson, Abraham	709
Gibson, Eliza	558
Gibson, Elizabeth	426
Gibson, George	426
Gibson, Henrietta	426
Gibson, Hester	558
Gibson, Jeremiah	774
Gibson, John	668
Gibson, Sarah	564
Gibson, Susan	558
Gibson, Thomas	426, 558
Gibson, William	558
Gieson?, Betts	119
Gilbert, Luke	422
Gilliam, Anna	306
Gillis, Harry	342
Gillis, Mary	342
Gilroy, John P. (Dr.)	227
Ginnell, William	893
Gittings, Benjamin E.	364, 368
Gittings, Christian	599
Gittings, Jedediah	260, 599
Gittings, P. H. C.	72
Gittings, Thomas	260, 368, 599
Gladden, Ellen	330
Gladman. See Gladmon.	
Gladmon, Ann	419
Gladmon, Darius T.	419
Gloyd, Rebecca	198
Goddard, E.A.C.	45
Goddard, Francis M.	45
Goddard, Margaret A.	45
Godey, Walt?	103
Godey, Walter	595
Goins, George	130
Goins, Malinda	130
Golden, Catharine	476
Golden, Catharine A.	477
Golden, F.	476, 477
Golden, William P.	476, 477
Goodall, Emily	183
Goodall, Milly/Milley	183
Goodwin, Henry R.	222
Goodwin, Perry	29
Goodwin, Susan A.	222
Gordon, Alexander	181
Gordon, Charles	99
Gordon, Clement	345
Gordon, David	723
Gordon, George	345
Gordon, Harriet	723
Gordon, Jane	345
Gordon, Jerry	345
Gordon, Lucy	345
Gordon, Rosanna	181
Gordon, Vincent	345
Gordon, William	181
Gormley, Margaret	277
Gormley, Philip	277
Gott, Mary E.	369
Gough, Elizabeth	789
Gough, Georgiana/Georgianna	789
Gough, Stephen	789
Gover, Charlotte	495
Gozler, Elizabeth	870
Graham, Aloysius	620
Graham, Beckie	345
Graham, Charity	345
Graham, Charley	345
Graham, Eliza	345
Graham, James Duncan (Maj.)	239
Graham, Joanna	345
Graham, Lucy	345
Graham, Matilda	232
Graham, Peter	345
Graham, Robert	345
Grammer, Christopher	515
Grammer, Gottlieb C.	515
Grammer, Julius E.	515
Grant, Hannah	210
Grant, Mary	210
Gray, Abraham Dixie	185
Gray, Benjamin	54
Gray, Caroline	88, 185, 796
Gray, Charles	796
Gray, Drusilla	54
Gray, Eliza	796
Gray, Frank	185
Gray, Grace	796
Gray, Henny	796
Gray, Jennie/Janna	185
Gray, John Asbury	796
Gray, Lucy	185, 742
Gray, Nebraska Bill	185
Gray, Orlando	796
Gray, Phebe	185
Gray, Reverdy	796
Gray, Sarah B.	209
Gray, Walter	796
Grayson, Caroline	703
Grayson, George W.	703
Green, Alexander	459
Green, Ammon	732
Green, Andrew	866
Green, Ann	52
Green, Ann/Anne	780
Green, Anna	807
Green, Bill	807
Green, Charles H.	501
Green, David	923
Green, Eliza	807
Green, Elizabeth	238
Green, Ellen	796
Green, Florence	807
Green, Gassaway	796
Green, George	459

250

Name	Page
Green, German Ignatius	97
Green, Henry	97, 501
Green, Henry, Jr.	250
Green, Henry Robert	97
Green, Henry, Sr.	250
Green, John	12, 459, 780
Green, Jonas (Dr.)	219
Green, Leona	796
Green, Maria	93, 780
Green, Martha	52
Green, Mary	52
Green, Michael	469
Green, Nancy	796
Green, Paris	241
Green, Samuel	52
Green, Sarah	200
Green, Susan	52
Green, William	796
Greenfield, Alice	618
Greenfield, Betsy	618
Greenfield, George	618
Greenfield, Louisa	618
Greenfield, Rachel	618
Greenleaf, Morganna	259
Greenleaf, William C.	253
Greenleaf, Winna Ann Cecelia	259
Greenwell, Betty	789
Greenwell, Charlotte	789
Greenwell, Emily	789
Greenwell, Emily, 2nd	789
Greenwell, Frederick J.	105
Greenwell, Louisa Jane	789
Greenwell, Martha	789
Greer, Alexander A.	682
Greer, Mary E.	682
Greeves, John	259
Greeves, Sarah Ann	259
Grey, Elsie	744
Grey, Horace	429
Grey, James	429
Grey, John	429
Grey, Nancy	429
Griffith, Lyde	570, 788
Griffith, Nacy	185
Grinful, Ann	250
Grinful, Henry	250
Gross, Basil	406
Gross, Isaac	666
Gross, Laura	198
Gross, Margaret	198
Gross, Maria	198
Gunnell, Anna	442
Gunnell, Charles	442
Gunnell, Florida	442
Gunnell, Leonard C.	30
Gunnell, Ludwell	952
Gunnell, Robert	442, 876
Gunnell, William H.	199
Gunton, William	775
Gunton, William A.	775
Gustus, Charlotte	281
Gutridge, Albert	627
Gutridge, Basil	627
Gutridge, Charles	627
Gutridge Eveline	627
Gutridge, Francis	627
Gutridge, Henrietta	627
Gutridge, Henry	627
Gutridge, Sally	627
Gutridge, Virginia	627
Guttrich, Mary	171
Guttridge, Cornelius	813
Guttridge, Margaret	813
Guttridge, Sarah Frances	813
Guy, Betty	213
Guy, Harriet	213
Guy, John Henry	213
Guy, Lila	213
Guy, Martha	213
Haddox, Minnie	534
Hagan, Stephen	464
Hager, William H.	890
Hagner?, (Dr.)	260
Haislip, Mary Ann	182
Hall (Mrs.)	419
Hall, Aaron	608
Hall, Absalom A.	757
Hall, Ann F.	171
Hall, Baruch	754, 755, 757
Hall, Benjamin H.	265
Hall, Caroline	137
Hall, Charles	869
Hall, D. A.	77
Hall, E.G.W.	611
Hall, E.J.	349
Hall, Edward	507, 757
Hall, Elisha J.	758
Hall, Eliza	619, 788
Hall, Fanny W.	77
Hall, Hannibal	669
Hall, Harry W.	755
Hall, Henry	581
Hall, Henry Lowe	615
Hall, Jacob	754, 755
Hall, Jane	869
Hall, Jerelina	137
Hall, Jeremiah	137
Hall, John	171, 669
Hall, John Wesley	137
Hall, Lavinia	374
Hall, Margaret	265, 438
Hall, Martha T.	509
Hall, Mary	377
Hall, Mary A.	374
Hall, Mary Ann	181
Hall, Matilda	581
Hall, Minta	137
Hall, Richard Henry	142
Hall, Robert L.	420
Hall, Rosa E.	754
Hall, Suckey	869
Hall, Thomas	509, 669, 757
Hall, William A.	130
Hall, William W.	918
Hall, Zilphia	669
Haller, George W.	671
Halley, Henry S.	325
Hallowell, Benjamin	834
Hamilton (Mrs.)	746
Hamilton, Ann L.	384
Hamilton, Anna M.	881
Hamilton, Isaac	879
Hamilton, John	635, 746
Hamilton, John C.C.	963
Hamilton, Margaret A.	846
Hamilton, Mary	344
Hamilton, Mary C.	713
Hamilton, Mary H.	713
Hamilton, Matilda	963
Hamilton, P.H. (Dr.)	285
Hamilton, Samuel	415, 881
Hamilton, William E.	443
Hammack, John D.	726, 739
Hammond, Debora	679
Hammond, Edward	679
Hammond, Henry	375
Hammond, John	77
Hammond, Margaret	747
Hammond, Robert	679
Hammond, Susan	679
Hampton, Cornelia	115
Hampton, Toby	116
Hancock, Andrew	498
Hancock, Maria	144
Handy, Ann	841
Handy, Dennia	571
Handy, Gathy	571
Handy, Hannah	571
Handy, Joe	571
Handy, Sanuel K. (Dr.)	554
Hanson, Amanda	637
Hanson, Clara	637
Hanson, Edward	637
Hanson, Grafton	405
Hanson, Harriet	38
Hanson, Henrietta	532
Hanson, Henry, Jr.	61
Hanson, Jane Rebecca	356
Hanson, John	356
Hanson, Lewis	846
Hanson, Margaret	356
Hanson, Milla	356
Hanson, Sarah D.	457
Hanson, Sophia	637
Hanson, William	846
Harbaugh, Ann	256
Harbaugh, D.	698
Harbaugh, John Randolph	256
Harbaugh, Joseph	15
Harbaugh, Leonard	698
Harbaugh, Winifred Sophia	698
Harbin, Catharine A.	552
Harbin, George F.	552
Harbin, Julia A.	552
Harbin, Sarah P.	552
Harbin, Walter	552
Harding, Andrew J.	721
Harding, Edward	91, 522
Harding, John	721
Harding, Joseph	522
Harding, Josiah	521
Hardy, (Dr.)	274
Hardy, William G.	904
Harley, James	600
Harley, John	600
Harley, Susan	600
Harman, Henry M.	676
Harper, Chrisa	604

Name	Page	Name	Page	Name	Page
Harper, Hannah	604	Haw, John S.	800	Hewitt, Mary A.	427
Harper, Harvey	604	Hawkins,. Fanny	857	**Hickey, William**	408
Harper, Julia Frances	604	Hawkins, Abraham Lincoln	857	Hickman, Albert	465
Harper, Levinia	604	Hawkins, Charles	153	Hickman, Daniel	935
Harper, Margetta	604	Hawkins, David	266	Hicks, Mary	235
Harper, Maria	604	Hawkins, Dick	860	Higgins, Charles A.C.	369
Harper, Susannah	604	Hawkins, Ellen	153	**Higgins, Lucretia R.**	654
Harper, Trecy/Trece	176	Hawkins, Emily	153	**Higgins, Samuel**	820
Harris, Alice	661	Hawkins, George	153, 691, 857	Higgins, Thomas L.F.	654
Harris, Amanda Augusta	510	Hawkins, Harriet	444, 523	Hill, Alice	357
Harris, Arnold	912	Hawkins, Henry	153	Hill, Ann	383
Harris, Betty	458	Hawkins, Isaac	153	**Hill, Ann M.**	472
Harris, Charles	71	Hawkins, James	153	Hill, Annie	815
Harris, Charles Asbury	510	Hawkins, John	708	Hill, Bruce	887
Harris, Cornelia	614	Hawkins, John H.	102	Hill, Cely	887
Harris, Cornelius Hunt	510	Hawkins, Lewis	153	Hill, Charles	357
Harris, Josephine	458	Hawkins, Louisa	472	**Hill, Clement**	434
Harris, Judy	71	Hawkins, Lucinda	523	Hill, Daniel	357
Harris, Kitty	510	Hawkins, Malinda	153	Hill, Eliza Jane	352
Harris, Linda	62	Hawkins, Martha	153	Hill, J.	653
Harris, Martha E.	937	Hawkins, Mary Ann	857	Hill, James David	352
Harris, Mary Ann	364	Hawkins, Mathias/Matthias	153	Hill, John	357
Harris, Noble	177	Hawkins, Sophy	860	Hill, Joseph	352
Harris, O.C.	225	Hawkins, Susan	233	Hill, Mary Ellen/Elen	352
Harris, Susan W.	912	Hawkins, Virginia	523	Hill, Rebecca	357
Harrison, Ann	520	Hawkins, William	813	Hill, Susan	815
Harrison, Benjamin	517	Haxall? (Mrs.)	89	Hill, William	434
Harrison, James E. (Capt.)	793	Hayes/Hays, Davy	785	Hill, William Henry	352
Harrison, Joseph Cornelius	520	Hayes/Hays, Elizabeth	785	Hill, William W.	37
Harrison, Kate	342	Hayes/Hays, Lewis Preston	785	Hillary, Henry	198
Harrison, Louisa	520	Hays, George	686	Hilleary, Ann T.	880
Harrison, Mary	890	Hazel/Hazle, Harriet Ann	479	**Hilleary, Eleanor B.M.**	879, 880
Harrison, R.H.	653	Hazel/Hazle, Zachariah	41, 479, 802	**Hilleary, Elizabeth A.**	132
Harrison, Rachel	517	Heiskell, P.H. (Dr.)	887	Hilleary, Henry	302
Harrison, Rebecca S.	832	Helen, Walter	517	**Hilleary, Leonard**	134
Harrison, Sarah	334	Henderson, Ann Velinda/Verlinda	57	Hilleary, S.O.	813
Harrison, William H.	130	Henshaw, J.L.	591	**Hilleary, Sarah A.**	133
Harrison, William Henry	507, 701	**Henshaw, Susanna G.**	591	Hilleary, Tilghman	879
Harrod, William	504	Hensley, John	857	Hilleary, Washington	701
Harry, John	1	Hensley, Lawrence	619	Hilliary (Mr.)	746
Harshman, Lettisha	678	Hensley, Sophia	619	Hilton, John P.	675
Harvey, Anna P.	145	Henson, Caroline	464	**Hines, Jacob**	290
Harvey, Henry	471	Henson, Delilah	822	**Hinsley, John**	634
Harvey, James S.	251	Henson, Ellen	91	Hinton, Eliza	470
Harvey, Mary Ann	471	Henson, Rebecca	125	Hinton, Emily J.	470
Harvey, Thomas	251	Henson, Thomas	770	Hinton, George J.	470
Harwood, Mary	718	Hepburn, Frank	616	Hinton, Hanson	470
Harwood, Tom	718	Hepburn, Frederick	276	Hinton, James H.	470
Haslup, J. Waters	70	Hepburn, Jenny	616	Hodges, B.? T.	525
Haslup, Mary Ann	70	Herbert, (female child)	434	**Hodges, Benjamin B.**	581
Hason, Mary Ann	545	Herbert, Ary	526	Hoffer, A.M.	241
Hasson, Henry	545	Herbert, Catharine A.	590	Hogan, Martin	106
Hasson, Mary	545	Herbert, Charles Henry	590	**Holcomb, Florence**	931
Haston, Abel	545	Herbert, Edmund	526	**Holcomb, Sarah M.**	931
Haston, Anna	545	Herbert, Emily	303	Holland, Amelia	606
Haston, John	545	Herbert, Frank	289	Holland, Ann	322
Haston, Mary	545	Herbert, Friday	732	Holland, Ann Amelia	606
Haston, William H.	545	Herbert, Henry	429	Holland, James S.	322
Hatton, Charlotte/Sharlott	216	Herbert, Levi	429	Holliday, Joseph	486
Hatton, George	61	Herbert, Martha	429	Hollyday, Albert	63
Hatton, George W.	781	Herbert, Peggy	434	Holman, E.	77
Hatton, Harriet	638	Herbert, Rebecca	289, 429	**Holmead, Mary A.**	899
Hatton, Henry	61	Herbert, T.F.	259	**Holmead, Matilda S.**	649
Hatton, Lavinia	216	**Herold, Adam G.**	592	Holmead, Sarah	649, 705
Hatton, Martha	61	**Herold, Alice King**	592	Holmes, Arena	893
Havenner, Peter	741	**Hesse, Frederick Godfrey**	243	Holmes, Harriet	573

Holmes, Henry	573	Hues, Sarah	198	Jackson, Catherine (Kate)	857
Holmes, Irene	573	**Hughes, Sarah T.**	633	Jackson, Charlotte	275
Holmes, Jefferson	573	**Hughes, Susanna**	263	Jackson, Darkey	902
Holmes, Jefferson D.	893	Hughes, Thomas	633	Jackson, Dolly	275
Holmes, John Wesley	893	**Hume, Anna M.**	262	Jackson, Eliza	197, 692
Holmes, Mary J.	259	**Hume, Charles**	262	Jackson, Elizabeth	286
Holmes, Nancy	573, 893	Hume, Eliza Priscilla	262	Jackson, Emeline/Emmeline	943
Holmes, Stephen	573, 893	Hume, Fannie Ella	262	Jackson, Fanny	731
Holmes, Thomas	573, 893	Hume, Francis	262	Jackson, Frederick, Jr.	275
Holmes, Wesley	573	Hume, Ida May	262	Jackson, Frederick, Sr.	275
Holmes, William	328	Hume, J.M.	262	Jackson, George	94
Holmes, William (Mrs.)	328	Hume, Mary Ann	262	Jackson, Harriet	957
Holt, Joseph	836	Hume, Suse Ellen	262	Jackson, James	288, 297
Holt, Thomas	836	Hume, Virginia Rawlings	262	Jackson, Jeremiah	68
Homiller, Charles	857	Humphreys (Mr.)	209	Jackson, John	562
Honesty, Lucy	702	Humphreys, Betty Ann	869	Jackson, Laura	235, 411, 625
Hood, J.H.	394	Humphreys, Edward	594	Jackson, Lucy	742
Hooe, Brother & Co.	217	Hunter (Mr.)	411	Jackson, Lydia	377
Hoover, Andrew P.	950	Hunter, George W., Jr.	240	Jackson, Martha Ann	121
Hoover, John	482	Hunton, Elizabeth E.	712	Jackson, Mary	197
Hopewell, James	429, 430, 681	Hurburt, Friday	732	Jackson, Mary Ann	68
Hopewell, Mary	536	Hurd, Sophia	735	Jackson, Mary Ellen	731
Hopewell, Rebecca	432	**Hurdle, Noble**	331	Jackson, Mary Jane	68
Hopkins, Casper Hauser	70	**Hurley, Anne M.**	559	Jackson, Millie	603
Hopkins, Charles	734	Hurley, Henry	259	Jackson, Patsy	18
Hopkins, Edgar	734	Hurley, William	558	Jackson, Polly	275
Hopkins, Eliza	734	Hurst, Jemima	876	Jackson, R.P.	16, 54, 55, 108, 202, 205, 546, 870
Hopkins, Eliza A.	26	Hutchins, David	367		
Hopkins, George W.	571, 883	Hutchins, Eliza	367	Jackson, Rachel	137, 284, 367
Hopkins, Hellen	734	Hutchins, George	367	Jackson, Richard P.	892
Hopkins, Henry	634	Hutchins, L.W.B.	906	Jackson, Sarah	197
Hopkins, John	571	Hutchins, Louisa	367	Jackson, Susan	799, 800
Hopkins, John S.	571	Hutchins, Mary	367	Jackson, Wesley	275
Hopkins, Sallie/Sarah	734	Hutchins, Rachel	367	Jackson?, Eliza	731
Hopkins, Sarah	734	Hutchins, Susan	367	**James, Charles H.**	649
Hopkins, William	734	Hutchins, Tobias	367	James, John	300
Hopp, Betty	893	Hutchinson, Ignatius	191	James, William	108, 275
Hopp, Charles	644	**Hutchinson, Margaret Ann**	188	Jamieson (Mr.)	891
Hopp, Rachel	644	Hutchinson, William	233	Jamison, Calvin	114
Horden, Elizabeth	601	Hutton, Eliza	313	Jamison, Lucy	632
Horden, Hannah	601	Hutton, Frank	313	Janifer, Nellie	846
Horseman, George	216	Hyatt (Mr.)	655	**Jarboe, Francis M.**	439
Horseman, George	638	Hyatt, C.C.	264	Jefferson, Anthony	163
Horseman, Jane E.	216	**Hyatt, Seth**	284, 579	Jefferson, Mary Louisa	447
Hoskins, Amos	499	Indian Queen Hotel	68	Jefferson, Richard H.	815
Howard, Edward Hepburn	616	Infant child of Louisa	520	Jenifer, Caroline	430
Howard, Ellick	741	Infant child of Winny Ann	589	Jenifer, Charlotte	430
Howard, Emily	741	Infant son of Fanny	514	Jenifer, Francis	677
Howard, George	741	Ingersoll, Frank	254	Jenifer, Gusty	660
Howard, Henny	616	Ingle, Edward	762	Jenifer, Neenah	430
Howard, Jackson	741	Ingle, John P.	762, 774	Jenifer, Richard	430
Howard, Lettie	741	**Ingle, Joseph**	806	Jenkins, Ann	752
Howard, Ned	390	Ingram, Phillis	655	**Jenkins, Eliza**	628
Howard, Phillis/Fillis	757	Ingram, Smith	655	Jenkins, Elizabeth	926
Howard, Tilly	741	Ingram, William	655	Jenkins, Ellen	366
Howard, Tom	741	**Ireland, Susan**	375	Jenkins, George	612
Howard, William E.	854	**Irwin, Aurelia H.**	411	Jenkins, Henrietta	53
Howell, Augustine N.Y.	777	Isaac (Mr.)	262	**Jenkins, Joseph T.**	629
Howle, Park/Parke G. (Maj.) 359, 777	358	**Isherwood, Martha**	823	Jenkins, Maria	53
		Isherwood, Robert	823	Jenkins, Mary	366
Howle, Peter C.	777	Jacks, Michael	275	Jenkins, Patty	38
Hoyle, William L.	540	Jacks, Rachel	198	Jenkins, Peter	366
Hubbard, J.S.	520	Jackson, Alice	197	Jenkins, Thomas	417
Hudley, Charlotte	934	Jackson, Andrew	197	**Jenkins, Thomas of Thomas**	417
Hues, Charles	94	Jackson, Ann	258, 800	**Johns, Jane E.**	760
Hues, Otho	94	Jackson, Caroline	121	**Johns, John S.**	811

Johns, Lucy M.	811	Jolson, Alfred	100	Joyce, Frank	962
Johnson, Aloysius	206	Jones, Addison	827	Joyce, Mary	212
Johnson, Ann	630	Jones, Adeline	59, 416	Joyce, Susan	116
Johnson, Arilla	89	Jones, Alice/Allice	707	Karna, Charles A.	228
Johnson, Baker W.	541	**Jones, Ann E.**	955	Karna, Daniel W.	228
Johnson, Charles	205, 463	Jones, Bill Hamilton	896	Karna, James W.	228
Johnson, Charlotte	89	Jones, Camilia	707	Karna, John H.	228
Johnson, Colonel	474	Jones, Caroline	59, 868	Karna, Mary C.	228
Johnson, Delilah	655	Jones, Charles	312	Keane, William	244
Johnson, Eliza A.	313	Jones, Charles Sumner	297	**Kearney, Louisa**	43
Johnson, Eliza J.	205	Jones, Charlotte	708	Kearns (Mr.)	891
Johnson, Ella	631	Jones, Christiana	59	Keech, Samuel	192
Johnson, Ellen	498	Jones, Cornelia	707	Keech, Susannah Harriet	192
Johnson, Frank	718	Jones, Daniel	782	Keefe, John A.	301
Johnson, George J.	862	Jones, Edward	868	Keefe, Martha Ann	301
Johnson, Hannah	206, 750	**Jones, Elisha**	868	Keene, Benjamin R.	948
Johnson, Harriet	34, 313, 533	Jones, Eliza	45, 893	**Keene, Susan**	948
Johnson, Henrietta	420	Jones, Eliza Ann	617	**Keese, Augustus E. L.**	88
Johnson, Jane	328, 814, 866	**Jones, Ellen C.**	441	Keffert, Leah	876
Johnson, Jemima	814	Jones, F.W.	441, 442	Keich, J.C.S.	962
Johnson, Jenny	491	**Jones, Frances J.**	421	Keith, James	715
Johnson, Jess/Jesse	440	Jones, Frederick W.	708	Keith, Mary Helen	715
Johnson, Joe	962	Jones, George	707	Kelleher and Pywell	351
Johnson, John	314, 694, 866	Jones, George H.	421	**Kelley, Ann**	101
Johnson, John Barnes	577	Jones, Gusty	725	**Kelley, John T.**	108
Johnson, John H.	28	Jones, Harriet	298	**Kendall, John W.**	934
Johnson, John Henry	841	Jones, Isaac	412, 655	**Kengla, Henry**	797
Johnson, Joseph	89, 361, 487, 959	Jones, Isaiah (Isaac)	412	Kennedy & Pugh	253
Johnson, Joshua	46	Jones, Jack	125	**Kennedy, Henrietta J.**	383
Johnson, Lewis	487	Jones, Jennie	416	Kennedy, J.C.	230
Johnson, Louisa	911	Jones, John	416, 955, 893	Kent (Col.)	150
Johnson, Lucinda	765	Jones, Jubah	689	Kent, Daniel	142
Johnson, Maria	465	Jones, Julia	59	Kent, Dewitt	739
Johnson, Maria Burley	80	Jones, Lloyd	507	Kent, Joseph	515
Johnson, Martha	436, 718	Jones, Louisa	297	Keppler, Isaac	701
Johnson, Martha Ann	508	Jones, Lucien	550	Kerby, George W.	962
Johnson, Mary	205, 463, 738, 962	Jones, Lucretia	868	Kerby, J. Owen	962
Johnson, Mary Clare	463	Jones, Lucy	125, 893	Kerr, Alexander	30
Johnson, Mary W.	296	Jones, Lucy Ann	650	Kerr, Archibald	395
Johnson, Minnie Ann	21	**Jones, Mary**	536	**Kerr, Henrietta**	30
Johnson, Nace	333	Jones, Mary Jane	427	**Kerr, Mary Ann**	30
Johnson, Rachel	765	Jones, Mary Verlinda	416	Key, Avonia	224
Johnson, Rebecca	911	Jones, Matilda	896	Key, Caroline	658
Johnson, Richard	898	Jones, Nelson	259	Key, Catharine Virginia	224
Johnson, Robert	962	Jones, Richard Isaac	397	Key, Charles Richard	224
Johnson, Sally	395	**Jones, Richard L.**	397	Key, Ellen	658
Johnson, Sarah	446	**Jones, Robert**	441	Key, H.G.S.	689
Johnson, Simeon M.	848	Jones, Robert C.	49	Key, Lucinda (Lucy)	224
Johnson, Susan	463	**Jones, Roger**	448	Key, Mary Alice	224
Johnson, Thomas	750	Jones, Roger (Gen.)	448	**Kibbey, William B.**	2, 482
Johnson, Washington	691	Jones, Rosanna	868	**Kidwell, John L.**	435
Johnson, William	154, 463, 654, 866, 959	Jones, Rosetta	427	Kiekoffer? (Mr.)	602
		Jones, Rosina	868	**Kilgour, Charlotte**	230
Johnson, William Alexander	888	Jones, Sally	565	Kilgour, Elizabeth	230
Johnson, Winnie Ann	21	**Jones, Sarah**	94, 749	**Kilgour, Isabella**	230
Johnston, Catherine	936	Jones, Susan	288	Kilgour, Martha	230
Johnston, Delilah	655	Jones, Thomas	859	**Kimmell, Abraham F.**	699, 902
Johnston, Dennis	827, 828, 829, 830, 938	Jones, Thomas W.	188	King, Charles	715
		Jones, William	627, 815	King, Elizabeth Ann	77
Johnston, Francis, Sr.	938	**Jones, William B.**	859	**King, Ellen J.**	852
Johnston, Horace S.	114	Jones, Z.	93	King, George	307
Johnston, Jane	830	Jordan, Eliza	722	King, Harriet	379
Johnston, Mary	827	Jordan, Milly	425	King, Henry	307
Johnston, William S.	828, 829	Jordan, Nelly	209	King, Jacob F.	893
Jokey, Betsey/Betsy	763	Jourdan, Milly	105	King, James	547
Jokey, John	763	**Joy, Helen L.**	756	King, Joe	884

King, John	547	Laskey, Richard H.	569	Lee, Wallace	508
King, John H.	852	Laughlin, Samuel H.	478	**Lee, William**	173, 583, 795
King, Lucien	547	Lawrence, Mary	259	Lee, William Arthur	842
King, Maria	307	Lawson, Catherine	664	Lee, William H.	233
King, Martha	128, 307	Lawson, Melinda	664	**Leiberman, Charles H.**	782
King, Nancy	547	Lazenby, Thomas A.	622	Leitch. *See Litch.*	
King, Ned	884	**Le Compte, Anna**	267	Leland, Luther L.	501
King, Peter	592	Le Compte, James L.	267	**Lenman, Charles**	944
King, Sarah E.	461	Leapley, P.N.	493	Lenman, Mary Elizabeth	720
King, Thomas A.	109	**Lear, Mary D.**	336	Leonard, Lucretia	515
King, Thompson	547	**Leddy, Owen**	126, 469	Letis, Kitty	816
King, William	547	Lee, Adam	948	Lewis, Alice	607
Kirby, Baptist	859	Lee, Addie	153	Lewis, Anthony	816
Kirkland, Jonathan	72	Lee, Alexander	842	Lewis, Belinda	816
Kirkwood (Mrs.?)	46	Lee, Alfred	737	Lewis, C.O.	701
Kirkwood Hotel	790	Lee, Alice	962	Lewis, Cora	607
Kitchen, Jesse W.	204	Lee, Amelia Jane	842	Lewis, Elizabeth	863
Kloeppinger, Christopher	602	Lee, Anthony	886	Lewis, George N.	2
Knode, Israel	493	Lee, Basil	314	Lewis, Geraldine	457
Knott, Charles	453	Lee, Bland (Mrs.)	447	Lewis, Harriet	816
Knott, Elenora/Ellenora	566	Lee, Charles	288	Lewis, Helen	607
Knowles, Thomas	791	Lee, Charlotte	508	Lewis, Jane	875
Kolp, Eliza	598	Lee, Clinton	508	Lewis, Lishy	863
Krafft, George S.	699	Lee, Dick	408	Lewis, Lizzie	457
Krafft, Mary C.	556	Lee, Edmonia	737	Lewis, Margaret	457
Krumbhaar, Sophia	504	Lee, Edward	163	Lewis, Maria	816
Kulp, John	141	Lee, Elias	506	Lewis, Marion	457
Kurtz, John	807	Lee, Eliza	583, 737	Lewis, Mary	2, 875
Kurtz, William H.	426	Lee, Eliza Ann	737	Lewis, Mashack	607
Lacy, Mary Jane	292	Lee, Ellen	233, 583, 794	Lewis, Oscar	607
Lacy, Robert A.	458	Lee, Fanny	615	Libbey/Libby, Joseph	300, 671, 930
Lacy, William B.	292	Lee, Francis X.	233	Lieberman. *See Leiberman.*	
Lacy, William B.	291	Lee, George	153, 794	Linch, Truman	930
Lambell, K. N.	181	Lee, Hannah	626	Lindsay, John G.	104
Lambell, William	902	Lee, Henny	384	Lindsay, Samuel D.	104
Lambert, John J.	82	Lee, Henry	46, 241, 574	**Lindsley, Eleazer**	86
Lammond, Peter	318	Lee, J.	450	Lingon?, Mary	152
Lancaster, Ammy	605	Lee, Jane	508	**Linthicum, Edward M.**	719
Lancaster, Eliza	8, 170	Lee, John	173, 233	Linthicum, Mary	719
Lancaster, F.H.	288	Lee, Julia	506	Linton, John A.	492
Lancaster, Henny	8	Lee, Juliet	84	**Linton, Martha A.**	707
Lancaster, Henrietta	170	Lee, Leslie	737	**Linton, William A.**	492
Lancaster, Henry	8, 170, 346	Lee, Lettie	737	Litch, John	788
Lancaster, James	170	Lee, Loretta	173	**Little, John**	744, 745, 746
Lancaster, John	8, 170	Lee, Louis	572	**Little, John O.**	745
Lancaster, Louis Napoleon Bonapart	170	Lee, Louisa	84	**Little, Julia A.**	746
Lancaster, Lucy	8	Lee, Margaret	583	Little, Samuel J.	745, 746
Lancaster, Matthew	8	Lee, Margaret Ann	233	Lloyd,	130
Lancaster, Nathan	8	Lee, Maria	220, 962	Lloyd, A.	489, 668
Lancaster, Rachel	8	Lee, Martha A.	233	Lloyd, Anthony	600
Lancaster, Susan	346	Lee, Mary	148, 173, 583, 794	**Lloyd, Asbury**	810, 877
Landreth, Sarah	319	Lee, Mary C.	233	**Lloyd, E.E.**	393
Landreth, Sarah A.	319	Lee, Mary Caroline	378	Lloyd, Edward	600
Landreth, Sarah Ann	62	Lee, Mary Eliza	737	Lloyd, H.M.	393
Lang, Eleanor R.	152, 153	Lee, Nancy	56	Lloyd, Henry	600
Lang, Emily	727	Lee, Price Birch?	617	Lloyd, Mary	600
Lang, Nathan	956	Lee, Richard B.	952	**Lloyd, Matilda**	903
Lang, Robert	727	Lee, Richard B. (Maj.)	442	**Lloyd, Richard B.**	393
Langley, William H.	21	Lee, Rosanna/Rosannah	153	Lloyd, Sarah	600
Lanham, Hezekeiah	711	Lee, Rose	934	Lloyd, Thomas E.	181, 280
Lanham, Julia	464	Lee, Rosie	842	Locke, Charlotte Ann	92
Lanham, Meekey	711	Lee, Sinah E.	607	Locke, Henrietta	68
Lanham, Richard	464	Lee, Susan	842	Locke, Lewis Washington	92
Larner, Christiana	107	Lee, Theodore	233	Lofflin, Samuel H.	478
Larner, Michael	107	Lee, Thomas Sim	450	Loggins, Jane	341
Lashley, Caroline	903	Lee, Thornton	842	Loggins, Margaret	341

Loggins, Mary	341
Loker, Thomas	723
Loker, W.	802
Loomis, Silas L.	488
Loughborough, Margaret A.	173
Loughborough, Margaret H.	173
Lounds, Leah	922
Lourge, Rachel	571
Lowe, Barbara	393
Lowe, Dennis	198
Lowe, Susanna	676
Lowndes, Samuel	883
Lowndes, Solomon	883
Lowrie, Margaret E.	437
Lowry, Ann	764
Lowry, George	371, 764
Lowry, George (Mrs.)	371
Lowry, Steptoe	764
Lucas, Caroline	181
Lucas, Eliza	205
Lucas, Kitty	712
Luckett, Penoply (Mrs.)	241
Luckett, W.	634
Ludlow, John	796
Lyddane, Edmund	835
Lyddane, Thomas	835
Lydock, Mary	394
Lyles, Albert	494
Lyles, Amelia	268
Lyles, Ariana	538
Lyles, Arianna J.	867
Lyles, Benjamin	494
Lyles, Catharine	494
Lyles, Dennis M.	867
Lyles, Elizabeth	494
Lyles, Emma	494
Lyles, Frank	387
Lyles, Leander	494
Lyles, Matilda	494
Lyles, Osceola	494
Lyles, Rachael	494
Lyles, Rebecca	494
Lyles, Sarah	387
Lynch, James	265
Lynch, Truman	930
Lynch, William	930
Lyons, Catharine S.	769
Lyons, Charles	690
Lyons, Jacob E.	690
Lyons, Joseph	769
MacDaniel, Albert	147
Macdaniel/McDaniel, Ann	211, 805
MacGill, Emily	195
Mackall, Benjamin F.	442
Mackall, Caroline	110
Mackall, Henson	572
MacKenny, Henry	670
Mackey, Mary	573
Mackey, Philip	573, 893
Macoy, Eliza	558
Maddox, Alexander	12
Maddox, Catharine A.M.	372
Maddox, Charles	319
Maddox, Edward	62
Maddox, Elizabeth	319
Maddox, Elizabeth Jane	373
Maddox, F.T.	455
Maddox, John	400
Maddox, Margaret Ann	399, 400
Maddox, Maria	319
Maddox, Mary Jane	12
Maddox, Notley	345
Maddox, Thomas	319
Maddox William A.T. (Capt.)	270
Maddox, William R.	372, 373
Magruder, Ann	255
Magruder, Daniel	145
Magruder, Dennis	117
Magruder, Eleanor	931
Magruder, Ellen	117
Magruder, Emeline	255
Magruder, Fielder	190
Magruder, Hezekiah (Dr.)	414, 615
Magruder, John	255
Magruder, Louisa	825
Magruder, Lucy Chase	145
Magruder, Ninian (Dr.)	885
Magruder, Thomas C.	124, 891
Magruder, William B.	349
Magruder, William H.	362
Magruder, Zadock	882
Maguder, Julian	882
Maguire, James	730
Maguire, Martina	730
Magurder, C.C.	422
Mahoney, Benjamin	569
Mahoney, Charles	732
Mahoney, Jane Ella	261
Maize, William	459
Mankin, John W.	537
Mann, Charles H.	578
Manning, F.	656
Manning, Ignatius	317
Manning, John	317
Manning, Martha	71
Manning, Mary	271
Manning, Mary M.	656
Manning, W.A.. (Dr.)	317
Manning, Wilfred A.	486
Mansfield, William	634
Marbury (Col.)	152
Marbury, Ann O.	184
Marbury, George	729
Marbury, J.C.	632
Marbury, John	184, 729
Marbury, John, Jr.	714
Marbury, William	506
Marks, Henry E.	919
Marks, Samuel A. H.	145
Marks, Samuel H.	913
Marks, William A.	913
Marler, Benjamin	962
Marlow, Margaret	713
Marlow, Mary (Lydia)	695
Marlow, Walter H.	327
Marriott, George H.	925
Marsh (Mr.)	538
Marsh, Otis W.	221
Marshal, Frank	877
Marshall, Bettsey	645
Marshall, Charles	645
Marshall, Charlotte	497
Marshall, Chloe	611
Marshall, Eleanor A.H.	697
Marshall, Ellen	107
Marshall, Hanson	867
Marshall, Harriet R.	697
Marshall, Julia Ann	250
Marshall, Martha	107
Marshall, Mary Ann	414
Marshall, Richard	644
Marshall, Thomas	816
Marshall, William	479, 465
Martin	674
Martin (Mr.)	287
Martin, Alexander	525
Martin, Brice	752
Martin, Davy	25
Martin, Fanny	25
Martin, George	184
Martin, Henry	191
Martin, Kitty	84
Martin, Lucinda	66
Martin, Moses	25
Martin, Rachel	525
Martin, Samuel	882
Martine, Andrew	423
Maryman, Horatio	802
Masi, Francis	155
Masi, Seraphim	155
Mason, Frank	653
Mason, Harriet	666
Mason, Isaac	549
Mason, Joseph	653
Mason, Lloyd	905
Mason, Lucinda	649
Mason, Priscilla	649
Mason, Rachel	649
Mason, Richard	43
Mason, Sarah	790
Mason, Sarah Frances	810
Mason, Sophia	790
Mason, Susan	715
Mason, William	790
Massey, George W.	474
Massey, Mary	910
Massi, *See Masi*	
Massi *See Massy*	
Massy, Dick	408
Massy, John	408
Masters, Nathan B.	353
Mathews, Alfred	288
Mathews, Charles	210
Mathews, Charlotte/Sharlotte	511
Mathews, George	210
Mathews, infant child of Lucinda	526
Mathews, John	288, 526
Mathews, Lucinda	526
Mathews, Maria	210
Mathews, Mary A.E.	921
Mathews, Henry C.	799, 800
Mathews, Lucinda S.	799, 800
Mathews, Milley	288
Mathews, Richard	210
Mathews, Sally T.	28
Mathews, Sarah	210
Mathews, Susan	848
Mathews, Teresa	288

Mathews, William	511, 526, 930	McKinsey, Charlotte K.E.	372	**Middleton, Erasmus J.**	724, 725, 749
Matthews, Alexander	799, 800	McKinsey, Mary E.	372	**Middleton, Lemuel J.**	761
Matthews, Charles M.	167	McKnew, Maria M.	178	Middleton, Minty	103
Matthews, Eliza	233	McKnew, Mary	683	Middleton, Nancy	753
Matthews, Henry C.	49, 587, 799, 800	**McKnew, Nathan C.**	87	Middleton, Polly	103
Matthews, Lucinda S.	799, 800	McKnew, Thomas	87	Middleton, Theodore	567
Matthews, Mary A.	438	**McKnew, William**	683, 956	Milburn, Benedict	873
Matthews, William	193	**McKnight, Catharine**	928	Miles, Adelaide	241
Matthews, William S.	438	McKnight, Martha H.	139	Miles, Ann	241
Mattingley, W.F.	314	McLain, Harriet Louisa	878	Miles, Dominick	241
Mattingly (Mr.)	200	McLain, Julia	878	Miles, Harriet	552
Mattingly, Edward	453	**McLain, William**	447	Miles, Lucy	241
Mattingly, George	241, 282	McLean, Eugene	878	**Miller, Catzarina**	394
Mattingly, John	454	McLean, Fanny	878	**Miller, Charles**	425, 686
Mattingly, Lucy E.	453, 454	McLeod, Mary Helen	73	**Miller, Eliza**	394
Maughon?, Sarrah E.	270	**McLeod, Matthew**	271	Miller, Eliza Ariss	174
Maury, Isabel	833	**McNantz, Patrick H.**	248	Miller, Ellen	425
Maury, John W.	833	McNeil, Duncan	219	**Miller, Francis**	394
Maury, Jourdan W.	696	McNeir, Sally Maria	696	**Miller, George**	394
Maxwell (Mr.)	384	McNeir, Thomas? S.	696	Miller, George W.	425
May, John Frederick	964	McPhearson, Priscilla	720	**Miller, Harriet**	174
McAlister, Caroline	753	McPherson, Charles	860	**Miller, Henry**	394
McBlair, Augusta	307	McPherson, Ginnie	3	**Miller, Lucy R.**	174
McBlair, J. Hollis	307	McPherson, Mary Ann	381, 884	**Miller, Margaret Ann**	752
McCeney, George	137	McPherson, Priscilla	720	**Miller, Maria**	174, 175
McCeney, Joseph	137	McPherson, Rebecca	860	Miller, Mary Ann	512
McClellan, George (Gen.)	286	**McPherson, Robert L.**	538	Miller, Matilda	800
McCormick (Mr.)	297	McQuay, Benjamin	525	**Miller, Thomas W.**	394
McCormick, A.G.? (Rev.)	451	McWilliams, Clement	155	**Miller, Washington**	316
McCormick, Hannah P.	451	McWilliams, John S.	471	**Miller, William**	174, 175
McCormick, Margaret L.	451	Mead, Kitty	925	Miller, William J.	335, 506
McCormick, Mary E.	451	Mealy, Alice	341	**Mills, Clark**	741
McCormick, Sophia	451	Mearing, George	570	Mills, E.B.	537
McCubbins, William	956	Mechlin, A.H.	534	**Mills, Eliza B.**	665
McDaniel, James W.	834	**Mechlin, Alexander H.**	399, 400	Mills, Eliza M.	169
McDaniel, Jemima	834	**Mechlin, Florence**	400	Mills, Emma	257
McDaniel, Lucy Ellen	834	**Mechlin, Georgie**	534	Mills, John	169
McDermott, Arthur	225	Meekins, Alexander	36	Mills, Nancy	169
McDermott, Francis	225	Meekins, Harrison	36	Mills, Robert	665
McDermott, James	225	Meekins, Mary Columbia	865	Mills, William	169, 274
McDermott, John	225, 226	Meekins, Rachel	726	Millstead, Ignatius	502
McDermott, Michael	226	Meekins, Robert	36	Minor, Ann M.	731
McDonald, James E.	77	Melvin, Charles B.	424	**Minor, Elizabeth**	731
McDonald, Stephen	318	**Melvin, Josiah**	10	Minor, George	39
McDowell, General	123	**Mercer of R., Andrew**	716	Minor, Jane	39
McElfresh (Mr.)	672	**Mercer, Thomas S.**	467	Minor, Marietta S.	519
McElfresh, John	716	Meredith, Alfred	1	**Minor, Smith**	386
McGill, John	512	Meredith, Charles	1	Mitchell, Jerry	270
McGinnis, Elizabeth	679	Meredith, Eveline	1	Mitchell, John	163, 502
McGinnis, John	679	Meredith, Henry	1	**Mitchell, Joseph T.**	958
McGregor, Roderick M.	301	Meredith, John	1	**Mitchell, Judson**	714
McGrunder/McGrundy James	209	Meredith, Kate	1	Mitchell, Kitty	163
McGuire, James C.	572	Meredith, Lizzie	1	Mitchell, Nelly	163
McGuire, Thomas	617	Meredith, Lydia	1	**Mix, Charles E.**	896
McHenry, John (Dr.)	665	Meredith, Maria	1	Mockabee, Ann	795
McIntire, Alexander	318	Meredith, Philip	1	Mockabee, Frank	795, 885
McIntire, John E.	318	Meredith, Richard	1	Mockabee, Henny	795
McIntire, Laura E.	318	Meredith, Rogers	1	Mockabee, Henry	795
McIntire, Mary Eliza	318	Meredith, Susan	421	Mockabee, Louisa	795
McIntire, Mary M.	318	Middleton & Beall	217	Mockabee, Mary	795
McIntire, William A.	318	Middleton, Alpheus	499	Mockabee, Rose	795
McKelden, John C.	540	**Middleton, Benjamin F.**	217, 499	Mockabee, Sarah	795
McKeldin, John	112	**Middleton, Charles S.**	567	**Mohun, Francis**	695
McKenney, John	808	**Middleton, Daniel W.**	762	Molden, Sarah Ann	465
McKenney, John, Sr.	808	Middleton, Ellen	945	**Monroe, Georgiana**	626
McKenzie, Geoffrey	744	**Middleton, Ellen Ross**	724, 725	Monroe, Lawrench	626

Monroe, Susanna	201	
Monroe, Thomas	201	
Montgomery, Abigail	280	
Montgomery, Adelaide	525	
Montgomery, Andrew	23	
Montgomery, Ann Maria	870	
Montgomery, Charles	852	
Montgomery, Elizabeth	97, 280	
Montgomery, Georgiana	280	
Montgomery, Isaac	280	
Montgomery, James	301	
Montgomery, Lucy	525	
Montgomery, Maria	557	
Montgomery, Sidney	525	
Moore, Benjamin	24	
Moore, Davis	168	
Moore, Eleanor C.	197	
Moore, Elizabeth	612	
Moore, Eveline	24	
Moore, Frederick	24	
Moore, George	586	
Moore, George M.	560	
Moore, Isaac	195	
Moore, James	600	
Moore, John	187	
Moore, John Lewis	586	
Moore, Lettice C.	197	
Moore, Lucy	586	
Moore, Mary	38	
Moore, Richard	586	
Moore, Sallie	24	
Moore, Simon	764	
Moore, William H.	480, 586	
Moran, Horatio	123	
Moran, John	123	
Morehead, A.H.	612	
Morehouse, Alanson	927	
Moreland, Eliza G.	95	
Moreland, Notley	333	
Morgan, E.C.	442	
Morgan, Evelina	442	
Morgan, James E. (Dr.)	657	
Morris, Henny	184	
Morris, Henry M.	359	
Morrison, William H.	220	
Morsell, Benjamin K.	5	
Morsell, James S.	609	
Morsell, Jane Gray	785	
Morsell, Joshua	785	
Morton, Archey/Archy	75	
Morton, Isabella	735	
Mosby, John G.	447	
Moseley, Anne E.	19	
Mosher, Eliza M.	885	
Mosher, Theodore	636	
Mosher, Theodore	886	
Moss, A.	448	
Moss, Robert B.	292	
Moulden, Notley	465	
Moulden, Sarah Ann	465	
Moxley? (Mr.)	287	
Moxley, Alberry	28	
Moxley, Mary	79, 81	
Mudd,	525	
Mudd, Catharine	283	
Mudd, Charlotte	707	
Mudd, Emily B.	618	
Mudd, George P.	707	
Mudd, Henry S.	861	
Mudd, J. H. Clay	618	
Mudd, Julia Ann	248	
Mudd, Mary	618	
Mullican, Cassy	669	
Mullihin, John B.	775	
Mullikin, Francis	76	
Mullikin, Samuel	457	
Muncaster, Harriet E.	882	
Muncaster, Otto Z.	882	
Munroe, Henry	403	
Munson, Cornelia	812	
Munson, Dolly	812	
Munson, Owen (Dr.)	812	
Murdock, Addison	233	
Murdock, William D.C.	233	
Murphy, Thomas	900	
Murray, Charles	928	
Murray, Mary	928	
Murray, Mary H.	713	
Murray, Sally	128	
Murray, Stanislaus	156, 285, 392, 713	
Myers, Charles	51	
Myers, Maria	896	
Nailor, Alison, Jr.	864	
Nailor, Allison	576, 726, 739, 865, 959	
Nailor, Dickinson	104	
Nailor, Lizzie R.	865	
Nailor, Thompson	465	
Nailor, Thompson	726	
Nailor, William	446	
Nailor. *See also Naylor.*		
Napa, Virginia	113	
Nash, Adelaide	459	
Nash, Arabella	459	
Nash, Archy	459	
Nash, George Ruffin	459	
Nash, Horace	459	
Nash, infant	459	
Nash, James	459	
Nash, Martha	459	
Nash, Mary E.	69	
Nash, Selima	459	
National Hotel	790	
Naughton, Milly	966	
Naylor, (Col.)	473	
Naylor, Allison	739	
Naylor, Ann	691, 841	
Naylor, Francis Y.	841	
Naylor, George	705, 706	
Naylor, Henry	403, 705, 706, 729, 841	
Naylor, James George	585	
Naylor, John Lawson	404	
Naylor, John Lawson (Capt.)	197	
Naylor, John T.	403	
Naylor, Judson	403	
Naylor, Van Deusen	403	
Naylor, Verlinda	404	
Naylor. *See also Nailor.*		
Nead, Winnefred	932	
Neal, Fannie	536n	
Neal, John	569	
Neal, Louis	536	
Neal, Margaret	569	
Neale, John E.	170	
Neale, Lewis	536	
Negro Abraham	125, 143	
Negro Adaline	9	
Negro Agnes	317	
Negro Aldezina	549	
Negro Alethe	317	
Negro Alexander	589	
Negro Alfred	317, 651, 844	
Negro Alice	83, 165, 628, 760	
Negro Aloysius	835	
Negro Amanda	70	
Negro Amelia	116	
Negro Anachy?	230	
Negro Ananias	387	
Negro Ann	129, 219, 689	
Negro Ann Maria	326	
Negro Anna	217	
Negro Anne	909	
Negro Annie	116, 907	
Negro Anthony	549, 867	
Negro Baptist	176	
Negro Barbara	947	
Negro Barney	387	
Negro Beckie/Becky	505	
Negro Benjamin	116, 191	
Negro Betsy	852	
Negro Betty	505, 549	
Negro Bill	482	
Negro Blanche	686	
Negro Bob	129, 171, 210	
Negro Boker/Booker	943	
Negro California	587	
Negro Caroline	14, 147, 465, 894, 794	
Negro Catharine	123, 528, 794	
Negro Catharine Louisa	874	
Negro Cato	787	
Negro Cecilia	86	
Negro Cecy	176	
Negro Charity	42	
Negro Charles	89, 143, 287, 325, 505	
Negro Charles Henry (Osceola)	86	
Negro Charles Montgomery	852	
Negro Charley	482	
Negro Charlotte	89, 143, 217, 317, 453, 549, 726, 752, 909	
Negro Chloe	846	
Negro Clement	884	
Negro Cline	35	
Negro Comfort	554	
Negro Cooper	554	
Negro Cora	120	
Negro Crissey	670	
Negro Cynthia	175, 393	
Negro Daniel	783	
Negro Delia	322	
Negro Delilah	70	
Negro Delozier	387	
Negro Dennis	787	
Negro Dinah	785	
Negro Dolly	199	
Negro Dominick	39	
Negro Douglass	191	
Negro Easter	697	
Negro Eddy	325	
Negro Ede	554	

Mathews, William	511, 526, 930	McKinsey, Charlotte K.E.	372	**Middleton, Erasmus J.**	724, 725, 749
Matthews, Alexander	799, 800	McKinsey, Mary E.	372	**Middleton, Lemuel J.**	761
Matthews, Charles M.	167	McKnew, Maria M.	178	Middleton, Minty	103
Matthews, Eliza	233	McKnew, Mary	683	Middleton, Nancy	753
Matthews, Henry C.	49, 587, 799, 800	**McKnew, Nathan C.**	87	Middleton, Polly	103
Matthews, Lucinda S..	799, 800	McKnew, Thomas	87	Middleton, Theodore	567
Matthews, Mary A.	438	**McKnew, William**	683, 956	Milburn, Benedict	873
Matthews, William	193	**McKnight, Catharine**	928	Miles, Adelaide	241
Matthews, William S.	438	McKnight, Martha H.	139	Miles, Ann	241
Mattingley, W.F.	314	McLain, Harriet Louisa	878	Miles, Dominick	241
Mattingly (Mr.)	200	McLain, Julia	878	Miles, Harriet	552
Mattingly, Edward	453	**McLain, William**	447	Miles, Lucy	241
Mattingly, George	241, 282	McLean, Eugene	878	**Miller, Catzarina**	394
Mattingly, John	454	McLean, Fanny	878	**Miller, Charles**	425, 686
Mattingly, Lucy E.	453, 454	McLeod, Mary Helen	73	**Miller, Eliza**	394
Maughon?, Sarrah E.	270	**McLeod, Matthew**	271	Miller, Eliza Ariss	174
Maury, Isabel	833	**McNantz, Patrick H.**	248	Miller, Ellen	425
Maury, John W.	833	McNeil, Duncan	219	**Miller, Francis**	394
Maury, Jourdan W.	696	McNeir, Sally Maria	696	**Miller, George**	394
Maxwell (Mr.)	384	McNeir, Thomas? S.	696	Miller, George W.	425
May, John Frederick	964	McPhearson, Priscilla	720	**Miller, Harriet**	174
McAlister, Caroline	753	McPherson, Charles	860	**Miller, Henry**	394
McBlair, Augusta	307	McPherson, Ginnie	3	**Miller, Lucy R.**	174
McBlair, J. Hollis	307	McPherson, Mary Ann	381, 884	**Miller, Margaret Ann**	752
McCeney, George	137	McPherson, Priscilla	720	**Miller, Maria**	174, 175
McCeney, Joseph	137	McPherson, Rebecca	860	Miller, Mary Ann	512
McClellan, George (Gen.)	286	**McPherson, Robert L.**	538	Miller, Matilda	800
McCormick (Mr.)	297	McQuay, Benjamin	525	**Miller, Thomas W.**	394
McCormick, A.G.? (Rev.)	451	McWilliams, Clement	155	Miller, Washington	316
McCormick, Hannah P.	451	McWilliams, John S.	471	**Miller, William**	174, 175
McCormick, Margaret L.	451	Mead, Kitty	925	Miller, William J.	335, 506
McCormick, Mary E.	451	Mealy, Alice	341	**Mills, Clark**	741
McCormick, Sophia	451	Mearing, George	570	Mills, E.B.	537
McCubbins, William	956	Mechlin, A.H.	534	**Mills, Eliza B.**	665
McDaniel, James W.	834	**Mechlin, Alexander H.**	399, 400	Mills, Eliza M.	169
McDaniel, Jemima	834	**Mechlin, Florence**	400	Mills, Emma	257
McDaniel, Lucy Ellen	834	**Mechlin, Georgie**	534	Mills, John	169
McDermott, Arthur	225	Meekins, Alexander	36	Mills, Nancy	169
McDermott, Francis	225	Meekins, Harrison	36	Mills, Robert	665
McDermott, James	225	Meekins, Mary Columbia	865	Mills, William	169, 274
McDermott, John	225, 226	Meekins, Rachel	726	Millstead, Ignatius	502
McDermott, Michael	226	Meekins, Robert	36	Minor, Ann M.	731
McDonald, James E.	77	Melvin, Charles B.	424	**Minor, Elizabeth**	731
McDonald, Stephen	318	**Melvin, Josiah**	10	Minor, George	39
McDowell, General	123	**Mercer of R., Andrew**	716	Minor, Jane	39
McElfresh (Mr.)	672	**Mercer, Thomas S.**	467	Minor, Marietta S.	519
McElfresh, John	716	Meredith, Alfred	1	**Minor, Smith**	386
McGill, John	512	Meredith, Charles	1	Mitchell, Jerry	270
McGinnis, Elizabeth	679	Meredith, Eveline	1	Mitchell, John	163, 502
McGinnis, John	679	Meredith, Henry	1	**Mitchell, Joseph T.**	958
McGregor, Roderick M.	301	Meredith, John	1	**Mitchell, Judson**	714
McGrunder/McGrundy James	209	Meredith, Kate	1	Mitchell, Kitty	163
McGuire, James C.	572	Meredith, Lizzie	1	Mitchell, Nelly	163
McGuire, Thomas	617	Meredith, Lydia	1	**Mix, Charles E.**	896
McHenry, John (Dr.)	665	Meredith, Maria	1	Mockabee, Ann	795
McIntire, Alexander	318	Meredith, Philip	1	Mockabee, Frank	795, 885
McIntire, John E.	318	Meredith, Richard	1	Mockabee, Henny	795
McIntire, Laura E.	318	Meredith, Rogers	1	Mockabee, Henry	795
McIntire, Mary Eliza	318	Meredith, Susan	421	Mockabee, Louisa	795
McIntire, Mary M.	318	Middleton & Beall	217	Mockabee, Mary	795
McIntire, William A.	318	Middleton, Alpheus	499	Mockabee, Rose	795
McKelden, John C.	540	**Middleton, Benjamin F.**	217, 499	Mockabee, Sarah	795
McKeldin, John	112	**Middleton, Charles S.**	567	**Mohun, Francis**	695
McKenney, John	808	**Middleton, Daniel W.**	762	Molden, Sarah Ann	465
McKenney, John, Sr.	808	Middleton, Ellen	945	**Monroe, Georgiana**	626
McKenzie, Geoffrey	744	**Middleton, Ellen Ross**	724, 725	Monroe, Lawrench	626

Monroe, Susanna 201	Mudd, Emily B. 618	**Neale, John E.** 170
Monroe, Thomas 201	Mudd, George P. 707	Neale, Lewis 536
Montgomery, Abigail 280	Mudd, Henry S. 861	Negro Abraham 125, 143
Montgomery, Adelaide 525	Mudd, J. H. Clay 618	Negro Adaline 9
Montgomery, Andrew 23	Mudd, Julia Ann 248	Negro Agnes 317
Montgomery, Ann Maria 870	Mudd, Mary 618	Negro Aldezina 549
Montgomery, Charles 852	Mullican, Cassy 669	Negro Alethe 317
Montgomery, Elizabeth 97, 280	Mullihin, John B. 775	Negro Alexander 589
Montgomery, Georgiana 280	Mullikin, Francis 76	Negro Alfred 317, 651, 844
Montgomery, Isaac 280	Mullikin, Samuel 457	Negro Alice 83, 165, 628, 760
Montgomery, James 301	**Muncaster, Harriet E.** 882	Negro Aloysius 835
Montgomery, Lucy 525	Muncaster, Otto Z. 882	Negro Amanda 70
Montgomery, Maria 557	Munroe, Henry 403	Negro Amelia 116
Montgomery, Sidney 525	**Munson, Cornelia** 812	Negro Anachy? 230
Moore, Benjamin 24	Munson, Dolly 812	Negro Ananias 387
Moore, Davis 168	Munson, Owen (Dr.) 812	Negro Ann 129, 219, 689
Moore, Eleanor C. 197	Murdock, Addison 233	Negro Ann Maria 326
Moore, Elizabeth 612	**Murdock, William D.C.** 233	Negro Anna 217
Moore, Eveline 24	**Murphy, Thomas** 900	Negro Anne 909
Moore, Frederick 24	Murray, Charles 928	Negro Annie 116, 907
Moore, George 586	Murray, Mary 928	Negro Anthony 549, 867
Moore, George M. 560	**Murray, Mary H.** 713	Negro Baptist 176
Moore, Isaac 195	**Murray, Sally** 128	Negro Barbara 947
Moore, James 600	**Murray, Stanislaus** 156, 285, 392, 713	Negro Barney 387
Moore, John 187	**Myers, Charles** 51	Negro Beckie/Becky 505
Moore, John Lewis 586	Myers, Maria 896	Negro Benjamin 116, 191
Moore, Lettice C. 197	**Nailor, Alison, Jr.** 864	Negro Betsy 852
Moore, Lucy 586	**Nailor, Allison** 576, 726, 739, 865, 959	Negro Betty 505, 549
Moore, Mary 38	**Nailor, Dickinson** 104	Negro Bill 482
Moore, Richard 586	Nailor, Lizzie R. 865	Negro Blanche 686
Moore, Sallie 24	**Nailor, Thompson** 465	Negro Bob 129, 171, 210
Moore, Simon 764	Nailor, Thompson 726	Negro Boker/Booker 943
Moore, William H. 480, 586	**Nailor, William** 446	Negro California 587
Moran, Horatio 123	Nailor. *See also Naylor.*	Negro Caroline 14, 147, 465, 894, 794
Moran, John 123	Napa, Virginia 113	Negro Catharine 123, 528, 794
Morehead, A.H. 612	Nash, Adelaide 459	Negro Catharine Louisa 874
Morehouse, Alanson 927	Nash, Arabella 459	Negro Cato 787
Moreland, Eliza G. 95	Nash, Archy 459	Negro Cecilia 86
Moreland, Notley 333	Nash, George Ruffin 459	Negro Cecy 176
Morgan, E.C. 442	Nash, Horace 459	Negro Charity 42
Morgan, Evelina 442	Nash, infant 459	Negro Charles 89, 143, 287, 325, 505
Morgan, James E. (Dr.) 657	Nash, James 459	Negro Charles Henry (Osceola) 86
Morris, Henny 184	Nash, Martha 459	Negro Charles Montgomery 852
Morris, Henry M. 359	Nash, Mary E. 69	Negro Charley 482
Morrison, William H. 220	Nash, Selima 459	Negro Charlotte 89, 143, 217, 317, 453, 549, 726, 752, 909
Morsell, Benjamin K. 5	National Hotel 790	
Morsell, James S. 609	Naughton, Milly 966	Negro Chloe 846
Morsell, Jane Gray 785	Naylor, (Col.) 473	Negro Clement 884
Morsell, Joshua 785	Naylor, Allison 739	Negro Cline 35
Morton, Archey/Archy 75	Naylor, Ann 691, 841	Negro Comfort 554
Morton, Isabella 735	Naylor, Francis Y. 841	Negro Cooper 554
Mosby, John G. 447	**Naylor, George** 705, 706	Negro Cora 120
Moseley, Anne E. 19	**Naylor, Henry** 403, 705, 706, 729, 841	Negro Crissey 670
Mosher, Eliza M. 885	**Naylor, James George** 585	Negro Cynthia 175, 393
Mosher, Theodore 636	Naylor, John Lawson 404	Negro Daniel 783
Mosher, Theodore 886	Naylor, John Lawson (Capt.) 197	Negro Delia 322
Moss, A. 448	Naylor, John T. 403	Negro Delilah 70
Moss, Robert B. 292	**Naylor, Judson** 403	Negro Delozier 387
Moulden, Notley 465	Naylor, Van Deusen 403	Negro Dennis 787
Moulden, Sarah Ann 465	**Naylor, Verlinda** 404	Negro Dinah 785
Moxley? (Mr.) 287	Naylor. *See also Nailor.*	Negro Dolly 199
Moxley, Alberry 28	Nead, Winnefred 932	Negro Dominick 39
Moxley, Mary 79, 81	Neal, Fannie 536n	Negro Douglass 191
Mudd, 525	Neal, John 569	Negro Easter 697
Mudd, Catharine 283	Neal, Louis 536	Negro Eddy 325
Mudd, Charlotte 707	Neal, Margaret 569	Negro Ede 554

258

Negro Edward	89, 146	
Negro Eliza	226, 291, 302, 443, 445, 606, 651, 711	
Negro Eliza Ann	589, 820	
Negro Eliza Jane	785	
Negro Elizabeth	26, 291, 317, 450, 719	
Negro Ellen	147, 439, 907	
Negro Ellenora	129	
Negro Elsey	225	
Negro Elvira	143	
Negro Emeline	287	
Negro Emely	210	
Negro Emily	143, 387, 793	
Negro Evelyn	19	
Negro Fanny	296, 360, 495, 514	
Negro Fanny Ann	310	
Negro Flora	453	
Negro Florida	424	
Negro, Frances	445	
Negro Francis	123, 453	
Negro Frank	549, 697	
Negro Frederick	146	
Negro Gabriel	743	
Negro George	89, 127, 143, 146, 147, 225, 296, 387, 453, 670, 696, 807, 909	
Negro George Albert	820	
Negro George Washington	589, 873	
Negro Gerard	846	
Negro Grace	120	
Negro Gracy	176, 282	
Negro Gusty	146	
Negro Hannah	120, 174, 296, 317, 369, 629, 697	
Negro Hanson	291, 317	
Negro Harriet	42, 94, 554, 669, 760	
Negro Harriet Ann	317	
Negro Harriot	210	
Negro Hennie	775	
Negro Henny	120	
Negro Henrietta	514	
Negro Henry	90, 143, 217, 295, 549, 616, 760	
Negro Hezekiah	852	
Negro Hillery	884	
Negro Horace	783, 784	
Negro Ibbey	783	
Negro Irving	554	
Negro Isaac	686	
Negro Isabella	174, 514	
Negro Isreal	697	
Negro Jacob	317	
Negro James	147, 412, 628, 760, 783	
Negro James Thomas	820	
Negro Jane	210, 219, 317, 369, 387	
Negro Jeannette	505	
Negro Jenny	49, 77, 317, 719	
Negro Jim	210, 909	
Negro Jinney	49	
Negro Jinny	606	
Negro Joanna	760	
Negro Johanna	917	
Negro John	210, 317, 322, 629, 696, 784, 785, 873, 907	
Negro John Calvert	589	
Negro John Henry	35	
Negro John Lincoln	909	
Negro John Thomas	820	
Negro Joseph	325	
Negro Josephine	226, 907	
Negro Joshua	775	
Negro Julia	116, 141	
Negro Julia Rouselle	589	
Negro Kate	120, 219	
Negro Kitty	4, 94, 129, 317, 629, 643	
Negro Landonia	41	
Negro Laura	101, 628	
Negro Laura Ann Virginia	820	
Negro Lavinia	687	
Negro Lawson	102	
Negro Leathy	317	
Negro Leonard	454, 549	
Negro Lethe	945	
Negro Lewis	710, 907, 959	
Negro Lidia	884	
Negro Lin	727	
Negro Littleton	783, 784	
Negro Liz	210n	
Negro Lizzie	146	
Negro Llewellen/Lewellen	296	
Negro Louisa	31, 83, 89, 120, 129, 317, 450, 846, 909	
Negro Lowder	783	
Negro Lucinda	820	
Negro Lucy	291, 820	
Negro Mady	783, 784	
Negro Magdelane	955	
Negro Many	628	
Negro Marcellus	39	
Negro Margaret	128, 326	
Negro Maria	165, 331, 401, 445, 519, 629, 651, 696, 736, 873	
Negro Mariah	120, 697, 846, 873	
Negro Marie	616	
Negro Marion	811	
Negro Martha	90, 127, 686, 719, 811	
Negro Mary	39, 77, 129, 165, 171, 212, 217, 227, 287, 317, 445, 453, 549, 669, 927, 947	
Negro Mary Ann	937	
Negro Mary Ellen	830	
Negro Mary Jane	505	
Negro Matilda	226, 302	
Negro Milley	317	
Negro Milly	26, 669, 830	
Negro Mingy	21	
Negro Miranda	128	
Negro Morgan	123	
Negro Moses	218	
Negro Nace	852	
Negro Nancy	174, 482, 760	
Negro Ned	287	
Negro Nelly	589, 683	
Negro Nelly Ann	317	
Negro Nicholas	434	
Negro Oscar	317	
Negro Osceola	86	
Negro Ottoway	953	
Negro Patty	77	
Negro Peggy	719	
Negro Penelope	687	
Negro Peter	453	
Negro Phillis	270, 959	
Negro Polly	670	
Negro Priscilla	55, 453, 651	
Negro Priss	55	
Negro Prudence	884	
Negro Rachael	441	
Negro Rachel	218, 387, 493, 651, 783	
Negro Randall	180	
Negro Rebecca	109	
Negro Reny Ann	917	
Negro Richard	836	
Negro Richard Thomas	927	
Negro Robert	218, 322, 439, 686	
Negro Rose	16, 90	
Negro Ruth	907	
Negro Sabra	783	
Negro Sally	39, 445, 606, 670, 813, 953	
Negro Sally Ann	785	
Negro Sam	83	
Negro Samuel	651, 784	
Negro Sandy	317	
Negro Sarah	325, 651, 783, 787, 812	
Negro Serena	83	
Negro Severn	554	
Negro Sidney	387	
Negro Sophia	86, 453, 846	
Negro Sophy	387	
Negro Sucky	511	
Negro Susan	90, 291, 482, 514, 628, 651, 811, 909, 953	
Negro Susanna	628	
Negro Tecumseh	86	
Negro Thomas	128	
Negro Thomas Sidney (Tecumseh)	86	
Negro Tom	947	
Negro Treacy/Treasy	192	
Negro Truman	83	
Negro Violetta	651	
Negro Violette	210	
Negro Wallis	147	
Negro Wesley	129	
Negro William	39, 75, 302, 317, 339, 393, 710, 785	
Negro William, Jr.	317	
Negro William Henry	783, 811	
Negro Willie	453	
Negro Willis	453	
Negro Winney	953	
Negro Winny Ann	589	
Negro Younger John	102	
Neill, George S.	295	
Neill, Sarah A.	295	
Nelson, Anna Virginia	714	
Nelson, Dudley	826	
Nelson, Fanny	485	
Nelson, Maria	423	
Nelson, Martha	674	
Nelson, Mary	146	
Nelson, Mary Jane	674	
Nelson, Minnie Ann	485	
Nelson, Nora	485	
Nelson, Polly	485	
Nelson, Reuben	138	
Nelson, Thomas H.	892	
Nelson, William	714	
Netter, Ellen	537	
Netter, Emma Rebecca	537	

Nevitt, Catzarina	394	Oliver, David	867	Patterson, Robert	640
Nevitt, Ellen	394	Oliver, John	867	**Patterson, Robert S.**	577
Nevitt, Robert K.	197	Oren, Thomas	716	Patton, James V.	199
Newlin, Joseph B.	34	Orme, Ann	945	**Paxton, John S.**	295
Newman, Henry	445	Orme, Caroline D.	945	Payne, Alice	915
Newman, James	106	Orme, Catharine	134	Payne, Ann	782
Newman, Thomas A.	274	**Orme, George W.**	236	Payne, Grace	130
Newman, William G.H.	304	Orme, Jeremiah	236	Payne, Jacob	782
Newton, Ann E.	148, 845	Orme, Susan	134	Payne, Mary Helena	277
Newton, Hanson	383	**Orme, Thomas**	712	Payne, Rosa	300
Newton, Susan	211	**Orme, William**	25, 449	Payne, Thomas	915
Newton, Tony	211	**Osborn, Margaret**	131, 246	Peacock, George	603
Nicholls, Virginia	687	Osborn, Susan	131	Peak, Jane	310
Nicholls, William S.	685	Osborne, Charlotte	711	**Peake, John A.**	652
Nichols, William A.	306	**Osbourn, Catharine**	189	Pearce, Edmund	530
Nichols, William S.	615	**Osbourn, Margaret**	246	**Pearce, Sallie E.**	530
Nicholson, A.A.	657	Osbourn, Susan	189	**Pearson, Catharine/Catherine**	162, 163
Nicholson, Somerville (Lt.)	657	**Osbourn, Susan W.**	247	Pearson, Elizabeth Worthington	162
Nickin, Philip Holbrook	680	**Osmun, Joseph**	151	Pearson, Joseph	162, 163
Nixon, Martha E.	895	**Ott, Eliza**	293	Peck, Anna	944
Noble, Eliza	172	Ott, Jacob	293	Peck, Asa	279
Noble, Ellen C.	441	Ott, John D.	293	Peck, Clement A.	279
Noble, George	441	Otterback, Philip	301	Peck, Elenora	944
Noble, Louisa	172	Ould, Henry	663	**Peck, Patience W.**	279
Noble, Sam	567	Ould, Robert	557	Peel, Clara	242
Noell (Mrs.)	321	**Owen, Edward**	523	Peel, Maria	242
Noell, William	321	Owen, Elisha D.	602	Peel, Richard	242
Nokes, David	279	Owen, J. (Dr.)	523	Peel, Sarah	242
Nokes, Henson	828	Owen, Stephen	215	**Peerce, Elizabeth C.**	167
Nokes, Maria	279	Owen, Washington (Col.)	253	Peerce, Joseph M.	167
Noland, Basil	36	Owens (Lt. Col.)	241	**Peirce, Joshua**	743, 774, 929
Noland, Betsy	36	**O'Brien, Sarah Jane**	13	**Peirce, Margaret Ann**	98
Noland, Hanson	36	**O'Hare, Christopher S.**	850	Penn, Harrison	506
Noland, Milley	36	**O'Neale, Anne R.**	905	**Penn, Jane C.**	506
Noland, Phillis	36	O'Neale, Timothy	905	Penn, Joanna	539
Norment, Samuel	83	**O'Reiley, Elizabeth**	164	**Pepper, John P.**	111
Norris, Clara	705	O'Reily, Margaret	277	Perrie, C.F.	302
Norris, Edward Francis	239	Padgett, Violetta	529	Perry (Mr.)	746
Norris, Ellen	239	Page, Edward	421	**Perry, Augustus E.**	724, 725
Norris, Ellen Virginia	239	Page, James, Jr.	421	Perry, Henderson/Henson	896
Norris, Susan/Susanna	282	Page, James, Sr.	421	Perry, Lemuel	324
Norris, William	716	Page, Nancy	19	**Perry, Louis F.**	622
Norton, Charles H.	436	Page, Susan	421	Perry, Margaret	580
Norton, Ellen	436	Page, Winifred Sophia	698	Perry, Mary	235
Norton, Lewis	436	**Paine, Mary A.**	268	**Perry, Mary Jane**	724
Norton, Winnean	521	**Palmer, Catharine**	286	Perry, Rachel	324
Nottingham, William	501	Palmer, J.N. (Gen.)	286	Perry, Ruth Ann	622
Noyes, H.C.	939	Parker, Caroline	901	Perry, Susan	324
Noyes, William	939	**Parker, Fannie**	99	**Perry, Thomas J.S.**	622
Nutt, William D. (Maj.)	544	**Parker, George**	99, 849, 916	Peter, Mary	311
Offut, Sarah R.	96	Parker, John	856	Peter, Thomas	549
Offutt, Hilleary L.	203	Parker, Juliet	54	Peters, J.H.	600, 601
Offutt, James Wesley	610	Parker, Marandy	901	**Peters, William**	338
Offutt, Lawson	405	Parker, Maria	452	Peterson, Henry	647
Offutt, Lois E.	553	**Parker, Nancy**	546	Pettibone, John	951
Offutt, Robert	610	Parker, Southey S.	332	**Peyton, Eliza**	388, 389
Offutt, Sarah	610	**Parker, Thomas**	257, 849	Peyton, Mary Elizabeth	388
Offutt, Sarah B.	553	Parker, William	546	Phenix, George	905
Offutt, Thomas B.	774	Parkman, Lucy	254	Phenix, Mary Ellen	584
Ogle, Ann	714	Parr, Michael	117	Phenix, Rebecca M.	549
Ogle, Benjamin R.	714	Patrick, Dinah	253	Phenix, Sarah	584
Ogle, Hannah	85	Patrick, John	253	Philip, William H.	162, 163
Ogle, R.L.	641	Patterson, Anna	853	Philips, George William	492
Ogle, Rachel	85	**Patterson, Carlisle P.**	162	**Pickett, James C.**	296
Ogle, William C.	636	Patterson, Margaret	577	**Pickrel/Pickrell, Ann**	518
Oliver, Caroline	867	**Patterson, Mary R.**	640	Pickrell, Esau	807

Pickrell, John F.	807	
Pierce, Abner	494	
Pigott, Jennings	18	
Piles, Rachel	776	
Piles, Richard	125	
Piles, W.H.	776	
Pindell, Catharine	407	
Pindell, Renaldo	407	
Pindle, William N. (Dr.)	177	
Pinkney, Ellen	137	
Pinkney, Joseph	387	
Pinkney, Laura	137	
Pinkney, Maria	137	
Pinkney, Martha	137	
Pinkney, Priscilla	137	
Pinkwood, Emanuel	891	
Pipes, Mary	382	
Pipsico, Henderson	133	
Pipsico, Letitia B.	133	
Pipsico, Louis Cass	133	
Pitts, Nace	104	
Plater, William (Dr.)	558	
Pleasants, Ailcey	314	
Pleasants, Anne	314	
Pleasants, George	314	
Pleasants, James	314	
Pleasants, Polly	314	
Pleasants, Samuel	314	
Pleasants, Susan	314	
Pleasants, Tom	314	
Plowden, Arthur	361	
Plowden, Charles	639	
Plowden, Charlotte	639	
Plowden, Lotty	639	
Plowden, Rebecca	361	
Plummer (Mrs.)	3	
Plummer, Edward	241	
Plummer, Edward S.	3	
Polk, James K.	581	
Pollett, Elizabeth	692	
Pool, Hampton/Hamilton	323	
Pool, Teresa	831	
Porter, A.P. (Capt.)	123	
Posey, Molly	227	
Posey, Peter D.	444	
Posey, Peter G.	797	
Posey, William E.	707	
Potts, John	904	
Powell, Lila	36	
Powell, Moses	499	
Powers, Jack	572	
Powers, Jennet	572	
Powers, Jennie/Jenny	572	
Powers, John T.	167	
Prather, James	499	
Prather, John C.	683, 956	
Prather, Joseph	662	
Prather, Nathan	956	
Prather, William	96	
Pressey/Pressy, William	820	
Preuss?	858	
Price, Andrew	627	
Price, Austin	477	
Price, Benjamin	144, 213	
Price, C.M.	668	
Price, George (Mrs.)	213	

Price, Joseph	144	
Price, Mahilda	476	
Price, Margaret Ann	144	
Price, Sally	627, 725	
Prior, Sarah	39	
Proctor, Richard	503	
Prout, Celest	744	
Prout, Delilah	744	
Prout, Hortense	744	
Prout, Jonathan	46	
Prout, Kalisti	744	
Prout, Leander	744	
Prout, Robert	40	
Prout, Rose	698	
Prout, Sarah	698	
Prout, Tabitha	744	
Pullison, Beverly	180	
Pulman, Peter	113	
Pumphrey, Ellen	391	
Pumphrey, Henry A.	121	
Pumphrey, James W.	660	
Pumphrey, John W.	481	
Pumphrey, Levi	391, 660	
Pumphrey, Thomas?	718	
Purcell, Mary F.E.	527	
Purcell, William F.	527	
Purnell, Benjamin	744	
Pursell, Mary Ann	513	
Pursell, Thomas	513	
Quad, Priscilla	609	
Quander, George	938	
Quander, Ned	938	
Queen (Mrs.)	518	
Queen, Ann	439, 627	
Queen, Charles Richard	439	
Queen, Elizabeth	627	
Queen, Frank	136	
Queen, Harriet	772	
Queen, Henrietta	33	
Queen, Henry	627	
Queen, Jim	417	
Queen, Maria	252	
Queen, Maria A.	91	
Queen, Mary	627	
Queen, Mary Jane	136	
Queen, Mary Marcelena	439	
Queen, Nelly G.	627	
Queen, Nicholas	617, 655	
Queen, Nicholas L.	354, 627, 725	
Queen, Rosena	439	
Queen, Steven	596	
Queen, Theodore	439	
Radcliffe, Caroline	766	
Radcliffe, Celia	766	
Ramsey, George D.	643	
Randall, T.	137	
Randolph, Eglantine	31	
Randolph, Emily C.	208	
Randolph, Margaret B.	208	
Randoy, John	57	
Ratchford, Philip	101	
Ratcliff, Ignatius	171	
Raux, B. (Mr.)	267	
Rawlings, Beckey	621	
Rawlings, David	59	
Ray, A. Ross	608	

Ray, Albert	608	
Ray, Deborah	606	
Ray, Enos	470	
Raymond, Elias	541	
Read, J.D.	642	
Read, Maria Louisa	125	
Read, Mary Eliza	739	
Read, Robert	642	
Redin, W.	598, 625	
Redin, William E.	235	
Reed, Bushrod W.	125	
Reed, Maria Louisa	125	
Reed, Nancy	207	
Reeves, Courtney	310	
Reeves, Elizabeth	176	
Reid, Philip	741	
Reily, Ellen T.	848	
Reily, James A.	536	
Reintzell, Henry	688	
Reintzell, Margaret	688	
Reintzell, Mary E.	688	
Rendler, Charlotte	191	
Renfro, James, Sr.	127	
Renfro, Skelton	127	
Renshaw, Margaret A.	382	
Reynolds, Binah	939	
Reynolds, Sam	482	
Reynolds, Thomas	209	
Rhodes, George	135, 565	
Rhodes, George, Jr.	313	
Rhodes, George, Sr.	313	
Rhodes, James	22	
Rhodes, Jane	546	
Rhodes, Louisa	546	
Rhodes, Thomas	774	
Rice, Mary J.	261	
Richards, A.	97	
Richards, Alfred	7, 33, 97, 250	
Richards, George F.	513	
Richards, Sarah A.M.	250	
Richards, Susanna	250	
Richards, Thomas A.	97, 250	
Richards, William	124	
Richards, William? H.	105	
Richardson, James	77	
Richardson, Judson	917	
Richardson, Judson F.	21	
Richardson, William	77	
Ridenour, Hugh H.	342	
Ridenour, J.W.	342	
Ridenour, J.W. (Mrs.)	342	
Ridenour, Jonathan	342	
Rider, Charles	304	
Ridgely, Sophia	558	
Ridgely, William G.	558	
Ridgley, Clara	367	
Ridgley, James H.	367	
Ridgley, William	367	
Ridgley, William G.	330, 789	
Ridout, John	718	
Riggs, George W.	478	
Riggs, Samuel of R.	788	
Rigney, Albert	526	
Rigney, Archibald	526	
Rigney, Charles Henry	526	
Rigney, Cornelius	526	

Rigney, David	526	
Rigney, Georgiana/Georgianna	526	
Rigney, Hester	526	
Rigney, Louis	526	
Rigney, Matilda	526, 744	
Rigney, Narcissa	744	
Rigney, Thomas	526	
Rigney, William	526	
Riley, John C.	358, 359	
Riley, Joshua	414	
Riley, Thomas Robinson	524	
Riley, Thomas W.	525	
Riley, William R.	280, 524, 734	
Ringgold, Eliza W.	29	
Ringgold, Mary D.G.	450	
Ringgold, William T.	28	
Ringold, Georgiana	912	
Ringold, John	292	
Ringold, Mary Ann	912	
Riordan, James	65	
Ritchie, Joshua	748	
Ritchie, Mary S.	748	
Rittenhouse, Fant & Co.	77	
Ritter, Henny	205	
Rives, John C.	262	
Rives, John C.	297	
Rixey, Smith H.	220	
Roach, Edward N.	4, 435	
Roberson, Betsy	460	
Roberson, John	460	
Roberts, Ann	723	
Roberts, John M.	722	
Roberts, John W.	723	
Robertson, Ann Eliza	47	
Robertson, Eleanor	847	
Robertson, Evelina	142	
Robertson, John C.	643	
Robertson, William Basil	710	
Robinson, Alfred Curtis	290	
Robinson, Alfred Y.	594	
Robinson, Alice Maria	290	
Robinson, Ann Eliza	47	
Robinson, Barbara/Barbary	6	
Robinson, Eliza Jane	290	
Robinson, Elizabeth	594	
Robinson, Frances H.P.	822	
Robinson, Francis V.	822	
Robinson, James Henry	290	
Robinson, John	576, 710	
Robinson, Margaret	822	
Robinson, Nancy	576	
Robinson, Robert	6	
Robinson, Roberta A.	965	
Robinson, Sally	290	
Robinson, Walter W.H.	822	
Roche, Winifred A.	848	
Rochford, Bartholomew	65	
Rogers, Ann	514	
Rogers, Rowland	377	
Rolles, Anna	514	
Rollins, Susan A.J.	540	
Rooker, Jabez	231	
Rosenthal?	287	
Rosier, Eliza	867	
Rosier, Hannibal	867	
Rosier, Henry	867	
Rosier, Sallie	867	
Rosier, William	521	
Ross, Ann	741	
Ross, Ann Maria	655	
Ross, Celia	324	
Ross, Elizabeth	724, 725	
Ross, Fanny	585	
Ross, Frances Ann	468	
Ross, George	669, 677	
Ross, Henry	387	
Ross, Jacob	468	
Ross, Keziah/Kessiah	468	
Ross, Lucinda	799	
Ross, Lucy	848	
Ross, Maria	677	
Ross, Mary	385, 474	
Ross, Mary Jane	724	
Ross, Nancy	324	
Ross, Phoebe	486	
Ross, Rachel	655	
Ross, Richard	724, 725, 734, 823	
Ross, Richard L.	734	
Ross, Sarah	111, 474	
Ross, Smith	655	
Ross, Sophia	669	
Ross, William	324, 677	
Rowland, John A.	934	
Ruff, John A.	831	
Runnels, Samuel	315	
Russell, L. (Mrs.)	495	
Rustin, Anna Maria	774	
Rustin, Jane	520	
Rustin, Louisa	520	
Rustin, Nancy	520	
Rustin, Nancy Catharine	259	
Rustin, Sarah Ann	520	
Rustin, Thomas	394	
Rustin, William Nicholas	774	
Ryan, Maria	422	
Ryan, Sandy	422	
Ryon, Richard J.	161	
Ryon, Thomas P.	161	
Sainsbury, John H.	21	
Sampson, Florence	28	
Sampson, Gertrude	28	
Sampson, Jinney	28	
Sampson, Laura	28	
Sampson, Lydia	28	
Sampson, Maria	28	
Sanders, Benedict J.	539	
Sanders, Caroline E.	616	
Sanders, Ellen	151	
Sanders, James	473	
Sanders, Nora	473	
Sanders, Rachel	473	
Sanders, William G.	616	
Sandriegle?, Mary	262	
Sansbury, John H.	508	
Sardo, Michael	196, 471	
Sasser, Sarah Ann	399, 778	
Sasser, William	63	
Saunders (Mrs.)	550	
Saunders, Jack	63	
Saunders, Louisa	63	
Savage, Alice/Allice	153	
Savage, Cornelia	153	
Savage, George	37	
Savage, Hamilton	153	
Savage, Harriet	153	
Savage, Hester	153	
Savage, William	153	
Scaggs, George B.	794	
Scaggs, Isaac	198, 433	
Scaggs, James	433	
Scaggs, Mary	560	
Scaggs, Selby B.	198, 484	
Schooler, John	190	
Schrivener, Thomas, Jr.	640	
Schwarz, Conrad	673	
Scifas, Thomas	887	
Scipio, Lewis	18	
Scott (Mrs.)	376	
Scott, Amelia	132	
Scott, Ann	117, 273, 533	
Scott, Caroline	871	
Scott, Elizabeth	871	
Scott, Elizabeth C.	750	
Scott, Ellen	750	
Scott, Florida	659	
Scott, George B.	919	
Scott, Jane	39	
Scott, Jane H.C.	463	
Scott, John D.	463	
Scott, Judson	247, 335	
Scott, Mary Ann	39	
Scott, Nancy	553	
Scott, Polador E.	581	
Scott, Richard M.	936	
Scott, Rose	39	
Scott, Thomas A.	620	
Scott, Virginia	936	
Scott, William B. (Maj.)	733, 893	
Scrivener, Thomas	62	
Scrivener, Thomas, Jr.	62, 319, 778	
Scrivenner *See Scrivener*		
Sears, James W.	645	
Sears, Rebecca	645	
Seibert, Ida	94	
Seibert, Louisa	94	
Seibert, Matilda	94	
Seibert, Thomas	94	
Selby, Ned	598	
Selden, Albert Augustus	532	
Selden, George L.	909	
Selden, James	532, 533, 909	
Selden, Margaret	532	
Semmes, Francis	222	
Semmes, George	670	
Semmes, Henrietta	884	
Semmes, John B.	884	
Semmes, Nelly	663	
Semmes, Rose Ann	222	
Semms, Jesse M.	394	
Semple, G.W. (Dr.)	306	
Sengstack, L. Kemp	671	
Sepas. *See Cepas.*		
Sewall, Robert D.	314	
Sewall, Sophia	776	
Sewell, Lucinda	756	
Sewell, Mary	756	
Seybolt, Elizabeth C.	337	
Shanks, Michael	278	

Name	Page
Sharer, John	460
Shaw, Caroline	724
Shaw, Dawson	725
Shaw, Gusty	725
Shaw, James	188
Shaw, Lucy	725
Shaw, Nicholas S.	215
Shaw, Rezin	215
Shaw, Sidney	725
Shaw, Verlinda	794
Sheckell, Owen	668
Sheckels and Company	853
Sheckels, Theodore	326, 543
Sheehy, Ann	957
Shekell, Benjamin O.	329, 690, 744, 781, 950
Shepherd, Alexander R.	779
Shepherd, Susan D.	637
Shepherd, William D.	216, 638
Sheriff, Charlotte Ann	711
Sheriff, Emeline/Emmeline	436
Sheriff, Levi	436, 437, 491
Sheriff, Samuel	275
Sheriff, Susan B.	275
Sheriff, Thomas	722
Sherman, Charles E.	795
Shields, Mary	20
Shiles, Emily	203
Shiles, Isabella	203
Shiles, Maria	203
Shinn, Stephen	241
Shoemaker, Edward	898
Shoemaker, Martha L.	748
Shoemaker, Pierce	494, 748
Shorter, Andrew	163
Shorter, Ann	343, 777
Shorter, Anna	648
Shorter, Benjamin	163
Shorter, Bosquet Henry	359
Shorter, Charles	56
Shorter, Charles Edwin	174
Shorter, Eliza	648
Shorter, Elizabeth	163
Shorter, Frank	163
Shorter, Hannah	648
Shorter, Harriet	343
Shorter, Henry	163
Shorter, Isaac	56
Shorter, Jacob	163
Shorter, John Joseph	174
Shorter, Joseph	56
Shorter, Lamartine/Lamertine	358
Shorter, Lewis	163
Shorter, Lucy	343
Shorter, Margaret C.	358
Shorter, Maria	551
Shorter, Mary	163
Shorter, Michael	56
Shorter, Nancy	56
Shorter, Rebecca	777
Shorter, Robert	343
Shorter, Sarah	163
Shorter, Thomas	163
Shorter, William	777
Shreve, Caleb	689
Shreve, James H.	689, 703
Shreve, Samuel	299, 689, 727, 898
Shreve, Samuel, Sr.	299, 850
Shreves, Barbara	702
Shulze, Francis S.	351
Shulze, M. Alice	351
Sifas, Alice	771
Silas/Silass, Gilbert	366
Silas/Silass, Kitty	366
Silas/Silass, Philip	366
Silas/Silass, William	366
Silvey, Maria Edmonia	853
Silvey, Verlinda	853
Simmes, Kate	437
Simmes, Laura	437
Simmes, Mary	437, 483
Simmons, Richard	589
Simmons, Serena	769
Simms, Anna	958
Simms, Elexius	376
Simms, Elizabeth	906
Simms, Euridice F.	376
Simms, Jerry	682
Simms, John	748
Simms, Joseph	494
Simms, Lewis	481
Simms, Lillie	746
Simms, Lucy	746
Simms, Mary	748
Simms, Mary Ellen	165
Simms, Patty	68
Simms, Rebecca	239
Simms, Jane	328
Simms, William H.	206
Simms, Willie	746
Simpson, James A.	564
Simpson, Sarah T.	564
Sims, Anna Maria	345
Sims, Charity	345
Sims, Charlotte	345
Sims, Clement	345
Sims, Daniel	345
Sims, Elias	345
Sims?, Gustavus	239
Sims, Henrietta	345
Sims, Henry	239
Sims, James	239
Sims, Jane	328
Sims, Joseph	345
Sims, Margery	345
Sims, Marion	345
Sims, Martha	345
Sims, Mary	345
Sims, Matilda	239
Sims, Protus	345
Sims, Sally	345
Sims?, Venus	239
Sims, William	345
Singleton, Clara	117
Singleton (Col.)	116
Singleton, George	893
Singleton, Martha	117
Sioussa, Charles	396
Sisson, Ann F.	171
Sisson, Jesse	171
Sister Mary Angela Harrison	569
Sister Mary Ellen	569
Sister Regina	569
Sisters of the Visitation	569
Skelley, Margaret E.	224
Skelley, William E.	224
Skinner, James	324
Skinner, Julius Caesar/Cesar	739
Slack (Mrs.)	142
Slack, William B. (Maj.)	142
Slaten/Slatten, Dorey/Dory	538
Slater, Henrietta	236
Slater, Marion	236
Sloan, Alfred A.	178
Smallwood, Ann	243
Smallwood, Bernard	243
Smallwood, Fannie	243, 500
Smallwood, Henrietta	243
Smallwood, Henry	243
Smallwood, John	282
Smallwood, Julia	243
Smallwood, Lucy	243
Smallwood, Mary	243
Smallwood, Moses	373
Smallwood, Nelly	243
Smallwood, William	243
Smilo, William Edward	678
Smith (Mrs.)	449
Smith, A. Thomas	257
Smith, Adaline/Adeline	862
Smith, Alfred	734
Smith, Andrew	684, 734
Smith, Anna Maria	724
Smith, Anthony	363
Smith, Bell	639
Smith, Benjamin P.	213
Smith, Billy	639
Smith, Caroline	734
Smith, Charity	24
Smith, Charles	639
Smith, Clement (Mrs.)	797
Smith, Dick	164
Smith, Elizabeth	667
Smith, Fanny	662
Smith, Frederick	828
Smith, George	686, 734
Smith, Harriet	210, 639
Smith, Helen	24
Smith, Henrietta	734
Smith, Henry	734
Smith, Hezekiah	260
Smith, J.B.H.	572
Smith, Jack	398
Smith, James	164
Smith, James R.	641
Smith, Jennie	639
Smith, John	237, 264
Smith, John A.	286, 549
Smith, John Chandler	773
Smith, Judy	201
Smith, Julia	734
Smith, Leannan	703
Smith, Leonard	734
Smith, Lewis	734
Smith, Louisa	639
Smith, Lucy	667
Smith, Margaret	150
Smith, Margery	639

Name	Page
Smith, Maria	676
Smith, Maria Ann	667
Smith, Martha A.	667
Smith, Mary	163, 164, 549, 862
Smith, Mary A.	943
Smith, Mary C.	549
Smith, Mary Jane	639
Smith, Matilda B.	213
Smith, Maurice	639
Smith, Richard	148
Smith, Robert	156
Smith, Rosina	734
Smith, Samuel P.	549
Smith, Susan Elizabeth	791
Smith, Teresa	156
Smith, Thomas	734, 943
Smith, Verlinda	480
Smith, William	150, 611
Smoot, Ann	528, 592, 958
Smoot, Harriet	135
Smoot, J.H.	589
Smoot, Jacob	857
Smoot, Jacob G.	589
Smoot, John H.	860
Smoot, Luther R.	875
Smoot, Margaret Ann	289
Smoot, Mary A.	438
Smoot, Mary B.	438
Smoot, Robert W.	289
Smoot, Samuel	135
Snell, Jenny	182
Snell, Mandy	182
Snell, William Henry	70
Snoden, Maria	804
Snowden, Darkey Ann	368
Snowden, Emma	368
Snowden, Maria	804
Snowden, Martha	885
Snowden, Richard Nicols	616
Snowden, Spencer	879
Snowden, Wesley	636
Snowden, William	67, 616
Snyder, J.M. (Dr.)	673
Sollers, Sarah E.	861
Solomon, Hester	597
Solomon, Julia	457
Solomon, Mary	457
Solomon, Sarah	483
Solomon, Thomas	457
Somers, Eliza Jane	799
Somers, Senior?	386
Somerville, James	435
Somerville, Mary	435
Sommers, Eliza	544
Sommervell, Elizabeth	184
Sommerville, John H.	872
Sommerville, Sarah J.	872
Soper, Ann V.	272, 273
Soper, Sallie	58
Sothoron, George M.	406
Sothoron, John W.	406
Sothoron, W. (Dr.)	406
Southern, Richard	544
Spalding, Ann Caroline	243
Spalding, Basil William	243
Spalding, Caroline V.	82
Spalding, John	243
Spalding, Mary Camilla	243
Spalding, W.E.	332
Spaulding (Mrs.)	387
Speake, Rufus H.	34
Speake, William F.	144
Speaks, Hilleary	669
Speaks, William Henry	544
Speiser, Frederick	402
Speiser, Maria	402
Spinks, James	498
Sprigg, Horace	849
Sprigg, Martha Ann	856
Sprigg, Mary Ann	754
Sprigg, Thomas	755
Stabler, George	34
Stanford, James E.	241
Stanford, Obadiah	445
Stanley, Amelia	415
Stanley, Charles A.	415
Stanley, Harriet	415
Stanley, Henry C.	415
Stanley, Thomas	415
Starrow, S.A. (Dr.)	412
Statesman, Margaret	767
Stephens, Jacob	561
Stevens, Jeremiah	531
Stevens, Matthew H.	369
Stevenson, George	286
Stevenson, Samuel	790
Steward, Ailsey	198
Steward, Albert	198
Steward, David	198
Steward, Edward	198
Steward, John	198
Steward, Lucy	198
Stewart, Alice	83
Stewart, Archibald Kerr	395
Stewart, Caroline	298
Stewart, Cecelia Caroline	12
Stewart, Charles	688
Stewart, Charles J.	651
Stewart, Charles W.	640
Stewart, Edmund	367
Stewart, Edward	437
Stewart, Eliza	915
Stewart, Fanny	492
Stewart, George W.	138
Stewart, H. Clay	138
Stewart, Harriet	956
Stewart, Helen L.	535
Stewart, James E.	395
Stewart, Jerry	95
Stewart, Jesse	95
Stewart, John	433
Stewart, Leathe	95
Stewart, Manuel	95
Stewart, Margaret C.	535
Stewart, Mary E.	138
Stewart, Mary R.	640
Stewart, Rebecca	640
Stewart, Robert	491
Stewart, Robinson Crusoe	492
Stewart, Serena	83
Stewart, Sophia	681
Stewart, Truman	83
Stewart, Walter	688
Stewart, William	83, 95, 437, 651
Stewart, William H.	395
Stoddard, Charlotte	247
Stoddard, Eliza	247
Stoddard, Frank	395
Stone, Ann Maria	405
Stoddert, Charlotte	247
Stoddert, Eliza	247
Stone, Anna E.	340
Stone, Anna Maria	405
Stone, Charles	405
Stone, John G.	339
Stone, John H.	915
Stone, Philip	202
Stone, Robert King (Dr.)	314
Stone, Sarah Ann	915
Stone, William James, Jr.	314
Stone, William James, Sr.	314
Stone, Woodford	704
Stonestreet, Samuel T.	795
Storm, Leonard	326
Stott, Samuel	157
Stott, Samuel, trustee	158
Strabit, Mary A.	234
Strider, John	278
Stuart, Anna	345
Stuart, Fanny	492
Stuart, Hamlet	345
Stuart, Margaret	345
Stuart, Mary	345
Stuart, Robinson Crusoe	492
Stutley, Elizabeth	208
Suite, John Smith	662
Sullivan, John T.	354
Sullivan, Luther O.	934
Summers, Ann Maria/Mariah	742
Summers, Nathaniel	742
Summervill, Sarah J.	771
Sutton, Frederic	863
Sutton, Nelly	336
Sutton, Robert M.	863
Swann, Jane E.	496
Swann, Richard	711
Swann, William	711
Swart, Bernard T.	474
Sweeny, Dennis	705
Sweeny, Eugenia	949
Sweeny, H.M.	232
Swinks?, Solony	702
Sword, Alexander	11
Sword, Mary E.	11
Swort, Barnet T.	474
Sybolt, William	799
Syphax, Nancy	307
Talbert, Henry	140
Talbert, Thomas	76
Talbert, Thomas, Jr.	76
Talboot, Ann	392
Talbot, Benjamin	761
Talbot, Sarah	761
Talbott, Ann	711
Talbott, Caroline	711
Talbott, Cecily/Cicily	639
Talbott, Harriet Ann	68
Talbott, Rachael	711

Talbott, Sarah Ann	711	Thomas, Ann Sophia	854	Throckmorton, Charles	686
Talbott, Walter M.	396	Thomas, Anna	186	**Throckmorton, Hugh W.**	18
Talburtt, George W.	288	Thomas, Betsey/Betsy	768	Throckmorton, John A.	190, 686
Taney, William	705	Thomas, Caroline Isabella	673	**Throckmorton, Mary**	686
Tanner (Mrs.)	234	Thomas, Catharine Jane	693	Throckmorton, Mordicai	18
Tate, Henry	940	Thomas, Cecelia	455	Thurburn, Joseph	146
Tate, Mary	940	Thomas, Celia	301	Tibbles, Lilly	723
Tayloe, Benjamin Ogle	664	Thomas, Clara	762	Tibbles, Lucinda	723
Tayloe, John (Col.)	664	**Thomas, Eliza**	90	Tidwell, Albert G.	604
Taylor, Alexander	591	Thomas, Elizabeth	446	Tighlman, Cecilia	569
Taylor, Ann	251	Thomas, Ellen	275	Tighlman, Charles	569
Taylor, Annie	260	Thomas, Ellen Amelie	673	Tighlman, Ignatius	569
Taylor, Annie E.	565	Thomas, Francis	222	Tighlman, Ignatius, Jr.	569
Taylor, Ben	482	Thomas, Francis Elizabeth	673	Tighlman, Jane	569
Taylor, Benjamin	90, 194	Thomas, Harriet	222, 490	Tighlman, Josephine	569
Taylor, Bridget	280	Thomas, Harriet Ann	693	Tighlman, Mary	569
Taylor, Catharine	627	Thomas, Helen	762	Tighlman, Mary Elizabeth	569
Taylor, Charles Edwin	174	Thomas, Henry	740	Tighlman, Rosalie	569
Taylor, Charlotte	627	Thomas, Hessey	693	**Tilghman, Amelia**	615
Taylor, Eben	764	**Thomas, Hope**	592	Tilghman, Charles	117
Taylor, Eliza	251	Thomas, James	49, 149, 765, 820	Tilghman, James	117
Taylor, Fanny	260	**Thomas, Jenkin**	55	Tilghman, John	615
Taylor, Fendall/Fendell	627	**Thomas, John**	90, 301, 366, 790. 820	Tilghman, Thomas	117
Taylor, Frances	627	Thomas, Josephine S.	187	Tilghman. *See also Tilghman.*	
Taylor, Gabriel	627	Thomas, L.	204	Tills, Margaret	384
Taylor, Isaac	796	Thomas, Levi	741	Tills, Sarah	384
Taylor, John	482	**Thomas, Lorenzo**	847	Tilman, Amelia	615
Taylor, John Wallace	10	Thomas, Louisa	487	Tilman, Ann	615
Taylor, Joseph P.	209	Thomas, Louisa Alley	673	Tilman, Charles	52
Taylor, Joshua T.	565	Thomas, Margaret	361	Tilman, Eliza	52
Taylor, Kitty	184	Thomas, Mary Ann	301	Tilman, Elizabeth	615
Taylor, Leonard	591	Thomas, Mary E.	17	Tilman, James	615
Taylor, Leonard, Jr.	591	Thomas, Nancy	87	Tilman, John	52, 615
Taylor, Lewis	321	Thomas, Ned	392	Tilman, Juliet/July	52
Taylor, Lloyd	627	Thomas, Rachel	741	Tilman, Mary	615
Taylor, Louis	627	Thomas, Robert	87	Tilman, Rosah	615
Taylor, Lucinda	452	Thomas, Robert S.	187	Tilman, Sarah	615
Taylor, Margaret	207, 597	Thomas, Sarah Baker	673	Tilman, William	615
Taylor, Margaret E.	260	Thomas, Susan	187, 490, 854	Tilman. *See also Tilghman.*	
Taylor, Marion M.	919	Thomas, Susan Virginia	673	Tinney, George	315, 315
Taylor, Mary Abbey	627	**Thomas, William**	4, 243, 301	Tinney, John	315
Taylor, Mary Elizabeth	428	Thomas, William H.	660	Tinney, Virginia	315
Taylor, Olivia	627	Thomas, William Henry	186	Tippins, Eliza	952
Taylor, Rachel	627	Thompson, Ann E.	272	**Tobias, Susannah Harriet**	192
Taylor, Robert E.	69	**Thompson, Anthony**	272	Todd, William B.	418, 564
Taylor, Sarah	10	**Thompson, Catharine**	547	Tolson (Mr.)	316
Taylor, Susan	256	**Thompson, Egbert (Lt.)**	618	Tolson, Ella	542
Taylor, V.J.	608	Thompson, Emily B.	618	**Tolson, Henry**	925
Taylor, Vincent	597	Thompson, James	908	Tolson, Isabel	542
Taylor, Vincent J.	565	Thompson, Jefferson	908	Tolson, John	670
Taylor, William Henry	284	Thompson, John	641	**Tolson, Mary Eleanor**	670
Taylor, Zachary (Gen.)	207	Thompson, John C.	59, 516	**Tolson, Rachel M.A.**	796
Tayman, Laura Virginia	596	Thompson, John E.	370	**Tolson, Sarah**	315
Tebbs, Daniel H.	298	Thompson, Lydia	226	Tolson, William	775
Tebbs, Martha	298	**Thompson, Mary**	255	**Tonge, John T.**	160
Teel, Robert L.	89	Thompson, Smith	422	Toogood, John	487
TenEyck, John C.	307	Thompson, Thomas	272	**Torbert, James M.**	388
TenEyck, Julia	307	Thompson, William	916	**Torney, Patrick J.**	603
Tenny, Harriet	915	Thompson, William B.	807	Toyer, Chapman	366
Thayer, Stephen	648	**Thomson, S. John**	150	Toyer, Daniel	366
Thom, Christopher N.	193	Thorn, Alexander A.	102	Toyer, Eliza	366
Thomas (Mrs.)	959	**Thorn, Benjamin T.**	102	Toyer, Henry	366
Thomas, Alice	854	Thorn, Matild	102	Toyer, Joseph	366
Thomas, Ann	740	Thornton, John Thomas	329	Toyer, Louisa	366
Thomas, Ann Eliza	673	Thornton, Joseph	434	Toyer, Sarah	366
Thomas, Ann Maria	186	Thornton, William Henry	512	Trapnell,	131

Name	Page
Travers, Elias	33
Travers, John T.	301
Travers, Martha Ellen	301
Triplett, James D.	220
Trisler, Peter	834
Trott, Thomas P.	935
Trowbridge, William P.	254
Trumbull, Jane	504
Trunnel, Henry	55
Trusty, Andrew	791
Trusty, Anna	791
Trusty, Henny	791
Trusty, Joe	791
Truxson, Rachel	11
Tschiffely, Frederick A.	474
Tuck, Clement T.	880
Tuck, Ruth A.	946
Tuck, William C.	946
Tuck, William H.	880
Tucker, James	14
Tucker, William	548
Turley, Ariana	268
Turley, Fanny	733
Turley, John	268
Turley, Martha	733
Turley, Mary Jane	733
Turley, William H.	268
Turnbull, Jane	413
Turner, Ann	409
Turner, Armistead/Armstead	805
Turner, Cecilia	805
Turner, Charles H.	409
Turner, Edward	603
Turner, Elizabeth	805
Turner, Frances H.P.	822
Turner, James Lewis	409
Turner, Lucy	805
Turner, Mary Jane	765
Turner, Millie	603
Turner, Nancy	327
Turner, Naomi J.	130
Turner, Rachel W.	6
Turner, Rebecca H.	765
Turner, Thomas	765, 805
Turpin, Isabella L.	496
Turton, John E.	796
Turton, Rachel M.A.	796
Turton, William H., Jr.	796
Tweedy, Arian	107, 877
Tweedy, Robert	877
Tyler, Ann Maria	639
Tyler, Berry	264
Tyler, Dennis Ellsworth	571
Tyler, Eliza	571
Tyler, Elizabeth	684
Tyler, Frank	518, 571
Tyler, George	758
Tyler, Henry	639
Tyler, Leah	571
Tyler, Margaret	264
Tyler, Mary	439
Tyler, Mary E.	264, 392
Tyler, Penelope	684
Tyler, Robert	210, 571
Tyler, Sarah A.	392
Tyler, Sarah A.M.	264
Tyler, Susan	316, 365
Tyler, Teresa	639
Utermaehle, Charles W.	265
Vallis, Josephine	162
Van Horn, W.?	190
Van Resnick, Thomas	274
Van Riswick, J.	487
Van Riswick, John	486
Vandrey, Martha	858
Vandrey, William	858
VanRiswick, Louisa J.	274
Vigall/Vigell, Richard S.	197
Vigel, Jane	706
Vigel, Susan	706
Vineyard, J.W.	309
Vinson, Ann	34
Vinson, Charles	36
Vinson, Thomas F.W.	610
Von Essen, Peter	152, 153
Vonessen, *See Von Essen*	
Wagener, Margaret S.	527
Wailer/Wailes, Dorothy	591
Walker (Mrs.)	387
Walker, Andrew	613
Walker, Augusta A.	532
Walker, Billy	309
Walker, Cecelia	509
Walker, D.S.	736, 738
Walker, Elizabeth	191, 613
Walker, George W. (Maj.)	637
Walker, Hannah M.	199
Walker, Isaac	683
Walker, Jane	169
Walker, John	199
Walker, Josephine	169
Walker, Lewis	613
Walker, Lucy B.	116, 669
Walker, Maria	309, 683
Walker, Mary	309, 637, 683
Walker, Sarah	116
Walker, Simon	613
Walker, Zachariah	669
Walker, Zacharias	116
Wall & Barnard	906
Wall, D.R.	508
Wall, Sarah J.	508
Wallace, Amanda	244
Wallace, Daniel	115
Wallace, Edwin	965
Wallace, Elizabeth	244
Wallace, Elizabeth B.	965
Wallace, Ellen	244
Wallace, Emeline	244
Wallace, Harriet	965
Wallace, Joanna	244
Wallace, Julia	115
Wallace, Lester	115
Wallace, Mary	407
Wallace, Mary E.	965
Wallace, Mary Key	590
Wallace, Noah	115
Wallace, Priscilla	407
Wallace, Richard	94
Wallace, Robert	590
Wallace, William A.	965
Wallace, Winna	244
Wallach, Richard	124
Wallack, Charles	934
Wallis, Fanny	616
Wallis, Harrison	918
Wallis, Kate	616
Wallis, Sallie	616
Walls, Jane	740
Walsh, Francis S.	143
Walter, Charles	227
Walters, Caroline V.	81
Walters, George D.	78
Walters, James	81
Walters, James	78
Walters, James, Jr.	80
Walters, James, Sr.	80
Ward, Alfred	403
Ward, Ann Amelia	455
Ward, Ann Emeline	455
Ward, Ellen	403
Ward, Emeline	69
Ward, George	403, 868
Ward, John Morsell	709
Ward, John S.	455
Ward, Sarah	709
Ward, Sophia	403
Ward, Tom	403
Ward, Ulysses	83, 456
Ward, Ulysses, Jr.	416
Ward, Ulysses, Sr.	416
Ward, William H.	564
Warder, John B.	260
Ware, Cagy	501
Ware, Juliet	262
Ware, Louisa	262
Ware, Richard	262
Waring, Ann	735
Waring, Charles Stone	405
Waring, Hanson Grafton	405
Waring, Marcus S.S.	596
Waring, Mary Jane	405
Waring, Ruth/Rutha	405
Waring, William	405
Warner, William	908
Warren (Mr.)	266
Warren, Columbus	657
Warren, Ellen	466
Warren, Henrietta	467
Warren, Henry	466, 487
Warren, John	657
Warren, Kate	531
Warren, Louisa	657
Warren, Maria	255
Warren, Nelly	255, 466
Warring, Anna M.	743
Warring, Ellen	429
Warring, Henry	743
Warring, Peter	797
Warrington, Henry	580
Warrington, Lewis	893
Warrington, Lewis (Comm.)	580
Washington, Aline	706
Washington, Ann M.	952
Washington, Ann T.	311
Washington, Anthony	636
Washington, Catherine J.	294
Washington, Clara	429

Washington, D.? (Mrs.)	241	Webster, William	122	**White, Mary**	246
Washington, Daniel	294	Weeden, Ann	291	**White, Rachael E.**	674
Washington, Eliza A.	429	Weeden, Benjamin F.	292	**White, Sophia M.**	131
Washington, George C.	311	**Weeden, Clement**	144	White, Stephen N.C. (Dr.)	289
Washington, Ida Mary	294	Weeden, Frisby	292	White, W.G.W.	674
Washington, John	706	Weeks, Levinia	846	**White, William G.W.**	641
Washington, John A.	130	Weems, Mary	332, 840, 907	Whiting, Harry/Henry	717
Washington, Joseph H.	279	Weightman, Sidney	387	Whiting, Kitty	717
Washington, Linah/Sinah	294	Weldon, Thomas	569	Whiting, Lucy	614
Washington, Louisa	175	Wells, Amelia	912	Whiting, Peter	717
Washington, Lucy	489	Wells, Elizabeth Susannah	701	Whitlock (Mrs.)	371
Washington, Margaret	680	**Wells, John**	701	Whitney, Lucy	640
Washington, Margaret A.	296	**Wells, John W.**	444	Widdecomb, George	245
Washington, Mary	475, 570	**Wells, Verlinda W.**	701	Widdecomb, Sarah	245
Washington, Mary Teresa	175	Wells, William	912	Wightt, Cary	627
Washington, Peter G.	680	Welsh, Edward	517	Wightt, John M.	627
Washington, Romulus	570	Werckmuller, Anna	267	Wilcoxen, Ellen	116, 962
Washington, Sally	706	West (Mr.	797	**Wildman, Cornelius G.**	887
Waters, Anna C.	364	West, Alexander	116	Wilkerson, Isaac	321
Waters, Eliza	665, 794	**West, Ann E.**	624	Wilkinson, Robert	30
Waters, Gustavus	228	West, Caroline	115	**Wilkinson, William**	119
Waters, Henry	750	West, Charles	880	**Willard, Caroline M.**	766
Waters, James	71, 794	West, Clement Alexander	318	**Willard, Henry A.**	301, 766
Waters, John	893	West, Eleanor	278	**Willard, Joseph C.**	301, 766
Waters, Julia	794	**West, Eliza M.**	169	Willard's Hotel	266, 301, 790
Waters, Lornezo	71	West, Ellen G.	822	Willcoxen, Sarah	403
Waters, Lucy	71	West, Hannah	116	Willett, Cephas T.	911
Waters, Margaret	263	West, Henny	689	**Willett, Marinus**	42
Waters, Mary Louise	71	**West, James W.**	169	Willett, Ninian	425
Waters, Nathan	364	West, Jane	672	Willett, Sarah	42
Waters, Sarah	71	West, John	689	William, James	729
Waters, Tabitha Mead	228	West, Julius	689	Williams, Adeline	190
Waters, Thomas	780	West, Kitty	705	Williams, Albert	35
Waters, William Joseph	71	West, Laura	689	Williams, Ann	62
Watkins, Benjamin	436	West, Margaret	822	Williams, Ann Dorinda	32
Watkins, C.M.	896	West, Mary Rebecca	318	**Williams, Barbara**	632
Watkins, Greenberry M.	926	West, Nancy	822	Williams, Caroline	76
Watkins, Harriet	436	West, Rose	949	Williams, Charles	190
Watkins, Margaret	728	West, Sillah	669	Williams, Charles S.	500, 713
Watkins, Robert	288	West, Susan	318, 434	Williams, Cynthia	262
Watson, Ann	279	West, William	434, 879	Williams, Dick	705
Watson, Maria	496	**West, William H.**	624	**Williams, Dorothy**	838
Watters, Henry G.	377	West, William Henry	949	Williams, Duke	190
Watterston, David A.	826	Whaley, William	336	Williams, Edward	35
Watterston, George	393	Wharton, Martha	959	**Williams, Elizabeth**	866, 941
Watterston, Maria	825, 826	**Wheeler, Elizabeth E.**	903	**Williams, Emma B.**	965
Watts, Eliza	314	Wheeler, Henry	167	Williams, Frank	705
Watts, Mary E.	767	**Wheeler, Hester A.**	303	Williams, Gertrude	1, 35, 76
Watts, Richard H.	767	Wheeler, Jesse	750	Williams, Harriet	136
Waugh, Eveline	212	**Wheeler, John P.**	610	Williams, Harriet Eliza	1
Waugh, Mary E.	240	Wheeler, Margaret Ann	201	Williams, J.A.	805
Waugh, Warren	212	Wheeler, Patsy	527	Williams, James	35, 308
Weaver, Dennis	18	**Wheeler, Theodore**	667	**Williams, Jesse**	32
Weaver, Henry	18	Whitaker, Laring	72	Williams, John	705, 708
Weaver, Henry	786, 787	Whitaker, Louisa M.	260	**Williams, John M.**	50
Weaver, Joseph	872, 873, 874	Whitaker, Marian	72	Williams, John Marsellas	32
Weaver, Rebecca S.	874	**Whitaker, Samuel**	495	Williams, Joseph	32
Weaver, Thomas	872	White, Amanda	778	Williams, Laura	35
Weaver, William V. W.	34	White, Benjamin	289	**Williams, Leonora M.**	708
Webb, Jane	207	White, Daniel	289	Williams, Lewis	35, 190
Webb, Joseph W.	504, 505	White, Griffith	70	Williams, Louisa	7
Webster, B. (Mrs.)	682	**White, Harriet**	526	Williams, Lydia	35
Webster, Elizabeth	122	White, Henry	778	Williams, Margaret	859
Webster, James G.	59	**White, Horace**	424	Williams, Maria	190, 307
Webster, John Lewis	123	**White, James**	778	Williams, Maria? Louisa	10
Webster, Sandy	123	White, James (Capt.)	526	**Williams, Marial H.**	84

267

Williams, Marion	35	
Williams, Mary Ann	910	
Williams, Mary Sophia	76	
Williams, Nancy	885	
Williams, Rebecca	790	
Williams, Richard	366	
Williams, Samuel S.	934	
Williams, Sarah	262	
Williams, Selina	35	
Williams, Susan K.	235	
Williams, Thomas	705	
Williams, Thomas W.	646	
Williams, Tom	705	
Williams, Virginia	859	
Williams, Walter	838	
Williams, William Elias	32	
Williams, William H.	562, 900	
Williams, William Hamilton	500	
Williams, William J.	876	
Williams, Zadock	249	
Willis, Priscilla	412	
Willliams, Harriet	792	
Willson, Charles Horace	229	
Willson, Ellen	229	
Willson, John Q.	229	
Wilson, Adelaide	490	
Wilson, Amelia	195	
Wilson, Charles	88	
Wilson, Charles Edward	896	
Wilson, Frank	371	
Wilson, Henry P.C.	554	
Wilson, John	138, 326, 675	
Wilson, John A.	928	
Wilson, John H.A.	490	
Wilson, John M.	468	
Wilson, John W.	276	
Wilson, Joseph H.	890	
Wilson, Kitty	964	
Wilson, Leah L.	783	
Wilson, Leah Lyttleton Gale	783, 784	
Wilson, Lucy	371	
Wilson, Marlborough	110	
Wilson, Martha	371	
Wilson, Mary G.	783	
Wilson, Mary Gale	783, 784	
Wilson, Priscilla	771	
Wilson, Samuel	429	
Wilson, Samuel Lyttleton	783	
Wilson, Susan H.	246, 247	
Wilson, William	951	
Wiltberger, Charles H.	813, 954	
Wiltberger, Verlinda Mary	813	
Windsor, Catharine	115	
Windsor, Elizabeth	355, 650	
Windsor, Lofton	115	
Windsor, Richard	355	
Windsor, Richard S.	115	
Winston, Harriet	798	
Winston, Robert	798	
Wise, John H.	60	
Wood, Ann M.	207	
Wood, Betsey	566	
Wood, Bill	705	
Wood, Caroline	27	
Wood, John T.	350	
Wood, Lethe	278	
Wood, Linda (Lucinda)	699	
Wood, Margaret A.	514	
Wood, Mary Eliza	810	
Wood, Peter, Sr.	350	
Wood, Phineas F.	810	
Wood, Robert S.	749	
Wood, Virginia S.	749	
Woodland, Joseph	671	
Woodland, Nancy	910	
Woodley, Bill	549	
Woodley, Sarah	861	
Woodward, John William	113	
Woodward, Kirby S.	232	
Woodward, Margaret	213	
Woodward, Sabra	232	
Woodward, Thomas	74	
Woodward, William R.	540, 614	
Wootten, Turner (Dr.)	681	
Wootton, Olivia C.	681	
Worthington, Fermore?	744	
Worthington, James	763, 804	
Worthington, Landon W.	897	
Worthington, Sallie	964	
Worthington, Sarah M.	896	
Worthington, Susan	763	
Worthington, William	158	
Worthy, Ellen	564	
Wren, Catharine A.	607	
Wren, George W.	607	
Wren, Sarah S.	607	
Wright, James M.	462	
Wright, Louisa M.	485	
Wright, Mary	718	
Wright, Mary R.	462	
Wroe, Everett	238	
Wroe, Everett	237	
Wroe, John A.	237	
Wroe, Samuel C.	34, 237, 238	
Wroe, Vanduden Marcella	237, 238	
Wylie, Andrew	547, 602	
Yates, Andrew	366	
Yates, Jane	366	
Yates, Judah	366	
Yates, Rezin	366	
Yates, Samuel	366	
Yates, Townley	366	
Yearby, Rachel	177	
Yerby, Mary S.	779	
Yerby, William	435	
York, George	190	
Young, Amanda	259	
Young, Amelia T.	77	
Young, Barbara S.	345, 816	
Young, Charles	590, 705	
Young, Clementina S.	818	
Young, Coleby	106	
Young, Daniel	413	
Young, Elizabeth L.	302	
Young, Filmore	259	
Young, Florence E.	811	
Young, Francis	381	
Young, George W.	816	
Young, George Washington	42, 345	
Young, H. Howard	811	
Young, H. M. L. (Mrs.)	42	
Young, Henrietta	51, 345, 646	
Young, Henry	51, 413	
Young, Hillary/Hilleary	905	
Young, Ignatius F.	889	
Young, J. Fenwick	816, 817, 818	
Young, Jane	884	
Young, Jennie	960	
Young, John	482	
Young, John B.	111	
Young, Kate	413	
Young, Lizzie	381	
Young, Mary	366, 730	
Young, Mary C.	817	
Young, Noble	8	
Young, Notley	344, 569	
Young, Notley (Rev.)	56	
Young, Robert	413	
Young, Sam	381	
Young, Sarah A.	106	
Young, Susan B.	275	
Young, Thomas	440, 767, 759	
Young, Washington	490	
Young, Willis	241	
Zell, Enoch F.	347	
Zimmerman, Matilda	262	
Zimmerman, Sarah Virginia	130	

www.ingramcontent.com/pod-product-compliance
Lightning Source LLC
Chambersburg PA
CBHW080731300426
44114CB00019B/2546